CONTEMPORARY STUDIES OF

Sexuality &
COMMUNICATION

Theoretical and Applied Perspectives

Jimmie Manning, Ph.D.
Carey Marie Noland, Ph.D.

Northern Illinois University • Northeastern University

Kendall Hunt
publishing company

www.kendallhunt.com
Send all inquiries to:
4050 Westmark Drive
Dubuque, IA 52004-1840

Graduate Awards

GRADUATE COLLEGE and IP AWARDS

Graduate College Post-Comprehensive Research Award
Michelle Colpean (Spring 2018)

Graduate College Summer Fellowship
Michelle Colpean

Graduate College Underrepresented Minority
Summer Research Fellowship
Lance Bennett

COUNCIL ON TEACHING

Outstanding Teaching Assistant Award
Michelle Colpean, Ashley Peterson

FALL 2017 DEPARTMENT AWARDS

Becker/Bowers/Bryant Awards
Lin (Veronica) Sun—Samuel L. Becker Award
Emily Buehler and Ashley Peterson—John Waite Bowers Award
Matthew Houdek—Donald C. Bryant Award

Gronbeck Collegiality Award
Ethan Chetkov; Chenthu Jayachandiran

Dissertation Research Awards
Michelle Coplean, Chenthu Jayachandiran, Raven Maragh,
Ashley Peterson, Heather Roy

SPRING 2018 DEPARTMENT AWARDS
(To be announced during the Ceremony)
Carroll Arnold Fellowship
Douglas Ehninger Prize for Teaching Excellence
Ramona Tomlin Mattson Fellowship
Carol Schrage Prize for Community Building

GRADUATE STUDENTS—PENDING DEGREE CONFERRALS

May, 2018 (MA)	alea adigweme
May, 2018 (PhD)	Matthew Houdek, Raven Maragh, Heather Roy, Christopher Thomas, Meg Tully
August, 2018 (MA)	Michelle Acevedo Callejas
August, 2018 (PhD)	Emily Buehler, Seung Min Hong

THE UNIVERSITY OF IOWA

COLLEGE OF LIBERAL ARTS & SCIENCES

Communication Studies

2018 Awards and Recognition Ceremony

◆

Friday, May 4, 2018

4:00 pm

Room 101—Samuel L. Becker
Communication Studies Building

Welcome—Timothy Havens, DEO

◆

Lambda Pi Eta Induction Ceremony

Omicron Kappa Chapter—University of Iowa

The Official Honor Society of the National
Communication Association

2018 New Members—Lambda Pi Eta

Brianne Erin Crouch

Elizabeth K. Flanagan

Grace Marie Harper

Megan E. Hill

Corrine Carolyn Jones

Jacquelyn Marie Judickas

Haesung Lee

Emily Nicole Meeks

Riley Jameson O'Day

Cassidy Elise O'Leary

Megan Nicole Rosenbrook

Margaret M. Santillan

Margaret A. Sperry

Elaine Joan Stewart

Rachel Maureen Valentine

Danni Zhang

Undergraduate Awards and Scholarshı

A. Craig Baird Award
Lauren Phalen

C. Jay Starr Award
Corrine Jones

Jerome & Marian Feniger Award
Alexis Tansey

Cristen M. Loza de Bighley Award
Stephanie Hesse
Emily Meeks

Sam Becker & Herb Meinert Scholarship
McKinsey Gartner
Emily Meeks

Joseph M. Sitrick Media Internship Award
Macy Anderson

Patrick & Kimberly Hatting Scholarship
Katherine Baer

Richard A. & Donna J. McKay Award
Alexus Atzen
Shiwen Zhou

Orville Hitchcock Award
Shiwen Zhou

Robert P. Newman Award
Morgan Jones

DEDICATION

To anyone who has ever been curious about sex; which is to say, to everyone. – J.M.

To my children Anneka and Erich. – C.N.

CONTENTS

v

Section 3: Rethinking Sexual Relationships 153

Section 4: Sexual Rights, Recognitions, and Equalities 237

Section 5: Sexual Health and Well-Being 339

Section 6: Sex, Media, and Popular Culture 419

ACKNOWLEDGMENTS

We would like to acknowledge the encouragement and support of Kendall Hunt at all stages of this project. We especially recognize the support of Shannon Roney who came to us with the great idea for this book. Our goal was to create a peer-reviewed volume that showcased scholarship about sexuality and communication. Although we wanted a collection that advanced current understandings in the field, we also wanted the collection to be accessible to those who do not research and write for a living. We believe we have accomplished this goal, and only because of the editorial support from Kendall Hunt. Thank you for your faith in us!

Jimmie would like to acknowledge his loving partner Adam for all the support he has given over the past few years. Writers and editors can sometimes be difficult people to love as they spend a little too much time in front of their computers, always want to talk about their latest projects, and sometimes never end up coming to bed after inspiration strikes. Through all of this, Adam has been unwavering in his love and support. Thanks so much, babe, for supporting who I am and who I want to be.

Jimmie also wants to thank his students who have given him so many good ideas about what to research both in the classroom and out. He especially thanks Kayleigh Grubb, Melanie Schlenker, Rebecca Johnson, Bradley Carerra, and Maureen Wieland who have assisted him with many other projects not related to this book over the past year. Without their support, the time directed at this project would not be possible. I look forward to seeing the articles, books, and chapters you write (or the movies you make, Kayleigh) as you all continue in your own journeys. Mad love!

He also wishes to thank the Society for the Scientific Study of Sexuality, the National Communication Association, and the International Association for Relationship Research. These organizations have not only facilitated good spaces for research regarding sexuality and communication, they have allowed many valuable connections to be made. Indeed, many of the authors who are in this book have benefitted from presenting their research via conferences sponsored by those organizations.

Finally, and to that end, he wishes to acknowledge the valuable intellectual stimulation and caring friendship provided by the many scholars and friends who have engaged in sometimes challenging, sometimes heated, but always interesting and productive conversations about sexuality and communication research. Tony Adams, Kristen Jozkowski, Kathy Denker, Jen Dunn, Charee Thompson, Danielle Stern, Andrea South, Amanda Denes, KT (Kathleen Turner), Chuck Morris, Tom Nakayama, Jacob Matig, Tina Coffelt, Michaela Meyer, Randy Caspersen, Lara Stache, Gust Yep, Alysa Lucas, Siobhan Smith, Kristen Myers, Laura Ellingson, Adrianne Kunkel, Tamara Afifi, and Sarah Chuzi, at some point during the work on this book you said something that inspired me or made me think about my work in a different way. Of course, Carey Noland was an excellent co-editor, too, always bringing organization, support, and—most important—great ideas to the table. Thanks for sharing your talents and friendship!

Carey would like to thank her family for giving her the all hours she spent on this book. My son, Erich, was born in the middle of this process (March 22, 2015), another labor of love that I went through. For Erich, who attended to a lot of conference calls without crying and slept on my chest while I edited chapters. I thank my husband Hans, who listened to my ideas about chapters, provided input on my chapter, and supported me by taking trips with the kids without me. To my beautiful daughter, Anneka, for being as patient as a 3-year-old can be and waiting for me to finish my current task before we went exploring. My mother, Donna Noland, had been a tireless system of support and encouragement, listening to my ideas, reading my materials, and just being all around fantastic. She even supervised my house move so I could finish the book. To my German family in Bretzfeld where I spent the summer in 2015: Manfred and Renata Röll and the entire extended Stellrecht familien, for being supportive and providing the best bread, beer, and company I could ask for on breaks. Especially for Sabrina Röll, host extraordinaire, for her friendship and company on our nightly hundwalks.

I would like to express my gratitude to dear friend Janet MacLeannan who inspired me to start researching the positive aspects of sex when I first started to branch out from health communication. I offer heartfelt thanks to my friends and colleagues Heather Carmack and Elise Dallimore for their support.

I would like to offer my most sincere appreciation to Jimmie Manning for co-editing this book with me. Thanks for taking this wonderful journey with me (again!). I was amazed at the insightful and clever edits that he made to each of the chapters; it was a pleasure to work with someone so smart. It was a joy to be able to work with such talented and giving authors, whose intelligence and creativity shined through in this project. You made research and writing fun.

Lastly, we would like to thank the numerous outside reviewers who spent valuable time providing feedback that made these book chapters even better.

INTRODUCTION

THINKING ABOUT SEXUALITY AND COMMUNICATION

Carey Noland, Ph.D.

Jimmie Manning, Ph.D.

Our quality of life is inextricably linked to the quality of our communication and the quality of our personal relationships. The quality of sexual relationships has a significant bearing on our wellness, too. As physician Charles Marwick notes, "As human beings our sexuality is inextricably linked to our overall health, happiness, and sense of wellness."[1] Thus, the study of human sexuality and sexual practices—and communicative elements in particular—are increasingly important to consider. For many decades, sex was thought of as a topic that was too personal and too private to be investigated in the public domain of research; but then many negative social consequences became painfully public because individuals' sexual choices have important consequences for personal and society welfare.[2]

As a result, both political and medical entities have taken a great interest in the consequences of private sexual relationships. However, political and medical entities are not best-positioned to study the mediating environment involved: human communication. Much of the research that has been done to understand, mediate, and control the consequences of human sexual relationships has been focused on information and education, not communication. Usually such research is also devoid of any consideration about the relational aspects of sex.

The title of this text is *Contemporary Studies of Sexuality and Communication: Theoretical and Applied Perspectives*. Although most people talk and joke about sex a lot, too few of us engage in meaningful communication about it. And although we might think about sex frequently, many people do not engage in the theoretical elements involved with sex and communication either. This observation extends beyond communication studies—theorizing about sexuality is limited across disciplines or areas of study. To that end, this text is an invitation to talk and think about sex in meaningful ways. Moreover, we hope to provide readers with the tools to transform understandings about sex and sexuality into practice, thus improving their relationships, their communities, their organizations, and their lives.

In an effort to encourage meaningful reflection and communication about sex, we have turned to top scholars across many disciplines to compile research about the most salient issues regarding communication about sex. We asked these experts to write in a way that still advances scholarly ideas about sexuality and communication—thus making a contribution to current theoretical and research bodies—but also to write in a way that is accessible to a diverse audience. As such, this book can be used by researchers for their own studies, students to learn in the classroom, and by other adult readers who want to learn more about sexuality and communication. By encouraging readers to think deeply about sex, sexuality, and sexual identities, we hope people will become more comfortable with their own sexualities and the sexualities of others as they have a larger knowledge and set of tools to deal with emerging or ongoing sexual concerns.

As teachers, we have found in our classes about interpersonal communication, media studies, or health that students are especially interested to talk about sexuality and learn more about what research has to say. It is little wonder that students crave such knowledge since the reality is that *most* people find it difficult to talk about sex in relationships. Whereas much of the public health education about sex focuses on developing practices of safer sex, this information often disregards the reality of our personal relationships and how they are developed and maintained. As sex researchers, we find that many people are interested in what we have learned from our studies, ranging from people on airplanes to good friends. They are often surprised to learn that people study sexuality and communication, as they often say they have only heard about sex research when in a sex education course. They also frequently remark that they feel sexual topics are off limits, and that it feels refreshing to talk about sex, sexuality, and sexual identity candidly.

As you will read in this book, there are a number of off-limits topics in sexual relationships, including the current state of sex satisfaction in a relationship, sexual activity outside of the relationship, what is normal, what feels normal for a particular person or couple, health issues, prior relationships, any topic about sex that might generate conflict, and self-disclosures perceived as unpleasant to discuss.[3] Furthermore, much of the space dedicated to education about sex focuses on the negative aspects of sexuality, such as sexually-transmitted infections and unplanned pregnancies. The things that can increase our sexual pleasure and relational intimacy are absent from these conversations. This text highlights the positive aspects of sex and introduces research about improving sexual satisfaction.

The tone of our book is exploratory, in that the communicative quality of sexual lives and identities are considered. Although every chapter is grounded in previous research, each chapter also makes a contribution to building ongoing knowledge. That includes original research studies, working literature reviews, and the development of new models or theories. We believe we need research and readings that explore communication about sex that avoids presuming negative aspects about sexuality itself and that can help people to have fulfilling sex lives—or not, if they are not interested in sexuality. By treating sex and sexual identity as a communicative form, we will delve into the interpersonal dynamics that significantly influence and determine the kinds of sexual relationships possible.

Endnotes

1. Charles Marwick, "Survey Says Patients Expect Little Physician Help on Sex," *Journal of the American Medical Association* 281 (1999).

2. Robert Michael, "Private Sex and Public Policy," in *Sex, love, and health in America: Private choices and public policies,* eds. Edward Laumann and Robert Michael (Chicago: University of Chicago Press, 2000), 465.

3. (Baxter & Wilmot, 1985) quoted in Ibid, 38.

Overview

Section One of the book invites readers to think about what sex means and how that influences how we think and talk about sex. In the first chapter, Brittnie Peck and colleagues present a research study showing how people define sex. This quantitative research study offers some surprising results that indicate people might mean a lot of different things when they say they "had sex." Then Katrina Pariera focuses on sexual norms, how they are communicated interpersonally, and the impact of different societal institutions on those interactions. In the third chapter Larissa Brian looks at how sexual consent has evolved in the United States. The belief that people have always had a say about whether they have a choice to have sex and how, is still an issue that plagues many cultures today, and Brian's chapter helps to add context to ongoing discussions. Finally, Randal Brown and Daniel Weigel author a chapter that presents a theoretical basis for thinking about sexual communication. Their *ecological systems* approach helps to illustrate ties between culture and individuals.

Section Two incorporates cultural perspectives to help illustrate that sex, sexuality, and sexual identities can be diverse. Chapter 5 by Gust Yep and colleagues offers a delightful and insightful view into the lives of Manuel and Daniel, two characters involved in an intercultural romance. In Chapter 6, Zelaika Clarke offers us a complex portrait of African sexuality. Unfortunately, most sex research happens in Western cultures, but as Clarke points out, we have a lot to learn from examining other cultures. Then Jimmie Manning offers an original model in Chapter 7 where he examines the complexities of coming out. This chapter considers how research from many different academic disciplines, including psychology and sociology, help to inform how people communicate about sexual identity. Continuing the theme of sexual identity, in Chapter 8 Linda Baughman and Michaela Meyer speak to the challenges of being bisexual/queer identified women in a culture that tends to see things in a binary—i.e., you are either gay or you are straight—kind of way.

Chapter 9 then looks at the complexities of gender. Shannon Criniti and Eli Green examine transgender identity, helping to illustrate the ways that gender and sexuality might or might not be related. Finally, Jenny Dixon examines a topic that is starting to gain more recognition in contemporary culture: polyamorous relationships. Although many people do not know much about polyamory, they often are skeptical about whether or not people can truly be in open relationships. Dixon's research review gives readers more to think about when it comes to understanding polyamory.

Section Three examines aspects of relationships people take for granted. Sarah Trask begins this exploration with her chapter on friends with benefits relationships. Can people be friends *and* lovers without it being a romantic relationship? Trask helps to answer this question through the presentation of qualitative data from people in such relationships. Then, in Chapter 12, Dan Strasser and Kathryn Hobson explore queer friendships. When queer people hang out together and relate, it can be quite different than friendships that are both heterosexual. In their theoretical piece, Strasser and Hobson help to illustrate why. Next, Jayson Dibble and colleagues discuss back burner relationships. Do we always keep someone in line in case a current relationship does not work out? And what does sex have to do with it? The chapter answers these questions and more. Chapter 14 examines something that most people probably do not think about, but that almost certainly has an impact on relationships: after-sex communication. Are you a chatter, a snacker, or a snuggler? Or do you roll over and go to sleep? Amanda Denes and Annika Speer review their published studies to consider what it all means. Finally, in Chapter 15 Jessica Kratzer uses a fictive case study to help illustrate the concerns older adults have about maintaining their sex lives.

Section Four focuses on sexual rights and recognition. This includes a compelling investigation from Kristen Jozkowski on why rape seems like a myth in contemporary United States culture. In addition to reviewing literature about rape being a myth, she reviews some compelling recent cases where whether someone was raped or not has been called into question. That is followed by Pamela Lannutti and Sandra Faulkner's chapter exploring a day-in-the-life of people in same sex relationships. In addition to a fictive case study, the authors examine research that helps to provide much-needed context about the experiences of many gay, lesbian, bisexual, or otherwise sexually-queer people. Roger Davis Gatchet and Amanda Davis Gatchet then examine rhetorical movements against marriage equality in Chapter 18. The authors provide many examples of these movements and offer an overview of what queer theory is and why it is important. Shinsuke Eguchi writes about his personal experiences as he examines many aspects of his Gay Asian Male (G.A.M.) identity and how they translate across Japanese and North American cultures in Chapter 19. That is followed by two chapters about sexuality in the workplace. Tim McKenna-Buchanan and Sara Baker offer an overview of microaggressions related to sexual identity in Chapter 20 while Tiffany Emerson and Jimmie Manning explore sexual harassment and consenting relationship policies in Chapter 21.

Section Five explores one of the most-researched areas of sexuality and communication, sexual health. Even though this area is highly researched, the authors bring new ideas and insights through these interesting chapters. This begins with Chapter 22 where Carey Noland explores sexual communication between doctors and patients by following an attending physician teaching medical students how to take a sexual history. That is followed by a chapter from Dayna Henry and Rose Hartzell-Cushanick who offer vignettes of people in sex therapy to help readers to understand what is involved with counseling and how it can be helpful for sexual relationships. Tina Coffelt then reviews research about how families talk about sex in Chapter 24. Her chapter especially offers many interesting insights about how parents talk to children about sex. Chapter 25 from Tobias Reynolds-Tylus and Lance Rintamaki introduces two concepts important to sexual health. First, they include information about the Health Belief Model, an oft-used model for sex research; and they tie that to condom use, an important consideration for sexual health. Finally, Diana Ivy examines a different kind of sexual safety in Chapter 26 where she reviews verbal and nonverbal consent. This important chapter helps to explain where confusion about consent might emerge and how understanding what consent is can prevent sexual assault and rape.

All good things must come to an end, but for the final section of this book we saved some of the most fun for last as we explore media and popular culture. Section Six begins with an entertaining exploration of sexuality in popular culture from Lara Stache. Exploring a range of topics from Amy Schumer's hilarious critiques of how women are sexualized (yay!) to the slut-shaming of popular Avengers character Black Widow (boo!), this chapter will engage readers as they think about what their favorite popular culture representations mean. Jennifer Mayo and Robert Alan Brookey then examine some of the problems with video game culture in Chapter 28, and Danielle Stern takes a deeper look at sexting in Chapter 29. Both of these chapters help shed light on contemporary challenges regarding sexuality and digital technologies. The final three chapters offer interesting and in-depth explorations of three different popular culture topics. Jennifer Dunn talks about her research interviewing the women who were seen on the HBO television series *Cathouse*. That allows her to make compelling arguments about people's attitudes toward sex workers and offer a glimpse behind the scenes of the popular show into the lives of these sex workers and how they feel about their profession. *American Horror Story* fans will love Kelly Wilz's exploration of how torture porn features into the series in Chapter 31. And, finally, in Chapter 32 Sean Robinson writes a love letter to Lady Gaga as he considers how her tweets might inspire queer youths.

As we hope you see, there is something for everyone in this collection. Whether you read it cover-to-cover, or if you only look at one or two chapters, we believe you will learn as much as we did. It is our hope that you turn the theoretical material and applied research presented here into action. This action might be instigating a meaningful conversation about the topics in this book with your sexual partner, your parents (and eventually, perhaps, your children), your physician, your friends, or your co-workers or human resource managers. It may mean that you stand up for someone at work who is being harassed about their sexual identity, or intervene at a party to prevent non-consensual sex, or tell your partner about your sexual preferences and invite them to talk about theirs, or make an effort to cuddle after sex, or even ask your doctor to take a complete sexual history because you found that you have never had one.

Although there are significant differences in sexual practices across cultures, it is an activity that unites humanity. The importance of sex cannot be downplayed. Why else would some of the most powerful politicians, corporate leaders, and even presidents risk everything for sex? Although they do not find the answer to that larger mystery here, the authors of these chapters do offer many practical answers about sexuality and communication as well as some compelling, evidence-based theories. We invite you to learn from all they have to offer!

ABOUT THE EDITORS

Jimmie Manning (Ph.D., University of Kansas) is Associate Professor of Communication Theory at Northern Illinois University where he also serves as Chair of Sexuality Studies. Dr. Manning's research focuses on relationships, typically in interpersonal, health, computer-mediated, or organizational contexts. Much of this work has focused on sexuality, including studies about sexting, coming out, purity pledges, turning points in sexual relationships, among others. His work has appeared in several top-tier journals including *Communication Monographs*, *Journal of Computer-Mediated Communication*, *International Journal of Communication*, *Journal of Social and Personal Relationships*, and *Journal of Family Communication*, among others. He is also the author or editor of five books including *Researching Interpersonal Relationships: Qualitative Methods, Studies, and Analysis* (co-authored with Adrianne Kunkel). His research and teaching have been recognized with many awards including the Society for the Scientific Study of Sexuality Early Professional Career Award; the International Association for Relationship Research Teaching Award; the National Communication Association Lambda Award; the Organization for the Study of Communication, Language, and Gender Feminist Teacher-Mentor Award; and the National Communication Association Outstanding Mentor in Master's Education Award. He has also received 14 top paper awards from regional, national, and international organizations. He currently resides in Chicago.

Carey Noland (Ph.D., Ohio University) is an award winning researcher and professor with over 25 years experience in the fields of health and sex. This is her third book on the topic of sex and communication. She has produced over 65 scholarly articles and professional papers on topics in health and sex communication. While she initially began her sex research investigating topics related to HIV and sexually-transmitted infections, she has become increasingly interested in the role of sex and sexuality in quality of life issues, social justice, and personal wellness. Dr. Noland holds a Ph.D. in communication studies from Ohio University, a Master's degree from the LBJ School of Public Affairs, University of Texas, Austin, and completed her undergraduate work in economics and statistics at Boston University. Dr. Noland joined the communication studies faculty at Northeastern University in 2002, where she is currently an Associate Professor. She was also an adjunct professor at Tufts University School of Medicine in the Department of Family Medicine.

CHAPTER 1

What Do People Mean When They Say They "Had Sex"? Connecting Communication and Behavior

Brittnie Peck, Jimmie Manning, Andrew Tri,
Daria Skrzypczynski, Morgan Summers, & Kayleigh Grubb

KEY TERMS

Defining sex	Sexual activity	Health
Intercourse	Sexual identity	Quantitative research

ABSTRACT

What do people mean when they say they "had sex"? The most-cited study regarding what activities are communicated as having "had sex" is now over 20 years old. This chapter provides findings from a study that replicated the original study's methods to provide an up-to-date understanding. An Internet survey completed by 380 women and 197 men from the United States was conducted. Results show that penile-vaginal intercourse was the sexual activity most likely to count as having "had sex," with 97.4% of participants indicating it as sex. Other common sexual activities measured include penile-anal intercourse, oral-genital contact, and manual stimulation of genitals. The findings suggest many attitudes represented in the original survey have changed. Implications and future studies are offered.

In their article "Would You Say You 'Had Sex' If...?" published in the *Journal of the American Medical Association*, researchers Stephanie Sanders and June Reinisch (1999) found that even though the phrase "had sex" might appear to have a single meaning that is commonly understood by everyone, participants in their study held "widely divergent opinions about what behaviors do and do not constitute having 'had sex'" (p. 275). Their research essay, inspired by a lack of research showing what behaviors the general public defined as sex, used data collected in 1991 from a survey given to a group of 599 eligible participants (Sanders & Reinisch, 1999) to help determine how people might indicate their sexual activities to others, especially physicians or potential sex partners. Since the initial publication of the study about 15 years ago, many have turned to the data to understand what people mean when they say they "had sex." Indeed, a citation count generated by Google Scholar in late 2015 demonstrates 36 citations since 2014, 114 citations over the past five years, and 435 citations total. Additionally, the same Google Scholar search reveals the article has been reprinted at least six times, indicating this data has been well used. As beneficial as these data have been, given that almost 25 years have passed since the initial data collection, an update is in order.

For the research study in this chapter, we sought to replicate the original methods used by Sanders and Reinisch to create an up-to-date data set. Although we followed the same survey methods used by the researchers, we made changes in recruiting procedures to get a more diverse, and thus more indicative of the general population, group of participants. The people who participated in the original study were limited to one Midwestern state university (Sanders & Reinisch, 1999). Additionally, they were younger in age (96% of the participants were between the ages of 18 and 25) and mostly politically moderate to conservative (79% of participants self-categorized in these categories) (Sanders & Reinisch, 1999). The cultural context for the study was also grounded in the then-current Clinton-Lewinsky scandal (see *JAMA*: Editor, 1999). At the time, President William Jefferson Clinton was at the center of a controversy where he claimed he "did not have sexual relations" with White House intern Monica Lewinsky (quoted in Nelson, 2013). Later, when it was revealed that he had intimate relations that included oral sex and genital stimulation, many questioned whether or not Clinton lied. Although they did not have penile-vaginal intercourse, what they did was clearly sexual—suggesting that the definition of *sexual relations* was in flux. The research study was, in many ways, a response to the scandal (*JAMA*: Editor, 1999).

Although the Clinton-Lewinsky scandal has long passed, the importance of understanding what people mean when they say they "have sex" can be beneficial for many reasons. It can help to establish what consent means (see Brian, this volume or Ivy, this volume) and perhaps prevent rape; it can help physicians to understand the range of activities different people might be indicating when they say they had sex (see Noland, this volume); and it can help to contextualize everyday talk about sex between friends (see Strasser & Hobson, this volume), families (see Coffelt, this volume), and people in a variety of relationships. In short, what "having sex" means is at the center of understanding sexuality and communication in many contexts.

Defining Sex

Sanders & Reinisch's (1999) original research study indicated that most participants considered penile-vaginal intercourse to be sex (99.5%); about 81% considered penile-anal intercourse to be sex; and only about 40% of individuals considered oral-genital contact as constituting sex. That means that most people counted traditional heterosexual penetration as sex, although many people counted penile-anal penetration as well. Other activities, such as oral sex, presented less possibility for agreement because there was less agreement from participants about whether it counted as sex or not.

After the study was published, other researchers (e.g., Pitts & Rahman, 2001; Taylor & Muscarella, 2002) also did research to try to understand what counted as sex, giving participants a similar list of sexual behaviors and asking them if that behavior would count as sex. Across these studies, findings were generally the same, with most participants in agreement about penile-vaginal intercourse being the most dominant understanding of having sex and considerable disagreement about whether oral or anal intercourse—when the most intimate behavior experienced during a physical encounter—counted. Also, similar to the original Sanders and Reinisch (1999) study, the researchers primarily relied on heterosexual, traditionally college-aged students to provide their data.

Although some scholars looked to replicate Sanders and Reinisch's work, others were critical of their findings. For example, Peterson and Mue-hlenhard (2007) noted that the design of the original study lacked an understanding of situation and context. They argued that certain people might have more of a motivation to count something as sex than others. For example, for men—who are often socially awarded for having more sexual activity—it would be of benefit to count more activities as sex. Women, on the other hand, might count less behaviors as sex because they are generally criticized more by others for their sexual activity. Sanders and Reinisch (1999) did acknowledge this somewhat in their study, suggesting that a "potential costs/benefits of labeling a behavior as having 'had sex'" (p. 277) might be at play. Denes (2013) extended Peterson and Muehlenhard's observation, pointing specifically to how the labeling of sexual activities can also be related to different aspects of an individual's identity. Other research backs up Denes' contentions. For example, Faulkner (2003) demonstrated a relationship between Latina women's definitions of sex to their culture, religion, and evaluation and presentation of self.

Additionally, differences in what behaviors gay men (Hill, Rahman, Bright, & Sanders, 2010) and lesbian women (Horowitz & Spicer, 2013) constitute having "had sex" compared to heterosexual men and women have been demonstrated. Specifically, research has found that gay men label anal sex as having had sex more often than they do penile-vaginal intercourse (Hill et al., 2010); and lesbian women more often label oral, manual, and use of sex aid for stimulation of genitals as having had sex (Horowitz & Spicer, 2013). Although these findings are not that surprising, they do establish empirical evidence for what people have long assumed in social science research. The findings also suggest that more diverse populations could lead to a more accurate set of results for learning what people mean when they say they "had sex."

Research Methods: Replicating the Original Study with More-Diverse Participants

Taking past research to heart, and especially being cognizant of McCormack's (2014) advice to be mindful of recruiting diverse sexual identities, we replicated Sanders and Reinisch's (1999) original research study, including their original research question:

R1: What behaviors do individuals define as constituting having "had sex"?

Participants

Participants were recruited through convenience sampling, predominantly by requests for participation posted to different Facebook groups. Additional participants were recruited through an offer of extra course credit for an undergraduate class in which they were currently enrolled. A total of 577 participants completed the survey and were included in analyses. The sample consisted of 380 women (65.9%) and 197 men, ranging in age from 18 to 74 years with 43.2% ranging in age from 18 to 24, 51.4% from 25-50, and 5.2% 50 years or older. The self-reported race/ethnicity of participants was 80.1% White, 6.4% of mixed race/ethnicity, 5.2% Hispanic or Latino, and 4.3% Black. Participants' self-reported sexual orientation consisted of 76.7% identifying as heterosexual and 24.3% identifying as gay, lesbian, or bisexual. The sample was highly educated, with 70.4% of participants having some college and 14.4% having graduate degrees. Participants were also more likely to be liberal, with 55.9% reporting being politically moderate to liberal.

Procedures and Instrumentation

Although five other measures were included in the questionnaire, the findings of this report are based solely on the original Sanders and Reinisch (1999) protocol. These items asked participants to respond to the question, "Would you say you 'had sex' with someone if the most intimate behavior you engaged in was…" by indicating "yes" or "no" to 11 behaviors. The items regarding behaviors that would constitute having "had sex" were presented in random order to prevent participants from identifying any preconceived hierarchy of sexual behaviors. The questionnaire was accessed online by clicking a link directed to a survey collection site. After reading the consent form explaining their rights, voluntary participation was indicated by continuing to the first portion of the questionnaire. Responses were anonymous and no identifying information was collected. If participation was for extra course credit, participants provided their name and class information by clicking on a link that directed them to a separate questionnaire so this information could not be linked back to individual responses. All participants were provided with contact information of the researchers and the university's Institutional Review Board should their participation raise any issues or questions they wanted to discuss.

Results

The research question asked what behaviors constituted having sex. As can be seen in Table 1, almost all participants (97.4%) were in agreement that penile-vaginal intercourse would qualify as having "had sex." Although the number of those who considered penile-anal intercourse was significantly lower, the level of agreement on this item still indicates a high level of shared agreement (85.4%). Interestingly, few individuals considered deep kissing (14.4%) or breast contact (17.5%) with a partner as having "had sex." However, these levels do differ substantially from those reported in the original Sanders and Reinisch (1999) study (2% and 3%, respectively). Additional notable findings were that 37.7% to 38.6% of individuals indicated that manual stimulation of the genitals (either given or received) would constitute having "had sex," another substantial departure from findings of the original study. Responses to the items concerning oral-genital contact show that 57.7% to 58.4% of individuals would say they had "had sex" if this was the most intimate behavior in which they engaged. These findings are in contrast to the original study, where only 40% of individuals indicated that either giving or receiving oral-genital contact would constitute having "had sex."

TABLE 1: *Percentages for Participants Answering 'Yes' to the question: "Would you say you "had sex" with someone if the most intimate behavior you engaged in was…"*

Behaviors	Percentage Indicating "Had Sex" (95% Confidence Interval)		
	Women *n = 380*	Men *(n = 197)*	Overall *n = 577*
Deep kissing (French or tongue kissing)?	**13.6** *(10.2-17.1)*	**15.7** *(10.6-20.8)*	**14.4** *(11.5-17.2)*
A person had oral (mouth) contact with your breasts or nipples?	**17.6** *(13.7-21.4)*	**17.2** *(11.9-22.5)*	**17.5** *(14.3-20.6)*
A person touched, fondled, or manually stimulated your breasts or nipples?	**15** *(11.3-18.6)*	**12.6** *(8.0-17.3)*	**14.2** *(11.3-17.0)*
You touched, fondled, or manually stimulated a person's breasts or nipples?	**9.7** *(4.7-14.6)*	**18.7** *(13.2-24.2)*	**14** *(11.2-16.8)*
You had oral (mouth) contact with another person's breasts or nipples?	**12.3** *(9.0-15.6)*	**22.3** *(16.4-28.2)*	**15.7** *(12.7-18.7)*
You touched, fondled, or manually stimulated a person's genitals?	**39.7** *(34.7-44.6)*	**34** *(27.3-40.6)*	**37.7** *(33.8-41.7)*
A person touched, fondled, or manually stimulated your genitals?	**41.8** *(36.8-46.8)*	**32.4** *(25.9-39.0)*	**38.6** *(34.6-42.6)*
You had oral (mouth) contact with a person's genitals?	**58.1** *(53.1-63.1)*	**56.8** *(49.9-63.8)*	**57.7** *(53.6-61.7)*
A person had oral (mouth) contact with your genitals?	**58.6** *(53.7-63.1)*	**57.8** *(50.9-64.8)*	**58.4** *(54.3-62.4)*
Penile-anal intercourse (penis in anus/rectum)?	**83.1** *(79.3-86.9)*	**89.8** *(85.6-94.1)*	**85.4** *(82.5-88.3)*
Penile-vaginal intercourse (penis in vagina)?	**97.3** *(95.7-98.9)*	**97.4** *(95.2-99.6)*	**97.4** *(96.1-98.7)*

Discussion

Comparisons and Contrasts to the Original Study

Although agreement regarding whether penile-vaginal intercourse was considered having "had sex" was higher than any other behavior, the current findings (97.4%) were slightly different than those of the original study (99.5%), and there was a slight increase for penile-anal intercourse (85.4%) compared to the original findings (81%). We suspect that both of these changes are related to our more-diverse population, as the inclusion of more gay or bisexual men could help to explain the increase of those counting penile-anal intercourse as sex. Changing public perceptions about same-sex activity (see Lannutti & Faulkner, this volume) could also account for the increase. Similarly, lesbians and bisexual women could also help to account for why less people reported penile-vaginal intercourse as having "had sex." Indeed, a self-identified lesbian participant included on another portion of the survey where open-ended data were collected, "I do not sleep with men. For penile-vaginal intercourse to happen, I would most likely call it rape."

The most interesting contrast in the findings of this study versus the findings of the original is the big increase in the number of people who counted the manual stimulation of genitals as having "had sex." This number ranged from 37.7% to 38.6% (given or received) in contrast to the findings of the original study where only 13.9% to 15.1% saw it as having "had sex." This change could be because of the number of older participants included in the study, as many older populations consider touching as more sexual than younger generations (see Kratzer, this volume). Oral-genital contact also saw big change from the 1999 study where 39.9% to 40.2% counted it as having "had sex." In the current study, that number increased to 57.7% to 58.4%. This increase might be, in part, because of lesbian or bisexual women participants, but it is also likely indicative of some other social change. Future research would be illuminating to help understand such a shift.

Other differences were found in responses to questions about deep kissing (14.4% compared to 2% reported in original study), oral contact with breasts or nipples by another individual (17.5% compared to 3% reported in original study), and manual stimulation of breasts or nipples by another individual (14.2% compared to 3.4% reported in original study). Again, these findings might be the result, in part, of older people participating in the study who are more likely to see touch activities as sexual (see Kratzer, this volume). These changes might also be the result of a shift in cultural values about sex, the inclusion of more ethnic/racial minorities as well as more sexual minorities in the current study, or participation from more liberal participants. To explore the causes of these differences, more research is in order.

Limitations: Considering the Sample and Their Motivations

Just as with Sanders and Reinisch's (1999) original study, we offer some cautionary notes for those who want to use this data. First, we note that although this study is more diverse in terms of sexual identities than the past study, it also has a larger percentage of gay, lesbian, bisexual, and transgender (GLBT) participants than can be found in the general population. Possible explanations for the substantial differences in responses to items regarding manual and oral stimulation of the breasts and genitals can probably be explained by the diverse sexual identities in the current sample. Past research also shows GLBT people are more likely to see activities that deviate from penile-vaginal intercourse as sex in comparison to heterosexual people (e.g., Hill et al., 2010; Horowitz & Spicer, 2013).

Although the current study stands as a much-needed update of what people might mean when they say they "had sex," it also has other limitations. First, similar to how the original study (Sanders & Reinisch, 1999) employed a highly educated sample, participants in this study were highly educated as well. Even though the demographics here represent a more-diverse level of education among participants, over 70% have had some college. Future research should strive to build a participant pool more reflective of diverse education levels.

Another possible limitation of this study is reflected in critiques of the original study about participant motivations that were made by Peterson and Muehlenhard (2007). To that end, these motivational factors should be considered in future research. Additionally, it might be helpful for communication scholars to consider motivations in terms of other contexts as well. For instance, the current study asks people to reflect on their own sexual behaviors. It would be interesting to explore whether those same behaviors are seen as having sex when it is another person—such as a romantic or sexual partner or a child—that is engaging them.

References

Brian, L. (This volume). A genealogy of sexual consent from the social contract to sex-positive feminism. In J. Manning & C. Noland (Eds.), *Contemporary Studies of Sexuality & Communication: Theoretical and Applied Perspectives*. Dubuque, IA: Kendall Hunt.

Coffelt, T. (This volume). Communication about sex in families: Educational and relational. In J. Manning & C. Noland (Eds.), *Contemporary Studies of Sexuality & Communication: Theoretical and Applied Perspectives*. Dubuque, IA: Kendall Hunt.

Denes, A. (2013). Engaging in pillow talk: The challenges of studying communication after sexual activity. *International Journal of Communication, 7,* 2495–2506.

Faulkner, S. L. (2003). Good girl or flirt girl: Latinas' definitions of sex and sexual relationships. *Hispanic Journal of Behavioral Sciences*, 25(2), 174–200. doi:10.1177/0739986303025002003.

Hill, B. J., Rahman, Q., Bright, D. A., & Sanders, S. A. (2010). The semantics of sexual behavior and their implications for HIV/AIDS research and sexual health: U.S. and U.K. gay men's definitions of having "had sex." *AIDS Care*, 22(10), 1245–1251.

Horowitz, A. D., & Spicer, L. (2013). "Having sex" as a graded and hierarchical construct: A comparison of sexual definitions among heterosexual and lesbian emerging adults in the U.K. *Journal of Sex Research*, 50(2), 139–150.

Ivy, D. (This volume). College students' sexual safety: The verbal and nonverbal communication of consent. In J. Manning & C. Noland (Eds.), *Contemporary Studies of Sexuality & Communication: Theoretical and Applied Perspectives*. Dubuque, IA: Kendall Hunt.

JAMA: Editor fired for timing of sex study. (1999, January). *California Healthline*. Retrieved from http://www.californiahealthline. org/articles/1999/1/19/jama--editor-fired-for-timing-of-sex-study?view=print.

Kratzer, J. (This volume). Sexual activity, intimacy, aging, and communication. In J. Manning & C. Noland (Eds.), *Contemporary Studies of Sexuality & Communication: Theoretical and Applied Perspectives*. Dubuque, IA: Kendall Hunt.

Lannutti, P., & Faulkner, S. (This volume). Everyday experiences of people in same-sex relationships. In J. Manning & C. Noland (Eds.), *Contemporary Studies of Sexuality & Communication: Theoretical and Applied Perspectives*. Dubuque, IA: Kendall Hunt.

McCormack, M. (2014). Innovative sampling and participant recruitment in sexuality research. *Journal of Social and Personal Relationships, 31*(4), 475–481. doi:10.1177/0265407514522889.

Noland, C. (This volume). Taking a sexual history. In J. Manning & C. Noland (Eds.), *Contemporary Studies of Sexuality & Communication: Theoretical and Applied Perspectives*. Dubuque, IA: Kendall Hunt.

Peterson, Z. D., & Muehlenhard, C. L. (2007). What is sex and why does it matter? A motivational approach to exploring individuals' definitions of sex. *Journal of Sex Research, 44*, 256–268. doi:10.1080/00224490701443932.

Pitts, M., & Rahman, Q. (2001). Which behaviors constitute "having sex" among university students in the U.K.? *Archives of Sexual Behavior, 30*, 169–176.

Sanders, S. A., & Reinisch, J. M. (1999). Would you say you "had sex" if . . . ? *Journal of the American Medical Association, 281*, 275–277. doi:10.1001/jama.281.3.275.

Strasser, D., & Hobson, K. (This volume). "You had sex, right?" Theorizing desire, identity, reciprocity, and sex in queer friendships. In J. Manning & C. Noland (Eds.), *Contemporary Studies of Sexuality & Communication: Theoretical and Applied Perspectives*. Dubuque, IA: Kendall Hunt.

Taylor, F., & Muscarella, F. (2002, November). *Sexual Attitudes: An examination of differences by ethnicity, gender, and year in college.* Paper presented at the annual meeting of the Society for the Scientific Study of Sexuality, Montreal, Quebec, Canada.

CHAPTER 2

The Communication of Sexual Norms

Katrina L. Pariera

 ## KEY TERMS

Sexual norms

Injunctive norms

Descriptive norms

Social norms approach

 ## ABSTRACT

This chapter describes sexual norms with a particular focus on the United States. The chapter examines three research-informed fictive case studies of people writing their private thoughts about their experiences communicating about and pondering sexual norms. Exploring their situations helps illustrate how sexual norms are often a private issue with public effects.

When it comes to sex we often cannot help but wonder if what we are thinking and doing is "normal." We might wonder if we are having more or less sex than other people. We might wonder if other people fantasize about the same things we do. On the one hand we might sometimes claim that being "normal" is mundane, but on the other hand we cannot help but ponder how we stack up to others when it comes to matters of sex. Many aspects of sex are private, so when we try to figure out what is normal, we usually have to guess based on what we hear from others. As we talk with partners, joke with friends, overhear strangers, read articles online, watch movies, and so on, we start to form an idea of what everyone is doing and thus what is normal. When we communicate about sex, we communicate sexual norms and for better or worse, these sexual norms have an effect on us. However, it turns out that we are not good at guessing what is normal. In fact, when we guess what other people are doing, we usually guess wrong. This chapter describes some common sexual norm misperceptions we have, how we communicate them, and the effect they have on our sexual well-being.

Sexual Norms

Norms are like codes of conduct. They are usually implicitly agreed upon by groups of people, but not always explicitly put into words. Norms change slowly over time, differ across cultures and sub-cultures, and are acted upon differently in different contexts. Norms "either prescribe or proscribe behaviors that members of a group can enact" (Lapinski & Rimal, 2005, p. 129), and hence understanding norms can tell us a lot about people's attitudes and behaviors. Humans have a complicated relationship with norms. Acting outside the norm can make us feel unique or rebellious, but can also make us feel isolated. Acting within the norm can make us feel ordinary, but it can also give us a sense of belonging and guide our behavior in uncertain situations. The extent to which we follow a norm usually depends on whether we think there will be some kind of repercussion for not following the norm, such as being made fun of, left out, or feeling bad about ourselves (Rimal & Real, 2003).

Although this chapter takes a social scientific perspective, it is important to note that norms are studied by both social scientists and critical-cultural scholars alike. Critical scholars tend to study collective norms, or those that operate on the larger social, structural level; whereas social scientists tend to study individual perceived norms (Lapinski & Rimal, 2005). Individual perceived norms are usually broken into two categories: injunctive and descriptive norms. Injunctive norms describe what we think most other people *approve* of, or what is socially acceptable. For example "Most people think you should use condoms when hooking up with a new partner" is an injunctive norm. Descriptive norms, on the other hand, describe what we think most other people are doing, or the prevalence of a behavior. For example, "Most people do not use condoms when hooking up with a new partner" is a descriptive norm. Even though descriptive norms are more commonly studied, each of the two types of norms goes hand in hand. For example, many college students think most of their peers drink a lot of alcohol (the descriptive norm) and many of them think that they should drink alcohol if they want to make and keep friends (the injunctive norm) (Rimal & Real, 2003). Sometimes these norms are at odds. For example, people who believe that most people disapprove of littering are still likely to litter if it seems that most other people are doing it (Cialdini, Kallgren, & Reno, 2000). Because norms give us guidance on how to behave, we are often scanning the environment and drawing on prior knowledge to try to figure out the norm. This is sometimes called our quasi-statistical instinct, wherein we make quick assessments about what the majority of people do or should do (Noelle-Neumann, 1993). We observe what others are doing or use information we have stored in our memories to make quick judgments about the prevalence of behaviors and attitudes. Any time we say to ourselves "most people probably…" or "the majority of people…" we are using our quasi-statistical instinct. However, it turns out human beings are not good natural statisticians. When we try to guess what everyone else is doing and thinking, we usually guess wrong.

Sexual Norm Misperceptions

When it comes to norms, perception is everything. This distinction between actual norms and perceived norms is a key starting point for a discussion of sexual norms. Actual norms refer to what most people actually do. For example, the average age of first intercourse for people in the United States is 17 years old (Mosher, Chandra, & Jones, 2005) and thus having first intercourse at 17 can be considered within the norm. It is worth noting that the concept of an actual norm can be problematic. It is important to keep in mind that a discussion of actual norms simply refers to what is common, not a value judgment about what should be common. Certainly having sex before or after age 17 does not make one "abnormal." However, understanding what is common and what most people do is helpful if we are to understand the main problem with sexual norms, which is how we perceive them. Perceived norms refer to what we imagine most people are doing. Perceived and actual norms are almost always mismatched, resulting in what is called misperceived norms. For example, try to guess what percentage of U.S. men have visited a pornographic website in the past month. What percentage of women in their 60s masturbate? What percentage of men in their early 20s have performed anal sex in the last year? The answers to these questions can be found by looking at large-scale, anonymous, nationally representative surveys of sexual behavior. Although people might occasionally be dishonest on surveys, most researchers take this behavior into account when conducting big surveys, so it is possible to get a good sense of the actual norm for many sexual behaviors. How many men did you guess visited a pornography website in the past month? It turns out about a quarter of men have done so (Buzzell, 2005). According to the National Survey of Sexual Health and Behavior (2010) almost a fifth of women in their 60s have masturbated in the past month. About 11% of men in their early 20s have performed anal sex. Maybe you guessed right on all of these, but chances are you overestimated the prevalence of most of these behaviors. In fact, 91% of studies on norms reveal a gap between our norm perceptions and the actual norm (Borsari & Carey, 2003). In the case of sexual norms, human beings consistently over-estimate the prevalence of sexual behavior in others. The actual norm (e.g., how much sex other people have) is usually less frequent than the perceived norm (e.g., how much sex we *think* other people have). Time and again studies show that we overestimate sexual behaviors. In one study, college students guessed that their peers have had oral sex with an average of five people, but in reality students in this study had oral sex with an average of two people. When asked how many people their peers had had any sexual experience with, they guessed the average number was about 16, but the actual number reported by students was 8 (Sullivan & Stephenson, 2009). These misperceived norms can have numerous, sometimes negative effects on our sexual well-being. Our sexual norm misperceptions can influence our sexual beliefs, attitudes, and even our behaviors.

Scholars have looked at norm perceptions for the prevalence of sexual activity, sexual attitudes, and gender roles in sex, to name a few (Barriger & Vélez-Blasini, 2013; Buunk & Bakker, 1995; Chia & Lee, 2008; Hall & LaFrance, 2012; Pariera, 2013; Sennott & Mollborn, 2011; Sullivan & Stephenson, 2009). Many studies have found that college students overestimate the prevalence of sexual behaviors, including oral sex, vaginal sex (Barriger & Vélez-Blasini, 2013); how often their peers have casual sex, and condom-less sex (Seal & Agostinelli, 1996); and the prevalence of sexually transmitted infections (STIs) and unplanned pregnancies (Scholly, Katz, Gascoigne, & Holck, 2005). College students also over-estimate permissive sexual attitudes, reporting that they think most of their peers are willing to have sex with people they are not emotionally involved with, even though they themselves do not feel that way (Cohen & Shotland, 1996).

Sexual norm misperceptions do not only affect young people. Men and women aged 18 to 80 overestimate all kinds of sexual activity, including how often other people view pornography, have anal sex, and engage in three-way intercourse (Pariera, 2013). The only time we seem to underestimate other people's sexual behavior is when it comes to elderly adults. Many people perceive a lack of sexual activity as totally normal for older couples (Ivey, Wieling, & Harris, 2000), even though large numbers of people over 70 are still sexually active (Herbenick et al., 2010). Older women even perceive that their peers are or should be asexual, even when they themselves are not (Jones, 2002). Studies show time and again that we are simply wrong when we guess what most people do and think when it comes to sex.

The Effect of Sexual Norms

Misconceptions about sexual norms are important because we use norm perceptions to guide our own behavior. "Underlying the formation of norms is the ubiquitous belief that there is a correct response for every situation" (Friedkin, 2001, p. 167). If there is a "correct" way to act or look or think, then not stacking up to others might cause anxiety and insecurity. Some researchers have found that the larger the gap between one's own sexual behavior and the perception of other people's behavior, the lower the person's sexual satisfaction (Sullivan & Stephenson, 2009). Other researchers have found that sexual norm misperceptions, though prevalent for all kinds of sexual behaviors, have no impact on satisfaction with one's sex life (Pariera, 2013). Although researchers have not been able to conclude how sexual norms affect our sexual satisfaction, feeling like we do not fall within the norm can certainly cause anxiety and affect our behavior.

There are some studies that suggest sexual norm misperceptions make us engage in more sexual activity. In other words, thinking that everyone else is doing it makes us feel like we should do it too and therefore we do it (Buunk & Bakker, 1995; Chia & Gunther, 2006). Young people in particular are much more likely to have sex if they perceive their peers to be doing so (Harper, Gannon, Watson, Catania, & Dolcini, 2004; Kinsman, Romer, Furstenberg, & Schwarz, 1998; Milhausen, Reece, & Perera, 2006; Sieving, Renee E., Eisenberg, Pettingell, & Skay, 2006). New college students who perceived casual sex to be common on campus tended to engage in more sexual activity during their time at college (Katz, Tirone, & van der Kloet, 2012). It might be tempting to think that people simply misperceive a norm in order to match their own behavior, but experimental and long-term studies have found that people adjust their behavior to fit the perceived norm over time (Berkowitz, 2004; O'Donnell, Myint-U, O'Donnell, & Stueve, 2003).

Descriptive norms seem to be the most influential when it comes to sexual behavior (Buunk & Bakker, 1995) and occasionally there is a disconnect between descriptive and injunctive norms. Many people believe that condoms should be used during sex with new partners, but many people assume others do not use condoms as often as they should. In one study on determinants of condom use among gay and bisexual men, researchers found that descriptive norms (thinking condom use was common) made men more likely to use condoms, while injunctive norms (thinking people should use condoms) did not have any effect (Franssens, Hospers, & Kok, 2009). Regardless of which type of norm is most influential, most researchers would argue that both types of norms influence our behavior, especially when combined (Lapinski & Rimal, 2005; Rimal & Real, 2003).

The Communication of Sexual Norms

Given the prevalence of misperceived norms, it is important to identify the origin of these misperceptions and examine how they are spread. Generally, norms are formed by direct observation, such as seeing what people do; passive observation, such as being told what someone else does; or complete inference, meaning guessing without any observation. Sexual norms are distinct from other norms because sexual behavior is almost always private, so norms are usually inferred from communication rather than direct observation. In other words, we learn about what is "normal" by communicating with others about sex and through media communication. Young people are more likely to have sex if they think their peers are having sex, which is influenced by peer communication. Sexual norms can also be communicated interpersonally by parents (Gillmore et al., 2002; Jaccard, Dittus, & Gordon, 2000; Sennott & Mollborn, 2011; Whitaker & Miller, 2000). When parents talk to their children about sex, their children are more likely to have positive attitudes and make more protective choices about sex (DiIorio, Pluhar, & Belcher, 2003). Young people whose parents do not talk to them about sex tend to rely more on communication with their peers to understand what is considered normal (Whitaker & Miller, 2000). While parent-child sexual communication has been shown to be beneficial in terms of promoting positive attitudes and better sexual health, parents also transmit norms about gender roles to their children. Parents tend to discuss sexual exploration more with their sons, but with their daughters they tend to discuss avoiding sex (Downie & Coates, 1999).

Scholars have also begun to accrue evidence that sexual norms are inferred from media consumption (Chia, 2006). Television provides a lot of information to viewers that can then be activated when using the quasi-statistical instinct to guess at the prevalence of something. Because sexual norms are less likely to be discussed openly in interpersonal situations, people might rely even more on mass media to assess sexual norms. The more people watch television, the more they perceive other people to be sexually active or have sexually permissive attitudes (Chia, 2006; Chia & Lee, 2008; Pariera & Sangalang, 2015). In one survey, a third of teens said that television and movies made sex seem more normal and about half said they learned about sex from these sources (The Kaiser Family Foundation, 1996). In fact, teens who watch a lot of television are more likely to initiate having sex (Collins et al., 2004). College students who watch reality dating television are more likely to endorse sexual double standards, believe dating is a game, and believe that men are purely sex-driven (Zurbriggen & Morgan, 2006). Television's communication of sexual norms is especially concerning because sex is often portrayed unrealistically and inaccurately. A quarter of sexual health storylines on primetime television portray the issue as stigmatized, and half of stories have moderate or weak information (Pariera, Hether, Murphy, de Castro Buffington, & Baezconde-Garbanati, 2014). Sex on television tends to reinforce gender norms and rarely portrays sexually responsible models (Brown, 2002).

Norms are communicated through social media, too. In one experiment, people who browsed a set of Facebook photos with a high prevalence of sexual content tended to perceive that their peers were more sexually active than people who browsed profiles with a low prevalence of sexual content (Young & Jordan, 2013). In a more positive example, media campaigns have been found to generate conversations about sex, which then have a normative effect, such as generating more positive attitudes about HIV prevention (Chatterjee, Bhanot, Frank, Murphy, & Power, 2009; Frank et al., 2012; Geary et al., 2007). Media campaigns have been able to promote responsible sexual behavior by increasing positive norm perceptions about contraceptive use, condom use, and delaying teen sexual activity (Keller & Brown, 2002).

Norms also influence communication about sex. Every culture has norms about who can talk about sex and what topics are appropriate. Some sexual communication norms might be negative. For example, when homophobic communication (i.e., using the term "gay" in a derogatory context) is perceived as normal, men are more likely to hold homophobic attitudes (Hall & LaFrance, 2012); and when adolescents rely on their peers and siblings for sexual communication, they are more likely to feel pressured to start having sex (Kornreich, Hearn, Rodriguez, & O'Sullivan, 2003; Sennott & Mollborn, 2011; Whitaker & Miller, 2000). However, most research finds that sexual communication is generally associated with positive outcomes. For example, when parent-child sexual communication is considered normal, parents are more likely to initiate it (Evans, Davis, Umanzor, Patel, & Khan, 2011; see also Coffelt, this volume). When communication about condoms is considered normal, people are more likely to use condoms (Elwood, Greene, & Carter, 2003; Geary et al., 2007; Limaye et al., 2012). Positive attitudes about sexual communication itself has been associated with more communication about sexual health and sexual pleasure (Alvarez & Villarruel, 2013). Normalizing communication between sexual partners is a key element to avoiding some of the unintended negative consequences of sex.

Promoting Sexual Well-Being With Sexual Norms

Because sexual norm misperceptions have some negative effects, there are many potential ways norms could be used to promote sexual well-being. For example, parents who perceive that talking to their child about sex is "normal" are more likely to do so; therefore, increasing this norm perception can result in more open sexual communication between parents and children. Some have suggested that teaching sexual communication skills to incoming college students could be an effective way to enhance sexual health and decrease sexual assault (Lindgren, Schacht, Pantalone, & Blayney, 2009). Moreover, because misperceived sexual norms seems to encourage people to engage in more frequent and riskier sexual activity, it might be possible to intervene by providing accurate information about the norm.

Social norms are so fundamental to human behavior that several communication theories include them as a key component, including The Theory of Planned Behavior (Ajzen, 1991), Spiral of Silence (Noelle-Neumann, 1993), Third-Person Effects (Davison, 1983), and Communication Accommodation Theory (Giles & Ogay, Tania, 2007), to name a few; but the most common theory used to promote sexual health is the Social Norms Approach (SNA). This theory posits that our behavior is influenced by what we think the norm is, and as we misperceive a norm, we incorrectly adjust our behavior to fit the norm. Therefore correcting the misperceived norm can lead to fewer risk behaviors and more healthy behaviors. The SNA researchers collect data about actual norms and provide that data to people to correct their misperceptions (Berkowitz, 2004; Wesley Perkins & Berkowitz, 2003). Providing information on actual norms, in a way that audiences find believable, can eliminate misperceptions about behaviors. Becoming more aware of our overestimation of other people's sexual behavior means no longer relying on our own biased guesses. For example, if a student entering high school believes that most of their peers are having sex, they are more likely to engage in sex than a student who does not share this perception. Informing the student that only a third of their peers have had sex by the end of ninth grade (CDC, n.d.) might remove some of the pressure to adhere to the misperceived norm.

Dozens of studies have shown that the SNA is effective in correcting misperceptions. Most of the research has shown that the SNA can decrease drinking on college campuses. Many college students overestimate the prevalence of binge drinking, and several colleges have been able to substantially reduce drinking by correcting these misperceptions (Perkins, 2007; Perkins, Meilman, Leichliter, Cashin, & Presley, 1999). Few studies have tried the SNA with sexual health topics, but one study found that it was possible to correct people's misperceptions about how much risky sexual behavior other people have, simply by giving them information about actual reported prevalence of behavior (Sullivan & Stephenson, 2009). There has also been success with this approach in encouraging college students to intervene in sexual assaults (Bruce, 2002; Kilmartin et al., 2008). Breaking down our norm misperceptions to increase sexual well-being has a great deal of potential, but we must also be aware of potential unintended consequences. Although many people fall within the norm more than they realize, some do not. In fact, campaigns aimed at correcting the misperceived norm could have a negative effect by further isolating some groups and individuals. Although researchers have not explored this potential, it is important to include sexual minorities, meaning people whose sexual identity, orientation, or practices differ from mainstream society, in research on sexual norms for this reason.

Where Do We Go From Here?

At this point it is clear that sexual norms are widely established through various communication channels, and they affect many aspects of our lives. Yet there is much that remains a mystery about how sexual norms work. When does sexual communication lead to norm misperceptions and when do we ignore it? For example, the next time you are watching television and sex is the topic, think about what sexual norms are being portrayed and whether you think they reflect reality. Even when watching fictional television shows we might say, "That is probably what most people think about sex" or we might say, "That is ridiculous and in no way reflects what people really think." Does it depend on who says it, how they say it, or how often they say it? If we understand exactly how we come to internalize sexual norms, we might be able to find ways to fend them off, especially those that are harmful or prejudicial.

It is also clear that sexual norms can be deeply entrenched, but we still do not know what kinds of social sanctions motivate us to follow a sexual norm. We tend to adhere to norms when we perceive there will be a social sanction if we do no not follow them (Rimal & Real, 2003), but this is more complicated with sexual behaviors because they are mostly private, and not subject to public scrutiny. For example, a couple might perceive that using female condoms is outside the norm, but it might not matter because no one else need know of their choice, and therefore no social sanction is imposed. However, proposing the use of a female condom to a new sexual partner might be strongly influenced by perceived norms, because the possibility of a social sanction from the new partner (rejection, being laughed at, etc.) is brought into the equation. The next time you are talking with a partner or friend about sex, think about what potential social sanctions could arise. Teasing, awkwardness, shaming, even ignoring a comment can be types of social sanctions that alter the way a person acts in the future. Which, if any, of these do you sometimes do to others or experience yourself? This question brings us to an important final point. Sexual norm communication research must be done with and by groups who face widespread social and even legal sanctions for their sexual attitudes or behaviors. Scholars, researchers, and individuals must continue to assess the impact of misperceived sexual norms on all groups of people. Ideally we would find ways to lessen the influence of misperceived norms, but as social creatures it is unlikely we will ever ignore sexual norms altogether. Although the existence of sexual norm misperceptions will probably never go away, we can still reflect on our own assumptions about what constitutes a normal behavior, whether or not we are wrong about what we think is normal, and how these beliefs affect us and those around us.

Dear Diary: Private Thoughts About Sexual Norms

The following research-informed fictional case studies illustrate how we sometimes think about, communicate about, and act on sexual norms. Three individuals privately reflect on their sex lives and compare themselves to what they think is normal.

Jamie. Fifteen-year-old Jamie is in the ninth grade and is happily dating Taylor, a boy she's had a crush on since junior high. Jamie and Taylor have been together for two months and have said "I love you" to one another. Jamie has never had vaginal intercourse and is contemplating doing so with Taylor. She writes in her anonymous blog: "Taylor is so sweet! He brought me a granola bar before class because he knows I always complain about how hungry I am during math. He's been doing a lot of stuff like that lately, and I think we're both feeling pretty into each other. I think I'm ready to have sex, but I'm worried two months isn't long enough to be with someone before having sex. Most of the other girls in my class talk about sex a lot, so I know it's not a big deal, but I don't want to be thought of as 'too young' or 'too old' to lose my virginity either. I also don't want to end up as one of these teen moms with all the drama, so I guess I have to get condoms from that clinic on 10th Street all the girls on my soccer team talk about. I wish someone could tell me exactly when the right time to have sex is and exactly what to expect."

Mateo. Twenty-seven-year-old Mateo has been in a relationship with Josh for a year. They just moved in together. This is the first time Mateo has lived with a boyfriend, but Josh lived with a serious boyfriend in the past. Mateo writes in his private online journal: "Just got the new dining room table today. Josh and I joked about having sex on it because that's what passionate couples in the movies do, but we didn't actually do it. I feel bad sometimes, like I'm supposed to be more spontaneous and adventurous with sex, but it doesn't work out that way. We did have anal sex recently, which I actually haven't done in a while. I feel like as a gay man I'm supposed to love it, but it's not my thing for some reason. I'm a little nervous that our sex life won't be as good as Josh's was with his ex. They were younger when they lived together, so they probably had more sex than we do, but that's not the kind of thing you're supposed to ask your boyfriend. Whenever we hang out with Tim and Alex, they seem so physically into each other and I'm like, wait, are we supposed to be like that too? I guess this is just part of being with someone for a long time."

Lori's diary. Lori's marriage ended in divorce last year at age 52. Although she wasn't entirely unhappy in her 28-year marriage, she is relieved the divorce is behind her. She did not think she would date again, but a co-worker asked her out a week ago and they hit it off right away. She writes in her journal: "I shouldn't even be saying this, but I'm quite interested in having sex with this new person in my life. I thought after the divorce I would go be an old lady and that would be the end of my sex life. I guess everyone assumes sex ends when you're 50 or when you start menopause, but here I am. I think a lot of men my age still want casual sex, but the women I know seem to disapprove. I don't even know what you're supposed to do these days, with texting and video-chatting and all that. I feel a little behind the times and like I'm going to make a fool of myself, but I guess I'll see what happens."

DISCUSSION QUESTIONS

1. Think about the way you communicate about sex when talking to friends, partners, parents, and when watching television. What sexual norms are brought up with these different groups of people? Do you think there are times you reinforce sexual norms in these conversations, and if so, how?

2. Consider the fact that we almost always "misperceive" other people's sexual behavior. What kinds of norm perceptions do you think would be the most difficult to change and why?

3. How do you think sexual norm communication affects groups whose sexual attitudes or behaviors are indeed outside the norm, (sex workers, for example)? How might people in these groups communicate about sexual norms differently or perceive different sexual norms?

4. After reading the diaries of Jamie, Mateo, and Lori, do you think any of them would benefit from having their norm misperceptions pointed out to them? Explain why or why not. Do you think they are more affected by descriptive or injunctive sexual norms?

5. Imagine you are designing a campaign to correct people's sexual norm misperceptions. Do you think the same strategies would work for Jamie, Mateo, and Lori? Explain why or why not. If applicable, how would you change your approach for each of the three case studies?

6. How do you think the advent of social media affects sexual norms? How does it affect the way people communicate about them? Is the way you communicate about sexuality on social media different than the way you communicate about it in other areas? If so, how?

References

Ajzen, I. (1991). The theory of planned behavior. *Organizational Behavior and Human Decision Processes, 50*(2), 179–211. http://doi.org/10.1016/0749-5978(91)90020-T.

Alvarez, C. P., & Villarruel, A. (2013). Sexual communication among young adult heterosexual latinos: a qualitative descriptive study. *Hispanic Health Care International, 11,* 101–110.

Barriger, M., & Vélez-Blasini, C. J. (2013). Descriptive and injunctive social norm overestimation in hooking up and their role as predictors of hook-up activity in a college student sample. *Journal of Sex Research, 50,* 84–94.

Berkowitz, A. D. (2004). *The social norms approach: Theory, research and annotated bibliography* (pp. 1–47). Retrieved from http://www.alanberkowitz.com/articles/social_norms.pdf.

Borsari, B., & Carey, K. B. (2003). Descriptive and injunctive norms in college drinking: A meta-analytic integration. *Journal of Studies on Alcohol and Drugs, 64,* 331.

Brown, J. D. (2002). Mass media influences on sexuality. *The Journal of Sex Research, 39,* 42–45. http://doi.org/10.2307/3813422.

Bruce, S. (2002). The "A man..." campaign: Marketing social norms to prevent sexual assault. Retrieved March 12, 2013, from http://www.socialnorms.org/CaseStudies/sexassaultprev.php.

Buunk, B. P., & Bakker, A. B. (1995). Extradyadic sex: the role of descriptive and injunctive norms. *The Journal of Sex Research, 32,* 313–318. http://doi.org/10.2307/3813355

Buzzell, T. (2005). Demographic characteristics of persons using pornography in three technological contexts. *Sexuality & Culture, 9,* 28–48. http://doi.org/http://dx.doi.org.libproxy.usc.edu/10.1007/BF02908761.

Centers for Disease Control and Prevention (CDC). (n.d.). CDC-Youth Online High School YRBS: Home Page. Retrieved March 8, 2013, from http://apps.nccd.cdc.gov/youthonline/App/Default.aspx?SID=HS.

Chatterjee, J. S., Bhanot, A., Frank, L. B., Murphy, S. T., & Power, G. (2009). The importance of interpersonal discussion and self-efficacy in knowledge, attitude, and practice models. *International Journal of Communication, 3,* 607–634.

Chia, S. C. (2006). How peers mediate media influence on adolescents' sexual attitudes and sexual behavior. *Journal of Communication, 56,* 585–606.

Chia, S. C., & Gunther, A. C. (2006). How media contribute to misperceptions of social norms about sex. *Mass Communication & Society, 9,* 301–320. http://doi.org/10.1207/s15327825mcs0903_3.

Chia, S. C., & Lee, W. (2008). Pluralistic Ignorance About Sex: The Direct and the Indirect Effects of Media Consumption on College Students' Misperception of Sex-Related Peer Norms. *International Journal of Public Opinion Research, 20,* 52–73.

Cialdini, R. B., Kallgren, C. A., & Reno, R. R. (2000). A focus theory of normative conduct: When norms do and do not affect behavior. *Personality and Social Psychology Bulletin, 26,* 1002–1012. http://doi.org/10.1177/01461672002610009.

Cohen, L. L., & Shotland, R. L. (1996). Timing of first sexual intercourse in a relationship: Expectations, experiences, and perceptions of others. *The Journal of Sex Research, 33,* 291–299.

Collins, R. L., Elliott, M. N., Berry, S. H., Kanouse, D. E., Kunkel, D., Hunter, S. B., & Miu, A. (2004). *Does Watching Sex on Television Influence Teens' Sexual Activity?* Retrieved July 21, 2015, from http://www.rand.org/pubs/research_briefs/RB9068.html.

Davison, W. P. (1983). The third-person effect in communication. *The Public Opinion Quarterly, 47,* 1–15.

DiIorio, C., Pluhar, E., & Belcher, L. (2003). Parent-child communication about sexuality: A review of the literature from 1980–2002. *Journal of HIV/AIDS Prevention & Education for Adolescents & Children, 5,* 7–32. http://doi.org/10.1300/J129v05n03_02.

Downie, J., & Coates, R. (1999). The impact of gender on parent-child sexuality communication: Has anything changed? *Sexual and Marital Therapy, 14,* 109.

Elwood, W. N., Greene, K., & Carter, K. K. (2003). Gentlemen don't speak: communication norms and condom use in bathhouses. *Journal of Applied Communication Research, 31,* 277–297. http://doi.org/10.1080/1369681032000132564.

Evans, W. D., Davis, K. C., Umanzor, C., Patel, K., & Khan, M. (2011). Evaluation of Sexual Communication Message Strategies. *Reproductive Health, 8,* 15–25.

Frank, L. B., Chatterjee, J. S., Chaudhuri, S. T., Lapsansky, C., Bhanot, A., & Murphy, S. T. (2012). Conversation and compliance: the role of interpersonal discussion and social norms in public communication campaigns. *Journal of Health Communication*, *17*, 1050–1067.

Franssens, D., Hospers, H. J., & Kok, G. (2009). Social-cognitive determinants of condom use in a cohort of young gay and bisexual men. *AIDS Care*, *21*(11), 1471–1479. http://doi.org/10.1080/09540120902883127.

Friedkin, N. E. (2001). Norm formation in social influence networks. *Social Networks*, *23*, 167–189. http://doi.org/10.1016/S0378-8733(01)00036-3.

Geary, C. W., Burke, H. M., Castelnau, L., Neupane, S., Sall, Y. B., Wong, E., & Tucker, H. T. (2007). MTV's "Staying Alive" global campaign promoted interpersonal communication about HIV and positive beliefs about HIV prevention. *AIDS Education and Prevention: Official Publication of the International Society for AIDS Education*, *19*, 51–67.

Giles, H., & Ogay, Tania. (2007). Communication Accommodation Theory. In B. B. Whaley & W. Samter (Eds.), *Explaining Communication: Contemporary Theories and Exemplars* (1st ed., pp. 293–310). Mahwah, N.J: Lawrence Erlbaum.

Gillmore, M. R., Archibald, M. E., Morrison, D. M., Wilsdon, A., Wells, E. A., Hoppe, M. J., … Murowchick, E. (2002). Teen sexual behavior: applicability of the theory of reasoned action. *Journal of Marriage and Family*, *64*, 885–897.

Hall, J., & LaFrance, B. (2012). "That's gay": sexual prejudice, gender identity, norms, and homophobic communication. *Communication Quarterly*, *60*, 35–58. http://doi.org/10.1080/01463373.2012.641833.

Harper, G. W., Gannon, C., Watson, S. G., Catania, J. A., & Dolcini, M. M. (2004). The role of close friends in African American adolescents' dating and sexual behavior. *Journal of Sex Research*, *41*, 351–362. http://doi.org/10.1080/00224490409552242.

Helms, S. W., Choukas-Bradley, S., Widman, L., Giletta, M., Cohen, G. L., & Prinstein, M. J. (2014). Adolescents misperceive and are influenced by high-status peers' health risk, deviant, and adaptive behavior. *Developmental Psychology*, *50*(12), 2697–2714. http://doi.org/10.1037/a0038178.

Herbenick, D., Reece, M., Schick, V., Sanders, S. A., Dodge, B., & Fortenberry, J. D. (2010). Sexual Behavior in the United States: Results from a National Probability Sample of Men and Women Ages 14–94. *The Journal of Sexual Medicine*, *7*, 255–265. http://doi.org/10.1111/j.1743-6109.2010.02012.x.

Ivey, D. C., Wieling, E., & Harris, S. M. (2000). Save the young—the elderly have lived their lives: ageism in marriage and family therapy. *Family Process*, *39*, 163–175.

Jaccard, J., Dittus, P. J., & Gordon, V. V. (2000). Parent-teen communication about premarital sex. *Journal of Adolescent Research*, *15*, 187–208. http://doi.org/10.1177/0743558400152001.

Jones, R. (2002). "That's very rude, I shouldn't be telling you that": Older women talking about sex. *Narrative Inquiry*, *12*, 121–143. http://doi.org/10.1075/ni.12.1.18jon.

Katz, J., Tirone, J., & van der Kloet, E. (2012). Moving in and hooking up: women's and men's casual sexual experiences during the first two months of college. *Electronic Journal of Human Sexuality*, *15* (March). Retrieved from http://www.ejhs.org/volume15/Hookingup.html.

Keller, S. N., & Brown, J. D. (2002). Media interventions to promote responsible sexual behavior. *The Journal of Sex Research*, *39*, 67–72. http://doi.org/10.2307/3813427.

Kilmartin, C., Smith, T., Green, A., Heinzen, H., Kuchler, M., & Kolar, D. (2008). A real time social norms intervention to reduce male sexism. *Sex Roles*, *59*, 264–273. http://doi.org/10.1007/s11199-008-9446-y.

Kinsman, S. B., Romer, D., Furstenberg, F. F., & Schwarz, D. F. (1998). Early sexual initiation: the role of peer norms. *Pediatrics*, *102*, 1185–1192.

Kornreich, J. L., Hearn, K. D., Rodriguez, G., & O'Sullivan, L. F. (2003). Sibling influence, gender roles, and the sexual socialization of urban early adolescent girls. *The Journal of Sex Research*, *40*, 101–110. http://doi.org/10.2307/3813774.

Lapinski, M. K., & Rimal, R. N. (2005). An explication of social norms. *Communication Theory*, *15*, 127–147. http://doi.org/10.1111/j.1468-2885.2005.tb00329.x.

Limaye, R. J., Rimal, R. N., Mkandawire, G., Roberts, P., Dothi, W., & Brown, J. (2012). Talking about sex in Malawi: toward a better understanding of interpersonal communication for HIV prevention. *Journal of Public Health Research*, *1*, 117–125. http://doi.org/10.4081/jphr.2012.e17.

Lindgren, K. P., Schacht, R. L., Pantalone, D. W., & Blayney, J. A. (2009). Sexual communication, sexual goals, and students' transition to college: implications for sexual assault, decision-making, and risky behaviors. *Journal of College Student Development*, *50*, 491–503. http://doi.org/10.1353/csd.0.0095.

Milhausen, R. R., Reece, M., & Perera, B. (2006). A theory-based approach to understanding sexual behavior at Mardi Gras. *Journal of Sex Research, 43*, 97–106.

Mosher, W. D., Chandra, A., & Jones, J. (2005). *Sexual behavior and selected health measures: Men and women 15–44 years of age, United States, 2002* (No. 362). CDC.

Noelle-Neumann, E. (1993). *The spiral of silence: public opinion, our social skin* (2nd ed). Chicago: University of Chicago Press.

O'Donnell, L., Myint-U, A., O'Donnell, C. R., & Stueve, A. (2003). Long-term influence of sexual norms and attitudes on timing of sexual initiation among urban minority youth. *Journal of School Health, 73*, 68–75. http://doi.org/10.1111/j.1746-1561.2003.tb03575.x.

Pariera, K. L. (2013). Misperceived social norms about taboo sexual behavior. *Electronic Journal of Human Sexuality, 16*. Retrieved from http://www.ejhs.org/volume16/Norms.html.

Pariera, K. L., Hether, H. J., Murphy, S. T., de Castro Buffington, S., & Baezconde-Garbanati, L. (2014). Portrayals of reproductive and sexual health on prime-time television. *Health Communication, 29*, 698–706. http://doi.org/10.1080/10410236.2013.774653.

Pariera, K. L., & Sangalang, A. (2015). The relationship between parental media consumption and parent-child sexual communication. In G. L. Kreps & J. M. Alpert (Eds.), *Proceedings of the 2015 DC Health Communication Conference*. Fairfax, VA: Center for Health Risk and Communication. Retrieved from https://mail.google.com/mail/u/0/#inbox.

Pariera, K. L., & Sangalang, Angeline. (2015, April). *Parents' Media Consumption and Parent-Child Sexual Communication*. Conference Presentation presented at the DC Health Communication Conference, Fairfax, VA.

Perkins, H. W. (2007). Misperceptions of peer drinking norms in Canada: Another look at the "reign of error" and its consequences among college students. *Addictive Behaviors, 32*, 2645–2656. http://doi.org/10.1016/j.addbeh.2007.07.007.

Perkins, H. W., & Berkowitz, A. D. (Eds.). (2003). Applications of social norms theory to other health and social justice issues. In *The social norms approach to preventing school and college age substance abuse: a handbook for educators, counselors, and clinicians* (1st ed, pp. 259–279). San Francisco: Jossey-Bass.

Perkins, H. W., Meilman, P. W., Leichliter, J. S., Cashin, J. R., & Presley, C. A. (1999). Misperceptions of the norms for the frequency of alcohol and other drug use on college campuses. *Journal of American College Health, 47,* 253–258. http://doi.org/10.1080/07448489909595656.

Rimal, R. N., & Real, K. (2003). Understanding the influence of perceived norms on behaviors. *Communication Theory, 13,* 184–203. http://doi.org/10.1111/j.1468-2885.2003.tb00288.x.

Scholly, K., Katz, A. R., Gascoigne, J., & Holck, P. S. (2005). Using social norms theory to explain perceptions and sexual health behaviors of undergraduate college students: An exploratory study. *Journal of American College Health, 53,* 159–166. http://doi.org/10.3200/JACH.53.4.159-166.

Seal, D. W., & Agostinelli, G. (1996). College students' perceptions of the prevalence of risky sexual behavior. *AIDS Care, 8,* 453–466. http://doi.org/10.1080/09540129650125641.

Sennott, C., & Mollborn, S. (2011). College-bound teens' decisions about the transition to sex: Negotiating competing norms. *Advances in Life Course Research, 16,* 83–97. http://doi.org/10.1016/j.alcr.2011.05.001.

Sieving, Renee E., Eisenberg, M. E., Pettingell, S., & Skay, C. (2006). Friends' influence on adolescents' first sexual intercourse. *Perspectives on Sexual and Reproductive Health, 38,* 13–19.

Sullivan, K. T., & Stephenson, K. R. (2009). Social norms and general sexual satisfaction: The cost of misperceived descriptive norms. *The Canadian Journal of Human Sexuality, 18,* 89.

The Kaiser Family Foundation. (1996). Teens on Sex: What They Say About the Media as an Information Source. Retrieved September 27, 2013, from http://kff.org/hivaids/teens-on-sex-what-they-say-about/.

Whitaker, D. J., & Miller, K. S. (2000). Parent-adolescent discussions about sex and condoms. *Journal of Adolescent Research, 15,* 251–273. http://doi.org/10.1177/0743558400152004

Young, S. D., & Jordan, A. H. (2013). The influence of social networking photos on social norms and sexual health behaviors. *Cyberpsychology, Behavior and Social Networking, 16,* 243–247. http://doi.org/10.1089/cyber.2012.0080.

Zurbriggen, E. L., & Morgan, E. M. (2006). Who wants to marry a millionaire? Reality dating television programs, attitudes toward sex, and sexual behaviors. *Sex Roles, 54,* 1–17. http://doi.org/10.1007/s11199-005-8865-2.

A Genealogy of Sexual Consent from the Social Contract to Sex-Positive Feminism

Larissa A. Brian

KEY TERMS

Sexual consent
Sex-positive feminism

Feminist history
Sexuality and law

Incapacity and disability

ABSTRACT

Historically, sexual consent laws have made assumptions that humans are rational, autonomous beings with a will and a capacity for speech. However, repeated instances of sexual violence against women and the proliferation of what we have come to call "rape culture," have called that presumed capacity into question. This particular chapter traces conceptions of consent throughout history by showing its evolutionary tract from 17th century political theory to feminist critiques that have spanned the course of several decades. This historical overview, also called a *genealogy*, will demonstrate the sexual oppression that women have experienced in being able to communicate sexual consent, and highlight the more recent feminist push towards enthusiastic or "affirmative" consent. The chapter ends with a closer look at the Affirmative Consent Law that has been implemented on California's college campuses and an actual court case that exemplifies the ways in which nonverbal communication complicates our understandings of sexual consent.

The human capacity for building sexual relations with others is underpinned by a capacity to communicate. Communication's relationship to the erotic life rests on the concept of sexual consent, the social and legal measure by which we deem sexual encounters as lawful or unlawful acts. The pervasive force of "rape culture," a term that has come to signify the normalization and everydayness of sexual violence, has instigated recent discussions about the definition of sexual consent, making it a frequent and urgent topic for public discussion. Questions about what consensual sex *is* and what it is *not* have, of late, become prominent issues of social concern. But even amidst this public conversation, these questions are not new. Discussions on sexual consent have long been fraught with debates about *who* can consent and what exactly it means *to* consent to another person. Such contestations are based primarily on criticisms towards consent's historical ties to the social contract that was thought to legitimate the origin of civil society. In the simplest terms, the social contract is a nonverbal contract that the individual has with the state (political/government apparatus). To protect one's property, an individual obeys certain rules that are conferred by the state, thus giving the state authority over the individual but also creating a tacit contract between the two.

Consent, as a contemporary communicative signifier for the legitimacy of sexual relationships, is derived from the origination of the social contract, a political model constructed in the 17th century for understanding the beginning of civil society as being formed through the *tacit*, or implied, consent of the governed. The notion of implied consent has lingered throughout our political and historical landscape, with consent coming to be understood largely as *silence*—particularly for women, who were thought to always be consenting to sexual activity, even without the verbal utterance of any kind of language. In this chapter, you will find a brief historical overview of women's capacity to express sexual consent, from the formation of the social contract to what we now call "sex-positive feminism," or feminism that focuses on women's sexual empowerment and reclamation of sexual desire in their own terms. Indeed, the concept of consent has come to function as a universal marker of sexual relations that shapes our most intimate experiences. Not only a theory, consent also serves as an ethical communicative practice, a foundation for negotiating and articulating one's desires to others. Key to our understandings of sexuality, consent holds great importance to our everyday lives.

The Beginning of Silence as Consent

When we think of the definition of sexual consent, we probably tend to think of it as *mutually* agreed upon sexual activity, an encounter that involves both parties agreeing to a particular sexual experience through talking and negotiating with one another through a combination of various modes of communication: verbal language, nonverbal body language, or even other communicative signs of some kind. However, historically speaking, this was not always the case. In an American context, well before the 20th centuries, and even into the 20th century, sexual consent for women was thought to be given by the nature of the marriage contract in which women became property to men. This meant that a woman's consent to get married also served as a perpetual and everlasting consent to sexual activity with her husband. Therefore, if a woman uttered "no" to sex with her husband, and it occurred anyways, it would not be looked at as rape, for a woman was perceived as always already saying "yes" to sex. As a signifier of consent, silence, indeed, meant "yes" at the time. Yet there is more here to the historical story of silence and how it came to signify *consent*.

The close relationship between silence and consent emerged out of the Enlightenment period, a historical era from the 17th to 18th centuries that privileged human reason, rationality, the acquisition of property, and individual autonomy. Intrinsic to this period was a focus on what was called the "social contract." For Enlightenment philosophers like John Locke (1689), Thomas Hobbes (1651), and Jean-Jacques Rousseau (1762), the social contract was a vision for how civil society came into being. These theorists thought that humans transitioned from a state of nature[1] into civil society so as to become citizens, have their rights protected by the government,

---

1. "State of nature" is another phrase that means a society without laws. Therefore, "civil society" means a society that is organized, governed, and internally structured by laws.

and to live cooperatively amongst others in a community (Hobbes, 1981; Locke, 1966; Rousseau, 1968). Such a vision was predicated on the idea of hypothetical consent—that if people were originally surveyed, they would have actively consented to being a part of civil society. But because this kind of original form of consent was not possible (since society was already formed), the social contract was framed in terms of *tacit* consent—that because people were living in a community of laws that protected human rights, they implicitly consented by virtue of carrying on their everyday activities and being a citizen of society. Unless one actively resisted or fled the country, then consent was assumed to be present, even in silence. Thus, humans were assumed to have made a contract with society so as to live safely and cooperatively with others in a shared community. Although each political theorist—now regarded as "contractarian" theorists—differed somewhat in his views on the actual social contract, all of them agreed on tacit consent as the ground for a political society. The concept of tacitness (being understood without being directly stated) translated to consent being largely understood as *silence*, which manifested most prominently in the arena of sexual consent.

Women's Struggle to Express Sexual Consent

Still don't understand the social contract...

Many feminist critiques that have laid significant charges against both the origination of the social contract and its implications on how we have come to interpret and define sexual consent. Over the past several decades, and even before, feminists and critical race theorists alike have challenged the underlying assumptions of the social contract, arguing that it not only justified silence as a form of sexual consent, but was also predicated on an exclusionary principle that omitted women and people of color. Moreover, such criticism highlighted the fact that women were unable to give any form of active sexual consent since silence constituted consent, thereby legally sanctioning rape and sexual violence against women. This is shown in suffragist Elizabeth Cady Stanton's claim in the *Declaration of Sentiments*, a document signed at the Seneca Falls Women's Rights Convention in 1848, that the marriage contract was a sanction for rape, in that a woman's consent to the institution of marriage signified her enduring consent to every sexual act thereafter (Stanton, 1848). Meaning, a woman could not sexually refuse her husband, for spousal rape was not considered rape at the time. To Stanton and other women's rights activists, women were unjustly thought to always already be consenting to sex, as silence (a lack of *yes* and *no*) was read as consent—a manifest reality of the social contract's emphasis on *tacit* consent. The feminist criticisms against the inherent patriarchal nature of the social contract are well woven through the 19th to 21st century.

Following Stanton, there were key historical moments where definitions of consent were contested as a result of the perceived injustice of tacit consent that originated in the social contract. These contestations are mostly situated in feminist and critical race theory that emerged most pervasively in the mid to late 1980s, a period in history that has been referred to as "second-wave feminism." Key feminist, political, and legal scholars have identified the problematic form of sexual consent, noting the ways in which the legal structure of consent is set up in such a way that women were *incapable* of expressing consent, particularly in a heterosexual context. Political theorist Carole Pateman (1988) has critiqued the social contract for upholding a fiction that women were included in civil society, when they were actually excluded from the beginning. In *The Sexual Contract* Pateman details the ways in which silence has come to define sexual consent for women as well as the ways in which the social contract was built on a sexist agenda intended to regard women as solely wives, and thus, as property (1988). During this time, feminist theorists like Andrea Dworkin (1987) and Susan Brownmiller (1975) argued that a woman's sexual consent to a man was impossible, given that the internal structure of consent maintained the patriarchal oppression of women, rather than equality or reciprocity. Feminist legal theorist and lawyer Catharine MacKinnon (1983) made similar claims, stating that the law's framing of consent was based on a sexist ideology of dominance and submission, and that without true equality, women could only be victims of rape, rather than autonomous sexual beings. Critical race theorists[2] expanded on this relationship between oppression and the social contract, noting that the formation of civil society was also built on a foundation of racism. Charles Mills' *The Racial Contract* (1997) explains the ways in which injustice, such as racism, was written into the social contract so as to build and maintain a society based on the terms of a white supremacy. Legal theorist Kimberlé Crenshaw (1991) made an

---

2. "Critical race theory" is a term within the scholarly area of study known as legal theory. It refers to the analysis of the relationship between race/racism and the law.

argument from a similar platform, contending that women of color were not deemed capable of being raped under the law, as they were seen to always be consenting to sex, a result of both racist stereotypes of Black (hyper)sexuality[3] and the residual impact of master-slave relations left over from plantation slavery. Critical race theory leaves us with the idea that people of color stand outside the social contract, and because of this, they are historically caught in a contradiction of not being capable of consent at the same time that they are seen as always already consenting. Taken together, these scholars have noted that historically, the legal structure of consent has excluded women, especially women of color, from having a legal capacity to express sexual consent. As such, these feminist scholars have argued that sexual consent was a term largely removed from the realm of women's experience in that they could not fully articulate desire in ways that were recognized and accepted by law.

Sex-Positive Feminism and Consent

Following these criticisms of the social contract and consent, sex-positive or what has also been called pro-sex feminism that emerged out of the feminist "sex wars" in the late 1980s attempted to return a sense of sexual agency to the conversation. Instead of seeing an impossibility of consent, like many feminists mentioned previously, sex-positive feminists do not see consent's historical ties to silence to be such a totalizing obstacle for women's sexual freedom. Rather, they encourage women to cultivate languages of consent that are empowering, explicit, and true to their desires. Feminists such as Gayle Rubin (1984) and Carol Queen (1997) have sought to reclaim and embrace female sexuality, and in doing so, encouraged women to speak about their desires. The end of this chapter will show the effects that sex-positive feminism has had on contemporary discussions and understandings of consent, especially with the publication of books like *Yes Means Yes* (2008) and *What You Really Really Want* (2011) that

---

3. The term "hypersexuality" refers to the cultural perception that some bodies (generally Black), are overly sexualized. This is largely due to racist historical myths about Black sexuality that white people conjured during chattel plantation slavery to justify the rape of Black women by White masters. In other words, if Black women were thought to always be consenting to sex (because of their "overly" sexual nature), then they could not, in effect, be raped.

advocate for an enthusiastic model of consent—where only "yes" indicates consent to a sexual act, not silence or the absence of a "no," what has also been referred to as "affirmative consent."

A leading text in the world of sex-positive culture, Carol Queen's *Real Live Nude Girl* (1997) has furthered this conversation on sexual autonomy and consent. Emerging out of San Francisco's sex-positive scene, and the erotic communities and subcultures therein, Queen discusses sexual consent by way of BDSM subcultures[4]. For instance, she embraces and celebrates all forms of sexual desire that women may have, including the desire to be sexually dominated. In this text, Queen personally recounts her participation in and experiences with public sex parties in San Francisco, asserting that the concept of "safe sex" and the most effective, and realistic conversations about sex, take place in S/M subcultures where contracts, negotiation skills, and "safe words" are celebrated. Queen implicitly advocates for enthusiastic consent and the importance of articulating one's desires, particularly through a "yes, no, maybe" list (a classic negotiation tool in S/M subcultures) where all parties involved can express what they erotically wish to do, what they would maybe like to do ("soft limits"), and what they would absolutely not wish to do ("hard limits") (Queen, 1997, p. 128).

This sex-positive model of consent that gestures towards an affirmative/enthusiastic model, has become most apparent in *Yes Means Yes: Visions of Female Sexual Power in a World Without Rape* (2008), the first book that really prompted the "yes-means-yes" consent campaign that we now see permeating several college campuses. In this book, a series of essays are dedicated to empowering women through the use of language to prevent sexual violence. "Beyond Yes or No: Consent as a Sexual Process," an essay in this pivotal book, sets out to (re)imagine the relationship between consent, power and what it means to have both language and a body in the world (Bussel 2008). In Rachel Bussel's essay, she attempts to think beyond the yes/no framework of consent, demonstrating that the articulation of sexual desire encompasses more than a simple yes or no response. As an alternative, she looks to the use of the yes/no/maybe list that is enacted by BDSM subcultures to negotiate forms of sexual play that push edges of

---

4. The term "BDSM" is an abbreviation that stands for Bondage-Discipline/Sadomasochism-Masochism. It is a term attributed to the sexual practices of particular subcultures that desire to more fully, and physically, experience the complex relationship between erotic pleasure and pain. Sadomasochism-Masochism is also sometimes referred to as "S/M", which you will see throughout this chapter.

both pain and pleasure. Invoking the Antioch College Consent Policy that worked to abolish the long-standing historical framework that equates silence with consent, Bussel advocates for affirmative consent, claiming that women need to become more vocal about what they want in their sexual lives. For Bussel, it is only through such verbal affirmation that erotic creativity, invention, and discovery can come into being; that is, it is only through language and the embrace of "consent as sexy," that a true partnership can emerge. Bussel states that, in order to transcend the yes/no dichotomy of consent, we must *play* with the language we've been given so as to change the conditions of historical constraint that women have to conditions of erotic possibility (2008).

A similar communicative model appears in Jaclyn Friedman's publication of *What You Really Really Want: The Smart Girl's Shame-Free Guide to Sex and Safety* (2011). In this honest, provocative, and funny guidebook, Friedman sets out to define sexuality in positive terms for women of all ages, demographics, and sexual orientations. Attending to the cultural norms that tend to slut-shame and guilt women into thinking that their sexual desires are dirty, perverse, and immoral, Friedman introduces a pedagogical step-by-step guide for how to reclaim female sexuality in a society that constantly seeks to dilute, eschew, or foreclose it. In the chapter entitled "Let's Talk About Sex Baby," Friedman broaches the communicative aspects of sexuality, arguing that there is a "dangerous" silence around sex for both women and men in which women are deemed "sluts" when they articulate their sexual desires, where men are socially conditioned to "conquer" their partners, sexually, rather than communicate with them (Friedman, 2011, p. 188). In light of this, Friedman writes that women can only express what they "really really want" through *direct* communication that departs from the normative narrative that views sex as something that just happens to us, as something that is deprived of agency and the discovery of pleasure. The direct communication that Friedman envisions can only be characterized by one's *enthusiastic* verbal expression of their own turn-ons, turnoffs, STD status, safe-sex practices, consent and boundaries, and expectations to their partner. She also argues that mutual risk and the willingness to be vulnerable in front of another are crucial components to effectively communicate about sex. She even lists key strategies for how to communicate in the sexual life when words do not come easily.

Consent in Real Life

To demonstrate an applied example of consent, this chapter will close with the recent implementation of the affirmative consent model across college campuses, with a focus on California's Affirmative consent law (SB 927) that was passed in the fall of 2014. In September of 2014 Governor Jerry Brown of California signed legislation that, in order for public colleges and universities to continue receiving state funds, they are required to implement policies on sexual assault and rape under the banner of "student safety." This state law is the first to fully respond to President Obama's initiative to end sexual assault and rape on college campuses. Looking closely at the text of the bill, one can see that the legal task in establishing a standard of "affirmative" consent is actually a task in *clarification* and creating a definitional argument for what, in fact, *consent* should constitute. The definition of affirmative consent is explained in the following excerpt from the bill:

> An affirmative consent standard in the determination of whether consent was given by both parties to sexual activity. "Affirmative consent" means affirmative, conscious, and voluntary agreement to engage in sexual activity. It is the responsibility of each person involved in the sexual activity to ensure that he or she has the affirmative consent of the other or others to engage in the sexual activity. Lack of protest or resistance does not mean consent, nor does silence mean consent. Affirmative consent must be ongoing throughout a sexual activity and can be revoked at any time. The existence of a dating relationship between the persons involved, or the fact of past relations between them, should never by itself be assumed as an indicator of consent. (Counsel Digest, 2014).

The law goes on to explicitly state that affirmative consent cannot be given from one who is "intoxicated," "asleep," "unconscious," or "unable to communicate due to a mental or physical condition." (Counsel Digest, 2014). In a court of law, rape is thought to have occurred if the "accused" did not make communicative efforts in receiving and ascertaining an affirmative "yes" from the complainant. It becomes clear in the language of the law that patterns of recognition are expected to emerge in sexual encounters between people when it comes to how they communicate sexual fantasy and desire. One could say that the law assumes that there is a communicative repertoire available to each individual, a box of terms, codes, and words available that can be easily communicated and understood by another. Unless otherwise *incapacitated* due to the aforementioned reasons, the law asks for the cultivation and establishment of "common" language that can render sexual desire fully knowable and "unambiguous" to the individual who can then articulate that clearly to another. However, we can only assume and imagine that language cannot always account for personal desires and that what we feel may not always be communicated so easily—through *words*—to others in a sexual encounter. In other words, communication may not always live up to the standards of this particular law, as verbal meaning can change from the personal to the social.

To reflect this expectation of clear communication, the affirmative consent law has created a new standard for sexual activity on college campuses in California, requiring that *each* sexual act be verbally and mutually consented to so as to prevent instances of sexual violence and rape. Calling for "clear" and "unambiguous" language, the affirmative consent model intervenes into the historical norm of tacit consent that was explained at the beginning of this chapter—the norm that silence constitutes a "yes" response. Instead, this particular model calls for the actual utterance of a "yes," to indicate consent, so that someone's silence is not misinterpreted as a signal of desire or intention. A measure like this one is predicated on what has been deemed "communicative sexuality," a model of consent that seeks to replace the social contract, by encouraging clear and ongoing conversation that can be easily understood by each person involved in a sexual encounter. If the conversation does not exist, or someone did not actively or verbally consent, then the encounter is read as rape.

The following is a summary of a court case that involves the rape of a woman with cerebral palsy who was unable to verbally consent, allowing us to more fully contemplate the effectiveness of something like affirmative consent in a real-life setting. Please take time to review it, as several of the discussion questions will ask you to think about how affirmative consent might be expressed in situations where difficulties in communication are present.

In a 2012 court case *Fourtin v. Connecticut*, a man was acquitted for raping a woman (in her mid-twenties) who has cerebral palsy and is unable to walk or verbally communicate. Attending an adult day care daily, the woman wrote out on a chalkboard to her care-taker that she had been sexually assaulted by her mother's boyfriend (Orlando, 2012). Fourtin was at first convicted of sexual assault but then appealed to the State Supreme Court that overturned the prior ruling on the grounds that the victim was not actually "physical helpless" in that she could communicate through "biting, scratching, moaning, hitting" or other modes of nonverbal communication to resist an unwanted act (Orlando, 2012). For Connecticut courts, "physical helplessness" usually involves a situation in which the victim is incapacitated due to alcohol, drugs, or some kind of physical unconsciousness. In this case, however, the victim was deemed *capable* of consent, even though she had an incapacity for speech and the court could find no "physical evidence" that the sexual act was unwanted. Testimonies from nurses at the day care only served to confirm the fact that, if the victim really wanted to resist something, she would struggle nonverbally (as she had done with the workers when she did not want to eat certain food or perform a certain activity).

[handwritten marginal note: "Disgusting" with arrows]

DISCUSSION QUESTIONS

1. Reflecting on the affirmative consent law, come up with a scenario in which you think something like affirmative consent would work effectively, and a scenario in which you think it may not work effectively. Explain your reasoning behind each.

2. Think of an example in the media (television, movies, songs, news, etc.) where consent was not communicated at all, or not easily communicated between people. What can we learn from this example and what communication advice would you give the individuals in this encounter?

3. How is the affirmative consent law challenged or complicated by situations where verbal communication cannot be made due to incapacity or disability (like in the situation with the woman with cerebral palsy)?

4. Think about your own personal circles of friends, family, or significant others. Is consent talked about and discussed? If so, how? If not, why do you think this is the case?

5. How do you see the relationship between silence and consent manifesting today? Think back to key moments in history that are explained above where silence (as tacit consent) served as a way to sexually oppress women.

6. What are your overall thoughts on affirmative consent? Do you think the feminist focus on "enthusiastic consent" can offer positive change and help lessen (or even end) continued instances of rape and sexual violence? What other communicative tools might we need to cultivate for this to happen?

References

Brownmiller, S. (1975). *Against our will*. New York: Simon and Schuster.

Bussel, R. K. (2008). Beyond yes or no: Consent as sexual process. In J. Friedman & J. Valenti (Eds), *Yes means yes: Visions of female sexual power and a world without rape* (pp. 43–52). Berkeley: Seal Press.

Crenshaw, K. (1991). Mapping the margins: Intersectionality, identity politics, and violence against women of color. *Stanford law review, 43.6*, 1241–1299.

Dworkin, A. (1987). *Intercourse*. New York: Free Press.

Friedman, J. (2011). *What you really really want*. Berkeley: Seal Press.

Hobbes, T. (1981). *Leviathan*. London: Penguin Books.

Legislative Counsel's Digest. (2014). Senate bill no. 967. *California's legislative information*, Retrieved from https://leginfo.legislature.ca.gov/faces/billNavClient.xhtml?bill_id=201320140SB967.

Locke, J. (1966). *The second treatise of Government*. J.W. Gough (Ed.). Oxford: Basil Blackwell.

MacKinnon, C. A. (1983). Marxism, method, and the state: Toward feminist jurisprudence. *Signs, 8.4*, 635–658.

Mills, C.W. (1997). *The racial contract*. Ithaca: Cornell UP.

Orlando, J. (2012) Summary of state v. fourtin. *OLR Research Report*. Retrieved from http://www.cga.ct.gov/2012/rpt/2012-R-0474.htm.

Pateman, C. (1988). *The sexual contract*. Stanford: Stanford UP.

Queen, C. (1997). *Real live nude girl: chronicles of sex-positive culture*. San Francisco: Cleis Press.

Rousseau, J. J. *The social contract*. (1968). M. Cranston (Ed). London: Penguin Books.

Rubin, G. (1984). Thinking sex: Notes for a radical theory of the politics of sexuality. In C. Vance (Ed), *Pleasure and danger: Exploring female sexuality*. London: Routledge and K. Paul.

Stanton, E. C. (1848). Declaration of sentiments. *Princeton University*. Retrieved from http://www.princeton.edu/~achaney/tmve/wiki100k/docs/Declaration_of_Sentiments.html.

CHAPTER 4

Beneath the Tangled Sheets: Examining Sexual Communication through Ecological Systems

Randal D. Brown & Daniel J. Weigel

 KEY TERMS

Sexual communication
Interpersonal communication

Relationship communication
Ecological systems theory

 ABSTRACT

Traditionally, sexual communication studies have mostly focused on the individual relationship partners or the interaction between them, but this limits our understanding because sexual communication is impacted by more than only individual or relationship factors. Rather, sexual communication occurs within broader social contexts. This chapter will examine the importance of these different social contexts using the framework of Ecological Systems Theory. We use a research-informed fictive case study to illustrate the complex, interacting components at each level of context, or system, that influence sexual communication. Weaving the case study through the Ecological Systems framework encourages us to consider external, often unnoticed or "behind-the-scenes" factors that influence the way a couple communicates about sex. We hope readers will walk away from this chapter with a wholesome appreciation of the complex dynamics that influence sexual communication between relationship partners.

Meet James and Zach

Our story begins with James and Zach, a couple in their mid-twenties who have been together since their early undergraduate years in college. Now, James and Zach live together as James pursues his graduate degree in advertising and Zach works for a local technology start-up. In general, both James and Zach are satisfied with their relationship. One morning, after reading an article from an online news source about the importance of communicating about sex with one's partner, Zach realized that he and James, while being intimate with one another since shortly after they started dating, had never really talked about sex together in a meaningful way. Sure, they had joked with one another and alluded to sex, but they never talked directly about whether or not they were happy with their sex life. Zach decided to broach the topic during breakfast.

"Babe, I just read this article and I realized—we've never talked about sex together."

James hesitated for a moment. "Well, do we need to? I mean, I think we both have fun during sex…"

"Right," said Zach, "but I don't think we've ever talked about being satisfied with …"

"We've been together for five years. We're spending our life together. I don't think now is the time to talk about it," James interrupted, bothered by the conversation.

"I don't mean to imply that we …"

"If you don't think we have a problem, then why even bring it up?"

"Because I just want to make sure you're satisfied, you know, sexually," said Zach, trying to calm the tone of the conversation. "I'm satisfied with our sex life, but I want to make sure that you're satisfied, too. And if you're not, we can talk about how to switch things up so you are. I'm only bringing this up because we've never talked about it."

"Obviously, I'm fine," James responded angrily. "Now, let's finish breakfast so we can meet up with Kristi and Shawn."

As Zach washed the dishes, he could not get his mind off of their conversation. *Why did James seem so unwilling to talk about sex with me? Doesn't he trust me? Is he unsatisfied and afraid to say it?* Zach finished the dishes hoping that James' shutting down the conversation was not a sign that he was becoming disengaged in their relationship.

Sexual Communication and Ecological Systems Theory

Though there are many different kinds of sexual communication, in this chapter we use the term sexual communication to describe the verbal or nonverbal interaction regarding sexual topics between partners in a romantic and/or sexual relationship. This definition includes discussing sexual preferences, desires, and fantasies; ways to improve each partner's sexual satisfaction; suggesting new sex acts or positions; or even asking a partner to "move a little to the left." Studies suggest that sexual communication is an important component of relationship and sexual satisfaction (e.g., Coffelt & Hess, 2014; Byers, 2005; Cupach & Metts, 1991). Despite this importance, many couples have sex before having a conversation about it (Ryan, Franzetta, Manlove, & Holcombe, 2007).

Through communicating about sex, partners learn more about one another by sharing thoughts, preferences, and suggestions that can enhance their relationship both sexually and emotionally. Accordingly, sexual communication has been given a lot of attention by researchers, though the majority of this research examines sexual communication from an individual or relationship standpoint. Following scholars including Duck (2011), Baxter (2011), and Manning (2014a, 2014b), we wish to challenge and thus extend previous research by acknowledging that communication does not simply occur between the partners in a romantic relationship. Instead, a couple's sexual communication is the result of each partner's beliefs, experiences, and the environment in which they exist. In the following sections we illustrate how environmental factors affect comfort with sexual communication and willingness to communicate about sex, ultimately determining the quality of a couple's sexual communication.

Take our fictive case study: Zach is left believing that James is becoming disengaged from their relationship because of James' unwillingness to talk about their sex life. This conclusion, while logical, is inadequate because it only focuses on James' reaction to that particular conversation. Zach is not considering broader explanations for why James avoids talking about sex. If we left the story here, we might conclude that Zach and James are heading toward a big argument or that James is unhappy with his sex life. However, we would only be giving ourselves a portion of the story, and in order to be accurate in our assessment, we need to paint a more complete picture.

To help us paint this more complete picture, we use Bronfenbrenner's Ecological Systems Theory, or EST (1977, 1986). Jones and colleagues (2011) used a classical representation of EST in their paper about sex therapy to identify multiple systems of influence on sexual dysfunction, arguing for therapy that looks at sexual problems within broader social context and emphasizes understanding instead of blame and guilt. We use Jones and her colleagues' application of EST to sexuality to build our case for EST's applicability to sexual communication.

A widely known theory in developmental psychology, EST affords a complete, all-encompassing, holistic lens through which we can examine human experience. EST proposes five different systems to help us understand how interactions between people take place. The five systems are the microsystem, containing the individual and people they interact with; the mesosytem, describing the interaction between microsystems; the exosystem, or institutional influences; the macrosystem, containing cultural and social norms, beliefs, and conventions; and the chronosystem, representing time. These five systems are nested within one another, such that the microsystem is contained in the mesosystem, the microsystem and mesosystem are contained in the exosystem, and so on.

EST extends our knowledge of relationship processes by wholly recognizing factors that affect our sexual communication. Often the factors outside of our romantic relationships are subtle, operating in the background. For example, most people would not recognize how their middle school sex education class affects their sexual relationships in college. Applying EST to sexual communication enhances our knowledge by recognizing the contributions of the different systems and illustrating that there is much more to an interaction than what is immediately present.

The Microsystem and the Mesosystem

The microsystem contains each partner, the people they interact with, and the relationship between each partner and the people with whom they interact (Bronfenbrenner, 1977; Jones et al., 2011). In our case study, this includes James, James' parents, James' friends, Zach, Zach's parents, and Zach's friends. The microsystem also contains the relationships between James and Zach, James and his parents, James and his friends, Zach and his parents, and Zach and his friends. A simpler way to think about the microsystem is that it not only includes various individuals, but also the relationships among those individuals. The second system of EST, the mesosystem, defines the interaction between microsystems, explaining how an individual's relationship with one person is influenced by the relationship they have with another (Bronfenbrenner, 1977; Jones et al., 2011). For example, the mesosystem explains how one person's communication with his parents impacts his communication with his partner. In this way, the microsystem is nested within the mesosystem. Another way to compare these two systems is to say the microsystem is where different people and relationships exist, and the mesosystem is where these different relationships are reconciled with one another.

To illustrate the complexity of the microsystem and mesosystem, we pick up with James and Zach. They have returned from a day of fun and laughter with their friends and are both in good spirits, though it is safe to say that the morning's discussion has not entirely faded from either of their minds. Zach decided to approach the topic again.

"Hey babe," he said. "I was wondering—could we talk a bit more about how we left things this morning? I don't like the way we left off."

"Sure, what's up?" replied James, cautiously open to the discussion.

"Well, when I brought up wanting to discuss our sexual satisfaction, you kind of put a stop to it. And I just want to find out—why did that make you uncomfortable?"

James hesitated, deciding that Zach was genuinely trying to understand instead of start an argument. "Yeah, I know. I guess I was caught off guard because I worry about what that means. We've been together for five years, and like—my parents have always said that 'relationships should be easy, not work,' and it looks like our friends—just look at Kristi and Shawn! They never talk about their relationship, it seems, let alone about sex. Isn't sex just supposed to happen? If we have to talk about sex, doesn't that mean something is wrong?"

Zach smiled, communicating his support for James. "I see, so you are assuming that—because I wanted to check in—that something must be wrong, based on what your parents have told you and what you see our friends doing?"

"Yes. And your bringing up the topic made me uneasy because it seems like everyone who is in a happy, healthy relationship doesn't need to talk about it."

"Well, I can tell you without hesitation that I am beyond satisfied, both emotionally and sexually. But I brought it up because we've never talked about it, and I figured it couldn't hurt to check in. I wanted to because I love you, not because I suspect we aren't on the same page."

James gave a weak smile. "I see that now. Thanks."

This interaction taught us that James' family's views on relationships and sexual communication (e.g., "relationships should be easy") and his perceptions of Kristi and Shawn's communication (e.g., "they never talk about anything") have led to James' discomfort resulting in his retreat from their earlier conversation. For James, if Zach wants to talk about their sex life, it must mean that something is wrong. This knowledge challenges Zach's previous suspicions and reassures him that James was not pulling away from their relationship.

However, so far we have only discussed two systems. As we are about to see, the microsystem and mesosystem are only two parts of a complex, dynamic equation.

The Exosystem

The exosystem contains institutions such as schools and the media (Bronfenbrenner, 1977; Jones et al., 2011). In school, sex education programs have an effect on students' sexual outcomes. As compared to abstinence-only sex education programs, which emphasize abstaining from any sexual activity whatsoever, comprehensive sex education programs, or those that teach students about contraception, have consistently led to better outcomes (e.g., increased sexual satisfaction and use of safe sex practices; Garcia-Retamero & Cokely, 2015; Jones et al., 2011). This evidence helps us consider how sex education might impact sexual communication. It could be that comprehensive programs lead to positive student outcomes as a result of candid discussion about sexual topics. Talking openly about sex in the classroom may lead to more comfort with talking about sex, resulting in increased sexual communication in their romantic relationships.

The media is another component of the exosystem, serving to communicate what is appropriate sexually. Through portrayals of sex scenes in movies and TV shows, song lyrics, and the presentation of idealized body types in magazines (e.g., Downing, Scrimshaw, Antebi, & Siegel, 2013; Lever, Frederick, & Peplau, 2006), the media presents an idea of what sexuality looks like in our culture. Depending on how well a person matches media depictions, the media can promote comfort or discomfort with one's sexuality, leading to comfort or discomfort with communicating about sex. If a person is not comfortable with her or his sexuality and with talking about sex, she or he is probably going to have poor-quality sexual communication as compared to someone who is comfortable.

Our couple's conversation continues:

"So, what else do you think might have made you shy away from talking about our sex life?" Zach asked kindly. He wanted to learn about James' prior experiences communicating about sex so that he could help James feel more comfortable discussing such things with him.

"Well, I mean, I don't know," replied James, shrugging. "I guess sex wasn't talked about much when I was growing up."

"Not even in school?" exclaimed Zach. "Like, you had sex ed, right?"

James paused before speaking. "Well, yes, but they really didn't talk about sex except that it was for having kids, how your body changes, and the only way to be safe with sex was to avoid it until you got married."

Zach nodded. "Were you taught about gay relationships at all? Were they at least mentioned?"

"Not really. Sex was talked about as something you do when you want to have kids. If it wasn't, then it was just the negative stuff, like chlamydia and unplanned pregnancy. And the only time gay couples were mentioned was when they talked about HIV… 'gay sex will likely lead to serious infections,' they said."

"Wow," said Zach. "I guess that would make sex a tricky thing to talk about. My school did a good job talking about all kinds of relationships…very different experience."

Over the next week, James and Zach left the topic of sexual communication alone, although Zach did start making connections between James' previous experiences and his current response to sexual communication. He normally would not think anything of these connections, but now they seemed obvious. When watching movies and television shows together, they usually watched shows involving straight couples: boy meets girl, girl falls in love with boy, boy and girl get married, have babies, and live happily ever after. Few shows they watched had openly gay characters involved in long-term relationships and those that did tended to portray them as stereotypical, flamboyant men who existed primarily for comic relief. These representations were different than those from Zach's adolescence, when he watched a number of indie films about gay couples with his parents. It became clear to Zach that not only was James neglected the comprehensive sex education that fostered comfort with sexuality, but he also lacked a proper model of what a gay man and a gay relationship is, instead left with stereotypes and stigma. In turn, this lack of positive representation might increase James' discomfort with being gay, which will make him less comfortable communicating about related topics such as sex with his romantic partner.

In other words, James' exosystem highlighted heterosexual relationships, with gay relationships only talked about in a negative manner in school. The media that James consumed perpetuated this negativity, endorsing stereotypes through its depiction of gay characters. On the other hand, Zach's exosystem exposed him to positive sexual communication through discussions of orientation in sex education and watching gay-friendly films with his parents. In the exosystem, sexual communication is influenced by different institutions and their endorsements of different perspectives. This can result in comfort or discomfort with sexuality and sexual communication. Zach grew up in an environment that was comfortable with gay relationships, which translates to his willingness to communicate with James. James' negative experiences resulted in his unwillingness to talk about sex. As a result, James shut down the conversation with Zach.

The Macrosystem

The macrosystem is made up of broad cultural and social influences, such as gender roles and religious doctrines (Bronfenbrenner, 1977; Jones et al., 2011). The macrosystem contains the overarching norms proscribed by society, culture, and religion that then guide the exosystem. Society has been criticized as deeming legitimate only those same-sex relationships that correspond with conventional heterosexual norms, such as being emotionally and sexually monogamous (Kleinplatz & Diamond, 2014) and religious debate over the legality of same-sex marriage (Herek, 2006). Further, a person's sexuality is interconnected with their gender identity (Impett, Muise, & Peragine, 2014), suggesting that cultural differences in gender norms will also affect how an individual expresses him or herself sexually. Gender norms are exemplified in Western cultures, where masculinity proscribes men as being strong and emotionally non-expressive (Worth, Reid, & McMillan, 2002). If you do not follow these conventions, you risk social stigmatization. As with the exosystem, the macrosystem likely influences individuals' sexual communication in an indirect manner by way of comfort with and willingness to communicate. To explore these ideas, we again return to our couple.

While enjoying lunch together on a sunny afternoon, Zach decided to share his realizations with James. James, hesitant at first, was amazed by the connections Zach was able to make.

"This all makes so much sense," said James. "I never identified with those characters on TV! I wondered if I'd been doing gay all wrong! I really haven't been comfortable with my sexuality because I felt it wasn't something that could be expressed—I was told it was bad to be who I was. From the religious perspective at least. It was like I couldn't be a real man and be gay."

"Well, I think that's a big component," Zach replied. "I know you had a hard time with religion. I can't really contribute, because religion was on the outskirts of my upbringing. But I get what you're saying about being a man—one time my dad caught me walking around in my mom's heels as a kid. Dad paused and stared. And then he said, 'You look good.' And at dinner we talked about becoming a boy and a girl and all that….and how it didn't matter as long as you were yourself."

"I wish I'd had that from a young age," replied James. "Your family is amazing."

This interaction helps illustrate the power of the macrosystem. James' discomfort with sexual communication can be traced back to his conflict with his religious upbringing and what he thought he ought to be as a man. This discomfort can translate into poor sexual communication. After all, how productive can a conversation be if you are feeling somewhat ashamed by the topic altogether? Zach's experiences contrast with James', preparing him for purposeful communication about sex resulting from his learned comfort with talking about sexual topics.

The Chronosystem

The last system is the chronosystem, best represented by time. Time includes different values such as historical period and relationship length, among others (Jones et al., 2011; Rosa & Tudge, 2013). When it comes to sexual communication, historical time period can dictate one's comfort with communicating sexually. For example, during the repression of the 1940s, couples might be considerably less likely to communicate about sex than in the freedom of the 1970s (Canaday, 2009; Pettit & Hegarty, 2014; Hammack, Mayers, & Windell, 2011; Mustanski, Kuper, & Greene, 2014). As such, it is appropriate to assume that James and Zach's sexual communication would look very different in the 1940s than it does today. Similarly, couples might be less likely to disclose their sexual preferences at the start of their relationship when they are still guarded and getting to know one another compared to when they have been together for a number of years (see Byers & Demmons, 1999). Time can influence how couples talk about sex within their relationships, from the greater social norms of the decade to the amount of time romantic partners have been together. Although James and Zach still have difficulty communicating about sex after five years together, the communication discrepancies can be resolved in an easier manner because of their commitment to and investment in each other.

"Babe, you know, after five years together I'm surprised that we've never talked about this," James said kindly. "But I'm really, really glad we did."

"Me too," replied Zach. "I just hope that we can keep the doors open. And that you can feel comfortable talking with me about anything, including what we do in the bedroom." He winked.

"I will," said James. "If anything else, I think these things we've talked about don't need to negatively affect our relationship. We've been together for five years where nothing but value and appreciation has grown. It's time to let that happen with sex, too."

It is here that we leave James and Zach. After five years together, the couple is very much in love and continues to learn a great deal about each other. By communicating about sex, they learned why each of them initially approached sex talk as they did. Zach was open and ready to talk about sexual topics because his relationships with parents, friends, and experiences in school and with the media led to a greater comfort with sexuality, both in general and as it applied to himself and his interpersonal relationships. James was avoidant and uncomfortable with talking about sex as a result of his parents' avoidance of the topic, negative representations in sex education, and negative experiences with the media and religion. This contributed to James' discomfort, both with his own sexuality and with sex in general. Sexual communication is so much more than the exchange of words between James and Zach: it is the product of the influence and interaction of the five Ecological Systems.

Conclusion

With the help of our fictive case study, we emphasized the importance of acknowledging the multiple systems that affect the quality and quantity of a couple's sexual communication. As we have seen, factors in each of EST's five systems create a complex dynamic within which a couple interacts and communicates. It is our hope that readers will be mindful that the person and persons they are communicating with are bringing much more to the conversation than is immediately present. This is particularly true for topics littered with cultural and social taboos, such as sexual communication.

DISCUSSION QUESTIONS

1. This chapter provided examples of factors influencing sexual communication at each system, but the list is by no means comprehensive. What factors were not discussed that might impact a couple's sexual communication?

2. What are the barriers to successful sexual communication?

3. How can these barriers be addressed in order to aide in successful sexual communication?

4. In what ways is sexual communication similar to more general (non-sexually specific) relationship communication? In what ways are they different?

5. Is sexual communication important? Is it important to talk about sex before having sex?

References

Baxter, L. A. (2011). *Voicing relationships: A dialogic perspective.* Thousand Oaks, CA: Sage.

Bronfenbrenner, U. (1977). Toward an experimental ecology of human development. *American Psychologist, 32,* 513–531.

Bronfenbrenner, U. (1986). Ecology of the family as a context for human development: Research perspectives. *Developmental Psychology, 22,* 723–742.

Byers, E. S. (2005). Relationship satisfaction and sexual satisfaction: A longitudinal study of individuals in long-term relationships. *Journal of Sex Research, 42,* 113–118.

Byers, E. S., & Demmons, S. (1999). Sexual satisfaction and sexual self-disclosure within dating relationships. *Journal of Sex Research, 36,* 180–189.

Canaday, M. (2009). *The straight state: Sexuality and citizenship in 20th-century America.* Princeton, NJ: Princeton University Press.

Coffelt, T. A., & Hess, J. A. (2014). Sexual disclosures: Connections to relational satisfaction and closeness. *Journal of Sex & Marital Therapy, 40,* 577–591.

Cupach, W. R., & Metts, S. (1991). Sexuality and communication in close relationships. In K. McKinney & S. Sprecher (Eds.), *Sexuality in close relationships* (pp. 93–110). Hillsdale, NJ: Lawrence Erlbaum Associates.

Downing, M. J., Schrimshaw, E. W., Antebi, N., & Siegel, K. (2013). Sexually explicit media on the Internet: A content analysis of sexual behaviors, risk, and media characteristics in gay male adult videos. *Archives of Sexual Behavior, 43,* 811–821.

Duck, S. (2010). *Rethinking relationships.* Thousand Oaks, CA: Sage.

Garcia-Retamero, R., & Cokely, E. T. (2015). Simple but powerful health messages for increasing condom use in young adults. *Journal of Sex Research, 52,* 30–42.

Hammack, P. L., Mayers, L., & Windell, E. P. (2011). Narrative, psychology, and the politics of sexual identity in the United States: From "sickness" to "species" to "subject." *Psychology and Sexuality, 4,* 219–243.

Herek, G. M. (2006). Legal recognition of same-sex relationships in the United States: A social science perspective. *American Psychologist, 61,* 607-621.

Impett, E. A., Muise, A., & Peragine, D. (2014). Sexuality in the context of relationships. In D. L. Tolman & L. M. Diamond (Eds.), *APA Handbook of Sexuality and Psychology* (vol. 1, pp. 269–316). Washington, DC: American Psychological Association.

Jones, K. E., Meneses da Silva, A. M., & Soloski, K. L. (2011). Sexological Systems Theory: An ecological model and assessment approach for sex therapy. *Sexual and Relationship Therapy, 26,* 127–144.

Kleinplatz, P. J., & Diamond, L. M. (2014). Sexual diversity. In D. L. Tolman & L. M. Diamond (Eds.), *APA Handbook of Sexuality and Psychology* (vol. 1, pp. 245–268). Washington, DC: American Psychological Association.

Lever, J., Frederick, D. A., & Peplau, L. A. (2006). Does size matter? Men's and women's views on penis size across the lifespan. *Psychology of Men & Masculinity, 7,* 129–143.

Manning, J. (2014a). A constitutive approach to interpersonal communication studies. *Communication Studies, 65,* 432–440.

Manning, J. (2014b). Exploring family discourses about purity pledges: Connecting relationships and popular culture. *Qualitative Research Reports in Communication, 15,* 92–99.

Mustanski, B., Kuper, L., & Greene, G. J. (2014). Development of sexual orientation and identity. In D. L. Tolman & L. M. Diamond (Eds.), *APA Handbook of Sexuality and Psychology* (vol. 1, pp. 597–628). Washington, DC: American Psychological Association.

Pettit, M., & Hegarty, P. (2014). Psychology and sexuality in historical time. In D. L. Tolman & L. M. Diamond (Eds.), *APA Handbook of Sexuality and Psychology* (vol. 1, pp. 63–78). Washington, DC: American Psychological Association.

Rosa, E. M., & Tudge, J. (2013). Urie Bronfenbrenner's theory of human development: Its evolution from ecology to bioecology. *Journal of Family Theory & Review, 5,* 243–258.

Ryan, S., Franzetta, K., Manlove, M., & Holcombe, E. (2007). Adolescents' discussions about contraception or STDs with partners before first sex. *Perceptions on Sexual and Reproductive Health, 39,* 149–157.

Worth, H., Reid, A., & McMillan, K. (2002). Somewhere over the rainbow: Love, trust and monogamy in gay relationships. *Journal of Sociology, 38,* 237–253.

SECTION 2

Sexuality, Culture, and Identity

CHAPTER 5

Intercultural Same-Sex Relationships: Masculinities, Sexualities and Communication across Borders

Gust A. Yep, Ryan M. Lescure, & Jace Allen

 ## KEY TERMS

Gay male relationships	Intercultural communication	Sexual systems
Gender systems	Racialization	

 ## ABSTRACT

With the emergence of new communication technologies, increasing global presence of gay and lesbian identities, and the creation of niche markets for gay and lesbian travel, intercultural same-sex relationships are becoming more visible than ever before. Through the interplay and collision of different local cultural meanings and global gay identities and movements, communication in intercultural same-sex relationships is rife with possibilities and pitfalls. Following two moments (Mexico City and Los Angeles) in the lives of a fictional same-sex intercultural couple—Juan Manuel, a masculine man from urban Mexico, and Daniel, an androgynous man originally from rural United States—we explore, in this chapter, some of these intercultural communication dynamics. More specifically, we examine different sexual and gender systems (e.g., cultural conceptions of sexual identity based on gender object choice and sexual aim; cultural conceptions of masculinity and gender performance) as well as racial and class systems (e.g., different racialization processes in Mexico and the United States; class assumptions based on race and culture) as Juan Manuel and Daniel travel across cultural and national borders with Oso, their sensitive and affectionate dog.

In recent years, the availability of new communication technologies (e.g., the Internet, smartphones, email, video chatting, social media) have made geographical constraints to communication less significant, facilitating interpersonal contact between people around the world. While these technologies have increasingly connected individuals who have access to them, they have also positively and uniquely transformed the way that lesbian, gay, bisexual, transgender, and queer (LGBTQ) individuals form and navigate relationships, community, and culture. Prior to the advent and widespread use of the Internet, certain physical spaces like bars, clubs, community centers, adult bookstores, and bathhouses were prominent sites for interaction between LGBTQ individuals. These spaces were often not ideal due to issues related to access, physical harm, police harassment, and the distinct possibility of being publicly outed (Grov, Breslow, Newcomb, Rosenberger, & Bauermeister, 2014). New communication technologies have opened virtual spaces for communication, which tend to be less stigmatized, less public, and more accessible than physical ones (Grov et al., 2014; Ross, 2005). Additionally, in the form of cybersex, the Internet allows for sexuality without close proximity and the physical presence of bodies (Ross, 2005).

New communication technologies also create new pitfalls for LGBTQ relationships. For example, the Internet facilitates the spread of what Halberstam (2012) describes as a distinctly urban, monolithic, and decidedly Western "global gay" identity. This could be understood both as a potentially liberating sexual discourse and as an imperialistic cultural imposition. Additionally, the Internet facilitates global gay and lesbian travel, which potentially advances Western imperialism and neoliberalism while also increasing intercultural contact and the visibility of LGBTQ identities (Coon, 2012; Mitchell, 2011; Puar, 2002). In this chapter, we aim to extend this discussion by focusing on two moments in the life of a fictional intercultural same-sex couple.

Scene 1: Mexico City

After spending several nights entertaining buyers from Buenos Aires, Lima, Rio, and Santiago, Juan Manuel Rosales, a top executive for a European clothing designer, was ready to take a few days off. Cruising in his brand-new red BMW through the heavy Friday evening traffic in Mexico City, Juan Manuel—heading back to his penthouse in La Condesa—was hoping for a quiet evening while ignoring the pings coming from his digital devices. His dashboard clock read 6:20 when he pulled into the garage.

Oso, his affectionate Keeshond, greeted him excitedly as he started peeling off his Prada suit. Consuela, his maid, had fresh flowers everywhere and a note greeting him: "Welcome home, Señor Juan Manuel. Oso was restless today so I took him on a long walk after I fed him at 5. He should be tired now. Your dinner is in the refrigerator. Next to this note is a bottle a Chilean red, which, I've been told, will go nicely with your dinner. I know you don't want dessert... but I left you some flan—made from Carlota's recipe!—just in case you feel like indulging. I'll pick up your clothes from the cleaners when I come back on Monday morning. In case you want to wear your leather pants this weekend, they should be ready by tomorrow morning. If you need anything, please call. I'll be at Aunt Carlota's house. Have a wonderful weekend! C."

Juan Manuel smiled and felt grateful. Consuela has been working for him for several years and Carlota was Juan Manuel's family maid for almost three decades until she retired. Oso followed Juan Manuel around the house when he heard another series of pings on his iPad. After a few more, he realized that it was Daniel who was trying to reach him.

By all accounts, Daniel Norris was an outsider, both in his early life and adolescence. Born into a white farming family in the small town of Burlington, Wisconsin, Daniel often sought to escape the vacuity of his everyday life. His escape mainly came in the form of books, painting, and going for long walks on the farm. Although he loved and was good at schoolwork, he hated going to school. There, his classmates would tease him incessantly about his lisp, his lanky build, his long blonde hair, and his androgynous demeanor. Daniel eventually left everything behind when he was accepted into the Architecture and Urban Design program at UCLA after finishing high school. When he graduated *summa cum laude* with a Bachelor's degree, he was anxious to enter the job market. Daniel submitted countless applications and was invited to interview several times, but he never landed a position as an architect. After fruitlessly searching for six months, his patience and his money ran out. Friendless and broke, Daniel applied for a job at a clothing boutique for plus-size women. The owner of the boutique was impressed with Daniel's gentle, kind demeanor. She hired him immediately and Daniel got promoted to assistant manager in a matter of months. Though he was the only male employee at the boutique, Daniel found himself fitting in perfectly with his coworkers. In fact, he finally felt at home.

Juan Manuel and Daniel started as "cyber fuck buddies." Magnetically drawn to each other—Daniel to Juan Manuel's dark hair, olive skin, and sculpted muscles and Juan Manuel to Daniel's slender build, hazel eyes, and boyishness—their first online encounter was intense. Soon they were learning a lot about each other. Daniel saw pictures of Oso and Juan Manuel's mother. Daniel confessed about the shame he felt about his lisp and the torment he experienced at school, which Juan Manuel found heartbreaking. Juan Manuel was drawn to Daniel's honesty and vulnerability while Daniel was attracted to Juan Manuel's protectiveness and confident masculinity. When Daniel's friends invited him to join them in Puerto Vallarta, he decided to finish his vacation in Mexico City with Juan Manuel.

It was magic. When Juan Manuel and Daniel met in person, it felt like no one else existed in the world. Oso approved and would sit between them to get a double petting. A few months later, they became partners.

Although it was only a lateral move in the international design house, Juan Manuel decided to pursue it so that he and Daniel can finally live together. Juan Manuel was excited that he and Daniel would get to be with each other without the dreaded anticipation of imminent departure and weeks without long embraces in bed as they shared dreams, hopes, and secrets.

Juan Manuel's mother decided to have an intimate bon voyage dinner for him and to welcome Daniel into the family. For this occasion, she asked Carlota to come back to prepare a special meal with Consuela's help. For a family that was legendary for large and memorable parties, this was a small group of eight: the mother; Juan Manuel's best childhood friend Agustín and his girlfriend; Juan Manuel's best college friend Julio and his boyfriend; Juan Manuel's younger sister Ana Cecilia; and Juan Manuel and Daniel, the guests of honor. Oso was happy to see everybody together and the prospect of savoring Carlota's cooking again.

As the guests arrived, they all commented on the warm and enchanting setting—the entire house was lit with candles of all shapes and sizes. Conversation over dinner was lively and, at times, boisterous—but Daniel felt welcome and included. When Carlota brought out Juan Manuel's favorite desserts, his mother spoke. She directed her gaze to Juan Manuel. "I'm going to miss you," she said, before addressing Juan Manuel and Daniel together. "I want to welcome Daniel, Juan Manuel's special friend into the family. May you be very happy in California."

The rest raised their glasses and said, "Yes, to Daniel, Juan Manuel's special friend!"

Although Daniel felt comfortable with the family, he was unaccustomed to be called a "special friend." "Why not 'boyfriend'?" he wondered after noticing Agustín's girlfriend being referred to as such. Juan Manuel didn't seem to mind and Daniel started doubting his reaction. Getting ready to retire for the evening, Juan Manuel's mother announced, "It's getting late for this old lady but please stay and enjoy each other" before turning to Juan Manuel and Daniel with some motherly instructions, "You two should stay here tonight. I hope Juan Manuel's old bed is not too small for the two of you. Carlota and Consuela will make your favorite breakfast in the morning." After hugging and kissing everybody, the mother said, "I love you" and the couple responded, "We love you too and have a good night." Immediately after, Carlota left for her old room while Consuela presented the group with after-dinner drinks.

Agustín, who has been drinking the most over dinner, turned to Daniel, "Are you a good cook?" He continued, "Juan Manuel won't have Consuela to look after him in LA."

"I cook, but nobody can do it like Carlota," Daniel responded graciously.

"We must talk to Carlota in the morning to get her to share her secret recipes with you. And Consuela to tell you how to take care of Juan Manuel, the man of the house."

Agustín's girlfriend interrupted, "Agustín, Daniel is not a maid. They are a couple."

"I know. But didn't Milagros do all that?" Agustín responded.

Looking puzzled, Daniel asked, "Who is Milagros?"

"Milagros was Juan Manuel's girlfriend. They talked about getting engaged, but Milagros broke it off." Agustín took another sip of his after-dinner drink.

"That was a long time ago," Juan Manuel clarified, feeling a little embarrassed.

"Yes, but you are still good friends. This shows the kind of man you are, Juan Manuel. I couldn't stay friends with a woman who breaks up with me," confessed Agustín as his girlfriend squeezed his hand to get him to stop talking.

Julio's boyfriend jumped in, "It's not the same for us, Agustín. We don't have a woman and a man—we are two men." He quickly added, "If Julio and I decide to get married one day, we are 'husband and husband'—not 'husband and wife.'"

"But aren't you the *pasivo* (sexual bottom)?" Agustín earnestly asked Julio's boyfriend, who is undeniably the less masculine one in the couple.

"Yes, but I don't cook and clean for Julio," said the boyfriend. Then he added, "This doesn't mean that Juan Manuel is the *activo* (sexual top) and Daniel is the *pasivo!*"

Annoyed, Ana Cecilia asked, "Haven't you heard of *internacionales* (sexual versatile)?"

"For me, it is about what partners like. It is about pleasure… and love," Juan Manuel spoke holding Daniel's hand. Daniel nodded and smiled.

The conversation continued late into the night. When Oso led the couple to Juan Manuel's old bedroom, Daniel, feeling the warmth of the candlelight and Juan Manuel's family, wondered about living as a gay man and a gay couple in Mexico City.

Interplay and Collision of Cultural Meanings: Sexual and Gender Systems

Sexual meanings are culturally specific. When individuals from different cultures come together, such meanings play with and against each other during interaction and with potential consequences. These consequences can range from an expanded worldview, where intercultural understanding and new ways of relating emerge, to a rigid and calcified perspective of the world, where ethnocentrism can create and solidify intercultural misunderstanding, conflict, and xenophobia.

For intercultural same-sex couples, the interplay and collision of cultural meanings attached to sexuality are particularly salient. Through the "globalization of sexualities," local and global meanings circulate within and across cultures to produce complex sexual systems (Binnie, 2004, p. 8). To put it differently, local cultural meanings of sexuality (e.g., understandings of sexuality in Mexico) are influenced by multiple historical, geographic, economic, and political forces (e.g., globalization of gay and lesbian identities, sex tourism, gay travel). In addition, meanings do not travel across cultural boundaries evenly (e.g., understandings of same-sex sexuality in Mexico are more likely to be influenced by the United States than the other way around). With this in mind, we discuss sexual systems in the United States and Mexico.

The dominant sexual system found in U.S. culture focuses primarily on sex and gender. Within this system, sexuality is organized through the use of *object choice*; that is, individuals' sexualities are categorized and understood through comparing their sex and gender identities to those of whom they desire (Almaguer, 1998). In the eyes of dominant U.S. culture, "*All* men who engage exclusively in sex with men are presumed to be 'gay' or 'homosexual' regardless of their femininity or masculinity, or whether they are receptive or insertive during anal intercourse" (Carrillo & Fontdevila, 2014, p. 922). In this sexual system, sexuality is constructed dichotomously and hierarchically. The master category, heterosexuality, and its subordinated category, homosexuality, are positioned as opposites, with bisexuality existing somewhere between (Almaguer, 1998; Sedgwick, 1990). Dominant U.S. cultural discourses work to facilitate the perception of heterosexuality as natural, stable, and normal (Yep, 2003). Heterosexuality is not simply normative in U.S. culture. Indeed, it is compulsory, institutional, and responsible for organizing social life (Seidman, 2009; Yep, 2003).

The dominant sexual system found in Mexico focuses on sexual roles, organizing sexuality through *sexual aim* rather than *object choice* (Almaguer, 1998). Sexual aim focuses on specific erotic practices during sexual interaction when categorizing, defining, and interpreting sexuality (e.g., person who penetrates—or *activo*; person who is penetrated—or *pasivo*). Therefore, in the context of this sexual system, it is possible for individuals to engage in same-sex sexual acts without being considered homosexual, as would be the case in U.S. culture. This is especially true of men who act as the *activo* (Carrier, 1985). Although sexual acts between men do not necessarily designate homosexuality within the context of this system, stigma does factor in. According to Alonso and Koreck (1999), the masculinity and sexuality of a male who acts as an *activo* tends not to be diminished or stigmatized as a result of his intercourse with other men. While *activos* tend not to be stigmatized, *pasivos* tend to be perceived as effeminate, which leads to social ridicule (Carrier, 1985). Although *pasivos* are stigmatized in dominant Mexican culture, they do not experience the same kind of marginalization that gay men in the U.S. do. Instead, they tend to be more often perceived as "objects of pity and amusement than of horror and avoidance" (Alonso & Koreck, 1999, p. 274). Feeling pity for someone who deviates from culturally prescribed gender performances of "normal men," or just simply "men" (Carrillo, 2002, p. 38), is distinctly different from U.S. cultural definitions of homophobia.

Masculinity and sexuality interact, both similarly and differently, in U.S. and Mexican cultural systems. In terms of similarities, these cultures are heteropatriarchal; that is, both U.S. and Mexican societies maintain an overarching system of male dominance through institutionalized heterosexuality (Carrillo, 2002; Yep, 2003). As such, both endorse and celebrate traditional performances of masculinity—in the forms of physical (e.g., virility, muscularity), psychological (e.g., dominance, protectiveness), and socioeconomic (e.g., wealth, status) power, among others (Alonso & Koreck, 1999; Irwin, 2003; Kivel, 2013). In addition, U.S. and Mexico, as well as many other cultures, often conflate gender performance with sexuality, such as equating male effeminacy with homosexuality (Yep, Russo, & Allen, 2015). However, there are also cultural differences. Although there is a common preference for and celebration of masculinity, a gay man in the United States can perform his gender in multiple ways, ranging from hyperfeminine to hypermasculine. In Mexico, the range of gender expressions is different. Male effeminacy and cross-dressing are equated with homosexuality, and homosexuals are expected to be the *pasivo* in sexual interactions (Almaguer, 1998; Prieur, 1996). On the other hand, masculine men can penetrate women and men and retain the normative social status of heterosexuality (Alonso & Koreck, 1999; Prieur, 1996). To return to Juan Manuel and Daniel, we can see the interplay and collision of cultural meanings attached to masculinity and sexuality. Performing more traditional masculinity in terms of physical, psychological and socioeconomic power, Juan Manuel, not surprisingly, is expected, at least by Agustín, to be the *activo* and "the man of the house" and Daniel the *pasivo* and "the gay man." As the couple moves across cultural borders, other meanings emerge.

Scene 2: Los Angeles

Oso was feeling anxious. After a long evening walk, he would watch Juan Manuel and Daniel get on their electronic devices to find a house to live. When they thought they found a perfect place, Daniel would call right away but nobody called back. "Was it my lisp?" Daniel wondered as his own feelings of inadequacy resurfaced. Juan Manuel decided to be the caller but the results were the same. Juan Manuel was perplexed—he was used to immediate responses in Mexico. Now, he was hearing silence. Daniel thought about the U.S. prejudices against non-European accents but decided to keep it to himself. He suggested that he would respond to rental ads by using email exclusively. He told Juan Manuel, "I know the area better so let me do this. This way, you can spend more time with Oso."

Daniel's strategy worked. Mr. Singer responded to Daniel's inquiry and they set up an appointment to view the property. With his much higher income and impeccable credit score, Juan Manuel suggested that he should be the primary leaseholder and Daniel agreed. Juan Manuel had his assistant get his financial papers ready so that he could sign the lease if the house was right.

Wearing a tight V-neck T-shirt and J brand jeans that emphasized his masculine physique, Juan Manuel enjoyed maneuvering his BMW through the rustic curviness of Laurel Canyon with Daniel next to him and Oso in the back seat. They got to the house early and Daniel suggested that Oso stay in the car. The house looked perfect—it was a charming Spanish-style cottage—and Daniel decided to explore the surrounding area. Juan Manuel was mesmerized by the beautiful rustic front door when he heard a somewhat condescending voice addressing him.

"*Hablas ingles?* We are not looking for a gardener." It was Mr. Singer.

When Mr. Singer saw Daniel appear, he said, "You must be Mr. Norris. You have a beautiful car. It looks like a limited edition!"

Daniel shot a quick glance at Juan Manuel before shaking Mr. Singer's extended hand. Smiling awkwardly, Daniel responded, "The car is Juan Manuel's. Please call me Daniel." He quickly added, "Juan Manuel is my partner and we absolutely love the house."

After a tour, Mr. Singer addressed Daniel, "If you like it, we can take care of the lease right now. A personal check from you will do it."

Juan Manuel noticed that Mr. Singer hadn't looked at him since his initial condescending comment. Sensing Daniel's approval, Juan Manuel spoke, "Yes, we are ready to sign. I'll be the primary leaseholder," as he handed his financial file to Singer. "I'll write the check."

Mr. Singer looked stunned when he examined Juan Manuel's financial records. As Juan Manuel pulled out his checkbook, Singer vacillated, looked at the ground, and said, "I need a cashier's check from you. It's company policy—I hope you understand."

Daniel was getting upset but Juan Manuel responded quickly, "No problem. I'll call my assistant Trina right now."

With her stereo playing "Panic" by The Smiths, Trina, a curvaceous self-identified Chicana transwoman, arrived in less than 20 minutes. She smiled at Juan Manuel before handing him the check, "It should cover everything plus an extra one thousand dollars."

Mr. Singer was pleased that he was getting a larger deposit. His eyes lingered on Trina's dress as he and Juan Manuel exchanged signatures and papers. Handing the keys to Daniel, Mr. Singer said, "I hope you and your roommate enjoy living here."

Sensing Juan Manuel's amazement at her speedy arrival, Trina announced, "As someone who faces prejudice and discrimination daily, I asked your bank to issue a cashier's check yesterday." Looking at Juan Manuel but intending for everyone to hear, she said, "As people of color, we have to be prepared to face other people's prejudices in this country." Ignoring Singer, she added, "Mr. Rosales and Mr. Norris, welcome to your new house and new life in LA!"

Silently wondering, "Am I a 'person of color' now? A 'gay Latino' as I often hear Daniel's friends call me?" and pleased with the house, Juan Manuel gave Daniel a hug and a kiss. Witnessing this tender moment, Oso let out a single bark. As he started the car, Juan Manuel wondered about living as a gay man and a gay couple in Los Angeles.

Interplay and Collision of Cultural Meanings: Racial and Class Systems

Like sex, gender, and sexuality, the meanings of race and class are also culturally specific. For example, cultures have different racial classification systems. As individuals travel across cultural borders, they experience different racialization processes; that is, they might be given different racial designations as they go from one culture to another. For example, a white person in Mexico becomes a person of color in the U.S., which creates potential conflict between avowed (how a person self-identifies, such as white in Mexico) and ascribed (how others identify the person, such as a person of color in the U.S.) identities. In addition to drastic changes of identities and treatment in the social world, the process of becoming a person of color also homogenizes diverse and distinct non-White people (e.g., African, Latin American, Middle Eastern, etc.) into a singular group. One of the ways to recover a degree of distinctiveness of Mexican culture in the U.S. is through a Latino identity (Flores & Benmayor, 1997).

In LGBTQ communities in the United States, the category of "gay Latino" has been used to designate the intersection of cultural and sexual identity, which can be a valuable tool for political and cultural organizing (Roque Ramirez, 2011). However, as Cantú (2011) accurately points out, "gay Latino" homogenizes Latino culture—that is, the differences between, say,

Mexican, Argentinian, Brazilian, and Cuban cultures, among others, are erased by the Latino umbrella—and depicts it as static, unchanging, and exotic. As a result, a Mexican gay man, for example, loses his own cultural identity through the Latino designation and his culture might be deemed as "other"—exotic and "backward" (p. 151). Further, gay Latinos in the U.S., according to Han (2013), "are invisible or exist only as props for white male consumption" (p. 372).

On the other hand, the category of "gay man" suggests whiteness and middle- to upper-classness (Bérubé, 2001). This notion appears to be true both locally (Bérubé, 2001) and internationally (Puar, 2002). In other words, the whiteness and perceived affluence of gay identity travel across cultural borders while Mexican gay identity, for example, takes on different meanings in Mexico and the United States. To put it differently, a white U.S. gay man is likely to uphold his racial and class privileges in both cultural contexts while a Mexican gay man is more likely going to lose his privileges in the United States.

In addition, masculinity and sexuality interact with race and class. A masculine gender performance by a Mexican man, for example, might be read as *macho*, a term imbued with multiple and contradictory meanings (Gutmann, 1996; Irwin, 2003; Mirandé, 2010). Focusing on how *macho* is given meanings based on race, class, and culture, Mirandé (2010) astutely observes:

> When applied to entertainers, athletes, or other "superstars," the implied meaning [of macho] is clearly a positive one that connotes strength, virility, masculinity, and sex appeal. But when applied to Mexicans or Latinos, "macho" remains imbued with such negative attributes as male dominance, patriarchy, authoritarianism, and spousal abuse. (p. 27)

Inhabiting these complex intersections, a masculine Mexican gay man—such as Juan Manuel—might be potentially viewed as desirable or undesirable, oppressor or protector, charming seducer or aggressive lecher, depending on the interactant, the local setting, and larger cultural context.

To conclude, as intercultural same-sex couples become more visible and travel across cultural and national boundaries, it is important to understand how culturally based sexual, gender, racial, and class systems shift and change. Through such understanding we can develop a deeper appreciation of these individuals' complex adjustments and experiences as they navigate changes in their social world, including identities, privileges, and relationships.

Note: Gust A. Yep would like to thank Juan Fernando Gutiérrez, a friend, artist, and native informant, for sharing some of the realities of gay life in Mexico City, and Yogi Enzo and Pierre Lucas, my sweet and affectionate Pomeranian companions, who inspire me with their inquisitiveness, playfulness, and creativity.

DISCUSSION QUESTIONS

1. After reading about Juan Manuel and Daniel, how would you describe their identities? How might your own identity and cultural background influence your response?

2. How did you see Juan Manuel and Daniel experiencing discrimination and privilege as they interacted with other people in each cultural context? What do you think this says about identity, culture, and power?

3. How might Juan Manuel and Daniel's sexual and gender identities be understood in the United States and in Mexico? How might other aspects of their identities (such as race, social class, and appearance) influence how they are understood in each context?

4. How does the fact that Juan Manuel and Daniel's identities are likely to be labeled and understood differently as they move across cultural boundaries, complicate how you think about identity itself?

5. How might Juan Manuel and Daniel's relationship be affected by the fact that sexual meanings from U.S. culture permeate cultural boundaries more easily than sexual meanings from Mexico do? How can intercultural relationships expand the way that people think about race, gender, and sexuality?

References

Almaguer, T. (1998). Chicano men: A cartography of homosexual identity and behavior. In P. M. Nardi & B. E. Schneider (Eds.), *Social perspectives in lesbian and gay studies: A reader* (pp. 537–552). London: Routledge.

Alonso, A. M., & Koreck, M. T. (1999). Silences: "Hispanics," AIDS, and sexual practices. In R. Parker & P. Aggleton (Eds.), *Culture, society and sexuality: A reader* (pp. 267–283). London: UCL Press.

Bérubé, A. (2001). How gays stay white and what kind of white it stays. In B. R. Rasmussen, E. Klinenberg, I. J. Nexica, & M. Wray (Eds.), *The making and unmaking of whiteness* (pp. 234–265). Durham, NC: Duke University Press.

Binnie, J. (2004). *The globalization of sexuality*. London: Sage.

Cantú, L. (2011). Entre hombres/between men: Latino masculinities and homosexualities. In M. Hames-García & E. J. Martínez (Eds.), *Gay Latino Studies: A critical reader* (pp. 147–167). Durham, NC: Duke University Press.

Carrier, J. M. (1985). Mexican male bisexuality. In F. Klein & T. J. Wolf (Eds.), *Bisexualities: Theory and research* (pp. 75–85). New York: Haworth.

Carrillo, H. (2002). *The night is young: Sexuality in Mexico in the time of AIDS*. Chicago: University of Chicago Press.

Carrillo, H., & Fontdevilla, J. (2014). Border crossings and shifting sexualities among Mexican gay immigrant men: Beyond monolithic conceptions. *Sexualities, 17*(8), 919–938.

Coon, D. R. (2012). Sun, sand, and citizenship: The marketing of gay tourism. *Journal of Homosexuality, 59*(4), 511–534.

Flores, W. V., & Benmayor, R. (Eds.). (1997). *Latino cultural citizenship: Claiming identity, space, and rights*. Boston: Beacon.

Gutmann, M. C. (1996). *The meanings of macho: Being a man in Mexico City*. Berkeley, CA: University of California Press.

Grov, C., Breslow, A. S., Newcomb, M. E., Rosenberger, J. G., & Bauermeister, J. A. (2014). Gay and bisexual men's use of the Internet: Research from the 1990s through 2013. *The Journal of Sex Research, 51*(4), 390–409.

Halberstam, J. J. (2012). *Gaga feminism: Sex, gender, and the end of normal*. Boston: Beacon.

Han, C.-S. (2013). They don't want to cruise your type: Gay men of color and the racial politics of exclusion. In M. S. Kimmel & M. A. Messner (Eds.), *Men's lives* (9th ed., pp. 368–380). Boston: Pearson.

Irwin, R. M. (2003). *Mexican masculinities.* Minneapolis, MN: University of Minnesota Press.

Kivel, P. (2013). The act-like-a-man box. In M. S. Kimmel & M. A. Messner (Eds.), *Men's lives* (9th ed., pp. 14–16). Boston: Pearson.

Mirandé, A. (2010). "Macho": Contemporary conceptions. In M. S. Kimmel & M. A. Messner (Eds.), *Men's lives* (8th ed., pp. 26–36). Boston: Pearson.

Mitchell, G. (2011). TurboConsumers™ in paradise: Tourism, civil rights, and Brazil's gay sex industry. *American Ethnologist, 38*(4), 666–682.

Prieur, A. (1996). Domination and desire: Male homosexuality and the construction of masculinity in Mexico. In M. Melhuus & K. A. Stolen (Eds.), *Machos, mistresses, madonnas: Contesting the power of Latin American gender imagery* (pp. 83–107). London: Verso.

Puar, J. K. (2002). Circuits of queer mobility: Tourism, travel, and globalization. *GLQ: A Journal of Lesbian and Gay Studies, 8*(1-2), 101–137.

Ross, M. W. (2005). Typing, doing, and being: Sexuality and the Internet. *The Journal of Sex Research, 42*(4), 342–352.

Roque Ramirez, H. N. (2011). Gay Latino cultural citizenship: Predicaments of identity and visibility in San Francisco in the 1990s. In M. Hames-García & E. J. Martínez (Eds.), *Gay Latino Studies: A critical reader* (pp. 175–197). Durham, NC: Duke University Press.

Sedgwick, E. K. (1990). *Epistemology of the closet.* Berkeley, CA: University of California Press.

Seidman, S. (2009). Critique of compulsory heterosexuality. *Sexuality Research & Social Policy, 6*(1), 18–28.

Yep, G. A. (2003). The violence of heteronormativity in communication studies: Notes on injury, healing, and queer world-making. In G. A. Yep, K. E. Lovaas & J. P. Elia (Eds.), *Queer theory and communication: From disciplining queers to queering the discipline(s)* (pp. 11–59). Binghamton, NY: Harrington Park Press.

Yep, G. A., Russo, S. E., & Allen, J. K. (2015). Pushing boundaries: Toward the development of a model for transing communication in (inter) cultural contexts. In L. G. Spencer & J. C. Capuzza (Eds.), *Transgender communication studies: Histories, trends, and trajectories* (pp. 69–89). Lanham, MD: Lexington.

CHAPTER 6

African Sexualities: Exploring Ọ̀ṣunality

Zelaika S. H. Clarke

KEY TERMS

Afrocentric communication theory	Ọ̀ṣunality Phallocentrism	Ecosexuality Vaginas

ABSTRACT

Ọ̀ṣunality is a postcolonial, Africa-centered sex-positive paradigm that supports diversity in sensuality and eroticism, inclusive of all forms of sexual pleasure. Historically, the fields of human sexuality and communication have been shaped by Westocentrism, a dominating bias toward European and North American colonialistic hegemony. This tradition privileges phallocentrism while oppressing and silencing "other" perspectives. Learning about Ọ̀ṣunality can provide insight into non-Western theories of communication and narratives that disrupt phallocentric views of sex. This includes the devouring vagina, which assigns primary agency in coitus to the vagina; and ecosexuality, the erotic love of nature.

The fields of human sexuality and communication have been dominated by Western theories and perspectives, which silence voices and "Other" perspectives. As Miike (2007) notes, "Eurocentric theory has unduly overstated the global significance of its own local knowledge. The time is long overdue for the Western mind to lend an ear to unheard and silenced voices from elsewhere" (p. 277). Learning about Others' perspectives can be thought provoking and provide insight into our own sexosophy,[1] or our personally-experienced eroticisms and sexualities. Many default schemas within sexosophy have been dominated and even tainted by Western constructions. The Europeanization of human ideas (Asante, 2006), due to Western imperialism, legitimized the theories and values of the colonizers while silencing the colonized. Westocentrism privileged heterosex between one man and one woman, with an emphasis on procreation. Alternative perspectives of sexualities and communication are available outside Westocentrism.

Both fields of human sexuality and communication need to be rethought outside Westocentrism to include voices that have historically been silenced. Postcolonial paradigms are created by the taking back of self-determination by historically oppressed peoples. They "[enable] us to rethink communication through new visions and revisions, through new histories and geographies" (Shome & Hegde, 2002, p. 249). Different paradigms offer different narratives, sexual schemes, normalities, and sexosophies of human sexualities. One way of reconceptualizing sexuality within the postcolonial paradigm is Ọ̀ṣunality.

Ọ̀ṣunality is a neologism coined by Nkiru Nzegwu in 2010. Ọ̀ṣunality is an empowering, postcolonial, sex-positive, and African-centered paradigm that "affirms the normality of sexual pleasure and the erotic" (Nzegwu, 2011, p. 256). All forms of pleasure are considered normal: from traditional, procreative heterosex to pathologized paraphilias. There is no value judgement placed on any eroticism, sexual behavior, or fantasy. A simple translation of Ọ̀ṣunality is Ọ̀ṣuna-sexuality or African sensuality-sexuality and eroticism (Nzegwu, 2010). Studying Ọ̀ṣunality increased my awareness of alternative forms of communication beyond Western communication theories and into Afrocentric and Asiancentric communication theory.

---

1. Sexosophy is the body of knowledge that comprises the philosophy, principles, and knowledge that people have about their own personally experienced eroticism and sexuality as well as that of other people both singly and collectively (Money, 1982).

By immersing myself in Candomblé, an Afro-Brazilian religion, while conducting decolonizing autoethnographic research (Diversi & Moreira, 2009) in Brazil, I was able to unlearn colonial constructs and seriously consider a postcolonial paradigm. In other words, I realized sexual knowledge can be interpreted, understood, and experienced in a number of different ways. During my decolonizing experiences, I committed to auto-decolonization (i.e., decolonizing of self) by focusing on *concientization*, or developing critical thinking skills (Friere, 1970). This practice involved deconstructing and reconstructing discursive imperialism, or discourse that values "self-interest, in-group favoritism, and ethnocentrism (van Dijk, 1993, p.160). It also involved practicing mindfulness as a way of achieving *neurodecolonization*, or decolonization of the mind (Yellow Bird, 2013). When I say I work toward decolonizing my mind, I mean mentally engaging in a process where I change the way I view the world by unlearning negative effects of colonialism such as internalized oppressions like misogyny, ageism, genderism, etc.

To that end, communication and sexuality are not monolithic: there are multiple ways to interpret, perceive, and experience both. Communication ethics are always historically, materially, politically, and socially situated, and yet the universalizing framework though which they are often constructed is largely Western (Rao & Wasserman, 2007). In response to this lack of diverse perspectives, Qin Cao (2007) recommends "opening up spaces for new voices or different truths to be in dialogue with existing, often dominant, ones" (p. 117). For him, this allows "a productive and empowering engagement in resisting essentialist representation of the Other" (p. 117).

Afrocentric Communication and the Value of Ọ̀ṣunality

Afrocentric communication theory repositions Africans in the center of their own historical experiences, rather than on the margins of European experiences (Asante, 1999). Ọ̀ṣunality is an African-centered paradigm that I used to free my mind from hegemonic thinking about sex and communication. When I say my thinking was hegemonic, I mean accepting of prevalent colonial philosophies—in a word: Western. While exploring Ọ̀ṣunality, a pleasure-embracing sensuality, I actively engaged my critical thinking skills and self-reflexivity, and that allowed me to foster the decolonization of sexualities and communication. Ishii (2009) recommended scholars of intercultural communication develop a "non-self-centric, non-anthropocentric and holistic worldview and ethical thought" (p. 58). I took this recommendation into consideration as I observed communication between people and forces of nature in the Afro-Brazilian spiritual paradigm of Candomblé. With an open, non-judgmental mind, I witnessed communication expand beyond the interpersonal to include human-to-nature interactions.

This human-to-nature perspective exemplified that there are different forms of communication that can be experienced outside conventional Western interactions. The Buddhist paradigm acknowledges that communication can emphasize "non-anthropocentric and 'deep-ecological' human-to-nature relationships" (Ishii, 2009, p. 51). For example, Candomblé practitioners who are called "horses" are considered to be "mounted" by forces of nature and "ridden"; they have a special relationship and communication with a non-human entity. Although this perspective represents an Asiancentric position, the same perspective is utilized in some African-centered religions that have a deep relationship and connection with nature.

The Candomblé paradigm actively engages in non-anthropocentric (i.e., humans are not at the center of everything), ecological, and human-to-nature relationship forms of communication. Candomblé is an afro-Brazilian religion that honors orishas, as do other African-centered religions such as Ifá of Nigeria, Santeria, Lucumí, Regla de Ocha of Cuba, Oyotunji of the United States, and Shango Baptist of Trinidad and Tobago. Orishas can be conceptualized as deities in the Yorùbá (Nigerian) religious pantheon associated with forces of nature (Edwards & Mason, 1985). As Love (2012) explains, "As a summarizing symbol, the orisha represents a personality archetype, a divinity, a force of nature, an aspect of God, or an energy matrix" (pp. 9-10). Orishas (Yorùbá) are similar to the Abosom (Akan), Neteru (KMT/Ancient Egyptian), Vodun (Fon and Ewe), Lwa/loa (Haitian) and Kami (Japanese). In my studies, I focused on the orisha Ọ̀ṣun. Ọ̀ṣun is the force of nature (orisha) associated with fresh waters. Ọ̀ṣun represents sexual knowledge and agency (Nzegwu, 2011). As Badejo (1996) notes, "Ọ̀ṣun is a powerful, indeed empowering, Yorùbá goddess" (p. xvi). She is the divinity of love, sensuality, fertility, femininity and beauty, to name a few. Researching about Ọ̀ṣun provided me with a new awareness of the complexities and sensual-sexualities.

Ọ̀ṣun and Female-Centered Sexuality

Ọ̀ṣun "represents a pronatalist, female-centered, life-transforming energy that courses through and animates life" (Nzegwu, 2011, p. 258). In other words, Ọ̀ṣun stands for African female sexual knowledge and agency. This energy is shared with other women (Abimbola, 2001; Abiodun, 2001; Ogungbile, 2001; Washington, 2005) and is located in the female creative organs (i.e., reproductive and genitalia) (Nzegwu, 2011). As Castellanos (2001) points out, "Fertility, reproduction, and human sexuality are also notions intimately associated with the theme of life … [Ọ̀ṣun] is the owner of female genitalia and the female egg" (p. 42). Ọ̀ṣun is imperative for sustaining life.

Ọ̀ṣun is a powerful force that can promote growth and/or change, as "the activation of Ọ̀ṣun's 'concealed power' or Ọ̀ṣunality, revitalizes and renews life….the act of copulation spiritually and psychologically activates this force of change, transformation and growth, and the feeling of sexual fulfillment it produces ensures social harmony and stability" (Nzegwu, 2011, p. 259). In simplified terms, Ọ̀ṣunality is African sensuality-sexuality that goes beyond eroticism (Nzegwu, 2010) and into self-conceptualization and -actualization. In short, "Ọ̀ṣunality affirms the normality of sexual pleasure and the erotic" (Nzegwu, 2011, p. 258).

Ọ̀ṣunality provides a non-phallocentric narrative of sexual intercourse—i.e., a narrative that sheds the bond of privileging the male member. In this context, women are positively affirmed, and the vagina is perceived as an important organ. In Ọ̀ṣunality, agency is assigned to the vagina, which is absent in Western notions of the erotic. Instead of the penis being an organ of dominance, a measure of passivity is assigned to the penis (Nzegwu, 2010). In other words, it is not a penis that conquers a vagina, but instead a vagina that surrounds a penis and demands its surrender.

Consider the many modern American/Western colloquialisms used to describe sex: "bang," "beat it up," "hit it," "screw," "smash," and "slam," among others. Often, these words have undertones of violence associated with them. The expression of "losing" one's virginity implies that it is something that a penis "takes away." Further, etymology of the word *vagina* indicates that it comes from Latin meaning "sheath" or "scabbard"—more commonly known as a sword holder. This history implies that the penis is the "sword" or a weapon. In heteronormative Western culture (see Manning, this volume), men are assigned the roles of dominant sexual beings. As Nzegwu (2011) explains, "The penis is represented as the central and dominating copulatory organ; the vagina is merely a sheath for the penetrating penis, a passive receptacle that receives the invading penis that drives deep into the woman" (p. 265). Based on Nzegwu's read, she questions why Western narratives of the penis is depicted as an organ that can give pleasure and a weapon. Morgan (1977) contends that the Western heterosexual "male sexual style" which emphasizes "genital sexuality, objectification, promiscuity, emotional non-involvement" (p. 181) is problematic. Instead, she argues for a female-centered sexuality, which would place a "greater trust in love, sensuality, humor, tenderness, commitment" (Morgan, 1977, p. 181). In other words, she argues for a move from phallocentrism and toward a female centered paradigm.

Òṣunality holds potential as one of those paradigms. One of the core concepts of Òṣunality is the "devouring vagina" (Nzegwu, 2011). The devouring vagina comes from the aesthetic interpretation of the penis being enveloped, swallowed, and made to disappear during intercourse. The withdrawing of the penis is seen as an act of resistance from being pulled in (re-swallowed) by the demanding vagina. The engulfing of the penis by the vagina reverses normative Western sexual wisdom by putting the male in a subordinate position (Nzegwu, 2011). The position used for execution (e.g., if the man is on top) does not imply a superior physical or psychological position, considering that the impact can be just as powerful from the underside. Nzegwu (2011) explains, "After all, to devour or to eat something is to assert one's power or will over it, yet the act does not deny power to that which is eaten, because what is eaten provides nourishment to the eater. Indeed, the penis' frantic activity of withdrawal, being pulled in (re-swallowed) and withdrawing again might appear as resistance, but its effort is really futile because its seed is pulled from it by the demanding vagina" (p. 264).

Western Culture's Resistance to the Ọ̀ṣunic Paradigm

The devouring vagina's association with characteristics of ingestion might spark Western fear of its power. In the West, the ideas often hint at the "castration" of males. Freud wrote in his book, *Fetishism* (1927), "probably no male human being is spared the terrifying shock of threatened castration at the sight of the female genitals" (p. 154). The imagery of the devouring vagina also might stir memories of the Western myths of the "vagina dentata," which describes a woman's vagina as having teeth—implying that sexual intercourse might result in injury or castration for the man involved (see Wiltz, this volume). These cautionary tales might have been told to warn of the dangers of unknown women and/or to discourage rape (Rankin, 2010). In a bestseller titled *Sexual Personae*, Paglia (1991) warned that, "the toothed vagina is no sexist hallucination: every penis is made less by every vagina, just as mankind, male and female, is devoured by mother nature" (p. 47). In his book, *The Wimp Factor*, Stephen J. Ducat (2004) expressed a similar view: that these myths articulated the threat sexual intercourse poses for men who, although entering triumphantly, always leave diminished.

Copulation, in this context, is interpreted as a unidirectional consumption because only men give something up of themselves (Nzegwu, 2011). After semen is extracted by the demanding vagina, the depleted male is drained emotionally and physically. This aspect is echoed in Taoism, particularly during the Han dynasty in China, in which men aimed to develop their power through the containment of *jing*, or seminal essence, which could be lost during ejaculation. As a result, they devised techniques to prevent ejaculation, so as to not lose their *jing*, but rather to build up *jing*, to retain *yang* during a spiritual engagement of intercourse (Gregersen, 1996).

The act of eating food can be comparable to the act of devouring. Ordinarily, eating involves something's demise, but there is no death in the devouring act of the vagina—except for the seeds that are absorbed and die. While one eats food, it becomes a part of the body, to be processed, integrated, and transformed into energy. "In the heat of the moment the owner of the penis relishes the consumption, oblivious to the cycle of life and death and to the energy expended in each act, the end of which leaves him emotionally drained and compliant. Copulation forces the man to replenish speedily his viral force so he can function as a man, even when procreation is not the goal of intercourse. The script of extraction and expulsion, the disappearance (symbolic death) and re-emergence (symbolic re-birth) of the penis chronicles the drama of life and death" (Nzegwu, 2011, p. 264). The penis role in copulation does not have to be undermined. The devouring vagina provides an alternative narrative to coitus outside Western frameworks.

Other androcentric notions pervade Western narratives, even in scientific interpretations of conception. In addition, Western narratives have permeated even scientific interpretations of conception. Gender stereotypes are hidden within the scientific language of reproductive physiology (Martin, 1991). For example, although attempting to be objective in the fields of biology and physiology, sometimes cultural narratives and interpretations ascribe human characteristics to their analysis: "may the best strongest sperm win," assigns sperm perceived masculine characteristics, as they "fight their way toward an egg." The egg (ovum) is therefore perceived to be passively waiting for the aggressive sperm. Alternative narratives are available for the same event. It could be postulated that the egg "chooses" which sperm it selects and contains the power and intuitive wisdom to lock out all other competitors that are drawn to it (Clarke, 2015). Or perhaps the egg acts as a magnetic force and pulls in the sperm, aimlessly flapping their tails. The cervix has been known to dip and create a suction-like reaction as a physiological response to orgasm (Ladas, Whipple & Perry, 2005); this could be indicative of the pulling force that supports an aspect of the devouring vagina.

People I have talked to in my studies also realize the potentials for Òşunality, a pleasure affirming paradigm, can be considered in their own cultures. For example, one interviewee found the gynocentric view of sex too limiting: "Homosexuals don't have a devouring vagina. It's about the whole body, not just the vagina." Another interviewee, a Candomblé priest, reminded me that "sex does not have to be a phallic act," nor does the definition of intercourse have to revolve around a penis. I explore this idea in my final section.

Ọ̀ṣunality Beyond Penises and Vaginas

Although Ọ̀ṣunality increased my awareness of non-phallocentric and androcentric views of conception and sex by introducing a gynocentric narrative of penile-vaginal intercourse (PVI) as a valuable alternative, I learned other things as well. For example, I learned that conceptualizing sex as a whole body experience is key to expanding eroticism beyond the genitals. Sex does not even need to involve a penis or a vagina. Sex does not have to be limited to involving other humans. When sex is outside phallocentrism, there are still many creative avenues for sexual pleasure and expression. When we have the freedom to make our own meanings and define concepts for ourselves, creative possibilities can emerge. For example, another Candomblé priest that I interviewed suggested "to make sex with the wind, it's so good. It is truly powerful!" By this, he meant that powerful sexual pleasurable experiences can occur in human-to-nature relationships. This recommendation, among others, reminded me that sex can be defined in many different ways outside Western phallocentric notions.

Ecosexuals are capable of making love with different aspects of nature. They can experience "sex" without humans or the involvement of genitals. Ecosexuality serves as an excellent example of expanding the definition of sex beyond phallocentric, gynocentric, and anthropocentric conceptualizations. My co-researcher described an ecosexual experience as follows:

> While I was laying appreciating and loving the sun in an erotically enriching way, it felt as though the sunrays were penetrating my skin; and it was sensuous and enjoyable. My skin became the prominent sex organ. The rays pleased my skin as the sunshine penetrated my body. I used sun screen for protection and thought about it as a type of condom in this love affair. In the erotic moment, when my body was flushed, aroused, and receptive, I produced a liquid that looked like semen which came through my erotically inclined skin. The sweat was my pleasure liquid that squeezed out of my open pores after the sun penetrated me. It was euphoric, joyous, and pleasureful. I felt connected, erotic, sexual, sensual, aroused, pleased, and fulfilled.

This type of sexuality did not involve the genitals, nor another human, but was reported to be as satisfying. Some might have branded my co-researcher a heliophiliac—heliophila is love of sun or sunlight—with the pleasure they derived from basking in the sun. However, from the paradigm of Ọ̀ṣunality, which affirms the normality of sensual-sexual pleasure and the erotic, finding erotic pleasure from the sun does not have to be pathologized (or named with a -philia, as many psychologists tend to do), nor produce feelings of shame and guilt. Rather, Ọ̀ṣunality involves eroticism being experienced in a number of different ways.

Conclusion

There are many different ways of interpreting sexuality that do not have to be limited by phallocentric viewpoints that dominate Western ideology. Humanity should make room for respecting multiple views and opening themselves up to new possibilities. As Kabat-Zinn (2005) articulates, "When we do not limit ourselves to one way of knowing, or one vocabulary, or one set of lenses through which to look, when we purposefully expand our horizon of inquiry and curiosity, we can take delight in all the various ways we have of knowing something" (p. 589-90). By learning about other paradigms, one has the opportunity to better understand their own narratives and sexosophy and to celebrate differences, otherness, and plurality found in human experiences of sexualities. Thinking about phallocentrism and ecosexuals can remind us that communication and sexuality can mean different things to different people.

DISCUSSION QUESTIONS

1. Do you believe there is one right way to view sex? Why or why not?

2. What messages have you received about the penis and vagina? How do they make you think about your own sexual organs?

3. How is sex culturally constructed? That is, how do you see sex as a part of everyday life?

4. Were you familiar with the idea that Western ways of thinking about sex differ from Asian or African ways of thinking? Why is it that Western ways might seem normal to you whereas other paradigms may not?

5. What is your personal sexosophy? Did reading this chapter make you reconsider it?

References

Abimbola, W. (2001). The bag of wisdom: Òşun and the origins of Ifá divination. In J. M. Murphy & M. Sanford (Eds.), *Òşun across the waters: A Yoruba Goddess in Africa and the Americas* (pp. 141–154). Bloomington, IN: Indiana University Press.

Abiodun, R. (2001). Hidden power: Òşun, the 17th Odù. In J. M. Murphy & M. Sanford (Eds.), *Òşun across the waters: A Yoruba Goddess in Africa and the Americas* (pp. 10–33). Bloomington, IN: Indiana University Press.

Asante, M. K. (1999). An Afrocentric communication theory. In J. L. Lucaites, C. M. Condit & S. Caudill (Eds.), *Contemporary rhetorical theory: A reader* (pp. 552–562). New York, NY: Guilford Press.

Asante, M.K. (2006). The rhetoric of globalization: The Europeanisation of human ideas. *Journal of Multicultural Discourses, 1*(2), 152–158. doi:10.2167/md054.0

Badejo, D. (1996*). Òşun Şéégésí: The elegant deity of wealth, power and femininity.* Trenton, NJ: Africa World Press.

Castellanos, I. (2001). A river of many turns: the polysemy of Ochún in Afro-Cuban tradition. In J. M. Murphy, & M. Sanford (Eds.), *Òşun across the waters: A Yoruba Goddess in Africa and the Americas* (pp. 34–45). Bloomington, IN: Indiana University Press.

Cao, Q. (2007). Western representations of the Other. In Shi-xu (Ed.), *Discourse as cultural struggle* (pp. 105–122). Hong Kong: Hong Kong University Press.

Clarke, Z. H. (2015). *Coming to my senses: A decolonizing autoethnographic exploration of osunality.* (Unpublished doctoral dissertation). Center for Human Sexuality Studies, Chester, PA.

Diversi, M., & Moreia, C. (2009). *Betweener talk: Decolonizing knowledge production, pedagogy and praxis.* Walnut Creek, CA: Left Coast Press.

Ducat, S. J. (2004). *The wimp factor: Gender gaps, holy wars, and the politics of anxious masculinity.* Boston, MA: Beacon Press.

Freud, S. (1927). Fetishism (J. Strachey, Trans.) In *The complete psychological works of Sigmund Freud* (Vol. XXI, pp. 147–157). London: Hogarth and the Institute of Psychoanalysis.

Freire, P. (1970/2007). *Pedagogy of the oppressed.* New York, NY: Seabury.

Gregersen, E. (1996). *The world of human sexuality: Behaviors, customs, and beliefs.* New York, NY: Irvington Publishers.

Ishii, S. (2009). Conceptualising Asian communication ethics: A Buddhist perspective. *Journal of Multicultural Discourses, 4*(1), 49–60. doi: 10.1080/17447140802651645.

Kabat-Zinn, J. (2005). *Coming to our senses: Healing ourselves and the world through mindfulness.* London: Piatkus.

Kuokkanen, R. (2007). *Reshaping the University: Responsibility, indigenous epistemes, and the logic of the gift.* Vancouver, BC: UBC Press.

Ladas, A. K, Whipple, B., & Perry, J. D. (2005). *The g spot and other discoveries about human sexuality.* New York: Owl Books.

Love, V.E. (2012). *Divining the self: A study in Yoruba myth and human consciousness.* University Park, PA: The Pennsylvania State University.

Manning, J. (This volume). Identity, relationships, and culture: A constitutive model of coming out. In J. Manning & C. Noland (Eds.), *Contemporary Studies of Sexuality & Communication: Theoretical and Applied Perspectives.* Dubuque, IA: Kendall Hunt.

Martin, E. (1991). The egg and the sperm: How science has constructed a romance based on stereotypical male-female roles. *Journal of Women in Culture and Society, 16*(3), 485–501.

Miike, Y. (2007). An Asiacentric reflection on Eurocentric bias in communication theory. *Communication Monographs, 74*(2), 272–278. doi: 10.1080/03637750701390093.

Money, J. (1982). Sexosophy: A new concept. *Journal of Sex Research, 18*(4), 364–366.

Morgan, R. (1977). *Going too far.* New York, NY: Random House.

Nzegwu, N. (2010). "Osunality," or African sensuality-sexuality: Going beyond eroticism. *Jenda: A Journal of Culture and African Women Studies,* (16), 1–24.

Nzegwu, N. (2011). 'Osunality' or African eroticism. In S. Tamale (Ed.), *African sexualities: A reader* (pp. 253–270). Cape Town, SA: Pambazuka.

Ogungbile, D. O. (2001). Eerindinlogun: The seeing eyes of sacred shells and stories. In J. M. Murphy (Ed.), Òsun *across the waters: A Yoru-*

ba goddess in Africa and the Americas. Bloomington, IN: Indiana University Press.

Paglia, C. (1991). *Sexual Personae: Art and decadence from Nefertiti to Emily Dickinson.* New York, NY: Vintage.

Rankin, L. (2010). *What's up down there?: Questions you'd only ask your gynecologist if she was your best friend.* New York, NY: St. Martin's Press.

Rao, S., & Wasserman, H. (2007). Global media ethics revisited: A postcolonial critique. *Global Media and Communication, 3*(1), 29–50.

Shome, R., & Hegde, R. S. (2002). Postcolonial Approaches to communication: Charting the terrain, engaging the intersections. *International Communication Association, 12*(3), 249–270.

Van Dijk, T. A. (1993). *Elite discourse and racism.* Newbury Park, CA: Sage.

Washington, T. N. (2005). *Our mothers, our powers, our texts: Manifestation of Ajẹ́ in Africana literature.* Bloomington, IN: Indiana University Press.

Yellow Bird, M. (2013). Neurodecolonization: Applying mindfulness research to decolonizing social work. In M. Gray, M., J. Coates, M. Yellow Bird, & T. Hetherington, T. (Eds.), *Decolonizing social work.* Farnham Surrey: Ashgate.

CHAPTER 7

Identity, Relationships, and Culture: A Constitutive Model of Coming Out

Jimmie Manning

KEY TERMS

The closet
Sexual identity

Homophobia
Coming out

Sexual orientation

ABSTRACT

For several decades, researchers across many disciplines have developed a large body of research exploring the topic of coming out. This research has provided many insights about what it means for gay, lesbian, and bisexual people to acknowledge their sexualities and to share their sexual identities with others. As helpful as this research has been, little has been done to move scholarship toward a holistic theory of coming out. This chapter provides a step in that direction by offering a constitutive model of coming out. This three-level model proposes that culture informs a person's viewpoints and personal acceptance regarding sexuality; and that both culture and a person's personal viewpoints impact how sexual identities are shared with others. Data from qualitative research studies about coming out help to illustrate the concepts associated with the model.

Unless people do or say something to show that they are gay, most people assume that they are straight. The notion that people are often considered to be heterosexual until proven otherwise, known as *compulsory heterosexuality*, happens both because most people have sexual longings and behaviors that align with heterosexuality; but also because non-heterosexual orientations have been and continue to be shamed or stigmatized in many cultures (Rich, 1980). Of course, many people are not heterosexual and are attracted to people of the same sex. Because of cultural expectations about sexuality, gay, lesbian, bisexual, and otherwise sexually queer (GLBQ) people often find themselves in a situation where they must come out about their sexualities. Rust (2003) characterizes coming out as "the process by which individuals come to recognize that they have romantic or sexual feelings toward members of their own gender, adopt lesbian or gay (or bisexual) identities, and then share these identities with others" (p. 227). This chapter offers a model that explores that definition of coming out, specifically examining cultural, cognitive, and relational aspects.

Because coming out can be tough, many researchers have tried to understand what it entails. These studies have happened mostly in three contexts. First, many *cultural studies* have examined how cultures and societies create rules about sex and sexuality. These studies have primarily focused on two contexts: heteronormativity and the closet. *Heteronormativity* is the idea that people are either heterosexual or not; and that those who are heterosexual are privileged (Plummer, 1992). People are often not even aware of their heteronormative assumptions. These assumptions include that people in general are heterosexual; that men act masculine and women act feminine; and that until someone does something to disrupt these ideas, heterosexuality is the norm.

Queer theory is a body of theory that examines, among other things, how gender and sexuality are disciplined when they do not meet heteronormative cultural expectations (Yep, 2003). One way that people with non-conforming gender or sexualities is punished is through the fear of violence. As Yep (2003) points out, many physical threats have been aimed at GLBQ people. Moreover, the fear of such violence encourages people to try and conceal their sexuality; or, if people are open about their sexuality, they know that there are threats. Beyond physical threats, those include being fired from work, rejected from houses of worship, or banished from families. Because this risk can be intense, many GLBQ people choose to stay in what is referred to as *the closet*. As will be explored later in this chapter, the closet is a metaphorical cultural construction where people are encouraged to hide aspects of their identities that others do not want to see.

Whereas studies of heteronormativity and the closet deal more with cultural constructions, a second body of research has dealt more with how people think about themselves and see their own identities. These *cognitive studies* have helped to explain how people understand their own sexuality as well as the feelings and emotions that accompany those understandings. Much of the research in this area has been used to develop models that can help GLBQ people as they come out, especially people who might be struggling with self-acceptance or acceptance from others. Although these models have been and continue to be helpful for GLBQ people, they continue to be developed today, as the original studies that helped build these models often did not account for cultural differences, especially in terms of ethnicity (see Gonzales & Espin, 1996 or Greene, 1994). The models also generally ignored bisexuality (Rust, 1996). One of the most discussed cognitive models of coming out (Cass, 1979) will be explored in-depth later in this chapter.

Most recently, a new line of research exploring coming out has examined how people interact regarding their sexual identities. As Manning (2015a) notes, in many instances people explored the cognitive aspects of coming out while assuming the communication that surrounds those processes. Unfortunately, this communication is often filled with anxiety, uncertainty, and stress even in affirming or accepting environments (Manning, 2015b). As such, it is important to consider coming out at the relational level: how do people communicate their sexual identities with others? Because communication involves cognitive processes and because it is situated within a culture, it is included as the middle-level in the *Constitutive Model of Coming Out* (Figure 7.1) presented here that combines all three strands of research. Because culture has an impact on both relating and cognitive processes, it is at the outer edge of the model. The model is labeled as *constitutive* because rather than any level having a direct effect or impact on the other, all three combine to create a constitutive sense of coming out. Similarly, research across all three areas—cultural studies, cognitive studies, and interactive relational studies—constitutively inform a person's coming out experiences. The rest of this chapter explains each level and provides concrete examples.

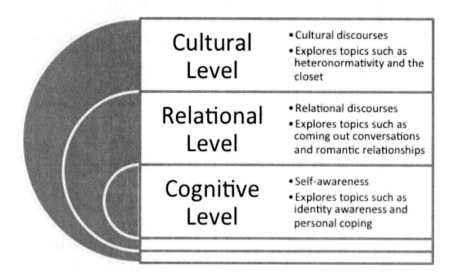

FIGURE 7.1 *A Constitutive Model of Coming Out*

Cultural Level
- Cultural discourses
- Explores topics such as heteronormativity and the closet

Relational Level
- Relational discourses
- Explores topics such as coming out conversations and romantic relationships

Cognitive Level
- Self-awareness
- Explores topics such as identity awareness and personal coping

The Cultural Level

The outer edge of the model—the level that engulfs the other two—is the *Cultural Level*. Research at this level reflects how a culture informs, impacts, or otherwise influences the people and relationships within it. Culture is not a container, however; rather, it is a circulating sense of meaning that happens across collected people, artifacts, and ideas across a particular place and space. Within a particular culture, identities and relationships are defined. In addition to being defined, some identities are rewarded, punished, controlled, limited, or contested within a given culture—especially sexual identities (Manning, 2013). Because some identities or relationships are not valued—and, in fact, might be open to cultural scrutiny and punishment—people might choose to hide these identities. This notion of *the closet* is important to a constitutive model of coming out, as the closet is what allows for the idea that people come out.

Many who study the closet, point to Eve Kosofsky Sedgwick's (1990) highly-influential book *Epistemology of the Closet* as the starting place for considering how cultures create aspects of identity that must be hidden. Even though many social scientists use ideas generated by Sedgwick in that text, the book itself relies more on humanistic approaches to literary criticism to make its arguments. To that end, works of literature from writers such as Proust or Melville are considered in terms of how gender and sexuality are established; and how such constructions or representations inform the idea that people are either homosexual or heterosexual. As Sedgwick argues, only having two categories is too simple. One of the most intriguing ideas she explores in the book is how some aspects of identity might always remain closeted. For example, if someone were to come out of the closet as a lesbian, what would that mean? Does that label itself tell you much about the person's whole identity (e.g., lesbians are often different) or even their sexual (e.g., lesbians have different kinds of sex) or gendered (e.g., lesbians have different gender performances) identities? She also asks good questions about why people are so interested in the closet being mostly about sex. As she suggests, many aspects of a person's identity beyond gender or sexuality have the potential to be closeted.

Although many scholars in many different academic disciplines explore aspects of coming out at the cultural level, Sedgwick's (1990) notion of the closet is often at the foundation as it pushes thinking about how a larger social order, or the people who watch us as we relate with others (see Duck, 2011), impinges on our sexual relationships as well as who we are as gendered people. These explorations of sexual or gender identity often intersect with other identity categories such as race, ethnicity, nationality, social class, religion, or age. In the communication discipline, many scholars use rhetorical or media criticism to examine cultural aspects of the closet (e.g., Eguchi, Calafell, & Files-Thompson, 2014) and coming out (e.g., Manning, 2015c), although autoethnography—a combination of ethnography and autobiography (see Ellis, 2004) where researchers examine their own lives as they are culturally situated—is quite common as well. Perhaps the most notable autoethnographic work exploring coming out at the cultural level—research that, similar to Sedgwick's work, asks good questions about how cultures construct closets—is that of Tony E. Adams.

In Adams' (2011) *Narrating the Closet*, he considers how people interact with each other in terms of sexual identity, considering a wide range of cultural influences from modern popular culture representations of LGB people to how people interpret religious texts. In terms of coming out, Adams describes what he calls *situational paradoxes* within a culture, or the culturally-constructed rules of coming out. As he explains,

> Paradox occurs when a person with same-sex attraction is held accountable—by self and others—for taking a wrong course of action, making the wrong move: there are consequences for a person who comes out or does not, who comes out too soon or not soon enough, who completes the coming-out process or finds completion impossible, or who comes out most of the time, some of the time, or never at all (Adams, 2011, p. 112).

As that quotation implies, in many ways the decision to come out—if it is a decision at all—is often filled with turmoil, even in circumstances when others are supportive.

In many ways, Adams' (2011) nine paradoxes of the closet serve as a perfect illustrator for coming out at the Cultural Level. As such, I close this section by reviewing each. First, Adams notes that being attracted to someone of the same sex is instantly connected to the closet. That is because, as he explains in his second paradox, that attraction is not immediately visible. So even though people who are attracted to the same sex might be present, they probably are not realized as being present until they give some sort of indication they are there. Third, because of the second paradox, the world is heteronormative in nature. That is, as Adams says, people are "heterosexual until proven otherwise" (p. 112). That leads to his fourth paradox, that if people want to be recognized as full sexual beings, then they must come out. Fifth, coming out is dangerous, both because some people are hostile toward those who are attracted to people of the same sex but also because people are suspicious about how or why someone was private about their sexuality. That is, a person's reason for not coming out is under scrutiny and might even be viewed as deceptive or dishonest.

Yet, as he points out in his sixth paradox, people are expected to come out because doing so is not being culturally constructed as mature, honest, healthy, and politically responsible. Those who do not come out might be labeled as self-hating, immature, secretive, or foolish. Yet, at the same time, other members of a culture will see coming out as insensitive, attention-seeking, or even selfish. To that end, the seventh paradox examines how some people will suggest that coming out is disrespectful to others, and a sign that a person does not care. That might cause some people to come out to some people and not to others. Along those lines, Adams' (2011) eighth paradox suggests that coming out can be discrete, in that there is an end to the process (e.g., "I came out!"). Yet, at the same time, because coming out is not self-evident, every time someone new is met, coming out has to happen with that person again. As such, the final cultural paradox suggests that coming out never ends.

The Cognitive Level

Even though the Cultural Level is not directly connected to the Cognitive Level on the model, it is presented after the Cultural Level because culture has a direct impact on the way people understand themselves and others (see Brown & Weigel, this volume). The *Cognitive Level* of coming out involves the psychological processes involved with how GLBQ people understand their sexual identities as well as how they feel about them. The foundational research for understanding cognitive coming out practices was developed by Vivienne Cass (1979, 1984), whose Homosexual Identity Formation Model (HIM) is widely cited and recognized. Although many coming out researchers are now dismissive of the model, suggesting that coming out research has moved far beyond Cass' work, it does not change the fact that HIM started the conversation and has influenced virtually all coming out research that has followed. Moreover, it has great heuristic value. As Manning (2014) notes, it is widely used in brochures, pamphlets, websites, and self-help guides to help GLBQ people think about their identities.

HIM is a stage model, meaning that it suggests that people go through different phases. Specifically, Cass' (1979) model suggests that people move from being confused about their sexual identity to, if all goes well, figuring out how to synthesize it with a largely heterosexual culture. The six stages a GLBQ person goes through—Identity Confusion, Identity Comparison, Identity Tolerance, Identity Acceptance, Identity Pride, and Identity Synthesis (see Figure 7.2)—are goals of sort that allow people to "acquire an identity of 'homosexual' fully integrated within the individual's overall concept of self" (Cass, 1979, p. 220). Simply put, for someone to try to have good mental health related to sexual identity, progressing through all six stages would be beneficial.

FIGURE 7.2 *Cass' (1979) Stages of Homosexual Identity Formation*

Stage	Description	Representative Thought Process
Identity Confusion	Realizing you do not have a heterosexual identity	"Okay, there's no more denying it. I have a crush on Amanda. Am I a lesbian?"
Identity Comparison	Comparing your sexual identity to heterosexuality	"If I marry a girl, though, I could have kids and a normal life."
Identity Tolerance	Presenting your sexual identity to others	"Mom said she'd love me no matter what. I might as well tell her and see how that goes."
Identity Acceptance	Sharing your sexual identity more openly and starting to hang out with other GLBQ people	"Sorry, I can't make it to drinks with you all after work today. I play poker with the other lesbians on Thursdays."
Identity Pride	Celebrating your identity, perhaps even pitting it against heterosexuality	"I love that most gay guys don't get all bent out of shape when their boyfriends check out someone else. Being heterosexual and dealing with that jealousy must suck."
Identity Synthesis	Seeing how your identity is, in many ways, similar to others and recognizing that you are a unique part of culture	"I never thought I'd want to get married. But here I am, ready for the ring and kids and the whole shebang."

Even if Cass' (1979) model is helpful for people to think about their sexual identities, other researchers have rightly pointed to some of its problematic aspects. For example, Troiden (1988, 1989) was skeptical that people had to go through each of the six stages one-by-one, and instead thought that people might go back and forth through various stages at different points in their lives. His research, and the work of others, confirmed that he was right. Coming out, in the self-acceptance sense, if probably more like a spiral than a line where people might go up and down the stages as life changes. Taking a completely different approach, D'Augelli (1994) hypothesized that coming out was tied to a person's life span. Through his research, he developed a model that emphasizes six areas where sexual identities are malleable as a person grows and develops: 1) exiting heterosexual identity; 2) developing a personal gay identity status; 3) developing a gay social identity; 4) becoming a gay offspring; 5) developing a gay intimacy status; and 6) entering a gay community.

In doing his work, D'Augelli (1994) tried to be more sensitive to culture, too. Past models were rightly criticized for being too focused on White people or people with a middle-class lifestyle. D'Augelli recognized that different environmental factors could impact development. For example, it might be harder for someone in Southwest Kansas to accept his or her sexual identity than it would be for someone from suburban Chicago. Even then, a person's family or school might also have an impact. D'Augelli calls these "interindividual differences" (1994, p. 321), recognizing that even though models are good at giving general guidelines, they cannot account for each individual person in the same way. That, in general, is a widely-recognized flaw with cognitive research and models: they often put a single person at the center of the analysis. Scholars have also noted that they lack diversity (e.g., Diamond, 2003; Peplau & Garnets, 2000), even though in the mid-1990s some scholars were exploring how racial and ethnic differences impacted coming out experiences (e.g., Greene, 1994). Finally, many cognitive models assume how people communicate or interact with others, something that was not addressed until recent communication scholarship.

The Relational Level

The Relational Level, located between the cultural and cognitive level because of its strong connections to both, focuses on interpersonal relationships. This level is essential both because it demarcates general social relationships from close relationships such as friendships, family, and romantic relationships. Research studies examining the Relational Level tend to explore *proximal discourses*, the things people say to each other (Manning, 2014). These proximal discourses draw from *distal discourses*, the larger pool of intelligible ideas that allow people to organize a conversation and make it intelligible. In that sense, the Relational Level connects to the cultural level because proximal coming out disclosures and the conversations that precede and follow are informed by larger cultural understandings of coming out. As I explained in an earlier essay,

> [I]f someone says, "I'm gay," that proximal disclosure ties into a larger, distal idea of "coming out." Depending on an individual's experiences and ideas about coming out, he or she will respond with another proximal utterance that draws from a distal discourse. That could be, "You know it's an abomination" (drawing from a distal discourse of religion); "God made you perfectly, and if that's gay then so be it" (drawing from a different distal discourse of religion); "But you don't act gay!" (drawing from a distal discourse that suggests LGB people behave a particular way); or, as was common for the participants of this study, "Are you being careful sexually?" (drawing from a distal discourse that gay or bisexual men are at risk to contract sexually transmitted diseases or infections) (Manning, 2014, p. 34).

The idea that coming out conversations involve proximal discourses that draw from distal cultural discourses is inspired by the second iteration of Leslie A. Baxter's relational dialectics theory (Baxter, 2011). Baxter's theory assumes that conflict and contradiction are a natural part of dialogue, and that different, competing discourses—both at the proximal and distal level—can result in conversational tensions. These tensions can be productive, in that they allow those involved with the conversation to learn, grow, or reconsider their viewpoints. They can also be difficult, disheartening, or even destructive. Manning's (2015b) typology of positive and negative communicative behaviors, developed from research with GLBQ participants from diverse backgrounds, illustrates these possibilities (see Figures 7.3 and 7.4).

Although every coming out conversation is different, they tend to follow patterns in terms of how they happen and what details are involved. Drawing from over 260 coming out narratives from GLBQ people of different ages and from around the world, Manning (2015a) developed a typology that helps to illustrate some of the most common ways that coming out conversations occur. The typology is non-exclusive, meaning that in some cases a single conversation can fall into two different categories. This typology revealed that coming out conversations are often pre-planned, emergent, coaxed, forced, romantic, and/or educational/activist (see Figure 7.5).

FIGURE 7.3 *Positive Communicative Behaviors in Coming Out Conversations (Manning, 2015b)*

Receiver Behavior	Defined	Representative Dialogue or Action
Open Communication Channels	Inviting future discussion regarding relationships and sexual identity	"I hope you know you can always talk to me about this. I want to know about you and your life!"
Affirming Direct Relational Statements	Directly and explicitly expressing care, respect, and affection	"I love you so much. I am proud to be your father!"
Laughter and Joking	Use of gentle humor to show acceptance	"Well, now I know why you are always spending the night at your 'best friend's' house! I can't wait to meet him!"
Nonverbal Immediacy	Use of appropriate touch to show affection	Hugs; comforting rubs on back, shoulder, or arms; holding a hand

FIGURE 7.4 *Negative Communicative Behaviors in Coming Out Conversations (Manning, 2015b)*

Receiver Behavior	Defined	Representative Dialogue or Action
Expressing Denial	Insistence that the person is not GLBQ or is confused	"I think you want attention. I don't believe for a second that you're really a lesbian."
Religious Talk	Invoking religion as a critique of identity or actions	"Well, you know I don't agree with it. But love the sinner, hate the sin."
Inappropriate Questions, Comments, or Concerns	Asking questions, making comments, or expressing concerns that violate privacy or invoke authority	"You're not the girl, right? I mean, you don't let him, you know… put it there?"
Shaming Statements	Direct admonishment and/or judgment	"We have done so much for you, and this is how you repay us. You should be ashamed of yourself!"
Aggression	Physical or verbal behaviors that are threatening, hostile, intimidating, or violent	"Maybe if I gave it to you right here, you'd see what a woman is supposed to like! Is that what you want?"

Conversation Type	Defined	Representative Dialogue
FIGURE 7.5 *Manning's (2015a) Non-Exclusive Typology of Coming Out Conversations*		
Pre-planned	The GLBQ person decides to arrange a conversation	Bianca: Mom, I invited you over tonight for dinner because I want to talk to you about something.
Emergent	The GLBQ person decides to come out based on an ongoing conversation	Geoff: Sorry to dump all my problems on you. It's just that I don't know anyone who's gay. Bianca: Well, you know me. Geoff: What? You mean… Bianca: Yes, I'm a lesbian. Feel free to invite me for a conversation any time.
Coaxed	The GLBQ person is encouraged to come out by another	Imi: Bianca, you are my cousin and I sense that you are holding back. You know you can tell me anything. Bianca: I know that, Imi. Imi: So if you ever want to tell me anything about your love life, and who you love, know I'm ready.
Forced	The GLBQ person is coerced to come out	Grandpa: I see you with that girl, Bianca. Girls don't behave that way! So you tell me now—so help me or I will write you out of the will. I won't be a fool anymore! Tell me!
Romantic	The GLBQ person comes out by making romantic or sexual advances	Bianca: I know we're best friends. And you probably only see us that way. But… but I want to kiss you so bad right now.
Educational/ Activist	The GLBQ person comes out in order to educate or encourage others, usually in front of an audience	Bianca: Thank you for coming to our Safe Zone panel tonight. My name is Bianca, and I am an out lesbian, and I want to help you learn about what it means to be an ally tonight!

Although the typologies presented in this section are helpful, much more research is needed about how people communicate in their relationships after coming out. As both the Cultural and Cognitive Levels indicate, coming out is a process. It makes sense that as people in a relationship continue to consider their sexual and romantic identities, that the relationship itself will continue to change. Although many studies that would fall into the Cognitive Level have explored how people think and feel about their relationships post-coming out (e.g., Cramer & Roach, 1988; Griffith & Hebl, 2002), few have examined the actual communication in those relationships. More research about communication in relationships after coming out is in order. It is also helpful to consider that each time a person comes out to a friend, family member, or even a romantic partner, that it typically involves three steps: a pre-announcement or introduction that sets the stage ("There's something I want to tell you"); a disclosure ("I'm gay"); and then a reaction or series of reactions in the form of a conversation (Manning, 2014).

Conclusion

As this constitutive model of communication indicates, coming out can be conceptualized in three different ways: culturally, as societies and their communities continue to forge understandings about what GLBQ identities involve and that work together to create frameworks for how those identities are understood and communicated; cognitively, as individuals realize who they are sexually and romantically and how that is likely to be received; and relationally, as GLBQ people share their identities with others. Even though great progress has been made in many cultures, even the most liberated often set the stage for GLBQ people to spend a great deal of mental energy being in the closet and worrying about revealing their identities to others as well as discursive energy having to explain who they are and how they know. With continued research about coming out—as well as continued education about how individuals and cultures can be supportive of a broad spectrum of relationships and sexualities—it might soon be that coming out as gay, lesbian, bisexual, or sexually queer is not necessary as diverse sexual and romantic identities are expected and respected in society.

DISCUSSION QUESTIONS

1. Has someone ever come out to you? If so, did you enact any of the behaviors listed on the positive communicative behaviors chart? How about the negative communicative behaviors chart? If no one has ever come out to you, what behaviors from the two charts would you be more likely to exhibit? Why?

2. Think about someone coming out in your workplace. What about your workplace would make it easy? What would make it difficult? What would be the ongoing impact for the person who came out?

3. Why might someone be scared to come out, even in a supportive culture or relationship?

4. When someone comes out, does it change how they are viewed? Why or why not?

5. This chapter examines GLBQ coming out. What identities besides sexual identities might be concealed or uncertain until a person discloses that identity? Try to list at least five, and then look at each and decide: If someone revealed that identity to you, would you say they were coming out?

References

Adams, T. E. (2011). *Narrating the closet: An autoethnography of same-sex attraction*. Walnut Creek, CA: Left Coast.

Baxter, L. A. (2011). *Voicing relationships: A dialogic perspective*. Thousand Oaks, CA: Sage.

Cass, V. C. (1979). Homosexual identity formation: A theoretical model. *Journal of Homosexuality, 4*(3), 219–235.

Cass, V. C. (1984). Homosexual identity: A concept in need of a definition. *Journal of Homosexuality, 10*, 219–235.

Cramer, D. W., & Roach, A. J. (1988). Coming out to mom and dad: A study of gay males and their relationships with their parents. *Journal of Homosexuality, 15*, 79–91.

D'Augelli, A. R. (1994). Identity development and sexual orientation: Toward a model of lesbian, gay, and bisexual development. In E. J. Trickett,

R. J. Watts, & D. Birman, (Eds.), *Human diversity: Perspectives on people in context* (pp. 312–333). San Francisco: Jossey-Bass.

Diamond, L. M. (2003). Was it a phase? Young women's relinquishment of lesbian/bisexual identities over a 5-year period. *Journal of Personality and Social Psychology, 84*, 352–364.

Duck, S. (2011). *Rethinking relationships.* Thousand Oaks, CA: Sage.

Eguchi, S., Calafell, B. M., & Files-Thompson, N. (2014). Intersectionality and quare theory: Fantasizing African American male same-sex relationships in *Noah's Arc: Jumping the Broom. Communication, Culture & Critique, 7*(3), 371-389. doi:10.1111/cccr.12054.

Ellis, C. (2004). *The ethnographic I: A methodological novel about autoethnography.* Walnut Creek, CA: AltaMira.

Gonzales, F., & Espin, O. M. (1996). Latino men, Latina women, and homosexuality. In R. P. Cabaj, & T. S. Stein (Eds.), *Textbook of homosexuality and mental health* (pp. 583–602). Washington, D.C.: American Psychiatric.

Greene, B. (1994). Lesbian women of color: Triple jeopardy. In L. Comas-Diaz, & B. Greene (Eds.), *Women of color: Integrating ethnic and gender identities in psychotherapy* (pp. 389–427). New York: Guilford.

Griffith, K. H., & Hebl, M. R. (2002). The disclosure dilemma for gay men and lesbians: "Coming out" at work. *Journal of Applied Psychology, 87*(6), 1191–1999.

Manning, J. (2013). Interpretive theorizing in the seductive world of sexuality and interpersonal communication: Getting guerilla with studies of sexting and purity rings. *International Journal of Communication, 7*, 2507–2520. Retrieved from http://ijoc.org/index.php/ijoc/article/view/2250/1023.

Manning, J. (2014). Coming out conversations and gay/bisexual men's sexual health: A constitutive model study. In V. L. Harvey, & T. H. Housel (Eds.), *Health care disparities and the LGBT population* (pp. 27–54). Lanham, MD: Lexington Books. doi:10.13140/2.1.1867.8089.

Manning, J. (2015a). Communicating sexual identities: A typology of coming out. *Sexuality & Culture, 19*(1), 122–138. doi:10.1007/s12119-014-9251-4.

Manning, J. (2015b). Positive and negative communicative behaviors in coming-out conversations. *Journal of Homosexuality, 62*(1), 67–97. doi:10.1080/00918369.2014.957127.

Manning, J. (2015c). The rhetorical function of laugh tracks in situation comedies: Examining queer shame in *Will & Grace* and *Roseanne*. *Relevant Rhetoric, 6*, 1–15. Retrieved from http://relevantrhetoric. com/LaughTracks.pdf.

Peplau, L. A., & Garnets, L. D. (2000). A new paradigm for understanding women's sexuality and sexual orientation. *Journal of Social Issues, 56*(2), 330–350.

Plummer, K. (1995). *Telling sexual stories: Power, change, and social worlds.* New York: Routledge.

Rich, A. (1980). Compulsory heterosexuality and lesbian existence. In H. Abelove, M. A. Barale, & D. M. Halperin (Eds.), *The lesbian and gay studies reader* (pp. 227–254). New York, NY: Routledge.

Rust, P. C. (2003). Finding a sexual identity and community: Therapeutic implications and cultural assumptions in scientific models of coming out. In L. D. Garnets, & D. C. Kimmel (Eds.), *Psychological perspectives on lesbian, gay and bisexual experiences* (pp. 227–69). New York: Columbia University Press.

Sedgwick, E. K. (1990). *Epistemology of the closet.* Berkeley, CA: University of California.

Troiden, R. R. (1988). Homosexual identity development. *Journal of Adolescent Health Care, 9*(2), 105–113.

Troiden, R. R. (1989). The formation of homosexual identities. *Journal of Homosexuality, 17*(1-2), 43–73.

CHAPTER 8

Challenging the Closet: Living the Politics of Identity as Bisexual/Queer Identified Women

Linda Baughman & Michaela D. E. Meyer

KEY TERMS

Bisexuality   Autoethnography   Sexual identity
Queer   Closet

ABSTRACT

Our chapter explores the idea that bisexual/queer identified individuals experience a particular and specific communicative challenge regarding the closet. At times, the closet, which is conceptualized as almost universally negative for gay and lesbian identities, can provide a political space that benefits bisexual/queer identities. In this chapter, we employ collaborative autoethnography to explore sexual identity formation. Through this approach, we illustrate the complex communicative features of the closet using our own bisexual/queer-identified experiences as primary data for analysis. Ultimately, our work seeks to expand discussions of sexuality identity beyond the heterosexual-homosexual binary and challenge current thinking about identity politics.

In contemporary discussions of sexual identity, the closet is a salient and powerful discursive metaphor. The exact origin of the use of the term "closeted" for sexual identity is muddy at best (Guittar, 2014), though, most commonly, the phrase is linked to discourses of family secrets as "skeletons in your closet" (Sedgwick, 2008). These skeletons could damage the social status of the entire family, and therefore the closet becomes a metaphorical holding place for secrets (McCune, 2014). "The closet" is a tough metaphor to unpack—it comes from something negative (hiding family secrets that could be harmful if they came to light) but it is also something positive (a phrase that is used to claim public space for someone's identity). As long as our society is heteronormative, or a society that generally assumes people are heterosexual, people with same-sex attraction will continue to be defined through that attraction. This cultural assumption is why the metaphor of the closet is a common cultural troupe used to understand disclosure of non-heterosexual identities. Individuals who identify as heterosexual do not often conceptualize sexual identity as central to their individual identity (Diamond, 2008). In short, individuals who identify as heterosexual often take sexual identity for granted as something that is just "known" and thus needs no additional consideration. The opposite is true for those with same-sex attraction. For us, "who we are" is bound intricately to our sexual identity. Individuals who do not identify as heterosexual spend a large amount of time considering how to define their sexual identity and how it impacts their daily existence. So, if you are not straight, you are probably familiar with the closet. You have a secret about whom you are that you sometimes keep from others.

This conundrum is where communication plays a key role in understanding sexual identity and the closet. As Dinno (1997) notes, "Our culture has a very strong sense of the gay or lesbian person. These are part of our cultural iconography or typology of persons. Whether or not they are presented in detail or as positive or negative, they are available for the developing youth to grasp and manipulate" (p. 205). Gays and lesbians can "come out" of the closet because these identities already exist as common currency in the cultural lexicon of identity (see Manning, this volume). This lexicon of identity is far more challenging for individuals who identify as bisexual, queer, pansexual, omnisexual, or by another non-heterosexual identity. In other words, our cultural construction of the closet works nicely to explain gay and lesbian experience, but is perhaps problematic when examining other types of sexual identities. Perhaps the closet is a tough metaphor for more than just its history—the closet actually isn't a one-size-fits-all place.

If how we conceptualize the closet is problematic for those who do not easily identify as heterosexual or homosexual, then how are sexual others constructed in relation to this cultural discourse?

LINDA: So in high school, I was messing around with girls, but I didn't take it seriously. It was something I did, like eat too much sugar, it wasn't who I was. Eventually I realized I was noticing this girl who was in technical theater. But I didn't really think about it. I didn't understand what that meant. And then there was this moment where I'm working on a cat-walk, 100 feet in the air, trying to hang a huge light. I've got this wrench and I'm tightening this light. The theater is dark and I think I'm alone, but Michelle Barnes leans down behind me and puts her arms around me, presses her breasts against my back and whispers in my ear, "Let me help you." …It was like "Oh My God! This is the best thing ever! Please don't let her ever move." But I was kind of awful. Because I didn't take her seriously. We had sex, a lot of sex. But she was a woman, you know and I was dating a guy… that was *real*. I liked to have sex with her, but that wasn't real. So I totally compartmentalized my behavior and attraction. I drank too much, I did drugs. I drove too fast, and … I fucked Michelle. It was one of my vices. It had nothing to do with who I was.

MICHAELA: I grew up in Nebraska. I had a lot of cues that there were people that were not straight but for some reason it didn't translate to me until I went to college. And so the first year I was in college, I was in a theatrical production with this one woman and she was like, "well, why would you limit yourself to being just with dudes? When you could have a woman!!" And I was like "Ohhh, interesting, there's other people out there who are homosexual. But it's not me. Clearly I'm heterosexual. I only date dudes, Catholic dudes." So my senior year I met Ari, who ended up being my on and off girlfriend for quite some time. But it was the first time I met a woman that I was like, "Oh…wait, maybe I'm not straight." Because before it was hypothetical, and I didn't care so much about it when it was hypothetical. I was like, "Yeah, I mean, if I was interested in women, I guess I would be interested in them, but I'm not, so it's not an issue." But at that point, for some reason I was like, "I'm interested in YOU—in like, a not friends way." And even then, when it happened, when I got into a relationship with her, I didn't know what to call it. Because I wasn't lesbian. I only understood gay and lesbian. When I finally had bisexual as a term, I was like, "Oh, thank God!" Give me something I can actually say, "this is me!" this is my person.

Complicating Sexual Identities

One of the primary problems with our cultural discussions of sexual identity is that we are firmly wedded to a binary discourse where heterosexuality exists, and homosexual identity is the opposite of heterosexuality.[1] Sexuality scholars have articulated bisexuality as an identity where individuals remain capable of feelings for and/or sexual contact with both women and men, but these attitudes or behaviors do not necessarily constitute their sexual practices or patterns of attraction (Rodriguez Rust, 2002). Savin-Williams (2005) observes at least nine different types of bisexuality recognized by sexuality literature that can be grouped into three general themes as articulated by Meyer (2010): *sexuality as (situational) behavior*, *sexuality as (negative) identity*, and *sexuality as (constitutively) relational*.

First, bisexuality can be explained as a specific set of sexual behaviors often resulting from certain subject positions and constraints. For example, in *situational bisexuality*, heterosexuals engage in same-sex behavior given extenuating restrictive circumstances, such as being incarcerated in a same-sex prison. If this behavior continues beyond situational constraints, individuals are said to exhibit *transitional bisexuality* where the goal is to bridge an identity change from heterosexual to homosexual. In the end, the individual "discovers" that they are homosexual through sexual experimentation. Rosario, Schrimshaw, Hunter, and Braun (2006) found through a longitudinal report of 156 lesbian, gay, and bisexual youths, nearly one-fifth utilized transitional bisexuality as a means of eventually adopting a gay or lesbian identity (see also Savin-Williams, 1998). In some cases, heterosexuals may engage in *chic bisexuality* (or heteroflexibility) where same-sex behavior is used as a means of cultivating social acceptance, such women engaging in same-sex kissing to obtain the attention of (usually male) others. This behavior is labeled as socially acceptable within the context it occurs and is not necessarily related to personal sexual identity claims. In each of these instances, the individual uses bisexual behavior as a liminal

---

1. While homosexual behavior has existed as long as there have been living organisms on this planet, the term was not coined until 1892. When translating Krafft-Ebing's medical text on sexual deviance, *Psychopathia Sexualis*, Charles Gilbert Chaddock coined the term "homosexuality" as a means to describe a German concept of Krafft-Ebing's (Halperin, 1990). The term "heterosexual" came into being at about the same time, but at first it meant someone who has sexual interest in both sexes, what we now call bisexuality (Katz, 1983). Heterosexual did not come to mean someone who is interested in only the opposite sex until around 1900 (Halperin, 1990).

space when still determining how to label their identity, and the end result of the behavior is an identity as heterosexual or homosexual.

A second set of scholarship identifies bisexuality as primarily an identity concept. Often when an individual recognizes that their desire and behavior are bisexual, they actively refuse to accept bisexuality as an identity category or label. This refusal is related to negative cultural stereotypes of bisexuality, and these forms tend to privilege heterosexuality and heteronormativity. *Historic bisexuality* occurs when an individuals' sexual history includes behaviors and/or fantasies contrary to their current sexual identification (e.g., Linda's story about her first same-sex experiences). Historic bisexuality is often aligned with being closeted because the subject is often constructed as denying their true identity. *Technical bisexuality* occurs when an individual has sex with men and women but prefers to be identified as straight, lesbian, or gay rather than bisexual. Perhaps the strongest example of technical bisexuality comes from the research on the "Down-Low" phenomenon among African-American men (e.g., Heath & Goggin, 2009; Lapinski, Braz, & Maloney, 2010; McCune, 2014; see also Yep, Lescure, & Allen, this volume). Men on the Down Low have sex with other men, but often adamantly refuse to identify as anything other than heterosexual. Finally, *cop-out bisexuality* occurs when individuals want the "best of both worlds" without having to commit themselves to a particular partner or lifestyle. This form of bisexuality is most frequently associated with individuals participating in swinger culture (Cooper, 2003; deVisser & McDonald, 2007) where individuals have sex with both men and women, but attribute this to playful behavior that is not inconsistent with a heterosexual identity.

Finally, a third set of scholarship indicates that bisexuality is best defined by relational choices and romantic attachments. This theme relates to our cultural understanding of bisexuality as driven by futuristic choices in attraction and sexual behavior, primarily with respect to the "option" of both sexes as sexual partners (Meyer, 2003). In this category, *sequential bisexuality* occurs when individuals create consecutive relationships with different sexes over time such that at any one point they are involved with only one partner. This notion is quite similar to the idea of serial monogamy, and as a result, these individuals are often not socially recognized as bisexual. Instead, their sexual identity is viewed as contingent on the sex of their current romantic partner (if a woman is dating a woman, she is a lesbian—

even if she identifies as bisexual). In contrast, *concurrent bisexuality* occurs when an individual maintains relationships with both sexes at the same time, often refusing to accept monogamy as a social construct. Polyamory, or the meaningful formation and maintenance of relationships with multiple partners, is one example that can embody concurrent bisexuality (Aviram, 2007; Kleese, 2006; Ritchie & Barker, 2006; see Dixon, this volume). In some cases, individuals engage in *experimental bisexuality* as means of testing relationships with more than one sex at a time to see which sex and/or gender performances appeal to them the most. This idea is similar to transitional bisexuality, but the individual involved accepts that s/he is bisexual and they engage in this behavior to learn about sexual preferences.

If we do not readily identify as heterosexual or homosexual, how do we decide how to label our sexual identities?

LINDA: It wasn't until I got to grad school that things changed. I met Sarah—we started going out. She identified as a lesbian at that time, and she kind of laid it on the table—"I'm not having sex with you just for fun. I've got two kids. I'm a grown-up. I can't be bothered—if you're not in this, leave me alone." So I had to kind of take seriously the fact that I liked women for the first time. And it changed everything. Because suddenly now I have to be this person. Instead of accepting it as behaviors for fun, now it's like I'm this person—I was this new identity: a queer woman. I had to step up. If I didn't step-up, she wasn't giving me the time of day.

MICHAELA: Oh, my gosh, that was so not my experience. Ari also hadn't identified as bi or queer and wasn't really sure about who she was. So we were like a classic case of missed opportunities. So I'd be like, "I'm flirting with you" and she'd be like, "peace out" and I'd be like, "shit, she doesn't like me." And then she'd be like, flirting with me. And I'd be like, "I gave up on that." And then later I was like, "Ohhh wait, I messed that up." Our dynamic was totally influenced by that because we couldn't quite figure out how to communicate. And I think about that a lot, if I had had the language... if I knew...but neither one of us had been with other women so we didn't know how to start it. We were like, "I'd be cool with it, if you are but I don't know what to do." And when we talked about it later (we're still friends), she was like, "I expected you, because you were older, to know what to do." And I was like, "I didn't know what to do! I assumed when you hit on me, you would know what to do!"

The Unique Experience of Bisexual/Queer Otherness

Coming out as bisexual or queer is not easy. The stereotypes about bisexual women and men can be ugly (see especially Burleson, 2005; Hutchins & Kaahumanu, 1991; McCune, 2014; Mulick & Wright 2002). Bisexuals are greedy—that is, we can't settle for one kind of sexual partner, we need them all. Bisexuals aren't trustworthy or monogamous because they want to sleep with everyone. Members of the gay community sometimes distrust us because they think we will "turn straight" and turn our backs on the community at the first opportunity. Members of the heterosexual community often believe we will steal husbands or wives. And there's more negativity: we are liars. We claim to be bisexual when we really are just gay (or straight).

This last point is at least a little understandable. Gay men and lesbians often claim a bisexual identity as a part of the coming out process. There is a long history of gay individuals claiming a bisexual identity first, then coming out as gay or lesbian later. Guittar (2014) calls this use of bisexuality a "transitional identity" (p. 43). Some gay individuals feel, often incorrectly, that if they come out as bisexual first, it will soften the blow when their actual gay identity is revealed (Guittar, 2014). This use of the bisexual "white-lie" makes it difficult for bisexual women and men to be taken seriously as a sexual minority. When coming out as bisexual, we are often not believed; bisexuality is viewed with skepticism by both the heterosexual and homosexual communities (Burleson, 2005; Diamond, 2008). For this reason, it is common for bisexuals to have to come out more than once (Land & Kitzinger, 2005). Families often assume that the bisexual identity disappears when the adult child comes home with a partner. If a woman brings home a male partner, she is often seen as putting away the "bisexual phase" and has "become straight." Similarly, if the new partner is a woman, the female child is now a lesbian. In either case, when an adult child takes a partner, families and friends often assume the bisexual identity was simply a phase, which is now over (Garber, 2000; Land & Kitzinger, 2005). So, while coming out is a life-long process for all sexual minorities, it is doubly so for bisexuals as we are often, incorrectly, identified by our partners of choice, rather than the sexual identity we continue to claim (Angelides, 2001; Burleson, 2005). Bisexuals must often remind their friends and family that while, yes, they are in a relationship, they are still bisexual.

When bisexuals come out and are believed, there are often negative consequences not present when gay men and lesbians come out. Bisexuals are often negatively judged by *both* heterosexual and homosexual communities (McLean, 2008; Mulick & Wright 2002; Weinberg, Williams, & Pryor, 1994). Plummer (1995) noted that coming out is a story-telling process that can help a person join a community, or become more honest with a community of origin. Coming out can help gay men and lesbians bond with other same-sex attracted persons and can bring them into a wider community. This is not the always the case when coming out as bisexual. Many members of the gay community are hostile to bisexuals. Biphobia is a unique type of oppression. As Eisner, and others have noted (Burleson, 2005; Eisner, 2013; Garber, 2000; McCune, 2014), bisexuals are often dismissed as illegitimate members of the queer community. Like many heterosexuals, gay men and lesbians will sometimes argue "bisexuality doesn't exist" (Eisner, 2013, p. 59). This statement is not the same as thinking bisexuality is "just a phase." The it's just a phase argument recognizes that bisexuality exists, but assumes the person speaking isn't really bisexual. This is a judgment about our ability to understand who we are and what we feel; it denies our identity. Coercive passing is another form of biphobia existing in the queer community; this misconception occurs because some members of the gay community believe bisexuals aren't "gay enough." Because a bisexual can "choose" to live in a heterosexual pairing, some members of the gay community believe we do not have to experience the fear and rejection often present in the lives of gay men and lesbians (Burleson, 2005; Garber, 2000; Weinberg, Williams, & Pryor, 1994). The notion that bisexuals don't experience discrimination is, of course, incorrect. When a gay man or lesbian comes out to members of the gay community, they can expect a welcoming atmosphere and a sense of in-group belonging. Bisexuals do not have that privilege, because coming out as bisexual often alienates a person from both straight and gay communities (McLean, 2008; Mulick & Wright 2002).

So, given that bisexuals are often not believed when we tell people about our sexual identities, and when we disclose them, both straight and gay individuals often judge us negatively, why bother?

LINDA: That summer when I went to Michigan—I have—my mother's side of the family is *Duck Dynasty* without the money. I have a cousin who bought a machine gun. He shoots deer out of his bathroom window at two in the morning because he saw a "huge buck." And I have this, I don't know, this second or third cousin—and she's gay. She's a lesbian. And this is the side of the family...they are homophobic red-neck, dick-head ass-holes. Unless you're family—if you're family, you're in. This is OUR QUEER!

Queers ruined America, but you're our faggot. So you're okay. But coming home as bisexual? Bisexual doesn't make sense to people. Because Stacey is a lesbian. They get that. She makes sense. But because I date boys and girls—I can't commit.

MICHAELA: Yeah, no one knows what to do with you. It sucks. I wish I were lesbian. Given my politics and how I think about things. When I broke up with my ex-husband, I assumed I'd be with a woman. My brother and my sister-in-law were like, "Yeah, we realized things with him were bad. But we thought they were bad because you hadn't come to terms with the fact that you're a lesbian." And then I started dating my current husband and they were like "NOooooo!" They all didn't like him at first. My whole family. Because my brother and sister-in-law had convinced my whole family that I just needed a good woman. Because that notion of bisexuality is so off the radar—that you're making a mistake.

Challenging the Closet: Finding Space for Sexual Others

For the many individuals, experiencing their sexuality as a state in-between heterosexuality and homosexuality is not the biggest problem—Western civilization is saturated with binary thinking, and our social world loves binaries. Levi-Strauss (1963) changed how we view anthropology by explaining how the Western world works hard to put ideas, things, and humans into categories of opposites: male/female; light/dark; good/bad; raw/cooked (food). But, he noted that some items are hard to define, they lived in neither category, or straddled both categories and upset the system. Take for example fish—in the United States, are they pets or food? According to our social classifications, animals are supposed to be pets OR food, not both—yet fish can be both food and household pets. This binary is why sexual others have difficulty coming out—they expose the problematic construction of the heterosexual/homosexual binary. Some people must declare a sexual life as a bisexual, a queer woman (or man), a pansexual, an omnisexual, because they do not feel heterosexual or homosexual. It simply isn't who they are.

Many human beings are sexually fluid, that is, they can enjoy sex with partners of both sexes and various sexual identities. As far back as Kinsey's studies in the 1940s and 50s, science was examining these phenomena. According to the well-read book, *Sexual Behavior in the Human Female*, Kinsey and his fellow authors found that 8–10% of married women, 11–20% of unmarried women, and 14–17% of previously married women reported homosexual encounters, as well as satisfying heterosexual experiences (Kinsey, Pomeroy, Martin, & Gebhard, 1953). During that same time period, men who slept with women experienced a much higher percentage of homosexual encounters, coming in at 50% (Kinsey, Pomeroy, & Martin, 1948). In a more recent examination of sexual identity, Diamond (2008) found that most women who identified in their teens and early 20s as bisexual or lesbian did not change their minds later; instead, 75% of them still identified as bisexual or lesbian five years later. Of the other 25%, only half determined they were heterosexual and the other half declined to label themselves at all (Diamond, 2008). This finding indicates that most of these women felt that the term bisexuality indicated a stable identity for them. People who live between the heterosexual and homosexual binary find life full and exciting, as well as difficult and troubling. It is hard to deny who you are, no matter how you label that identity.

If the metaphor of the closet doesn't work for sexual others, and is instead largely tied to experiences of a hetero-sexual/homosexual binary, how might we re-think the closet?

LINDA: I came from this position…this incredibly naïve position. I thought the closet had nothing to do with me because I was a straight woman having sex with women. And then when I got my eyes opened, I actually had to make a decision to step *into* the closet. Because I think many people who identify as lesbian or gay, as soon as they recognize that identity, they are IN the closet. But for me, it was like, people already know most of who I am. They already know the heterosexual side of my identity. So, the closeted part of my identity was only a piece of who I was. For me the closet is weird. Usually when people identify as lesbian or gay, they come out that same way all the time—"I am gay," "I am lesbian." But for me, as queer, how I come out depends on the audience. When I come out to straight friends, I have to come out as some who is sexually attracted to women. But when I come out to gay friends, I have to come out as being a part-time boy lover. So my closet is different from a gay closet.

MICHAELA: Yes—it is so situationally constrained! So, I live in this old historic house. And I kid you not, one of the things that drives me nuts about it is my bedroom closet door. Because of how it is hinged, and its latching, it's like, never closed. You close it hard—click—and then 30 minutes later someone breathes the wrong way and it pops ajar. But it doesn't fully open either—like in the morning, I go in to get some clothes out and throw the door wide open, but the hinges naturally just ease back and suddenly the door is like hitting your butt. Almost forcing you into the closet. So if I was going to explain the metaphor of my closet, it would be that way—when I want it closed, it sometimes pops ajar, and when I want it open, something is always forcing me back in. That's what it's like to try to claim being bisexual as my stable sexual identity. I'm not closeted. I'm so out—on my website, in my professional life. But, it's this weird dynamic, where sometimes people decide what they want to know and what they don't want to know. I have to sometimes "remind" people that I'm bisexual. Especially when they view my life in a married, opposite-sex partnership. And we are the weird couple on the block with the stay at home dad and working mom. So we don't really fit in with the religious stay-at-home mom culture, but gay people do not want to hang out with us because our life looks so heterosexual. Plus, my husband is super ridiculously hot. Every gay person we meet is like, "your husband is hot!" The last time we went to gay pride, I got a lot of "oh, honey" because the gay men all thought he's the one who is gay! I'm seen as the straight one. So my bisexuality is actually subsumed under his supposed homosexuality! He makes me seem more straight, not less so. So even though I'm very open with who I am, it's very public, I am still perceived to be closeted. And what's worse, the assumption is that because I married a guy and had a kid, you've done this to yourself. You closeted yourself.

Looking to the Future

Articulating sexual identity through the closet metaphor produces "weighty and occupied and consequential epistemological space" in contemporary culture (Sedgwick, 2008, p. 77). Adams (2011) outlines seven interrelated conditions that culturally construct the closet, explaining that "when a person is said to be 'in the closet,' she or he is thought to possess a wild-but-hidden, potentially troubling secret" (p. 40). As a result, one of the defining features of the closet is the awareness that communicative disclosure about non-heterosexual identity invites negative criticism from others, ultimately threatening your primary interpersonal relationships with family, friends, and acquaintances. So communication plays an imperative function in how we construct the closet (see also Cheseboro, 1981; Chirrey, 2003; Dindia, 1998; Meyer, 2005; Yep, 2003), and as such, is one aspect of sexual identity that is largely constituted (or defined) by communication.

Bisexual or queer people aren't completely in hiding before they come "out of the closet." Part of their sexual identity has always been on display. The person was never entirely "in the closet." If a bisexual man dates another man, people know he likes men, they just don't know he likes women too. You are paradoxically on sexual display and hidden simultaneously, and the closet as a metaphor does not work well for this situation. When we use the closet as the primary metaphor for how non-straight people exist and figure out who we are, we inadvertently confuse some people. If we had other ways of communicating about working through one's sexual identity, it might make it easier for some of us to figure out who we are. We aren't saying we need to leave the closet metaphor behind, but perhaps it is time to think of other metaphors for growing into one's sexual identity. Even if we simply start with the awareness that closets can be cracked or ajar just as easily as they can be open or closed.

DISCUSSION QUESTIONS

1. What does it mean to be part of a heteronormative society? How do we understand sexuality within a heteronormative context?

2. In this chapter, the authors discuss how bisexuality is a complicated sexual identity because there are multiple types of bisexuality identified in sexuality scholarship. What is your reaction to these different types of bisexuality? How do they complicate your understanding of sexual identity?

3. The authors used a collaborative autoethnographic method in this chapter—offering analysis of academic scholarship juxtaposed with personal narrative. How did you respond to this type of methodological framing for this research? What does the use of autoethnography add to our understanding of sexual identity?

4. What does the term "closeted" mean to you? Given the authors' discussion of the metaphor of the closet as it relates to sexual identity, how might you understand the closet and its articulation through communication?

5. At the end of the chapter, the authors call for a broader understanding of the closet and suggest that we begin to develop new metaphors for sexual identity. What might a new metaphor be? How could we better conceptualize sexual "others"—bisexuals, queers, pansexuals, etc.—through communication?

References

Adams, T. E. (2011). *Narrating the closet: An autoethnography of same-sex attraction*. Walnut Creek, CA: Left Coast Press.

Angelides, S. (2001). *A history of bisexuality*. Chicago: University of Chicago Press.

Aviram, H. (2007). Make love, not law: Perceptions of the marriage equality struggle among polyamorous activists. *Journal of Bisexuality, 7*(3/4), 261–286.

Burleson, W. (2005). *Bi-America: Myths, truths, and struggles of an invisible community*. New York: Harrington Park Press.

Chauncey, G. (1994). *Gay New York: Gender, urban culture, and the gay male world 1890–1940*. New York: Basic Books.

Cheseboro, J. W. (1981). *Gayspeak: Gay male and lesbian communication*. New York: The Pilgrim Press.

Chirrey, D. A. (2003). "I hereby come out": What sort of speech act is coming out. *Journal of Sociolinguistics, 7*, 24–37.

Cooper, C. (2003). Swing it baby! *Journal of Bisexuality, 3*(3/4), 87–92.

Diamond, L. (2008). *Sexual fluidity: Understanding women's love and desire*. Cambridge, MA: Harvard University Press.

Dindia, K. (1998). "Going into and coming out of the closet": The dialectics of stigma disclosure. In B. M. Montgomery & L. A. Baxter (Eds.), *Dialectical approaches to studying personal relationships* (pp. 83–108). Mahwah, NJ: Lawrence Erlbaum Associates, Inc.

Dinno, A. B. (1997). From the perspective of a young transsexual. In G. E. Israel & D. E. Tarver II (Eds.), *Transgender care: Recommended guidelines, practical information, and personal accounts* (pp. 203–207). Philadelphia: Temple University Press.

Eisner, S. (2013). *Bi: Notes for a bisexual revolution*. Berkeley, CA: Seal Press.

Garber, M. (2000). *Bisexuality and the eroticism of everyday life*. New York: Routledge.

Guittar, N. (2014). *Coming out: The new dynamics*. Boulder, CO and London: First Forum Press.

Halprin, D. (1990). *One hundred years of homosexuality*. New York: Routledge.

Heath, J., & Goggin, K. (2009). Attitudes towards male homosexuality, bisexuality, and the Down Low lifestyle: Demographic differences and HIV Implications. *Journal of Bisexuality, 9*, 17–31.

Hutchins, L., & Kaahumanu, L. (Eds.). (1991). *Bi any other name: Bisexual people speak out*. Los Angeles: Alyson Books.

Katz, J. N. (1983). *Gay/lesbian almanac: A new documentary*. New York: Harper & Row.

Klesse, C. (2006). Polyamory and its 'others': Contesting the terms of non-monogamy. *Sexualities, 9*, 565–583.

Kinsey, A., Pomeroy, W., & Martin, C. (1948). *Sexual behavior in the human male*. Bloomington: Indiana University Press.

Kinsey, A., Pomeroy, W., Martin, C., & Gebhard, P. (1953). *Sexual behavior in the human female*. Bloomington: Indiana University Press.

Land, V., & Kitzinger, C. (2005). Speaking as a lesbian: Correcting the heterosexist presumption. *Research on Language and Social Interaction, 38*, 371–416.

Lapinski, M. K., Braz, M. E., & Maloney, E. K. (2010). The Down Low, social stigma, and risky sexual behaviors: Insights from African-American men who have sex with men. *Journal of Homosexuality, 57*, 610–633.

Legate, N., Ryan, R. M., & Weinstein, N. (2012). Is coming out always a good thing? *Social Psychology and Personality Sciences, 3*, 145–152.

Levi-Strauss, C. (1963). *Structural anthropology*. (C. Jacobson & B. G. Schoepf., Trans.) New York: Basic Books.

McCune Jr., J. (2014). *Sexual discretion: Black masculinity and the politics of passing*. Chicago: University of Chicago Press.

McLean, K. (2008). Inside, outside, nowhere: Bisexual men and women in the gay and lesbian community. *Journal of Bisexuality, 8*, 63–80.

Meyer, M. D. E. (2010). Representing bisexuality: Exploring intersectionality in television targeted to emerging adults. *The Journal of Bisexuality, 10*(4), 366–387.

Meyer, M. D. E. (2005). Drawing the sexuality card: Teaching, researching and living bisexuality. *Sexuality & Culture, 9*, 3–13.

Meyer, M. D. E. (2003). Looking toward the interSEXions: Examining bisexual and transgender identity formation from a dialectical theoretical perspective. *Journal of Bisexuality, 3*(3/4), 151–170.

Mulick, P., & Wright, Jr., L. W. (2002). Examining the existence of biphobia in the heterosexual and homosexual populations. *Journal of Bisexuality, 2,* 47–64.

Orne, J. (2011). You will always have to 'out' yourself: Reconsidering coming out through strategic outness. *Sexualities, 14,* 681–703.

Plummer, K. (1995). *Telling sexual stories: Power, change and social worlds.* London: Routledge.

Ritchie, A., & Barker, M. (2006). 'There aren't words for what we do or how we feel so we have to make them up': Constructing polyamorous languages in a culture of compulsory monogamy. *Sexualities, 9,* 584–601.

Rodriguez Rust, P. C. (2002). Bisexuality: The state of the union. *Annual Review of Sex Research, 13,* 180–240.

Rosario, M., Schrimshaw, E. W., Hunter, J., & Braun, L. (2006). Sexual identity development among lesbian, gay, and bisexual youths: Consistency and change over time. *The Journal of Sex Research, 43,* 46–58.

Savin-Williams, R. C. (2005). *The new gay teenager.* Cambridge, MA: Harvard University Press.

Savin-Williams, R. C. (1998). *"...And then I became gay": Young men's stories.* New York: Routledge.

Sedgwick, E. K. (2008). *Epistemology of the closet.* Berkeley: University of California Press.

de Visser, R., & McDonald, D. (2007). Swings and roundabouts: Management of jealousy in heterosexual 'swinging' couples. *British Journal of Social Psychology, 46,* 459–476.

Weinberg, M., Williams, C., & Pryor, D. (1994). *Dual attraction: Understanding bisexuality.* Oxford: Oxford University Press.

Yep, G. A. (2003). The violence of heteronormativity in communication studies: Notes on injury, healing, and queer world-making. In G. A. Yep, K. E. Lovaas, & J. P. Elia (Eds.), *Queer theory and communication: From disciplining queers to queering the discipline(s)* (pp. 11–60). Binghamton, NY: Harrington Park Press.

CHAPTER 9

Understanding Transgender Identities & Experiences

Shannon Criniti & Eli R. Green

KEY TERMS

Biological sex
Gender identity
Gender expression

Gender roles
Transgender

Pubertal suppression
Medical transition

ABSTRACT

Transgender people are those who have a gender identity that is different than the sex that they were assigned at birth. American culture is currently generally hostile toward transgender people, who experience pervasive and severe prejudice. To help better understand what it means to be transgender, this chapter explains the differences between biological sex, gender identity, gender expression, gender roles, and sexual orientation. Narratives of transgender children, teens, and adults are explored to help better understand the experiences of transgender people. Finally, examples of bystander interventions are used to demonstrate how to be better allies and advocates for transgender people.

An estimated 700,000 transgender people live in the United States, which is more than the total population of Boston, MA (Gates, 2011, Oliver, 2015). Stereotypes might imply that transgender people primarily live in large liberal cities, but in fact, transgender people live in all areas of the United States including suburban and rural places. Transgender people also come from all sorts of different backgrounds, including every age, ability, ethnicity, race, religion, socioeconomic status, and political party (Erickson-Schroth, 2014).

More people are becoming familiar with transgender people because of the increased positive coverage of transgender individuals in the media—both real actors and activists, such as Laverne Cox, Janet Mock, Chaz Bono, and Caitlyn Jenner; and fictional characters on award-winning popular television shows such as *Transparent* and *Orange is the New Black*. However, outside of pop culture only 14% of people report having a friend or a family member who is transgender, compared with 85% of people who report having a friend or family member who is lesbian, gay, or bisexual (Green, 2014). Many people assume that all transgender people are "visibly" transgender, but in reality it is likely that you have met a transgender person before and did not know. Chances are that there are transgender people living in your hometown, going to school on your campus, working at your place of employment, or in your extended family or friends circle.

Even as acceptance and rights for LGBQ (lesbian, gay, bisexual, and queer) people advance in the United States, people who are transgender face pervasive, persistent, and severe discrimination in their daily lives. A 2011 national study of transgender people's experiences of discrimination found that 63% of transgender people experienced an act of discrimination that had a major negative impact on their lives and jeopardized their personal safety, security, and ability to sustain themselves financially and emotionally (Grant et al., 2011). Some examples of prejudice and discrimination (*anti-transgender prejudice*) toward transgender people include: being prohibited from using a public bathroom; facing severe verbal or physical bullying in school; being physically attacked or sexually assaulted; not being hired for a job; being denied housing, medical care, or social services—all because the person is transgender. Due to the intersections of racism and anti-transgender prejudice, this discrimination is amplified for transgender people of color—reporting far higher levels of discrimination and related negative outcomes than white transgender people (Grant et al., 2011).

Much of this discrimination is rooted in ignorance, misinformation, and misconceptions about transgender people. To help increase understanding and awareness about the lives of transgender people, in this chapter we explain what it means to be transgender, what transgender people navigate in the world, and some real life and representative fictional examples.

What is Transgender?

In order to understand what it means to be transgender, it is important to understand that all people have a *biological sex*, a *gender identity*, a *gender expression*, and a *sexual orientation* (Green & Maurer, 2015). A person's biological sex is their combination of chromosomes, genitals/gonads, and hormones (Rudacille, 2005). A majority of people's biological sex can be categorized as *male* or *female*. Someone who is assigned male at birth usually has a combination of XY chromosomes, a penis and testicles, and testosterone as their dominant hormone. Someone who is assigned female at birth usually has a combination of XX chromosomes, a vulva, vagina, uterus and ovaries, and estrogen as their dominant hormone.

In about .02% of the population, a person's biological sex cannot be easily categorized into male or female, which is known as *intersex* (Intersex Society of North America, 2008). Intersex is when a person is born with a different combination of chromosomes, genitals, and hormones than what we expect of someone who is male or female. Intersex has sometimes been referred to as being a "hermaphrodite," but that word is considered outdated and offensive.

Gender Identity

While a person's biological sex is entirely physical, a person's *gender identity* is internal. Gender identity refers to an individual's innate sense of identifying as male, female, or some other gender (American Psychological Association, 2015; Kessler & McKenna, 1978; Rudacille, 2005). Some people describe their gender identity as being in their brain, while others describe it as being a part of their heart or their soul. For a majority of people, their gender identity is congruent with, or matches, the sex that they were assigned at birth. This is called *cisgender* (Green, 2006). Because a cisgender person's gender identity and biological sex are congruent, they might not realize that these are two separate parts of a person's gender (Stryker, 2008).

For some people the sex that they were assigned at birth is incongruent with, or does not match, their gender identity (American Psychological Association, 2005, Namaste, 2000; Serano, 2007; Stryker, 2008). This is called *transgender*. Transgender people who were assigned female at birth but have a gender identity of being male are known as *transgender men*. Transgender people who were assigned male at birth but have a gender identity of being female are known as *transgender women*. Some transgender people's gender identities are not easily categorized as male or female (Serano, 2007). These individuals may identify themselves using other terms, such as *genderqueer, genderfluid, bigender,* or *non-binary.*

A transgender young woman named Jazz Jennings describes her identity as "I have a girl brain, a boy body, I think like a girl, but I have [male] parts" (Jennings, 2012). She and her parents explain that ever since she was little, she has always known that she was a girl on the inside and wanted to have the body of a girl, so that her body would match her heart and mind. Jazz explains that she has never been confused about her gender, but that other people were confused, and that it took a few years for people to understand that she was a girl.

Like Jazz, transgender children will often repeatedly say that they identify as a different gender than their sex assigned at birth (Reed, Cohen-Kettenis, Reed, & Spack, 2008). These children often want to express themselves by wearing clothing and hairstyles that reflect their innate gender identity, rather than the sex they were assigned at birth. They might express frustration or disappointment with having the "wrong" body parts, or might inquire when their bodies will change to reflect their true gender. These patterns are consistent, persistent, and insistent (Brill & Pepper, 2008).

Many transgender people describe their experience as knowing in their brain, heart, or souls that are not the sex they were assigned at birth (American Psychological Association, 2015). Some transgender people know that they are transgender from a young age (2-3 years old) or around the time of puberty (8-10 years old). Other people realize that they are transgender

The narratives used in this section are fictional composite representations meant to illustrate the experiences of some transgender individuals and their families.

later in their lives. Although we do not know what causes a person to be transgender, we do know that transgender people have existed all over the world and throughout history. Transgender people come from all different backgrounds and have different races, ethnicities, socioeconomic statuses, religions, and abilities.

AJ, Age 3

AJ, age 3, and Paige, age 5, were bathing together when AJ stood up in the bath and said "Mommy, when can I get my 'gina? I don't want dis penis."

Alicia hesitated. AJ had been talking for months now about wanting to grow up to be a girl. AJ frequently chose clothes from Paige's wardrobe and refused to wear a short hairstyle. AJ was always asking to be included when Paige played games with her girl friends and wanted to be considered one of them. Alicia and her partner—AJ's dad—thought it was a phase at first, but lately AJ has been more insistent, getting upset if they tried to brush it off.

"Well," she started, "you were born with a penis. If you decide when you are a grown-up that you don't want it anymore and that you want a vagina, you can talk to a doctor about changing your body."

"But penises are pretty cool too," Alicia continued. "You might decide when you are older that you want to keep it."

"No," answered AJ. "No like it. Me a girl, not a boy!" AJ threw a bath toy out of the tub in anger.

Alicia had recently brought this up with a close friend, someone who she had known since childhood. Her friend did not think that Alicia's strategy of validating AJ's gender-variant behaviors was a good idea. She suggested that Alicia should steer AJ toward more traditional boy activities and take away his favorite princess dresses. But when Alicia talked to her child about giving away the dresses, AJ fell on the floor sobbing. She didn't have the heart to follow through with it.

Gender Expression

In addition to having a biological sex and a gender identity, all people also have a *gender expression*. Gender expression is how a person communicates or displays their gender to the world (Rudacille, 2005; Serano, 2007). Gender expression is usually a combination of different visual cues and mannerisms. This behavior includes the types of clothing and shoes that a person wears, how they style the hair on their head, if they have hair on their face, what type of jewelry or makeup they wear, and how they walk, talk and carry themselves. Gender expression is usually divided into two categories, *masculine* and *feminine*. Generally speaking, people assigned male at birth are expected to be masculine, while people assigned female at birth are expected to be feminine. People who express a gender that is different than the sex they were assigned at birth (or are not traditionally masculine or feminine) are known as *gender nonconforming* (Grant et al., 2011).

Gender Roles

From the time a person is born—and sometimes even before they are born—people make assumptions about who a person will be or become based on sex assigned at birth. These assumptions usually include ideas about the way they will express their gender, the types of activities they will enjoy, and the career that they will choose. These are frequently shaped by expectations of *gender roles*. Gender roles refer to the social expectations for the way boys/men and girls/women are expected to act and behave (Kessler & McKenna, 1978). For example, usually girls are expected to be quieter, empathetic, and nurturing, while boys are expected to be more "rough and tumble," outspoken, and less emotional. These expectations are enforced through social and cultural interactions. Individuals aligning with gender roles are often praised or supported, while those going against gender roles might be shamed or ridiculed. This negative reaction is particularly true for people who are gender non-conforming and people who are transgender.

Sexual Orientation

A person's *sexual orientation* is about who someone is physically, sexually, emotionally, romantically, and psychologically attracted to (Green & Maurer, 2015). More simply put, sexual orientation is about attraction to and desire to be in relationships with other people. Transgender is not a sexual orientation. Transgender people also have sexual orientations (Erickson-Schroth, 2014). Some people who are less familiar with transgender identities can often get tripped up when trying to figure out how to label a transgender person's sexual orientation. The trick is to ignore the sex that someone was assigned at birth and focus on their gender identity as the most important piece of information. So, similar to a cisgender woman who is attracted exclusively to women would likely label herself a lesbian, we would also label a transgender woman who is attracted exclusively to women a lesbian. Likewise, a transgender man who is attracted exclusively to men would likely identify as gay. A transgender man who is attracted to women and transgender women who are attracted to men are heterosexual. Transgender people who are attracted to all genders might identify as bisexual, pansexual, or queer, and transgender people who are not sexually attracted to people may identify as asexual.

Medical Interventions

Many transgender people experience what is known as *gender dysphoria*, which is a profoundly intense discomfort with and stress resulting from having the physical attributes of the sex someone was assigned at birth (American Psychological Association, 2015). Being transgender is not considered to be a mental health issue, in the same way that being lesbian, gay, or bisexual is not considered a mental illness. However, the significant stress that results from gender dysphoria and cultural prejudice against transgender people is considered to be an extra and unnecessary strain on a transgender person's life and emotional well-being.

The widely accepted best practice to reduce gender dysphoria is to use hormonal and surgical interventions to change someone's body to be more aligned with their gender identity (American Psychological Association,

2015; WPATH, 2012). This process is known as *medical transition*. Although not all transgender people wish to medically transition, many of those who desire to do so are unable to afford the costs, which can be tens of thousands of dollars (Serano, 2007). Generally speaking, medical transition is not covered by medical insurance, and it is too expensive for many people to be able to pay out of pocket. As a result, many people who are transgender are forced to live in bodies that cause them intense psychological discomfort. For many transgender individuals, this results in increased rates of anxiety and depression; engagement in high-risk sexual activities; self-medication through drug and alcohol abuse; and self-harm behaviors such as ritual cutting (American Psychological Association, 2015; Grant et al., 2011).

Another treatment option for transgender young people is to stop their body from going through puberty. This can be done by use of hormone blockers that suppress the physiological development of secondary sexual characteristics (such as breast development in girls, and facial hair growth and voice deepening in boys) that occurs during puberty, which reduces the need for medical interventions to reverse these changes down the line. This process is known as *pubertal suppression*, and can be used for a few years prior to deciding whether the young person should go through male or female puberty (Spack et al., 2012). Providing opportunities for transgender children to undergo pubertal suppression—which is fully reversible—is a relatively low-risk way to reduce the psychological distress that often accompanies puberty for transgender youth. It also allows them and their parents more time to make decisions about how to navigate puberty.

Suppressing puberty has been shown to be a highly effective form of helping transgender youth who have not yet entered puberty and do not wish to go through puberty as the sex that they were assigned at birth (de Vries, Steensma, Doreleijers, & Cohen-Kettenis, 2011). Young people who have been able to use this medical intervention to delay puberty and then go through a puberty that is consistent with their gender identity report being much happier and healthier than their transgender peers who had to go through puberty of the sex they were assigned at birth.

Corey, Age 11

> Corey looked into the mirror with concern. His nipples looked
> a little bigger than normal, and he felt a little hard bump under

them. His best friend Olive from school, also aged 11, was already wearing a bra and several of their female classmates had bragged about getting their periods.

Cory was assigned female at birth, but began asserting himself as a boy at age 2. At first, his parents were at a loss of how to react and tried to brush it off as normal gender play, but it persisted and Cory became more and more insistent that they treat him as a boy. After consulting with their pediatrician and counselors at their local LGBT community center, they decided to support his gender identity and expression. Cory then began calling himself a boy and living as a boy full-time. He started first grade at a progressive school that had a Gay-Straight Alliance and a principal who supported students' freedom of expression and enforced a strong anti-bullying policy. Although Cory's best friend knew he was transgender, there were many kids at school who didn't know he had been assigned female gender at birth.

Cory's pediatrician had prepared him for puberty at his annual well visit last year. She told him that once he began showing early signs of puberty—such as breast buds—that he should come in to talk about taking hormone blockers. The thought of having large breasts like his mom and grandmother made Cory feel sick to his stomach. He was hoping to begin looking more manly like some of his male classmates. It seemed as if a lot of the boys in Cory's class had shot up several inches over the summer and some were even shaving their faces now! Cory was worried that his body was never going to look masculine enough to pass muster in high school. He started to get dejected at the thought of dating girls if he himself looked like a girl. Would that make him a lesbian? He didn't think of himself as a lesbian—he thought of himself as a straight guy who happened to be born with female body parts.

Blake's Story

Blake Brockington made national headlines in 2014 when he was nominated by his peers for prom king at his North Carolina high school (Comer, 2015). The story became a media sensation because many considered the idea of Blake being prom king to be controversial because he was transgender. Blake had come out as transgender when he was a sophomore in high school. Although his step-mom was supportive of his being transgender, his father rejected him, and he was forced to enter foster care. At the same time, he faced intense bullying and harassment from some of his peers at school, and found that the school counselors who he expected to support him and advocate on his behalf would not accept him as a boy:

> "It was pretty black and white; there was no gray area," says Brockington. "It was either they were really supportive or really not supportive, and it's still like that. … I've had a hard time with counselors. They're like, 'You're not a boy. This isn't your name. We're not going to call you that.'" But, Brockington says he's known he is transgender since he was child. He didn't know what it was called, but always remembers identifying as a boy. He and his mother, he says, had "a very heated discussion" when she told him he was a girl at 6 years old. Eventually, though, he found the words to express how he felt. "It was winter break my sophomore year and I was on Tumblr," he says. "I found out what transgender was and said, 'Okay, that sounds like me.'" He came out gradually to friends and then attended the Queer Youth Prom held by Time Out Youth Center, a local LGBT youth support and services organization. "After that, I was like, 'I don't have to do this anymore—I don't have to hide anymore or not be myself,'" he says. "I came to school my junior year and said, 'Hey, I'm Blake.'" (Comer, 2014).

After receiving support and accolades from people around the country, Blake won the title of prom king, becoming one of the first transgender people to ever hold the title in the United States. Blake's response was heartwarming: "This means a lot to me because I know that for me, this is a dream that has finally been made and for others this is an inspiration. I hope this makes everybody know that they can be themselves regardless of what anybody else says. You can do anything you set your mind to."

Although the support that Blake received was encouraging, Blake also became a target of extensive online bullying and harassment from people around the United States who were prejudiced against transgender people. This, combined with his struggles with depression, navigating the world as a Black transgender man, and the rejection from his family proved to be too much to bear. Blake took his own life less than year after winning the title of prom king.

Leelah's Story

Leelah Alcorn is another transgender young person who was lost to suicide due to isolation and a lack of support from her family. In her online suicide note, Leelah explained:

> When I was 14, I learned what transgender meant and cried of happiness. After 10 years of confusion I finally understood who I was. I immediately told my mom, and she reacted extremely negatively, telling me that it was a phase, that I would never truly be a girl, that God doesn't make mistakes, that I am wrong. If you are reading this, parents, please don't tell this to your kids. Even if you are Christian or are against transgender people don't ever say that to someone, especially your kid. That won't do anything but make them hate them self. That's exactly what it did to me (Alcorn, 2014).

Having been raised in a conservative Christian household was a significant factor in Leelah's life. After she came out, her parents sent her to a Christian therapist practicing *conversion therapy*, which is a practice that tries to change a person's gender identity to be consistent with the sex assigned at birth. (This practice is also used to try to make a lesbian, gay, bisexual, or queer [LGBQ] person be heterosexual.) Just as a therapist could not make a cisgender person become transgender or make a heterosexual person become lesbian, gay, bisexual, or queer, it is not possible to make a transgender person identify as cisgender. This practice is increasingly considered to be abusive toward LGBTQ people. Appropriate and affirming therapeutic responses focus on helping a transgender person navigate the challenges of being transgender in a world that is not accepting.

Families' reactions are often a significant source of stress for transgender people, and being rejected by one's family dramatically increases the other challenges that person will face in the world (Ryan, 2010). Rejection can come in many forms. For some it is being kicked out of their homes or being told that they cannot dress or live as their true gender while living in the home. Other rejecting responses include cutting off contact, ignoring or avoiding discussing the person's transgender identity, requesting that a person not tell other people, being excluded from family events, or being told that their transgender identity is a phase.

Thankfully more and more families are responding in affirming ways when their loved ones come out as transgender. Affirming responses include using the name and pronouns that are consistent with the person's gender identity; providing clothing, shoes, makeup, or jewelry that helps the person express their true gender; helping with costs of medical transition; advocating for the loved one in areas where they experience related challenges; and helping to educate other people about transgender identities and people.

Vanessa & Jordan, parents to Mikey, age 8

Vanessa & Jordan had never even heard of transgender when they had their third child, who was assigned female sex at birth and named Ruby. Jordan explained that by the time she was 3-4, Ruby was asking us to use the name "Mikey" and insisted on living as a boy.

> "At first, we feared for his soul and sought advice from our church," said Vanessa. "Our pastor told us it would be a sin to support our child as gender variant. We really struggled with what to do, but then Mikey started getting so depressed. He used to love school, but didn't want to go anymore. He talked about wanting to hurt his body."

> "As his parents, we couldn't sit by and let our child think that his life was not worth living," said Jordan. "We found an online support group for parents of transgender kids and it changed our perspective. We told Mikey that we loved him just as he was and that we would support him unconditionally. Eventually, we found a new church that welcomed Mikey and supports our whole family. And they've even helped us work with the school to do transgender education and enforce a no-bullying policy. Now Mikey is a generally happy child who acts like a typical 8-year-old boy. We are doing everything we can to make sure that he knows that we love him no matter what, and that he gets to enjoy his childhood."

Transgender people in the world

Blake and Leelah's stories are tragic and unfortunately not unusual. Although there is increasing support for and acceptance of transgender people, a vast majority of transgender people still report experiencing daily prejudice and discrimination. For many transgender people, even simple everyday actions like walking down the street, going grocery shopping, and using the bathroom become potential safety risks (Grant et al., 2011; Westbrook & Schilt, 2014). For example, many people report fearing for their physical safety in public, and over 47% of transgender people report having experienced physical violence (Lombardi et al., 2001). This principle holds true for all areas of life where transgender people interact with cisgender people, including: as K-12 and college students, while getting medical care, during interactions with police, and while trying to find housing (Grant et al., 2011). One area where there is an especially negative impact is when transgender people are trying to find jobs. One study reported that 42% of transgender people were denied jobs solely because they were transgender (Make the Road New York, 2010). As of 2015, there are no federal legal anti-discrimination protections, so this type of discrimination is legal in most places (National Center for Transgender Equality, 2015).

In order to make the world a safer place for transgender people, it is essential that cisgender *allies* stand up for transgender people (Green & Mauer, 2015). Allies are people who advocate for and intervene in instances where they witness prejudice toward transgender people (which is also known as a *bystander intervention*). Anyone can be an ally. For example, allies might make it a point to show kindness to a transgender person, like smiling or holding open a door, as a way of helping to counter the negativity received from others. Or, an ally might tell a friend that it is not okay to tell a prejudiced joke about a transgender person, or, correct someone when they use derogatory or offensive language. Allies can also help raise awareness about transgender people's experience by sharing information on social media, or participating in related events on campus. Another important task for allies is to develop and support policies—in schools, in businesses, and in local, state, and federal government—that protect the human and civil rights of transgender individuals.

Here are a few examples of how to be an ally and intervene as a bystander when you see that a transgender person is not being treated with respect:

Setting: In the checkout line at a store, after a transgender person has walked away but is still in hearing range.

Checkout Clerk: "Can you believe that freak? What a mess. I don't know who they think they are fooling."

Ally: "That's not an okay thing to say. Transgender people are human and deserve respect. How would you feel if someone said something like that about you?"

Setting: In class, where classmates roll their eyes and give looks to each other when a transgender student enters the classroom and purposely ignore them.

Ally: "Hey, your hair looks great today—I love that style. Do you want to come sit over here?"

Setting: Hanging out with friends, watching a late night TV show that makes a negative joke about transgender people

Friend A: "Transgender people are just weird. Why would someone even choose to do that to themselves?! What kind of mental illness causes that anyways?"

Friend B: "I know, right? And then they are always trying to trick people into having sex with them. I can't even."

Ally: "Oh, actually we talked about transgender people in class. Did you know that there are transgender kids, who know from the time that they are really young that they are transgender? I saw this documentary about a kid named Jazz. She was amazing and it was super cool. It made me realize that these jokes about transgender people are hurtful."

Conclusion

As U.S. policies and culture slowly move toward greater acceptance of LGBQ individuals and protection of their human and civil rights, great disparities and discrimination still exist for transgender individuals.

Transgender youth in particular are at high risk for suicide, depression, harassment, and physical and sexual violence due to hostility to their gender identity and gender expression. A deeper understanding of the constructs of gender identity, gender expression, gender roles, and sexual orientation may help to address the ignorance, misinformation, and misconceptions that exist about transgender individuals. Allies can play an important role in eliminating anti-transgender prejudice through providing social support, policy advocacy, and bystander interventions.

DISCUSSION QUESTIONS

1. What are some of the ways that your culture enforces gender norms? What are the pros and cons of these enforcements?

2. What are some of the ways that you choose to express your own gender, and how do you think this influences the way people interact with you?

3. What do you think might be some of the negative impacts of forcing a transgender child to go through puberty of the sex that they were assigned at birth, rather than in accordance with their gender identity?

4. Why do you think it is important to make sure that transgender people are able to access medical transition? What might be some of the drawbacks to not being able to access hormonal and surgical interventions?

5. This chapter has focused a lot on the negative reactions and discrimination that transgender people face. What might be some things that you could do to help support transgender people?

References

Alcorn, Leelah (December 28, 2014). "Suicide Note." *Tumblr.* Archived from the original on January 1, 2015. Retrieved from: https://web.archive.org/web/20150101052635/http://lazerprincess.tumblr.com/post/106447705738/suicide-note.

American Psychological Association. (2015). *Guidelines for Psychological Practice with Transgender and Gender Nonconforming People.* Retrieved from: http://www.apa.org/practice/guidelines/transgender.pdf.

Brill, S., & Pepper, R. (2008). *The Transgender Child: A Handbook for Families and Professionals.* San Francisco; Cleis Press.

Collier, K. L., van Beusekom, G., Bos, H. M. W., & Sandfort, T. G. M. (2013). Sexual Orientation and Gender Identity/Expression Related Peer Victimization in Adolescence: A Systematic Review of Associated Psychosocial and Health Outcomes. *Journal of Sex Research, 50*(3-4), 299–317. doi:10.1080/00224499.2012.750639.

Comer, M. (2015). Young transgender activist Blake Brockington mourned. Retrieved from: http://goqnotes.com/34689/young-transgender-activist-blake-brockington-mourned/.

Comer, M. (2014). Transgender Charlotte student nominated from homecoming king. Retrieved from: http://goqnotes.com/27350/transgender-charlotte-student-nominated-for-homecoming-king/.

de Vries, A. L., Steensma, T. D., Doreleijers, T. A., & Cohen-Kettenis, P. T. (2011). Puberty suppression in adolescents with gender identity disorder: A prospective follow-up study. *The Journal of Sexual Medicine, 8*(8), 2276–2283.

Erickson-Scroth, L. (2014). *Trans bodies, trans selves: A resource for the transgender community.* New York, NY: Oxford University Press.

Grant, J., Mottet, L., Tanis, J., Harrison, J., Herman, J., & Keisling, M. (2011). *Injustice at every turn: A report of the National Transgender Discrimination Survey.* Retrieved from http://endtransdiscrimination.org/PDFs/NTDS_Report.pdf.

Green, E. R. (2006). Debating trans inclusion in the feminist movement: A trans-positive analysis. *Journal of Lesbian Studies, 10*(1/2), 231–248.

Green, E. R. (2014). Does Teaching Transgender Content Effectively Reduce Anti-Transgender Prejudice? The Assessment Findings from a National Study. (Unpublished doctoral dissertation). Widener University, Chester, PA.

Green, E. R. & Maurer, L. (2015). *The Teaching Transgender Toolkit: A Facilitator's Guide to Increasing Knowledge, Decreasing Prejudice and Building Skills.* Ithaca, NY: Planned Parenthood of the Southern Finger Lakes: Out for Health.

Intersex Society of North America. (2008). How common is intersex? Retrieved from: http://www.isna.org/faq/frequency.

Jennings, J. (2012, December 17). I am Jazz: A family in transition. [Video file]. Retrieved from http://www.transkidspurplerainbow.org/featured/i-am-jazz-a-family-in-transition/.

Kessler, S.J. & McKenna, W. (1978). *Gender: An ethnomethodological approach.* Chicago, IL: The University of Chicago Press.

Lombardi, E.L., Wilchin, R.A., Preisling, D. & Malouf, D. (2001). Gender violence: Transgender experiences with discrimination and violence. *Journal of Homosexuality, 42*(1), 89–101.

Make the Road New York. (2010). Transgender need not apply: A report on gender identity job discrimination. Retrieved from http://www.maketheroad.org/pix_reports/TransNeedNotApplyReport_05.10.pdf.

National Center for Transgender Equality. (2015). Know your rights: Employment (General). Retrieved from: http://transequality.org/know-your-rights/employment-general.

Roberts, A. L., Rosario, M., Corliss, H. L., Koenen, K. C., & Austin, S. B. (2012). Childhood Gender Nonconformity: A Risk Indicator for Childhood Abuse and Posttraumatic Stress in Youth. *Pediatrics, 129*(3), 410–417. doi:10.1542/peds.2011-1804.

Reed, B. W. D., Cohen-Kettenis, P. T., Reed, T., & Spack, N. (2008). Medical care for gender variant young people: Dealing with the practical problems. *Sexologies, 17*(4), 258–264.

Roberts, A. L., Rosario, M., Slopen, N., Calzo, J. P., & Austin, S. B. (2013). Childhood Gender Nonconformity, Bullying Victimization, and Depressive Symptoms Across Adolescence and Early Adulthood: An 11-Year Longitudinal Study. *Journal of the American Academy of Child and Adolescent Psychiatry, 52*(2), 143–152. doi:10.1016/j.jaac.2012.11.006.

Rudacille, D. (2005). *The riddle of gender: Science, activism and transgender rights.* New York, NY: Pantheon Books.

Ryan, C., Russell, S. T., Huebner, D., Diaz, R., & Sanchez, J. (2010). Family acceptance in adolescence and the health of LGBT young adults. *Journal of Child and Adolescent Psychiatric Nursing, 23*(4), 205–213.

Serano, J. (2007). *Whipping girl: A transsexual woman on sexism and the scapegoating of femininity.* Berkely, CA: Seal Press.

Stryker, S. (2008). *Transgender history.* Berkeley, CA: Seal Press.

Spack, N. P., Edwards-Leeper, L., Feldman, H. A., Leibowitz, S., Mandel, F., Diamond, D. A., & Vance, S. R. (2012). Children and adolescents with gender identity disorder referred to a pediatric medical center. *Pediatrics, 129*(3), 418–425.

Westbrook, L., & Schilt, K. (2014). Doing gender, determining gender: Transgender people, gender panics, and the maintenance of the sex/gender/sexuality system. *Gender & Society, 28,* 32–57.

World Professional Association for Transgender Health. (2012). Standards of Care, v7. Retrieved from: http://www.wpath.org/site_page.cfm?pk_association_webpage_menu=1351&pk_association_webpage=3926.

CHAPTER 10

Polyamory, Sex, and the Communication of Commitment

Jennifer Dixon

KEY TERMS

Polyamory
Commitment

Relationship rules
Relationship identities

Sexual stigma

ABSTRACT

Polyamory, the ideology and/or practice of maintaining multiple romantic and/or sexual relationships with consenting partners, presents an interesting position from which to explore the communication of commitment in sexual relationships. Due to the multiple possible relational structures, polyamorous relationships lack a clear trajectory as well as the typical narrative of fidelity often found in monogamous relationships. As a result, the communication of commitment is amplified in polyamorous relationships to ensure that clear rules are established and that the legitimacy of the relationship is adequately relayed to those outside the relationship.

Sex is unavoidably bound to relationship status. Even if both parties explicitly agree that there is no relationship, the sexual experience is guided by the cultural grammar of this (lack of a) relationship status. Phrases such as *casual sex* and *hook-up culture* denote sexual relationships that are often depicted as "no strings attached," or "just for fun" (Heldman & Wade, 2010). In contrast, the committed sexual relationship is generally assumed—if not explicitly defined—as two people who have agreed to only have sex with each other. Casual sex was at one time, and somewhat still is, stigmatizing—especially for women (Wood, 2012). Even where non-exclusive sex is accepted, it lacks the social approval of a committed romantic sexual relationship. In many a lifetime narrative, nonexclusive sex occurs at a stage that precedes the more respectable stage of settling down and committing to one, and only one, sexual partner. Sex at the intersection of relational commitment brings us to an intriguing crossroads for considering dominant assumptions of what it means to be in a healthy, responsible, and respectable sexual relationship. A prime opportunity for reflecting on these assumptions is by considering sexual relationships that are founded on commitment but *not* exclusivity: polyamory.

Defined as responsible non-monogamy, and grounded in the capacity to love many partners (Klesse, 2006; Ritchie & Barker, 2006), polyamory is the practice of having multiple sexual relationships with each relationship partner consenting to the other(s). Polyamory has also been defined as an identity, rather than a practice (Robinson, 2013), acknowledging those who are in a relationship with only one person, but still subscribe to polyamorous ideals. Put another way, people can "be poly" if they believe that having open, honest, sexual relationships with more than one person at a time "is a valid lifestyle choice for some people" (McGarey, 2001, p. 4).

Furthermore, polyamory may be considered a type of open relationship, but not all open relationships espouse the values of relational commitment that are found in polyamory. For example, many polyamorous couples actively avoid the label *swingers*. Swinging is characterized as being in a romantic relationship while engaging in recreational sex with other partners (Cook, 2005). In swinging arrangements, extra-relational sexual encounters are devoid of commitment. In polyamorous relationships, each sexual partner holds a level of commitment similar to those seen in sexual relationships in which partners decide to be sexually exclusive. In these relationships, the communication of commitment has implications for multiple relational partners.

In contrast to monogamous relationships that generally include two people, polyamorous relationships can take on a number of different structural models. For example, Labriola (1999) refers to the *Primary/Secondary Model* as a common relational formation in which there is a primary relationship that takes on many of the characteristics of a monogamous relationship: The couple may live together, share financial responsibilities, be married, and have children. Each member of this primary relationship may also have one or more secondary relationships. These relationships are generally bound by rules set forth by both members of the primary relationship. Though many polyamorous relationships use the Primary/Secondary Model, some dislike its inherently hierarchical structure. Many secondary relationships experience strain as a result of meaning "less" than the primary relationship. Additionally, incidences in which secondary relationships vie for—or perhaps usurp—primary status are not unheard of. As a result of the occasionally political nature of the Primary/Secondary Model, some polyamorists adopt the *Multiple Primary Relationships Model* in which all partners experience a somewhat equal amount of relational commitment and intimacy. Those who adopt this model tend to forge sexual relationships with multiple partners, allotting an equal amount of rule-negotiating power to each partner. Though other models exist (see Labriola, 1999), the common element of all polyamorous structures is the communication of rules.

Communicating About Polyamory Within the Relational Constellation

On the surface, healthy communication within poly relationships looks strikingly similar to communication practices used to maintain monogamous relationships. In the *Polyamory Communication Survival Kit*, McGarey (2001) advises readers to ask open-ended questions, maintain a win-win attitude, and practice active listening. Each piece of advice, intended for polyamorous readers, would benefit monogamous couples. However, communication differs in both frequency and in the language used to establish rules, boundaries, and goals.

Monogamous relational partners may choose not to discuss exclusivity because they want to avoid appearing clingy or placing undo pressure on the relationship. Baxter and Wilmot (1984) examine the covert practices (monogamous) couples use to determine whether their relationships have reached exclusive status. Interestingly, these researchers found that monogamous couples engage in secret tests: *Jealousy Tests* gage a partner's reaction to descriptions of possible alternative mates; it can also involve the physical presence of another viable partner (Baxter & Wilmot, 1984). Also, *Fidelity Checks* were described as one partner setting up a situation in which the other partner is given a clear opportunity to be unfaithful (non-exclusive) (Baxter & Wilmot, 1984). Though this study is now 30 years old, monogamous couples still generally avoid overtly "checking in" with partners to confirm that their sexual relationship is, indeed, exclusive. Polyamorous partners must communicate, openly, about rules and expectations because there is no master narrative guiding the trajectory of the relationships.

Adding a new paramour is always a little tricky. It basically means saying to your partners, "hey, I'm really interested in this person—so much so that I'm willing to spend less time with you in order to get to know them better." Yep. Tricky. I don't dare lay on the old "I hope the two of you can become good friends" line. I think my best bet is to be completely open and honest and hope for the best.

Relationships are communicated into being (Duck, 2011). In other words, the rules, values, and criteria of relating are established through talk. Therefore, it makes sense that "communicate, communicate, and then communicate more!" is a popular mantra within the polyamorous community (Wosik-Correa, 2010). Some polyamorous couples even reflect that they spend more time talking about their relationship(s) than they otherwise spend with their partners. Polyamorous relationships require consistent and open communication about the parameters of sexual relationships with others. These conversations must occur at least as often as when a new partner enters the picture. Amid this communication is language that illuminates the goals of polyamorous couples while allowing distance from monogamous counterparts.

A New Language for Commitment

The language people use on a daily basis is embedded in what Duck (2011) refers to as social order. Most couples in western cultures consider exclusivity to be an essential aspect of a healthy relationship (Barash & Lipton, 2001; Baxter & Bullis, 1986), and thus exclusivity is often demanded to be presented by people to the social order. In other words, when people show their relationships to others, they have to live up to the expectations others have about what a relationship should be. Exclusivity is such a compulsory function of the ideal committed sexual relationship that it is difficult to know where to begin in presenting an alternative. Common phases such as *cheating*, *sleeping around*, and *philandering* would have us believe that non-monogamy is inherently wrong. After all, there is no common word for *sleeping around* with the blessing of one's committed sexual partner.

To respond to the dominant understanding that all acceptable and respectable romantic relationships are monogamous, people in polyamorous relationships use terms that aid in constructing legitimacy. For example, polyamorous couples use *breaking the rules* rather than *cheating* to describe a breech in established relationship boundaries. The word *cheating* is avoided because it suggests that having multiple sexual partners is inherently wrong (Wosik-Correa, 2010). Another form of mononormative language is *jealously*. While polyamorous people do at times experience jealousy, many feel that it is more productive to focus on the opposite of jealousy. *Compersion*, or the genuine feeling of happiness at seeing one's partner basking in the glow of another relationship (Cook, 2005), is a far more productive point of focus than jealousy and is often considered the key to happy and healthy polyamorous relationships.

Word choices such as *compersion* (rather than jealousy) and *breaking the rules* (rather than cheating) help foster productive dialogue in the rule-making process. Rules established by polyamorous couples can vary greatly, although many rules cater to the health and safety of all partners. A participant in Wosik-Correa's (2010) study of agreements and rules in polyamorous relationships provided the example "that there has to be STD testing before any sexual contact with a new partner. That means no impulsive going to clubs to hook up and have sex" (p. 51). Other rules might serve to delineate primary from secondary relationships. For example, a primary couple might agree that secondary partners can visit their house, but cannot have sex in the primary couple's bed. Often, polyamorous couples also have rules about how (or whether) the relationship is to be communicated to other people.

Communicating Polyamorous Identity

Sometimes communicating commitment in polyamorous relationships puts us in some precarious situations. From vigilant STD/I testing, to buying two romantic Valentine's Day cards, to even deciding who to kiss at midnight on New Year's Eve, polyamorous people are continually reminded that we are living in a monogamists culture. Conspicuous situations such as these also make it necessary to negotiate polyamorous identity in everyday interactions. In addition to avoiding the swinger label, polyamorous people also resist the label *promiscuous* in that there is an assumption that the quest for multiple relationship partners is inspired by an accentuated thirst for sex. Belaying this assumption means communicating commitment not only to the people in the relationship, but to friends and family as well.

My friends have been overwhelmingly supportive of my polyamorous lifestyle. They are kind and welcoming to Lex and Jody, and they are always interested in hearing about a possible new partner. (I can't wait to tell them all about my weekend with Graham!) But I get this boulder in my stomach when I think of telling my parents. I've even toyed with the idea of not telling them, but my partners are a big part of who I am and I can't imagine keeping Lex and Jody from them forever. I'll take a deep breath, and try to explain that I am in two loving, committed relationships with two wonderful and talented people who respect and honor one another all the while having my best interests at heart. Do you suppose I can say that all in one breath?

Being polyamorous usually means being out or in the metaphorical closet often depicted in LGBT studies (see Manning, this volume). Some people who are gay and polyamorous explain that it was easier to come out as gay than to come out as polyamorous in that there is at very least a general awareness of what it means to be attracted to someone of the same sex. Just as polyamorous couples adopt a non-mononormative language when establishing rules with each other, it makes sense that they must return to monogamist language when explaining polyamory to friends and family. For example, effort is often made to ensure that friends and family understand that nobody is cheating and that—while jealousy does sometimes occur—partners feel happy for their partner's other relationships. In an effort to avoid the promiscuous label, many emphasize the mutual commitment established for each relationship. However, many people who are polyamorous choose not to come out at all—at least not at work.

An important contrast between polyamory and monogamy emerges in how one is able to talk about one's private life in the workplace. People generally like talking about their families—and therefore their relational partners—at work. Sharing stories about loved ones helps make non-work lives important and meaningful (Clark, 2002). Talking about one's personal life at work creates a site for self-advocacy. In other words, by being able to talk about one's personal life at work, people are therefore able to discuss non-work obligations with the hope of having those obligations accommodated when needed. When working adults feel that they cannot talk about their families at work, they often find themselves working around—or yielding to—the needs of employees who do communicate about family at work (Dixon & Dougherty, 2014).

It is an extremely rare luxury for working adults in polyamorous relationships to be able to talk about their partners at work. This situation creates the difficult circumstances of deciding which partner to talk about and who to bring along to workplace events where significant others are invited. Some choose to pass as single, while others might talk about a primary relationship and relegate secondary relationships to the title of family friend. Though this is in no way an ideal representation of one's family structure, many polyamorous people remain optimistic for a more inclusive future.

> When I look idealistically into the future, I see a world where polyamory is just another relational category. I imagine parents who wonder if their children will grow up to have just one romantic love in their lives or many. I imagine workplaces that seamlessly include polyamorous working adults in their call for more diverse personnel. As for me, I look forward to starting a family with Jody, and maybe with Lex, too. I look forward to proving to people that this isn't a fad or a phase or an opportunity to be avant-garde. And, as a basis for all of these hopes and aspirations, I look forward communicating polyamory into legitimacy—both within my relationships and beyond.

DISCUSSION QUESTIONS

1. How does the language used in communicating within polyamorous relationships differ from monogamist language? Does avoiding words such as *jealous* really help prevent feelings of jealousy?

2. The chapter states that people in polyamorous relationships must communicate about their relationships with a depth and frequency that monogamous couples often don't usually experience. For example, a monogamous couple might not regularly discuss the meaning or importance of exclusivity, because both people feel exclusivity should go without saying. What other aspects of sexual relationships often "go without saying"? How might individuals and/or relationships benefit from communicating about these aspects?

3. What communication strategies would you advise friends to adopt who are polyamorous and want to tell their parents? What might be the most important point to emphasize?

4. The chapter mentioned dilemmas such as deciding whom to kiss at midnight of New Year's Eve. What other customs communicate a mono-normative culture?

5. Why might communicating about one's polyamorous relationships at work (in a respectful and appropriate manner, of course) be important? What advantages do people who can communicate freely about their families while at work enjoy?

References

Barash, D. P., & Lipton, J. E. (2001). *The myth of monogamy: Fidelity and infidelity in animals and people.* New York: W. H. Freeman and Company.

Baxter, L. A., & Bullis, C. (1986). Turning points in developing romantic relationships. *Human Communication Research, 12*(4), 469–493. doi: 10.1111/j.1468-2958.1986.tb00088.x.

Baxter, L. A., & Wilmot, W. M. (1985). Taboo topics in close relationships. *Journal of Social and Personal Relationships, 2*(3), 253–269. doi: 10.1177/0265407585023002.

Clark, S. C. (2002). Communicating across the work/home border. *Community, Work, & Family, 5*(1), 23–47. doi: 1080/13668800020006802.

Cook, E. (2005). Commitment in polyamorous relationships. (Unpublished master's thesis.) Regis University, Denver, CO.

Dixon, J., & Dougherty D. S. (2014). A language convergence/meaning divergence analysis exploring how LGBTQ and single employees manage traditional family expectations in the workplace. *Journal of Applied Communication Research, 42*(1-2). doi: 10.1080/00909882.2013.847275.

Duck, S. (2011). *Rethinking relationships.* Thousand Oaks, CA: Sage.

Heldman, C., & Wade, J. (2010). Hook-up culture: Setting a new research agenda. *Sexuality Research and Social Policy, 7,* 323–333. doi: 10.1007/s13178-010-0024-z.

Klesse, C. (2006). Polyamory and its 'others:' Contesting the terms of non-monogamy. *Sexualities, 9*(5), 565–583. doi: 10.1177/1363460706069986.

Labriola, K. (1999). Models of open relationships. *Journal of Lesbian Studies, 3*(1-2), 217–225. doi: 10.1300/J155v03n01_25.

Manning, J. (This volume). Identity, relationships, and culture: A constitutive model of coming out. In J. Manning & C. Noland (Eds.), *Contemporary studies of sexuality & communication: Theoretical and applied perspectives.* Dubuque, IA: Kendall Hunt.

McGarey, R. (2001). *Polyamory communication survival kit: The essential tools for building and enhancing relationships.* Austin, TX: The Human Potential Center.

Ritchie, A., & Barker, M. (2006). 'There aren't words for what we do or how we feel so we made them up': Constructing polyamorous language in a culture of compulsory monogamy. *Sexualities, 9*(5), 584–601. doi: 10.1177/1363460706069987.

Robinson, M. (2013). Polyamory and monogamy as strategic identities. *Journal of Bisexuality, 13*(1), 21–38. doi: 10.1080/15299716.2013.755731.

Wood, J. T. (2012). *Gendered lives* (10th ed.). Boston, MA: Cengage.

Wosick-Correa, K. (2010). Agreements, rules, and agentic fidelity in polyamorous relationships. *Psychology & Sexuality, 1*(1), 44–61. doi: 10.1080/19419891003634471.

SECTION 3

Rethinking Sexual Relationships

CHAPTER 11

Why Can't We Be Friends (with Benefits)?

Sara L. Trask

KEY TERMS

Casual sex
Cross-sex friendships

College life
Friends with benefits

Relational ambiguity

ABSTRACT

Friends with benefits relationships (FWBRs) are becoming more prevalent, especially on college campuses. Researchers are finding that over 50% of students report having had at least one FWBR over the course of their college career (Bisson & Levine, 2009; Owen & Fincham, 2011; Puentes, Knox, & Zusman, 2008). These types of relationships appear to be popular due to the ease of obtaining sexual intimacy, without being in an exclusive relationship with their sexual partner. By examining previous research, real world experiences from over 400 college-aged students, and a case study, this chapter examines what types of FWBRs exist, allows for a better understanding of both the advantages and disadvantages of these types of relationships, explores the communication that occurs within these relationships, and describes how these relationships end or progress into more committed, romantic relationships.

Meet Quinn and Reese: One of Many FWB Stories

Quinn and Reese met at a party and hit it off almost instantaneously, realizing that they knew many of the same people and appeared to hang out in the same social circle. After an amazing time at the party, they ended up going back to Quinn's apartment and having sex. Two weeks later, they saw each other again at a party and ended the night the same way, going back to Quinn's place and having sex. Being in the same social circle made it easy for Quinn and Reese to end up at the same places. Once there, they would find each other at the end of the night and go home together. This pattern went on for about three months, and they both felt comfortable in their situation: knowing they were engaging in sex with a partner they trusted.

However, after three months Quinn started to develop feelings for Reese. One night, Quinn asked Reese if they could start to see each other more frequently and exclusively. Reese was shocked, as he thought what they were doing was perfect and he wasn't ready to be in a committed relationship. Reese told Quinn he didn't feel the same way. Quinn was devastated, and although she knew their relationship was based on sex, she thought eventually their relationship would progress into something more. After her talk with Reese, she called her best friend, Ashton. Quinn told Ashton the story and asked what she could have done differently. Ashton didn't seem surprised; pointing out that the only time she and Reese ever saw or spoke to each other was when they were at the same places with their friends.

Ashton asked if Quinn and Reese had ever talked about this type of relationship, how they should maintain it, and where it was headed. Quinn realized that she and Reese never had a conversation about their relationship. She was too afraid to put Reese on the spot about what they were doing and did not want to jeopardize what they had. Plus, her friends had explained how to handle a "friends with benefits" relationship. Despite their advice, she hoped that continuing to have sex would help nudge her into a deeper relationship with Reese. Ashton asked Quinn what she planned to do now that she knew Reese didn't feel the same way about her. Despite her initial desire to continue to have sex without a commitment, she later decided to end it with Reese.

Friends with Benefits

College is a time of transition and identity exploration (Arnett, 2000), where relational commitment is decreasing and sexual exploration is increasing (Bogle, 2008). Therefore, it is not surprising that 50-60% of college students admit to having engaged in at least one friends-with-benefits relationship (Bisson & Levine, 2009; Owen & Fincham, 2011; Puentes, Knox, & Zusman, 2008). Traditional notions of romantic relationships, with courting and deep connections preceding sexual interaction, seem to be something of the past; nowadays, it appears to be more acceptable for individuals meet at a party, through mutual friends, or in a class and instead of falling madly in love, they end up falling madly in….bed?

Westernized culture has seen its share of popular films, *No Strings Attached* (2011) and *Friends with Benefits* (2011) with themes that seem to encourage individuals to avoid commitment and explore their sexuality, but ultimately depict characters that fall madly in love. Happy endings do come true, right? Unfortunately, previous research shows FWBRs do not always have a fairy tale ending as popular culture often leads us to believe. In this chapter, data from a study involving 435 individuals, ages 18-23 is presented. Participants were asked to help define friends with benefits, list the advantages and disadvantages to FWBRs, detail how much communication occurs in this type of relationship, and describe how these relationships end. Combining previous research, real world experiences, and examining Quinn and Reese's relationship, this chapter will examine how FWBRs appear to function in the college setting.

Are We Really Having Sex With a Friend?

The Definition and Typologies of FWBRs

FWBRs are a unique sexual relationship due to the lack of romantic commitment. There are varying definitions of what constitutes a FWBR; however, previous research would indicate two consistencies across definitions. First, FWBR are those relationships in which the sexual encounter happens more than once (Furman & Shaffer, 2011; Gusarova et al., 2012; Hughes, Morrison, & Asada, 2005; Mongeau et al., 2013; Olmstead, Billen, Conrad, Pasley, & Fincham, 2013). This key aspect sets FWBRs apart from other non-committed sexual relationships, such as hook-ups or one-night stands. In those instances, a sexual encounter only happens once. Second, individuals who engage in a FWBR report experiencing intimacy within the relationship but lack commitment to the relational partner. In fact, over 80% of those surveyed describe FWBRs as relationships in which there is sex without love (Puentes, Knox, & Zusman, 2008), and individuals desire nonexclusivity in their relationship, meaning they have the freedom to be romantically involved with others (Stafford, Price, & Reynolds, 2014). Thus, based on previous research regarding FWBRs, FWBRs are defined here as "relationships in which sexual encounters occur numerous times, in which at least one individual in the relationship feels a lack of commitment and romantic love in the relationship" (drawing from Trask, 2015).

When Mongeau and colleagues (2013) asked college students to define the term "friends with benefits," they found that individuals differ in how well they know their FWB partner. Some individuals report initiating sexual encounters shortly after meeting someone, while others report having some type of prior relational investment. In the same study, participants defined the term "friends" within a FWBR in a variety of ways: true friends, just sex, network opportunism, and romantic intent. *True friends* were described as individuals who interacted in a variety of settings and trusted, loved, and respected their sexual partners. These individuals pointed to their friendship as true because it existed before the FWBR occurred. Afifi and Faulkner (2000) found that approximately half of their heterosexual college student sample had engaged in sexual activity in a platonic cross-sex friendship, indicating "true friends" might be a common type of FWB. Stafford and colleagues (2014) found individuals in this type of FWBRs consider their friendship as the most important aspect of the relationship by interacting outside of sexual activity. This potentially relates to why many individuals in this type of relationship note the emotional connection they feel with their FWB partner (Stafford et al., 2014). According to the 435 individuals asked, typically these relationships were characterized by statements such as, "We were always friends, but one thing led to another" or "We met over the summer and started out as really good friends, then eventually started hooking up, but both didn't want a relationship."

Others define their FWBR as *just sex*, solely connecting with the person in order to arrange sexual interaction. These individuals did not report having deep invested feelings or caring for their partner. Rather, they indicated their relationship was strictly sex without meaningful communication. Limited communication also occurs outside of the sexual relationship. Some examples of statements regarding this FWBR type include, "I met him at a party and we would occasionally hook up when we saw each other at parties," or "We were acquaintances, then we would go home together every once in a while when we were at the same parties." Some participants even pointed to how technology was used to facilitate this form of FWBR with statements such as, "We met on Tinder, we would get together and do physical stuff."

Those who described a *network opportunism* relationship would discuss interacting or having connections through a larger group in which they can encounter each other outside of their sexual interactions. In this FWBR type, they reported engaging in sexual activity if neither person had found a different sexual partner for the night. These individuals report initiating their relationship through mutual friends or, more specifically, "through hanging out with the same group of people," after having "hung out in groups with our other friends a lot, or went to parties together," or after they "met through mutual friends and saw each other around at many of the same social meetings and parties." They might even use a friend as a mediator, such as the participant who described, "She contacted me through a friend about being friends with benefits." Quinn and Reese's relationship would qualify as this type of FWBR, having mutual friends helped facilitate their meet-ups and when they were at the same places they would end up with each other at the end of the night.

Those with *romantic intent* were described in three ways: *transitioning in*, *failed transitioning in*, and *transitioning out*. Transitioning in individuals define these FWBR as having a stronger emotional bond than true friends due to the desire to transition into a romantic relationship. People who described this FWBR type made statements such as, "It was like any other friendship, only difference is that we liked each other. The only reason it didn't lead to anything more is because I wasn't sure if he was looking for a relationship and afraid to ask." For someone who did transition in, "My most recent FWB actually turned into a relationship after about four months." Others described their sexual partners as a previous romantic partner in which they were transitioning out of the romantic relationship by continuing to engage in sexual activity. For example, one person said, "We began as a relationship, then broke up but continued to hook up."

In addition to the varying perceptions of "friends," there is also little consistency in how individuals define "benefits." In other words, FWBRs are not only defined in different ways, but have varying levels of sexual activity. A prior study indicated a varying degree of the sexual activity that occurred between participants and their FWB partner with 2.7% indicating they only engage in oral sex, 1.3% engage in genital touching, 22.7% engage in intercourse only, 8% engage in all but intercourse, 56% engage in all types (oral, genital touching, intercourse), and 9.3% engage in some combination of the above mentioned (Bisson & Levine, 2009).

Although individuals appear to define friends with benefits differently depending on the type of relationship they experienced, many individuals report facing the same advantages and disadvantages in FWBRs.

Are There Benefits to Having a FWBR?

The Advantages and Disadvantages of FWBRs

Individuals in FWBRs experience positive and negative emotions before, during, and after a FWBR has occurred. Individuals report advantages of FWBRs including having sex with a trusted partner in a safe environment. As we saw with Quinn and Reese, they felt comfortable in their relationship because they could engage in sex with someone they trusted. More than experiencing comfort and trust in a FWBR, FWB partners appear to take more sexual precautions than romantic relationships. Lehmiller, Vanderdrift, & Kelly (2014) report that people in FWBRs are more likely than those in romantic relationships to engage in condom or barrier use during both oral sex and intercourse. Additionally, individuals like the aspect of avoiding a romantic commitment (Bisson & Levine, 2009). Owen and Fincham (2011) found that less than half of individuals in FWBRs, only 25% of men and 37% of women, report wanting their FWBR to progress into

160

a committed relationship. Further, Lehmiller and colleagues (2011) found commitment to the sexual and friendship aspects of the relationship did not differ for men and women. The lack of gender differences suggest, in some regard, some men and women view the commitment in FWBRs similarly.

However, participants report numerous disadvantages to these relationships. Owen and Fincham (2011) found that men (54.3%) are more likely than women (42.9%) to engage in FWBR. Additionally, men listed sex as the most common motivation for beginning a FWBR, whereas women indicated the emotional connection as the most common motivation (Lehmiller, Vanderdrift, & Kelly, 2011). The divide in this finding suggests some women entertain the idea of engaging in a FWBR because they hope for something more, while some men are more likely to enter these relationships strictly for the sexual intimacy. Examining Quinn and Reese's relationship, we see that Quinn could not help but want more in the relationship; however, Reese wanted the relationship to remain strictly sexual in nature. An alternative explanation is that women are more likely to report emotional investment, because women are viewed less negatively by society if there is emotional involvement with her partner (Lehmiller et al., 2011). This notion could also help explain why there is a disproportionate distribution of rewards and regrets for men versus women when it comes to casual sex. Women appear to have a greater likelihood of regret after the sexual encounter (Gusarvo et al., 2012; Owen & Fincham, 2011). Though these differences do not exist in a gender vacuum, previous research on predominately heterosexual relationships indicate that men and women do experience some differences in how they feel about FWBRs.

Previous research identified three main disadvantages to FWBR: 1) individuals identify developing unrequited feelings for the other, 2) getting hurt emotionally, or 3) experiencing jealousy (Bisson & Levine, 2009; Gusarova et al., 2012). Individuals acknowledge how FWBRs invite complications by saying, "Its random, being too involved invites unwanted or unreciprocated feelings." One expressed how unrequited feelings develop in FWBRs, "It ended because I started to have feelings for him and he didn't like me in that way." Other individuals expressed how they ended up getting hurt emotionally, with statements such as, "I had feelings and he didn't, so it ended badly." Quinn experienced both developing unrequited feelings, as well as getting hurt emotionally when she told Reese she had feelings for him and he explained he did not feel the same. Feeling emotionally drained, Quinn enlisted the advice of her friend Ashton, who made Quinn think about the lack of communication that had occurred in her and Reese's FWBR. Similar to Quinn, many other FWBRs experience this lack of communication and often times acknowledge how "very important it is to discuss these things, but we didn't really talk about it."

Are We Communicating in FWBRs?

The Role of Communication in FWBRs

Hughes, Morrison, and Asada (2005) reported that 40.6% of participants listed "communication rules" (e.g., honesty) as important to the maintenance of FWBRs. Similarly, Weaver, MacKeigan, and MacDonald (2011) reported that openness and honesty were important features of successful FWBRs. Individuals in FWBRs find it easier and are more likely to communicate about other sexual relationships more than romantic partners (Lehmiller et al., 2014). Although individuals engaging in FWBRs recognize the importance of communication, individuals in FWBRs do not often engage in communication regarding ground rules that should occur within the relationship (Bisson & Levine, 2009, Hughes et al., 2012). Bisson and Levine (2009) found that 77% of partners report there was no discussion of ground rules or conversations about relational maintenance in their FWBR. Additionally, FWB partners communicate less about their sexual desires, sexual boundaries both within and outside of the relationship, and some safe-sex issues than romantic partners (Lehmiller et al., 2014). Knight (2014) began to explore the communicative strategies (or lack thereof) used in FWBRs and found that individuals do not engage in relational maintenance talk because it appears to become problematic in the relationship and it is face threatening to the FWB partner. Therefore, individuals avoid open discussion of their sexual relationship in an effort to protect the relational status quo. As we saw with Quinn and Reese, there was no communication surrounding what each of them wanted out of the relationship or how to maintain their FWBR. Quinn thought that her idea of what a FWBR was, and what her friends had explained was enough to inform her of the ground rules surrounding her relationship. Plus, she was afraid that if she asked Reese about the relationship, it might have jeopardized what they had.

Taken together, this previous research would suggest although there are rules surrounding FWBRs (i.e., relationship exclusivity, sexual boundaries, etc.), these rules are not explicitly discussed within the relationship. Out of the 435 individuals surveyed about their FWBR, only one individual mentioned explicitly discussing rules. She reported that there were guidelines surrounding the issue of jealousy, the individual remembers telling her ex-boyfriend, "He couldn't get jealous or show that he was jealous if I talked to or dated other guys and there would be no feelings involved. If the rules were broken, the FWB relationship would end. It lasted about a month. He gradually showed signs of being jealous and told me he wanted more than this. I ended it."

Although individuals believe openness and honesty are important aspects in engaging in a successful FWBR, usually there is little to no communication that occurs, causing relational vagueness about status and the future of the relationship. As previous relational research has shown, FWB relationships are particularly vulnerable to relational ambiguity and communication issues (Knight, 2014). This ambiguity can either encourage FWBs to talk about what they want out of the relationship, as Quinn and Reese did, or continue to avoid the conversation.

Are We Going Anywhere in a FWBR?

Implications of FWBRs

Only 10-20% of FWBR progress into exclusive romantic relationships (Bisson & Levine, 2009). One individual recalled how her FWBR turned into something more, which was not what she had planned, "We started hooking up after a while and after some time he asked me out. It was pretty unexpected." Although a progression into a romantic relationship is possible, individuals engaging in FWBRs suggest that the progression is not common (Stafford et al., 2014). Quinn and Reese's relationship is one such instance where although one wanted a more committed relationship, it was unlikely that romantic relationship status would ever be achieved. One individual recalls how "the relationship was strictly sex, but then I started to like him, and when I told him I wanted to stop because I actually liked him, he told me he liked me too. We tried to hang out and not have sex, but I soon figured out he wasn't interested in anything besides that. It's ended."

With such a low percentage of individuals in FWBRs progressing into a committed, romantic relationship, that leaves a larger number of dyads who are faced with the choice of continuing the nonexclusive, sexual relationship or end the sexual relationship completely. Some acknowledge they could not sustain the strictly sex relationship so there was no other choice but to end the relationship. As one individual recalls, "Both of us realized that we care too much for the other person for this to just be kept causal, therefore we ended it and have split ways by attending different colleges." Others suggest that, with the nature of FWBRs, there is never an ending. One individual believes, "The beauty of FWB is that you don't really have anything to end. That's the point."

However, once a FWBR is no longer sexual, can individuals go back to being friends without a sexual relationship? A majority of individuals report staying friends on some level (81.5%), with some stating they remained friends and were as close as they were before they started having sex (35.4%), and some reporting they were even closer than before (14.6%) (Owens, Fincham, & Manthos, 2013). One acknowledges that the relationship was confusing and there was uncertainty surrounding next steps, so they "ended the relationship by returning to the status of being friends." Another individual also recognizes how she and her best friend remained best friends, "We are still best friends, just do not have any extra 'benefits' involved. It is not awkward at all, it picked up as if we have always just been best friends."

Not all FWBRs go back to being friends. Owen et al. (2013) found that 31.5% remained friends but were less close than they used to be and 18.5% of the participants said they were no longer friends at all. One individual recalls how they "were friends that were attracted to one another... became intimate and it ruined the friendship."

Although it does appear that FWBRs can return to friendship, if a friendship existed in the first place, there is a chance that the relationship might not be as strong as before. Some considered FWBR negatively, with 30% of individuals indicating they would never enter a FWBR again. Other people seem to have had positive (38%) or at least neutral (32%) experiences with FWBRs (Gusarova, Fraser, & Alderson, 2012), suggesting there are both positives and negatives to this type of relationship.

FWBRs appear to be a prominent type of relationship that is infiltrating college campuses, which helps explain why individuals can easily identify when they are in a FWBR. However, the college population is often studied, comprised of mostly heterosexuals, and a FWBR extends far beyond this type of sample. Although recent work by Stafford and colleagues (2014) has begun to examine non-college aged samples, future research needs to begin to look at how these relationships exist in adult populations as well as homosexual, bisexual, and transgender relationships. Additionally, previous research has shown that FWBRs can provide both advantages and disadvantages in relationships. The lack of communication about ground rules, but the understanding of implicit rules (i.e., do not talk about the relationship), might be a starting point for understanding how people in this type of relationship choose to stay in it, advance the relationship to a more committed relationship, or end it. More recent work on FWBRs (Knight, 2014) has begun to explore the communicative strategies surrounding FWBRs. This type of work needs to continue to be able to fully understand the intricate working of a FWBR. Ultimately, work still needs to be done to allow for a better understanding of FWBRs; as personal experiences such as Quinn and Reese are not enough to help researchers know if we can be in a FWBR and experience both friendship and relational benefits.

DISCUSSION QUESTIONS

1. Are there times it would be better to follow the "unspoken rules" of being in a FWBR? If so, why? Why do you think there is a disconnect between what individuals want and their ability to communicate their needs in a FWBR?

2. In addition to the advantages and disadvantages mentioned in the text, are there additional costs and benefits associated with FWBRs?

3. Men and women report different intentions for engaging in a FWBR, why do you think there are gender differences in how men and women view FWBRs?

4. There are several "types" of FWBRs from true friends to transitioning out of a relationship. Do you think each of these types of FWBRs engage in their relationships in the same way? If so, why? If not, why not?

5. There are mixed reviews on whether individuals can go back to being "just friends." How can *true friends* go back to being just friends after sexual intimacy has occurred? How might the sexual intimacy change a friendship? Do you think those who initiate their FWBRs as *just sex* ever end up being friends in the end?

References

Afifi, W.A., & Faulkner, S.L. (2000). On being 'just friends:' The frequency and impact of sexual activity in cross-sex friendships. *Journal of Social and Personal Relationships, 17*, 205–222, doi: 10.1177/0265407500172003.

Bisson, M. A., & Levine, T. R. (2009). Negotiating a friends with benefits relationship. *Archives of Sexual Behavior, 38*, 66–73, doi: 10.1007/s10508-007-9211-2.

Bogle, K. A. (2008). *Hooking up: Sex, dating, and relationships on campus.* New York: New York University Press.

Furman, W., & Shaffer, L. (2011). Romantic partners, friends, friends with benefits, and casual acquaintances as sexual partners. *Journal of Sex Research, 48*(6), 554–564, doi:10.1080/00224499.2010.535623.

Gusarova, I., Fraser, V., Alderson, K. G. (2012). A quantitative study of "friends with benefits" relationships. *The Canadian Journal of Human Sexuality, 21* (1), 41- 59, doi: 10.1080/00224499.2011.623797.

Hughes, M., Morrison, K., Asada, K. J. K. (2005). What's love got to do with it? Exploring the impact of maintenance rules, love attitudes, and network support on friends with benefits. *Western Journal of Communication, 69*(1), 49–66, doi: 10.1080/10570310500034154.

Karlsen, M., & Traeen, B. (2013). Identifying "friends with benefits" scripts among young adults in the Norwegian cultural context. *Sexuality & Culture, 17*, 83–99, doi: 0.1007/s12119-012-9140-7.

Knight, K. (2014). Communicative dilemmas in emerging adults' friends with benefits relationships: Challenges to relational talk. *Emerging Adulthood, 2* (4), 270–279, doi: 10.1177/2167696814549598.

Lehmiller, J. J., VanderDrift, L. E., & Kelly, J. R. (2014). Sexual communication, satisfaction, and condom use behavior in friends with benefits and romantic partners. *The Journal of Sex Research,* 51(1), 74–85, doi: 10.1080/00224499.2012.719167.

Lehmiller, J. J., VanderDrift, L. E., & Kelly, J. R. (2011). Sex differences in approaching friends with benefits relationships. *Journal of Sex Research, 48*(2-3), 275–284, doi: 10.1080/00224491003721694.

Mongeau, P. A., Knight, K., Williams, J., Eden, J., & Shaw, C. (2013). Identifying and explicating variation among friends with benefits relationships. *Journal of Sex Research, 50*(1), 37–47, doi: 10.1080/00224499.2011.623797.

Puentes, J., Knox, D., Zusman, M. E. (2008). Participants in "friends with benefits" relationships. *College Student Journal, 42*(1), 176–180.

Olmstead, S. B., Billen, R. M., Conrad, K. A., Pasley, K., Fincham, F. D. (2013). Sex, commitment, and casual sex relationships among college men: A mixed-methods analysis. *Archives of Sexual Behavior, 42,* 561–571, doi: 10.1007/s10508-012-0047-z.

Owen, J., & Fincham, F. D. (2012). Friends with benefits relationships as a start to exclusive romantic relationships. *Journal of Social and Personal Relationships, 29* (7), 282–996.

Owen, J. & Fincham, F. D. (2011). Effects of gender on psychological factors on "friends with benefits" relationships among young adults. *Archives of Sexual Behavior, 40,* 311–320, doi: 10.1007/s10508-010-9611-6.

Stafford, L., Price, R., & Reynolds, M. (2014). Adults' meanings of friends with benefits relationships: A romantic relationships-oriented study using focus groups and values coding. In J. Manning, & A. Kunkel (Eds.), *Researching Interpersonal Relationships, Qualitative Methods, Studies, and Analysis* (1st Ed, pp. 87–91). Thousand Oaks, CA: Sage Publishing Company.

Trask, S. L. (2015). The (dys)functionality of deceptive affection: Using a goals-based approach to understand the process of deceptive affection and its connection to relational health in friends with benefits and other intimate relationships (Doctoral Dissertation).

CHAPTER 12

"You Had Sex, Right?" Theorizing Desire, Identity, Reciprocity, and Sex in Queer Friendships

Daniel S. Strasser & Kathryn Hobson

KEY TERMS

Autoethnography	Friendship
Queer theory	Identity

ABSTRACT

As friends, our love for one another exists in a system that works to prioritize monogamous sexual relationships in a hierarchy over other relationships. However, in this chapter we challenge the cultural ideas of "normal" relationships and offer our own concept of *queering friendship*, which provides a more fluid and open understanding of relationships. Specifically, we explore how the areas of desire, identity, reciprocity, and sex make up the foundation of queer friendships, particularly when talking about sexual communication. Individual, community-based, and political perspectives of queer friendship and sexual identity are explored to challenge and resist the normative understandings of relationships.

Where and how does friendship begin? As children we are socialized at home and school how to make friends to the best of our abilities. We work to find those individuals who are most like us and then form tight, often long-lasting bonds with them. These bonds offer us companionship, guidance, comfort, and fun while making our way through the world. In these friendships we learn who we are, what to do, and what not to do. And, as a result, as Rawlins (1992) suggests, we tend to move through the world with friends that are like us in terms of gender, race, and age. These friends help us to solidify who we are and make us feel like we are a part of the culture we identify with and that identifies us. But how does friendship and relationship building work within the queer community? Does it mirror the process of "normal" friendship construction or does it take on a new form? More importantly, why does this matter?

Although scholars have examined the intersections of gender and sexuality in friendship (Muraco, 2012; Tillman, 2015; Tillman-Healy 2001, 2003) in the past, their scholarship surrounding friendship, intimacy, sexuality, and desire lacks a *queer* perspective of sex and relationships. Research often focuses on gay male friendships with heterosexual women or lesbian and bisexual women's relationships with straight men. Yet, the lines of gender, gender identity, and sexual orientation are not always so clear-cut. As we have come to understand, sex is the physiological/genetic characteristics that we are born with; gender is the socially and culturally constructed performances associated with masculinity and femininity; gender identity is our sense of self—how we self-identify our gender; and sexual orientation is who we desire sexually and romantically (Wood, 2015). With so many variations of sex and gender identification, there are also many ways that people can be considered deviant, different, or queer. But what binds those different performances of queerness together when creating friendship? And, again, why is this important?

With these questions in mind, we use queer theory and autoethnography to explore our relationship and our connection to "queering" friendship. From the perspective of two self-identified queer people, we acknowledge that our friendship is a queer friendship. We also acknowledge that queer and queering can mean and incorporate many ideas, peoples, cultures, and relationships. So when asking, "what is queer friendship," the answer, like queer itself, is also not so cut and dry. For a friendship to be queer, the people involved should self-identify as queer, or must relate to each other in ways that queer traditional relationships. This might happen between two gay men, or two lesbian women, or a questioning straight man and lesbian woman, or a group of current and former lovers, and the list could go on and on. Queer friendships also involve relationships in which individuals relate to each other in ways that queer traditional relationships, be engaged with communities of marginal identities of which they are a part, and be willing to keep each other accountable to being self-reflexive to their multiple identities. It also means that queerness is most likely a part of more relationships than just between people of marginalized sexual identities. However, in this chapter we use our experiences as a queer man and woman with non-normative identities to serve as one example of how queer friendship can operate within relationships.

Below we offer a more in-depth description of what "queering" a relationship means, and offer our experiences of a queer friendship. Furthermore we offer the core ideas of our framework for understanding queer friendships—sexuality and sexual identity, desire, reciprocity, and sex—via "four dates" that exemplify the core of queer friendships. Using this framework, we argue that queering friendships allows us to resist heterosexual, monogamous relationship ideals. That, in turn, opens up the possibilities for various personally valuable and culturally significant ways of relating. To begin, we cover some basic definitions and concepts as well as our theoretical and methodological frameworks.

Queering and Queer Theory

What does it mean to be queer? From our perspective, when discussing queer people or the queer community, we are talking about individuals whose gender performance and/or sexual orientation/identity are outside of what traditional society deems normal. As queer people, a cisgender queer-femme woman (identified as K throughout the chapter) and a cisgender queer man (D), we are both White and from working class backgrounds. Our friendship and our love for one another exist within normalizing systems of gender, sex, and sexuality (see Lannutti & Faulkner, this volume, or McKenna & Baker, this volume). Within these systems, and especially from our vantage point of White, middle-class people, we are taught to act like a boy or girl, to date someone of the opposite sex, to go to college after high school, to get married after college, and to have two children, a house with a picket fence, and a dog named Rover. Through mass media, our families, schools, and religious institutions, these traditions are perpetuated making them societal norms (see Manning, this volume). These norms are not only what we are supposed to do; they are supposed to make us happy. However, this system also works to prioritize monogamous sexual relationships over other relationships in people's lives by policing relational norms. As Kreps (2000) notes, "The dominant culture establishes normative rules for acceptable behavior within social systems, forcing all members to either adopt these prescribed norms, or be isolated, alienated, and punished" (p. 182).

One way that those who do not conform to traditional heterosexual norms are punished is through questions: "When are you going to settle down?" "When are you going to get married?" "When are you going to start a family?" Although some people may not want anything to do with these traditions, these questions are still asked. We challenge a system that sustains normative relationships; relationships that are socially approved and legally backed often at the expense of stigmatizing "other" people and their non-normative relationships. Thus, focusing on queering friendships opens up the possibility to challenge the stigmas and resist the norms in ways that are positive and productive for people and their lives.

So where does queering and queer theory come into this system? Queer theory examines the power dynamics within cultural systems and helps to better understand the positions of others who perform outside of the norms. In order to get a better understanding of what we mean by queer/queering, Berry (2014) suggests that:

> To queer is to disrupt taken-for-granted and "common sense" presumptions about cultural lives and beings. Moreover, queering entails (re)considering selves as being more situated, fluid, and complicated than fixed, static, and uniform . . . make[ing] possible and necessary different, more inclusive understandings of identities and ways of relating (p. 92).

Berry (2014) explains that queering is an active, identity-making process that often challenges the traditions socialized through most of our lives. Thus, queer is not simply something we are, and queer friendships are not something that we are merely in with another person, but something we continuously do. At the same time, while queerness is fluid and contextual, it is also an identification that happens through and with the body. As a result of different bodies, different individuals have different experiences of queerness (e.g., a gay black man will experience queerness differently than a lesbian white woman). Cohen (2005) even suggests that queer refers to all people outside of normative, white, heterosexual, middle-to-upper class, monogamous marital relationships. This includes people of various racial, class, ethnic, nationality, and relationship structures. With this in mind, many communication scholars assert that identities work intersubjectively, or intersectionally. Much like two or three or four streets cross to create an intersection, an individual's race, sexual orientation, class, and relationship structures cross to create their intersectional identities. For example, Moreman and McIntosh (2010) maintain "that the discourses of race, gender, and sexuality work not as separate entities but within and through each other" (p. 116).

How do we experience and define ourselves as queer? Is our identity defined by who we have sex with? Do the friends we have define it? Is it not being married or not wanting children? Does being queer reside in dating men and women, or just women? Is it having sex with multiple partners? Or is it about abstaining from sex altogether? Or is it talking with a lisp or with your hands or is it about how we dress? Each of our experiences inform our identities as queer people. For D this resides in his individual understanding of self, or our self-identification. In self-identifying, in finding your own identify, you are able to make this distinction by yourself and for yourself. For K, her queer identity is tied to her gender expression as femme and her participation in queer communities and activism. Thus, our identities as queer, white, cisgender, male and female work together to produce our varied experiences. While our queerness is a marginal identity, we also have privileged identities. Looking at our identities as queer and intersectional allows us the opportunity to root through what queering a friendship means and engage this experience both theoretically and in everyday life.

Throughout the chapter we refer to our identities, relationship, and community as queer, as well as the process of our negotiating and challenging normativity, or politicizing, normative relationships as queering, adhering to Berry's concept of queer as an *act of doing*, rather than simply being. Moving forward with our approach to friendship we employ an autoethnographic methodology to make sense of our experiences. This approach is discussed more specifically below.

Autoethnography

Autoethnography is a method of writing about your self and your own personal experiences in order to make sense of those experiences as a form of research. Autoethnography helps us understand who we are while connecting our experiences with others. Like queer theory, autoethnography goes against the grain of other more traditional methodologies; and, as Adams and Holman Jones (2008) suggest, *autoethnography is queer* (p. 377, italics in original).

In this project we write an autoethnographic narrative introducing ourselves, and then from there we write four autoethnographic scenes using an interwoven personal narrative style from which we theorize our four-date system of desire, identity, reciprocity, and sexual identity and desire. We then connect our four narratives to the larger cultural systems of which they are a part, advocating for an expansive understanding of how we may all be acting queer in our relationships at various times.

This approach best represents and explores our social positionalities, sexuality, and friendship in ways that disrupt "normal" assumptions of how friendships "ought" to exist. We begin with a narrative introducing our relationship.

It's Who We Are Now

> K: We greet each other, kisses on the cheeks and a long embrace. It's one of those hugs that envelops you. I smell Calvin Klein Eternity on your neck. "I've missed you," I say.

> D: "I've missed you more." My hand lingers on your back easing you toward the bar. Fiercely femme for our night out as usual: red lipstick and form fitting outfit. I step back, admiring, and let you walk ahead.

> Dimly lit with music playing in the background, the bar is our place. Amber, our regular bartender walks around the bar to give us a hug, and asks if we would like our "usual." We nod and smile back. We sit close to each other on the stools lining the granite bar top, our usual drinks poured before us: Tito's vodka,

soda, and lime in our 40 oz., brightly painted, self-decorated mugs. It isn't a special drink order, but it's special to us.

Legs dangling from barstools, arms brushing, we sing along to a 90s boy band song. While sometimes we sit for hours talking, laughing, commiserating, theorizing, and teasing, tonight we are just being us. It is getting to that part of the song when Justin Timberlake hits the high note, and you grab my arm, pulling me toward you singing into a microphone, which is really just your fist balled up in front of your face. Raising my fist similarly, I push our fists together to give us both enough space to sing and right as we are getting to the climax—

"You two would make a perfect couple," Amber cackles.

K: "We get that a lot," I say, and you laugh.

She pushes on, "I mean, even if you're not dating, *you've had sex, right?*"

The cloud of ambiguity swirls between all three of us, as we avoid each other's eyes. Eventually Amber is called away to pour shots for a bride-to-be, and we go back to sitting, to dangling, to brushing.

In this moment, Amber, a white, heterosexual, working-class, cisgender woman, symbolizes the subtle policing embedded in the cultural construction of supposed heteronormative relationships. Insisting that we must be a romantic couple, or at least pushing for our disclosure on whether or not we have had sexual contact with one another pushes us from a "normal" relationship to "abnormal." From D's point of view, asking this question is a dismissal of our queer identities, as it is an attempt to reinforce the cultural notion that a man and a woman who are friends should be in a relationship with one another. While similar comments may be exchanged with people who are self-identified heterosexual, for those whose are queer, it serves to be a reminder that whatever our relationship is in this moment is less important than the romantic relationship it could be if we could overcome our queerness.

From K's perspective, Amber knows that we both identify as queer, and so Amber may embody a representation of a more queer understanding of relationships. While maybe not having the language to put to it, she recognizes what Berry (2014) is suggesting, that queerness is a fluid notion of identity and relating with others. Maybe we have had sex, maybe we haven't, but because we are queer, we are open to the notion that people would think we were past lovers or that we might at any point become future lovers. The danger of queer friendship lies in its unpredictability, in the not knowing where it will go next. Because we have cultivated an intimacy beyond a traditional friendship, as reflected in our four dates, sexuality and sexual identity, desire, reciprocity, and sex, it is not surprising that she might sense that our friendship is indeed a queer one.

So, we are caught in flux, theorizing our queer friendship as it existed in the past, as it exists now, how we see it existing in the future, and knowing full well that we may have differing interpretations of the scenarios because our experiences differ, too. In the next section we conceptualize the four-date system and illustrate how instances in our relationship help us better understand the culture of relating that perform in and (re)create.

The Four-Date System

Although we acknowledge the normative friendship construction processes stated above, we argue that because queerness is a process that forming our friendship and other friendships with queer people takes different trajectories, or paths, than most other relationships and that queer individuals experience many aspects of life in different time frames and trajectories (Halberstam, 2005; Johnson, 2010). With this in mind, because individuals come out at different times in the life cycle, or become a part of the queer community in others ways (e.g., straight ally, transgender male/female friend), making friends who are similar to them can be problematic. Even if you are out of the closet and comfortable, locating other queer people and finding your way into a group of friends may be a bit daunting. Much like navigating the playground when a child, this new adult playground can be a daunting place, too. Cliques of jocks, cool kids, or geeks are replaced by femmes, butches, and bears or other labels depending on the context. Thus, when trying to make your own way through the playground of friendship, we offer what we call a four-date system where we began to get to know each other and eventually became, now, lifelong friends. Although queer theory suggests that there is no set trajectory or method to forming and maintaining relationships (Halberstam, 2005), we have found that these four principles can better help us understand the creation and importance of queer friendships and relationships. Although we write these four categories as initial guidelines, we also note that they are assumptions, and that there is room for movement, challenge, and change within them.

The rest of this chapter is framed as four dates, which correspond to four different elements that make up queer friendships. We utilize the metaphor of "dates" as a working example of queering. Here we are queering the normative construct of heterosexual, monogamous "dating" in which the end goal or resolution of a certain number of dates (i.e., after three dates it's "okay" to have sex) is sexual intercourse. Rather, our "dates" correspond to the four different elements we see as constituting queer friendship.

First Date, How It Started: Desire

D: You slide into a chair close to me. You were *just* across the patio, and now your slender arm is on my chair, your eyes looking through my eyes, and with a smile you simply said, "I think that we should be friends." Taken aback by the forwardness of your confidence and demeanor, my intrigue and awareness shifts to you. Mixing drinks, jokes, scholarship, and flirtatious glances, I wonder about you, wanting to know more; wanting more.

K: Not butterflies, but wasps bounce around my stomach as I choose my outfit, plan my hair, decide it all looks terrible, and stop at *Target* on the way to your house. As I pull up to your place I smooth my new tank top, adjust my sweater, take a deep breath and text, "I'm here." You look nice, and I am attracted to you. I thread my arm through yours as we walk, listening to you through nervous heartbeats. Your voice is quiet, and sometimes words mumble together, but I don't care because desire, blurred by end of summer sun and breeze has taken hold.

D: Was it my dimly lit apartment across from the park; the music we took turns picking; vodka, limes, and ice clinking the shaker? A kiss, hands going here and there, bodies pressing. A disruption of boundaries—yet, safety too. Eye contact and flush bring us back. We laugh, shrug, and you retire to my bed—and I, the couch.

Above, in our interwoven narrative, we explored the intricacies of desire in our first meeting and our first date. Within queer relating, meeting another person for the first time with whom you feel propelled toward thrusts individuals into a closeness and intimacy that circumvents the "normal" trajectory of friendship building. Although many friendship scholars, such as Tillman Healy (2003), articulate the murky lines that friendship can take, within queer friendships these boundaries are even less clear. The lack of clarity that often emerges in these friendships results in part from desire within these friendships, in which attraction, sexual attention, and wanting authentic human connection combine to create not only an undefined and chosen relationship, but also a compulsion toward one another.

As another example of how queer friendship can look, Gingrich Philbrook (2008) explains his own queer desire experiencing sexual arousal from his female friend, although he is queer and primarily attracted to men saying, "desire is an encounter with the unforeseen . . . in the course of experiencing our desire, we fail to fully anticipate its effects, effects that die when we routinize desire, prefigure, mythologize, or empty it into law" (Gingrich-Philbrook, 2008, p. 356). Much like our experience, and Gingrich-Philbrook's encounter of the unforeseen, that night was led by spiraling desire; desire for companionship, love, lust, release, closeness, comfort, and affection—and also shrouded by what we did not know yet of each other. Queer relationships, unlike normative friendships, do not always follow a linear course, and we find ourselves negotiating the unforeseen in rocky terrain with no concrete path, pattern, or prototype on which to build. In our relationship, much like other relationships with queer people, whether those relationships are between two gay men, a gay man and a lesbian woman, a bisexual man and transgender woman, or even a heterosexual ally and a femme, etc., the concept of desire is expanded as we move to (re)consider the taken-for-grantedness that desire only entails sexual attraction and lust for another.

Although some traditional friendships may be marked by similar elements of desire, it is our identification as queer people that mark this murky terrain as a queer friendship. In our budding relationship, we not only desired each other sexually in that moment, but we also desired to have the comfort of understanding that the other person is queer, too. This attraction and desire is situated in being sexually and/or romantically attracted to someone but also attracted to their ability to understand a vital part of who you are, your identity, and how it shifts in the moment and how it changes over time.

Second Date: Identity

K: It is ladies night at the gay male bar downtown. It is advertised as open and inclusive space, so we go together. As we enter, music shatters our conversation. Inside bodies sweat from (s)queer-dancing, two-stepping, and grinding to old school hip hop. Each section of the bar offers a buffet of different bodies, sounds, and fog-frame forms. I have long hair, a sexy vintage thrift dress, and bright red lipstick to compliment my pale complexion. My femme is in full force because I have a date with my future partner that night.

D: V-neck black T-shirt, form-fitting jeans, and stringless grey chucks—your femme eclipses my attempt to dress for the space. But this is how I always dress. For me, comfort and confidence is sexy; for you, sexy is sexy. Tim McGraw's twang fills the large dance floor, and before a chance to buy a beer comes, a masculine-expressing woman's body almost meets mine. She shouts, "What are you doing here? You're not gay! You shouldn't be here!"

I am sweating, flush, heart-beating fast, and I'm afraid. I look around for you, for someone I know who can vouch for me. With shaky, stuttering voice, downward gaze, and closed body, muffled, unrecognizable utterances stumble clumsily out of my mouth as my body begs to be saved.

K: I grab your arm and pull you toward me. I am not shocked that this happened, as most spaces, even if they are queer, are not inherently safe. All I can think is, "Now you know part of what it means to be queer." To be questioned and to be unwanted in a space more often than not accompanies queer identification. I also know that when you experience this, sometimes all you really have to count on are the comforts of a good friend to pull you through. Our group of queer friends, who primarily identify as dykes, warmly embrace you. "He's with us." I demand.

D: My panic eases, now that I have found our people—people with whom I share very few identities, but through differences, we find ways to authentically relate with one another.

＊ ＊ ＊ ＊

Who are you in relationship to the people around you? Do they offer support, comfort, and do they reinforce who you are and want to be? These may seem like simple questions to answer. But when forced to identify yourself in a hostile environment, or even if forced to come out or defend a queer friend, those who stand with you become vital in determining the person you are. For D, questioning your own queerness while your queerness is being questioned puts an individual in a position of not knowing fully who they are or where they belong. These instances make us feel deviant, or different, or less than. They make us feel queer. In these moments of questioning and struggle, identification becomes unique in queer relationships. Queer friendships reinforce who you are in the times and spaces of great challenge and of great celebration. Being able to be yourself with other queer people gives comfort and satisfaction in those relationships.

For K, in queer friendship, there are feelings of security in identifying who you are in relation with others who are different from you. Engaging with differences is vital for understanding yourself as queer as part of a larger community of different queer people. Much like Healy-Tillman (2003) when talking about allies, cross-group friends, and social justice, we agree that friendships across lines of difference are not only beneficial for the individual, but they are also beneficial to communities engaging in the work of social activism.

In this way, queer relationships become homeplaces. Bell hooks (1999) describes homeplace as a space of political resistance and yearning for those in marginalized positions to find places of identification, comfort, and safety against acts of racism, sexism, homophobia, and cissexism. In our relationship we were able to accept each other for who we were/are and guide each other as well. In queer friendships this becomes a vital portion of building trust and understanding within the relationship. As each of us comes to the relationship with different intersections, and different points of entry into the queer community, we acknowledge those portions of our identities and navigate them just as we would other characteristics.

Coming to see yourself as queer may take different paths. For example, when feeling different from others growing up, finding yourself attracted to men and women, living in the "taken-for-granted" culture and not being able to explore those feelings until you are older, relating to someone who may identify with your experiences validates who you are. In this, we acknowledge that there are no degrees of queer within our identities (e.g., I am not more or less queer than you) and support each other while embarking on our unique queer paths, while still holding each other accountable for our privileges based on our different identifications with queer. Although we hold privilege in our cisgender, white, middle-class performances, articulating identities and positionalities remains essential to queer friendships. As we deepen our knowledge of each other's identities and disclose our changing relationships with queerness, our relationship is made and re-made queer.

In the next date we explore reciprocity in our relationship and the particular need in queer friendships to be able to acknowledge vulnerabilities, shortcomings, affection, and the ability to return those embodied characteristics equitably.

Third Date: Reciprocity

> D: Walking out of the coffee shop on 17th Street over-caffeinated, roasted coffee permeates my clothes. I unlock my Vespa from the bike rack and singe my legs on the hot black seat. Dressed in a halter-top, flowing, beaded skirt and a bandana for the gypsy theme of the day, Billy steps in and embraces me with a huge hug. "You got your coffee fix, but forgot something," he teases. I gladly hug back, smile, and tell Billy I might see him later—there is a fundraiser for the queer organizing group being held in the city tonight and I have a ticket. Cruising through the city on my way home, I can't stop smiling and immediately want to call K to ask about writing, tonight, and him.

> K: My partner and I had to do some cajoling, but we finally got three-fourths of our fundraising table filled. You took some full out convincing. "If you are going to identify as queer, you have to show up for the community. It's not all about flirting with cute boys at the coffee shop," I tease. "I'm broke," you say. "It's a sliding scale—no excuses," I reply. "Fine," you reply. "What are you wearing?"

> The tables are filled with various bodies: fat and thin, brown, black, white, tan, all in an array of clothing choices, hairstyles, and makeup looks. The three of us (my partner, you, and me) walk in together, so that we now look to be part of a triangular

polyamorous relationship—we are okay with that. Tonight we are celebrating the strength and resilience of our smaller grass-roots, queer organization, which works to educate public entities about LGBTQ issues. We hear presentations, watch DIY film projects, bid on silent auction items, laugh and talk. It is about us, but to be queer is bigger than only our relationship, it is about being engaged in our community.

Within relationships the law of reciprocity, or reciprocity, suggests that if an individual brings something into a relationship, the person with whom that thing is shared will share something too. For example, if I tell my friend a story about my first sexual experience, in order to maintain and continue the friendship the person with whom I shared that information then would share a story of value with me. Although we know that this is not always true for all scenarios, to be put more simply, to create and then maintain a relationship, one behavior begets another. As the first dates focus on theorizing desire and identity, there also remains a unique application of reciprocity in queer friendships that exists in addition to communication and related disciplines. However, when framing the roles within our own interactions, we ask: How do we use reciprocity in order to strengthen our queer relationship? And what is different about reciprocity in queer relating?

Reciprocity, as we explore through our third narrative, takes on an additional meaning. We offer an new perspective, suggesting that reciprocating *within* our friendship (i.e., internal reciprocity) also includes making sure that each of us remains accountable not just to the friendship, but also *to those identities and communities that make us queer*. In this external reciprocity, we advocate for each other, for our own friendship, for our own romantic/sexual relationships, and thus deepen our relationship through reciprocity while simultaneously advocating for people of various queer identities, communities, and, relationalities. To do this, we are constantly remaining self-reflexive in our interactions in order to maintain our relationship that we desire, while remembering our privilege and marginalization within a larger system of power relations that we intentionally challenge in our friendship.

The reciprocity is not just in the interpersonal; it is in the political. Just as relationships are set up to have a give and take with regards to reciprocity, there needs to be reciprocity within the queer community itself. Although not the case for all queer individuals, as certain queer performances are policed even within the queer community, ideally, we would like to think that queer communities offer places of inclusion and some comfort. Although queer communities are not inherently safe spaces (Hobson, 2013), they are places where people of varying identities can gather and express their complicated and often contradictory identities. Therefore, reciprocal action of going to events, offering comfort, offering support for each other *and* the community is vital to not only the queer relationship that we are in, but the queer community itself.

Having explored the first three components to queer friendship and addressing the intricacies that are present in queer friendships with regards to these components, below we enter into the last date, sex.

Fourth Date: Sex?

"You've had sex, right?" The question rings through our collective ears. This time it is our queer friends Rae, Billy, and Heidi that are asking us. We are sitting on Rae's porch, the hot sun pounding down upon us. We are discussing how we all became friends. "Well, I was dating Rae when I introduced her to Dan, and I met Heidi because Rae and Heidi used to date each other, but now they are friends with benefits sometimes."

Billy chimes in, "When I moved in upstairs from Rae, we all met on this porch that very night. I thought Dan and Kathryn were a couple because Moe, Kathryn's partner, was away on business. That bummed me out because I thought Dan was so cute."

"I definitely thought you two were 'more than friends' when I met you guys that night," Rae looks at us. "I mean, you just act like you've had sex before, so I always assumed that you had."

D: Caringly winking at you across Rae's stone porch, we smile and shrug our shoulders. There is comfort in the question, comfort in my identity, in yours, and with our friends. Just like Tito's vodka, soda, and lime has become "our drink," or *I Remember You* (Skid Row, 1989) has become "our song," *all* of the rituals that have become ours, the question too has become a part of our friendship and our queer relating.

The question stems from social expectations that sex, specifically heterosexual intercourse, needs to be the final goal or accomplishment in a successful relationship. Sex, sexual orientation, communicating explicitly about sex, and openness surrounding sex are imperative to our relationship and the relationship that we have with the queer community. Of course, sex is important in relationships; but for us, sex is not the only thing that propels our relationship.

In this final date, the issues that come from this question frame the relationship from a heteronormative perspective but bear little on our queer relationship itself. Instead, it is important to draw upon the importance of intimacy Wood (2015) and queer relationality (Pattisapu & Calafell, 2012) as opposed to sexual intercourse as the norm for indicating relational satisfaction and accomplishment to distinguish queer friendships from other types of relationships.

Conclusion

In exploring the four dates, we highlight the importance of queering sexuality and friendships. Queer friendships, as we see them, are relationships formed between self-identified queer people, and/or encompass relating to each other in ways that queer traditional relationships. We focus on these friendships, and more specifically our friendship, as having the ability to engage with communities of marginal identities of which they are a part, and remaining accountable to being self-reflexive to their multiple identities. Each of the four dates adds a different dimension to the complexities of how queer friendships are formed and maintained, and how Berry's (2014) *act of doing* is represented within our narratives. By presenting these, we advocate for a queer relational style that accounts for the various, sometimes intricate, relationships that form throughout our lives. In thinking about our own relationship and through writing our narratives above, we continuously question and examine our own sexual identities and the friendship that guides, challenges, reinforces, and alters those identities.

Now, we ask you to not only do the same by considering the following questions. Do your relationships have some or all the elements of queer friendships in them? Do you challenge your friends and friendships to think and act more inclusively and openly to queer people and communities? What would it mean for you to think of some of your relationships as queer? Last, what empowerment and social change can result in learning more about these, and perhaps your own, queer relationships? Perhaps in reading this chapter and through thinking critically about the concepts of queering friendship, you can more deeply question how you perform in your own friendships. Through those considerations we hope that no matter what kind of friendships you may have, that you continue to work to improve, challenge, and reinforce those relationships and how you interact with those closest to you.

DISCUSSION QUESTIONS

1. In the chapter we concentrate on queering friendship. What does queering friendship mean to you? How you can include this concept into your own friendships?

2. After reading the chapter and learning about our challenges, how has *your* sexual identity been challenged? What practices have you used to reinforce your own identity?

3. How do you see the author's relationship as being like "friends with benefits"? How is it different?

4. Why do you think U.S. American culture is so preoccupied with sexual intercourse in relationships?

5. Why do you think people feel it is okay to ask some people about the sex they are or are not having? Is it a good or a bad thing to feel as if you can ask others about their sex lives?

References

Adams, T., & Holman-Jones, S. (2008). Autoethnography is queer. In N. K. Denzin, Y.S. Lincoln, & L. Tchiwai (Eds.), *Handbook of Critical and Indigenous Methodologies* (pp. 373–390). Thousand Oaks, CA: Sage.

Berry, K. (2014). Introduction: Queering family, home, love, loss/relational troubling. *Cultural Studies <=> Critical Methodologies, 14*, 91–94. doi:10.1177/1532708613512258

Bolar, R., & Sabo, D. (1989). I remember you. [Recorded by Skid Row]. On Skid row. [CD]. NYC, United States: Atlantic Records.

Cohen, C. J. (1997). Punks, bulldaggers, and welfare queens: The radical potential of queer politics? *GLQ: A Journal of Lesbian and Gay Studies,* 3(4): 437–465. doi: 10.1215/10642684-3-4-437.

Gingrich-Philbrook, C. (2008). Queer theory and performance. *Journal of Homosexuality,* 45(2),353–356.

Halberstam, J. (2005). *In a queer time and place: Transgender bodies, subcultural lives.* New York: New York University.

Hobson, K. (2013). Performative tensions in female drag performances. *Kaleidoscope: A Graduate Journal Of Qualitative Communication Research, 12*35–51.

Hooks, b. (1999). *Yearning: Race, gender, and cultural politics.* Boston, MA: South End Press.

Johnson Jr., M. (2010). "Just getting off": The inseparality of ejaculation and hegemonic masculinity. *The Journal of Men's Studies, 18*(3), 238–248.

Kreps, G. (2000). Disability and culture: Effects on multicultural relations in modern organizations. *Handbook of Communication and People with Disabilities: Research and Application.* Eds. Braithwaite, Dawn O., Thompson, Teresa. Lawrence Erlbaum Associates Publishers, Mahwah: NJ.

Lannutti, P., & Faulkner, S. (This volume). Everyday experiences of people in same-sex relationships. In J. Manning & C. Noland (Eds.), *Contemporary Studies of Sexuality & Communication: Theoretical and Applied Perspectives.* Dubuque, IA: Kendall Hunt.

McKenna-Buchanan, T., & Baker, S. (This volume). "You are on your own": Magnifying co-cultural LGB/TQ microaggressions in the workplace. In J. Manning & C. Noland (Eds.), *Contemporary Studies of Sexuality & Communication: Theoretical and Applied Perspectives.* Dubuque, IA: Kendall Hunt.

Manning, J. (This volume). Identity, relationships, and culture: A constitutive model of coming out. In J. Manning & C. Noland (Eds.), *Contemporary Studies of Sexuality & Communication: Theoretical and Applied Perspectives*. Dubuque, IA: Kendall Hunt.

Moreman, S., & McIntosh, D. (2010). Brown scriptings and rescriptings: A critical performance ethnography of Latina drag queens. *Communication and Critical/Cultural Studies, 7*(2), 115–135.

Muraco, A. (2012). *Friendships at the Intersection of Gender and Sexual Orientation*. Durham, NC: Duke University Press.

Pattisipu, K., & Calafell, B. (2012). (Academic) families of choice. In N. Bardhan & M. Orbe (Eds.), *Identity research and communication: Intercultural reflections and future directions* (pp. 51–67). Lanham, MD: Lexington Books.

Rawlins, W. K. (1992). *Friendship matters: Communication, dialectics, and the life course*. New York: Aldine de Gruyter.

Tillman, L. (2015). *In solidarity: Friendship, family, and activism beyond gay and straight*. New York: Routledge.

Tillman-Healy, L. (2003). Friendship as method. *Qualitative Inquiry, 9*(5), 729–749.

Tillmann-Healy, L. M. (2001). *Between gay and straight: Understanding friendship across sexual orientation*. Lanham: AltaMira.

Wood, J. T. (2015). *Gendered lives: Communication, Gender, and Culture*. Boston, MA: Wadsworth, Cengage Learning.

CHAPTER 12: "You Had Sex, Right?" Theorizing Desire, Identity, Reciprocity, and Sex in Queer Friendships

187

CHAPTER 13

A New Look for the "Little Black Book": Prospective Sex Partners, Back Burner Relationships, and Modern Communication Technology

Jayson L. Dibble, Narissra M. Punyanunt-Carter, Anita Morris, & Richelle Hair

KEY TERMS

Back burners
Relationship alternatives

Casual sex experiences
Romantic relationships

Interpersonal communication

ABSTRACT

Back burners are romantic and/or sexual prospects with whom people stay in touch for purposes of keeping or establishing a romantic and/or sexual relationship. People maintain back burner relationships in order to have an available alternative should they desire to change their current romantic/sexual situation. At one time, this practice was known as keeping a "little black book," a list of potential dating or sex partners. Communicating with prospective romantic/sexual partners is not a new trend, but scholars have recently begun to study how people communicate with their prospects. Whether the little black book was real or metaphorical, data show that people are communicating with back burners, and that they are using modern electronic communication technologies to do so. Moreover, singles as well as those in committed romances keep prospects " simmering" on the back burner. The current chapter presents back burners as a concept for understanding modern sexual life, discusses what is known about the prevalence of back burner communication, addresses some implications of back burners for singles and those in committed relationships, and highlights the electronic technologies people are using to communicate with their back burners.

Chris and Kelly are students who happen to be partying at the same dance club near the college they both attend. At some point in the night, the two cross paths, find themselves attracted to one another, and trade phone numbers before heading home separately. They even "friend" each other on Facebook the next morning. As the months go by, Chris and Kelly date around, go in and out of exclusive romances with others, and spend time being single, but never date (much less commit to) one another. However, every few weeks, Kelly text-messages Chris. These exchanges are harmless enough—*Hey stranger how r u?*—and Kelly isn't particularly interested in dating Chris at the moment, but Kelly does like knowing Chris' dating situation in case Kelly's current romantic life ever needs to change. Through text messages and the occasional private message on Facebook, Chris and Kelly stay in touch—not so close as to initiate a full-on dating relationship, yet not so distant in the event either wishes to escalate a stronger romantic connection with the other.

Researchers use the term *back burner* to describe a potential romantic/sex partner to whom one is not presently committed and that one communicates with in order to keep or establish the possibility for future sexual/romantic involvement (Dibble, Drouin, Aune, & Boller, 2015). Back burner situations themselves are not new, but they are quite common—especially among college students—and researchers are only now beginning to study them. In the opening narrative, Chris and Kelly would qualify as a back burner of each other.

We view back burners as part of the landscape of human sexual life, and here discuss what is currently known about them. Specifically, we address the situation where people will use communication to cultivate and maintain a source of potential sex and/or romantic partners, whether or not sex or romance actually occurs. We organize our presentation around four key questions: 1) What are back burners? 2) How prevalent are back burners? 3) Why do people maintain back burners? and 4) How are people using technology to connect with their back burners?

Defining Back Burners

As was the case for the terms *hookups* and *friends with benefits*, the term *back burner* emerged from the popular culture (Married Jake, 2009; Midlifebachelor, 2008). For example, the popular Internet site Urbandictionary.com defines back burners as "Friends that you are attracted to, that you flirt with and stay close to, so if in the future you're interested in hooking up there's the option to." Although we would hesitate to rely on this definition for scientific purposes, it does illustrate the presence of the concept in the popular culture, and we use it as a basis for our discussion. In this section, we lean on what little scholarship exists to address the defining features of back burner situations, returning to the popular definition where necessary.

Whether or not they are already in committed relationships, it is common for people to keep tabs on the availability and suitability of alternative romantic/sexual partners (Fletcher, 2002; Kelley & Thibault, 1978). As was the case with Kelly and Chris in the chapter's opening, sometimes people will reach out to their alternatives in order to keep open the possibility of future romantic/sexual involvement. The term back burner suggests a metaphor. People communicate with their back burners so as to fan the "embers" of romantic and/or sexual attraction, while simultaneously keeping them away from the "central flame" of their current relationship situation. In other words, the alternative partner "simmers on the back burner" while the admirer manages his or her primary romantic situation (which can include being single). Some college students have also described their back burners as a back-up plan that they might access should they desire. As we discussed earlier, Kelly and Chris are romantically and/or sexually interested in one another, and they stay in touch to maintain that romantic/sexual interest. Thus, Chris can be considered a back burner of Kelly's and vice versa.

Back burners are defined by at least two key conditions. First, there must be a degree of romantic and/or sexual desire on the part of one person (whom we'll call the admirer) for another person (the back burner). Chris and

CHAPTER 13: A New Look for the "Little Black Book": Prospective Sex Partners, Back Burner Relationships, and Modern Communication Technology

191

Kelly are attracted to each other in this way, and so they satisfy this condition. Furthermore, Chris and Kelly probably know of their attractions for one another, and are aware that they are back burners to each other, but mutual awareness is not necessary. A back burner may not always be aware of the admirer's desires, and may not even know that they are a back burner. In other words, some back burners are aware of the admirer's romantic and/or sexual motivations (and may even respond in kind), while other back burners are unaware of the admirer's motivations. Note that our conceptualization differs from the Urban Dictionary definition that does not specify whether the back burners are aware of each other's intentions. We believe any of these situations could be theoretically interesting. Until new research suggests otherwise, we define back burners as being instantiated from the admirer's perspective, and that the presence of the admirer's romantic and/or sexual motivations is sufficient for the target to be a back burner. That is, the condition of romantic/sexual interest in the other need only be present in one of the parties. For example, if Chris were interested in Kelly, but Kelly was not interested in Chris, it would still be possible for Kelly to be a back burner of Chris'—provided the next condition is met.

The second key condition is communication. We agree with the Urban Dictionary definition that back burners cannot exist without some measure of communication between the admirer and the back burner. This communication can range from veiled flirting to overt flirting, but can also be platonic in appearance. For example, college students had back burners with whom they exchanged overt romantic and/or sexual messages, as well as back burners with whom they exchanged only platonic-appearing messages (Dibble et al., 2015). In other words, even though the admirer's ambitions must be of a romantic and/or sexual nature, the *messages* people send to their back burners can range in form from explicitly sexual and/or romantic to platonic (e.g., *Hey stranger how r u?* from our opening example). Thus, people can use both romantically/sexually-charged messages and platonic messages to communicate with their back burners.

Furthermore, those same college students were able to differentiate their back burners from other sexually-desirable alternatives with whom they did not communicate (Dibble et al., 2015). This finding suggests that people do not automatically consider everyone they are romantically or sexually interested in to be back burners. People can be sexually/romantically attracted to lots of others, but only some of those targets count as back burners.

Because of their rooting in popular culture and relevance to human sexuality, back burners might be related to casual sexual experiences like hookups and friends with benefits (Aubrey & Smith, 2013; Bisson & Levine, 2009; Claxton & van Dulmen, 2013). Moreover, in certain situations we might even expect some overlap between back burners and these other relationships. For example, a couple might end their exclusive dating relationship, but remain back burners while they explore other relationship options. Alternatively, hookup partners or friends with benefits could morph into back burners (and vice versa). That is, some back burners happen to be others with whom people have had a sexual/romantic past. Importantly, however, people can also have back burners with whom they've had neither sex nor any romantic commitment, such as was the case above with Chris and Kelly. Thus, back burner relationships can exist apart from hookups and friends with benefits because sex is necessary for hookups and friends with benefits to occur. Whether or not sex has occurred between the people involved, back burners are ripe for exploration and deserve to be studied. Having spent some time discussing what back burners are, let's turn our attention to what we know about the prevalence of keeping back burners.

The Prevalence of Back Burners

Because people keep a continuous eye on their romantic and sexual prospects regardless of commitment status to somebody else (e.g., Fletcher, 2002), then we have little reason to believe that communicating with back burners is necessarily restricted to certain kinds of people. We speculate that many kinds of people have back burners. Nonetheless, college students are known to embrace a culture characterized by an acceptance of and preference for hookups and friends with benefits experiences over committed romantic relationships (Garcia, Reiber, Massey, & Merriwether, 2012; Levine & Mongeau, 2010; Townsend & Wasserman, 2011). Given that casual sex researchers expect college students to have the most casual sex experiences, we suspect that college students and young adults are maintaining the most back burners. Therefore, college students represent a sensible starting group for studying back burners.

Research about back burners is only beginning, but two prior studies give us an early picture. In the first study, 66% of 374 students sampled reported

CHAPTER 13: A New Look for the "Little Black Book": Prospective Sex Partners, Back Burner Relationships, and Modern Communication Technology

193

having at least one back burner, and of those who reported at least one, the average was 5.56 (Dibble et al., 2015). In a separate study, Dibble and Drouin (2014) found mean numbers of back burners to be higher for students who were single ($M = 6.74$) than for those who were in committed romances ($M = 4.53$), but this difference was not statistically significant. However, men ($M = 8.32$) averaged more back burners than did women ($M = 3.78$).

For this book chapter, we introduce a new set of data that has yet to be published. This study includes 762 students (71% female, 29% male) at a large southern university. Based on the results of the Dibble et al. (2015) study, we provided students with the following description:

> Back burners are people we are romantically and/or sexually interested in, who we're not currently committed to, and with whom we keep in contact in the possibility that we might someday connect romantically and/or sexually. People can have back burners whether or not they're already in a committed romantic relationship with someone else. Back burners can also take different forms. For example, back burners could be former romantic/sexual partners or current sexual partners, provided we're not committed to them, we still desire them romantically and/or sexually, and that this desire is one of the reasons we keep in touch with them. Finally, we may end up getting together with some of our back burners, while we may never get together with others.

The college students read this description then looked through the contact list of the electronic communication channel they reported using most (e.g., mobile phone calling, text messaging, Facebook friends list) to determine how many of these contacts they considered to be back burners.

Our results corroborated the earlier studies. Over 75% of our sample reported at least one back burner, and for those who reported at least one, the average was 9.41. Similarly, we found no statistically significant difference between singles and those who were already committed to another romantic partner. With regard to gender, Dibble et al. (2015) found men to have more back burners than did women. Our data revealed the same pattern: Men ($n = 204$; $M = 18.51$, $SD = 85.35$) reported having more back burners than did women ($n = 486$, $M = 5.59$, $SD = 26.86$).

We should note that back burners have not yet been studied using random representative samples, and that our data come only from college students. That said, about three-fourths of our sample reported at least one back burner, with 5–9 back burners being typical. Similar to Dibble et al. (2015), our participants reported back burners whether or not they were already in a committed relationship, and being in a committed romance didn't relate substantially to the number of back burners one maintained.

Prior research also suggests people with back burners communicate with at least one of their back burners somewhat frequently, with over 48% doing so on at least a weekly basis (Dibble et al., 2015). In our current sample, about 26% communicated with a back burner on a weekly basis or more frequently (roughly 2% reported communicating with a back burner every day). It seems reasonable to believe that back burner communication is a common and regular occurrence.

Also, people do not readily tell their current partner about their back burners. In the Dibble et al. (2015) sample, only about 15% reported that their partners knew about all of their back burners. Our sample revealed a similar result: only 11% of those who had back burners disclosed all of them to their partner. However, we do not know how much detail people give their partners about their back burners. We can easily imagine partners reacting differently to a back burner who is reported to be *just a friend* versus *a back burner of mine*. Unfortunately, the available studies were not set up to answer this question. More research is needed, but communication with back burners seems to be something of a secretive endeavor that people do not readily make known to their current relationship partner.

Reasons Why People Maintain Back Burners

In short, people maintain back burners to preserve access to sex partners in the event that such a partner is wanted. Social exchange perspectives like interdependence theory (Kelley & Thibault, 1978) and its extension the investment model (Rusbult, 1980) can help us understand back burners. These perspectives hold that individuals establish relationships in part by identifying available alternative partners with whom to form a relationship. As we already noted, people continue to monitor their relationship

CHAPTER 13: A New Look for the "Little Black Book": Prospective Sex Partners, Back Burner Relationships, and Modern Communication Technology

195

prospects whether or not they are already in a committed relationship (Fletcher, 2002). Interestingly, individuals monitor alternatives whether or not those alternatives are already in a committed relationship, as the vast literature on mate poaching indicates (e.g., Fisher, 2012; O'Sullivan & Ronis, 2013; Schmitt & Buss, 2001; Sunderani, Arnocky, & Vaillancourt, 2013). That is, just as people who are already committed to another person can have back burners, people who are already committed to another person (e.g., those who are "taken") can also *be* a back burner. From an evolutionary viewpoint, activities like mate poaching increase an individual's mating success by providing access to mates who would ordinarily be unavailable (Schmitt & Buss, 2001). To summarize, for singles and those in committed relationships, connecting with back burners facilitates access to prospective sex partners, even if the admirer's sexual/romantic ambitions are never actually carried out.

Technology Use in Back Burner Communication

Keeping in touch with romantic/sexual prospects is probably as old as humankind. Even if the label back burner is new, having back burners is probably not new. In fact, the proverbial little black book likely refers to what we are labeling back burners today. Our observation is that this phrase is going out of vogue, and people may not be keeping a list using paper and pen, but that people's contact with their back burners indeed continues through contemporary channels. In the current landscape, people are staying in touch with back burners using mobile phone calls, text messages, and various Internet-based applications like Facebook, Instagram, Snapchat, and Skype (Dibble & Drouin, 2014; Dibble et al., 2015). Thus, the little black book of days of yore has converted to mobile phone contact lists, Facebook "friends" lists, and so forth.

Technology has made connecting with back burners easier, more efficient, and to a large extent more private. In the United States, there are a large and growing number of individuals that have near-constant Internet access through computers as well as portable handheld devices (Hargittai, 2004). For many people, this means that they are available to be contacted nearly

24 hours a day. There has been a move away from landline telephones and a move toward having a personal mobile telephone. These changes have fostered a new generation of individuals who are almost constantly in contact with other individuals, and the preferred method of communication is often text messaging as opposed to phone calls (Leonardi, 2003; Smith, 2011). Indeed, text messaging was the mode of choice for more than half of our student sample, as well as that of Dibble et al. (2015). Hence, this allows for easier access to transmit messages and multi-messages to a variety of back burners.

At the time of this writing, Facebook continues to be the most prominent social networking platform (Duggan, Ellison, Lampe, Lenhart, & Madden, 2015), and students use Facebook to keep in touch with back burners (Dibble & Drouin, 2014; Dibble et al., 2015). Facebook allows people to renew old friendships; communicate with friends; and obtain information about interests, opinions, and activities of friends (Ellison, Steinfield, & Lampe, 2007). At the same time, Facebook has been linked to negative outcomes regarding romantic relationships that include conflict, infidelity, and jealousy (Clayton, Nagurney, & Smith, 2013; Drouin, Miller, & Dibble, 2014; Muise, Christofides, & Desmarais, 2009). Moreover, the information exposed on social networks can reveal to others the existence and identities of one's back burners, which may fuel rumination, surveillance behaviors, and/or other relational negatives (Fox & Warber, 2014).

This begs the question of whether the business of maintaining back burners is good or bad for an individual or for a relationship. Interestingly, the available data do not necessarily spell doom and gloom. Although it was true that many students who were already in committed relationships reported keeping in touch with at least one back burner, Dibble and Drouin (2014) found no relationship between the number of back burners the student kept and how committed that student was to her/his partner. That is, having back burners itself does not automatically imply anything about the quality of a romantic relationship, at least when looking at commitment. Consistent with these findings, some early unpublished data indicated that although students could identify more back burners when looking at Facebook than if they had to generate a list from memory, the back burners identified using a Facebook friends list did not relate to their investment in, or satisfaction with, their current romantic relationships (Drouin, Miller, & Dibble, in press). Thus, two early studies did not find a link between the

CHAPTER 13: A New Look for the "Little Black Book": Prospective Sex Partners, Back Burner Relationships, and Modern Communication Technology

197

number of back burners students maintained using electronic technology and the relationship variables commitment, investment, and satisfaction. Perhaps it's not the number of back burners that make the difference, but some other aspect of the back burner situation, e.g., the intensity of the connection with one or more particular back burner. To be fair, researchers so far have only looked at commitment, investment, and satisfaction. Future research may find other relational variables that are significantly impacted by back burners.

Still, we wonder, as did these researchers, whether the ubiquity of electronically mediated communication such as text-messaging and social networking has somehow normalized back burner communication to the point where people do not necessarily associate their back burner activity as having anything to do with their real romantic relationships. In a time before mobile phones and the Internet, the family's single telephone was often located in a high-traffic area of the house (e.g., kitchen), so using the phone was rarely a private experience. In contrast, every person can now possess her or his own private mobile phone, which can now allow access to a wider array of communication channels through which to contact their back burners. Indeed, Chris and Kelly from our opening example would periodically send each other a quick text message that nobody else would have to know about. If reaching out to one's back burners is now easier and more private, perhaps the practice has somehow become normalized to the point where people fail to automatically associate their communication with back burners with the way they feel about their current partners. This is only our speculation, and even if it turned out to be true, we don't yet know what it would mean for romantic relationships in general.

To summarize, early studies are showing that back burner communication is common, and that people use available technologies to maintain contact with back burners, with social networking sites and mobile text messaging being most popular. However, the impact of technology use to maintain back burners is less clear, with sound arguments to be made that operating in an increasingly public social networking environment will damage romantic relationships, and/or that technology is simply making it easier to do what humans have always done and that the existence of back burner communication itself should not trigger concern.

Conclusion

A significant amount of research regarding sexual and romantic relationships is focused on hook-ups and friends with benefits, particularly research involving college students. To this body of work we introduce the back burner concept (Dibble & Drouin, 2014; Dibble et al., 2015) to describe romantic/sexual prospects people communicate with in order to establish or maintain a potential sexual and/or romantic liaison. Studying back burners helps to expand the picture of human sexual life by attending to communication events that can (but do not have to) lead to a sexual or romantic encounter or relationship.

Similar to previous research, our data showed that most people communicate to some extent with at least one person they consider a back burner, and that they use modern electronic technologies to do so. However, the research reviewed in this chapter showed no link between the number of back burners students communicated with via electronic technology and levels of partner commitment, involvement, or satisfaction. For now, we pass along the recommendation of Dibble et al. (2015) to use discretion and care before automatically assuming that one's relationship is in jeopardy if either or both partners talk to back burners. Although people vary in their sensitivity to this topic, we simply do not yet know enough about how back burners impact existing relationships. So perhaps the best advice we can offer is to consider each relationship on a case-by-case basis and focus on other markers of relationship health while we wait for more research to fill in the picture.

DISCUSSION QUESTIONS

1. Back burner relationships require a delicate balance of being close, but not too close. What communicative strategies do you think people engage in to maintain this balance?

2. Chris and Kelly's situation illustrates just one way back burners can develop. What are some others?

CHAPTER 13: A New Look for the "Little Black Book": Prospective Sex Partners, Back Burner Relationships, and Modern Communication Technology

199

3. How would you feel if you discovered you were a back burner? What are some ways that people might find out or suspect that they are back burners?

4. What sorts of ethical considerations go along with maintaining back burners? Should people talk openly to their back burners about the back burner aspect of their connection? What other ethical issues deserve consideration?

5. In your opinion is it healthy to have back burners? Are there positive aspects to the back burner concept? How has technology influenced and changed back burner relationships?

References

Aubrey, J., & Smith, S. E. (2013). Development and Validation of the Endorsement of the Hookup Culture Index. *Journal of Sex Research*, *50*, 435–448. doi:10.1080/00224499.2011.637246.

Bisson, M. A., & Levine, T. R. (2009). Negotiating a friends with benefits relationship. *Archives of Sexual Behavior*, *38*, 66–73. doi:10.1007/s10508-007-9211-2.

Claxton, S. E., & van Dulmen, M. H. M. (2013). Casual sexual relationships and experiences in emerging adulthood. *Emerging Adulthood*, *1*, 138–150. doi:10.1177/2167696813487181.

Clayton, R. B., Nagurney, A., & Smith, J. R. (2013). Cheating, breaking up and divorce: Is Facebook use to blame? *Cyberpsychology, Behavior, & Social Networking*, *16*, 717–720.

Dibble, J. L., & Drouin, M. (2014). "Using modern technology to keep in touch with back burners: An Investment Model Analysis." *Computers in Human Behavior*, *34*, 96–100. doi:10.1016/j.chb.2014.01.042.

Dibble, J. L., Drouin, M., Aune, K. S., & Boller, R. R. (2015). Simmering on the back burner: Communication with and disclosure of relationship alternatives. *Communication Quarterly*, *63*, 329–344. doi:10.1080/01463373.2015.1039719.

Drouin, M., Miller, D. A., & Dibble, J. L. (in press). Facebook or memory—which is the real threat to your relationship? *Cyberpsychology, Behavior, and Social Networking*.

Drouin, M., Miller, D. A., & Dibble, J. L. (2014). Ignore your partners' current Facebook friends; beware the ones they add! *Computers in Human Behavior, 35*, 483–488.

Duggan, M., Ellison, N. B., Lampe, C., Lenhart, A., & Madden, M. (2015). Social media update 2014. Pew Research Center. Retrieved from http://www.pewinternet.org/2015/01/09/social-media-update-2014/.

Ellison, N. B., Steinfield, C. & Lampe, C. (2007). The benefits of Facebook "friends": Social capital and college students' use of online social network sites. *Journal of Computer Mediated Communication, 12 (4)*, 1143–1168.

Fisher, H. E. (2012). Serial monogamy and clandestine adultery: Evolution and consequences of the dual human reproductive strategy. In S. C. Roberts (Ed.), *Applied evolutionary psychology* (pp. 93–111). New York, NY: Oxford University Press.

Fletcher, G. J. O. (2002). *The new science of intimate relationships.* Malden, MA: Blackwell.

Fox, J., & Warber, K. M. (2014). Social networking sites in romantic relationships: Attachment uncertainty and partner surveillance on Facebook. *Cyberpsychology, Behavior, & Social Networking, 17*, 3–7.

Garcia, J. R., Reiber, C., Massey, S. G., & Merriwether, A. M. (2012). Sexual hookup culture: A review. *Review of General Psychology, 16*, 161–176.

Hargittai, E. (2004). Internet access and use in context. *New Media & Society, 6*, 137–143. doi:10.1177/1461444804042310.

Kelley, H. H., & Thibault, J. E. (1978). *Interpersonal relations: A theory of interdependence.* New York, NY: Wiley.

Leonardi, P. M. (2003). Problematizing "new media": Culturally based perceptions of cell phones, computers, and the Internet among United States Latinos. *Critical Studies in Media Communication, 20*, 160–179. doi:10.1080/07393180302778.

Levine, T. R., & Mongeau, P. A. (2010). Friends with benefits: A precarious negotiation. In M. Bruce & R. M. Steward (Eds.) *College sex: Philosophy for everyone* (pp. 91–102). Oxford, UK: Wiley-Blackwell.

Married Jake. (2009, September 25). Do you have a back burner? [Web log post]. Retrieved from http://www.glamour.com/sex-love-life/blogs/smitten/2009/09/do-you-have-a-back-burner.html.

Midlifebachelor.com (2008, September 1). Front burner, back burner dating strategy. Retrieved from http://www.midlifebachelor.com/articles/frontburnerbackburner.html.

CHAPTER 13: A New Look for the "Little Black Book": Prospective Sex Partners, Back Burner Relationships, and Modern Communication Technology

201

Muise, A., Christofides, E., & Desmarais, S. (2009). More information than you ever wanted: Does Facebook bring out the green-eyed monster of jealousy? *Cyberpsychology & Behavior, 12,* 441–444. doi:10.1089/cpb.2008.0263.

O'Sullivan, L. F., & Ronis, S. T. (2013). Virtual cheating hearts: Extradyadic and poaching interactions among adolescents with links to online sexual activities. *Canadian Journal of Behavioural Science, 45,* 175–184.

Rusbult, C. E. (1980). Commitment and satisfaction in romantic associations: A test of the investment model. *Journal of Experimental Social Psychology, 16,* 172–186. doi:10.1016/0022-1031(80)90007-4.

Schmitt, D. P., & Buss, D. M. (2001). Human mate poaching: Tactics and temptations for infiltrating existing mateships. *Journal of Personality and Social Psychology, 80,* 894–917. doi:10.1037/0022-3514.80.6.894.

Smith, A. (2011). Americans and text messaging. *Pew Internet & American Life Project.* Retrieved from http://pewinternet.org/~/media//Files/Reports/2011/Americans%20and%20Text%20Messaging.pdf.

Sunderani, S., Arnocky, S., & Vaillancourt, T. (2013). Individual differences in mate poaching: An examination of hormonal, dispositional, and behavioral mate-value traits. *Archives of Sexual Behavior, 42,* 533–542.

Townsend, J. M., & Wasserman, T. H. (2011). Sexual hookups among college students: Sex differences in emotional reactions. *Archives of Sexual Behavior, 40,* 1173–1181. doi:10.1007/s10508-011-9841-2.

CHAPTER 14

Chatting, Snacking, and Snuggling: An Overview of Research on Post-Sex Communication

Amanda Denes & Annika Speer

KEY TERMS

Post-sex communication	Sexual communication
Pillow talk	Afterplay

ABSTRACT

With a focus on scholarship produced in the past 10 years, this chapter provides a brief synopsis of the current literature on communication after sexual activity. The chapter offers an overview of verbal and nonverbal behaviors following sexual activity, predictors of post-sex communication (such as orgasm and relationship status), outcomes of post-sex communication (including bonding, emotional intimacy, and increased relationship satisfaction) and future directions for post-sex communication research. Given that post-sex communication is a relatively new line of research, further exploration may offer insights into a variety of factors that contribute to overall relationship maintenance, satisfaction, and well-being.

In the past decade, researchers have begun to more closely examine the behaviors that occur after sexual activity and their potential importance to relationship functioning (e.g., Denes, 2012; Denes & Afifi, 2014; Muise, Giang, & Impett, 2014). Although research exploring behaviors after sexual activity is fairly new, the potential effects of individuals' post-sex communication on relationship functioning has been noted for decades. In 1979, Halpern and Sherman introduced the concept of afterplay. Afterplay focuses on the ways individuals "exit" a sexual episode. In other words, afterplay is what occurs immediately after sexual activity. Halpern and Sherman (1979) suggest that afterplay contributes to sexual satisfaction even more than other components of sexual interactions, such as foreplay, orgasm, and even sex itself. They also note that the interactions immediately following sexual activity are probably affecting both individuals' sexual satisfaction as well as their overall relationship satisfaction. Research such as this has encouraged scholars to better understand communication after sexual activity and its potential link to relationship well-being.

This chapter will cover several key topics relevant to communication and *after sexual activity*: an overview of behaviors after sexual activity, predictors of post-sex communication, outcomes of post-sex communication, and future directions for post-sex communication research. Additionally, we will complement this literature review with an inside look at Denes and Afifi's (2014) study, "Pillow Talk and Cognitive Decision Making Processes: Exploring the Role of Orgasm and Alcohol on Communication After Sexual Activity" that appeared in the research journal *Communication Monographs*. Overall, this chapter will introduce readers to the developing area of study on post-sex communication.

An Overview of Post-Sex Behavior

Research exploring interactions after sex has focused both on verbal and nonverbal behaviors between partners. Verbally, scholars studying post-sex behavior have focused on "pillow talk," or the moments of shared verbal intimacy following sexual activity (Denes, 2012). Scholars have examined pillow talk both by exploring dimensions of post-sex disclosures, such as the valence (i.e., the positivity or negativity), intentionality, magnitude, and amount of such communication (Denes, 2012; Denes &

Afifi, 2014) as well as by investigating the duration of post-sex intimate talk (Muise et al., 2014).

Several studies from this line of work have focused on self-disclosure after sexual activity. Self-disclosure involves "any information exchange that refers to the self, including personal states, dispositions, events in the past, and plans for the future" (Derlega & Grzelak, 1979, p. 152). Expressing feelings and emotions is often cited by communication scholars as one of the primary goals of self-disclosure (Derlega & Grzelak, 1979). Derlega and Grzelak (1979) explain that individuals often self-disclose with the goal of expression [of emotions and feelings] or for relationship development. For example, individuals may say, "You make me so happy," or, "I'm really angry right now," as a way of disclosing emotions and feelings.

Much of the research on post-sex communication has focused on the valence of disclosures after sexual activity (e.g., Denes, 2012; Denes & Afifi, 2014). The term "positive relational disclosures" captures this idea, as such disclosures involve sharing "positive aspects of the relationship between the two partners such as declarations of love, affection, and intimacy," and are thus positively valenced (Denes, 2012, p. 95). Exploring positive relational disclosures after sexual activity is important, as several scholars have suggested that this is a pivotal time for bonding and sharing emotions (e.g., Halpern & Sherman, 1979; Veenestra, 2007). Though positive relational disclosures have been measured broadly by asking study participants about the valence of the information they disclosed after sexual activity, such disclosures may also include saying "I love you," or other positive emotional expressions. Communication, and self-disclosure in particular, after sexual activity may thus be one way that individuals obtain the goal of emotional expression and pair-bonding. In sum, studies investigating verbal communication after sexual activity have primarily focused on self-disclosure and different dimensions of disclosure.

Nonverbally, scholars have focused on a plethora of post-sex behaviors, including kissing, cuddling, spooning, caressing, snacking, and sleeping (Hughes & Kruger, 2011; Muise et al., 2014). For example, Muise et al. (2014) discovered that higher relationship satisfaction was reported by couples who spent more time interacting intimately, which included nonverbal (e.g., snuggling) and verbal (e.g., speaking affectionately) behaviors. They also found that sexual satisfaction mediated the relationship between post-sex affection and relationship satisfaction. In other words, post-sex affection was associated with sexual satisfaction, which in turn was associated with relationship satisfaction. Hughes and Kruger (2011) have also explored these behaviors in their investigations of the post-coital time interval (PCTI) (Kruger & Hughes, 2010). The PCTI denotes the time period subsequent to sexual activity or physical intimacy that precedes one partner sleeping or leaving and is deemed a significant attribute of romantic relationships (Kruger & Hughes, 2010).

Kruger and Hughes' line of research has been lauded as reinvigorating the "science of the post-coitus" (Ryder, 2012), opening up future avenues of research for scholars interested in post-sex communication. Such studies have more intricately explored nonverbal behaviors that occur immediately following sexual activity. For example, many times, partners may touch one another and snuggle after sexual activity. We go deeper into this growing line of research in the following sections.

Predictors of Post-Sex Communication

Several studies have sought to understand the various factors that may influence post-sex behavior. A developing line of research indicates that orgasm is an important predictor of individuals' likelihood of sharing positive feelings with their partners after sex (Denes, 2012; Denes, under review; Denes & Afifi, 2014). These studies have suggested that the hormones released during orgasm—particularly the hormone oxytocin—may influence individuals' perceptions and subsequent disclosures. Oxytocin is sometimes called the "trust hormone" or "love hormone," as studies have found that increases in oxytocin are associated with greater feelings of trust, increased prosocial behavior, a better ability to read nonverbal cues, and decreased fear responses (Domes et al., 2007; Guastella, Mitchell, & Dadds, 2008; Huber, Veinante, & Stoop, 2005; Kirsch et al., 2005; Kosfeld et al., 2005; Lim & Young, 2006). In other words, oxytocin often makes people feel good and bond with others. Several studies have also revealed that oxytocin is released in large amounts when people orgasm (Blaicher et al., 1999; Carmichael et al., 1987). Taken together, it is possible that the flood of hormones after sexual climax causes people to perceive the time immediately after orgasm as one that is safe for disclosing feelings.

Though research has yet to directly measure oxytocin and its potential effect on post-sex communication, both Denes (2012) and Denes and Afifi (2014) found that individuals who orgasmed reported disclosing more positive feelings for their partners after sexual activity than those who did not orgasm. Denes and Afifi (2014) further found that individuals who orgasmed also reported disclosing information of greater depth and perceived greater benefits to disclosing post-sex information than those who did not orgasm. Though these studies have focused primarily on young adults, the findings suggest that orgasm influences individuals' verbal communication after sexual activity.

Though oxytocin has yet to be investigated, new research is investigating the link between another hormone—testosterone—and post-sex communication (Denes, Afifi, & Granger, 2015). Denes et al. (2015) found that the higher the individuals' (which included women and men) testosterone levels, the fewer benefits and greater risks they perceived to disclosing to their partners after sexual activity, even after controlling for sex. Higher testosterone levels were also associated with less intentional and less positively valenced post-sex disclosures, and these associations were mediated by risk-benefit assessments. Denes et al. (2015) also found an interaction between testosterone and orgasm—higher testosterone levels were associated with more negatively valenced disclosures for individuals who did not orgasm, but not for those who orgasmed. Testosterone is thought to dampen the effects of oxytocin (Taylor et al., 2002), and the authors therefore suggest that individuals with high testosterone levels who do not orgasm may not experience the positive effects of orgasm on post-sex communication.

Another important predictor of post-sex behavior involves individuals' relationship status. For example, Denes (2012) found that individuals in monogamous/committed relationships engaged in more positive relational disclosures (i.e., sharing positive thoughts and feelings with their partners) after sexual activity than those in casual/open relationships. Hughes and Kruger (2011) also investigated differences in individuals' post-sex behaviors depending on whether individuals were in long-term or short-term partnerships. They found that the following five factors emerged from long-term partners' reported behaviors after sexual activity: intimacy and bonding (e.g., engaging in intimate talk, cuddling), extrinsic rewards (e.g., smoking a cigarette, drinking alcohol), continuing sex (e.g., continuing penetration, oral sex), hunger (e.g., eating, snacking), and sanitary practices (e.g., using the bathroom, showering). However, a different set of factors emerged in short-term partnerships. Short-term partners demonstrated the factor of intimacy and bonding like long-term partners, but the other behaviors loaded onto a different set of factors. Short-term partners' behaviors grouped into pleasure-seeking (e.g., continued sexual activity, snacking/eating), partner departure (e.g., leaving and/or not falling asleep with the partner, leaving to shower, use the bathroom, or snack), alternative motives (e.g., drinking/smoking, asking for things from the partner), and sleep (e.g., going immediately to sleep), in addition to intimacy and bonding (Hughes & Kruger, 2011).

A final important predictor of post-sex behavior involves biological sex. Kruger and Hughes (2010) found that during the PCTI, males perceive their female partners as having more interest in discussing relationship issues than they [men] do. Compared to males, females in long-term relationships also place more value on post-sex behaviors that indicate intimacy and closeness with their partners, and are more likely to initiate such behaviors (Hughes & Kruger, 2011). Similarly, women report initiating more kissing after sex than men. Across both long- and short-term relationships, women have been found to initiate more bonding behaviors, while men initiate behaviors that may promote further sexual activity or offer some extrinsic reward (e.g., smoking, drinking, leaving; Hughes & Kruger, 2011).

Outcomes of Post-Sex Communication

Multiple scholars have argued that the time after sexual activity is crucial for partner bonding and emotional intimacy (e.g., Halpern & Sherman, 1979; Veenestra, 2007), and thus, may have important effects on relationship well-being. The period of time subsequent to sexual activity is frequently deemed as one of elevated affection or intimacy in which partners exhibit behaviors necessary for bonding, such as sharing or disclosing feelings verbally as well as demonstrating nonverbal affection (Halpern & Sherman, 1979; Veenestra, 2007). Such research suggests that post-sex behavior may influence other areas of relational functioning. This possibility was tested in a study by Muise et al. (2014) examining the amount of time individuals (ages 18 to 64) spent engaging in certain behaviors after sexual activity. As noted earlier, Muise et al. (2014) discovered that couples who spent more time interacting intimately (i.e., snuggling, speaking affectionately, etc.) also reported higher relationship satisfaction, and that sexual satisfaction mediated the relationship between post-sex affection and relationship satisfaction. In other words, engaging in affectionate behavior increased sexual satisfaction, which in turn increased relationship satisfaction. Furthermore, current research (Denes, under review) reveals that the more benefits individuals assess to disclosing feelings to their partners after sexual activity, the higher their reported relationship satisfaction. Together, studies such as these suggest that the positive effects of post-sex behavior may extend beyond the sexual episode itself and into other facets of couples' communication.

Though causal links between post-sex communication and relationship outcomes have yet to be established, the research described above suggests that what happens after sexual activity may influence couples' relationships in important ways. For example, intimate talk and affectionate behavior after sexual activity may help couples maintain their closeness and intimacy, which may ultimately increase the longevity of their relationships. It is also possible that pillow talk helps couples increase their positive communication and increase their communication efficacy (i.e., an individual's belief that s/he can communicate a particular message; Bandura, 1977), which may aid them in other facets of relational communication and help with everyday communication. Though speculative, couples that have already built a certain level of intimacy and closeness in the bedroom may find themselves better equipped to deal with conflict, and communicate with more care and consideration when discussing stressors.

Future Directions

Although current research deals primarily with individuals' reports about their communication following sexual activity, a direction for future research is to investigate qualitative differences in what couples say to one another after sexual activity (i.e., examining the perceptions of *both* parties in the relationship). Such research could take two approaches. First, a valuable future direction involves couples recording their post-sex communication. This approach would allow researchers to code the conversations and gain a better understanding of the interpersonal exchanges that occur post sex and the content of such communication. A second approach involves conducting interviews with couples about their post-sex communication. By conducting interviews with both members of the couple regarding their mutual or differing perceptions about their post-sex behavior, researchers can better assess the dyadic nature of the verbal and nonverbal communication after sexual activity and better understand why partners may differ in their post-sex goals and outcomes.

As noted above, it would also be beneficial for scholars to investigate the long-term effects of post-sex communication. What types of post-sex communication have the most positive effects on couples' relationship satisfaction? Do couples that consistently express positive emotions for their partners stay together longer than couples that do little to no communicating after sexual activity? Additionally, do couples view pillow talk as a relationship maintaining behavior? It is possible that some individuals use this time of intimacy and closeness as one that helps them maintain their relationship with their partners, while others may see it as less important to their relationship. Understanding individual differences that influence outcomes of pillow talk would help scholars understand when and for whom pillow talk is most beneficial.

Translated Research Study

The last section of the chapter will now focus on the applied aspects of Denes and Afifi's (2014) article, *Pillow talk and cognitive decision making processes: Exploring the role of orgasm and alcohol on communication after sexual activity*. The study explored the effects of orgasm and alcohol on post-sex communication over a two-week period, with a sample of primarily young adults ranging in age from 18 to 45 years old (with an average age of 21). The study revealed that individuals who orgasmed perceived greater benefits to disclosing to their partners after sexual activity, and disclosed more positive feelings for their partners and information of greater depth. The study also revealed that the more alcohol individuals consumed across the two-week timespan of the study (but not how much they consumed on any one occasion), the fewer benefits they perceived to disclosing. Similarly, individuals who consumed more alcohol across the two-week study also disclosed less deep and more negatively valenced information after sex, and their post-sex disclosures were more unintentional.

The findings of this study, particularly those involving alcohol consumption, were somewhat surprising. They suggest that it does not really matter how much alcohol an *individual* drinks on any one occasion, but rather what matters are the patterns of alcohol consumption *in relationships*. The study did not reveal any significant differences in terms of the positivity or depth of the disclosures depending on how much someone drank on any one occasion; but, rather, the results revealed that individuals who drank more before sexual activity *in general* (across the two-week diary study) disclosed information of less depth and less positively valenced information. In other words, consistently consuming more alcohol before sex was associated with less positive and less deep post-sex communication.

One takeaway of this study is that couples need to be aware of the way they are using alcohol in relationships and the patterns they are developing. If a person always feels the need to drink before sexual activity, it may imply that alcohol is "subbing in" for intimacy. Establishing such a pattern appears to have a negative effect on pillow talk and may be preventing individuals from building intimacy and closeness with one another. It is also important to note that participants in Denes and Afifi's (2014) study were fairly young, and the results may differ in older adult populations or in longer-term relationships (on average, individuals in their study reported being in their current relationship for 21 months).

Though research has yet to test the "dos" and "don'ts" of pillow talk, below is an offering of further thoughts and advice on post-sex communication. Much of the following information is derived from the research discussed in this chapter, while other advice is speculative in nature and remains to be tested by future researchers. First, there is a range of topics couples may discuss during pillow talk, some of which are potentially more productive than others. Topics that would likely be healthy to discuss during pillow talk involve expressing positive feelings for a partner, such as feelings of love or telling a partner how much they mean to them (if that is appropriate for where a person is in her/his relationship; see Denes, 2012). Another healthy topic may involve sharing sexual preferences with one's partner. It has been suggested that sexual self-disclosure (i.e., disclosing sexual likes and dislikes) increases the perceived sexual rewards of a relationship and relationship satisfaction, which in turn increases sexual satisfaction (Byers & Demmons, 1999). Therefore, if something felt good during the sexual activity, this could be a good time to reinforce that sexual preference to one's partner and compliment them on that experience. Another healthy behavior could involve showing nonverbal affection by cuddling, spooning, or kissing, as such behaviors have been linked to sexual and relationship satisfaction (Muise et al., 2014). There are numerous ways to convey affection without using words. Lastly, this may be a good time to open up with a partner—share experiences, let one's guard down, engage in banter or joking. Because pillow talk can be a time when individuals are willing to be more open and vulnerable, it may be a good time to share thoughts, feelings, and experiences.

As for the don'ts, or unhealthy behaviors, this is probably not a good time to air grievances. Though a person may feel comfortable opening up to a partner post sex, it may not be the best time to complain or engage in conflict. This may be a time to bring up sexual likes and preferences, but it is probably not the time to bring up dislikes or to be overly critical of a partner's performance. This can be a sensitive time for many, and such critiques could be hurtful. Lastly, though pillow talk may be a good time to share experiences and stories with a partner, it is probably best to make sure one's partner is also on board with such conversations. Bringing up topics unrelated to the relationship (such as discussing family issues, friends, work, etc.) might seem like venting rather than connecting, so it is wise to be cognizant of a partner's communication needs and responses.

Conclusion

This chapter offered an introduction to a developing line of research. Most of the studies cited in this chapter are from the last 10 years, demonstrating the relevance of this area and its growing popularity among both communication and sex scholars. For communication scholars, this area of research is of interest due to its potential links to both the physiological underpinnings of communication as well as relationship well-being. Understanding post-sex communication may help scholars more fully understand the multitude of factors that contribute to successful relationships and the ways that communication in a specific context (in this case, after sexual activity) may have a larger influence on communication patterns in the relationship in general.

For sex researchers and therapists, this body of work suggests that the communication surrounding sexual episodes—and not just sex itself—plays an important role in relationships. For sex therapists in particular, such work may suggest that therapies be aimed at increasing verbal and nonverbal expressions of intimacy and closeness after sexual activity, which may in turn increase sexual satisfaction and relationship satisfaction. Given the newness of this research domain, there are a multitude of research ideas and topics yet to be explored, and we hope that scholars will be encouraged to conduct research in this growing area of study. There are many exciting questions and future directions for exploring post-sex communication and its role in romantic relationships.

DISCUSSION QUESTIONS

1. Kruger and Hughes (2010) found that during the PCTI, males perceive their female partners as having more interest in discussing relationship issues than they [men] do. How much of this perception is potentially related to gendered societal stereotypes? (Is it possible that men see women as more relationship driven because that is a standard media-driven portrayal?)

2. What are some of the potential difficulties in conducting research on post-sex communication?

3. Hughes and Kruger (2011) investigated differences in individuals' post-sex communication depending on relationship longevity. How might relationship longevity affect areas of verbal communication, such as disclosure?

4. Much of the research on post-sex communication thus far seems to focus predominantly on heterosexual relationships. How might this research differ if it highlighted same-sex partnerships?

5. How might post-sex communication differ between hook-ups, casual dating relationships, new relationships, or long-term partnerships (such as marriage)?

6. Is there a dark side to pillow talk? How might pillow talk be used to deceive or manipulate a partner?

References

Bandura, A. (1977). Self-efficacy: Toward a unifying theory of behavior change. *Psychological Review, 84*, 191–215. doi: 10.1037/0033-295X.84.2.191.

Blaicher, W., Gruber, D., Bieglmayer, C., Blaicher, A.M., Knogler, W., & Huber, J. (1999). The role of oxytocin in relation to female sexual arousal. *Gynecological and Obstetric Investigation, 47*, 125–126. doi:10.1159/000010075.

Byers, E.S., & Demmons, S. (1999). Sexual satisfaction and sexual self-disclosure within dating relationships. *The Journal of Sex Research, 36*, 180–189. doi:10.1080/00224499909551983.

Carmichael, M.S., Humbert, R., Dixen, J., Palmisano, G., Greenleaf, W., & Davidson, J.M. (1987). Plasma oxytocin increases in the human sexual response. *Journal of Clinical Endocrinology and Metabolism, 64*, 27–31. doi:10.1210/jcem-64-1-27.

Denes, A. (2012). Pillow talk: Exploring disclosures after sexual activity. *Western Journal of Communication, 76*(2), 91–108. doi: 10.1080/10570314.2011.651253.

Denes, A. (under review). Toward a post sex disclosures model (PSDM): Exploring the associations among orgasm, self-disclosure, and relationship satisfaction.

Denes, A., & Afifi, T. D. (2014). Pillow talk and cognitive decision-making processes: Exploring the influence of orgasm and alcohol on communication after sexual activity. *Communication Monographs, 81*(3), 333–358. doi:10.1080/03637751.2014.926377.

Denes, A., Afifi, T.A., & Granger, D. (2015). The physiology of pillow talk: Exploring the relationship between baseline testosterone levels and communication during the post sex time interval. Paper presented at the annual meeting of the International Communication Association in San Juan, Puerto Rico.

Domes, G., Heinrichs, M., Michel, A., Berger, C., & Herpertz, S. (2007). Oxytocin improves "mind-reading" in humans. *Biological Psychiatry, 61*, 731–733. doi:10.1016/j.biopsych.2006.07.015.

Guastella, A.J., Mitchel, P. B., & Dadds, M.R. (2008). Oxytocin increases gaze to the eye region of human faces. *Biological Psychiatry, 63*, 3–5. doi:10.1016/j.biopsych.2007.06.026.

Halpern, J., & Sherman, S. (1979). *Afterplay: A key to intimacy*. New York: Stein & Day Publishers.

Haxby, J.V., Hoffman, E.A., & Gobbini, M.I. (2000). The distributed human neural system for face perception. *Trends in Cognitive Science, 4*, 223–233. doi: 10.1016/S1364-6613(00)01482-0.

Huber, D., Veinante, P., & Stoop, R. (2005). Vasopressin and oxytocin excite distinct neuronal populations in the central amygdala. *Science, 308*, 245–248. doi:10.1126/science.1105636.

Hughes, S.M., & Kruger, D.J. (2011). Sex differences in post-coital behaviors in long- and short-term mating: An evolutionary perspective. *Journal of Sex Research, 48*(5), 496–505. doi:10.1080/00224499.2010.501915.

Kirsch, P., Esslinger, C., Chen, Q., Mier, D., Lis, S., Siddhanti, S., Gruppe, H., Mattay, V.S., Gallhofer, B., & Meyer-Lindenberg, A. (2005). Oxytocin modulates neural circuitry for social cognition and fear in humans. *Journal of Neuroscience, 25*, 11489–11493. doi:10.1523/JNEUROSCI.3984-05.2005.

Kosfeld, M., Heinrichs, M., Zak, P.J., Fischbacher, U., & Fehr1, E. (2005). Oxytocin increases trust in humans. *Nature, 435*, 673–676. doi:10.1038/nature03701.

Kruger, D.J., & Hughes, S.M. (2010). Variation in reproductive strategies influences post-coital experiences with partners. *Journal of Social, Evolutionary, and Cultural Psychology, 4*(4), 254–264.

Lim, M.M., & Young, L.J. (2006). Neuropeptidergic regulation of affiliative behavior and social bonding in animals. *Hormones and Behavior, 50*, 506–517. doi:10.1016/j.yhbeh.2006.06.028 doi:10.1016/j.yhbeh.2006.06.028.

Muise, A., Giang, E., & Impett, E. A. (2014) Post sex affectionate exchanges promote sexual and relationship satisfaction. *Archives of sexual behavior, 43* (7) 1391–1402. doi: 10.1007/s10508-014-0305-3.

Ryder, K. (2012). *After the climax.* Retrieved from http://www.salon.com/2012/03/15/after_the_climax/.

Taylor, S.E., Lewis, B.P., Gruenewald, T.L., Gurung, R.A.R., Updegraff, J.A., & Klein, L.C. (2002). Sex differences in biobehavioral responses to threat: Reply to Geary and Flinn (2002). *Psychological Review, 109*, 751–753. doi: 10.1037/0033-295X.109.4.751.

Veenestra, M. (2007). Afterglow. In F. Malti-Douglas (Ed.), *Encyclopedia of sex and gender* (Vol. 1, pp. 39–40). Detroit, MI: Macmillan Reference.

CHAPTER 15

Senior Citizens, Sexual Activity, and Communication

Jessica M. W. Kratzer

KEY TERMS

Sexual communication   Aging   Intimacy
Senior citizens   Later-life

ABSTRACT

For most people, the goal in life is to live as long as possible. We may not want to be old but in order to live a long life we must *get* older. Youth is valued in American culture much more than aging so there is a great focus on younger people, especially when discussing sex. In order to understand how aging affects our relational, communicative, and sexual lives, information regarding senior citizen sexual communication must be explored.

This chapter focuses on sexual activity and communication in our aging population. It includes five areas of aging sexuality: 1) language used to describe the aging population, 2) a review of contemporary senior citizen sexual and romantic relationships, 3) changes in sexual activity as one ages, 4) creating and redefining intimacy, and 5) college students' perspectives on aging and sex. The chapter concludes with a fictive case study.

Being a Senior Citizen

"Senior citizen," "aging," and "later-life" are all terms used to describe older people. The term "senior citizen" was coined in the 1930s as a euphemism for an older person and was meant to describe elderly people, or those who were oldest in the community. The life expectancy for an American in the 1930s was 58 for men and 62 for women (Social Security Administration, 2015). This is a stark difference for current generations whose life expectancy for men and women is 78.8 years of age (Centers for Disease Control, 2015). Therefore, the use of the term senior citizen still often represents people in their 60s, as it was intended, but people in this age range are not often considered elderly as they once were. People in their 70s-100s are considered senior citizens as well and may also be considered elderly. The term elderly is often used for people who not only look older but also act older and may have disabilities related to aging. The terms aging and later-life are equivalent to the use of senior citizen in our culture. In the current time period, labeling people as senior citizens is done differently by different groups. For example, people can begin receiving senior citizen benefits from the American Association of Retired People (AARP) starting at the age of 50. According to the Social Security Administration (SSA) (2015), the current full retirement age varies, depending on year of birth, from ages 65-67. Additionally, some research studies that purport to examine later-life individuals have participants that would culturally be defined as middle-aged. For example, some studies on sexuality in later-life used participants as young as 45 years old (e.g., DeLamater & Moorman, 2007; Hinchliff & Gott, 2004).

Later-life romantic relationships come in many forms. Contemporary romantic relationships popular among senior citizens include marriage, dating, remarriage after death of partner or divorce, living alone together (LAT), and cohabitation. Aging couples value intimacy in their relationships just as they did when they were younger (e.g., earlier in their marriages or in past romantic/sexual relationships) and their intimacy can be expressed in many ways (e.g., Kratzer, 2013). For some people, being in a long-term marriage is ideal; however, divorce and death can change the form of future romantic relationships.

As one ages, companionship becomes more important. In our younger years, we have friends, partners, and family members to spend time with.

These aspects of our lives continue to be important as we age but our interests and priorities may vary from those of our children or grandchildren, so having a partner to go to the movies or have dinner with, makes life more enjoyable. After a long-term marriage ends, single folks may seek companionship, which is a large reason senior citizens date (Cooney & Dunne, 2001), remarry (Talbott, 1998), and cohabit. Some senior citizens prefer to have relationships where they live apart together (LAT). These relationships consist of each person having their own place to live (e.g., house, apartment, condominium) but they spend the night at each other's places regularly (de Jong Gierveld, 2002). This relationship gives each person the opportunity to be in a monogamous relationship with the benefits of sexual and emotional intimacy, without having to sacrifice personal space and belongings.

Some folks maintain LAT relationships for the sake of their grown children. They may not want to sell the family home or may want to keep the illusion of a friendship rather than a romantic relationship. Most of these relationships and living situations allow people the freedom of privacy to participate in intimate acts that may vary from having sex, to holding hands and cuddling. Communication Privacy Management theory (Petronio, 2002), states that people create rules when it comes to their private information. Senior citizens in LAT relationships may decide on specific privacy rules with their partners that protect their family members from knowing the details of their romantic relationship. LAT relationships can be used to camouflage the intimate aspects of a relationship in order to keep others from knowing about the level of intimacy being expressed. As senior citizens continue to age, their living situations may change.

Residential Options

Older people may live in a variety of homes. Many senior citizens live in their own homes or with family members. Others live in facilities such as independent living, assisted living, or nursing homes. Independent living facilities consist of residents having their own apartment or condominium. They are expected to maintain the residence with little assistance. Some independent living facilities offer residents the option of purchasing a maid service, laundry service, nurse visits, and a meal plan. Assisted living facilities offer more assistance to their residents. They usually offer three meals each day, regularly schedule visits with an on-duty nurse, medication assistance, and help with daily routines such as bathing, if needed. Both independent and assisted living facilities offer privacy too. Residents can lock their apartment doors and may choose from an efficiency style apartment with one room or a larger apartment with a few rooms such as a bedroom, living room, and kitchen/kitchenette. Nursing homes offer much more assistance and much less privacy. Residents are monitored around the clock, meals are scheduled, medical staff visits daily, medication is distributed regularly, and residents cannot lock their doors for privacy. Residents are also assisted with eating, bathing, and going to the bathroom. Some nursing home residents may have mental conditions such as dementia that affect their cognition and understanding of their environment, whereas independent living and assisted living residents are expected to be able to function cognitively. Some folks may have early stages of dementia or Alzheimer's disease but those with advanced stages are often not permitted to reside at independent and/or assisted living facilities.

Sex and Aging

Extensive research points to the challenges that some senior citizens confront regarding their abilities to perform sexual acts or that might impede their sexual desires. Challenges for seniors include physical problems, partner availability, general health and medication use, and living in a nursing home. Several physical problems might also occur for aging men and women. For men, common sexual dysfunctions include early ejaculation, inability to achieve orgasm, lack of interest, and erectile dysfunction (Nicolosi et al., 2004). For women, common sexual dysfunctions also include the inability to achieve an orgasm and lack of interest but they also experience a lack of proper lubrication and pain (Nicolosi et al., 2004).

Whether or not a person has physical challenges, they may also face relational challenges. For many older adults, having an available partner may determine how important they believe sexual intimacy to be. One study found that 78% of men between the ages of 75-85, as compared with 40% of women, had a spouse or other intimate relationship (Lindau et al., 2007). Factors explaining the disparity between the percentage of men and women who have intimate relationships included age because, on average, men marry younger women, and men pass away earlier than women. This means that there are more single senior women than there are senior men, making it easier for men to find a relational partner.

Older women's sexual desire has also been found to be associated with her relationship status. According to DeLamater and Sill (2005), having a partner was a significant predictor of sexual desire for later-life women. This study also found that women who have a partner are more likely to have sexual desire (83%), and women without a partner were less likely to experience sexual desire (78%). Turner and Adams (1988) found that sexual activity patterns of older women usually depend on their marital status. A sub-set of participants in a study by Gott and Hinchliff (2003) did not have a current partner, typically due to widowhood, and considered sex as no longer important. These particular participants also did not think they would form new sexual relationships in their lifetime.

Medication Use That Improves Sexual Functioning

Several medications can improve male sexual functioning by helping men achieve and maintain an erection for sexual activity. You have probably seen the commercial for Viagra with a group of men singing about their erections, "Viva Viagra!" Commercials like this one explicitly target men who have sexual functioning problems, and women who may have partners with these issues. In a study by Lindau and colleagues (2007), nearly one in seven men used an erectile dysfunction medication to improve their sexual functioning. Although men have considerably easy access to erectile dysfunction medications, there are currently no medications on the market that improve women's sexual desire and functioning. However, "Viagra for women" came under review by the Federal Drug Administration (FDA) in 2015 as a likely option for women who want to increase their libido and improve their sexual functioning. The FDA had yet to make a final decision at the time of this publication.

There are mixed emotions when it comes to sexual functioning medications. Research has been conducted on women's attitudes about these medications. Some senior women are excited about these medications and are enjoying a renewed sex life, but some women are not as enthusiastic. A study by Loe (2004) found that some women had enjoyed their hiatus from sex and did not like the rise of sexual activity that erectile dysfunction medications had caused. These women felt that they had done their duty as wives for much of their lives and enjoyed a break from the task of fulfilling their partner's sexual desires. There are two sides to the coin when it comes to erectile dysfunction medication use. Some people are excited to get back on the horse, while others would rather not.

Nursing Homes

Some senior citizens may live in nursing homes to assist with a multitude of possible health issues. Since most people aged 65 and older live alone or are married, finding a secluded place for sexual activity is not difficult; however, for those in nursing homes, sexual activity has been repressed (Levy, 1994). For the most part, senior citizens and elderly residents of nursing homes are restricted from sexual activity although more than half of both senior men and women, in a study by Richardson (1995), stated that they would like to be close or intimate with someone of the opposite sex. Stiffl (1984) suggested some conditions to remember when discussing institutionalized senior citizens: sensory deprivation and isolation, the need for touch for social reasons, the acceptance of masturbation, and opportunities to meet and mingle with others. Mayers and McBride (1998) suggested sexuality training for nursing home workers so that sexuality between residents can be handled in a professional, acceptable manner. They also suggested that one problem noted by many elderly residents was the lack of privacy in nursing homes, and that barrier could be removed by allowing conjugal visits and allowing doors to be shut. Not many nursing homes accommodate senior citizens in this way.

Sexually Transmitted Infections

Finally, a sexually related challenge that not all seniors consider is that of sexually transmitted infections. As mentioned earlier, many senior citizens choose to be in varying forms of monogamous relationships. However, there are also many seniors who choose not to be in monogamous relationships. Some of these folks choose abstinence, while others choose to have multiple sexual partners. Some populations are overlooked when it comes to education, prevention, and treatment of sexually transmitted diseases, yet an explosion of infection is expected as the Baby Boomers age and as people with HIV/AIDS live longer (Levy-Dweck, 2005). One study found that 20% of adults in a community home over 78 years of age were engaging in some sexual activity (Williams & Donnelly, 2002). A study of 55 community-residing senior women (aged 58-93) found that 60% of single participants had been sexually active in the past 10 years and had not used a condom (Lindau, Leitsch, Lundberg, & Jerome, 2006). Since pregnancy is often associated with the use of condoms, many older adults assume it is harmless to have unprotected sex because they do not have to worry about having a baby (Lindau et al., 2006; Williams & Donnelly, 2002). However, in 2011, approximately 26% of the 1.2 million people in the United States with HIV were people aged 55 and older (CDC, 2015).

(Re)Defining Intimacy

At any age, many people can usually find many benefits for participating in intimate acts. Sexual activity for senior citizens can boost self-esteem, which in turn increases life satisfaction (Johnson, 1998). For seniors who have experienced medical issues, such as a hysterectomy, having a healthy sex life can make them feel healthy (Johnson, 1998). The healthier a person feels, the more likely they are to want to participate in sexual activity and feel sexually adequate. As we learned above, people who have health challenges that impede sexual intercourse may have lower self-esteem and be less likely to participate in other forms of sexual play. One study reported that, of their 158 participants, 66% of men and 57% of women under the age of 70 desired sex two or more times a week, and 55% of men and 48% of women over the age of 70 also desired sex two or more times a week (Wiley & Bortz, 1996). For many aging couples, having sex continues to be an important part of being in a romantic relationship. However, some couples may no longer be participating in sexual intercourse and find other ways of expressing intimacy.

Many seniors redefine intimacy when dealing with sexual complications that hinder sexual intercourse. Intimate behaviors such as kissing, hugging, touching, and cuddling can be central to aging romantic relationships

(Kratzer, 2013). For both aging couples that have sexual intercourse and those that do not, showing love and reassurance through varying intimate behaviors other than sex is important (Hinchliff & Gott, 2004). For some people, the intimate relationship they had with their partner is so deep and they knew each other so well, that sex is not important, but knowing what is in each other's heart is the most intimate they could be (Kratzer, 2013).

According to Kratzer (2013), senior citizen participants stated that they had open communication with their romantic partners but happened to be closed when discussing sex. Many seniors experience sexual challenges, such as one partner having erectile dysfunction, and most said they did not discuss how these challenges affected their partner or their sexual relationship. Kratzer (2013) also found that when the male partners were unable to have an erection, most couples no longer participated in sexual acts such as intercourse or heavy petting. Most of the women stated that they were no longer interested in sex once their male partner could no longer get an erection so they found other ways to be intimate, such as kissing, hugging, holding hands, and other forms of showing affection.

College Students' Perceptions of Sex and Aging

Traditional college students are between the ages of 18-22 and, therefore, many readers of this chapter may be asking themselves why it is important to know about senior citizen sexuality. There are a few reasons. First, as mentioned earlier, if we want to live for a long time, we must get older. Second, this may help you think about the expectations you have for your own sexual activity as you age, and how you think about other people's sexual activity as they age (e.g., family members). People may expect to find ageism when discussing this topic but some researchers discovered some interesting results. A study by Floyd and Weiss (2001) expected to discover "sexual ageism" among college students about senior citizen sexuality but found that many college students expect to continue to be sexually active throughout their lives. Male college students were more likely to report anticipation of more sexual activity, interest, less guilt, and fewer sexual problems than women at the projected age of 70.

The college students also rated themselves, at the projected age of 70, as being more sexually active than an older friend and even more sexually active than an older relative. These results show that young participants are expecting sex lives that will last even while they are senior citizens. This attitude toward self as a sexually active senior citizen can result in both positive and negative outcomes.

People often talk about "growing" and "developing" but those terms change to "aging" after a person turns 40. This is important to consider. We are constantly growing and developing and with that comes aging, but we are still ourselves. We often still like the same types of music, television shows, and activities. We still enjoy spending time with our romantic partner, our family, friends, and pets. So, consider yourself at 70 years of age. You will still be you, but just an older version with some interesting life lessons learned. Consider your parents at 70, 80, or 90 years old. As a potential caregiver for your parents, consider how you will address sexual issues for them in repressive environments like nursing homes. In the case study below you are going to read about several friends talking about their sexual relationships. While reading this case study, imagine these folks not as just "old people" but as people who have lived a long life and are still themselves, in many ways as they were when they were younger.

The case study below is a fictive response to research I conducted at a Midwestern senior citizen day center where folks went to socialize with friends, play pool and cards, and have lunch. Many of the seniors I talked with dealt with issues of erectile dysfunction, loss of partners, and had varying attitudes about their past and current sex lives. The senior citizens I spoke with, and who are reflected in the case study below, were retired, middle class, Caucasian, and all but one was heterosexual (one woman was bisexual).

Fictive Case Study

"Hi Ron, how are you today?" Jeremiah asked as he entered the Senior Center on a Thursday afternoon. Ron volunteered at the center every week answering phones and greeting guests. Jeremiah, a 70-year-old man who has been married for 49 years, comes to the Senior Center at least once a week to eat lunch and play pool. As Ron and Jeremiah greeted each other, J. J. also entered through the glass door. J. J. is 79 years old and has been married for 52 years. He and his wife come to the Senior Center each week as well.

"Hey there Jeremiah. Ron. Nice day, isn't it?" Both men nod their heads in agreement. "Anything exciting going on today?"

"Not so far. Why? You plan on causing some excitement?" Ron asked playfully.

"Not any more than usual!" J. J. replied as the three men laugh loudly. They enjoy joking around with each other and know that everyone has been talking about the guest speaker that gave a talk about aging and sex the evening before. The center had invited a young college professor from the local university with expertise on communication, sexual intimacy, and aging to give a talk to those who were interested. The talk focused on how issues associated with aging—such as medication use, physical disabilities, and the like—could affect sexual interest and ability. The professor also gave the seniors tips on how to communicate with their partners about sexually related concerns.

"I heard you talked to the professor afterward. How did it go?" Ron asked slyly. "Did she learn a lot?"

"I really liked it," J.J. replied, laughing. "I mean, I like sex and so I also like hearing about it too."

"I went too. It wasn't bad. It was personal, but it was okay," Jeremiah added, taking a more serious tone.

"Well, I didn't go!" Ron exclaimed, laughing. "The Mrs. wouldn't let me anyway. Plus, I think that kind of stuff should stay between a husband and wife. But that's just my opinion."

"I guess some people are just more modest than others," Jeremiah replied. "Well, I'm going to get some lunch."

"I'll join you," said J. J. The two men nod good-bye to Ron as they walk to the lunch room where the hot food has just begun to be served. They pay for their lunch tickets and head over to the line that has formed at the buffet. They get plates full of food including fried chicken, mashed potatoes with gravy, Brussels sprouts, salad, soda, and a piece of pecan pie. When their trays are full the two men head over to a table where their friend Bill is sitting. Bill is 73 years old and has been dating Barb for the past five years.

"Hey Bill, how's it going?" asked Jeremiah.

"It's going quite well," Bill responded. "Lunch looks good, huh?"

"It certainly does," replied J. J. "Hey, did you like the speaker last night?"

"Well," Bill grinned, "she talked about some pretty personal stuff but I didn't mind. I'm pretty open about things."

"I figured you would be," Jeremiah stated. "Was her information relevant to your life?"

"Oh, I see, now we're going to share our stories," Bill said as he chuckled. "Well, Barb and I talk about sex much more than I ever did in my previous relationships. We kind of have to talk about it sometimes. I had prostate surgery, which makes a difference in sexual capacity. Very recently we started in the direction of having sex, but then I couldn't continue and so that was a short discussion. It's no secret and I'm not ashamed of it."

"Wow, I can't believe you just told us that. You should have shared last night," J. J. replied with a small laugh.

"I don't think so," Bill replied, also with a laugh.

"I know what you mean. I do pretty well for 79 but I've had bladder cancer. Radiation treatments killed a nerve in there for 11 months. So, I have to use a vacuum pump now," J. J. said.

"What exactly does the vacuum pump do?" asked Jeremiah.

"Um, well, it's basically a plastic tube I put over my penis and I pump it so it creates a vacuum that draws blood to my penis so that it gets hard. Then I have to put a little band at the base of my penis to keep the blood in it so it stays hard for sex," J. J. explained.

"I'm glad that I haven't had to deal with that yet," stated Jeremiah. "No offense, but it sounds uncomfortable and I wouldn't want it to get in the way of having sex all the time."

"Well, it can be but you have to be open with each other, and Barb and I are," Bill replied kindly. "By the way, how often are you having sex to be so concerned with it getting in the way of having sex ALL THE TIME!" Bill laughingly joked.

"You know what I mean," Jeremiah shot back. "But, I'm pretty happy. It's not near as important as it was when we where young, but we still have sex at least once a week. If it was up to me I'd do it five days a week, but for her it's only once a week. I mean, I'm old but I'm not dead."

"Yeah, Judy and I have sex about every five or six days. But, we've also been married for 52 years and Jeremiah's been married for what, 49 years. Bill, you and Barb have only been together for five years so that may also make a difference," J. J. stated.

"That's true," Bill replied.

They sat silently for a minute or two, eating their hot meal. Then, J. J. asked, "Do either of you think it's important for couples to talk about sex at our age?"

"I think it depends on the relationship. Barb and I have to talk about it due to my prostate problem but I do think it is important for all couples to have some communication about it," Bill answered. "Back in my professor days, I couldn't stress enough how important it is to talk about sex in a relationship."

"I think it can also depend on your partner," Jeremiah responded. "We talk about it to a degree, but mostly if I get her to talk about it, I have to bring the subject up more than once, and she'll finally communicate with me."

"I was just thinking that I don't know that I need her to talk about it. To me she's just a prudish person," J.J. stated with an irritated tone of voice. "I'd say her mother was the same way and the whole family was probably that way. She's not going to change now."

"Could be," Bill said. "But, you know, sometimes the more you talk about something, the easier it is. It could be she's not used to it, and so she—and you—need a little practice."

"As I've gotten older, it's gotten easier," Jeremiah responded. "But, then, as I've gotten older I find that sex isn't as important. Just sitting on the couch having a glass of wine is nice. You've got to still cuddle with your wife, even though you're not sexually motivated, you know what I mean? You can get as much pleasure out of that as you can any other way."

"I agree," Bill responded. "Holding hands is nice. Just going out for a walk is nice. Sitting and looking at the moon is nice. That all takes on a different meaning."

"That's true. I like doing a lot of things with my wife. We've been dancing together a lot lately and we both enjoy spending that time together. I can see where you are both coming from," J. J. replied.

"I'm inclined to say that sex doesn't have the importance that it did when we were younger. Deciding to have sex is much more casual. It's sort of like asking her if she wants to go to Walmart," Bill said, laughing at such an odd comparison. J. J. and Jeremiah laughed loudly with him as they continued to enjoy their meal together.

A few tables over, a group of four women had just sat down with their trays of food. As they adjusted their chairs and situated the items on their trays, Diane said, "Do you hear what those men are talking about? They're talking about sex! I heard one of them say that it isn't that important any more. I don't know about them but I strongly disagree."

"Quit listening to others' conversations, nosey!" Rhonda said jokingly. Rhonda is a 70-year-old widow who was married for 32 years.

"I can't help it when they're talking about something I'm so interested in!" Diane laughingly replied, her eyes widening with expression. Diane is a 63-year-old woman who has never been married but has been in two long-term relationships. She tends to be quite open about her sex life and is a very sexual person.

"Well, I'm interested in it too, but that doesn't mean I'm doing it," Elizabeth replies. Elizabeth is 68 years old and has been married for 38 years.

"I'm not doing it either, since Neil died," Nita Marie stated matter-of-factly. Nita Marie was married for 50 years and her husband passed away five years ago.

"I know," Elizabeth responded, thinking about how happy Neil and Nita Marie were. "I don't know what to do about Marcus, though. He seems so uninterested in sex these days. I mean, he's impotent, but he wears a pessary."

"A what?" Rhonda asks. "I've never heard of that before."

"It's a little thing that wraps around the end of the penis and keeps the blood flow up in the penis to keep it hard. He also takes Cialis, which helps him get an erection too. My goodness, we've only had sex three times in more than six months."

"And, with all of that medication and everything, he still doesn't want to do it?" asked Rhonda.

"Well, I guess it's too much work. And, uh, he's very fast. So, I think that is disappointing for both of us," Elizabeth responded, blushing a bit.

"In all of the relationships I've had, I've never had a man that has had to deal with that. I'm so sorry for you," Diane shared. "I mean, Donald was still wanting sex until a few months before he passed away. That's pretty good for a 101-year-old man!"

"Wow, that's impressive," Elizabeth stated.

"But, Dave, the man I lived with for 15 years back in my 30s. He was not very interested in sex at all," Diane admitted. "I would try to do it, but he was so into his work that he really wasn't that interested. So, I can understand your frustration."

"I can't say that that was ever a problem in my marriage," Nita Marie interjected. "I mean, we never really talked about it and we would just have sex when we wanted to."

"So, he was never uninterested and neither were you?" Diane questioned.

"Not that I can remember. If he wanted to have sex then he would just be more attentive and loving throughout the day. And, into the evening," Nita Maria replied with a sheepish smile. "And then we would do it that night. It was just simultaneously when we wanted to. And things were like that until he passed away."

"Did any of you actually talk about sex with your husbands?" Diane asked.

"Well, Rick and I both had kids and we were each other's second marriages so we had some life experience," Rhonda stated. "I think that made both of us more open about sex although I can't really remember a specific time that we talked about it. It was a lot like Nita Marie explained. A lot of it is nonverbal. It's just the way you behave, and of course that's communication just as well."

"Ed and I had to talk about it," Elizabeth said. We had trouble getting pregnant so we had to ask the doctor about it. So, that made us talk about it more."

"I can't think of a time that Neil and I talked about sex. I really don't think we ever did," replied Nita Marie.

"Well, Donald and I didn't talk about it at all either. It may have been because we weren't married," Diane said, beginning to giggle at some memories. "He would just come toward me with his hands out and I knew what that meant. He was older, though, so I didn't approach him for sex. I let him approach me."

"Rick and I used to have sex a few times a week," Rhonda said matter-of-factly. "But, as you get older your sexual desires decrease. You never lose them, but they do decrease."

"That's true. I was very sexual when I was younger but I am very grateful now that I don't have that sex drive," Diane admitted. "It was the boss. I think when you go through menopause you get more selective and less driven. But, I've had a great sex life!"

"Well, I agree that your desires decrease and that other things become more important," Elizabeth said. "We still sleep in a double bed and we cuddle so that's good. He says he likes me there next to him. He gets very upset if I go sleep downstairs or let the dog in or anything. He likes me to be with him."

"I agree, cuddling and just spending time together is really important as you get older. And, now that Rick is gone, I miss those special times together," Rhonda said sadly.

"I know what you mean," Nita Marie responded.

"Well, at least we have each other's company. Are any of you going to play cards after lunch?" Diane asked. The other three women nodded their heads in unison.

"Did I hear you all say you're going to play cards?" asked J. J.

"You sure did. Are you playing too?" Diane asked.

"We sure are!" J. J. exclaimed.

"Well, quit talking about sex so much and get moving!" Diane said laughing loudly. "We don't want them to start without us."

"So, you were listening to our conversation, huh?" Bill asked smiling.

"You bet," Diane said, still laughing.

"Well, we were listening to you all as well," J. J. said slyly. They all laughed together as they headed to the other room to play cards.

DISCUSSION QUESTIONS

1. What are your perceptions of sex among older people? How does the case study portrayal of senior citizens talking about sexual issues challenge or compliment your views of aging people? How does it affect the view you have of aging people you know such as your parents and/or grandparents?

2. How does the portrayal of sexual communication among senior citizens presented in the case study differ from other portrayals of senior citizens' intimate relationships on television or in the movies? How is it similar? Why do these differences and/or similarities exist?

3. What do you think about the suggestion in the literature of educating nursing home staff on how to handle conjugal visits? Do you think sexual intimacy should be allowed among nursing home residents? Why or why not?

4. What are some reasons it may be difficult to discuss sexually transmitted diseases with senior citizens? What are some ways to effectively educate senior citizens about sexually transmitted diseases?

5. How do you imagine yourself being when you are a senior citizen (70 or 80 years old)? Do you imagine yourself being very different or similar to how you are now? What changes and what stays the same?

References

Centers for Disease Control and Prevention. (2015). *HIV among people aged 50 and older.* Retrieved from http://www.cdc.gov/hiv/risk/age/olderamericans/.

Centers for Disease Control and Prevention. (2015). *Life expectancy.* Retrieved from http://www.cdc.gov/nchs/fastats/life-expectancy.htm.

Cooney, T. M., & Dunne, K. (2001). Intimate relationships in later life: Current realities, future prospects. *Journal of Family Issues, 22,* 838–858. doi: 10.1177/019251301022007003.

de Jong Gierveld, J. (2002). The dilemma of repartnering: Considerations of older men and women entering new intimate relationships in later life. *Ageing International, 27,* 61–78. doi: 10.1007/s12126-002-1015-z.

DeLamater, J., & Moorman, S. M. (2007). Sexual behavior in later life. *Journal of Aging and Health, 19*, 921–945. doi: 10.1177/0898264307308342.

DeLamater, J. D., & Sill, M. (2005). Sexual desire in later life. *The Journal of Sex Research, 42* (2), 138–149. doi: 10.1080/00224490509552267.

Floyd, M., & Weiss, L. (2001). Sex and aging: A survey of young adults. *Journal of Sex Education and Therapy, 26*, 133–139. doi: 10.1080/01614576.2001.11074393.

Gott, M., & Hinchliff, S. (2003). How important is sex in later life? The views of older people. *Social Science & Medicine, 56*, 1617–1628. doi: 10.1016/S0277-9536(02)00180-6.

Hinchliff, S., & Gott, M. (2004). Intimacy, commitment, and adaptation: Sexual relationships within long-term marriages. *Journal of Social and Personal Relationships, 21*(5), 595–609. doi: 10.1177/0265407504045889.

Johnson, B. K. (1998). A correlational framework for understanding sexuality in women age 50 and older. *Health Care for Women International, 19*, 553–564.

Kratzer, J. M. W. (2013). Gender and Power: A Thematic Analysis of Senior Citizen Sexual Communication. *Carolinas Communication Annual, XXIX*, 24–49.

Levy, J. A. (1994). Sexuality in later life stages. In A. S. Rossi (Ed.), *Sexuality across the Life Course* (pp. 313–339). Chicago, IL: The University of Chicago Press.

Levy-Dweck, S. (2005). 'HIV/AIDS fifty and older', *Journal of Gerontological Social Work, 46*, 37–50. doi: 10.1300/J083v46n02_04.

Lindau, S. T., Leitsch, S. A., Lundberg, K. L., & Jerome, J. (2006). Older women's attitudes, behavior, and communication about sex and HIV: A community-based study. *Journal of Women's Health, 15(6)*, 747–753.

Lindau, S. T., Schumm, L. P., Laumann, E. O., Levinson, W., O'Muircheartaigh, C. A., & Waite, L. J. (2007). A study of sexuality and health among older adults in the United States. *The New England Journal of Medicine, 357 (8)*, 762–774. doi: 10.1056/NEJMoa067423.

Loe, M. (2004). Sex and the senior woman: Pleasure and danger in the Viagra era. *Sexualities, 7*, 303–326. doi: 10.1177/1363460704044803.

Mayers, K. S., & McBride, D. (1998). Sexuality training for caretakers of geriatric residents in long term care facilities. *Sexuality and Disability, 16*, 227–236. doi: 10.1023/A:1023003310885.

Nicolosi, A., Laumann, E. O., Glasser, D. B., Moreira, E. D., Paik, A., & Gingell, C. (2004). Sexual behavior and sexual dysfunctions after age 40: The global study of sexual attitudes and behaviors. *Adult Urology, 64 (5),* 991–997.

Petronio, S. (2002). *Boundaries of privacy: Dialectics of disclosure.* Albany, NY: SUNY Press.

Richardson, J. P. (1995). Sexuality in the nursing home patient. *American Family Physician, 51,* 121–124.

Social Security Administration. (2015). *Life expectancy for social security.* Retrieved from http://www.ssa.gov/history/lifeexpect.html.

Social Security Administration. (2015). *Retirement planner: Benefits by year of birth.* Retrieved from http://www.socialsecurity.gov/retire2/agereduction.htm.

Stiffl, B. (1984). Sexuality and the aging. In B. Stiffl (Ed.), *Handbook of Gerontological Nursing* (pp. 450–464). New York: Van Nostrand Reinhold.

Talbott, M. M. (1998). Older widows' attitudes towards men and remarriage. *Journal of Aging Studies, 12,* 429–449. doi: 10.1016/S0890-4065(98)90028-7.

Turner, B. F., & Adams, C. G. (1988). Reported change in preferred sexual activity over the adult years. *The Journal of Sex Research, 25 (2),* 289–303. doi: 10.1080/00224498809551460.

Wiley, D., & Bortz II, W. M. (1996). Sexuality and aging – Usual and successful. *Journal of Gerontology, 51A (3),* M142–M146.

Williams, E., & Donnelly, J. (2002). Older Americans and AIDS: Some guidelines for prevention. *Social Work, 47,* 105–111.

SECTION 4

Sexual Rights, Recognitions, and Equalities

CHAPTER 16

Why Does "Rape" Seem Like a Myth?

Kristen N. Jozkowski

KEY TERMS

Consent
Culture

Public perception
Gender roles

Sexual assault

ABSTRACT

Sexual assault remains a salient public health problem and social issue in the United States. Approximately 1 in 5 women will experience sexual assault during their lifetime. Despite such high statistics, many are unaware sexual assault is such a problem and some believe that rates, such as the 1 in 5 statistic, are inflated. As such, critics argue that the frequency and magnitude of sexual violence have been exaggerated. There are myriad reasons why it *seems* as if sexual assault is an uncommon occurrence. However, in reality, sexual assault is, unfortunately, quite common. The question, thus, remains— why might it *seem* as though sexual assault is not common if it is, in fact, so common? In this chapter, I examine a number of factors, including how sexual assault is defined, issues associated with reporting, victim blaming, and cultural conceptualizations of sexual assault, which contribute to perpetuating the false belief that sexual assault is rare.

Evidence from peer-reviewed studies has been supplemented with anecdotes from current events discussed in the mainstream media to frame the discussion and articulate main points.

In 2014, the White House Council on Women and Girls published *Rape and Sexual Assault: A Renewed Call to Action* addressing the high rates of sexual assault in the United States and specifically at American colleges and universities. According to the report, approximately 20% of women experience rape during their lifetime and "college students are particularly vulnerable: 1 in 5 women has been sexually assaulted while in college." The report cites the 2007 Campus Sexual Assault (CSA) Study commissioned by the U.S. Department of Justice for the 1 in 5 statistic. The CSA study is an Internet-based survey completed by 5,446 undergraduate students from two major public universities (Krebs et al., 2007). The merits of this study, and thus the 1 in 5 statistic, have been questioned and even condemned by some. In fact, an article published by TIME.com identified "1 in 5" as the "most controversial sexual assault statistic" (June, 27, 2014). Critics argue that the 1 in 5 statistic might be inflated and potentially misleading because the CSA study was based on a two-university sample with a potentially low response rate (42.2–42.8%). This, critics argue, could lead to unnecessary panic and "exaggerated claims of victimization" (Sommers, quoted in *Time* magazine).

If one were to reflect on this statistic—1 in 5 women experience rape—it would seem like everyone *should* know someone who has experienced sexual violence. Perhaps you are saying to yourself—I don't know anyone who has been raped, so maybe the 1 in 5 statistic is false?

Accurately measuring rates of sexual assault/rape is challenging. There are myriad reasons why it might *seem* as if sexual assault/rape does not occur often, but the 2007 CSA study is not the only study to find such high rates of sexual assault. In fact, other national studies have found similar rates of sexual assault (e.g., Daigle, Fisher, Cullen, 2008; Sinha, 2013) and other studies, utilizing convenience, community or clinical samples, report similar or even higher rates of sexual assault (e.g., Rothman et al., 2011; Satinsky & Jozkowski, 2013). Nevertheless, the question remains—if 1 in 5 women truly experience sexual violence, why doesn't it *seem* that way?

In this chapter, I examine several aspects of contemporary American culture, with increased attention paid to American college culture, which contribute to perpetuating the false belief that sexual assault is rare. I have framed my argument around sexual assaults in which women are victimized and men perpetrate. At this juncture it is important to note that men experience sexual assault and are victims of sexual violence and women can and do perpetrate assault. However, the overwhelming majority of sexual violence in the United States includes a female victim and male perpetrator (e.g., Acierno, 1997; Koss, Gidycz, & Wisniewski, 1987). As such, this chapter addresses sexual assault in this context.

Inconsistent Definitions

Some of the major organizations or entities considered to be authorities on sexual violence lack clear, consistent definitions of sexual assault and rape. For example, the Jeanne Clery Disclosure of Campus Security Policy and Campus Crime Statistics Act (referred to as the Clery Act) utilizes a unique language when defining crimes of a sexual nature; the Act identifies four specific sex crimes. Of primary interest to this discussion is the use of the word "forcible" to describe these crimes: "*forcible rape,*" "*forcible sodomy,*" and "*forcible fondling.*" The final category defined by the Clery Act is "*sexual assault with an object.*" Although this latter term does not contain the word forcible, the Clery Act defines all four of these behaviors as sexual contact obtained via *force*. Alternatively, according to the Clery Act, incest and statutory rape are defined as "*non-forcible sexual assaults*" (Clery Act Regulations, 2014). The use of the word force in these contexts is somewhat problematic. When relegating a particular act as *forcible* rape, the implication, thus, is that other rapes are *not forcible*, which in and of itself, is confusing. Furthermore, it seems inappropriate to suggest, through definition, that victims of incest or statutory rape are compliant, as such acts are defined as *non-forcible.*

The Federal Bureau of Investigation's (FBI) Uniform Crime Report (UCR) provides a narrower definition compared to the Clery Act. According to the UCR, rape is defined as acts that are: 1) forcible, 2) include vaginal penetration, and 3) of a woman. According to the UCR, rape can only be perpetrated via vaginal penetration; thus other types of forced sex would not be considered rape (I will discuss conceptualizations of rape in terms of sexual behavior and force at a later point in the chapter).

Alternatively, the Centers for Disease Control and Prevention (CDC) define sexual assault in terms of acts perpetrated against both men and women (CDC, 2012). The CDC's definition differs from that provided by the UCR as both women and men may be victims of sexual assault. The CSA study mentioned earlier and cited the White House Task Force's *Not Alone* report utilizes a fairly complicated and comprehensive approach to measuring sexual assault. The CSA attempts to differentiate between sexual assaults that occurred on campus as well as before students arrived on campus and asks about a range of sexual behaviors in addition to vaginal penetration. Finally, researchers also utilize different nomenclature to discuss sexual assault. Most notably, Koss et al. (2007) created a comprehensive measure to assess rates of sexual assault via the Sexual Experience Survey (SES). The SES assesses the frequency and age at which individuals might have experienced various forms of nonconsensual sex differentiating between adult sexual assault and child sexual assault (see Koss et al., 2007).

According to Yung (2015), because these entities (as well as others not cited here) define sexual assault in different ways, reconciliations of the results remain challenging. When different definitions of sexual assault are utilized, it is difficult to come to a consensus regarding what "counts" as sexual assault; thus, rates inevitably fluctuate. Unfortunately, when people see fluctuating rates of sexual assault, they might question the legitimacy of how sexual assault is reported and, in turn, question its occurrence, leading to the perception that it does not occur in high frequency, when in reality, it certainly does.

Problems with Reporting

In addition to defining acts of sexual violence, there are several challenges in the mechanisms through which sexual assaults are reported in the United States. In this section I have highlighted different aspects related to reporting sexual assault and have explained how they could contribute to masking the magnitude of this problem.

Underreporting. When a crime occurs, the initial reaction by most is to involve the authorities; this typically includes the police. However, according to the Justice Department's National Crime Victimization Survey (2008-2012), 68% of sexual assaults are not reported to the police. This means only 32 out of 100 rapes that occur get reported. Among those that do get reported, approximately seven will result in an arrest (FBI: UCR, Arrest Data, 2006-2010) and only two will result in a conviction with the perpetrator spending time in jail (Department of Justice, Felony Defendants in large Urban Counties, 2009). As such, the extent to which this crime is reported to police and then prosecuted through the typical channels of the criminal justice system is minimal (Rennison, 2002).

Specifically, in regard to institutions of higher education, college women are at an increased risk for experiencing sexual assault compared to the general population (Daigle, Fisher, & Cullen, 2008; Krebs et al., 2007). When sexual assault is perpetrated against a woman while she is attending a university, the campus administration sometimes acts as an authority in that particular context, playing somewhat of a judiciary role. Unfortunately, similar to police, research suggests, that sexual assaults experienced by college students often go unreported to university officials as well (Fisher, Daigle, Cullen, & Turner, 2003). Additionally, and perhaps even more concerning, is that universities seem to be underreporting sexual assaults that occur on their campus. Yung (2015) found that "the sexual assault data supplied by schools [to the Department of Education] is likely severely undercounting the number of reported incidents on campuses." Underreporting, in turn, can result in policymakers, school administrators, campus and municipal police, and the general public underestimating the frequency and severity of sexual assaults perpetrated against university students and potentially "short-circuiting" investigations of sexual assault. Furthermore, if universities are underestimating sexual assault occurrences, it is likely the case that resources allocated to address sexual assault are inadequate. According to Yung (2015), actual rates of sexual assault are approximately 44% higher than what is being reported to the Department of Education in compliance with the Clery Act, which mandates that universities accurately report and make public rates of sexual assault occurring at institutions of higher education in the United States.

If Yung (2015) is accurate and universities are underreporting—what is the motivation for being disingenuous? One reason could be that universities do not want to develop a "bad reputation" or become known as the university where rapes occur; this would certainly result in poor public relations and potentially impact student enrollment (even though rape likely happens at all universities). However, by inaccurately reporting such crimes, not only will inadequate resources be allocated, but the illusion that sexual assault is *not* a problem could be perpetuated. In fact, Diane Moyer, Legal Director of the Pennsylvania Coalition Against Rape stated that "This will sound counterintuitive, but I actually tell parents to send their kids to the college or university with the highest number of sexual assaults reported through the Clery Act because these schools are probably most aware of the campus sexual assault problems" (Police Executive Research Forum, 2012). If sexual assaults are being underreported to police/university officials and universities are underreporting occurrences of sexual assault to the Department of Education, it is easy to see how the general public's understanding of the magnitude of this problem can become distorted.

False reporting. In addition to underreporting, false reporting of sexual assault contributes to the illusion that sexual assaults are uncommon. According to the National Sexual Violence Resource Center (2012), a false report is defined as "a reported crime to a law enforcement agency that an investigation factually proves never occurred." False reports of sexual assault sporadically emerge in news stories. Recently, *Rolling Stone* magazine retracted a story published about a college student given the alias Jackie (Coronel, Coll, & Kravitz, 2015, April 5). According to the (now discredited) *Rolling Stone* article, Jackie was sexually assaulted by a group of men at a particular fraternity at the University of Virginia. From the story's onset, many were skeptical of Jackie's account. After further investigation, *Rolling Stone* retracted the piece and apologized for misleading the public with the story, which they deemed to be false. Some believe that Jackie might have experienced a traumatic event, but based on the evidence from the investigation, it seemed to be the case that her depiction of the assault was fabricated.

Unfortunately, highly publicized cases of false reports of sexual assault, such as the example described above, create panic and concern that false reporting is common. False reports generally result in superfluous media attention; news media will generally report on a false accusation at least twice: once when the initial allegation was made and then a second time when the story is deemed false. As such, people might be exposed to false reports at higher frequencies than general allegations, giving the perception that they are more common. Based on several large scale, longitudinal studies, however, the prevalence of false reporting is between 2–10% (Heenan & Murray 2006; Lisak et al., 2010; Lonsway, Archambault, & Lisak, 2009), indicating that it is statistically uncommon. Misperceptions regarding the frequency of false reporting could also arise from conflating false reports with reports of sexual assault that might be unsubstantiated, meaning that insufficient evidence was available (Archambault, n.d.). It is important to note that if a case is deemed unsubstantiated, that does not necessarily mean a sexual assault did not occur (unsubstantiated reports will be discussed in a subsequent section). Rather, it means there is not enough available evidence, according to a prosecuting attorney, to move forward in bringing charges against a potential perpetrator.

Retracting Sexual Assault Allegations. Another factor that contributes to why the occurrence of sexual assault *seems* uncommon is related to situations in which allegations of sexual assault are made, but then later recanted by the victim. Note: I am not describing situations in which women report sexual assault to the police, but the authorities cannot arrest and/ or charge the perpetrator with the crime because of a lack of evidence. I am specifically referring to situations in which women recant initial allegations of sexual assault, later claiming that the sexual assault did not happen. The retraction of sexual assault allegations is a difficult topic to disentangle as adequate evidence regarding whether the woman was lying about the assault or lying when she recants is often lacking. Nonetheless, the topic is worth addressing.

There are two potential situations that might lead to sexual assault allegations being made and then recanted. First, an individual could falsely claim she has been victimized, get caught in her lies, and then recant in favor of telling the honest truth. Such situations are problematic as they are generally emotionally troubling for the accused and are wasting the time and effort of authorities such as police and prosecuting attorneys, investigators, and others. As discussed in the previous section, though, false reporting of sexual assault is statistically uncommon.

There is a second scenario, however: A victim might be assaulted, she might report the assault to the authorities, but then feel pressured, blamed, humiliated, and/or forced to recant her initial allegation of sexual assault and thus do so. It is difficult to know how often this scenario actually occurs. It might be a more likely scenario when the alleged perpetrator is a high-status or high-profile individual and there is a lack of "hard proof" available to support the allegation. Additionally, if a victim is intoxicated or drugged, she might be unable to provide a clear account of the assault, which can result in suspicion and victim blaming. In these situations, victims might be pressured, persuaded, or otherwise coerced into recanting their allegations particularly when adequate evidence to substantiate the sexual assault is lacking. Therefore, in this latter example, women accurately report experiences of sexual assault, but because adequate evidence does not exist for prosecution resulting in the victim feeling public humiliation, she might opt to recant. This leads into another challenge with reporting of sexual assaults: unsubstantiated allegations.

Unsubstantiated Sexual Assault Allegations. As previously stated, unsubstantiated allegations of sexual assault occur when an individual reports experiencing a sexual assault, but there is insufficient evidence to support the occurrence of the crime. An example of an unsubstantiated sexual assault allegation was described in the recent documentary, *The Hunting Ground*. According to *The Hunting Ground*, in 2012 Ms. Erica Kinsman, a female freshmen student (at the time of the incident), at Florida State University (FSU) maintains she was sexually assaulted by a stranger at a local bar, later identified by Ms. Kinsman as Mr. Jameis Winston, who was at the time a star on the rise on the FSU football team. Winston was the 2015 number one NFL draft pick. According to Ms. Kinsman, after the perpetrator was identified as Jameis Winston, the police heavily dissuaded her from pressing charges through low-level threats because of Mr. Winston's notoriety as a football star in the football crazed college-town. Ms. Kinsman recently filed a civil lawsuit against Mr. Winston.

Ms. Kinsman maintains she was victimized by Mr. Winston, although the district attorney in the case never pressed charges, citing lack of evidence. Mr. Winston has consistently maintained that he did not commit this crime. Unfortunately, in such situations, it is difficult to know what truly transpired between Ms. Kinsman and Mr. Winston. According to Ms. Kinsman's account (as described in *The Hunting Ground)* she was mistreated by the local authorities due to Mr. Winston's status. Similarly, according to an article published in *The New York Times* (Bogdanich, 2014, April 16), the police might have mishandled evidence and Ms. Kinsman might not have received fair treatment because of Mr. Winston's status as a football star. Certainly Mr. Winston's athletic achievements were not overshadowed by the sexual assault allegations as he won the 2013 Heisman trophy, recognizing his on-field accomplishments (while ignoring his potential off-field behavior). If we assume that Ms. Kinsman was sexually assaulted, her alleged treatment by the local police would be indicative of what some women experience when reporting sexual assault to the authorities—not being believed, being blamed, and being dissuaded from pressing charges—particularly when the accused is a high profile individual like Mr. Winston.

If retracted reports and unsubstantiated reports are seen as additional examples of false reports and generally false reporting seems more common than it is, there could be profound social consequences. First, victims might be more reluctant to report sexual assault because they feel ashamed and humiliated, common feelings associated with being victimized. That leads to underreporting, as previously discussed. Additionally, women believe it is "not worth it" to come forward. To unpack this a bit further, let us consider the sexual assault allegations surrounding comedian and television star, Bill Cosby.

Cosby has publically been accused of sexually assaulting nearly 50 women dating back to the 1970s; in some of these instances formalized reports were made to police. Of course compared to the 1970s, access to information has dramatically increased so public awareness of the earlier allegations was likely less widespread. However, Cosby has long denied these allegations, often publically shaming the alleged victims and maintaining they are liars. One could assume that because Cosby maintained success in his career, generally people believed that perhaps the alleged victims were falsely accusing Cosby. Additionally, because of Cosby's notoriety, some women have felt direct or implicit pressure not to report for fear of being stigmatized and victimized. These fears could have been amplified by the fact that criminal charges were not brought against Cosby in earlier allegations. It could be the case that at the time of some of the assaults, evidence was inadequate to prosecute (i.e., unsubstantiated cases). If that is the case, some women might have rationalized that there was no point in coming forward. Additionally, many people (including friends, family, and his wife) have long supported Cosby and too maintained that the alleged victims were lying. If we are to believe that Cosby did sexually assault at least some of the women who have made allegations against him (civil court documents seem to suggest Cosby admitted to these actions in some cases) the decades through which these women were deemed liars, compounded by the fact that criminal charges were not brought up, could both dissuade victims of sexual assault and mute the overall problem of sexual assault more broadly. This underscores the main point of this chapter: sexual assaults are occurring, but it seems as though they are not.

Victim Blaming

I have already alluded to the concept of victim blaming above regarding recanting allegations of sexual assault. Victim blaming occurs when the alleged victim of a sexual assault (or any crime/wrong doing) is held partially or entirely responsible for the situation occurring and, in particular, for the harm that befell her/him (Canadian Resource Centre for Victims of Crimes, 2009). Victim blaming can occur when women report sexual assaults, but are then dissuaded from reporting because authorities or others suggest that the victim's earlier actions make her somewhat responsible for the assault. As previously discussed, such actions result in women recanting initial allegations of sexual assault. Victim blaming can occur in the context of any crime, but is frequently associated with sexual assault. In fact, there are several accounts that exemplify victim blaming, but for the purposes of this chapter, I will discuss a recent situation in which direct victim blaming attempted to raise suspicion regarding whether an assault had actually even occurred (despite reasonably indisputable evidence).

In 2013, two high school students and football players from Steubenville, Ohio, Trent Mays and Ma'lik Richmond, were convicted of the 2012 rape of a female high school student from a neighboring town. Mays and Richmond were aspiring athletes and stars of the Steubenville football team; the team is well-known in the state as a football powerhouse. The sexual assault occurred during the night of August 11, 2012 at a party attended by many Steubenville students. Alcohol was consumed in large quantities by the perpetrators, Mays and Richmond, the victim, and other party attendees. What made this incident so unique (and likely contributed to the guilty verdict) was the fact that photographs of the assault were posted to social media websites such as Twitter, Facebook, and Instagram.

Interestingly, despite such indisputable evidence, a tremendous amount of blame was placed on the victim by Steubenville community members, students attending Steubenville High School, parents of children attending Steubenville High School, and even Steubenville High School football coaches. In fact, allegations were made that parents and school officials contributed to covering up this incident and perhaps related issues of sexual violence involving the football team in order to avoid marring the football program. The victim was harassed and bullied, via social media and other mechanisms; she even received death threats. For example, Nate Hubbard, one of the volunteer assistant coaches at the time of the incident stated: "*The rape was just an excuse, I think…What else are you going to tell your parents when you come home drunk like that and after a night like that?...She had to make up something. Now people are trying to blow up our football program because of it.*" This quote represents quintessential victim blaming—rather than acknowledging the criminal actions perpetrated by Mays and Richmond, Hubbard hones in on the behaviors of the victim. Myriad research demonstrates that women's behaviors are scrutinized in situations of sexual assault while men's behaviors might be ignored (as the excerpt from Hubbard demonstrates) or condoned as "boys will be boys." I will address this latter point again toward the end of the chapter.

Victim blaming is extremely problematic as it serves to make women feel ashamed and humiliated when they are victimized and it also serves to dissuade individuals from reporting incidents of sexual assault as discussed in the previous section. It is particularly upsetting and disappointing, though, when someone in an assumed position of authority makes disparaging remarks that blame the victim, such as those made by Hubbard. In the Steubenville community, someone in Hubbard's position is seen as an authority and role model. The cultural endorsement of victim blaming is made particularly evident when such remarks are made publically in light of the available evidence. And blaming the victim seems all that more acceptable when a person in a position of authority (such as a football coach) engages in blaming the victim. Unfortunately, such examples demonstrate how facts can be distorted via victim blaming which perpetuate the myth that rape is uncommon.

Cultural Conceptualizations of Sexual Assault

There are several different lenses used to define and conceptualize sexual assault and rape based on our cultural interpretation of these terms and our perception of their place in society. I have already addressed some of the different ways in which defining specific acts of sexual violence pose challenges. In the following section I will address some of the broader ways in which sexual assault has been culturally defined or framed and explain how these conceptualizations can lead to general confusion about sexual assault that in turn, can lead to the misperception that rape is an infrequent occurrence.

Politicians' Framing of Rape. Different terminologies have been utilized to describe sexual assault by politicians. These terminologies range from uninformed to disgraceful. It is particularly disparaging, though, that political leaders are making such remarks because they are supposed to be role models and figures of authority. As previously alluded to, if individuals in such positions of power and authority use terminologies and make remarks that undermine women's experiences of sexual assault, it should come as no surprise that these issues of sexual violence perpetrated against women remain ignored.

In the 2012 election, several local/state and federal politicians made distasteful remarks about sexual assault and rape in debates that were actually about access to safe, legal abortion. Most notably, Todd Akin, republican candidate for Congress from Missouri, stated, "*If it's a **legitimate rape**, the female body has ways to try to shut that whole thing down*" (August 20, 2012, emphasis added). Similarly, Ron Paul, a republican congressmen and presidential candidate from Texas, was also quoted as saying: "*If it's an **honest rape**, that individual should go immediately to the emergency room; I would give them a shot of estrogen*" (February 3, 2012, emphasis added). Although these remarks occurred fairly recently, politicians have a history of making offensive statements in regard to sexual assault and rape. For example, republican candidate for Governor from Texas Clayton Williams stated, "*If it's inevitable* [being raped], *just relax and enjoy it*" (March 25, 1990).

These statements reflect either a lack sensitivity regarding issues of sexual violence, at best, or a flagrant disregard for victims/survivors of rape or any sexual violence advocate and ally, at worst. Additionally, they might also more generally speak to the cultural disregard for the severity of sexual assault. To identify certain rapes as "legitimate" or "honest" suggests that other rapes are consequently "illegitimate" or "dishonest." Although Akin, Paul, and Williams were widely criticized for their comments and ultimately lost their respective elections, these individuals are not in isolation. Approximately 173 politicians, including Akin and Paul Ryan (former vice-presidential candidate), co-sponsored the "No Taxpayer for Abortion Act" which was aimed at prohibiting federal funding for abortion services; the bill passed the House of Representatives on May 4, 2011. Because it was projected not to pass the Senate, the bill has yet to come up for a vote, though it has remained a topic of debate.

The legislation received criticism from women's groups for the language utilized to describe "exceptions" to the funding allowances. In other words, the legislation stated that federal monies could not be used to fund abortions, with the exception of certain circumstances. The legislation allowed for federal funding for abortion in instances of "forcible rape" or if a minor experienced "an act of incest." Critics such as politician Debbie Wasserman-Schultz (democrat representative from Florida) argued that the bill was more than insensitive, describing it as "*a violent act against women in and of itself.*" She argued, "*Rape is when a woman is forced to have sex against her will, and that is whether she is conscious, unconscious, mentally stable, not mentally stable*" (Kapur, 2011). I would like to emphasize the importance of language in these examples. When politicians, leaders of the government, suggest that some rapes are legitimate and honest, (with the implicit messaging indicating that others are not), it is easy to see how the general public might begin to disregard the severity of sexual assault too. Wasserman-Schultz's critique highlights the implicit victim blaming underlying the language used in the legislation; this language is echoed in comments made by politicians such as Akin, Paul, Williams, and others (Richard Mourdock—republican senate candidate from Indiana; Rick Santorum—republican senator and presidential candidate; Linda McMahon—republican senate candidate from Connecticut). To delineate rape in this way serves to undermine the issue which further contributes to the myth that it is not a real problem.

Conceptualizing Rape: Force versus Consent. As described above, inconsistencies in how various institutions (e.g., UCR, CDC, CSA, Clery) operationally define sexual assault exist. For example, the Clery Act and the UCR define sexual assault as force whereas the SES and CSA define sexual assault via non-consent. According to Muehlenhard and Peterson

(2007), both conceptualizations pose challenges. However, people tend to accept sex obtained via extreme violence or physical force as a more acceptable form of sexual assault compared to nonconsensual sex in which one person verbally or nonverbally objects to the sexual behavior and the other person ignores the refusals progressing in sex. In most states, both circumstances qualify as sexual assault, but the former represents a "socially disvalued" form of sexual assault because it includes physical violence and force whereas the latter represents a somewhat "socially valued" form of sexual assault as people tend not to consider progressing in sex post-refusal to be severe (Levine, 1959, Muehlenhard & Peterson, 2004).

Disvalued versions of sexual assault have been deemed culturally unacceptable by general societal norms and thus in essence, are considered "real." For example, sexual acts that are obtained via physical force with a weapon or through other violent tactics are generally considered disvalued form of sexual violence (Muehlenhard & Peterson, 2007). Alternatively, valued forms of sexual violence meet an operational definition of sexual assault, but due to lack of physical force or violence, people might not consider the assault "real" (Estrich, 1987). For example, nonconsensual sex that occurs in the absence of physical force or coercion that involves guilt, manipulation, forms of blackmail, and/or emotional threats, or when someone is highly intoxicated might not be considered "real" acts of sexual assault or rape by some individuals because they believe that the victim could have done something more to ward off the assault or prevent it from happening to begin with by not being present in a particular situation. Victim blaming generally coincides with valued forms of sexual assault perpetuating the cultural acceptance of these forms of sexual violence. Support for this framing is evident in the remarks from some politicians described above. For example, consider the language used and sentiment driving the No Taxpayer for Abortion Act. Certainly this legislation was aimed at restricting women's access to abortion services. Delineating that public funding could be used for abortions for situations in which a woman becomes pregnant from "forcible rape" implies that these rapes are "real" whereas others are not real, as discussed above. Relevant to this discussion, it also suggests that forcible rape (which is perhaps culturally understood as rape that includes extreme physical force and violence) is a culturally disvalued form of sexual assault while sexual assaults that do not include physical violence are not disvalued.

To articulate this concept, let us imagine two scenarios. In the first scenario, Jane, an under-age female college student attends a party, but only to watch out for her girlfriends. Jane has never engaged in sexual intercourse and does not plan to consume any alcohol during the party. However, a man at the party secretly drugs Jane; while she is passed out, he sexually assaults her. This scenario clearly matches a culturally disvalued form of sexual coercion; Jane was not doing anything "wrong"—she was trying to be a good friend by watching out for her girlfriends and was secretly drugged and taken advantage of.

Now, imagine another situation in which Kara, another under-age female college student has been partying at a fraternity house with a group of her female friends. Although she does not know the specific directions to the fraternity party, she feels safe because she is with a large group her friends. Unfortunately, over the course of the party, she has been separated from her friends and is intoxicated. Without her friends, she finds that she does not have transportation to get home. John, a member of the fraternity invites Kara to sleep in his room for the night. John attempts to engage in sexual intercourse with her once they are alone in his bed. Kara initially refuses verbally and nonverbally but John continues to attempt post refusal.

At this juncture Kara has two options: 1) leave the fraternity house without knowing where she is, or 2) stay at the fraternity house. If she decides to leave, she could get lost, arrested for public intoxication or under-age drinking, or be victimized on the way home. Alternatively, if she stays, John might force sex on her. While intoxicated, Kara needs to weigh her options and decide whether to stay in a location where sexual violence could potentially happen or, if she can manage, leave but then be at risk for experiencing other negative outcomes. This decision is difficult, particularly when someone is intoxicated, because both options are not ideal. In this situation, it *appears* as if Kara has a choice: to leave (but face potential negative outcomes) or to stay (and potentially be sexually assaulted by John). In reality, regardless of which option Kara selects, she is likely to experience negative outcomes (see Lamb 1996).

Although I fabricated Kara's scenario, the events are far from fictitious. In fact, in their ethnographic study following female freshmen students from a large mid-west university over a five year period, Armstrong, Hamilton, and Sweeney (2006) highlight the frequency with which young college women experience nonconsensual sex as a result of what they termed "low-level coercion" consistent with the scenario described above. Armstrong et al. (2006) maintain that university policies orchestrate situations in which women are put in difficult situations consistent with what I described above. In brief, Armstrong et al argue that university polices to restrict alcohol consumption on campus, endorse Intra-fraternity council (IFC)/Panhellenic regulation over the Greek fraternity/sorority system, and discourage women from reporting sexual assaults experienced when they are under the influence of alcohol in conjunction with the social expectation to consume alcohol and party, act as a "push factor" contributing to sexual violence on campuses (for additional information regarding rape culture on college campuses in the U.S., see Armstrong et al., 2006; DeSantis, 2007; Jozkowski, 2015; Murnen, Wright, & Kaluzny, 2002).

Returning to our example—if Kara decided to stay and John forced sex on her, I would certainly argue she experienced sexual assault. However, some people might argue that Kara was responsible for facilitating the assault because 1) she could have left to avoid the assault, 2) she should not have gotten so intoxicated as to be unable to leave, and/or 3) she should not have gone out partying to begin with and thus avoided the situation altogether. By blaming Kara, rather than blaming John for forcing sex, we excuse and even disregard the sexual assault, reinforcing such disvalued forms of sexual violence. As an aside, this scenario also provides another example of the links between victim blaming and under reporting, concepts addressed earlier in the chapter. The more often women are blamed and made to feel at fault or responsible for their own sexual assault, the less we realize that the problem of rape is systematic and exists because of rapists, not because women consume alcohol or party. It is my hope that the reader is beginning to see the connection between these elements demonstrating how rape culture is institutionally constructed and maintained through many factors.

Unacknowledged rape. Previous research indicates that some women experience nonconsensual sex that meets a legal definition for sexual assault or rape; however these women do not define the experience as sexual assault or rape (e.g., Fisher et al., 2003; Koss, 2011; Peterson & Muehlenhard, 2004; Muehlenhard & Peterson, 2011). Reasons women do not identify these experiences as rape are varied, though a few consistent themes seem to emerge. First, some women characterize rape as a highly violent act that occurs between strangers. As such, they might not conceptualize their experience as rape because it does not match their stereotypical (albeit potentially false) characterization of what "most rape" looks like. Additionally, some women do not want to think of themselves as a "rape victim" or the person who perpetrated the rape as a "rapist." Therefore, they might not consider the experience to be rape. The term "unacknowledged rape" has been applied to such situations to make explicit the fact that these experiences *do* meet a legal definition of sexual assault or rape, but are unacknowledged with such terminology by the victim. It might seem obtuse for researchers or advocates to place a label on an individual (i.e., rape victim, rape survivor) or experience (i.e., rape, sexual assault) which that person does not identify with or apply to herself. Regardless of the terminology, no one should experience sex they did not consent to.

Conclusion: "Good Boys Don't Rape"

The term "rape culture" is being used with increased frequency as of late. Rape culture exists in settings in which sexual violence is common and in which prevalent attitudes, norms, practices, and media normalize, excuse, tolerate, or even condone rape. Over the course of this chapter, I have described several aspects of contemporary culture, with a focus on college culture, that contribute to the false perception that sexual assault is a myth. I conclude by discussing a final example of rape culture that warrants attention: the cultural fallacy that "good boys don't rape." I am using this phrase to refer to instances in which allegations of rape arise, and in response to the allegations, friends and family of the accused, defense attorneys, and sometimes even complete strangers argue that the accused could not have committed the crime because he is a "good boy." The implicit and sometimes explicit endorsement of the various aspects of rape culture previously articulated likely serve as main reasons or contributing factors for why this cultural fallacy even exists. Let us unpack this fallacy with two specific examples: 1) the 2012 Steubenville, Ohio case in which Trent Mays and Ma'lik Richmond were found "delinquent beyond reasonable doubt" for the rape of a 16-year-old girl from West Virginia (Mays was also convicted of the dissemination of child pornography because he took and distributed pictures of the victim) and 2) the 2013 Vanderbilt University case in which Brandon Vandenburg and Cory Batey were found guilty of multiple counts of sexual battery and aggravated rape.[1]

---

1. In June of 2015, Davidson County Judge Monte Watkins, the ruling judge in this trial, declared a mistrial, citing that the jury foreperson was the victim in a statutory rape case and did not disclose this information during jury selection. The prosecutors in the office of District Attorney General Glenn Funk indicated they would request a new trial "as soon as possible."

Both of these cases were fixtures in the national media for a few reasons: 1) the nature of the crimes, 2) the fact that Mays, Richmond, Vandenburg, and Batey were high profile athletes from top football programs (high school and college), and most memorably, 3) the fact that the crimes were made public via photographs of the crime posted to social media (Steubenville) and videos of the crime were obtained from surveillance and cell phone footage (Vanderbilt). The pictures of the Steubenville rape and videos of the Vanderbilt rape are largely credited to the convictions of the defendants in both cases. However, despite the availability of what seemed like largely indisputable evidence, during both trials, proponents for the defendants (including the boys' parents, friends, coaches, and even community members/football fans) argued that the young men were good boys and thus could not have committed these crimes. In fact, the head coach for the Steubenville football team testified as a character witness for Mays and Richmond.

I have no doubt that all four young men are talented football players. Perhaps it is the case that all four men are relatively "nice guys" on and off the football field—maybe they hold the door for people entering a building behind them, maybe they answer all questions with "yes sir" or "no ma'am," perhaps they are good sons, brothers, friends, and students. It could be the case that they are polite to their professors, their coaches, and their priests, pastors, or ministers. But, it is also the case that they committed a crime: they are perpetrators of sexual assault. This is something that we grapple and need to come to terms with as a culture: Men can be "good" in certain contexts, yet simultaneously perpetrators of sexual assault. Culturally, we need to stop thinking of rapists as "creepy men" who lurk in dark places. Instead, we need to realize that perpetrators of sexual assault can look like the "boy next door." Unfortunately, the boy next door is more likely to perpetrate rape compared to the creepy man lurking in the bushes. The creepy man rarely exists: 83-90% of victims know and have a relationship with their perpetrator prior to the assault (Abbey, 2000). The fact that our friends, boyfriends, husbands, fathers, grandfathers, brothers, etc. are likely the individuals committing sexual assault, as opposed to the mentally ill, serial rapist, makes conversations about sexual assault and rape difficult to have.

Let me be clear, I am not stating, nor am I even insinuating, that all men are rapists. That is certainly *not* the case. The point I am trying to make is that our perception of what a rapist looks like needs to change in order for us to begin to acknowledge the magnitude of this issue. Additionally, we need to realize that cultural norms exist which serve to perpetuate false ideas regarding what rape and rapists look like. This chapter is one attempt at deconstructing some of these issues; continued dialogue is necessary. But dialogues about rape and consent can be tense. In part, this could reflect contemporary American culture's general discomfort confronting issues related to sexuality, particularly women's sexuality. After all, if we still live in a culture that chastises women for expressions of sexual desire (e.g., we call them "sluts," "whores," and "hos") we do not respect women's right to say "yes" to sex. And if we do not respect a woman's right to say "yes" to sex, it is no wonder that the epidemic of sexual assault remains controversial. It is also difficult to begin conversations about rape that support individuals who have been victimized without sounding as though one is attacking men. Rather than shying away from these discussions, however, we need to embrace them and continue to have them with friends, family, and especially young people.

DISCUSSION QUESTIONS

1. Compare and contrast the different ways in which rape/sexual assault have been defined. How do these definitions fit into your conceptualizations of rape and sexual assault?

2. Describe three different aspects discussed in this chapter related to the reporting of sexual assault which contribute to people thinking that sexual violence is uncommon. Were you surprised by this discussion? Why or why not?

3. How do you define "*sex*"? How do you define "*rape*"? Do you believe your definition of the term "sex" influences your perception of the term "rape"?

4. What is meant by the terms "disvalued forms of sexual violence" and "valued forms of sexual violence"? Do you see these being accurate to experiences in your life?

5. What do you think the author's point was regarding her final discussion: "good boys don't rape"? Can you think of examples in which sexual violence has been framed in this way? Do you agree with the author? Why or why not?

References

Acierno, R. (1997). Health impact of interpersonal violence. 1: Prevalence rates, case identification, and risk factors for sexual assault, physical assault, and domestic violence in men and women. *Behavioral Medicine, 23,* 53–64. doi:10.1080/08964289709596729.

Archambault, J. (n.d.). Unfounded cases and false reports: A complex problem [PowerPoint slides]. Retrieved from the Iowa Coalition Against Sexual Assault: http://www.iowacasa.org/UserDocs/A3,_A4_Archambault_FALSE_REPORTS.pdf.

Armstrong, E. A., Hamilton, L., & Sweeney, B. (2006). Sexual assault on campus: A multilevel integrative approach to party rape. *Social Problems, 53*(4), 483–499.

Berenson, T. (2014, June 27). 1 in 5: Debating the most controversial sexual assault statistic. TIME.com Magazine. http://time.com/2934500/1-in-5%E2%80%82campus-sexual-assault-statistic/ Retrieved March, 20, 2015.

Bogdanich, W. (2014, April, 16). A Star Player Accused, and A Flawed Rape Investigation. *The New York Times.* Retrieved from: http://www.nytimes.com/interactive/2014/04/16/sports/errors-in-inquiry-on-rape-allegations-against-fsu-jameis-winston.html.

Centers for Disease Control and Prevention. (2012). Sexual assault facts at a glance. Retrieved from http://www.cdc.gov/violenceprevention/pdf/sv-datasheet-a.pdf.

Clery Act, 20 U.S.C. § 1092(f) (West 1990).

Clery Act Regulations, 34 C.F.R. 668.46 (West 2014).

Coronel, S., Coll, S., & Kravitz, D. (2015, April, 5). Rolling Stone and UVA: The Columbia University Graduate School of Journalism Report. 'A Rape on Campus' What Went Wrong? *Rolling Stone.* Retrieved from: http://www.rollingstone.com/culture/features/a-rape-on-campus-what-went-wrong-20150405.

Daigle, L. E., Fisher, B. S., & Cullen, F. T. (2008). The violent and sexual victimization of college women: Is repeat victimization a problem? *Journal of Interpersonal Violence, 23,* 1296–1313. doi:10.1177/0886260508314293.

Department of Justice, Felony Defendents in Large Urban Counties: 2009.

DeSantis, A. (2007). *Inside Greek U: Fraternities, sororities, and the pursuit of power, pleasure, and prestige.* Lexington, KY: University Press of Kentucky.

Estrich, S. (1987). *Real rape*. Cambridge, MA: Harvard University Press.

Fisher, B. S., Daigle, L. E., Cullen, F. T., & Turner, M. G. (2003). Reporting Sexual Victimization To The Police And Others Results From a National-Level Study of College Women. *Criminal Justice and Behavior*, 30(1), 6–38.

Gavey, N. (1999). "I wasn't raped, but…" Revisiting definitional problems in victimization. In S. Lamb (Ed.) *New versions of victims: Feminists struggle with the concept* (pp. 57–81). New York: New York University Press.

Heenan, M., & Murray, S. (2006). Study of reported rapes in Victoria 2000–2003: Summary research report. Retrieved from the State of Victoria (Australia), Victoria Police: http://www.police.vic.gov.au/retrievemedia.asp?Media_ID=19462.

Jozkowski, K.N. (2013). The influence of consent on college students' perceptions of the quality of sexual intercourse at last event. *International Journal of Sexual Health*, 25, 260–272.

Jozkowski, K.N. (2015). Yes Means "Yes"? Sexual consent policy and college students. *Change: The Magazine for Higher Learning*, 14(2), 16–23.

Justice Department, National Crime Victimization Survey: 2008–2012.

Kapur, S. (2011, February 1). Exclusive: Wasserman Schultz calls GOP abortion bill 'a violent act against women'. http://www.rawstory.com/2011/02/wasserman-schultz-gop-rape-violent-women/ Retrieved May, 2, 2015.

Kingkade, T. (2014, September 4). KU students outraged over soft punishment in rape case. *The Huffington Post*. Retrieved from http://www.huffingtonpost.com/2014/09/04/ku-rape-students_n_5767824.html.

Koss, M. P. (2011). Hidden, unacknowledged, acquaintance, and date rape: Looking back, looking forward. *Psychology of Women Quarterly*, 35, 348–354.

Koss, M. P., Abbey, A., Campbell, R., Cook, S., Norris, J., Testa, M., White, J. (2007). Revising the SES: A collaborative process to improve assessment of sexual aggression and victimization. *Psychology of Women Quarterly*, 31, 357–370.

Krebs, C. P., Lindquist, C.H., Warner, T.D., Fisher, B.S., Martin, S.L. (2007). The Campus Sexual Assault (CSA) study. National Institute of Justice. NIJ Grant No. 2004-WG-BX-0010.

Lamb, S. (1996). The trouble with blame: Victims, perpetrators, and responsibility. Cambridge, MA: Harvard University Press.

Levine, R. (1959). Gusii sex offenses: A study in social control. *American Anthropologist, 61*, 965–990.

Lisak, D., Gardinier, L., Nicksa, S. C., & Cote, A. M. (2010). False allegations of sexual assault: An analysis of ten years of reported cases. *Violence Against Women*, 16, 1318–1334. doi:10.1177/1077801210387747.

Lonsway, K. A., Archambault, J., & Lisak, D. (2009). False reports: Moving beyond the issue to successfully investigate and prosecute non-stranger sexual assault. *The Voice*, 3(1), 1–11. Retrieved from the National District Attorneys Association: http://www.ndaa.org/pdf/the_voice_vol_3_no_1_2009.pdf.

Martin, S. L., B. S. Fisher, T. D. Warner, C. P. Krebs, and C. H. Lindquist. 2011. Women's sexual orientations and their experiences of sexual assault before and during university. *Women's Health Issues*, 21, 199–205.

Muehlenhard, C.L., & Peterson, Z.D. (2007). Conceptualizing Sexual Violence: Socially acceptable coercion and other controversies. In A.G. Miller (Ed.) *The Social Psychology of Good and Evil*. The Guildford Press: New York.

Murnen, S. K., Wright, C., & Kaluzny, G. (2002). If "boys will be boys," then girls will be victims? Ameta-analytic review of the research that relates masculine ideology to sexual aggression. *Sex Roles*, 46(11/12), 359–375.

Peterson, Z. D., & Muehlenhard, C. L. (2004). Was it rape? The function of women's rape myth acceptance and definitions of sex in labeling their own experiences. *Sex Roles*, 51, 129–144. doi:10.1023/B:SERS.0000037758.95376.00.

Peterson, Z. D., & Muehlenhard, C. L. (2007). What is sex and why does it matter? A motivational approach to exploring individuals' definitions of sex. *Journal of Sex Research*, 44, 256–268. doi:10.1080/00224490701443932.

Peterson, Z.D., & Muehlenhard, C.L. (2011). A Match-and-Motivation model of how women label their nonconsensual sexual experiences. *Psychology of Women Quarterly*, 35(4), 558–570.

Rennison, C. A. (2002). Rape and sexual assault: Reporting to police and medical attention, 1992–2000 [NCJ 194530]. Retrieved from the U.S. Department of Justice, Office of Justice Programs, Bureau of Justice Statistics: http://bjs.ojp.usdoj.gov/content/pub/pdf/rsarp00.pdf.

Satinsky, S.A., & Jozkowski, K.N. (2013). Sexual coercion and behavior among a sample of sexual minority women. *Women & Health*, 54(2), 77–93.

Sinha, M. (2013). Measuring violence against women: Statistical trends (Component of Statistics Canada catalogue no. 85-002-X). Retrieved from http:// www.statcan.gc.ca/pub/85-002-x/2013001/ article/11766-eng.pdf.

Uniform Crime Reporting Statistics. (2010). Table building tool. Retrieved from http://www.ucrdatatool.gov/.

White House Task Force to Protect Students From Sexual Assault (U.S.). (2014). Not alone: The first report of the White House Task Force to Protect Students From Sexual Assault.

Yung, C.R. (2015). Concealing campus sexual assault: An empirical examination. *Psychology, Public Policy, and Law*, 21(1), 1–9.

CHAPTER 17

Everyday Experiences of People in Same-Sex Relationships

Pamela J. Lannutti & Sandra L. Faulkner

KEY TERMS

Discrimination

Everyday experiences

Minority stress

Relational context

Romantic same-sex relationships

Social stigma

ABSTRACT

This chapter examines similarities and differences between same-sex and different sex couples in the form of changing social and legal contexts. The everyday experiences of same-sex romantic partners within their social network of family, friends, and co-workers influence experiences of support and challenge. In addition, the shifts in the status of same-sex couples at the social, cultural, and legal levels may create dynamic change in even stable same-sex couples' experiences.

One way of understanding romantic relationships is to examine the experiences that couples have in their daily lives. Many social scientists believe that examining unique, different, and often dramatic episodes in our lives is important, but champion a focus on the ordinary, or "everyday" experiences rather than on the extraordinary experiences of relationships in order to fully understand such relationships and the individuals involved. For example, Tracy and Robles (2013) argue that everyday communication in our relationships is the primary way in which our identities, expected behaviors, and rituals are established. Carl and Duck (2004) contend that it is the everyday interactions in our relationships that form the basis of our understanding of our social world and general information processing. Given the significance of everyday experiences and communication, this chapter focuses on the everyday experiences of people in same-sex relationships. We note that the majority of the data on the everyday experiences of same-sex couples discussed in this chapter is derived from studies of same-sex couples in the United States (to learn about couples' experiences on a more-international level, see Yep, Lescure, & Allen, this volume or Eguchi, this volume).

Before taking a closer look at various aspects of the everyday experiences of people in same-sex relationships, we call attention to two important themes in the research about same-sex couples. First, in many ways, the everyday experiences of people in same-sex relationships are similar to the everyday experiences of people in different-sex relationships. Kurdek (2005) reviewed the literature examining relational quality and factors that affect relational quality and concluded that same-sex couples were more similar to than different from different-sex couples. The "more similar than different" theme is echoed in various studies comparing everyday aspects of same-sex and different-sex couples' lives. For example, Gottman et al. (2003) examined couple conflict and found that emotional qualities of conflict related to relational stability and satisfaction is similar for same-sex and different-sex couples. Haas and Stafford (1998, 2005) found that same-sex and different-sex couples used many of the same relational maintenance behaviors.

Although much of the research comparing same-sex and different-sex couples points to more similarities than differences between the couple types, important information can be learned from the differences between the two types of couples. Some differences between same-sex and different-sex couples indicate positive relational processes for same-sex couples. For example, where Kurdek (2005) did uncover differences in relational quality factors between same-sex and different-sex couples, same-sex couples tended to behave more positively than different-sex couples in that same-sex couples resolved conflict more constructively and shared housework more evenly than did different-sex couples. However, the majority of differences found between same-sex and different-sex couples are indicative of the social stigma, discrimination, and minority stress that same-sex couples often experience. Because the majority of the differences between same-sex and different-sex couples stems from the stigma, discrimination and stress experienced by same-sex couples, it is important to look more closely at the experiences of support and challenge that same-sex couples experience every day.

The social stigma, discrimination, and minority stress that same-sex couples often experience brings to the forefront a second theme about the everyday experiences of people in a same-sex relationship: a context of change. Interactions within relationships take place within a context, or environment, that is made up of many layers including cultural, psychological, sociological, temporal, relational, and physical aspects (see Manning, this volume or Brown & Weigel, this volume). The context of our interactions influences our relationship, while at the same time, our interactions influence aspects of the context. Contemporary same-sex couples are living in a context of drastic and dynamic social change regarding their relationships, for example, the right to marry and greater social acceptance of same-sex relationships. Although cultural, legal, and social factors differ from country to country and within countries, the last five decades have been times of great change for same-sex couples; the general trend has been toward greater acceptance of and recognition for same-sex couples; yet same-sex couples still experienced significant oppression, stigma, and discrimination during this time. Importantly, contemporary same-sex couples are likely to have been engaged in their relationships while changes in the social, cultural, and legal status of same-sex relationships were changing and continue to change. Thus, even a stable same-sex couple might experience dynamic change in their everyday experiences due to shifts in the status of same-sex couples at the social, cultural, and/or legal levels.

With the themes of "more similar than different" and "context of change" as a foundation, the rest of this chapter will highlight findings from the research literature on the everyday experiences of people in a same-sex relationship. Everyday experiences of support and challenge for same-sex couples will be discussed first. Then, attention will be given to the changing status of relationship and family civil and legal recognition experienced by same-sex couples. Throughout the discussion, we offer an illustrative example from the everyday experiences of a lesbian couple, Carrie and Sarah.

Carrie and Sarah: The First Year

Carrie and Sarah stood on the edge of the field watching a small group of women gather around the woman holding the football. Carrie had talked Sarah into trying out for their city's new team in the women's flag football league—"Come on Sarah, we need to meet some other lesbians! It will be fun."

Carrie was not so sure it was actually going to be fun now that they were there with all of those lesbians. She started to sweat from the sidelines, the questions silently asked playing on repeat: *What if they figure out I haven't dated any other women? That I am new at this? What should we talk about? Why did I want to join 'this' team?* Sarah was Carrie's first female partner. She felt exhilarated and scared to see so many women openly into other women. She and Sarah needed to make some lesbian friends to get out of the suburbs and into the city's LGBT community. They had been dating for two months, but Carrie had not told her religiously conservative family. Trying out their relationship in a safe public environment—assuming flag football with 25 lesbian, bisexual, and straight (only 2!) women was safe—seemed like a good move. Sarah's sister was happy they were dating, but Sarah still hadn't taken Carrie as her girlfriend to any of her coworker's parties. Carrie couldn't figure out how to tell her family about dating a woman. Getting covered in mud and banged up with other women who could relate to them seemed a good way to begin.

Everyday Experiences of Support and Challenge

Same-sex couples have been stigmatized and discriminated against in ways that increase the stress—often referred to as minority stress—experienced by people in a same-sex relationship (Meyer, 2003). Thus, when thinking about the everyday experiences of people in a same-sex relationship, it is important to consider the ways that these individuals are supported and challenged by others and how interactions with others increases and decreases their minority stress. Interestingly, the research on the support and challenges experienced by same-sex couples in their daily lives indicates that many interactions and relationships, including those with family members, friends, and coworkers, can serve as a source of both support and challenge (Rostosky, Riggle, Gray, & Hatton, 2007).

Carrie and Sarah: The First Five Years

Carrie was busy getting the grill ready for the party. She protected her engagement ring as she scrubbed, admiring the shine. She smiled when she thought about Sarah and remembered how they cried as they watched the first couples line up at city hall to get married. It had been a year since it was legal for her and Sarah to get married in New Jersey. They talked about what marriage would mean to them, to their families, how they never thought marriage would be a possibility for them or their other coupled lesbian friends. *Should they do it? What does it mean to get married as a same-sex couple?* The talk in their circle was how they should be the first to do it, to get married. After all, *they had been together the longest. They were the happiest.* When Sarah asked Carrie to marry her, she said yes.

As she continued to clean for the engagement party, Sarah wondered how they would tell Carrie's family. Carrie's father still referred to Sarah as Carrie's "roommate." How would Carrie's dad explain to his friends that his daughter was marrying her roommate? She decided to stop thinking about the negatives, what family would say, what could happen with her and Carrie once they got married, and focus on the party and the wedding.

***

Family of origin members are often a source of challenge and support for same-sex couples. The research suggests that, unfortunately, family of origin members are more likely to be a source of challenge for same-sex couples than support, so same-sex couples often rely on a "family of friends" for social support more so than on their family of origin (Rostosky et al., 2007; Weston, 1991). Challenges from family of origin members have led some same-sex couples to conceal their relationship status from some or all family of origin members (Rostosky et al., 2007) or to be only fully accepted as a couple by some family members (Lannutti, 2014). Still, when family of origin members are supportive of same-sex couples, their support is significant in reducing the minority stress experienced by couples (Feinstein, Wadsworth, Davila, & Goldfried, 2014).

As noted above, friends may be especially important to same-sex couples because they may serve the functions of family members in the absence of family support or in addition to mixed support from families (Rostosky et al., 2007; Weston, 1991). Friends might be the main source of social support and relationship recognition for same-sex couples. Friends serve other important functions in the daily lives of same-sex couples as well. For example, friends often serve as caregivers for midlife and older gay, lesbian, bisexual, and transgender (GLBT) people (Croghan, Moone, & Olson, 2014). However, friends can also be a source of challenge for people in a same-sex relationship. For example, same-sex couples considering marriage reported that both heterosexual and GLBT friends challenged the couple about their decision to marry and their relationship itself (Lannutti, 2014).

Finally, people in same-sex relationships experience support and challenge from everyday interactions with those with whom they have more context-specific, limited, or looser social ties. The everyday interactions between GLBT people and coworkers can be a source of support and challenge for people in same-sex relationships. Rumens (2010) showed that while some organizations can be particularly challenging environments for gay workers, coworkers often serve as a source of support for gay men. Horan and Chory (2013) compared perceptions of heterosexual coworkers and GLBT coworkers and found mixed results for support and challenge among people in same-sex relationships and their coworkers. Horan and Chory's (2013) results indicate what while GLBT coworkers relationships may be characterized by less deception and more caring that those with heterosexual coworkers, people did not view workplace romantic relationships between GLBT people positively.

Other looser or limited social ties may also impact the everyday support and challenge experiences of people in same-sex relationships. Lannutti (2011) described both supportive and unsupportive interactions about amendments banning same-sex marriage between same-sex couples and extended social network members, such as neighbors, friends of friends, and other acquaintances. For example, same-sex couples described interaction where people they had met only once or twice stopped them on the street to tell them they were against the same-sex marriage bans and supported same-sex couples. Other same-sex couples described conversations in which other guests at a party rudely denigrated same-sex marriage in their presence (Lannutti, 2011).

Relationship and Family Civil Recognition

For American same-sex couples, it is only in the last decade that civil and legal recognition for their relationships in the form of marriage had the possibility of being part of everyday life. As discussed above, same-sex couples are engaging in their relationships in a context of dynamic change regarding the civil and legal status for such relationships. The civil and legal status of same-sex partnerships affects the legal and civil protections that are available for families centered upon a same-sex couple. The new developments and changing status of protections for same-sex relationships is an important part of the everyday experience of contemporary same-sex couples whether or not the couple opts for civil recognition in the form of marriage or other legal bond.

The legal status of same-sex marriage in the United States has changed relatively rapidly and dynamically. When the first draft of this chapter was written, same-sex couples in the United States who wanted to have a civil marriage could do so in 35 states and Washington, DC. When the second draft was written, the Supreme Court of the United States had ruled that same-sex marriage must be recognized in all 50 states. It is false, however, to see the trajectory of same-sex marriage in the U.S. as smoothly moving toward greater acceptance. During the time when Massachusetts became the first state to recognize same-sex marriage and the recognition of same-sex marriage in all 50 states, there were also many ballot initiatives, legislation, and court cases aimed at banning same-sex marriage. The Supreme Court's decision leading to legal recognition of same-sex marriage nationwide has been met with opposition from some pundits, political figures, and social leaders. Thus, same-sex couples experienced and continue to experience the fallout from political debates, campaigns, media coverage, and shifting legal status pertaining to their relationships as a part of their everyday experiences. As such, the legal recognition of same-sex marriage and the surrounding debates form a new relational context for same-sex couples (Lannutti, 2014).

This new relational context of same-sex marriage influences and is influenced by the everyday interactions of same-sex couples. Over a series of studies, Lannutti (2014) investigated the impact of legally recognized same-sex marriage and the surrounding debates on same-sex couples and their social networks. People who are entering into or are in the early stages of a same-sex relationship now have the possibility of civil marriage in mind as they form and build their relationship. Established same-sex couples may face the decision of whether or not to seek the new legal option of same-sex marriage as part of their relationship. Same-sex couples who do opt to marry must figure out how this new civil recognition fits into the patterns of relational maintenance already established within their relationship with each other and within their relationships with their families, friends, and other social network members. Same-sex couples who do not opt to marry may also have to negotiate how to communicate about their non-married but committed relationship with each other and members of their social networks such as family members and friends. Thus, whether a same-sex couple wants to marry or not, the new relational context formed by same-sex marriage impacts their everyday experiences.

Legally recognized same-sex marriage, and the debates that surround it, are related to other civil and legal protections for families centered upon a same-sex relationship. Legal marriage often makes previously debated issues about same-sex parenting clearer under the law and may make having or adopting children easier for same-sex couples. Additionally, same-sex couples see important links between forming and protecting their families and same-sex marriage. Same-sex couples list increased legal protection and social acceptance for having children or wanting to have children as attractions to same-sex marriage (Lannutti, 2008) and as a benefit of being legally married (Badgett, 2009). In one study, 93% of married same-sex couples with children believed that their children were happier, better off, more secure, had a greater sense of stability, and saw their families as more validated by society as a result of the couple being married (Ramos, Goldberg, & Badgett, 2009). Thus, same-sex marriage not only impacts the everyday experiences of people in a same-sex relationship, but it affects the everyday experiences of their families as well.

Carrie and Sarah: The Last Day

Sarah stared out at the group of mourners still feeling a sense of disbelief. She wanted to tell Carrie how lucky they were to have friends like family, but then she remembered where she was and why. *How am I going to live without Carrie? Who knew I would be planning a funeral so soon after a wedding?* Sarah thought. She remembered how she gripped Carrie's hand when the doctor explained the test result to them and all of their friends in the ICU. Carrie yelped from the grip as the doctor talked. No one could speak. It had been just a few months since they celebrated Carrie's 40th birthday—with a pick-up flag football game and cook-out, of course—and now the doctors were explaining that Carrie's cancer was fast moving and incurable.

She only managed to hold it together because of her friends. They stopped by the hospital, texted and called her every day. They camped out in the ICU waiting room and convinced the doctors that a visit from Sarah and Carrie's dog—Sappho—would be okay. She couldn't talk about death or think too much about hospital and funeral bills, but at least she didn't have to argue with doctors or her employer about being Carrie's partner. *Wife can be a useful word.* She choked up when she thought about what the hospital staff told her. *Your love for each other shows. Wish we all had that.* But for now, she needed to get through this impossible day. The everyday details of bills and planning could wait. She and her friends—no, scratch that, her family—needed to tell the stories of Carrie and Sarah and their community.

DISCUSSION QUESTIONS

1. What does a focus on everyday experiences in same-sex relationships help us understand about communication processes in these relationships?

2. How do everyday experiences such as supportive and unsupportive relationships with family members, friends, and co-workers help and/or hinder same-sex couples abilities to cope with discrimination,

minority stress, and social stigma? How does civil recognition help and/or hinder same-sex couples' abilities to cope with discrimination, minority stress, and social stigma?

3.   Discuss the themes of "more similar than different" and "context of change" as a foundation for understanding differences and similarities between same-sex and different-sex couples.

4.   When we consider similarities and differences between same-sex and different-sex couples, what similarities are most important and why? What differences are most important and why?

5.   Describe how Carrie and Sarah's experiences with friends, co-workers, family, and health care personnel were influenced by their social and legal context. Would things have been different if they were not legally married? Why or why not?

References

Badgett, M.V. L. (2009). *When gay people get married: What happens when societies legalize same-sex marriage.* New York: New York University Press.

Brown, R. D., & Weigel, D. J. (This volume). Beneath the tangled sheets: Examining sexual communication through ecological systems theory. In J. Manning & C. Noland (Eds.), *Contemporary Studies of Sexuality & Communication: Theoretical and Applied Perspectives.* Dubuque, IA: Kendall Hunt.

Carl, W. J. & Duck, S. (2004). How to do things with relationships...and how relationships do things with us. *Communication Yearbook, 28,* 1–34.

Croghan, C. F., Moone, R. P., & Olson, A. M. (2014). Friends, family, and caregiving among midlife and older lesbian, gay, bisexual, and transgender adults. *Journal of Homosexuality, 61,* 79–102.

Eguchi, S. (This volume). Sexual and cultural difference(s): A case for theorizing "doing" queer foreignness. In J. Manning & C. Noland (Eds.), *Contemporary Studies of Sexuality & Communication: Theoretical and Applied Perspectives.* Dubuque, IA: Kendall Hunt.

Feinstein, B. A., Wadsworth, L. P, Davila, J., & Goldfried, M. R. (2014). Do parental acceptance and family support moderate associations between dimensions of minority stress and depressive symptoms among lesbians and gay men? *Professional Psychology: Research and Practice, 45,* 239–246.

Gottman, J. M., Levenson, R. W., Gross, J., Frederickson, B. L., McCoy, K., Rosenthal, L., Ruef, A., & Yoshimoto, D. (2003). Correlates of gay and lesbian couples' relationship satisfaction and relationship dissolution. *Journal of Homosexuality, 45,* 23–43.

Hall, G. (2005). "These are my parents": The experiences of children in same-sex parented families during the first year of marriage legalization in Massachusetts. In *What I did for love, or benefits, or...: Same-sex marriage in Massachusetts. Wellesley Centers for Women, Working Paper No. 422.* (pp. 35–45). Wellesley, MA: Wellesley Centers for Women.

Haas, S. M. & Stafford, L. (1998). An initial examination of maintenance behaviors in gay and lesbian relationships. *Journal of Social and Personal Relationships, 15,* 846–855.

Haas, S. M. & Stafford, L. (2005). Maintenance behaviors in same-sex and marital relationships: A matched sample comparison. *Journal of Family Communication, 5,* 43–60.

Horan, S. M. & Chory, R. M. (2013). Relational implications of gay and lesbian workplace romances: Understanding trust, deception, and credibility. *Journal of Business Communication, 50,* 170–189.

Kurdek, L. A. (2005). What do we know about gay and lesbian couples? *Current Directions in Psychological Science, 14,* 251–254.

Lannutti, P. J. (2008). Attractions and obstacles while considering legally recognized same-sex marriage. *Journal of GLBT Family Studies, 4,* 245–264. doi: 10.1080/1550428080209691.

Lannutti, P. J. (2011). Examining communication about marriage amendments: Same-sex couples and their extended social networks. *Journal of Social Issues, 67,* 264–281.

Lannutti, P. J. (2014). *Experiencing same-sex marriage: Individuals, couples, and social networks.* New York: Peter Lang Publishing.

Manning, J. (This volume). Identity, relationships, and culture: A constitutive model of coming out. In J. Manning & C. Noland (Eds.), *Contemporary Studies of Sexuality & Communication: Theoretical and Applied Perspectives.* Dubuque, IA: Kendall Hunt.

Ramos, C., Goldberg, N.G., & Badgett, M.V.L. (2009). *The effects of marriage equality in Massachusetts: A survey of the experiences and impact of marriage on same-sex couples.* Los Angeles, CA: The Williams Institute, UCLA.

Rostosky, S. S., Riggle, E. D. B., Gray, B. E., & Hatton, R. L. (2007). Minority stress experiences in committed same-sex couple relationships. *Professional Psychology: Research and Practice, 38,* 392–400.

Rumens, N. (2010). Firm friendships: Exploring the supportive components in gay men's workplace friendships. *The Sociological Review, 58,* 135–155.

Tracy, K. & Robles, J. S. (2013). *Everyday talk, 2nd Edition: Building and reflecting identities.* New York: Guilford Press.

Weston, K. (1991). *Families we choose: Lesbians, gays, kinship.* New York: Columbia University Press.

Yep, G. A., Lescure, R. M., & Allen, J. (This volume). Intercultural same-sex relationships: Masculinities, sexualities, and communication across borders. In J. Manning & C. Noland (Eds.), *Contemporary Studies of Sexuality & Communication: Theoretical and Applied Perspectives.* Dubuque, IA: Kendall Hunt.

CHAPTER 18

Undoing Marriage: Conservative "Protect Marriage" Rhetoric and the Symptoms of Gender Trouble

Roger Davis Gatchet & Amanda Davis Gatchet

 KEY TERMS

Queer theory   Gender binary
Same-sex marriage   Proposition 8

 ABSTRACT

This chapter explores the same-sex marriage debate through the lens of queer theory and the insights it offers regarding the relationships between gender, sexuality, and communication. Taking the 2008 Proposition 8 campaign in California as its case study, this chapter 1) introduces queer theory and its key arguments; 2) explains what some queer theorists argue are the negative consequences of the demand for state and legal recognition of relationships in the form of same-sex marriage; and 3) illustrates an alternative perspective that appears to challenge the queer critique of same-sex marriage. In the end, this chapter's focus on a contemporary social movement sheds light on some of the struggles that activists face when attempting to influence public perceptions of sexuality.

In the November 4, 2008 general election, California voters narrowly passed ballot measure Proposition 8, also known as the "California Marriage Protection Act," by a margin of nearly 4.5% (California Secretary of State, 2009). Much like the similarly titled 1996 Defense of Marriage Act that was signed into federal law by then president Bill Clinton, Prop. 8 amended the California Constitution by defining marriage as a legal arrangement that can only exist between a man and a woman. The new ballot initiative, which received the support of over seven million voters at the polls, effectively overturned the California Supreme Court's 2008 decision in *In re Marriage Cases*, where the Court found that any ban on same-sex marriage was a violation of the state Constitution. The passage of Prop. 8 coincided with the approval of similar voter initiatives around the country at the time, including those in the states of Florida, Arizona, and Arkansas, with the latter prohibiting same-sex couples from adopting children. Unlike those initiatives, however, the political struggle surrounding Prop. 8 garnered a significant amount of national attention. A record $73 million was spent both in support of and opposition to Prop. 8, making it the most expensive marriage ballot initiative of its time.

The constitutional amendment proposed by Prop. 8 supporters was especially controversial because it essentially took away a fundamental right that had previously been established by the California Supreme Court, and its passage prompted a series of lawsuits challenging the constitutionality of same-sex marriage bans. In June of 2013, the ruling by the U.S. Supreme Court in *Hollingsworth v. Perry* ultimately left the original district court ruling that had overturned Prop. 8 as the final ruling in the case and established same-sex marriage as legal once again in California. Two years later, in *Obergefell v. Hodges*, the legal right to marry was granted to same-sex couples nationwide when the Court ruled in a 5–4 decision that all 50 states in the country be required to license and recognize such unions.

You might think the U.S. Supreme Court's 2015 decision in *Obergefell v. Hodges* suggests that questions regarding the legality of same-sex marriage in the U.S. are now moot. However, the battle over Prop. 8 (and other similar state initiatives) demonstrates how same-sex marriage has become one of the most contentious public issues in the gay and lesbian community's struggle for recognition and equality, successfully rallying supporters and, simultaneously, mobilizing resistance from conservative political and religious groups. The controversy over marriage equality has not been limited to the outcry from conservatives and evangelical Christians, however. Although it has received less publicity in the media, some researchers who identify with a scholarly tradition known as queer theory have questioned whether same-sex marriage is ultimately a useful goal. Rather than challenging the state's power to regulate the institution of marriage, queer theorists argue that same-sex marriage only further empowers the state by creating a new social norm that renders "unthinkable" a whole array of sexualities, relationships, and identities that the state will not recognize (Butler, 2004, p. 106; see also Warner, 1999; Seidman, 2001; Brandzel, 2005; Grindstaff, 2003).

The same-sex marriage debate is, therefore, an ideal topic for exploring queer theory's insights regarding the relationship between sexuality, gender, and communication, especially in light of the 2015 Court's landmark ruling that legalized same-sex marriage nationwide. Taking the same-sex marriage debate and the Prop. 8 campaign in California as its primary case study, this chapter will 1) introduce queer theory and its key arguments; 2) explain what some queer theorists argue are the negative consequences of the demand for state and legal recognition of relationships in the form of same-sex marriage; and 3) illustrate an alternative perspective that appears to challenge the queer critique of same-sex marriage through an analysis of the language of the conservative movement that supported Prop. 8. It is our hope that this application of queer theory to a contemporary social movement will illuminate some of the struggles that activists face when attempting to influence public perceptions of sexuality.

Performing Gender: A Primer on Queer Theory

Scholars who identify with the diverse area of scholarship known as queer theory hail from a broad range of disciplines, including history, philosophy, English, cultural studies, and, of course, communication and rhetorical studies. Although the term "queer" brings with it a long history of pejorative connotations targeted against those who challenge the notion that heterosexuality is "natural" or "normal," members of the LGBTQ (lesbian-gay-bisexual-transgender-queer) community have effectively reclaimed it as a term of empowerment. In Zita's (1994) words, it is now a "pragmatically generic and diffuse category" that encompasses a shifting terrain of identities and scholarship (p. 258). The term *queer* currently has been widely adopted not only by gays, lesbians, and others who self-identify as queer, but also by scholars who investigate issues related to gender, sexuality, and identity. Yep, Lovaas, and Elia (2014) have described queer theory as "one of the most significant intellectual movements of the last two decades" (p. 2) for the way it "challenges the modern system of sexuality as a body of knowledge that structures and organizes the personal, institutional, and cultural life of individuals in Western societies" (p. 4). Along these lines, one of queer theory's central objectives—as it is applied not only in scholarship, but also in community organizing and social activism—is "to continuously destabilize and deconstruct the notion of fixed sexual and gender identities" (Lovaas, Elia, & Yep, 2006, p. 6).

Queer theory's overt political stance differentiates the scholarship in this area from other, more social scientific approaches to studying sexuality and communication. In other words, queer theorists attempt to not only *describe* the complex relationship between sexuality and identity, but also to *change* our understanding of that relationship in ways that empower marginalized groups. It has become a popular theoretical lens in the communication discipline because it offers a nuanced perspective on how individuals and communities use signs and symbols (such as language or visual images) to navigate the complex waters of human sexuality. Scholars from a wide variety of sub-disciplines in communication have used queer theory in their work, including those focusing on queer perspectives in the rhetoric of popular culture (King & West, 2014; King, 2010; Shugart & Waggoner, 2008); gender, law, and citizenship (West, 2013); history and public memory (Morris, 2004; Black & Morris, 2013); activism and agency (Rand, 2014); game studies (Shaw, 2015); interpersonal and relational communication (Elia, 2003; Manning, 2015); and intercultural communication (Eguchi, 2015). Studies in queer theory and communication can help us better understand how we communicate about sexuality, especially those messages that influence and shape (consciously or unconsciously) the ways in which we categorize ourselves and others.

Although all queer theorists share a commitment to challenging normative understandings of sexuality—that is, beliefs related to sexuality that establish a cultural norm—it is nearly impossible to offer a singular description of the term *queer* or provide a single example of how it is used in the theoretical work that happens under the banner of queer theory. Indeed, doing so would go against the anti-essentialist perspective that queer theory embraces, as Sullivan (2003) succinctly illustrates when she calls it "a discipline that refuses to be disciplined" (p. v). Nonetheless, Nealon and Giroux (2012) provide a helpful description of one of the central arguments that some queer scholars make with regard to sexuality, namely, that "there is no 'natural' relation between anatomical equipment and what that equipment is supposed to mean or do in a given context" (p. 186). Similarly, Beemyn and Eliason (1996) observe that queer theory's emphasis is on "the constructedness of sexuality" (p. 5). For example, in many cultures around the world, the perception that there are only two unambiguous genders (male and female) and that men and women only should be involved in romantic or sexual relationships if they are with a member of the opposite sex is widely perceived as common sense, despite the fact that this perception does not accurately describe the reality for those whose identities and sexualities do not fall within such a narrow definition of "normal" (see, for example, Fryer, 2010). Although queer theory resists such normative thinking, its critique goes beyond sex. As Fryer (2010) notes,

> It is also about how we relate to our own bodies and identities and the meanings we attach to them. So the modified body challenges the unadorned one; the transsexual body challenges the unaltered one; and the transgendered identity (that of people who fall into neither transsexual or transvestite categories nor single-gendered ones) challenges the traditional one (p. 5).

Queer theory, in short, collectively challenges the dominant discourses that promote such limiting worldviews at the expense of those who live on the margins of the mainstream.

One prominent example of this kind of scholarship is the work of feminist and queer theorist Judith Butler. In her landmark book *Gender Trouble: Feminism and the Subversion of Identity* (originally published in 1990), Butler (1999) offers a sophisticated critique of what she calls the "heterosexual matrix," a "binary framework for both sex and gender" that is one of many "regulatory fictions that consolidate and naturalize the convergent power regimes of masculine and heterosexist oppression" (p. 44). Throughout this book and in her later work, Butler argues that the restrictive male/female and heterosexual/homosexual binaries at the center of the heterosexual matrix are symbolic ruses or deceptions. She argues that instead of *being* male or female in an essential or biological sense, we *perform* those gender roles in ways that alternately conform to or challenge preexisting cultural codes. For example, the unconscious "pull" to dress in a certain manner or style one's hair in a certain way because that is the "appropriate" thing to do if one is a man or woman is a simple illustration of the gender performances that Butler describes. Her arguments regarding gender performance also extend to sexuality. As Nealon and Giroux (2012) explain, "One is not born a man or woman or a homosexual; one becomes a man or woman or homosexual (becomes recognizable as such) only in the context of performing or not performing certain acts" (p. 188). This theoretical stance has important political implications, as the next section will show.

Marriage Trouble: Queer Theory and Same-Sex Marriage

Queer theorists' commitment to performances that challenge binary arrangements of sex, gender, and sexuality leads them to adopt a critical stance toward same-sex marriage, a position that might, at first, appear to be counterintuitive. Upon closer examination, however, this opposition to the institution of marriage itself is in alignment with queer theory's broader critique of any system that preserves marginalization or oppression. For example, Richardson (2005) argues that "contemporary struggles for 'equality' help to reaffirm the regulatory power of the state by reinforcing the authority of the institutions . . . which confer rights and responsibilities" (p. 532). Brandzel (2005) similarly argues that "same-sex marriage rights merely expand the number of beds that can be 'approved' by the state" while still preserving the primary "mechanism by which the state ensures and reproduces heteronormativity" (p. 195). Few queer theorists capture this stance as succinctly as Warner (1999), who argues that, no matter what form it takes, "marriage sanctifies some couples at the expense of others. It is selective legitimacy" (p. 82).

What are the implications of queer theory for those invested in contemporary social movements such as the movement for same-sex marriage? By entering into dialogue with the state, antagonistically or otherwise, and often for important pragmatic reasons that might include securing health insurance or survivor pension benefits for a loved one, gay and lesbian partners must submit to the very discourses and definitions that limit the social and political power of those whose sexual practices do not conform to the dominant categories of normative, male-female heterosexual partnerships. As Butler (2004) explains,

> on the one hand, living without norms of recognition results in significant suffering and forms of disenfranchisement that confound the very distinctions among psychic, cultural, and material consequences. On the other hand, the demand to be recognized, which is a very powerful political demand, can lead to new and invidious forms of social hierarchy . . . and to new ways of supporting and extending state power (p. 115).

For Butler and other queer theorists, the way out of this pickle is not to avoid social activism or confrontations with the state—although queer theorists generally are critical of social movements whose tactics include persuasive messages that restrict the number of identity categories that individuals can ascribe to—but rather to refrain from "taking a single stand in such debates" (Butler, 2004, p. 129).

This vision of political activism that does not take a singular stand on a given social issue is one that sees struggle as a never-ending process; the very idea of working for a specific end and a specific cause tempts "the violence of foreclosure that stabilizes the field of activism" and limits possibilities for pursuing a livable life (Butler, 2004, p. 108). So, how then does one translate theoretical critiques such as those posed by queer theorists from the page or the classroom to the streets? This continues to be a central question for LGBTQ activists and academics alike. Butler (2004) recognizes this difficulty, and yet, despite the attention she gives to questions of social transformation and same-sex marriage in her work, it often remains unclear how social and political activists might accomplish such interventions. Contrary to what queer theorists might argue, is it possible that the activists who advocated for same-sex marriage in the struggle over Prop. 8 in California participated in a collective intervention that did in fact challenge the heteronormative binary of…? The remainder of this chapter will address this very question.

Fear of a Genderless Society: The Rhetoric of the "Yes On 8" Coalition

Social and political support for Prop. 8 can be traced back to 2004, when then San Francisco mayor Gavin Newsom authorized same-sex marriage in the city. Newsom's actions challenged Proposition 22, a 2000 voter initiative restricting marriage to a man and a woman (Goldberg, 2009). The California Supreme Court ultimately concluded that Proposition 22 was unconstitutional, thus allowing same-sex couples the right to marry under California law (Goldberg, 2009). In response to this ruling, the Protect Marriage coalition formed in 2005 with the goal, "to place a constitutional amendment before voters to define marriage as an institution between a man and a woman" (Hubbell, 2005). The coalition, that included conservative political and social groups such as the California Family Alliance, Focus on the Family, and the Family Research Council, was unable to collect a sufficient number of signatures for such an amendment until three years later. The coalition waged a successful petition campaign in 2008 that generated over one million signatures—well over the 694,354 required by California state law.

Secretary of State Debra Brown issued a press release on June 2, 2008, stating that Prop. 8 was certified to appear on the November 2008 ballot. The ensuing fundraising frenzy generated millions of dollars in donations for both sides. According to Leff (2009), the proponents of the measure (headed by a group called Protect Marriage) received nearly $40 million from various religious and political groups and individual donors. Moreover, it is estimated that a significant portion of that sum (between 50–70%) came from donations made by members of the Church of Jesus Christ of Latter-Day Saints, making the church one of the principal religious organizations contributing to the success of the "Yes on 8" movement (McKinley & Johnson, 2008; Kuruvila, 2008; Moynihan, 2008).

The well-funded campaign in support of Prop. 8 yielded a rich body of persuasive images and messages. Although a number of different conservative groups and churches participated in this campaign, this case study focuses primarily on the discourse of Protect Marriage and the LDS Church. Protect Marriage was the primary umbrella organization that lead the successful conservative effort to pass the measure, and the LDS Church, as mentioned above, played an influential role by motivating its extensive member base to donate time and funds to Protect Marriage.

Although several themes emerge from the rhetoric of the Protect Marriage coalition, perhaps the most striking is the discourse expressing intense fear that same-sex marriage will lead to a society in which the male/female gender binary no longer holds. For example, in the video "Preserving Traditional Marriage" (n.d.) that was originally posted to PreservingMarriage.org, a website maintained by the LDS Church, a woman observed, "This [voting for Prop. 8] is the most important thing that our generation will do because it will determine the structure of our society for the rest of our lives."[1] Even more telling is the LDS Church's (2008) assertion that traditional marriage increases the likelihood that children "will be able to form a clear gender identity, with sexuality closely linked to both love and procreation." By contrast, the Church (2008) explained, "the legalization of same-sex marriage likely will erode the social identity, gender development, and moral character of children." The Church (2008) went on to argue that,

> Strong, stable families, headed by a father and mother, are the anchor of civilized society. When marriage is undermined by gender confusion and by distortions of its God-given meaning, the rising generation of children and youth will find it increasingly difficult to develop their natural identity as a man or a woman. Some will find it more difficult to engage in wholesome courtships, form stable marriages, and raise yet another generation imbued with moral strength and purpose.

Similarly, Protect Marriage's youth-targeted website, iProtectmarriage.com, argued that, "Prop. 8 prevents the slow crumbling of civilization if marriage is redefined" ("What is Prop. 8?," 2008).[2]

We draw attention to two final examples of this theme, one in an interview with two senior LDS Church elders that predates Prop. 8 (but was posted to the Church's website during the debate over the proposition) and another from a video that was archived at PreservingMarriage.org. In an interview

---

1. At the time of this writing, www.preservingmarriage.org redirects to the URL http://www.mormonnewsroom.org/article/the-divine-institution-of-marriage.
2. Although www.iprotectmarriage.com is no longer an active website, UCLA's digital collections archive provides access to a functional archival version of the site at http://digital.library.ucla.edu/websites/2008_993_111/index.htm.

with Elders Dallin H. Oaks and Lance B. Wickman on the topic of same-sex attraction and marriage, Wickman argued,

> Either there is marriage as it is now defined and as defined by the Lord, or there is what could thus be described as genderless marriage. The latter is abhorrent to God, who . . . Himself described what marriage is—between a man and a woman (Church of Jesus Christ of Latter-Day Saints, 2006).

An almost identical statement is offered by one participant in the video titled, "Preserving Traditional Marriage." She states that, "I feel it's important for my children's future. I don't want my children to grow up in a genderless society" (Church of Jesus Christ of Latter-Day Saints, n.d.).

Gender Trouble or Not?

The above case study offers several examples that suggest, at minimum, that the proponents of Prop. 8 believe that same-sex marriage will challenge, if not dismantle altogether, the heterosexual matrix that queer theorists critique. But is this the case? In a 2008 interview at the Barcelona Center for Contemporary Culture, Judith Butler discussed the topic of same-sex marriage. "Of course," she said, "if marriage exists, then homosexual marriage should also exist; marriage should be extended to all couples irrespective of their sexual orientation; if sexual orientation is an impediment, then marriage is discriminatory" (Birulés, 2009). However, Butler also questioned the same-sex marriage movement's end game. "[T]he right to homosexual marriage runs the risk of producing a conservative effect of making marriage an act of normalisation," she explains,

> and thereby presenting other very important forms of intimacy and kinship as abnormal or even pathological. But the question is: politically, what do we do with this? I would say that every campaign in favour of homosexual marriage ought also to be in favour of alternative families, the alternative systems of kinship and personal association. We need a movement that does not win rights for some people at the expense of others. And imagining this movement is not easy (Birulés, 2009).

This critique is an important one, especially in light of the U.S. Supreme Court's 2015 decision that legalized same-sex marriage throughout the country. Although the evidence presented in the preceding case study seems to suggest that the demand for same-sex marriage is more radical than some queer theorists admit, by fighting for the right to marry, gay and lesbian couples ultimately reaffirm the state's authority to recognize the legitimacy of certain relationships (which is, of course, the same authority the state has used historically to discriminate against gays and lesbians). In doing so, the state is empowered as an arbiter in matters dealing with the distribution of resources that accompany a sanctioned marriage and that, many argue, should be made available universally regardless of one's marital status. Queer theorists envision a world in which the state does not have such power of recognition, and some might argue that themes such as the fear of a genderless society only demonstrate, at best, how same-sex marriage challenges conservative attachments to "traditional" gender norms.

Of course, activists who support the legalization of same-sex marriage might point out that, whatever conservative effect the demand for same-sex marriage might have, it needs to be juxtaposed to the long-term goals of the broader LGBTQ movement, to its members' often pressing need for the resources and benefits that come with state-sanctioned marriages, and perhaps more important, to the way same-sex marriage decenters the heteronormative male-female couple that continues to define marriage in many places around the world.

Cott (2002) observes that marriage "is the vehicle through which the apparatus of state can shape the gender order," and that what "we call *gender* relies on and to a great extent derives from the structuring provided by marriage" (p. 3, emphasis in original). Although same-sex marriage may not dismantle the structure of marriage, it does restructure it. Brandzel (2005), for example, has argued that "a questioning of the presumption of heterosexuality in marriage results, albeit fleetingly, in a disruption of the gender/sexuality binary system" (p. 184). Regardless of where one stands on this complex issue, queer theory offers a particularly useful framework for exploring gender, sexuality, and identity, and more important, how human actors communicate about them in our daily lives and relationships.

DISCUSSION QUESTIONS

1. Queer theory is concerned with critiquing and dismantling gender and sexuality binaries, or the idea that gender and sexuality fit into neat categories of male/female and heterosexual/homosexual. Can you think of other binaries that we use to categorize our understandings of daily life? How might you critique or dismantle those binaries?

2. Some scholars believe that style is one of the primary ways in which we engage in performances of gender and sexuality. For example, we often make judgments about individuals' gender or sexuality based entirely on the clothes they wear, their use of makeup, or their nonverbal communication (including tone of voice, posture, and gestures). In what ways do the many facets of our style become avenues for performing gender roles or sexuality?

3. This chapter presented evidence that the "Yes on 8" movement believes that legalizing same-sex marriage will lead to a genderless society. Is this evidence strong enough to suggest that the legalization of same-sex marriage is a social reform that queer theorists should support?

4. Consider another prominent social movement that is concerned with identity and is currently active at the time you read this chapter (you might want to visit the homepage of a popular news website such as npr.org or cnn.com for ideas). What might a queer theorist argue about the goals, strategies, and potential short- and long-term consequences of this movement?

5. In what ways does a queer perspective on gender and sexuality contrast with some of the other theoretical frameworks presented in this book? Which perspective do you find most useful for exploring your own identity, and why?

References

Beemyn, B., & Eliason, M. (Eds.). (1996). *Queer studies: A lesbian, gay, bisexual, and transgender anthology*. New York: New York University Press.

Birulés, F. (2009, May 16). Interview with Judith Butler: Gender is extramoral. Retrieved from http://mrzine.monthlyreview.org/butler160509.html.

Black, J. E., & Morris, C. E. (Eds.). (2013). *An archive of hope: Harvey Milk's speeches and writings*. Berkeley: University of California Press.

Brandzel, A. L. (2005). Queering citizenship?: Same-sex marriage and the state. *GLQ, 11*(2), 171–204.

Butler, J. (1999). *Gender trouble: Feminism and the subversion of identity*. New York: Routledge.

Butler, J. (2004). *Undoing gender*. New York: Routledge.

California Secretary of State. (2009, April 10). Statement of vote: 2008 general election. Retrieved from http://www.sos.ca.gov/elections/sov/2008_general/contents.htm.

Church of Jesus Christ of Latter-Day Saints. (n.d.). Preserving traditional marriage. Retrieved from http://www.preservingmarriage.org.

Church of Jesus Christ of Latter-Day Saints. (2006). Same-sex attraction. Retrieved from http://newsroom.lds.org/ldsnewsroom/eng/public-issues/same-gender-attraction.

Church of Jesus Christ of Latter-Day Saints. (2008, August 13). The divine institution of marriage. Retrieved from http://newsroom.lds.org/ldsnewsroom/eng/commentary/the-divine-institution-of-marriage.

Cott, N. F. (2002). *Public vows: A history of marriage and the nation*. Cambridge, MA: Harvard University Press.

Eguchi, S. (2015). Queer intercultural relationality: An autoethnography of Asian–Black (dis)connections in White gay America. *Journal of International & Intercultural Communication, 8*, 27–43.

Elia, J. P. (2003). Queering relationships: Toward a paradigmatic shift. In G. A. Yep, K. E. Lovaas, & J. P. Elia (Eds.), *Queer theory and communication: From disciplining queers to queering the discipline(s)* (pp. 61–86). Binghamton, NY: Harrington Park Press.

Fryer, D. R. (2010). *Thinking queerly: Race, sex, gender, and the ethics of identity*. Boulder, CO: Paradigm.

Goldberg, N. (2009, March 1). Gay marriage on trial. *Los Angeles Times*. Retrieved from http://articles.latimes.com/2009/mar/01/opinion/oe-goldberg1.

Grindstaff, D. (2003). Queering marriage: An ideographic interrogation of heteronormative subjectivity. *Journal of Homosexuality, 45*(2/3/4), 257–275.

Hollingsworth v. Perry, No. 12-144 (U.S. 2013).

Hubbell, J. M. (2005, April 28). Coalition seeks male-female marriage definition. *SFGate.com.* Retrieved from http://www.sfgate.com/cgi-bin/article.cgi?file=/c/a/2005/04/28/BAGM6CGHTT1.DTL.

In re. Marriage Cases, 43 Cal.4th 757 (2008).

King, C. S. (2010). Un-queering horror: *Hellbent* and the policing of the "gay slasher." *Western Journal of Communication, 74,* 249–268.

King, C. S., & West, I. (2014). This could be the place: Queer acceptance in *Lars and the Real Girl. QED: A Journal in GLBTQ Worldmaking, 1,* 59–84.

Kuruvila, M. (2008, October 27). Mormons face flak for backing Prop. 8. *SFGate.com.* Retrieved from http://www.sfgate.com/bayarea/article/Mormons-face-flak-for-backing-Prop-8-3264077.php.

Leff, L. (2009, February 3). Donors pumped $83M to Calif. gay marriage campaign. *Associated Press.* Retrieved from http://www.lexis-nexis.com/.

Lovaas, K. E., Elia, J. P., & Yep, G. A. (2006). Shifting ground(s): Surveying the contested terrain of LGBT studies and queer theory. *Journal of Homosexuality, 52*(1/2), 1–18.

Manning, J. (2015). Paradoxes of (im)purity: Affirming heteronormativity and queering heterosexuality in family discourses of purity pledges. *Women's Studies in Communication, 38,* 99–117.

McKinley, J., & Johnson, K. (2008, November 14). Mormons tipped scale in ban on gay marriage. *New York Times.* Retrieved from http://www.nytimes.com/2008/11/15/us/politics/15marriage.html.

Morris, C. E. (2004). My old Kentucky homo: Lincoln and the politics of queer public memory. In K. R. Phillips (Ed.), *Framing public memory* (pp. 89–114). Tuscaloosa: University of Alabama Press.

Moynihan, C. (2008, November 13). At Mormon temple, a protest over Prop. 8. *New York Times.* Retrieved from http://cityroom.blogs.nytimes.com/2008/11/13/at-mormon-temple-thousands-protest-prop-8/?scp=1&sq=lds%20church%20proposition%208%20donations&st=cse.

Nealon, J., & Giroux, S. S. (2012). *The theory toolbox: Critical concepts for the humanities, arts, & social sciences* (2nd ed.). Lanham, MD: Rowman & Littlefield.

Rand, E. J. (2014). *Reclaiming queer: Activist and academic rhetorics of resistance.* Tuscaloosa: University of Alabama Press.

Richardson, D. (2005). Desiring sameness?: The rise of a neoliberal politics of normalisation. *Antipode, 37*(3), 515–535.

Seidman, S. (2001). From identity to queer politics: Shifts in normative heterosexuality and the meaning of citizenship. *Citizenship Studies, 5*(3), 321–328.

Shaw, A. (2015). Circles, charmed and Magic: Queering game studies. *QED: A Journal in GLBTQ Worldmaking, 2,* 64–97.

Shugart, H. A., & Waggoner, C. E. (2008). *Making camp: Rhetorics of transgression in U.S. popular culture.* Tuscaloosa: University of Alabama Press.

Sullivan, N. (2003). *A critical introduction to queer theory.* New York: New York University Press.

Warner, M. (1999). *The trouble with normal: Sex, politics, and the ethics of queer life.* Cambridge: Harvard University Press.

West, I. (2013). *Transforming citizenships: Transgender articulations of the law.* New York: New York University Press.

What is Prop. 8? (2008). Retrieved from http://iprotectmarriage.com/prop-8/.

Yep, G., Lovaas, K. E., & Elia, J. P. (Eds.). (2014). *Queer theory and communication: From disciplining queers to queering the discipline(s).* New York: Routledge.

Zita, J. N. (1994). Gay and lesbian studies: Yet another unhappy marriage. In L. Garber (Ed.), *Tilting the tower: Lesbians, teaching, queer subjects* (pp. 258–276). New York: Routledge.

CHAPTER 19

Queer Foreignness and Intersectionality: A Case for "Doing" Sexual and Cultural Mixing and Mingling across Borders

Shinsuke Eguchi

KEY TERMS

Queer intercultural communication
Foreignness
Intersectionality

Borders
Globalization/Transnationalism

ABSTRACT

Through my personal account, I examine how my embodied performance of sexual and cultural differences is repeatedly marked as *foreign* within and beyond the U.S.-Japan transnational borders. I am interested in paying attention to my G.A.M. (a.k.a., Gay Asian Male) identity modes of *foreignness* as a theoretical lens to show complex, contradictory, and dynamic processes and practices of intersectionality. With this line of thinking, I hope to write that the communication of sexuality is an always already cultural phenomenon in the intersected webs of socio-historical, political, and economic contexts.

> *Borders are set up to define the places that are safe and unsafe, to distinguish us from them. A border is a dividing line, a narrow strip along a steep edge* (Anzaldúa, 2012, p. 25).

It has taken almost 15 years for me to *enjoy* my privilege to go back and forth between Japan and the U.S. During this time, I have questioned the extent to which I identify with my Japanese culture and my American culture, and if I am becoming Americanized. However, I recently began to realize that I am *neither* becoming American(ized) *nor* remaining Japanese. I have been always already living with queer (or non-heteronormative) modes of *foreignness* within the context of intersectionality. By intersectionality, I mean how multiple identities such as sexuality, race, class, gender, and other differences simultaneously play into my everyday intercultural interactions (Muñoz, 1999). In other words, I assert that intersectionality refers to the ways our many social identities intersect in the historical and ideological contexts (Eguchi, 2015). My everyday performances of intersectionality, include but are not limited to Asian, Japanese citizen, U.S. permanent resident, gay (sexual identity), queer (political identity), effeminate/flamboyant, and cisgendered male, constantly *foreignize* (or differentiate) my embodiment of culture(s). I am *forever foreign* in a queer intercultural borderland in-between and in-betwixt the U.S. and Japan.

Through this personal account, I unpack taken-for-granted ideas and social relations related to the communication of sexuality and culture in this essay. Specifically, I examine how my embodied performance of sexual and cultural differences is repeatedly marked as *foreign* within and beyond the U.S.-Japan transnational borders. I am interested in paying attention to my G.A.M. (a.k.a., Gay Asian Male) identity modes of *foreignness* as a theoretical lens to show complex, contradictory, and dynamic processes and practices of intersectionality. With this line of thinking, I hope to write that the communication of sexuality is an always already cultural phenomenon in the intersected webs of socio-historical, political, and economic contexts.

Expanding Queer Intercultural Communication Studies

In the discipline of communication, there has been a disconnection between the study of sexuality and communication and the study of intercultural communication. Much of the scholarship on sexuality and communication overlooked the effects of culture on sexuality; and, simultaneously, the intercultural communication scholarship ignored the critical and crucial roles of sexuality and sex/gender in processes and practices of cultural identity. Over the last decade, however, a number of communication scholars put extensive efforts to create a forum for examining simultaneous functions of sexuality, sex/gender, and culture.

For example, Yep, Lovaas, and Elia (2003) emphasized that sexual identities are "multiple, unstable, and fluid social constructions intersecting with race, class, and gender, among others" (p. 4). Despite their theoretical emphasis, a number of scholars (e.g., Eguchi, Calafell, & Files-Thompson, 2014; Johnson, 2001; McCune, 2008) have critiqued that most communication scholarships on sexuality do not pay careful attentions to how the complex and fluid intersections of race, gender, class, and other identity markers produce sexual and cultural differences among LGBTQ (lesbian-gay-bisexual-transgender-queer) people. Additionally, Lee (2003) raised a following concern: "sexual minorities who are not white, male, and affluent remain relatively invisible in their different localities" (p. 160). Moreover, Chávez (2013) maintained that sexuality and communication scholars must examine concerns and needs outside of U.S. American, white, middle-class genders and sexualities.

With this line of thinking, Chávez (2013) has added the queer to the intercultural to propose a field of study called *Queer Intercultural Communication*. She called into question connections among queer identities, performances, politics, and globalization. More specifically, she called for examining particularized and nuanced meanings of non-heteronormative genders and sexualities from non-western/white/U.S. American gazes. To interrogate complex and dynamic natures of queer intercultural communication, Yep (2013) further proposed the concept of think intersectionalities as a mode of analysis. He defined that think intersectionalities are:

> complex particularities of individuals' lives and identities associated with their race, class, gender, sexuality, and national locations by understanding their history and personhood in concrete time and space, and the interplay between individual subjectivity, personal agency, systemic arrangements, and structural forces. (Yep, 2010, p. 173)

With this concept of think intersectionalities, I move to unpack my modes of *foreignness* as a way to show my non-western/white/U.S. American processes and practices of sexuality with particular attention to race, class, gender, and the body. Next, I offer four scenarios that identify how simultaneous functions of my intersectionality produce nuanced, ambivalent, and ambiguous meanings of who I am and what I do both in the U.S. and Japan.

Scenario 1: A TSA Office in a U.S. Southwestern City

As a U.S. permanent resident (a.k.a, green card) holder, I was excited to walk into a designated office in a Southwestern city to apply for a TSA (Transportation Security Administration) pre-check program in April 2014. It allows the registered passengers to go through the least security check at the airport. While waiting, I saw that the white female agent called other applicants by their first names for their registrations. Then, she looked at the waiting list for a bit long and stared at me. So, I realized it must be my turn. I asked her, "Are you looking for Shinsuke?" She responded, "Yes. I couldn't pronounce your name. How do you say it?" As I taught her how to pronounce my first name, we sat down in her office. I handed her my red-colored Japanese passport along with my green card. She made a strange face. Then, she said, "You are not eligible. This is only for Americans." I replied, "Well, according to your website, the U.S. permanent residents/green card holders are eligible. I was even able to pre-register myself for this meeting online. That is why I have an appointment with you." She replied, "Well, let's try and see if the system allows you to register." Then, *of course*, the system allowed her to register my case to the TSA pre-check program. In the process of registering, the agent began to talk about her traveling experience to Hong Kong while she was in the U.S. military. Although I am not from Hong Kong, I assumed that she was trying to relate to me over something about my "Asian" identity to cover up her lack of knowledge about the TSA pre-check program. Then, she inquired about my occupation. As I mentioned that I teach in the college, she responded, "Are you teaching Math or Language?" I said, "Actually, I teach communication and sexuality." She said, "ha," looking so, so confused. Later, as I was leaving the office, she said, "By the way, I love your purse."

This scenario of a queer intercultural encounter mirrors how I am everyday incorporated into the historical racialization and foreignization of Asian/Americans in the U.S. As Nakayama (2012) and Ono (2005) critiqued, people of Asian descent have been historically represented as *foreigners* regardless of their locations of origin and/or family citizenship status. Said (1979) reinforced that the implication of Asia as *Orient* mirror the erasure of differences among Asian cultures, ideas, and people. Asians are socio-culturally, ethnically, linguistically, and politically homogenized as one racial group. This separates Asian/Americans from their full belonging to the U.S. nation-state in which whiteness is a normative U.S. American membership. In this context, my body is a clear indication of Asia as the *Orient*. That easily ignores and erases my "living in queer intercultural borderland." However, I actually finished my undergraduate and graduate educations and then obtained my current employment in the U.S. Quite honestly, I think I have been here long enough. Yet, my *in-between-ness* is simply and essentially translated as *foreign*. Therefore, I can never say that I can become an *American* no matter how long I have been here.

Scenario 2: My Interactions with Gay/Bisexual/Queer Men in the U.S.

At the same time, I recognize that I have adapted the U.S. Americanization of G.A.M. identity over the years. As Sekimoto (2014) argued, "To be Americanized means to be racialized, to be incorporated into the very fabric of racial relations in the United States" (p. 393). To expand this line of thinking, by the U.S. Americanization, I mean that I repeatedly imitate, adapt, and perform who I am and what I do according to the racialized, gendered, sexualized, and foreignized framing of a gay Asian man as feminine and sexually submissive. So, I can pass through the socio-historical context of racial relations in the U.S.

One day in July 2015, for example, I met an African American man at a bar in a Southwestern city. He was in his early 40s, 5' 11" tall, and about 200 pounds who appeared to be masculine. He started a conversation with me by saying, "Where are you from?" As I assumed that he probably meant which foreign country I am from, I responded, "I am from Japan." He immediately said, "Oh, nice. I used to be based in one of the military bases in Japan. I enjoyed being in Japan." Then, we began to get to know each other. Shortly after I finished my first drink, he mentioned that "men in Japan are so feminine. From an American perspective, their fashion styles are kind of like women." I did not want to "lecture" him when I was not on campus. So,

I said, "Oh okay," and moved to order my second drink. Shortly after I got my drink, he started to question me, "What kind of guys do you like?" So, I answered the question without answering the question by saying, "Well, you can tell me your preference first." He said to me, "I am mostly into a guy like you. Soft, feminine, and exotic. Someone like me is a turnoff."

In this communicative moment, I recall that I have always already received the comment, "*you are so feminine, soft, and exotic,*" from gay/bisexual/ queer men on numerous occasions since I first moved to the U.S. in 2001. As Han (2006) argued, "Much like the way that women are 'rewarded' for playing the feminine role, gay Asian men are 'rewarded' by the dominant [the western/U.S. American] gay community for performing their pre-scribed gender roles" (p. 17). With this cultural expectation of gay Asian male-femininity, others' reactions to my body rhetorically implicate what Lim (2014) observed, that "Asian boy is a subcultural category referencing the racialized fetishes of an older white male for the diminutive and effem-inized Asian male" (p. 27). Given that the beauty standard among gay men normally centers on white masculinity and youthfulness, I struggled with the second-class citizenship status associated with the mainstream framing of gay Asian/American men (Eguchi, 2011). To "escape" from the racial-ized struggle, I have shifted to situate myself around men of color, particu-larly African American men, as I feel that I am no longer a second-class citizen in such queer intercultural relationality (Eguchi, 2015). My affect was directed of our shared experiences as *non-white others* in mainstream gay communities. Although my feminine positionality never disappeared from the background of such interactions, I could avoid myself from be-coming and being a racialized fetish of an older white male.

However, I reflect that my gravitation toward men of color is also my es-cape from my intercultural encounters with American-born Asian gay/ bisexual/queer men who look like me. My interactions with them have been an ironic reminder that I am actually an *authentic foreigner*. For ex-ample, I remember that my American-born gay Vietnamese roommate often helped me to pronounce certain words and understand convoluted American idioms when I lived in San Francisco during my undergraduate studies. Although I appreciated his help, I was constantly reminded that I would never be able to speak English like an Asian American because I was not born and raised here. Quite honestly, I could not neutralize my foreign accent no matter how much I tried. Still, my inability to speak English like an Asian American was a clear indication of my foreignness. I learned that I could never be an American. I am always going to feel *foreign*. Therefore, I have gravitated toward other men of color because my race/ethnicity is far more significant than my linguistic ability in such color-to-color relations. In these intercultural spaces, I felt that I could imitate the stereotypical scripts of "gaysian [gay Asian] fabulosity" (Lim, 2014, p. xiii)—Asian American versions of gay fashion, beauty, and lifestyle—as I was temporarily able to *forget* my foreignness.

Scenario 3: Shopping in Tokyo, Japan

Simultaneously, I assert that my physical reentries to Japan have become a contested and contradictory zone of paradox in which I must shift to say, "I am not Japanese enough!" As Hao (2012) suggested, "each returnee is unique in how she or he understands home spaces and what these spaces mean—culturally, socially, and politically" (p. 84). I see my own *failure* to perform the Japanese social conformity every time I reenter to Japan.

For example, I was shopping in the Tokyo metropolitan area by myself one day in December 2012. Buying clothes is always on the top of my list when I return to Japan. I enjoy that the standard Japanese clothing sizes are a good fit for my G.A.M. body—5' 7" and 130 lbs. I buy medium-size clothes in Japan whereas I buy extra small/small-size clothes in the U.S. So, I tried on a number of coats, jackets, and pants in the designer's store for about a half hour. The male sales-associate and I were making small talk. As he gave me the last pants I was going to try on, he suddenly asked, "Do you live abroad?" I instantly knew he meant abroad by the west. But, I awkwardly responded, "yes…," as I did not expect the question. So, I quickly closed the door of the dressing room and then moved to try on the pants. As I was making the payment, I questioned him about why he asked me if I lived abroad. He explained, "You sound like you live in the U.S. or somewhere in the west. Especially, your pronunciations of certain words and phrases do not sound Japanese."

In this moment, I recognized how long I had been physically away from Japan. Apparently, it is inevitable that my speaking English affected my practices of speaking Japanese. As Kinefuchi (2008) asserted, "The tradition has fostered the view that Japanese society and Japanese identity are ethnically homogeneous, naturally unified, constant phenomena" (p. 96).

In this historical and ideological context, the sales-associate differentiated me even though I was born and raised in Japan. Because of my transnational experience, the sales-associate read my performance of Japanese national cultural identity as *questionable*. This is what Goodman (2012) called henna-nihonjin (変な日本人, literally the strange Japanese) returning from living abroad and *arrogantly* displaying foreignness through their verbal and non-verbal communication (e.g., voice, touch, distance, and body language). At the same time, I argue that the meaning of Japanese society and Japanese identity cannot be that particularized today as I believe that people are increasingly aware of transnationalism. By transnationalism, I mean that global movements of people, ideas, and commodities take place across multiple nation-state borders. Given this condition, I wondered if the sales-associate wanted to verbally solicit if I am gay or not through his awkward inquiry on my foreign resident status. Actually, it is possible that he might have used the culturally specific nuance of Japanese language, thought, and behavior to hint about his openness and/or curiosity about my non-heteronormative sexuality.

My speculation about his WHAT (interest or inquiry into my transnationalism) as I observed that the public discussion of same-sex desire generally remains a Japanese social taboo (Harada, 2001). The contemporary constructions of gay lifestyle are perceived as *western/U.S. American/foreign* materials although there have been historically local practices of same-sex sexual desire, attraction, and behavior in Japan (Suganuma, 2012). For example, a same-sex marriage is considered a western/U.S. American/foreign phenomenon. Also, a rainbow flag symbolizing LGBTQ equality is a western/U.S. American/foreign icon. In this regard, the western/U.S. American/foreign modernity of gay culture including fashion, beauty, and lifestyle is visible, showy, and out. However, this visibility generates the image of Japanese gender/sex and sexuality systems as *being behind* (McLelland, 2000). In this cultural context, I wonder if my G.A.M. performances of intersectionality might have translated as being a part of the *advanced* and *progressive* (gay) America as I interacted with the sales associate. Given my embodiment of G.A.M. identity, I might have appeared to reject the *backward* and *static* (queer) Japan. Thus, I wonder if the sales associate ambiguously communicated his openness and/or curiosity about my non-heteronormative sexuality.

Scenario 4: A Gay Bar in Tokyo, Japan

Furthermore, I assert that the ideological tensions between the *advanced* and *progressive* (gay) America and the *backward* and *static* (queer) Japan characterize how we talk about gay life in Japan. For example, I arrived at Tokyo's queer district Shinjuku Nichoume (新宿二丁目) around 6pm one day in June 2014. Since I was going to meet my friend Jay for dinner at 7pm, I stopped by one of the gay bars called *Dragon* to kill some time. As I sat down at the bar, a hip-hop dancer-looking host in his early 40s called Masa took my drink order. A few minutes after I got my drink, Masa began to speak with me by saying, "Are you visiting here?" While I was not sure what he meant by visiting, I replied to him that "yes, I am home for a short term." Then he asked, "Where do you live?" I said, "I now live in Albuquerque, New Mexico. But, I used to live in DC, New York, and San Francisco. I miss big gay cities though." Masa questioned, "I knew you lived abroad. My guess is right. How long have you been in the States?" I replied, "Since 2001." Then Masa began to talk about his living experience as a dancer in New York in the late 1990s. He apparently had a great time living in New York because he could always meet many different kinds of "openly out" gay men there. He continued that gay life in Japan is *not vibrant* as much as one in the U.S. because many remain disidentifying with same-sex sexual communities. They keep their non-heteronormative sexualities private. So, I said, "Well, a gay community in Albuquerque is small too." He immediately responded "but at least you can easily visit big gay cities like Los Angeles and San Francisco."

In this communicative moment, I re-realized why I have not permanently returned to Japan despite of currently living in a much smaller city in the Southwest. As I openly want to enjoy my adaptation of G.A.M. identity, I continue to stay in the U.S. For example, the idea of working in Japan was least desirable when I was about to finish my undergraduate in San Francisco in 2005. I observed a couple of my friends tried to train themselves to re/adapt elements of Japanese social conformity. Job candidates are expected to show how they perform unwritten and unspoken scripts of Japanese social conformity. As Gannon (2001) maintained, "To the Japanese, social conformity is not a sign of weakness but of strong inner self-control" (p. 42). Still, my observation of my friends reminded me of my high-school experience. I recalled how the high-school teachers had disciplined me when I had voiced my ideas and opinions. They told me, "You need to learn how to play along with others." They had wanted me to be *the same* as other students who obey superiors. However, I was never the same as others. I was *an effeminate/flamboyant gay boy* who disrupted the heteronormativity. This memory drives my desire to stay in the U.S. Because I do not live in Japan now, I get to be open and frank about my ideas and opinions as I socialize with my family and friends in Japan. They expect me to be direct and straightforward like *U.S. Americans* who are stereotyped in such manners. Moreover, effeminate queer men are always already represented as "bitchy," "frank," and "direct" in Japanese media and popular culture (Maree, 2008). In this condition, I recognize my irony that I am actually comfortable with my foreignness as I can temporarily excuse myself from my failure to conform to be Japanese. With my foreignness, I feel that I can be who I am in Japan.

A few minutes after Masa pointed out my ability to travel to big gay cities in the U.S., I decided to text my friend Jay to come to the Dragon to meet me first. Shortly after I texted him, Jay showed up to the bar and sat next to me. Jay is my black/African American friend in his early 30s who has been living in Japan for more than five years. After he ordered his drink, we began to catch up in English. Then, Masa interjected into our conversation and asked me, "What do you do?" I replied, "I teach at college." He continued, "Are you out at work?" I instantly replied, "Of course. Don't I look so gay?" Jay laughed at my comment. Then, he switched to Japanese and said, "Well, I do not talk about my sexuality at work here in Japan. Most Japanese gays whom I meet here [in the queer district] also told me that they do not talk about their sexualities at work either." Masa immediately said, "I think it is generally difficult for dousei-aisha (同性愛者, literarily the same-sex lovers) to come out at work. For those who want to come out tend to work in entertainment or night-life business."

In this communicative moment, I was again reminded of how privileged I am. I am always already *out* professionally. Although there remain historical prejudices against women, LGBTQ people, racial/ethnic minorities in the U.S. academy, I am simultaneously positioned in an academic space where I can use my knowledge as a way to identify with, speak about, and/or critique against possible prejudices (such as racism, hetero/sexism, homophobia, and/or xenophobia) imposed on my G.A.M. body. This paradoxical tension produces my on-going desire to live in the U.S. even though there have been many racialized, gendered, sexualized, and foreignized moments where I felt I should return to Japan. However, I am not saying that same-sex lovers cannot be *out* in Japan as some friends of mine are out at work. Given my living experience in Japan, at the same time, I speculate that there would be strong resistance against me because I would always already politicize and historicize cultural issues around same-sex sexual desire, attraction, and behavior in Japan. How I critique the system that marginalizes non-heteronormative sexual people would be construed as a loud and showy logo of disruption of Japanese social conformity. Thus, I am utilizing my privilege to stay in the U.S. and to distance myself from *backward* and *static* (queer) Japan. Therefore, I acknowledge that my foreignness is an indicator of my privileged proximity to the *advanced* and *progressive* (gay) America.

Concluding Remark(s)

In this essay, I have paid attention to my performative modes of intersectionality in the contexts of transnationalism. By focusing on my queer foreignness as a theoretical lens, I have attempted to show how socio-historical and contextual forces of power affect everyday communication processes and practices of sexual and cultural mixing and mingling. Particularly, I argue that my intersectionality explicates an on-going, complex, and dynamic interplay of multiple and messy tensions in-between and in-betwixt the U.S. and Japan. My practice of belonging has never been a linear and simple experience. From this personal account, I would like to end this essay by reiterating that the communication of sexuality is an always already cultural phenomenon in the intersected webs of socio-historical, political, and economic contexts.

DISCUSSION QUESTIONS

1. The concept of intersectionality has become popular among scholars who work on issues of sexuality and gender/sex. Why is the concept of intersectionality so important? How does the concept of intersectionality allow us to think about sexuality and gender/sex differently?

2. Eguchi has talked about the emergence of queer intercultural communication studies in this essay. What are queer intercultural communication studies? Why is this field necessary?

3. Eguchi has utilized the theoretical concept of foreignness as a way to critique the construction of G.A.M. identity. What may have driven him to pay attention to foreignness? What are the possibilities and limitations of foreignness to critique our views on sexuality and gender/sex?

4. Eguchi has discussed that "gay" identity markers symbolize the "western" thoughts. What are your assumptions about "gay" men? Where are they coming from? How do you challenge your own assumptions?

5. Eguchi has suggested that communication of sexuality is an always already cultural phenomenon in the intersected webs of socio-historical, political, and economic contexts. How do you agree or disagree with this statement? Share your everyday observations to discuss your reactions.

References

Anzaldúa, G. (2012). *Borderlands/la frontera: The new mestizo* (4th ed.). San Francisco: Aunt Lute Books.

Chávez, K. R. (2013). Pushing boundaries: Queer intercultural communication. *Journal of International and Intercultural Communication, 6*(2), 83–95.

Eguchi, S. (2011). Cross-national identity transformation: Becoming a gay 'Asian American' man. *Sexuality & Culture, 15*(1), 19–40.

Eguchi, S. (2015). Queer intercultural relationality: An autoethnography of Asian-Black (dis)connections in White gay America. *Journal of International and Intercultural Communication, 8*(1), 27–43.

Eguchi, S., Calafell, B. M., & Files-Thompson, N. (2014). Intersectionality and quare theory: Fantasizing African American men's same-sex relationships in *Noah's Arc: Jumping the Broom. Communication, Culture, & Critique, 7* (3), 371–389.

Gannon, M.J. (2001). *Understanding global cultures: Metaphorical journeys through 23 nations* (2nd ed.). Thousand Oaks, CA: Sage.

Goodman, R. (2012). From pitiful to privilege? The fifty-year story of the changing perception and status of Japan's returnee children (Kikokushijo). In R. Goodman, Y. Imoto, T. Toivonen (Eds.), *A sociology of Japanese youth* (pp. 30–52). New York: Routledge.

Harada, M. (2001). Japanese male gay and bisexual identity. *Journal of Homosexuality, 42*(2), 77–100.

Han, C-S. (2006). Geisha of a different kind: Gay Asian men and the gendering of sexual identity. *Sexuality & Culture, 10*(3), 3–28.

Hao, R. (2012). Cultural reentry: A critical review of intercultural communication research. In N. Bardhan & M. O. Orbe (Eds.), *Identity research and communication* (pp. 71–85). Lanham, MD: Lexington Books.

Kinefichi, E. (2008). From authenticity to geographies: Unpacking Japaneseness in the construction of Nikkeijin identity. *International and Intercultural Communication Annual, 31*, 91–118.

Johnson, E.P. (2001). "Quare" studies or (almost) everything I know about queer studies I learned from my grandmother. *Text and Performance Quarterly, 21*(1), 1–25.

Lee, W. (2003). Kuaering queer theory: My autocritography and a race-conscious womanist, transnational turn. In G.A. Yep, K.E. Lovaas, & J.P. Elia (Eds.), *Queer theory and communication: From disciplining queers to queering the discipline(s)* (pp. 147–170). Binghamton, NY: Harrington Park Press.

Lim, E-G. (2014). *Brown boys and rice queens: Spellbinding performances in the Asias.* New York: New York University Press.

Maree, C. (2008). Grrrl-queens: One-kotoba and the negotiation of heterosexist gender language norms and lesbo(homo)phobic stereotypes in Japan. In F. Martin, P. A. Jackson, M. McLelland, & A. Yue (Eds.), *Asiapacific queer: Rethinking genders and sexualities* (pp. 67–84). Urbana and Chicago, IL: University of Illinois Press.

McCune Jr., J. Q. (2008). "Out" in the club: The down low, hip-hop, and the architexture of Black masculinity. *Text and Performance Quarterly, 28* (3), 298–314.

McLelland, M. J. (2000). *Male homosexuality in modern Japan: Cultural myths and social realities.* New York: Routledge.

Muñoz, J.E. (1999). *Disidentifications: Queers of color and the performance of politics.* Minneapolis: University of Minnesota Press.

Nakayama, T. K. (2012). Dis/orienting identities: Asian Americans, history, and intercultural communication. In A. Gonzalez, M. Houston, & V. Chen (Eds.), *Our voices: Essays in culture, essay, and communication* (5th ed., pp. 20–25). New York: Oxford University Press.

Ono, K. A. (2005). From nationalism to migrancy: The politics of Asian American transnationalism. *Communication Law Review, 5*(1), 1–17.

Said, E. W. (1979). *Orientalism*. New York: Vintage Books.

Sekimoto, S. (2014). Transnational Asia: Dis/orienting identity in the globalized world. *Communication Quarterly, 62*(4), 381–398.

Suganuma, K. (2012). *Contact moments: The politics of intercultural desire in Japanese male-queer cultures*. Hong Kong: Hong Kong University Press.

Yep, G.A. (2010). Toward the de-subjugation of racially marked knowledges in communication. *Southern Communication Journal*, 75(2), 171–175.

Yep, G. A. (2013). Queering/quaring/kauering/crippin'/transing "other bodies" in intercultural communication. *Journal of International and Intercultural Communication, 6*(2), 118–126.

Yep, G.A., Lovaas, K.E., & Elia, J.P. (2003). Introduction: Queering communication: Starting the conversation. In G.A. Yep, K.E. Lovaas, & J.P. Elia (Eds.), *Queer theory and communication: From disciplining queers to queering the discipline(s)* (pp. 1–10). Binghamton, NY: Harrington Park Press.

CHAPTER 20

"You Are on Your Own": Magnifying Co-Cultural LGB/TQ Microaggressions in the Workplace

Tim McKenna-Buchanan & Sara Baker

KEY TERMS

Sexual identity management
Microaggressions

Co-cultural theory
LGB/TQ

ABSTRACT

Although organizations are becoming more attuned to the needs of their lesbian, gay, bisexual, trans (transgender), and queer (LGB/TQ) employees, workplace policies and practices can still discriminate against someone based on their sexuality. In this chapter, we discuss how LGB/TQ-based microaggressions are communicated in the workplace as a form of sexuality-specific discrimination. We focus on exploring four of these microaggressions (endorsement, heterosexism, exoticization, and denial) through the use of vignettes that describe composite accounts compiled from interviews with LGB/TQ working adults. Woven between each vignette are research-driven conversations emphasizing the pervasiveness of heteronormativity in organizational life; the (in)visible nature of sexual identity; and the basics of co-cultural theory. Our goal is to shine a light on how these microaggressions communicatively cultivate sexuality-specific discrimination in the workplace. We hope that this chapter increases awareness regarding organizational policies and practices—or lack thereof—that ostracize LGB/TQ employees.

I wish I would have known that truly there are no real protections for you. You are on your own. There may be laws and policies in place, but you know what? When it comes down to it, they don't count and you're on your own as far as how… you can't count on human resources and you can't count on other people to stop the harassment.

– Joe, a former airline employee

Joe's experiences at work left him feeling alone, on his own, and without the support from his organization and coworkers that he thought were in place. Whereas other social identities (e.g., sex, race, religion) are federally protected through the Civil Rights Act of 1964 and through the Equal Employment Opportunity Commission (EEOC, 2013), sexual orientation and gender identity do not generally benefit from such protections. Although the EEOC has, since 2012, interpreted anti-trans discrimination under the protected category of sex, lesbian, gay, bisexual, trans, and queer (LGB/TQ) employment discrimination is still legal in 29 states based on sexual orientation and in 34 states based on gender identity (HRC, Resources-Workplace, 2013). In other words, someone can legally be fired or discriminated against in the workplace due to their sexuality. For example, Catholic high school teacher Carla Hale was fired from her job in Ohio after her employer received an anonymous letter outing her as a lesbian after Hale's mother's obituary appeared in the town paper mentioning her partner (Brydum, 2013). And the General Social Survey (2008) reported that 42% of LGB individuals (some who were out at work, some who were not) had, at some point, experienced at least one form of employment discrimination based on their sexual orientation, with 27% reporting sexuality-based discrimination within the past five years (Gates, 2010).

Microaggressions are a subtle form of workplace discrimination that targets LGB/TQ employees. These messages are communicated through microassaults (i.e., calling someone a "fag" or "homo"), microinsults (i.e., telling an LGB/TQ person that they don't "act or look gay"), and micro-invalidations (i.e., labeling an LGB/TQ person as being "overly sensitive" or accusing them of pushing a "gay agenda") (Nadal, Issa, Leon, Meterko, Wideman, & Wong, 2011).[1] In this chapter, we examine how four LGB/TQ-based microaggressions (endorsement, heterosexism, exoticization, and denial) are communicated in the workplace. Below, we provide a series of vignettes that demonstrate how each microaggression is communicated. These stories are composites gathered from interviews with LGB/TQ working adults. Taken as a whole, the goal of this chapter is to increase awareness as to how sexuality-specific discrimination can be embedded in everyday workplace policies and practices.

Vignette 1: Endorsement

It was a warm spring day, one of the first of the year, and so Joan and Jay decided to take their lunch hour outside. Since joining Digi-Analytics, a marketing research firm, the two had been inseparable. They had bonded over their obsessions with cooking competitions and trashy TV. They came out at work together and supported each other through the process. Joan describes their being out at work as "we aren't flying a rainbow flag or anything, but we aren't hiding it either."

Now, as she unpacked her lunch, Joan kicked off her heels. "It's so nice to take these off," she said, rubbing her sore toes.

"Oh, yeah?" Jay said, looking over. "Trust me, these loafers aren't much better." He glanced over at his shoes that had been discarded as well.

"To be honest," Joan said. "I am not really into this whole professional dress thing." She gestured to her pencil skirt, button-up blouse, and suit jacket. "On the weekends you wouldn't catch me in heels or even a skirt. I'm a T-shirt and jeans kind of person. Oh, and I definitely wouldn't put on all this makeup."

---

1. There are seven categories of LGB/TQ-based microaggression: a) use of heterosexist or transphobic terminology, b) endorsement of heteronormative or gender normative cultures/behaviors, c) assumptions of a universal LGBT experience, d) exoticization, e) discomfort/disapproval with LGBT experience, f) denial of societal heterosexism and transphobia, g) assumption of sexual pathology/abnormality, and h) denial of individual heterosexism/transphobia (Nadal, Rivera, & Corpus, 2010). For the purposes of this chapter, we chose to focus on the four (endorsement, heterosexism, exoticization, and denial) that were most fully represented our data.

Jay chuckled. "Yeah, I don't dig the whole standard black and blue shirt and tie thing. So what would you want to wear to work?"

Joan froze. She was startled by Jay's question. "Honestly, I would want to dress a little more masculine, pants and loafers, maybe a button-up shirt and slacks. Dress more like you."

"Then why don't you?" Jay asked.

"Are you nuts?" Joan exclaimed. "I can't dress that way here."

"Why not?" Jay asked. "And what do you mean by 'that way'?"

"Um. Well. Uh," Joan stammered. "I mean, I can't dress masculine at work especially because, because…" she trailed off. "Because I'm a lesbian. You know. I think I would be under extra scrutiny."

"Oh." Jay said. "I understand, especially after what happened to that guy in advertising. He was put on notice about the amount of makeup he was wearing to work. I mean, I'm cool with him doing drag and all that, but you can't bring the bar culture into the workplace. You don't see me doing that do you?"

"No," Joan nodded. "You definitely can't bring that to the workplace. At least not here."

Heteronormativity in the Workplace

Despite the fact that Joan and Jay were open about their sexuality at work, they both still conformed to gender/sex stereotypes. This defines the microaggression *endorsement*, which occurs when LGB/TQ individuals adopt cisgender-normative cultures and/or behaviors (Nadal et al., 2010). *Cisgender* is a term that describes a person who believes that their gender identity aligns with what they were assigned at birth. So in other words, Joan and Jay can be out at work, but they still see the need to be read as stereotypically male and female. They are aware that other employees have been disciplined for non-cisgender behaviors, such as the male coworker in advertising who got in trouble for wearing too much makeup. They are aware that it is important to adhere to cisgender-normative ways of dressing, or that they "choose" to wear what their work colleagues and supervisors expect. Joan wears heels, skirts, and puts on makeup to go to work, even though she would prefer to dress differently. Jay admonishes the male colleague who was wearing make-up to work for "bringing the bar culture," yet at the same time is not content with the conservative suit and tie look he wears.

The tension that Joan and Jay are experiencing, *out, but cisgender-normative*, is indicative of the existence of heteronormativity in the workplace. Yep (2003) conceptualizes heteronormativity as "the (in)visible center and the presumed bedrock of society" (p. 18). What this means is that organizations' structures and processes uphold heterosexuality as the norm, the presumed sexual orientation of their workers. For instance, prior to marriage equality, numerous states excluded LGB/TQ couples from its definitions of marriage thus denying them access to spousal employment benefits.

Heteronormativity gains its power and pervasiveness due to its taken-for-granted, (in)visible nature. Wittig (1992) suggested that, "[t]o live in society is to live in heterosexuality" (p. 40), yet many people do not notice the ways that U.S. society, and by extension, the workplace, organizes around heterosexuality. From an early age, we are socialized to categorize and classify based on sex (women-men) and gender (feminine-masculine) linking women with femininity and men with masculinity. For instance, people tend to ask expecting families if they are having a "boy or a girl" and then buy gender-specific items like pink clothing for a girl and blue for a boy. These sex-specific dress codes continued into school with differing dress codes for boys and girls. And in the case of Joan and Jay, it is visible by a workplace that approves of cisgender-normative cultures and behaviors and disciplines those who go against them. This sends a subtle message that it is okay to be gay, just not too gay.

Vignette 2: Heterosexism

"Wait! Hold the door!" Tracy yelled.

Richard pushed the "door open" button and held the elevator. He recognized Tracy, one of the designers who worked on his team.

"Thanks," Tracy panted, catching her breath. She was carrying a large, oversized box along with her laptop bag. "T-shirts for the softball team," she explained.

They rode the elevator together down to the parking garage chatting about the upcoming season. When they got off, Tracy noticed that they had parked near each other. This gave Tracy the opportunity to ask a serious question.

"Richard, do you mind if I get your take on something?"

"Sure," he replied.

"I wasn't sure who to go to, or if this is even a big deal, but…" she trailed off.

"Go ahead, Tracy," Richard responded.

"I'm not comfortable with some of the language that I've been hearing from players. You know, the gay stuff. 'That's so gay,' or 'No homo.' Teasing each other about being a 'fag' or a 'sissy.' I know they don't mean it to be homophobic, but I don't think it's cool."

Richard stood in silence. Tracy continued.

"What if someone on the team was gay? Geez. I don't know everyone's sexuality. Someone could be."

Richard nodded. He understood where Tracy was coming from, but he knew that the other members of the team didn't mean those things as slurs. To them, that kind of language was a normal part of the game. That didn't make it okay, though, and clearly it wasn't okay with Tracy.

"I just felt like I needed to say something," Tracy said, getting into her car.

"I appreciate the heads up," Richard responded. "Have a good night."

(In)visibility as Constant Negotiation

What Tracy is encountering is the use of *heterosexist terminology,* language that degrades based on sexuality (Nadal et al., 2010). Specifically, Tracy's coworkers were using the terms "fag" and "sissy" to refer to one another, and phrases like "that's so gay," and "no homo." Although Richard felt confident that the guys did not mean what they were saying to be offensive, nonetheless that kind of language can isolate and single out LGB/TQ employees. Even if it is not intended, heterosexist language still communicates the message that "heterosexuality is normal" and that it is okay to talk negatively about LGB/TQ sexualities.

Heterosexist language is a difficult microaggression to combat because sexual orientation/identity is not always readily apparent, it is (in)visible. In essence, it is not visibly apparent on the surface level, yet it maintains present in the discourse. For example, Tracy mentions this when she justifies her concerns to Richard. She does not know everyone's sexuality. What if someone on the team was LGB/TQ? When heterosexist remarks are made, such as those from Tracy's colleagues, heteronormativity is reinforced. LGB/TQ employees receive messages that passing, or pretending to be heterosexual at work (Spradlin, 1998), might be the best means for navigating the workplace.

Additionally, being "out" is not a one-time event; it is a constant negotiation LGB/TQ working adults navigate (see Manning, this volume). Someone who identifies as LGB/TQ does not "come out" of the closet once. Rather, sexual orientation/identity is negotiated and managed at the grocery store, going out to eat, buying a car, heading to work, at home, and during many other every day, taken-for-granted experiences (Adams, 2011). For example, a gay individual may be out to a few colleagues, perceived as gay by other colleagues, and "closeted" on the softball team, especially when faced with heterosexist language.

Vignette 3: Exoticization

Happy to be home, Sam unlocked the door and walked into the apartment that she shared with her partner Emily. She was still in shock. Did that really happen?

"Hey Sam," Emily called out looking up from a stack of papers that she was grading. She did a double take and upon seeing Sam. "Is everything okay?" she asked.

"No," Sam said shaking her head and joining Emily on the couch. "Everything is not okay. I just got out of a very intense meeting with Amy."

Emily nodded. She knew Amy was the director of student affairs at the university where Sam worked.

"Apparently, I have been put on probation."

"What?" Emily gasped. She was puzzled. "Why?"

"Amy said she got poor performance reviews from Jamie," Sam responded. Jamie was Sam's supervisor, and together they oversaw the student organizations. "She specifically noted the time when I wasn't there to open the office. You know, the day that Jamie said he would cover, but then didn't show. Apparently, Jamie didn't put it in his report that he had agreed to work."

Sam had had a tenuous relationship with her boss Jamie from the start. They never really clicked. From day one, Jamie had made Sam's sexuality an issue. He frequently told Sam, even in front of students, that he didn't really believe she was bisexual. He claimed her relationship with Emily was a phase, and that she would eventually go back to having sex with men.

A few months ago, he really crossed the line. He surprised Sam with a trip to a strip club under the ruse of going to get pizza. He pulled into the parking lot and told Sam that he wanted to test if she was really bi. Sam did not report the incident, trying to maintain a professional atmosphere. She thought she was doing the right thing, but now her career was in jeopardy.

"I'm so frustrated," Sam said. "I don't know what to do. I haven't for a long time. The thing that upsets me the most is that Amy also seems to think that my sexuality is an issue. She kept talking about what was best for the students. I am really concerned that I am going to lose my job for being bi."

Linking Microaggressions to Co-cultural Theory

Sam's interactions with her supervisor Jamie reflect the microaggression of *exoticization*. Jamie is treating Sam's bisexuality as something to be studied, interrogated. In general, exoticization is communicated through prying questions that often involve graphic discussions of sex and genitalia

(Nadal et al., 2010). Jamie is constantly asking questions and challenging Sam's bisexuality. Despite Sam's attempts to keep things professional in the face of Jamie's inappropriate behavior, she finds her job in jeopardy and her sexuality once again a topic up for discussion.

Sam's case brings *co-cultural theory* (CCT) into the conversation as a useful lens for understanding how LGB/TQ persons respond to the communication of microaggressions. CCT highlights how co-cultural group members (marginalized and underrepresented individuals) use specific communicative tactics to navigate dominant structures and microaggressions. The focus is on the "preferred outcomes" or essentially, what communicative behavior leads to the effect one desires during interactions (Orbe & Spellers, 2005, p. 175).

The preferred outcomes that emerge for marginalized group members are assimilation, accommodation, and separation (Orbe, 1998). *Assimilation* attempts to eliminate cultural differences in an effort to be more like the dominant culture. *Accommodation* involves retaining some cultural uniqueness while acknowledging commonalities with the dominant society. And *separation* rejects the notion of establishing a common bond with the dominant culture. Take, for example, Sam's experience in the workplace. Sam separates herself by maintaining professional around Jamie and not engaging with him. Although she maintains communication to fulfill existing workplace expectations, she has yet to confront (accommodate) or dissociate (assimilate) from her sexual identity within the dominant culture. And now Sam finds herself in a predicament with her job on the line. If we look back at Jay and Joan, we can recognize assimilation in that Joan felt pressure to conform to dominant society through her dress code and eliminated any cultural differences as a lesbian woman. Or take for example Tracy, who never openly identified as LGB/TQ but chose to confront the situation by expressing her concern to her superior with hopes for accommodation and to help educate others about the microaggression. CCT helps us not only magnify the ways in which communication is embedded in hierarchy, privilege, and power, but recognizes the ways non-dominant members communicatively assimilate, accommodate, or separate in the face of microaggressions.

Vignette 4: Denial

"Knock knock," a man's voice said.

Hannah looked up from her computer screen to see Dylan, one of the company's developers. "Come in," Hannah smiled, greeting him. "Have a seat." Hannah was the Director of Human Resources for Innova-Comm, a brand consulting firm. Although she was familiar with some of Dylan's work, they had never had the chance to meet in person. "What can I do for you?" she asked, motioning him to take a seat.

"Thanks for seeing me," Dylan replied, shutting the door, and sitting down. "I wanted to talk to you about something, well, personal. That will, well, be noticeable at work."

"Okay," Hannah said, tentatively. "What's up?"

"Well, my partner and I have decided that we are ready to start a family."

"Wow, Dylan. That's great news. Congrats." Hannah exclaimed. "So how can I help you? Do you need information on our family leave policy?"

"That would be great. You see, I'm the one who is pregnant."

"Oh, I see," Hannah responded slowly. She had just been thrown for a loop. Up until now, she hadn't realized that there may be trans employees at Innova-Comm. Hannah had assumed that Dylan was a straight male. He looked the part of your typical web developer guy: jeans, T-shirt, squeaky voice, low key. He always used he/him/his pronouns to refer to himself and his paperwork listed his sex as male.

"I am not going to lie. I was nervous to come in here and tell you about it," Dylan continued, noticing that Hannah was a bit taken aback. "Most people here look at me as just the web developer guy, but now I am going to be the *pregnant* web developer guy. I thought it would be important to sit down and talk with you."

"Well Dylan, I'm glad you decided to come in and start the conversation," Hannah said.

"Thanks," Dylan said. "I know that the company is inclusive regarding sexual orientation, but there hasn't been much attention given to the needs of trans employees. I don't know if the company is even aware of its trans employees. There aren't many, but I'm not the only one. Gender identity isn't a protected category by the Federal or our state government, and gender identity isn't mentioned in our organizational documents and policies.

I know that some of my colleagues will think that it's weird, not natural. They were making fun of the guy in Oregon who had a baby a few years back. Called him a 'she-male' and made other transphobic remarks. They don't have a clue that I identify as a trans man. It's been easier that way, but once I start to show, well there will be no hiding it after that."

Hannah looked at Dylan. He was right. The company did not really actively seek to explore and address the needs of trans employees. Discussions of gender identity were absent from new employee orientation, wellness programs, and training and development opportunities. Hannah had assumed that if the company adequately addressed sexual orientation, that it was adequately addressing the needs of its LGBT workforce.

Hannah took a breath. "To level with you Dylan, I am not sure what the proper course of action is, but I will find out."

On Your Own

Dylan's experience reflects a sobering reality in terms of workplace equality. While the world of work is becoming more proactive in addressing matters of sexual orientation, discussions of gender identity have been less progressive. In Dylan's case, he is experiencing a *denial* of both societal and individual transphobia. Although Innova-Comm explicitly discusses matters of sexual orientation in its policies and practices, gender identity is absent from the conversation. This denial communicates transphobia through the absence of recognition.

On the individual level, Hannah is caught up in this denial as well—though not completely intentionally—but by failing to acknowledge the possibility of non-cisgender employees given her role in human resources. Hannah certainly did the right thing by recognizing Dylan as male, but she was not conscious about gender identity in the workplace. Furthermore, Dylan's coworkers are culpable through their use of transphobic terminology. Although people are becoming more aware of heterosexist terminology given an increase in openly gay workers, transphobic language (e.g., use of wrong pronouns; words such as *she-male* or *tranny*) can still be a matter of practice.

Putting Practice into Action

We hope that by sharing these stories, your understanding of sexuality-specific workplace discrimination has been deepened. Below, we engage each of the four LGB/TQ-based microaggressions through a discussion of potential communicative responses. We are aware that speaking up can be difficult, but we encourage you to find ways to be part of the change. Everyone deserves a comfortable, secure, and safe workplace.

First, we must recognize the endorsement of cisgender normative culture and behaviors in the workplace. These can present difficulties for non-gender conforming individuals to negotiate. One way that these negotiations can be made easier is through gender-neutral discussions of dress codes. This is an area where leadership and human resources become key for setting the tone. If dress codes are understood in a unisex manner, then it can give employees space to dress in the ways that are most comfortable to them. Also, those in supervisory or mentoring roles can do this informally with new employees by communicating these messages. For employees seeking change, look at the current dress code and create recommendations for how it can be amended to create a more affirming and comfortable workplace. Gather the support of your peers (e.g., petition, survey, etc.) and present your recommendations to the leadership.

Second, be aware of heterosexist and transphobic terminology. Not only in the language that you hear others use (e.g., "that's so gay," "fag"), but also in the ways that you may assume heterosexuality with your own language use. For instance, instead of asking if a person has a husband or a wife, ask about a partner. In terms of transphobic terminology, adopting gender neutral language is key. The use of the singular "they" can replace the need for he/she pronouns. We know this is not an easy transition, but in becoming more aware of your own language, you will begin to recognize the words that are exclusionary or limit an individual's sexuality.

Third, although it is natural for people to be curious about the unknown, it is important to be respectful. Do not ask prying questions of LGB/TQ individuals. Follow a rule of thumb that if you would be uncomfortable answering a question about your own sex life, do not ask someone else a question about theirs. Additionally, always consider your relationship to another person and the context in which you are having the conversation.

Do not assume that an individual is either gay or straight. If you assume that someone might be LGB/TQ, do not ask direct questions that force disclosure of sexuality. We believe that assumption-based questions are detrimental to creating inclusive and affirming workplaces. Always attempt to make space for inclusivity rather than placing someone in a box or challenging their sexuality.

Fourth, we as people can no longer be in denial of societal and individual heterosexism or transphobia. As a person of ability and conviction, we must recognize that heterosexism and transphobia are present in society and that individuals can perpetuate these discriminatory practices. This recognition does not mean that individuals who discriminate themselves are bad people, but that discriminatory structures and processes exist. We live in a society that privileges heterosexuality and cisgender identities. It is up to us to be aware of these structures and, through our communicative actions, seek to tear down these divisions and create the policies and practices that provide space for diverse sexualities and genders in the workplace and in society.

DISCUSSION QUESTIONS

1. Consider each of the microaggressions portrayed in this chapter: endorsement, heterosexism, exoticization, and denial. In what ways have you experienced or witnessed any of these in your own lives?

2. A 2011 study by researchers from Harvard and Boston University (Etcoff, Stock, Haley, Vickery, & House, 2011) revealed that women who wear makeup are seen as more competent, likable, and trustworthy. How might these findings explain Joan's struggle with cisgender dress codes?

3. Anti-discrimination policies in the workplace do not always protect LGB/TQ employees like we saw in Dylan's case. Still, workplace equality advocates believe that they are vital to have. So what is the role of anti-discrimination policies in organizations? Why are they considered valuable for combating workplace discrimination?

4. The stories presented in this chapter highlight how sexuality can be part of everyday organizational life. How do you feel about that? Have you experienced sex and sexuality as a topic of conversation in an organization (e.g., work, school, or community group)? How can we competently navigate discussions of sex and sexuality in the workplace? How can these discussions be inclusive of LGB/TQ sexualities?

5. How, in the future, might you respond to LGB/TQ-based microaggressions? What are some strategies illustrated in this chapter that you might use? What are some barriers to speaking up and speaking out about workplace discrimination?

6. This chapter drew on co-cultural theory to recognize the various ways in which marginalized individuals (LGB/TQ) communicate in dominant society. How might this theory apply to contexts outside of the workplace for LGB/TQ individuals?

References

Adams, T. E. (2009). *Narrating the closet: An authoethnography of same-sex attraction.* Walnut Creek, CA: Left Coast Press.

Brydum, S. (2013). Meet the people fired for being LGBT in 2013. *The Advocate.* Retrieved from http://www.advocate.com/year-review/2013/12/18/meet-people-fired-being-lgbt-2013?page=full.

Equal Employment Opportunity Commission (EEOC). (2013). *Overview.* Retrieved from http://www.eeoc.gov/eeoc/index.cfm.

Gates, G. (2010). *Sexual minorities in the 2008 General Social Survey: Coming out and demographic characteristics.* Los Angeles, CA: The Williams Institute.

Human Rights Campaign (HRC). (2013). *Resources-Workplace.* Retrieved from http://www.hrc.org/laws-and-legislation/federal-legislation/employment-non-discrimination-act.

Manning, J. (This volume). Identity, relationships, and culture: A constitutive model of coming out. In J. Manning & C. Noland (Eds.), *Contemporary Studies of Sexuality & Communication: Theoretical and Applied Perspectives.* Dubuque, IA: Kendall Hunt.

Nadal, K. L., Issa, M. A., Leon, J., Meterko, V., Wideman, M., & Wong, Y. (2011). Sexual orientation microaggression: "Death by a thousand cuts" for lesbian, gay, and bisexual youth. *Journal of LGBT Youth, 8,* 234–259. doi:10.1080/19361653.2011.584204.

Nadal, K. L., Rivera, D. P., & Corpus, M. J. H. (2010) Sexual orientation and transgender microaggressions in everyday life: Experiences of lesbians, gays, bisexuals, and transgender individuals. In D. W. Sue (Ed.), *Microaggressions and marginality: Manifestation, dynamics, and impact* (pp. 217–240). New York: Wiley.

Orbe, M. (1998). *Constructing co-cultural theory: An explication of culture, power, and communication.* Thousand Oaks, CA: Sage.

Orbe, M. P., & Spellers, R. E. (2005). From the margins to the center: Utilizing co-cultural theory in diverse contexts. In W.B. Gudykunst (Ed.), *Theorizing about intercultural communication* (pp. 173–191). Thousand Oaks, CA: Sage.

Spradlin, A. L. (1998). The price of "passing:" A lesbian perspective on authenticity in organizations. *Management Communication Quarterly, 11,* 598–605. doi:10.1177/0893318998114006.

Wittig, M. (1992). *The straight mind and other essays.* Boston: Beacon Press.

Yep, G. A. (2003). The violence of heteronormativity in communication studies: Notes on injury, healing, and queer world-making. *Journal of Homosexuality, 45*(2-4), 11–59.

CHAPTER 21

Sex and the Workplace:
Sexual Harassment and Consenting
Relationship Policies

Tiffany Emerson & Jimmie Manning

KEY TERMS

Sexual harassment	Consent	Workplace relationships
Sexual orientation	Romantic relationships	

ABSTRACT

This chapter examines sexual harassment. Ignored until the 1970s, sexual harassment continues to be a problem in many workplaces. To help identify what constitutes sexual harassment and to help prevent sexual harassment from occurring, two common types of sexual harassment are explored. These are *quid pro quo* and *hostile work environment* sexual harassment. Consenting relationship policies for the workplace are also reviewed. Finally, a case study examines a sexual harassment claim made by an employee in a restaurant.

One of the most interesting aspects of the critically-acclaimed and much-watched television series *Mad Men* is the way it reminds viewers that some of the things in the past were not so great. Notably, civil rights have seen great advances since the 1960s. Issues regarding race, ethnicity, sexual orientation, and ability, among others, have vastly improved in the United States even though many people struggle today for equal rights and recognitions. Perhaps because it is so different from what is expected in the present day, *Mad Men*'s depiction of women in the workplace is especially jarring. Bosses openly make sexual passes at or lewd commentary toward their secretaries; women are ignored or belittled in everyday interactions, certainly not seeing much in the way of promotions; and, dishearteningly, many women in the workplace seem to be more interested in a husband than a career. Those who seemed more interested in their work were bullied, dismissed, or ridiculed—even by other women.

Although times have changed remarkably, contemporary workplaces—both in the United States and in many other countries as well—are sites of struggle when it comes to gender and sexuality (see, for example, McKenna & Baker, this volume). Although the public groping of women depicted in *Mad Men* would be unexpected in the modern workplace, it does not mean that the *non*public groping of women—as well as men—is not happening. According to a recent survey, sexual harassment—or unwanted sexual commentary or advances in the workplace—has been experienced by an astounding 54% of those surveyed (Aware, 2015). Although a fair number of men reported being harassed, 79% of the respondents who reported sexual harassment were women. Of the people who were sexually harassed, 12% were told they would lose their jobs if they did not comply with sexual requests.

Unfortunately, the same survey also revealed that people were unaware of whether or not they had protection from sexual harassment behaviors. About two-thirds (66.6%) indicated they were not aware of any sexual harassment policies, even though about half (50.4%) said they had someone they could go to in their place of employment to seek counsel about sexual harassment (Aware, 2015). That sexual harassment continues to be a problem and remains unresolved is not surprising, as the United States has a long history of problems with sexual harassment. It was not until the 1970s that the term sexual harassment was even used to identify problematic behaviors in the workplace (Wise & Stanley, 1987). Even though workplaces were beginning to create or adopt sexual harassment policies, it was only in reaction to recommendations from legal experts who asserted such policies would protect organizations in court. A cultural breakthrough, at least in the U.S., came in 1991 when Clarence Thomas—who was nominated to serve on the Supreme Court—was questioned about many of his actions as part of his Supreme Court confirmation hearing. Anita Hill bravely pointed out the unwanted sexual advances he made when she worked for him as well as the lewd comments he would make (CBS News, 2010). Nevertheless, he was appointed to the Supreme Court.

Since the early 1990s, more attention has been paid to sexual harassment policies. Even so, many people who experience sexual harassment are unsure of how or why it happened (Lawson, Wright, & Fitzgerald, 2013). Some even question whether they were really sexually harassed or not (Lawson, Wright, & Fitzgerald, 2013). Still others are confused, believing the behaviors experienced at work constitute normal flirting when, really, the behavior is probably sexual harassment (Dougherty, Kramer, Klatzke, & Rogers, 2009). As the earlier statistics noted, women continue to be disproportionately targeted for sexual harassment. Women of color can be at even bigger risk (hooks, 1996). These findings suggest that education about sexual harassment is still needed. In order to clear up confusion about what sexual harassment is and to help prevent people from sexually harassing others, common definitions of sexual harassment are reviewed.

Sexual Harassment

Although different organizations have different policies that define sexual harassment—people should examine sexual harassment policies when they enter a place of work so they can be prepared if they are involved in a situation that involves sexual harassment. That can include being sexually harassed, seeing someone else be sexually harassed, or being the sexual harasser. Most organizations recognize two types of sexual harassment. The first of these is *quid pro quo* sexual harassment (Baker, 1994). In Latin, quid pro quo means "this for that." For example, a boss might tell his employee that he likes seeing her wear short skirts to work. "Keep wearing skirts that short, and I'll promote you to manager," he says. He offers a *quid*—wearing short skirts—in exchange for a *pro quo*—she will be promoted. Reading that example might make you feel uncomfortable. You might think, "Well, he could be joking." Even if he is, the statement reflects sexual harassment. The person hearing the words might believe it to be true. Even if she believes it is a joke, she could also feel offended that her boss is commenting on her body. It also puts the boss and his organization in a dangerous position—if she documented the words, and reported him, it would make the company look bad. More important, it could create an environment where she—and others—do not feel comfortable because they worry that they might be treated as sexual objects at work.

That leads to a second kind of sexual harassment: a hostile work environment. A hostile work environment is one where workers can feel uncomfortable because they fear that people will make inappropriate sexual remarks or advances (Paetzold & O'Leary-Kelly, 1993). A hostile work environment does not have to be related to things that are overtly sexual, however. In many cases, a hostile work environment is the result of inappropriate gendered language. For example, a boss calling all the waitresses in his bar "tits on a stick" might have nothing to do with him actually thinking of them sexually—but even so, by using sexualized language to refer to the women, he is dehumanizing them and reducing them to body parts. As another example, a boss might call her employee in for a meeting. Out of anger, she tells him she is going to "cut off his balls." Again, even though such a statement is not sexy, the use of language referring to genitals is demeaning and would create a hostile work environment for the employee. He would have every right to file a sexual harassment claim.

Many people are afraid to file sexual harassment claims, however. They fear retaliation (Bergman, Langhout, Palmieri, Cortina, & Fitzgerald, 2002), or they worry that no one will believe them. In other instances, they believe it is not worth the trouble (Bordo, 1997). Organizational policies are often unclear about what does or does not constitute sexual harassment—sometimes strategically—as well (Keyton & Rhodes, 1999); and so people worry about whether or not what they have experienced is truly sexual harassment. In many instances—including most court cases—determining what is or is not sexual harassment involves the *reasonable person standard*. The reasonable person standard involves asking, "Would a reasonable person see this as inappropriate behavior?"

So, for instance, if a woman claimed that a gay man was sexually harassing her because he had a photo of him and his husband on their wedding day in his cubicle, she would almost certainly be denied a sexual harassment claim. It is not reasonable to expect people to hide photos of their partners in the workplace. Even if the office had a policy about not displaying family photos, her claim would not be a sexual harassment claim because it has nothing to do with sex. Instead, it would be considered a simple policy violation regarding workplace photos. On the other hand, if she were to joke with him about all the hot sex gay men must have with each other, she would likely fail the reasonable person standard. It is not reasonable to think that someone has to listen to the person in the next cubicle talk about his or her sex life in the workplace. It could be annoying, demeaning, and offensive.

Consenting Workplace Policies

Even though unwanted sexual advances or commentary are inappropriate in the workplace, it does not mean that all workplace romance is forbidden. Some companies have *fraternization policies* that limit who people can have relationships with in the workplace. Some of these only prohibit managers or supervisors from dating other employees; others suggest that no one in the workplace is allowed to date. Cultural critic bell hooks (1996) refers to these policies as foolish. As she notes, many career-driven people only have time to meet others in the workplace. To pretend that people who are so dedicated to their work might see that work as a common interest— and as attractive—is denying the way many people function. Moreover, it sets a need for workers who are interested in each other to sneak around. That, in turn, can lead to bigger problems. For example, if a supervisor falls for someone she manages, they might eventually have a consensual relationship—one that they both agree they want to be a part of—and have to sneak around outside of the office to be together.

Most companies have these policies to protect the organization. If that relationship turns sour, however, it puts the company at risk. The supervisor could then be falsely accused of being coercive and forcing the employee to date her. Alternately, the employee could be punished by the supervisor after the break-up. Because of these problems that could occur, many companies adopt what are called *consenting relationship policies*. These policies ask employees who start to see each other romantically to report that they are dating each other. Colleges and universities—places where sexual harassment often occurs (hooks, 1996)—often have these policies in place as well, not only for university employees but also for students and professors. Many people find it curious or even unbelievable that a university would have a policy on hand that informs students and professors about how they can date. Such policies are important, however, as they can prevent professors from coercing students into continuing to date them (when coerced, students can go to the professor's chair and point out that they are not in a consenting relationship) or a student demanding good grades or other special treatment in exchange for not reporting the professor for dating him or her (because, if the policy is followed, the professor will already know about the relationship).

Whether it is a supervisor-employee or a student-teacher relationship, many consenting relationship policies require that while people are dating they have no official power over each other in the workplace. So, for instance, if a professor were dating a university student that was in her class, she would have to ask someone else to grade that student's work. If a manager was dating someone who worked his line in the factory, he would have to get someone else to approve overtime requests. Consenting relationship policies, when they work, can reduce the appearance and enactment of impropriety.

A Fictive Case Study Exploring Sexual Harassment

To help illustrate sexual harassment, here we offer a fictive case study. We believe that this case study especially illustrates how messy and confusing sexual harassment can be; and why a clear understanding of what is or is not sexual harassment is important.

Trouble at the Longhorn Roadhouse

The employees at the Longhorn Roadhouse in DeKalb, Illinois are in a state of confusion. An accusation of sexual harassment has been made by an employee and no one is exactly sure how it happened. The new district manager, Annaliese Grey, has been dispatched to the location to investigate the claim and to make a decision about how it should be handled. To begin her inquiry, she decides she needs to interview everyone who was present when the alleged violation occurred. She was given some basic facts about the incident to before the interviews.

First, she knows that a group of employees stayed after work on a Friday night to celebrate the birthday of Jane Duncan, the 20-year old woman who filed the claim against Calvin, her co-worker. Second, she knows that drinking was involved. Third, she knows the company policy: sexual harassment is considered to be when one employee asserts power over another to gain sexual favors; when someone approaches another employee with sexual or romantic interests in a way that is not appropriate by any reasonable standard; or when anyone intentionally touches another employee in a spot that is typically covered by underwear.

Finally, she also knows that the alleged sexual harassment behaviors happened in the restaurant's kitchen while no one else was around. To find out what everyone knows, Annaliese decides that she is going to begin by asking everyone to tell their version of what happened that night.

Jane

Okay, so basically it was my birthday. And, I know we're not supposed to drink on the clock, but because it was a special occasion we thought it might be okay. We didn't drink any of the restaurant's liquor, though. Teddy brought some stuff he had. He was only trying to be nice, like he usually does.

Anyway, Teddy brought the stuff in and then we had some music going, and then Ashleigh had a cake that she brought. So Verna lit the candles, and then I blew them out. Teddy joked that he was going to give me a "birthday girl spanking" and asked me how old I was. I laughed and said, "Teddy! You're so funny!" And then he pretended he was coming to spank me. So we all started playing around, and I said, "No! You're not spanking me!" And then, trying to be playful, I said, "But I'm spanking everyone else!"

And so I started giving light taps to all the girls. First Ashleigh, and then Tiana. But when I got to Verna it was weird. I mean, she's way older. We were surprised she even stuck around. And then I finally decided, "Okay, you have to make her included." So I kind of went in to spank her and she dodged it and somehow I ended up hitting Calvin on his side.

I thought that was kind of funny, but that's it. I mean, no one would have taken that as any more than me joking around. Teddy even looked at me and raised his eyebrows in a funny way to make fun of the absurdity of the situation. So I didn't even think then that Calvin would read more into it.

But then a few minutes later, when I went to go get plates so we could actually eat some cake, Calvin followed me into the kitchen. I didn't notice him at first, but as I was looking for the birthday paper plates in the back, Calvin started singing to me and doing this weird dance. I couldn't understand it, but something about him drinking a shake. Then he grabbed his crotch and wiggled it and ran away.

I came out of the kitchen. Teddy asked me what happened, and I started to tell him, and everyone laughed. As I kept trying to tell the story, they kept laughing harder and harder. It was humiliating! Verna kept trying to comfort me, and then she told me that what he did was sexual harassment. Said I should file a report before anything else happens.

So we called Jerry, and that's what I did. And now I'm here talking to you.

Ashleigh

I didn't really see a lot of it, to tell you the truth. Most of the time I was in the back, helping Mike to get stuff for the party. The last I remember, before I went back to the kitchen with Mike, was that we all did a shot. And then Teddy started flirting with Jane, telling her he was going to give her a "birthday girl spanking." He tried to play it off as a joke, but everyone knows they want each other. They flirt around all of the time.

So Jane came over and slapped me on the ass for some reason, and then Tiana. Then she runs up to Verna and just stood there. It was so awkward! I don't know if you know Verna or not, but she's this 60-year-old lady who I swear carries the Bible with her everywhere she goes.

But anyway, I thought it was all stupid so I asked Mike to help me get some stuff in the back. Then, I can't remember why, but we went to the back table and were sitting there talking. But then we heard Jane yell, and Mike runs out to see what is going on. I ran out after them, and he says, "Calvin did what?"

So him and Jane are laughing because Calvin started singing that "Milkshake" song and gyrating and stuff at her. Then he ran out. Like, don't ask me what that's about.

But then it got weird, because Jane went out and people were all by the door watching. And she told us about Calvin doing the dance, and people kept laughing. Tiana joked and said, "Slut! You know you wanted it!" And I joked that she wished it was Teddy, because she flirts with him all the time. And next thing I know, Jane is crying. Like, sobbing like a baby.

Then Verna, who was laughing as much as the rest of us before, comes up and grabs Jane and walks her over to a booth. That was the last I saw before they called the manager and we were all told to go home and not talk about it.

Verna

First of all, let me say I am so glad you are here. SOMETHING needed to be done, and Lord knows that Jerry isn't going to be the one to do it. Why you all chose him as manager is beyond me. He's more interested in getting home early and treating his friends to free steaks than he is anything else.

But anyway, it was Jane's birthday, and her and the kids decided they were going to celebrate. I heard Ashleigh tell her she bought her a cake. They were conspiring all night to bring in some vodka, and rum, and gin, and Lord knows what else. Mixers? Or whatever they call them.

Anyway, I overhear them, and I says to Ashleigh, I says, "So are you girls throwing a party tonight?" And I looked at her. And Ashleigh gives me this glare, and she rolls those makeup-crusted eyes, and she says, "Yeah, Verna. You want to come?"

So I thought, "Okay. I'll show you, you little witch. I'm gonna say yes, and I will come." So I told her yes, that I'd LOVE to be a part of the party. Besides, these kids needed some supervision. Lord knows our manager wasn't gonna be the one to give it. He was probably at home with that nasty wife of his.

So after we close, the kids bring in all their stuff. Teddy, of course, is the first one drinking. He's pouring a shot for this one, a shot for that one, making them all drink it. Jane, of course, is enjoying all the attention. She bends over, sticking her little fanny out, and blows out the candles. Then Teddy asks who is going to give her a birthday spanking, and she says, "Why do you care, Teddy? Do you want it to be you?"

Then somehow things go crazy and Jane is running around spanking the other girls. Then she came up to me, and I gave her this look like, "Go ahead, you little brat. I dare you to! I used to eat girls like you for breakfast when I was in high school!" I mean to tell you, Jane is pretty, and she's book smart. But I don't think the Lord gave her any common sense.

Then Tiana spilled a bottle of vodka on the carpet while trying to make her "party shot," or whatever she called it. So we started to clean that up, and Ashleigh goes to get some rags. Only she didn't come back, and so me and Tiana was trying to use napkins.

Next thing we know, Jane is running out of the kitchen screaming like she's on a roller coaster or something. We go to see what's going on, and she starts telling us some story about Calvin singing a song to her and being inappropriate. Evidently, he was going to pull out his you-know-what, but she told him to stop.

At first she tried to play it off like it was funny, but then as we were laughing and joking back with her she started crying. It was then that I knew this wasn't right, and it had to stop. So I told the kids to clean up, party's over. And I took Jane to the side and let her know what's what.

What he did wasn't right. It's sexual harassment. And I do expect you all to do something about it!

Mike

So, basically, we were going to have this birthday party for Jane. I don't really know Jane, or anyone here really, because I'm new. So I thought I should stick around and try to socialize a bit. Teddy told me that it would be okay as long as we clocked out before we started drinking and having cake and stuff.

The girls and Verna were finishing up their side work, and so me, Teddy, and Calvin were in the kitchen. Teddy had already brought in some vodka, and he wanted us to do shots. I went to clock out, and so did Calvin, and when we came back Teddy already had the shots poured. Calvin said he didn't want any, but I went ahead and had a drink. It was a hard night, you know?

After our shots, we joked around, and then it looked like everyone else was done with cleaning so we went into the dining room to cut the cake. Jane blew out the candles, and people were horsing around. Then Tiana spilled something, and Ashleigh grabbed my hand and took me to the back area. She, uh, started kissing me, and I wasn't so sure about it but I kind of went along with it.

Next thing we know, Jane screams and so I use that as an excuse to get away from Ashleigh. At first I thought it was nothing, because it looked like she was screaming in a funny way. She laughed and grabbed me on the shoulders and said, "You will not believe what happened! Best birthday ever!"

She must have been being sarcastic, though, because when she went into the dining room to tell everyone the story, people were laughing. But she started crying. I guess Calvin went up to her, when they were alone in the kitchen, and started singing the "Milkshake" song and grabbing his crotch. Verna kind of took her to the side to comfort her, and then they came back over to us and said they were calling the manager. We all got on the phone with him, and he told us to go home and not to talk about what happened. So I didn't.

Teddy

If you ask me, this whole thing has been blown out of proportion. It all started when Jane asked me to go to her birthday party after work. I actually had something else lined up—a date—and so I said I couldn't go. I mean, there's also the fact that Jane has a crush on me. She's nice and good looking and all that. But I don't want to lead her on.

But everyone said it wouldn't be as fun without me, so I said I'd stay. And I supplied some of the refreshments. But then we got a last minute rush, and so the girls were all doing their side work extra late, and one of the guys talked me into doing a shot or two while we were waiting. So I did a shot with Calvin and Mike. Calvin was already acting weird—or weirder than usual—but I didn't think much of it.

When things were finally getting started, Jane was cutting the cake. And, I don't know how else to say this, but she was flirting with me. Said she should give me a spanking for her birthday, or something like that. I'm pretty sure Calvin noticed that, because he started asking me questions about how he could impress Jane. Like, I think he thought he could turn that attention in his direction.

Next thing I know, Jane comes out of the kitchen. She was telling us how Calvin was doing some kind of sexy dance for her, and then Ashleigh called her a slut. That kind of pissed me off, because Ashleigh was all over Mike all night long. Very handsy. If anyone was sexually harassed, it was him. [Laughs.] Just kidding.

Seriously, though, I'd be concerned about Calvin. I know he's here with that special program or whatever, but I think he did something that made Jane break down. After we were supposed to go home, I went up to her. And, I guess I should tell you this, I gave her a kiss goodnight. I told her that I'd make sure she's safe at work. I mean, she walks out to her car in the dark at night. I don't want her to feel afraid of weirdos like Calvin. I want her to feel safe. That's just the kind of guy I am.

And so I guess I should let you all know that Jane and I are dating, like the rules say we should.

Tiana

Look, I don't have a lot to say. I'll own up to my part, and that's it. I was drinking. I didn't clock out. I spilled vodka in the dining room. I cleaned it up. I had nothing to do with the whole Jane and Teddy thing. I had nothing to do with the whole Jane and Calvin thing. The only thing I did was try to relax a bit after work.

And, even though I probably should keep my mouth shut about this, I don't think it's right that you all are handling the situation this way. I don't understand why we've had to come to work the past few days and not say anything about it. That doesn't make any sense.

So please leave me out of it. I own up to what I did, I don't have anything to say about the rest.

Calvin

Well, when it started out I was really excited. It was Jane's birthday, and she was turning 21, and I knew that we were supposed to have cake. Teddy said he was going to bring the party favors. He said I liked them a lot.

When I saw that the party favors were alcohol, my chest got kind of tight. I hadn't really drinked alcohol before. But Teddy called me over and said we should down some shots. I told him I didn't think so, but he told me he'd help me out and we'd have a real good time.

He then called Mike over and said we were all going to drink. Mike said we should wait for the others, but Teddy said they would take forever. So I did the shot, but I didn't like it. I told them that it burned.

Teddy just laughed and said that he would teach me to drink. He said, "Stick with me and I'll teach you all my secrets. Even how to get the ladies." I told him I didn't know of any ladies who would like me like that, and he goes, "Oh, I know of one."

I was surprised, so I said, "Who?" He told me that Jane always had a crush on me, only she was too shy to tell me. I—I kind of felt like my cheeks were hot. I always thought Jane was super nice, and she's really pretty. Sometimes I get confused, and she always helps me out. And one time, these really mean people came in and called me an idiot and said I was slow. She told them they were mean, and then she got Jerry to make them leave the restaurant.

Teddy goes, "Jane's all over me all the time. She's a good girl gone bad." I didn't get what he meant, so I asked. He said, "She pretends she doesn't like stuff. But she wants it. One time she told me a secret about you."

"What's that?" I asked.

"She said she would love to see you dance for her. She loves the song 'Milk-shake.' Do you know that song, Calvin?"

I did know that song, because they played it on the radio a lot when I was in high school. I sang it, and Teddy started laughing. He told me that he had a plan. That I should find a time when Jane and I were alone tonight and go and sing it for her. Then he said, "And you have to do this." He grabbed his private area and shook it.

I told him I didn't know. He said that of course I didn't know, because that's what men and women do when they want to be together. "Do you want to be a man?" he asked me, and then he raised his eyebrows up and down.

I was getting kind of embarrassed, so I told Teddy we should find Mike who went to go cut the cake with the girls. When we got out there, I saw how Teddy was acting. He was talking about giving Jane a birthday spanking, and then he would look at me and raise his eyebrows up and down. He kept saying things to Jane and giving me that look. I could tell that he was probably right, because Jane seemed really happy and was laughing.

Then Jane started to give Verna a birthday spanking, but she made that one face she makes when she's not happy. So she gave me a birthday spanking instead. I laughed because it was funny, but then I saw Mike and he was raising his eyebrows again. Jane saw, too, and she was laughing and looked happy.

Then Tiana spilled a bottle of vodka all over the carpet. Everyone was looking at it and getting it cleaned up. That's when Teddy came to me and told me that now was my chance. I should go in the kitchen, where Jane was now, and sing "Milkshake" for her and do the dance he taught me. I said I didn't know, but he said she was all alone in there. This was my chance.

So I went in and saw her. She goes, "What are you up to, Calvin?" and smiled at me. When she did, I thought she looked so pretty. So I started singing the song. I went, *My milkshake brings all the boys to the yard, and they're like – it's better than yours. Damn right, it's better than yours. I could teach you, but I'd have to charge.* She looked really surprised, and her eyes got big. She goes, "I'm really confused by what's happening." So, uh, I grabbed my, uh. I did what Teddy showed me. And, uh, she laughed at me.

I started to feel really embarrassed. I asked her if she liked it, but she laughed real loud. It sounded like she was almost screaming. I ran out of the kitchen. I didn't like it at all. When I ran out, Teddy goes, "Calvin, you wait right here." Then he went and brought Jane out, and he told her to say what happened. At first she was laughing, and then I heard Ashleigh call her a bad word that starts with *s*.

That made everyone laugh, and I started to tell them that she was not that word, and they shouldn't say it. You know, stand up for her like she stood up for me. But before I could do that, she started crying. Verna was standing by me, and she goes, "Calvin, you're a pig." Then she grabbed Jane and took her away.

Tiana came to talk to me. She asked what happened. I told her that I was trying to do a dance for Jane. She told me I shouldn't have done that.

Dear corporate office:

Because of our company policy, we had no choice but to fire Calvin Jones. We do not tolerate sexual harassment in any form at Longhorn Roadhouse stores. Clearly, what Mr. Jones did was sexual harassment. By any reasonable person's standards, it is not appropriate to approach an employee in a sexual manner and to perform dances of a sexual nature. It is especially inappropriate to touch one's self in the genital area as a way of flirting or indicating sexual interest in a colleague.

Others were drinking on the job, some while on the clock. Those who clocked out before drinking received a strong reprimand. Those who did not clock out were given a warning that if such behavior happens again they will be dismissed instantly. Letters were placed in each employee's file. I also thanked Verna Wheat for her leadership in helping to contain the matter.

During the investigation for this incident, Teddy Evans disclosed that he was dating Jane Duncan. I have put a note in each of their files. Given that no other company policies seem to have been violated, I am now closing this complaint. Based on everyone's expressed interests in moving past this incident, I suspect that company morale will not be an issue.

Sincerely,

Annaliese Grey

Annaliese Grey
Illinois District Manager
Longhorn Roadhouse

DISCUSSION QUESTIONS

1. Do you believe Calvin sexually harassed Jane? Why or why not? Do you believe he should have been fired for what happened?

2. According to company policy, Jane should be fired because she touched other employees in an area typically covered by underwear. Why do you believe Annaliese did not take this into consideration? Do you believe Jane should have been fired for what happened?

3. Do you believe that anyone else is guilty of sexual harassment in the case study? If so, who? Why? Are there other characters you are frustrated with? Why or why not?

4. Look up your university or workplace's consenting relationships policy. Does the policy (if they have one) surprise you? Why or why not? What do you think of consenting relationship policies in general?

5. What do you believe to be the difference between flirting and sexual harassment? How can someone tell when they are sexually harassing someone else? Or can they?

References

Aware. (2015). Workplace sexual harassment. *Association for Women and Action Research*. Retrieved from http://www.aware.org.sg/ati/wsh-site/14-statistics/.

Bergman, M. E., Langhout, R. D., Palmieri, P. A., Cortina, L. M., & Fitzgerald, L. F. (2002). The (un) reasonableness of reporting: Antecedents and consequences of reporting sexual harassment. *Journal of Applied Psychology, 87*(2), 230.

Bordo, S. (1996). Sexual harassment is about bullying, not sex. *Chronicle of Higher Education*, B6.

CBS News. (2010). Anita Hill versus Clarence Thomas: The back story. *CBS News.* Retrieved from http://www.cbsnews.com/news/anita-hill-vs-clarence-thomas-the-backstory/.

Dougherty, D. S., Kramer, M. W., Klatzke, S. R., & Rogers, T. K. (2009). Language convergence and meaning divergence: A meaning centered communication theory. *Communication Monographs, 76*(1), 20–46. doi:10.1080/03637750802378799.

hooks, b. (1996). Passionate pedagogy: Erotic student/faculty relationships. *Z Magazine*, 45–51.

Keyton, J., & Rhodes, S. C. (1999). Organizational sexual harassment: Translating research into application. *Journal of Applied Communication Research, 27*(2), 158–173. doi:10.1080/00909889909365532.

Lawson, A. K., Wright, C. V., & Fitzgerald, L. F. (2013). The evaluation of sexual harassment litigants: Reducing discrepancies in the diagnosis of posttraumatic stress disorder. *Law and Human Behavior, 37*(5), 337–347. doi:10.1037/lhb0000024.

McKenna-Buchanan, T., & Baker, S. (This volume). "You are on your own": Magnifying co-cultural LGB/TQ microaggressions in the workplace. In J. Manning & C. Noland (Eds.), *Contemporary studies of sexuality & communication: Theoretical and applied perspectives.* Dubuque, IA: Kendall Hunt.

Paetzold, R., & O'Leary-Kelly, A. (1993). The legal context of sexual harassment. In G. L. Kreps (Ed.), *Sexual harassment: Communication implications* (pp. 63–77). Cresskill, NJ: Hampton.

Wise, S., & Stanley, L. (1977). *Georgie Porgie: Sexual harassment in everyday life.* New York, NY: Pandora.

SECTION 5

Sexual Health and Well-Being

CHAPTER 22

Teaching Medical Students to Take a Sexual History

Carey Noland

KEY TERMS

Sexual history
Provider-patient communication

Sexual health
Medical school

ABSTRACT

Many people have a difficult time talking about sex and physicians are no exception. It is common for some medical doctors to experience embarrassment and discomfort when required to speak to patients about sex and sexual concerns. However, it is essential for the well-being of patients that their physicians speak to them about their sexual health. This chapter explores how medical doctors learn to take a sexual history. It follows a fictional physician, Jill Miller, who teaches at a medical school and her four students as she explains to them how to talk about sex with patients.

Patient: "Doctor, it's really painful when I have sex."

Physician: "Go on vacation, have a glass of wine, it will definitely work for you."

– Dr. Irwin Goldstein (San Diego Sexual Medicine clinic) recounting advice a physician gave to one of his patients. She left the clinic in tears, without a physical exam or any consultation about the problem.

The focus of sex in the United States has shifted from procreation to recreation, and most people have particularly high expectations for sex. Sex is now directly related to quality of life issues. In fact, numerous studies have confirmed that a close personal relationship with one other person is the most important factor in personal happiness, outranking career or financial achievement (Neto & Pinto, 2015). Research in human sexuality has found that engaging in sexual activity is good for the body both physically and psychologically (Smith, 2007). Physical benefits (from arousal and orgasm) include improvements to the respiratory, immune, circulatory, and cardiovascular systems. Psychological benefits include decreased stress, depression, and anxiety and increased levels of vitality.

Because sex is natural, most people assume that we should naturally know how to do it, how to talk about it, and how to solve problems associated with it. This is not the case. Many people need medical help. Over 40 million Americans are in sexless marriages. Even newlyweds have issues: A study showed that sexual problems rank among the top three problems in the majority of studies on newly married couples (Berkowitz & Yaeger-Berkowitz, 2007). When the newlywed couples were interviewed later in their relationships, the sex problems had not diminished; rather, they talked about them less often. This is a common trend, many people decide to live with sexual problems and not talk about them.

Research indicates that the medical community is aware of the need for better communication about sex between doctors and patients; however, there is a constant stream of survey results that indicate doctors do not address sex issues. In fact, 91% of Americans feel it is appropriate for a physician to take a sexual history (Ende, Rockwell, & Glasgow, 1984). When asked who people would prefer to talk about sex with (other than their sexual partner), the most frequent answer was physician, even more so than a close friend (Noland, 2013). People want to talk to physicians about sex. Yet it seems little information about sexual health and/or impetus to take a sexual history is trickling down into the actual office visit.

Patients do not expect their doctors to bring up sexual issues. The importance of this extends beyond facilitating positive communicative encounters; many significant sexual health issues such as sexually transmitted infections need to be addressed in the clinical setting. According to the American Medical Association Council on Scientific Affairs only 11% to 37% of primary care physicians routinely take a sexual history from new patients. However, this number increases to 76% if a specific complaint is sexual in nature (Wimberly, 2006). A large study found that only 14% of adults aged 40 to 80 years in the United States reported that a physician had asked about their sexual concerns within the past three years (Laumann, 2003).

Research shows that there are many reasons why physicians do not talk about sex with patients (Althof, 2013). These include: lack of training in this area, lack of communication skills, not enough time, fear of offending patient, reimbursement concerns, outside of area of expertise, lack of available or approved treatments, growing knowledge gap between improvements in sexual medicine and provider skills/knowledge, discomfort in asking sexual questions, particularly to opposite gender and discomfort in asking sexual questions to adolescents and the elderly. Medical doctor Charles Marwick wrote an article for *Journal of the American Medical Association (JAMA)* about a study regarding doctor-patient communication about sex. He found that over 85% of the adults polled indicated they would like to talk to their physicians about sexual problems, but most do not. He found that patients don't talk about sex because patients feared that physicians will dismiss concerns, that they would embarrass their physicians, that physicians could not help them anyway, because there was lack of opportunity to introduce the topic, they felt shame or embarrassment, or because of societal taboo to openly talk about sex.

So it seems neither patients nor physicians are good at addressing sexual health issues. It is important to realize that patient concerns about sex are not limited to the biological dimensions of sex such as contraception, infertility, and sexually transmitted infections. Realistically, physician skills in talking about sex vary. It has little to do with gender, age, or ethnicity. Some physicians are more comfortable talking about sex with their patients than others. Personal factors that influence a doctor's reluctance to talk about sex include conservative beliefs about sex, embarrassment, and the reluctance to intrude on a personal topic. Not surprisingly a study found that doctors with more liberal beliefs about sex were more likely to bring up sex with patients, and, this same study found that males were much more liberal about sexual beliefs than female doctors (Papaharitou, 2008).

A national self-report survey of ob/gyns reported their sexual history taking behaviors (Sobecki et al., 2012). It is important to note that ob/gyns discuss sex more with patients than any other specialty. The study found that only 63% of ob/gyns asked their patients about sexual activities, 40% asked about sexual problems, 28.5% sexual satisfaction, 27.7% sexual orientation/identity, 13.8% pleasure associated with sex. Unfortunately 25% reported that they expressed disapproval to their patients.

Medical schools vary greatly on how they teach students to take a sexual history and talk about sex. Because the medical school curriculum is so full, some schools do not teach any skills regarding the sexual history. The following case study is based on the experiences of a medical school professor who teaches medical students how to take a sexual history.

Case: Teaching Students to Take an Exam

Jill Miller is an attending physician at a large medical school affiliated with an urban hospital. She is an ob/gyn who has been tasked with teaching fourth-year medical students how to take a sexual history. Last week she gave a two-hour lecture on taking a sexual history to all the fourth-year students. Those students are now working in breakout groups. She has four students in her cluster. Jill knows how difficult it is to get students to feel comfortable taking a sexual history, especially since most will be younger than their patients. Her students today are Usha, Raj, Beth and Chris. In her lecture she explained that experts suggest for most patients, taking a comprehensive sexual history does not need to occur at every visit, but should happen at least once per year (Wimberly et al., 2006). Historically, men have received much more attention and better care than women when it comes to sexual health so she stressed that the same questions be asked to both men and women, taking a unified approach to the history.

"Okay folks, who remembers the key points to consider when obtaining a good sexual history according to the Sinha and Palep-Singh 2007 article in *Obstetrics, Gynecology, and Reproductive Medicine?*" Jill asked the students. Everyone raised their hands. She laughed—typical med students, she thought to herself. "Okay, Usha?"

"Yes, so, doctors should, make the patient comfortable, avoid embarrassment, allow sufficient time for interview, discuss the problem in detail, find out the most important cause of concern, discover the background history and work out a management plan in agreement with the patient that is tailor-made to an individual." Usha listed the key points in the exact order they appeared on the PowerPoint slide.

"Perfect Usha." Jill says taking in the students' eager faces. "As you know, it's a lot easier said than done. I know you remember some of your first experiences with physical exams during your second year, and those were with paid practice patients. It is more difficult with real patients. Okay, so my teaching style is 'see one, do one, teach one.' So let's start with the 'see one.' I have a video of myself conducting sexual histories with different patients. This way you can see what I am talking about before you have to do it yourself.

"Okay, first make sure the patient is physically comfortable. This means the patient is clothed and in a private area, especially if you practice in a hospital clinic. You know how in some exam rooms, such as in the Emergency Department, there is only a curtain for privacy. That isn't the best place to talk about sexual issues. Most patients feel more comfortable without observers in the room, so it is best to ask medical students, nurses, and others to leave, although the patient may request an escort. This is why you are watching a video rather than shadowing me in the hospital. Make sure it is the right time to talk about sex. For example, acute visits for a specific issue are not the time to talk about it. A follow-up comprehensive visit is a much more appropriate venue to begin the process. And do the talking before and after the physical exam so the patient is clothed and comfortable. The first thing I like to do is get permission to take a sexual history." Jill Miller finishes her lecture to the group and pushes the play button.

```
Dr. Miller: At this point in the exam I
            usually ask some question
            about your sex life. Is this
            Okay?

Patient:    Sure, that would be fine.

Dr. Miller: Are you sexually active?

Patient:    No.

Dr. Miller: How many partners have you
            had in the past year?
```

Jill stops the video at this point and asks, "Does anyone know why I am ask-ing about the number of partners if they said they were not sexually active?"

Beth remembered that even if a person says they are not sexually active, a good doctor will follow-up with a probing question. She says, "are you sexually active means different things to different people, so it is important to follow up with a question about number of partners in the past year."

Jill responds, "That is right. For example, some patients may say they are not sexually active if they have gone a week without sex, but have had nu-merous partners in the last month. Lets continue with this interview."

```
Patient:    None, I haven't had any
            partners. I have not had any
            sex in the last year, not
            even with my husband.

Dr. Miller: Is this by choice?
```

Jill tells the students that if the patient is not sexually active by choice, then they can move on to the next topic. If the patient indicates they are not fine with it or it is not by choice, then the physician has to take a complete sexual history to determine if and how they can help. She ends by explaining, "Also, remember, if the person says they are not sexually active, it is important to determine if they are comfortable with their situation. There may be some problems (with them or their partners) and you are providing them an opening to talk about it. Also remember, it is extremely important to ask this to all your patients. I have found that even ob/gyns have a hard time probing with these questions with older patients and patients that are younger than they are. If someone is 22 or 72, you should ask these follow-ups, regardless of their marital status.

"The hardest thing for new doctors seems to be talking about sex with patients. Experts say that using a system of questions starting with 'Are you sexually active?' helps physicians to be more comfortable and consistent when it comes to taking a sexual history. You need to develop a pattern, a system that rolls off of your tongue. This will make it second nature. This can help you to be comfortable and appear to be open to patients. If you are comfortable and matter of fact, then your patient may be more comfortable and reveal important information. However, experts suggest that asking 'Are you sexually active?' is not enough. The annual exam should also include the following questions at a minimum (Wimberely, 2006):

1) How many sexual partners have you had in the past year?

2) What do you know about the sexual practices of your partner(s)?

3) Do you engage in sexual activity with men, women, or both?

"Asking the third question demonstrates that you are open to gay and lesbian patients and that you do not assume that your patients are heterosexual. I tell my patients these are three questions that I ask all of my adult patients, regardless of their age, gender, or marital status. Never make assumptions about a person's sexuality. I still get surprised regularly and I have learned not to judge a book by its cover, especially when it comes to the age of the patient. A complete sexual history includes determination of the cause(s) of the problem(s), the biological and psychological impact of the problem(s) on the individual and the couple, and the influence of other health factors, medications, lifestyle, and diseases.

"As with any visit, the goal is obtain the necessary relevant information to accurately diagnose the process, however, experts on sexual health stress that the clinical relationship should not be sacrificed for information: It is essential to maintain rapport and empathy. Last week I taught you about the 5 Ps. They are a popular method to remember key factors that are important in a sexual history, mostly focusing on sexual risk. I think these are so important that I gave you a pamphlet with the 5 Ps and a summary of some opening questions. Do you have that pamphlet?"

Partners: For sexual risk, it is important to determine the number and gender of a patient's sexual partners. Avoid assumptions about partner gender in the initial history taking. It is recommended that you use the word "partner" rather than man or woman.

If there is a history of multiple partners, explore for more specific risk factors, such as condom use with partners and partners' risk factors, such as other partners, intravenous drug abuse, history of STIs, and drug use with sex. If the patient has a single partner, ask about length of time the couple have been together and about partner risk factors, such as other partners and intravenous drug abuse. You should also discuss the patient's and their partner's satisfaction with each others' sexual functioning.

Prevention of pregnancy: Based on information about the partner(s), you can easily determine if the patient is at risk of becoming pregnant or of causing a pregnancy. If so, determine if a pregnancy is truly desired.

Protection from STI: You should ask "What do you do to protect yourself from STIs and HIV?" This open-ended question allows different avenues of discussion, such as condom use, monogamy, patient's self perception of risk and perception of partner's risk.

Remember, even if you have determined that the patient has had a single partner in the past 12 months and that that partner has had no other partners, infrequent or no condom use would still merit risk reduction counseling.

Practices: If the patient has had multiple partners in the past year or a partner with other partners, you may want to explore this further in terms of sexual practices and condom use.

Past history of STD: A history of prior gonorrhea or chlamydia increases a person's risk of repeat infections. A recent or past history of STIs may indicate high-risk behavior. You can either ask the patient about this or obtain the information from the patients' chart.

The Opening Questions: Here are four potential opening questions to get the conversation going.

QUESTION 1

Doctor:	Are you sexually active?
Patient:	Yes, I do OK.
Doctor:	How many partners have you had in the past year?

QUESTION 2

Doctor:	Are you satisfied with the quality of your sex life?
Patient:	Umm, it's OK, it could be better.

If the patient reports low or medium levels of satisfaction you could follow-up with:

Doctor:	What might make it better?

OR, if you prefer an open-ended question rather than a closed yes/no question you can ask:

Doctor:	In what ways are you dissatisfied with the quality of your sex life?

QUESTION 3

Doctor:	Do you have any sexual concerns or worries you would like to talk about today?
Patient:	No, I don't think so.
Doctor:	Are you sure?

> **QUESTION 4**
>
> Sometimes people with (diabetes, depression, hypertension....) have sexual issues. Do you have any concerns you want to discuss with me?
>
> **OR,** if the patient recently started or switched medications you can ask:
>
> **Doctor:** After starting this new medication, did you notice any changes in your sexual enjoyment? Did it increase, decrease or stay the same?

Jill waited for her students to look the pamphlet over.

"Let's talk about question #3. It is important to give the patient some time to think about the answer. The automatic response to this question may be no, but asking again gives patients a needed opportunity to express concerns. Many medical schools today are teaching students and residents they need to repeat questions and ask follow-up questions such as 'are you sure you do not have any questions' in the general medical history."

"That makes a lot of sense," Usha said. "The last time I was at my doctor's, he asked me three times if I was sure that I didn't have any questions about a new medication I started taking."

"Yeah, I know it can be annoying, but so many patients say no the first time you ask and then really open up the second or third time you ask." Jill responded. "Lets talk about question #4 now. You can tailor this question to the patients' medical history. This also emphasizes that many people have this problem, universalizing the condition and reducing stigma.

"Once the patient has disclosed a sexual concern, you can ask a variety of follow-up questions. The next set of questions I am going to teach you about are from the International Consultation of Sexual Medicine Stepwise Diagnostic and Treatment Algorithm for Sexual Dysfunctions in Men and Women (Althof, 2006). Here is a handout, let's go over it together." Jill then hands each student some papers.

Next Step: Identifying the problem

"You can use the information obtained in the history to determine the major complaints and subtype of dysfunction. Dysfunctions may be lifelong or acquired, generalized (occurring with all partners) or specific (occurring with only one partner). Physicians are encouraged to explore all the biological (medical), psychological, and interpersonal aspects that may have contributed to its onset and continuance. It may be helpful to put the problem into a context—why patients are having these issues. Perhaps their partner has severe migraines, they are dealing with infertility issues, or their mother-in-law moved in." The students all laughed.

"Yeah, having my in-laws in the house…that would do it for me!" Chris joked.

THE SEXUAL HISTORY

Start by asking a patient about their satisfaction with their levels of:
- ☐ desire/interest
- ☐ arousal
- ☐ orgasm/ejaculation
- ☐ pain
- ☐ overall levels of satisfaction

Possible follow-up questions include:
How much does this problem bother you?
What barriers prevented you from coming into to talk about this sooner? (e.g., costs, side effects, embarrassment)
Have you sought treatment for this problem?
What is your partner's response to this problem?
Is your partner interested in resuming a sexual relationship?
Does your partner have any sexual problems?

Once you have completed some follow-up questions to the initial inquiry, there are specific questions that you can ask men and women.

Specific questions for women:
Are you satisfied with the level of your sexual desire or interest?
Are you satisfied with the frequency of lovemaking?
During sex do you have difficulty becoming mentally aroused?
During sex do you have difficulty with genital lubrication (wetness)?
During sex do you have difficulty achieving orgasm when you want to?
Do you experience pain during sex?
Are you satisfied with the overall quality of your sexual life?

Specific questions for men:
Are you satisfied with the level of your sexual desire or interest?
Are you satisfied with the frequency of lovemaking?
During sex do you have difficulty ejaculating?
Do you frequently ejaculate too quickly without wanting to?
Have you noticed any changes to the shape of your penis?
Do you experience pain during sex?
Are you satisfied with the overall quality of your sexual life?

Jill told her students a bit more about the sexual history, "Inquiries about sexual desire and interest should concentrate on frequency of sexual activity. It does not have to be intercourse, it could be oral/manual stimulation and does not have to lead to orgasm, whether it is by a partner or alone, frequency of sexual thoughts and fantasies, and how bothered the patient is with their reported level of function. I recommend that physicians use slang if they get the feeling that their patients are more comfortable using slang. It is essential is that you both understand one another and are on the same page."

"Okay, so what would you say to get a patient talking about a sexual problem, Chris?" Jill asked her student.

"Well, that article recommended that I say, 'I realize this is hard for you to talk about and it is embarrassing for you; but if we can treat the problem, it will be worth it.'"

"Yes, do you think you could say that to a patient?" Jill asked.

"I do. Yes, I could say something like that," Chris replied with a smile.

"Great. Another trick is to phrase an empathic reply that is in harmony with the feelings you have identified in the other person. Later in the conversation, you may be able to say something that will help that person have a better perspective or to resolve the particular concern. You should indicate your willingness to help or to be of service. If you cannot help the person, be prepared to refer them to someone who can help."

Jill continued. "So, I would say, 'I am glad you told me about this problem so we can get you some help. Unfortunately this is not in my area of expertise, but I can recommend Dr. Raj who can help you. I know you will have to go through the sexual history again and it will be hard to tell a stranger, but this person hears this all the time and can figure out what is going on.'"

Raj asked a question, "I know its bad to dismiss a patient or tell them you don't approve of their lifestyle, but what if you disagree with a person or if they are doing something dangerous?"

Students frequently asked this kind of question. Jill told them what she always tells people, "If you disagree with what the person expresses, you should be honest and state a difference of opinion. However, indicate that you acknowledge the person's right to her or his expression of that idea or feeling. For example, a lot of patients come in and want a prescription for Viagra or other drugs for erectile dysfunction but are not good candidates. Remember that video we saw last month about priaprism? It is not fun having a six-hour erection and then getting your penis drained in the emergency room before penile gangrene starts to set in."

"Yes, I think almost everyone was wincing during that video…" Raj replied.

"Right, so I would say something like this. 'I understand you may want a prescription for Viagra and you have a right to ask for it. I like that you are involved and proactive. But I think we should explore some other options first because….'"

Chris then asked another good question, "What do you say to patients who don't use condoms? Especially those at high risk for pregnancy or STIs?"

"I understand that condoms decrease your pleasure, but given your lifestyle, it is important for you to use one every single time you have sex because…" Jill just rattled this off because she says it to so many patients. "I think its important to acknowledge the reason they don't use condoms and then problem-solve or explain why it is so important to use a condom every time people have sex. Any other questions?"

"Yeah, so I have a friend who doesn't want to tell her husband that it really hurts when they have sex. What would you say to a patient in that case?"

"I get this one frequently, my patients seem to feel like it is something to be ashamed of. I usually say, 'I understand your reasons why you think you cannot tell your husband that having sex is painful. You are scared that he will think you are abnormal. But until we can get this problem resolved, I think you should try to tell him. Let's practice some things you can say.' And then we practice together. I have even role-played with patients before. When it comes to sex talk with patients, it's really important to try to avoid non-accepting behaviors: do not threaten, lecture, argue, ridicule, or make jokes. The more natural and matter of fact you are with patients, the better. They will appreciate it. I like to remind patients the important role that sex plays in their overall health and happiness."

Jill ends the session with these words for her students. "Overcoming barriers to communication about sex and sexuality with patients is a slow process. Although we have made great strides to have partnerships with patients rather than form paternalistic relationships, when it comes to sex, research shows it is up to physicians to bring up the topic. Doing so can strengthen the provider-patient relationship by showing that patient that you care about them and take their concerns seriously. Only you can provide them with a sense of hopefulness, support, and an understanding of their condition and potential outcomes" (Althof, et al., 2013).

Conclusion

Research shows that economic factors, such as recession, do not affect people's sex drive. However, stress and insomnia do. A 2009 *Consumer Reports* poll of 1,000 people found that 81% of adults aged 18–75 reported avoiding or delaying sex with their partners in the past year. The most common reasons that people reported for avoiding sex were tiredness (53%), illness

(49%), and not being in the mood (40%). Obviously, many of these reasons are health related and could be addressed by medical professionals. Approximately **half** of older women and **one-third** of younger and middle-aged women have sexual problems including difficulty lubricating and/or achieving orgasm, low desire, lack of pleasure during sex, or pain during sex (Wimberely, 2012). It is extremely important for patients' physical and mental health that physicians possess competence in communicating about sex, however, at the end of the day medical doctors are just people and get nervous and embarrassed. Unfortunately sexual health takes a back seat at many medical schools and training programs because of the stigma associated with sex that persists in our culture.

DISCUSSION QUESTIONS

1. In your opinion, regarding sexual issues, what should medical professionals be talking about with patients?

2. There is evidence that physicians are reluctant to talk about sex with their patients. What can we do to encourage their medical providers to engage in these conversations? What are some obstacles that would prevent physicians from doing so that you still foresee?

3. How important do you think it is for doctors to talk about sexual health issues with their patients?

4. Do you think most doctors need more training in sexual communication?

5. How well do you think the advice provided in this case study will work in real life?

6. Based on the research provided in this case study, it seems it may be up to you to broach the subject of sexual health with your physician. How would you do it?

References

Althof, S., Rosen, R., Perelman, M., & Eusebio Rubio-Aurioles, E. (2013). Standard Operating Procedures for Taking a Sexual History. *Journal of Sexual Medicine, 10,* 26–35.

American Medical Association Council on Scientific Affairs. (1996). "Health Care Needs of Gay Men and Lesbians in the United States." *Journal of the American Medical Association, 275,* no. 17.

Berkowitz, B., & Yaeger-Berkowitz, S. (2007). *He's Just Not up for It Anymore: Why Men Stop Having Sex and What You Can Do about It.* New York: HarperCollins.

Ende, J., Rockwell, S., & Glasgow, M. (1984). The sexual history in general medicine practice. *Archives of Internal Medicine, 144,* 558–561.

Haboubi, N.H.J., & Lincoln, N. (2003). Views of Health Professionals on Discussing Sexual Issues with Patients. *Disability and Rehabilitation* 25, 291–296.

Laumann, E., Paik, A., Glasser, D.B., Kang, J., Wang, T., Levinson, B., Moreira, E., Nicolosi, A., & Gingel, C. (2003). The Pfizer Global Study of Sexual Attitudes and Behaviors," Pfizer, http://www.pfizerglobalstudy.com/study/study-results.asp.

Laroche, C., & Rene de Grace G. (1997). Factors of Satisfaction Associated with Happiness in Adults. *Canadian Journal of Counselling, 31,* 275–286.

Marwick, C. (1999). Survey Says Patients Expect Little Physician Help on Sex. *JAMA, 281(23),* 2173–4.

Neto, F., & Pinto, M. (2015). Satisfaction with Love Life Across the Adult Life Span. *Applied Research Quality of Life, 10,* 289–304.

Smith, C.V. (2007). In Pursuit of 'Good' Sex: Self-Determination and the Sexual Experience. *Journal of Social and Personal Relationships, 24,* 69–85.

Papaharitou, S., Nakopoulou, E., Moraitou, M., Tsimtsiou, Z., Konstantinidou, E., & Hatzichristou, D. (2008). Exploring Sexual Attitudes of Students in Health Professions. *Journal of Sexual Medicine, 5,* 1308–1316. doi: 10.1111/j.1743-6109.2008.00826.

Sinha A., & Palep-Singh, M. (2007) Taking a sexual history. *Obstetrics, Gynaecology, and Reproductive Medicine,* 18, 49–50.

Sobecki, J., Curlin, F., Rasinski, K., & Tessler Lindau, S. (2012). What we don't talk when we don't talk about sex: Results of a national survey of U.S. Obstetrician/Gynecologist. *Journal of Sexual Medicine,* 9, 1285–1294.

Wimberly, Y. , Hogben, M., Moore-Ruffin, J., Moore, S., & Fry-Johnson, Y. (2006). Sexual history-taking among primary care physicians. *Journal of the National Medical Association, 98(12),* 1924–9.

CHAPTER 23

What to Expect in Couples Counseling

Dayna Henry & Rose Hartzell-Cushanick

KEY TERMS

Sexual health   Sex therapy
Sexual problems/dysfunction

ABSTRACT

Sexual health and satisfaction are important determinants of overall health. However, throughout their lifetime, many adults experience sexual problems or dysfunctions and some may seek out professional help to resolve these issues. The way sexual problems are defined and the causes of sexual problems impact the type of treatment that is offered. Research is presented on the various factors that can both cause and inform treatment include physiological, psychological and relationship factors. Certification requirements for sex therapists are presented along with several case examples informed by the author's own practice of sex therapy to stimulate discussion about the varying causes and potential treatments for sexual problems.

"Sex is perfectly natural but not naturally perfect."

– Sue Johanson, Author, Sex Educator & Counselor

The idea that sex and sexuality are natural and part of overall health is a common one supported by many national and international organizations (e.g., Sexuality Information and Education Council of the U.S., World Association for Sexual Health, World Health Organization, Centers for Disease Control and Prevention, American Psychiatric Association). The World Health Organization (WHO) presents a working definition of sexual health on their website as follows:

> Sexual health is a state of physical, emotional, mental and social well-being in relation to sexuality; it is not merely the absence of disease, dysfunction or infirmity. Sexual health requires a positive and respectful approach to sexuality and sexual relationships, as well as the possibility of having pleasurable and safe sexual experiences, free of coercion, discrimination and violence. For sexual health to be attained and maintained, the sexual rights of all persons must be respected, protected and fulfilled.

Sexual problems vary widely and can include a lack of interest in sex to a difficulty achieving aspects of the sexual response cycle (Laumann, Paik, & Rosen 1999; Lue et al., 2004). The American Psychiatric Association (APA) defines sexual dysfunction as "a heterogeneous group of disorders that are typically characterized by a clinically significant disturbance in a person's ability to respond sexually or to experience sexual pleasure" (APA, 2013). Sexual dysfunctions listed in the *APA's Diagnostic and Statistical Manual of Mental Disorders* 5th edition (DSM-5) include male hypoactive sexual desire disorder, premature (early) ejaculation, delayed ejaculation, erectile disorder, genito-pelvic pain/penetration disorder, female sexual interest/arousal disorder, female orgasmic disorder, substance/medication-induced sexual dysfunction, other specified sexual dysfunction, and unspecified sexual dysfunction. In order to determine whether someone meets the diagnostic criteria in the DSM-5, therapists typically assess if the sexual dysfunction has afflicted an individual their entire life (lifelong) or happened after a period of "normal" function (acquired). In addition, sex therapists will ask the individual questions in order to determine if the problem is present all of the time (generalized) or only under a specific set of circumstances (situational).

However, other sexual health professionals have critiqued the focus on "dysfunction" and reduction to physiological disturbances in a way that leaves out the contexts in which the problems occur, in particular, with respect to conceptualizing women's sexuality (Kleinplatz, 2012; The Working Group, 2000). They proposed that a sexual problem be defined as "discontent or dissatisfaction with any emotional, physical, or relational aspect of sexual experience." Sexual problems can occur as a result of many influencing factors including socio-cultural (e.g., religious beliefs, sexuality seen as taboo), economic or political factors (e.g., access to adequate information), partner and relationship factors (e.g., conflict, lack of communication), psychological factors (e.g., depression, past experience of trauma), and medical factors (e.g., chronic illness or pain, medication side effects, physiological dysfunction) (The Working Group, 2000). As a result of this critique, the diagnostic criteria for sexual dysfunction in the DSM-5 requires clinicians to consider these factors when making a diagnosis (APA, 2013).

In the Global Study of Sexual Attitudes and Behaviors (GSSAB), one of the few multi-country surveys to examine the sexual attitudes, beliefs, and health of middle and older adults, almost half of sexually active men and women reported experiencing at least one sexual difficulty within the past year (Moreira et al., 2005). The most common complaint by women is low sexual desire or a lack of interest in sex (Kleinplatz, 2012; Moreira et al., 2005). Additionally, women report issues with arousal, lubrication, orgasm, and pain (Hayes et al., 2008; Herbenick, Schick, Sanders, Reece, & Fortenberry, 2015; Moreira et al., 2005). The most common sexual problems reported by men include issues with ejaculation and erectile dysfunction, which can include difficulty achieving or maintaining an erection (Kubin, Wagner, & Fugl-Meyer, 2003; Laumann et al., 1999; Moreira et al., 2005; Porst et al., 2007). In national surveys of U.S. adults, an analysis of recent sexual encounters revealed that many, but not all, of the commonly reported sexual problems increase with age for both men and women (Herbenick et al., 2010; Laumann et al., 1999).

The causes of sexual dysfunction, dissatisfaction, or problems can vary. They include physiological, psychological, and relationship factors. Physiological factors such as chronic illness (Nusbaum, Hamilton, & Lenahan, 2003), cancers, medications, hormones, injuries, and health behaviors such as smoking can cause sexual problems (Institute for Sexual Medicine, 2010a). Sexual dysfunction or problems in both men and women are related to mental health concerns such as depression and lower self-esteem as well as relationship concerns such as lower partner, sexual, and relationship satisfaction and less communication (e.g., Kelly, Strassberg, & Turner, 2006; Leiblum, Koochaki, Rodenberg, Barton, & Rosen, 2006; Shifren et al., 2008; Shindel, Eisenberg, Breyer, Sharlip & Smith, 2011; Tan, Tong, & Ho, 2012). The majority of those experiencing sexual difficulties do not seek help nor advice from a professional (Moreira et al., 2005; Laumann et al., 2009).

For most states, there are no overarching licensing requirements in order to become a sex therapist. For professional recognition, therapists choosing to specialize in sex therapy often get certified as a sex therapist through the American Association of Sexuality Educators, Counselors, and Therapists (AASECT.org). In order to become an AASECT certified sex therapist, individuals must meet/complete a number of rigorous requirements including holding a graduate degree in a therapy field (e.g., social work, marriage and family therapy, counseling, etc.) be licensed as a therapist in the state in which they are practicing therapy, and complete a minimum of a 10-hour Sexual Attitude Reassessment (SAR) where they participate in a process-oriented exploration of their feelings, attitudes, values, and beliefs regarding human sexuality and sexual behavior. In addition, therapists must have completed academic coursework related to sexuality generally, specialized sex therapy training, and a specified number of supervised hours of sex therapy.

Sex therapists work in many diverse ways to help those seeking professional help for their sexual dysfunctions or problems (Binik & Meana, 2009). Generally, sex therapists work predominately from a psychological/psychosocial perspective (i.e., emphasizes the psychological, social, and relational causes and solutions) or work from a biopsychosocial (Biology + Psychology + Social Factors) approach with an interdisciplinary team that combines physiological and medical approaches with psychosocial approaches. Each of these perspectives is explained further below.

Prescription medications intended to treat male erectile dysfunction have been available for almost 20 years (Lue, 2000). These medications are called PDE-5 inhibitors and include drugs such as Viagra, Levitra, Cialis, & Stendra. Other common physical or medical approaches to treating sexual problems for both men and women can include injections into the genitals, medications applied to the genitals, surgery, hormone management, physical therapy, and medical management which may include prescribing medications intended to treat other conditions or changing existing medications to those with fewer sexual side effects (Institute for Sexual Medicine, 2010b).

Many of the psychosocial techniques used by sex therapists today are based on the work of Masters and Johnson and a combination of other psychotherapies including cognitive-behavioral and couple's counseling (Binik & Meana, 2009). Typical psychosocial interventions utilized in sex therapy interventions include cognitive restructuring (e.g., education, script modification), emotional regulation (e.g., anxiety reduction), stimulation control and desensitization (e.g., physical techniques, sensate focus), behavioral activation (e.g., new sexual behaviors, use of aids) and general relationship building and enhancement (e.g., communication skills) (Binik & Meana, 2009). Combination or biopsychosocial approaches that can also be thought of as multidisciplinary, involve the use of medical care along with psychosocial interventions (Althof, 2006; Binik & Meana, 2009; Schnarch, 1990).

In a review of controlled studies using psychosocial approaches to treating both male and female sexual dysfunction, the majority of the studies utilized the traditional "Masters and Johnson" psychosocial approach that includes sensate focus (i.e., pleasuring one another through touch but not necessarily for arousal), masturbation exercises and the stop-start technique, cognitive-behavioral therapy, or teaching communication and social skills (Berner & Gunzler, 2012; Gunzler & Berner, 2012). For treatment of men slightly less than half included medication or drug therapy (Berner & Gunzler, 2012). However, this type of therapy has had limited success in treating most types of female sexual dysfunction (Gunzler & Berner, 2012; Kingsburg & Woodard, 2015). The length of sex therapy treatment was typically 8-12 weeks (Berner & Gunzler, 2012; Gunzler & Berner, 2012).

To help get a sense of the types of problems that might bring someone to sex therapy and the diverse ways sex therapists might help people, we present three fictive case studies.

Case Study 1: 50 shades of ambivalence

"I began to wonder if this was all there is," Paulo expresses while looking sad. I had seen Paulo and his wife Angelica together for one session previously. They had originally come to me due to Paulo's infidelity. Although Paulo had committed different types of infidelity throughout their relationship in the past, Angelica had decided that the most recent incident was the last. She had given him an ultimatum: they either needed to seek therapy to work on their marriage and his infidelity; or she wanted a divorce. Like most straight couples, the woman was the one who called and initiated therapy.

"I love you," Paulo said, looking at Angelica. Then he turned to me. "Don't get me wrong. Angelica is the most amazing wife, and every aspect of our relationship is awesome EXCEPT for the sex. Every time we do it, it's so predictable. It's always in our bedroom, in the same positions, in the same order of things. After so many years of being together it's just...."

Paulo's voice drifted off and his face turned to the side to look out the window in my office. I followed his eyes and noticed the cherry blossoms has just bloomed and were looking particularly lovely today. Did he notice? I look at Angelica. Tears are rolling down her face. In the first session, she talked about not realizing there was a problem until the infidelity. Because they were their only sexual partners, Angelica assumed their sex life was just like any other after so many years. She thought after you become comfortable with someone sexually, you know what they like, so you get into a routine because it works well. The couple indicated that they had met in high school at 14 years of age and married right after graduation. It's interesting that so many of my clients met and married so young.

"So it sounds like you are saying you were bored with your sex life, is that right?" I asked. Paulo turned to look back at me, his body softened. "I don't think she would be interested in having the type of sex that I might be interested in."

Angelica wipes the tears from her cheeks and angrily shouts, "How the hell would YOU know?" Angelica shouts. She wipes the tears from her cheeks as her body is shaking. She continues. "Now I see what's going on. You were not happy but you didn't say anything! You had all these ideas, but you didn't say a damned thing. You ASSUMED things about me. Why? Because we've been together for 40 years? Because I'm a woman? WHY?"

Angelica stopped. It was evident she was angry. But she needed to get this out, and so I gave her the space. She continued, her voice softer.

"You know, I thought this was all my fault. Like… I did something, or didn't do something, and then you cheated because of me. Now I see, you cheated because of you!" I handed her a tissue as fresh tears were streaming down her face. Her cheeks and chest are flushed from the emotions.

Paulo looks shocked. It makes me wonder if Angelica typically communicates in this way. "So, Angelica, you are saying that you wished Paulo had talked to you when he wasn't happy with your sex life. Is that right?" I ask. "Yes" she says, wiping more tears.

"Do you and your wife ever talk about sex?" I ask Paulo.

"Talk about sex?" Paulo laughed uncomfortably. "No, I guess we don't. It's kind of an uncomfortable. Like she said, it's something we shouldn't have to talk about after being together so long."

Angelica interrupts. "Okay. It's uncomfortable. But you having sex with another woman is more comfortable?" "I was taught that women don't care as much about sex. You said so last session. You said that a routine was normal. That what we did was normal. Well, maybe normal for women, but not normal for me," Paulo says.

"I never said I didn't care as much about sex. I said I thought routines were normal. That is what I was taught," Angelica says. Then, after a brief pause, she has a breakthrough. "Or, maybe, I just assumed. And… Maybe I was also bored but didn't want to say anything. Because… I didn't want you to feel like less of a man."

Paulo seems frozen, his eyes fixed on Angelica. It's almost like he's embarrassed. I'm looking at him, but he doesn't want to look back. I see his eyes shift to me for a second and then back at her.

After some silence I decide to ask Paulo, "Do you think it's possible that Angelica might have been bored as well?"

"I guess," Paulo says. He's now looking at his feet. He definitely appears embarrassed. "You seem embarrassed, maybe?" I suggest. "What's going on?"

"It WAS my fault. What was I thinking? What was I doing? We talk about everything and we didn't talk about this, until now." Paulo says, looking sad. He turns to Angelica and reaches for her hand. She seemed to reluctantly allow him to take it. "I'm sorry," he says. "I'm sorry for not talking to you, for not asking you how you felt, for assuming you were happy, for cheating." Now they were both crying.

After validating their feelings, I ended the session with some homework. I told them to individually write down things they wanted to try or do sexually and then talk about what was on their lists. Then come to the next session with a common list—things they would both be interested in trying.

Two weeks later, Paulo and Angelica are in the waiting room. They are both smiling and holding hands. It seems a shift has happened. Back in my office, I start by asking the couple, "So what did you talk about?"

"We did the homework," Paulo says. "And I think it was a conversation we should have had a long time ago. We didn't or… I didn't think it was something she wanted to do and I was wrong." "It was hard," Angelica says. "People don't talk about sex so how do you know how to talk about it?"

"It sounds like you overcame some big barriers to have this conversation," I respond. "Tell me about the things you agreed to try."

Paulo starts. "It would be fun for Angelica to take the lead every once and awhile during sex, and for us to do some role play. It also would be fun to have sex in other areas of our house now that our kids are gone. I also thought it might be interesting to use some props every now and then— like vibrators, or handcuffs, or something like that."

Angelica interrupts. "Now that stuff, I am not sure about. The props. Do regular people do those things?" she asks me.

"People do lots of different things," I tell her. "I have many clients who try those things or others. Some like it, and others don't prefer it. It's really a personal preference. However, you both have to agree," I explain.

I think to myself, so many of my clients ask me if something is normal. We continued the session by talking about their homework and plans for next session.

Case Study 2: Permanently Injured?

"I'm still having trouble taking things to a higher level with women," Jason says. "I'll date, but once it looks as though things are going to progress sexually, I back off. I blow them off completely. I'm starting to question if it's even worth dating in the first place." "Tell me more." I say, as I attempt to sort through what's preventing Jason from moving forward in his relationships. He brushes some hair that has fallen into his face away from his eyes. I start to reflect on our first session together five months ago, when he told me how had injured his penis in a mountain biking accident. Shortly before working with me, Jason had also started seeing a sexual medicine physician who was managing his erectile symptoms medically. Around three months ago, he had surgery that physically restored his erectile function.

"It's frustrating… even though I know things are physically better, I'm still nervous that if I start to get intimate with someone I'm dating, I'm not going to get an erection." Jason looks down. "It's hard for me to forget and let go of the four years that I wasn't able to obtain an erection at all."

Although he's 24 years old, Jason looks much older to me. Perhaps from the years of engaging in outdoor extreme sports, or perhaps from the years of living with the weight of erectile dysfunction on his shoulders? "Those 'dark' years, were the worst years of my life," Jason mumbles, continuing to look down. "I feel like I lost my best sexual years to this stupid injury. I know things work now. I mean, I can tell during masturbation. But I don't have much sexual experience because of what happened. I don't even know where I should start sexually with someone, and I for sure don't know what I would do if I wasn't able to keep it up when I'm with someone else."

Jason and I sit in silence for a couple of moments while I gather my thoughts. I have to decide how I am going to proceed with him. Since I started working as a sex therapist five years ago, I've been surprised how many men like Jason I have seen. I've noticed that erectile dysfunction in young men not only negatively impacts their self-esteem, but can cause depression, and paralyze them when it comes to putting themselves out there in order to develop a deep relationship with a partner.

Case Study 3: Five million things to do and sex 'aint one

I look at the couple in front of me who I'm meeting for the first time. I know from their chart that they are in their late 30s. Janae is dressed in a long skirt and oversized top with no shape. Her hair is back in a messy ponytail and she looks older than her age. Dylan on the other hand is well groomed and appears very style conscious. Although Dylan's wearing shorts and flip flops, you can tell that a lot of effort went into the outfit. The shorts seem expensive and they are ironed. As a couple, they seem mismatched and I can already feel the tension in the air before we all sit down.

"We have some intimacy problems," Dylan says looking at the ground. I've worked as a sex therapist long enough to know that 'intimacy problems' often means sexual issues. "Janae just isn't interested in sex anymore," Dylan says, looking right at her.

"That's not fair and not true," Janae says, seemingly frustrated as she glares back at Dylan, and then at me. "We have three children, we both work full time, and ultimately there are only so many hours in a day. We just don't have the time we used to before we had kids. I'm still interested in sex, it just isn't as big of a priority to me anymore," Janae crosses her arms over her chest.

"You're right," Dylan shouts back, "it's not a priority to you, and I feel like I'm not a priority to you either. I feel like I'm the last thing you care about, and that everyone else's needs are more important than mine." With crossed arms, Dylan mumbles, "Sometimes I feel like an outsider in my own family."

We are five minutes into the session, and the couple is already plunging full force into therapy. Although it is snowing outside, the room is feeling especially warm.

"Hmmm…" I respond, to show I am being thoughtful with my words. "What is that like for you to hear?" I turn to Janae and ask. Janae looks dejected.

"It makes me feel sad. I don't want Dylan to feel like my last priority, but the truth is, I only have so much energy to give in a day." She looks over to Dylan, and then back at me. "I sometimes think about wanting sex, when

I'm not listing off in my head the 5 million other things I have to find time to do. I realize we should do it, but I don't want to force myself to have sex when I'm not feeling it."

"I don't want you to have sex with me if you don't want to either," Dylan interjects. "I want you to WANT me, and I want to feel like I'm important in your life!"

"This sounds like a good time to discuss goals," I interrupt the couple, not wanting to get too into treatment without knowing what they want out of therapy. "How would you know your journey with me is complete?" I ask.

DISCUSSION QUESTIONS

1. What do you think are the causes of the sexual issues of the clients presented in the fictive case studies? Do you think it's more physiological, psychological, or a combination and why? In what ways do the definitions of sexual problems impact the treatment provided by a therapist?

2. In couples, how is communication about sexual issues different or the same from other common issues that arise in relationships (e.g., money, parenting, religion, etc.)?

3. How does the portrayal of sexual issues in the case studies line up with or differ from what you see on television or in movies? How is this related to society's views about sex generally?

4. How does the portrayal of sex therapy in the case studies line up with or differ from what you see on television or movies? How does this impact someone's willingness to seek help for a sexual issue?

5. Do you feel that people with sexual issues are better served by someone with specialized training in sex therapy rather than a general practitioner? In what ways are sexual issues the same or different from other issues people might experience such as eating disorders, substance abuse, or mental health concerns?

6. Did you make any assumptions about the sexual orientation or identity of the clients in the fictive case study? Why or why not? How do you think sexual orientation or identity might impact sexual problems or sex therapy?

References

Althof, S. E. (2006). Sexual therapy in the age of pharmacotherapy. *Annual Review of Sex Research, 17*(1), 116–131. doi:10.1080/10532528. 2006.10559839.

American Psychiatric Association: Diagnostic and Statistical Manual of Mental Disorders, 5th Edition. (2013). Arlington, VA, American Psychiatric Association.

Berner, M. M., & Gunzler, C. (2012). Efficacy of psychosocial interventions in men and women with sexual dysfunctions – A systematic review of controlled clinical trials. Part 1—The efficacy of psychosocial interventions for male sexual dysfunction. *The Journal of Sexual Medicince, 9,* 3089–3107. doi: 10.1111/j.1743-6109.2012.02970.x.

Binik, Y. M., & Meana, M. (2009). The future of sex therapy: Specialization or marginalization? *Archives of Sexual Behavior, 38,* 1016–1027. doi: 10.1007/s10508-009-9475-9.

Centers for Disease Control and Prevention (CDC). (2014, December 2). *Sexual health.* Retrieved from http://www.cdc.gov/sexualhealth/.

Gunzler, C., & Berner, M. M. (2012). Efficacy of psychosocial interventions in men and women with sexual dysfunctions – A systematic review of controlled clinical trials. Part 2—The efficacy of psychosocial interventions for female sexual dysfunction. *The Journal of Sexual Medicince, 9,* 3108–3125. doi: 10.1111/j.1743-6109.2012.02965.x.

Hartmann, U., Heiser, K., Ruffer-Hesse, C., & Kloth, G. (2002). Female sexual desire disorders: Subtypes, classification, personality factors and new directions for treatment. *World Journal of Urology, 20*(2), 79–88. doi: 10.1007/s00345-002-0280-5.

Hayes, R. D., Dennerstein, L., Bennett, C. M., & Fairley, C. K. (2008). What is the "true" prevalence of female sexual dysfunctions and does the way we assess these conditions have an impact? *The Journal of Sexual Medicine, 5*(4), 777–787. doi: 10.1111/j.1743-6109.2007.00768.x.

Heiman, J. R. (2002). Sexual dysfunction: Overview of prevalence, etiological factors, and treatments. *The Journal of Sex Research, 39*(1), 73–78. doi: 10.1080/00224490209552124.

Herbenick, D., Reece, M., Schick, V., Sanders, S., Dodge, B., & Fortenberry, J.D. (2010). An event-level analysis of the sexual characteristics and composition among adults ages 18–59: Results from a national probability sample in the United States. *The Journal of Sexual Medicine, 79*(s5), 346–361. doi: 10.1111/j.1743-6109.2010.02020.x.

Herbenick, D., Schick, V., Sanders, S., Reece, M., & Fortenberry, J. D. (2015). Pain experienced during vaginal and anal intercourse with other-sex partners: Findings from a nationally representative probability study in United States. *The Journal of Sexual Medicine, 12*(4), 1040-1051. doi:10.111/jsm.12841.

Institute for Sexual Medicine. (2010a, February 27). *Sexual medicine diagnosis and treatments.* Retrieved from http://sexualmed.org/index.cfm/sexual-health-treatments/.

Institute for Sexual Medicine. (2010b, March 4). *Sexual health risk factors.* Retrieved from http://sexualmed.org/index.cfm/risk-factors/.

Johanson, S. (1992). *Sex is perfectly natural but not naturally perfect.* Penguin Group: Toronto.

Kelly, M. P., Strassberg, D. S., & Turner, C. M. (2006). Behavioral assessment of couples' communication in female orgasmic disorder. *Journal of Sex & Marital Therapy, 32*(2), 81–95. doi: 10.1080/00926230500442243.

Kingsberg, S. A., & Woodard, T. (2015). Female sexual dysfunction: Focus on low desire. *Obstetrics & Gynecology, 125*(2), 477–486. doi: 10.1097/AOG.0000000000000620.

Kleinplatz, P. (Ed.). (2012). *New directions in sex therapy: Innovations and alternatives* (2nd ed.). Routledge, Taylor & Francis Group: New York.

Kubin, M., Wagner, G., & Fugl-Meyer, A. R. (2003) Epidemiology of erectile dysfunction. *International Journal of Impotence Research, 15*, 63–71. doi:10.1038/sj.ijir.3900949.

Laumann, E.O., Glasser, D. B., Neves, R. C. S., Moreira Jr., E. D., & the GSSAB Investigators' Group. (2009). A population-based survey of sexual activity, sexual problems and associated help-seeking behavior patterns in mature adults in the United States of America. *International Journal of Impotence Research, 21*, 171–178. doi:10.1038/ijir.2009.7.

Laumann, E. O., Paik, A., & Rosen, R. C. (1999). Sexual dysfunction in the United States: Prevalence and predictors. *The Journal of the American Medical Association, 281*(6), 537–544. doi:10.1001/jama.281.6.537.

Leiblum, S. R., Koochaki, P. E., Rodenberg, C. A., Barton, I. P., & Rosen, R. (2006). Hypoactive sexual desire disorder in postmenopausal women: U.S. results from the Women's International Study of Health and Sexuality (WISHeS). *Menopause, 13*(1), 46–56. doi: 10.1097/01.gme.0000172596.76272.06.

Lue, T. F. (2000). Erectile dysfunction. *New England Journal of Medicine, 342*(24), 1802–1813. doi: 10.1056/NEJM200006153422407.

Lue, T. F., Basson, R., Rosen, R., Giuliano, F., Khoury, S., & Montorsi, F. (2004). *Sexual medicine: Sexual dysfunction in men and women.* Paris: Health Publications.

Moreira Jr., E. D., Brock, G., Glasser, D. B., Nicolosi, A., Laumann, E. O., Paik, A., Wang, T., Gingell, C., & the GSSAB Investigators' Group (2005). Help-seeking behavior for sexual problems: The global study of sexual attitudes and behaviors. *The International Journal of Clinical Practice, 59*(1), 6–16. doi: 10.1111/j.1742-1241.2005.00382.x

Nusbaum, M., Hamilton, C., & Lenahan, B. (2003). Chronic illness and sexual functioning. *American Family Physician, 67*(2), 347–354. Retrieved from http://europepmc.org/abstract/med/12562156.

Porst, H., Montorsi, F., Raymond, C. R., Gaynor, L., Grupe, S., & Alexander, J. (2007). The Premature Ejaculation Prevalence and Attitudes (PEPA) survey: Prevalence, comorbidities, and professional help-seeking. *European Urology, 51*(3), 816–824. doi:10.1016/j.eururo.2006.07.004.

Schnarch, D. M. (1990). *Constructing the sexual crucible.* New York: Norton.

Sexuality Information and Education Council of the United States (SIECUS). (n.d.). *About us.* Retrieved from http://www.siecus.org/index.cfm?fuseaction=Page.viewPage&pageId= 472.

Shifren, J. L., Monz, B. U., Russo, P.A., Segreti, A., & Johannes, C. B. (2008). Sexual problems and distress in United States women: Prevalence and correlates. *Obstetrics & Gynecology, 112*(5), 970–978. doi: 10.1097/AOG.0b013e3181898cdb.

Shindel, A. W., Eisenberg, M. L., Breyer, B. N., Sharlip, I. D., & Smith, J. F. (2011). Sexual function and depressive symptoms among female North American medical students. *The Journal of Sexual Medicine, 8*(2), 391–399. doi: 10.1111/j.1743-6109.2010.02085.x.

Tan H. M., Tong, S. F., Ho, C. C. (2012). Men's health: Sexual dysfunction, physical, and psychological health—Is there a link? *The Journal of Sexual Medicine, 9*(3), 663–671. doi: 10.1111/j.1743-6109.2011.02582.x.

The Working Group on a New View of Women's Sexual Problems. (2000). A new view of women's sexual problems. *Electronic Journal of Human Sexuality, 3*, Retrieved from http://www.ejhs.org/volume3/newview.htm#N_1_.

World Association for Sexual Health (WAS). (2013). Retrieved from http://www.worldsexology.org/.

World Health Organization (WHO). (2015). *Sexual and reproductive health: Gender and human rights, sexual health.* Retrieved from http://www.who.int/reproductivehealth/topics/gender_rights/sexual_health/en/.

CHAPTER 24

Communication about Sex in Families: Educational and Relational

Tina A. Coffelt

KEY TERMS

Family sexual communication	Incremental disclosures	Educational benefits
Sex education	Private information	Relational benefits

ABSTRACT

This chapter highlights sexual communication in family relationships by explaining an incremental approach to revealing sexual information, rather than relying on a single birds-and-bees conversation. The process approach unfolds during a child's development. As such, appreciable information has the potential to be divulged, and family members establish educational and relational benefits, which cultivate continued revelations of sexual information.

Deidra: Well, Mom's a nurse. So, right off the bat we learned, like, everything.

Maureen: …anatomy…

Deidra: Specific terms, yeah, you didn't call it any nicknames, that's what it was. And, so, I think that's part of it, like being educated in the field of sex. And then, I think if anything would have happened, I would definitely have to talk about it with Mom. So, that would be part of it, too.

Maureen: Yeah, and I see it, not so much as the physical part of it, but more…

Deidra: …mental…

Maureen: …relational, yeah, you know? Because the physical part of it, we never had to sit down and have the birds and bees talk because…

Deidra: …you already got the anatomy…

Maureen: ….they kind of knew the birds and bees stories type thing.

(Note: Names are pseudonyms where the M name is a mother and the D name is a daughter.)

This excerpt from an interview with mother-daughter members Maureen and Deidra captures some of the key issues in parent-child communication about sex. These issues are about content of conversations, such as sex education material, as well as the processing of information, such as using real terminology, recognizing relational and emotional aspects of sexual activity, and obtaining information at various times, not in one conversation. These and other elements have been studied under the canopy of *family*, *parent-child*, or *parent-adolescent sexual communication*. This chapter tackles some definitional issues with the hope of extending readers' ideas about the information that comprises sexual communication. The chapter also describes and critiques the prevalent birds and bees approach to sexual communication and advocates for a process model using incremental disclosures. Finally, the chapter mentions the educational and relational benefits of sexual communication. Each section includes excerpts from research conducted on sexual communication between mothers or daughters.

Defining Family Sexual Communication

> *Myrna:* There's more to sex than just how it works and what body parts you have.

Extensive parent-adolescent sexual communication research has been guided by a theoretical perspective called *socialization* (e.g., Lefkowitz & Stoppa, 2006), that identifies parents as sex educators for their children. In this role, researchers have tried to ascertain what sexual topics parents talk about, the age at which conversations occur, and the sexual behaviors adolescents practice. The agenda seems to be that if parents educate adolescents about sex, then teens' consensual sexual behaviors would be "less risky." *Risky sexual behaviors* are considered experimenting with sex at a young age, participating with multiple sex partners, or having unprotected sex, for example. Risky sex can lead to teenage pregnancy or sexually transmitted infections. Sexual activity has emotional and relational consequences, as well, but these seem to be identified or discussed less frequently than the physical outcomes of pregnancy or infections. Certainly, some parents adhere to this belief, as Muriel offers in this excerpt:

> *Muriel:* It's a very important subject to talk with your child about. I mean, hopefully if you keep talking to them about it, they'll know the dangers of it and like I mentioned before, um, and so they're not so naïve about it. And hopefully you can just have an open dialogue about it so it hopefully will prevent some problems. That's what you're hoping.

The socialization approach was critiqued (Warren, 1995) because the research showed that sex education by parents was not contributing to reductions in risky sexual behaviors. Rather than education, Warren and Warren (2015) suggested that family members needed to be involved in richer conversations about sex where they aspire to agree on the meaning of beliefs, attitudes, values, or behaviors. This alternate definition distinguished between *sex education*, where parents teach in a patronizing way, and *sexual communication*, a conversational approach geared toward reaching mutual understanding. Muriel's quote above alludes to richer conversations when she used the phrase *dialogue about it*. For example, the topic of birth control could be discussed from an educational perspective where parents introduce different methods and explain how they work. By contrast, parents could attempt to influence their offspring to use a specific birth control method and the child responds by indicating his/her attitudes about each method. The dialogue would involve turn-taking as each person shares a thought, which is responded to by the other, which prompts another turn, and so on.

Warren and Warren's (2015) definition for sexual communication has opportunities for enhancement because the concept is much too complex to be reduced to agreeing on beliefs, attitudes, values, or behavior or to be separated from education, as Deidra and Maureen discuss:

> *Deidra:* Like being educated in the field of sex. I think if anything would have happened, I would definitely have to talk about it with my mom, so that would be a part of it, too.

> *Maureen*: Yeah, and not so much the physical part of it, but more [*Deidra*: mental] relational, yeah, you know.

To illustrate, there are several ways birth control could be discussed by a parent or child. In addition to the educational information, a parent and child could engage in conflict about their beliefs about using birth control, a parent could self-disclose methods he/she has used, or the parent and child could engage in decision-making and select a method for the child. To be sure, there are several vantage points from which this or any sexual topic could be discussed. Indeed, sexual communication includes the educational element, as well as the influence strategies needed to create mutual understanding, and much more, such as social support, feedback, praise, dialogue, or privacy regulation, among other concepts. An updated definition for parent-child sexual communication must encompass both the content of the information and the ways in which this information is processed within family relationships. Because there are ample sexual topics parents and children could discuss, it may be useful to distinguish sexual information as that which is avoided and that which is private, an idea prompted by Monica and Debbie's interaction presented in the next excerpt and elaborated on in the following paragraph.

Monica: I think there's a privacy, to, you know, a lot of details if she's having sex with one certain person. I think everybody has their privacy.

Debbie: I'm really comfortable talking about anything with her. I think pretty much everything's open, except I mean like, I don't really tell her, like, when I have sex...

Monica: I don't want to talk about details.

Debbie: ...who I'm having sex with. Yeah, details like that. [*Monica:* That's a...] That's kind of like an unsaid rule, like, that I don't discuss with my mom.

Topic avoidance is a communication technique used to "purposefully evade [sic] communication with a partner about an issue" (Knobloch & Carpenter-Theune, 2004, p. 173). In other segments of Monica and Debbie's interview, they shared how some sexual information was not discussed at that time. Eventually, sexual information was brought up in conversation, suggesting that at earlier moments, the topics were avoided. Adolescents avoid topics for self-protection, relationship protection, partner unresponsiveness, social inappropriateness, or to establish autonomy (Guerrero & Afifi, 1995). The specific reasons why adolescents avoid the topic of sex have not been reported, although Guerrero and Afifi (1995) indicate that social inappropriateness could be an important reason. Adolescents may be concerned about avoiding punishment, judgment, or embarrassment. Parents may avoid sexual talks as well, because some adolescents were shown to respond with rejection, aggression, or nonverbal responses (Mazur & Hubbard, 2004). Perhaps another explanation for topic avoidance is the fear that private sexual information will be sought. Controlling private information has been suggested as a reason adolescents avoid topics (Petronio, 1994) and sexual experiences rank highest among several avoided topics in parent-adolescent relationships (Dailey & Palomares, 2004; Guerrero & Afifi, 1995). However, when Debbie and Monica, like other mothers and daughters in one study, differentiate the details of sexual experiences as private, they hint at a possible nuance in sexual communication definitions.

Private information has been broadly defined as any information that a person claims as belonging to him/her (Petronio, 2010). Through this lens, if sexual information is about one's own personal sexual activity, fantasies, or desires, for example, then individuals likely perceive the information as private. Even in mother-daughter relationships that are close and capable of managing considerable sexual communication, the "details" of sexual activity are deemed private and not shared with each other (Coffelt, 2010). The next excerpt from Michelle and Desiree further illustrates this notion.

> *Michelle:* I think there are probably some unspoken rules that Desiree and I have, that maybe out of respect, I don't know if it's respect or privacy. [*Desiree:* Yeah.] Yeah, that we don't ask. I think probably, while you may ask for information, or you may communicate about whether or not something is a positive or a negative experience, that, it goes beyond the bounds of privacy to ask for details about someone's relationship. That's not something that you discuss. I know Desiree doesn't want to hear about this, and I don't particularly feel some burning need to fill my children in on the details of my sex life.

Thinking about sexual information as either private or avoided may fragment the information in ways that temper the challenges associated with this topic and permit passage into parent-child conversations. So, when sexual information is presented as "not the personal, private information," some of the fear of discussing sex may be diminished because the personal aspects of one's sexual behaviors are allowed to remain protected by an individual.

This definitional consideration warrants additional discussion and debate; however, the distinction between privacy and avoidance offers new insights for parents and children, particularly during adolescence. A parent or child who wants to talk about sex and holds a privacy stance may need to rely on external prompts such as current events, movies, or websites to introduce information. Parents and children who hold an avoided topic stance present hope that discussions about sex are possible, but the conversations will take special effort. For this reason, the processing of sexual information warrants attention.

The Birds and the Bees

Interviewer: What was the birds and the bees conversation like?

Deanne: It was really funny. It's kind of like, you kind of already know some of the stuff, and then your parents try and be all serious and technical. It's just, it's kind of humorous, but, I remember. I think our grandma was with us too. The three of us kind of sat down and talked about everything. I don't remember exactly what all we talked about.

The birds and the bees conversation is understood to be a single discussion that a parent or parents have with a child around the time of puberty. The content of this conversation is educational in nature, describing the biological and physical processes of menstruation, erection and ejaculation, and sexual intercourse. The conversation is expected to include reproduction as the consequence of sexual activity. Some parents utilize this time to discuss prevention of pregnancy or sexually transmitted infections (STIs) while some also convey their hopes or expectations for their children such as abstinence, condom use, or birth control. This conversation, when characterized as formal, produces more anxiety in adolescents than informal conversations (Afifi, Joseph, & Aldeis, 2008).

Several research studies on sex education highlight the content of sexual topics parents discuss with their children as well as the frequency with which those subjects are discussed. There have been at least 35 different topics studied in several combinations across dozens of studies. Some of the common topics include pregnancy, intercourse, menstruation, STIs, AIDS, birth control, and using a condom. Some of the less common topics have been prostitution, masturbation, regret, sexual satisfaction, what others think about sex, sexual morality, or pornography, among others. Rosenthal and Feldman (1999) categorized these and other topics into four categories: development and societal concerns, sexual safety, experiencing sex, and solitary sexual activity. The extent of communication is defined as frequency and depth, although most research measures frequency, but not depth (Jaccard, Dittus, & Gordon, 1998). Extent of sexual communication has been ascertained by asking mothers, fathers, or adolescents to report on a Likert-type scale the extent to which a given sexual topic was discussed. Myriad approaches to measuring extent have shown that sex is discussed infrequently within families, even though a few studies have shown extensive sexual communication (e.g., Coffelt, 2010).

While measuring the sexual topics that have been discussed and to what extent, researchers have also examined the effects of parent-adolescent sexual communication on adolescent sexual behavior. To that end, results have shown no correlation, negative effects, or positive effects. For example, Fisher (1988) found no relationship between the extent of communication and premarital sex. By contrast, Clawson and Reese-Weber (2003) found that the greater the extent of sexual communication with fathers or mothers, the younger the adolescents were at first intercourse and the higher were the number of sexual partners. Other studies show that the extent of sexual communication with parents was lower among nonvirgins than among virgins (Karofsky et al., 2000), and when parents discussed sexual topics more frequently, then the children engaged in more safe-sex practices (Booth-Butterfield & Sidelinger, 1999).

Taken together, these examples show how measuring frequency of communication has led to a variety of results, often conflicting. Taken together, there is at least one reason why the results may fail to yield consistent findings. The extent of communication alone is not a good predictor of behavior because other variables influence behavior. The topics discussed or quality of conversation, among others, impact communication, while attitudes, peers, self-esteem, or the media also influence behavior. The extent of communication alone provides interesting descriptions about the nature of parent-adolescent sexual communication and illustrates that control over sexual information is quite diverse across families. Some families reveal information while others safeguard sexual information within impenetrable privacy boundaries. Relying on the tenets of *communication privacy management theory* (Petronio, 2002), a process approach to sexual communication shifts the stereotypical approach from a single birds and bees approach to a sequence of small conversations held over a number of years.

Incremental Disclosures: Little Bits and Pieces

Muriel: It's a very broad topic. It starts when they're young. You talk about it all the way.

I mean, they'll ask you. Especially if they ask, just... You know, especially about body parts and things. Let 'em know.

Monica: I think it's an ongoing thing because, uh. You change with age and you develop and you have different experiences. So I think it's always continual. So I think it changes all the time. I think it's always an ongoing, open, needs to be, communication.

Alternative approaches to the birds and the bees conversation have been suggested by researchers and sex educators (e.g., Coffelt & Olson, 2014). One of these approaches, in particular, encompasses a two-fold process approach that explains sexual communication over the course of the child's development. The first component of the process approach looks at sexual communication over time. The second component zooms in on each conversation and outlines the processing of sexual information. Let's look at each of these components.

First, the process approach advocates for conversations about sex to happen at multiple points as the child ages. With each interaction, the parent and child transport information from one to the other across a *privacy boundary*, a metaphorical border that contains information within it. For parents, the circumference of their privacy boundaries likely remains the same as the child ages. Their knowledge of sexual information and practices is likely fairly established by the time they become parents. However, the permeability of their boundaries may change. When children are young, parents likely maintain dense boundaries around sexual information, passing small bits of information at a time (Byers, Sears, & Weaver, 2008). As the child matures and additional conversations surface, the parents likely release more and more information (Beckett, Elliott, Martino, Kanouse, Corona, Klein, & Schuster, 2010), reflecting increasing permeability of their privacy boundary. For children, the circumference of the privacy boundary likely enlarges with age as information comes from parents as well as other sources such as peers, older siblings, or mediated messages. The permeability of their boundaries may expand and contract over time. For example, when children are young, they often ask uninhibited questions, showing a porous privacy boundary. However, as they approach the pre-teen and adolescent years, the privacy boundary may dam up as they protect their private information and seek to keep parents from invasion.

However, what makes this process approach distinct is that adolescents' privacy boundaries may exhibit some permeability so that information can pass to and from a parent because of previous interactions when sexual information was shared. When parents and children permit sexual information to flow between them, their co-owned privacy boundary containing sexual information expands.

Second, the management of sexual information within a given conversation acknowledges that the initiator of the message could be the parent or the child. Often, there is an external cue that prompts a conversation. For example, mediated sources leak sexual information frequently, older siblings or schoolmates speak about sexual things without considering younger audiences, mothers or other family members are pregnant, among many other possibilities. These circumstances may flag a parent to approach a child or conversely, a child might be prompted to ask a question. The ways in which these questions are handled signals to the child how they can approach future questions. Consider Mary's story about one of her daughters.

> *Mary*: I remember one of my daughters asking me, "Can you get pregnant by swimming in the same water as your brother or other boys?" I said, "No, no you can't." and then she asked, "Can you get pregnant by using a towel after a boy?" I said, "No, no you can't." She was just a little innocent and I thought, "Oh, that's so sweet."

Notice how Mary answers her daughter's yes/no question with a yes/no answer. She recognizes her daughter's naïve question and assures her daughter that it's okay to swim or share a towel with a male playmate or sibling and not get pregnant. In this way, the daughter is reassured by getting an answer and she learns that she can ask these questions without negative consequence. Notice the mother did not chastise the daughter for asking the question. The mother did not express un-ease or tell her daughter not to ask such things. Additionally, Mary did not use the question as a segue to describe the whole process of pregnancy in detail. Instead, Mary recognized her daughter's developmental age and readiness for sexual information and provided an appropriate amount of information. In this way, the daughter could see her mother as a trusted source of information who treats sexual information as a natural subject, answers questions about it, and moves on. The daughter can now recognize her mother as a resource whenever questions arise in the future.

Early teen years mark significant changes for children. Some teens ask questions, especially when they received validation or information when asking questions at an earlier age. Donielle was telling about junior high and remembered a time she went to her mom.

> *Donielle*: I would be like, "Hey, I read this book," and then be like, "What does it mean? What did they do?" And then she'd try to tell me in the best way she could without freaking me out I guess!

Donielle was cued from an external source and selected her mom as the confidant to seek answers to her questions. She remembers her mom providing an answer and doing so in a way that wasn't construed as an over-share. This process of an external cue, a question, and an answer, cycles repeatedly in the process approach to sexual communication. With each cycle, only information related to the external cue is disseminated, which satisfies the child's curiosity, establishes trust, and alleviates embarrassment. The information was called *little bits and pieces* by some mothers who were interviewed about sexual communication with their daughters. These incremental disclosures expanded the circumference of the co-owned privacy boundary around sexual information. Permeability of the privacy boundaries may open up as well. Dawn's disclosure reveals the potential for the extent of information shared between a parent and child.

> *Dawn*: I was having sex, probably six months until my mom found out that I was having sex. I knew she knew, but she didn't say anything. And so that was even more awkward to me, 'cause I'm like, "Why doesn't she say anything? Why isn't she bringing this up?" And then I thought, I just thought she'd be mad or something, but she wasn't. It's strange.

Dawn eventually told her mom that she was sexually active and Dawn's suspicions about her mom's knowledge were correct. Dawn later went on to discuss how the co-ownership of this information relieved tension in their relationship and built a clearing for even more sexual information to be shared between them.

In sum, the process approach relies on incremental disclosures made at several moments in a child's life, arguing that sharing sexual information in this way permits more information to be shared by both the parent and child, than if only one conversation were held. The process approach suggests that sexual communication results in both educational and relational benefits. A list of specific suggestions for parent-child sexual communication based on the ideas in this chapter includes:

- Respond to questions about sex when they asked with succinct, age appropriate answers.

- Share sexual information in little bits and pieces over time.

- Rely on cues from movies, books, current events, or websites, for example, to initiate a conversation.

- Suggest that sexual activity is a natural activity, and talking about it can have educational and relational benefits.

- Clarify that personal, sexual experiences are private and will not be asked about.

Benefits: Educational and Relational

Deanne: I think the biggest benefit is that, you're going to get honest, truthful information. I remember feeling a lot better and understanding a lot more once we started having those real conversations. I think that they've definitely helped a lot growing up.

Michelle: I want them to be happy. I want them to be healthy. I want them to enjoy their lives. I want them to grow up to be good partners, have good relationships, a healthy respect for their bodies, their sexuality, I mean, all of those things.

Parents and children benefit from sexual communication by receiving information and by enacting their mutual trust and closeness. Certainly, young people learn about sexual activity and its consequences from many sources. Deanne attributes her mom as a reliable source of educational information. With this knowledge, young people are empowered to make informed decisions about their own sexual practices. Parents also benefit by the reassurance of knowing their children obtain sexual information. Additionally, parents can impart their beliefs, attitudes, and values. Michelle recognized this benefit in her recollections of the benefits she received from talking with her daughter. Relational benefits were also found to be a benefit of parent-child sexual communication (Coffelt, 2010).

> *Dana*: The sexual talk, like, being able to talk to your parents about sex I feel like, you can talk about anything with your parents, but not being able to do that… if you can talk to your parents about sex, I think you can talk to your parents about anything.

Dana recognized relational benefits that stemmed from talking about sex. She attributed talking about sex as a hurdle or barrier that, once crossed, made other difficult topics seem manageable. To be clear, the closeness these mothers and daughters described does not mean that talking about sex *caused* the relational closeness. Indeed, there was no difference in relational closeness between parents and adolescents who talked about sex and those who did not (Afifi et al., 2008).

This chapter on family sexual communication was founded on research about communication between mothers and daughters. Mothers, more than fathers, are repeatedly shown to engage in more sexual communication with daughters and sons. However, other family members and relationship pairings are capable of managing sexual information. Fathers have been shown to talk to sons more than daughters (Wright, 2009). Like fathers, sons have participated in less research than daughters. Sibling relationships likely play an integral role in sexual communication, as well as parent-child relationships, and extended family members may also make helpful confidants. Indeed, grandparents, aunts, uncles, cousins, nieces, or nephews may be involved in conversations about sex. However, the management of the information could still operate in a similar manner introduced in this chapter—as incremental disclosures occurring at multiple moments in a child's life. This chapter provides one approach to conversing about sex in parent-child relationships. Not all parents or their children have the intent to talk about sex (Byers & Sears, 2012), thus it is important to acknowledge that this process approach does not claim to be the way for everyone to talk. The intent is to share the process approach used by mothers and daughters who talked about sexual information as they described it.

> *Dana*: Our relationship now, like me being in college is a lot more mature and a lot more developed. And I know, like, a lot more stuff. I trust her enough to tell her whatever.

Like Dana, educational and relational benefits can surface when family members share information with each other about sex. As a college student, you may be reflecting on the interactions you did or did not have with a parent. You may also begin to consider your prospective role as a parent. You are in a unique situation to look at parent-child interactions with an external lens. As you look through the window and see parents and children talking, what do you see? What is your vision for sexual communication in parent-child relationships?

DISCUSSION QUESTIONS

1. How would you define sexual communication? Do the educational, conversational, privacy, or topic avoidance concepts inform your definition?

2. Why might sexual topics be difficult for parents and children to discuss? What other topics, if any, are equally or more challenging?

3. This chapter was based on mother-daughter communication. How would sexual communication be similar/different in mother-son, father-daughter, and father-son relationships?

4. What was your reaction to some of the quotes from mothers and daughters included in the chapter? Were you surprised, uncomfortable, validated?

5. How would you qualify *effective* or *good* parent-child sexual communication?

References

Afifi, T. D., Joseph, A., & Aldeis, D. (2008). Why can't we just talk about it?: An observational study of parents' and adolescents' conversations about sex. *Journal of Adolescent Research, 23,* 689–721. doi:10.1177/0743558408323841.

Beckett, M. K., Elliott, M. N., Martino, S., Kanouse, D. E., Corona, R., Klein, D. J., & Schuster, M. A. (2010). Timing of parent and child communication about sexuality relative to children's sexual behaviors. *Pediatrics, 125*, 34–42. doi:10.1542/peds.2009-0806.

Booth-Butterfield, M., & Sidelinger, R. (1998). The influence of family communication on the college-aged child: Openness, attitudes and actions about sex and alcohol. *Communication Quarterly, 46*, 295–308. doi: 10.1080/01463379809370103.

Byers, E. S., & Sears, H. A. (2012). Mothers who do and no not intend to discuss sexual health with their young adolescents. *Family Relations, 61*, 851–863. doi:10.1111/j.17413729.2012.00740.x.

Byers, E. S., Sears, H. A., & Weaver, A. D. (2008). Parents' reports of sexual communication with children in kindergarten to grade 8. *Journal of Marriage & Family, 70*, 86–96. doi:10.1111/j.1741-3737.2007.00463.x.

Clawson, C. L., & Reese-Weber, M. (2003). The amount and timing of parent-adolescent sexual communication as predictors of late adolescent sexual risk-taking behaviors. *The Journal of Sex Research, 40*, 256–265. doi: 10.1080/00224490309552190.

Coffelt, T. A. (2010). Is sexual communication challenging between mothers and daughters? *Journal of Family Communication, 10*, 116–130. doi: 10.1080/15267431003595496.

Coffelt, T. A., & Olson, L. N. (2014). No more birds and bees: A process-approach to parent-child sexual communication. In E. L. Cohen (Ed.), *Communication Yearbook, 38* (pp. 207–240). New York: Taylor & Francis.

Dailey, R. M., & Palomares, N. A. (2004). Strategic topic avoidance: An investigation of topic avoidance frequency, strategies used, and relational correlates. *Communication Monographs, 71*, 471–496. doi:10.1080/0363452042000307443.

Fisher, T. D. (1988). The relationship between parent-child communication about sexuality and college students' sexual behavior and attitudes as a function of parental proximity. *The Journal of Sex Research, 24*, 305–311. doi: 10.1080/00224498809551429.

Guererro, L. K., & Afifi, W. A. (1995). Some things are better left unsaid: Topic avoidance in family relationships. *Communication Quarterly, 43*, 276–296. doi: 10.1080/01463379509369977.

Jaccard, J., Dittus, P. J., & Gordon, V. V. (1998). Parent-adolescent congruency in reports of adolescent sexual behavior and in communication about sexual behavior. *Child Development, 69*, 247–261. doi: 10.1111/j.1467-8624.1998.tb06146.x.

Karofsky, P. S., Zeng, L., & Kosorok, M. R. (2000). Relationship between adolescent-parental communication and initiation of first intercourse by adolescents. *Journal of Adolescent Health, 28*, 41–45. doi: http://dx.doi.org/10.1016/S1054-139X(00)00156-7.

Knobloch, L. K., & Carpenter-Theune, K. E. (2004). Topic avoidance in developing romantic relationships: Associations with intimacy and relational uncertainty. *Communication Research, 31,* 173–205. doi: 10.1177/0093650203261516.

Lefkowitz, E. S., & Stoppa, T. M. (2006). Positive sexual communication and socialization in the parent-adolescent context. *New Directions for Child & Adolescent Development, 112,* 39–55. doi:10.1002/cd.161.

Mazur, M. A., & Hubbard, A. S. E. (2004). "Is there something I should know?": Topic avoidant responses in parent-adolescent communication. *Communication Reports, 17,* 27–37. doi: 10.1080/08934210409389371.

Petronio, S. (2002). *Boundaries of privacy: Dialectics of disclosure.* New York: State University of New York Press.

Petronio, S. (2004). The road to developing communication privacy management: Narrative in progress, please stand by [Special issue]. *Journal of Family Communication, 4,* 193–208. doi: 10.1207/s15327698jfc0403&4_6.

Petronio, S. (2010). Communication privacy management theory: What do we know about family privacy regulation? *Journal of Family Theory & Review, 2,* 175–196. doi: 10.1111/j.1756-2589.2010.00052.x.

Rosenthal, D. A., & Feldman, S. S. (1999). The importance of importance: Adolescents' perceptions of parental communication about sexuality. *Journal of Adolescence, 22,* 835–851. doi: http://dx.doi.org/10.1006/jado.1999.0279.

Warren, C. (1995). Parent-child communication about sex. In T. J. Socha & G. H. Stamp (Eds.), *Parents, Children, and Communication: Frontiers of Theory and Research* (pp. 173–201). Mahwah, NJ: Lawrence Erlbaum.

Warren, C., & Warren, L. K. (2015). Family and partner communication about sex. In L. H. Turner & R. West (Eds.), *The Sage handbook of family communication* (pp. 184–201). Thousand Oaks, CA: Sage.

Wright, P. J. (2009). Father-child sexual communication in the United States: A review and synthesis. *Journal of Family Communication, 9,* 233–250. doi:10.1080/15267430903221880.

CHAPTER 25

Strategic Use of The Health Belief Model in Crafting Messages That Promote Condom Use

Tobias Reynolds-Tylus & Lance S. Rintamaki

KEY TERMS

Safer sex communication
Condoms

Sexually transmitted infections
(STIs)

Health Belief Model
Self-efficacy

ABSTRACT

Considerable research suggests speaking with sexual partners about condoms dramatically increases their use, but does not guarantee it. As such, the current chapter examines how the Health Belief Model provides theoretical insights on how one might strategically craft messages to promote condom use with sexual partners who are reluctant or ambivalent about condom use. In doing so, we include an overview of the Health Belief Model and its major components (perceived severity, perceived susceptibility, perceived barriers, perceived benefits, self-efficacy, and cues to action) with special attention paid to potential application for promoting condom use between sexual partners. After careful consideration of the Health Belief Model, we utilize a case study format (in this case, an informal discussion between friends) to better illustrate these concepts. We conclude the chapter by considering how the case study provided examples of how the Health

Belief Model can be utilized to strategically design messages to overcome some common objections to condom use.

The Centers for Disease Control and Prevention (CDC) estimates that approximately 20 million STIs (more commonly referred to as sexually transmitted diseases [STDs]) are spread among men and women each year in the United States (CDC, 2013). To put this into perspective, this number is nearly 13 times larger than the amount of students who graduate with a bachelor's degree each year in the U.S. (National Center for Education Statistics, 2011). The costs of treating these infections are staggering, estimated to approach $16 billion annually in direct medical costs alone (CDC, 2013). More important, the impact these infections can have on individuals' health and well-being is significant. In clinical terms, STIs negatively impact both *morbidity* and *mortality*. **Morbidity** refers to the negative health effects resulting from being infected with a disease. For example, the human papillomavirus (HPV), the most commonly contracted STI, is the number one cause of cervical cancer in women, accounting for approximately 80% of all cases. Likewise, other commonly spread STIs, including chlamydia, gonorrhea, and syphilis, can lead to severe reproductive health complications, such as infertility (CDC, 2014). **Mortality** on the other hand, refers to death resulting from a specific disease. HIV, for example, is by far the deadliest STI and is the leading cause of death of 18,000 people in the U.S. each year (CDC, 2013).

Despite the prevalence and severity of STIs, a relatively simple and feasible prevention method is available for most sexually active heterosexual individuals: Male latex condoms (henceforth, "condoms"). Consistent and correct use of condoms between sexually active partners is recommended by every major health organization in the United States as one of the most effective ways of preventing the transmission of STIs. Unfortunately, many individuals fail to consider condom use when engaging in sexual behavior, let alone use them properly and routinely.

One group at especially high risk for contracting STIs are young adults. Over half of new STI cases (10 million per year) occur among individuals between the ages of 15 and 24 (CDC, 2013). Despite their heightened vulnerability to STIs, consistent condom use among this population is rare. For example, in a review of a decade of research on the topic, researchers found that only a small minority (between 8% and 23%) of heterosexual college students used condoms consistently (Lewis, Malow, & Ireland, 1997). More recent evidence from a national survey of college students also suggests rather low rates of condom use. When asked about their condom use in the last 30 days, sexually active college students reported using condoms only 50.7% of the time for vaginal intercourse, 27.2% of the time for anal intercourse, and 4.6% of the time for oral intercourse (American College Health Association, 2014).

One of the fundamental ways to negotiate condom use and reduce your risk for STI transmission is to discuss risk-reducing behavior with your partner or partners (Allen, Emmers-Sommer, & Crowell, 2002). A landmark study looking at 44 different variables across 121 research studies found that communication about safer sex topics with one's partner was one of the strongest predictors of actual condom use (Sheeran, Abraham, & Orbell, 1999). More recent work analyzing data from additional studies has also found a consistent link between safer sex communication and subsequent condom use (Noar, Carlyle, & Cole, 2006). However, all communication isn't created equal. In fact, a rather large body of literature suggests that sometimes talking about safer sex topics, ironically, may actually lead to unsafe behaviors. For instance, research has shown that oftentimes when individuals discussed condom use practices with their partners, they would do so in a way that actually led to the couple choosing to *avoid* condom use (Bolton, McKay, & Schneider, 2010; Welch Cline, Freeman, & Johnson, 1990; Welch Cline, Johnson, & Freeman, 1992).

So what's going on here? A few things may be happening. To begin, many individuals avoid discussing safer sex topics with their partners enitrely, if not at least initially. Many individuals begin with the assumption that their partner is safe, as they rationalize that they'd avoid sex with someone who seems like a risk (Emmers-Sommer & Allen, 2004). However, the metrics that many individuals use to judge the safety of their partners is notoriously unreliable, including such superficial traits as the person's physical attractiveness, educational background, and perceptions of their general health (Masaro, Dahinten, Johnson, Ogilvie, & Patrick, 2008). Second, when these conversations occur, questions often are framed in ways that easily allow the partner to be less than truthful (Welch Cline et al., 1992; Metts & Fitzpatrick, 1992). For instance, asking your partner close-ended questions such as "do you have any STDs?" or "should I be worried about anything?" can easily allow him/her to skirt the conversation with a simple "no." The danger, of course, is that by not asking about or following up on detailed background information, such as a partners' sexual history, number of previous partners, or last date of testing, crucial information needed for accurate risk assessment is often overlooked.

So communication about safer sex topics is good... except when it's bad? Sounds confusing, right? Well, try thinking of it another way. Exercising is generally considered to be good for your overall health, but if you aren't careful, you could end up hurting yourself and being worse off than at the start. Stated another way, whereas the academic literature is quite clear on the importance of communicating with one's partner about safer sex topics, these conversations must be approached in the right way. Fortunately, existing theories, such as the Health Belief Model, illustrate core variables that drive health behaviors, which may prove useful in the crafting of messages that motivate sexual partners reluctant to use condoms to do so. Therefore, in the next section we begin with an overview of the Health Belief Model, and consider empirical research in the context of safer sex discussions about condom use, reflecting on how these findings highlight Health Belief Model constructs, as well as how these variables may be utilized to strategically communicate with sexual partners to maximize the likelihood of consistent condom use.

The Health Belief Model

The Health Belief Model is used for understanding health behavior and is one of the most commonly used theories in health promotion and education (Champion & Skinner, 2008). Initially, the Health Belief Model was developed in the 1950s by social psychologists at the United States Public Health Service to explain the widespread failure of individual participation in programs to prevent and protect against diseases (Hochbaum, 1958). In the decades since its original conception, the Health Belief Model has been used successfully to explain and predict a variety of health behaviors, including breast cancer screening (Silk et al., 2006), smoking cessation (Kazemi, Ehsanpour, & Nekoei-Zahraei, 2012), influenza vaccination (Blue & Valley, 2002), organ and tissue donation (Quick, LaVoie, Scott, Bosch, &

Morgan, 2012), among many others. The Health Belief Model is comprised of six components: a) *perceived severity*, b) *perceived susceptibility*, c) *perceived benefits*, d) *perceived barriers*, e) *self-efficacy*, and f) *cues to action* (Janz & Becker, 1984; Rosenstock, Strecher, & Becker, 1988). We will examine each construct of the Health Belief Model in turn, considering how the components are related to discussions with one's partner about sexual risk reducing behaviors, with an emphasis on condom use.

Perceived Severity

In the Health Belief Model, perceived severity is understood as an individual's belief(s) about the seriousness or severity of a disease. In order for an individual to engage in a recommended health behavior, the Health Belief Model theorizes that s/he must believe the consequences of the threat are grim (Hayden, 2009). Thus, according to the HBM, talking with a sexual partner about the seriousness of STIs is likely to promote subsequent condom use, so long as the partner believes the consequences of not taking precautions (i.e., contracting a STI) are severe. This reasoning explains why many college students report failing to discuss sexual precautions with their partners, because they underestimate the seriousness of STIs. It seems that for many college students, STIs often are (incorrectly) perceived as minor inconveniences rather than illnesses of potentially life-long significance (Barth, Cook, Downs, Switzer, & Fischhoff, 2002). For example, when asked what sexual health issue they felt was most concerning to them, twice as many college students said pregnancy was their number one concern compared to those who reported STIs as their primary concern (Emmers-Sommer, Warber, Passalacqua, & Luciano, 2010).

Perceived Susceptibility

According to the Health Belief Model, perceived susceptibility involves an individual's perception of the risk of contracting a disease. In general, the greater the perception of risk, the greater the likelihood individuals will engage in behaviors to reduce their risk (Hayden, 2009). However, studies consistently find that young people underestimate or disregard their own susceptibility to STIs (Ethier, Kershaw, Niccolai, Lewis, & Ickovics,

2003). For instance, Downing-Matibag and Geisinger (2009) found that college students underestimated their risk of contracting STIs for three primary reasons: a) by placing too much trust in their partners (e.g., believing something is "clean" because s/he is a good student), b) by placing too much trust in the local college community (e.g., underestimating prevalence of HIV/AIDs in the surrounding area), and c) by generally lacking knowledge on STI transmission (e.g., being unaware that STIs could be transmitted through oral sex). Furthermore, one of the most commonly used strategies for avoiding safer sex practices among college students is emphasizing to their partner that STI risk is not a major concern (Oncale & King, 2011). For instance, partners wishing to avoid condom use may say things such as "don't you trust me?" or "I just went to the doctor, I'm clean." However, by discussing your past sexual history with your partner(s), you can better understand your level of risk. Additionally, you can discuss getting tested together.

Perceived Benefits

In the Health Belief Model, perceived benefits is understood as a person's opinion of the value or usefulness of a new behavior in decreasing their risk for developing a disease. According to the Health Belief Model, in order for an individual to enact a health behavior, s/he must perceive the benefits of the behavior to be greater than the costs of the behavior (Hayden, 2009). In fact, perceived benefits often prove to be among the most significant factors in a person's decision to engage in a health behavior, making the benefits to using a condom a particularly important angle to discuss with sexual partners.

While one of the major benefits of discussing safer sex precautions is STI risk reduction, there are numerous other relational benefits to safer sex talk with one's partner. In particular, by discussing sexual likes and dislikes, sex can become more enjoyable for both parties. An abundance of research has shown that increased sexual communication with one's partner is related to higher sexual satisfaction in relationships (Ashdown, Hackathorn, & Clark, 2011; Widman et al., 2006). Additionally, sexual satisfaction in a relationship is a strong predictor of relational satisfaction and the duration of romantic relationships for both men and women (Heimen et al., 2011). Put simply, couples that discuss sexual topics are happier, healthier, and more likely to stay together.

Perceived Barriers

According to the Health Belief Model, perceived barriers refer to an individual's evaluation of the obstacles to adopting a new behavior. Barriers have been identified as the most crucial component of the Health Belief Model in determining behavior change (Janz & Becker, 1984). Like perceived benefits to a health behavior, perceived barriers proves to be one of the most important factors in people's decisions to engage in a health behavior. For that reason, finding ways to talk about and address barriers to engaging in condom use often proves critical in doing so.

There are many barriers that create challenges for those wanting to discuss safer sex behavior with their partner, for instance fear for negative outcomes such as embarrassment, anger from one's partner, or loss of a sexual opportunity (Allen et al., 2002). Not surprisingly, those who report greater fear in discussing sexual topics are less likely to discuss sexual precautions with their partner (Crosby et al., 2002). In addition to potential relational costs, many individuals complain that condoms can diminish sexual satisfaction. Fortunately, when used alone or in combination, modern condom technologies (e.g., ultra-thin condoms, flared-head condoms, and internally lubed-head condoms) have dramatically improved upon this drawback to older-style condoms.

Self-efficacy

Another important Health Belief Model construct, self-efficacy is defined as "a belief in one's own ability to do something" (Bandura, 1977). Even if individuals feel the adverse health outcome is severe, that they are susceptible to the threat, and that the benefits of the recommended health behavior outweigh the barriers, individuals must also believe they have the ability to adopt the recommended behavior. In the context of sexual communication, self-efficacy may refer to an individuals' perceived capacity to discuss condom use practices with their partner. Alternatively, self-efficacy may also refer to an individual's perception of their knowledge about condoms and how to use them. For instance, whereas individuals may believe they have the technical skills to use a condom correctly, they may find it hard to discuss their desire to use a condom with a partner. Although many individuals may feel nervous about engaging in these discussions, the discussions can often help build relational trust and foster intimacy between partners (Widman et al., 2006).

Cues to Action

The Health Belief Model also suggests that a behavior is influenced by cues to action. Perhaps the most difficult to conceptualize concept of the Health Belief Model, cues to action are defined as strategies to activate "readiness" for behavioral change. This can include events, people, or things that motivate individuals to change their behavior. Some examples of cues to action for condom use could include finding out a family member or friend has an STI, seeing a report on TV about a celebrity who became infected, being given a pamphlet from a local area health clinic about STI risks, or even reading this chapter! Perhaps most useful to a reader, however, is the fact that conversations with a sexual partner about condom use may, in fact, be one of the most potent cues to action of all.

Applying the Health Belief Model

Simply discussing safer sex with one's partner may not always necessarily translate to engaging in safer sexual practices. Remember, discussion is a negotiation, and your partner may have differing preferences in their sexual practices. In fact, as many as 30% of men and 41% of women report having had sexual partners try to prevent them from using a condom during a sexual encounter (Oncale & King, 2001). As such, thinking through how best to manage such negotiations is key, as forewarned is forearmed.

Building upon our own experiences talking with friends about condoms, we developed the following case study to depict a group of friends casually relaxing at the end of a long workweek, blowing off steam and having a laugh. Through their discussion, they depict communicative strategies they have employed with sexual partners to encourage (or down right require) condom use. As these strategies are presented, consider how they may map out across the Health Belief Model (HBM) or serve as the foundation for additional message strategies that may be used to promote safer sex behaviors. In addition, consider how combining specific message strategies may amplify their effectiveness, as research commonly reports how using HBM variables in tandem increases their impact on health behavior outcomes.

The Case

Bonnie loved nights like this. A warm summer evening, kicking back on the rooftop of their apartment building with her four closest friends, a bottle of wine shared between them. They'd known each other since middle school, grown up together and, despite spreading out to different colleges, regrouped after graduation when they all took jobs in the Big Apple. They felt more like family to her than friends, and much like siblings, teasing was a favorite pastime. One game Bonnie liked to play more than any other was tormenting Aisha, the most modest of the group, by placing her on the spot with some scandalous question sure to turn her dear friend scarlet from ear to ear. Eying her prey across the table, Bonnie leaned forward, crouched low for her attack, before demurely asking, "So tell me, Aisha, what is the best excuse a guy's ever given you for not wanting to wear a condom?"

The table erupted in guffaws as the jibe had its intended effect. Christine playfully cuffed Bonnie in the back of the head. "Oh, leave her alone! She's turning as red as the table cloth!" David and Jake joined in the teasing, ribbing their friend until she couldn't help but grin back. Aisha, her cheeks still hot, decided to turn the question back on her friend. "You go first, Bonnie. I'm sure your stories are better than mine!"

Bonnie leaned back in her chair, contemplating a moment. Before answering, she leaned forward again, eyeing the two men at the table and, in a rather high-pitched, whiny voice said, "but sex doesn't feel as good with a condom..." The last syllable of "condom" trailed off, accompanied by peels of laughter from her two female friends. Christine chimed in, "Oh! And how about this one?" Using a deep, husky voice, she said, "don't you worry baby, I'm clean..." Bonnie made a "yuck" sound at that, but answered with, "but if you love me, you won't make me wear a condom..." Christine laughed and gave her friend a high five. "And we have a winner!"

Jake and David looked at each other and grinned, taking in the performance. Each knew these to be common excuses to get out of wearing condoms. Jake, however, seemed intent on making a point. Laughing, he said, "Don't look over here as if it's all about us. You all pull some shenanigans, too. Do you know how many times I've had girls pout about me using a condom, tellin' me I'm not romantic and killing the mood and stuff?" David nodded and said, "He's right about that. I had a girl once try to talk me out of wearing a condom, saying it wouldn't be as *intimate*. I like it better without a condom, sure, but I don't want to catch some STD or get anyone pregnant. Hell, I've even had girls tell me not to worry about it cause they were on the pill, but that still leaves all kinds of stuff on the table. Sorry, but the jimmy is going *on*."

Bonnie raised a glass to her friends across the table, saluting them for their good sense, then paused for a moment, reflecting. What had started off as a joke meant to tease one friend had turned into something more somber, more serious. These were her dear friends, though, people around whom she felt the greatest trust. So, after a few moments of contemplating, she said simply, "What do you do when the other person doesn't want to wear a condom?"

Jake didn't hesitate for moment. "I'm pretty straight forward about it. I just say, 'I like you, but we gotta be careful. There are a lot of things out there that are going around, things you can't tell just by looking at someone. We both need to be smart about this and this'll keep us safe. So let's just enjoy this and let me take care of us both.' It works pretty good, man, talking about keeping us both safe from stuff out there."

David agreed. "I usually say something similar. Honestly, I think the odds are usually in my favor and I don't think something bad is likely to happen. But I bring up the possibility. I say, 'what if' and I say that catching something is a serious thing. You catch herpes and it's with you for the rest of your life. Hepatitis, HIV, same thing, only those are way worse. And how about if you get pregnant? Are you ready to raise a kid, starting right here and now? I mean, I gotta be careful or the night will be over, but if it comes right down to it, these days I'll walk before I have sex without a condom."

Christine nodded in agreement to David's stance. "I'm pretty much the same: No condom, no sex. Period. Every time. But I also think you can talk about it in less ultimatum-style terms. I've probably had the complaint about sex not feeling as good with a condom the most. What I've done is turn it into a game. What I do is basically say that it's important to me that they wear a condom, but I also say that I'll make a deal with them: They have to wear a condom, but it's my job to make it so good they can't tell the difference. I make it this playful challenge and it becomes more fun, more erotic. Then I break out some tricks." Christine looked up to see all eyes trained on her and laughed. "Oh, come on, these aren't any big mysteries! I'm talking about stuff that's been around for a long time. My favorite is simply putting a drop of lube in the tip of the condom, then rolling it on for him. I even like to take control of the situation, telling him to sit back and let me take care of him. By taking things out of their hands, so to speak, it gives 'em less to complain about, they worry less about doing it how I want, and I make sure it gets done right."

David was nodding in agreement. "I do the same thing with the lube. It's way better than regular old dry condoms. You can actually buy condoms with the lube built-in. Saves time."

"I've also found that when I tell them it turns me on to see them wearing a condom, it helps things out, if you know what I mean," Christine replied with a grin. "And just to be safe, I keep condoms handy in case he says, 'ugh, I don't got none on me…'"

Bonnie stopped for a moment and took a long look at Aisha, who had been quiet this whole time. Kidding aside, she asked her friend what she was thinking. Aisha, pausing only for a moment, said, "talk about how serious the risks are, how they could happen here and now if we're not careful, work through the barriers they throw at you, signal it's gonna happen, make it easy for 'em, show 'em the benefits of wearing a condom for you. I've been making mental notes so I can ask if you missed anything when I talk to my nana tonight on the phone."

With that, the mood shifted again and the friends began to laugh once more. "Hey," Bonnie said, "you never told us the best excuse you've been given for not using condoms."

Aisha, with only a hint of rose showing on her cheeks, said simply, "But I'm allergic to condoms!" As everyone laughed, Aisha smirked and said, "It's funny how often I hear people say that, when only 1% of the population has a latex allergy."

Feigning incredulousness, Bonnie protested, "Are you calling everyone who claims to have a latex allergy is a liar?"

Without batting an eye, replied, "No. Only the people I've slept with."

And with that, the group of old friends laughed and all raised their glasses to toast the finest comment of the night.

DISCUSSION QUESTIONS

1. Consider the message strategies the characters used in this case study to promote condom use with their sexual partners. Which of these do you feel correspond to aspects of the Health Belief Model? How so?

2. Before reading this chapter, were you aware of your risk for STIs? Have your views changed since reading this chapter?

3. What kind of education on safer sex communication, if any, did you receive in elementary/middle/high school?

4. Do you think schools should teach safer sex communication skills? Why or why not?

5. Which construct of the Health Belief Model do you think is most crucial for encouraging safer sex communication among partners and why?

References

Allen, M., Emmers-Sommer, T. M., & Crowell, T. L. (2002). Couples negotiating safer sex behaviors: A meta-analysis of the impact of conversation and gender. In M. Allen., R. W. Preiss., B. M. Gayle., and N. Burrell (Eds.) *Interpersonal communication research: Advances through meta-analysis* (pp. 263–279). Mahwah, NJ: Taylor & Francis.

American College Health Association. (2013). *American College Health Association national college health assessment: Spring 2013 reference group executive summary.* Hanover, MD: American College Health Association. Retrieved from http://www.acha-ncha.org/docs/ACHA-NCHA-II_ReferenceGroup_ExecutiveSummary_Spring2013.pdf.

Ashdown, B. K., Hackathorn, J., & Clark, E. M. (2011). In and out of the bedroom: Sexual satisfaction in the marital relationship. *Journal of Integrated Social Sciences, 2*(1), 38–55.

Bandura, A. (1977). Self-efficacy: toward a unifying theory of behavioral change. *Psychological Review, 84,* 191–215.

Barth, K. R., Cook, R. L., Downs, J. S., Switzer, G. E., & Fischhoff, B. (2002). Social stigma and negative consequences: Factors that influence college students' decisions to seek testing for sexually transmitted infections. *Journal of American College Health, 50*(4), 153–159.

Blue, C. L., & Valley, J. M. (2002). Predictors of influenza vaccine: Acceptance among healthy adult workers. *AAOHN Journal, 50*, 227–233.

Bolton, M., McKay, A., & Schneider, M. (2010). Relational influences on condom use discontinuation: A qualitative study of young adult women in dating relationships. The *Canadian Journal of Human Sexuality, 19*(3), 91–104.

Crosby, R. A., DiClemente, R. J., Wingood, G. M., Cobb, B. K., Harrington, K., Davies, S. L., & Oh, M. K. (2002). Condom use and correlates of African American adolescent females' infrequent communication with sex partners about preventing sexually transmitted diseases and pregnancy. *Health Education & Behavior, 29*(2), 219–231.

Centers for Disease Control and Prevention. (2014, Dec.). Reported STDs in the United States: 2013 national data for chlamydia, gonorrhea, and syphilis [Fact sheet]. *U.S. Department of Health and Human Services: Atlanta, GA.* Retrieved from http://www.cdc.gov/nchhstp/newsroom/docs/std-trends-508.pdf.

Centers for Disease Control and Prevention. (2013, Feb.). Incidence, prevalence, and cost of sexually transmitted infections in the United States [Fact sheet]. *U.S. Department of Health and Human Services: Atlanta, GA.* Retrieved from http://www.cdc.gov/std/stats/sti-estimates-fact-sheet-feb-2013.pdf.

Champion, V. L., & Skinner, C. S. (2008). The health belief model (pp. 45–66). In K. Glanz, B. K. Rimer, & K. Viswanath (Eds.), *Health behavior and health education: Theory, research, and practice.* San Francisco, CA: John Wiley & Sons.

Downing-Matibag, T. M., & Geisinger, B. (2009). Hooking up and sexual risk taking among college students: A health belief model perspective. *Qualitative Health Research, 19*(9), 1196–1209.

Emmers-Sommer, T. M., & Allen, M. (2004). *Safer sex in personal relationships: The role of sexual scripts in HIV infection and prevention.* Mahwah, NJ: Psychology Press.

Emmers-Sommer, T. M., Warber, K. M., Passalacqua, S., & Luciano, A. (2010). Communicating (and responding to) sexual health status: Reasons for STD (non) disclosure. *Psychology, 1*, 178–184.

Ethier, K. A., Kershaw, T., Niccolai, L., Lewis, J. B., & Ickovics, J. R. (2003). Adolescent women underestimate their susceptibility to sexually transmitted infections. *Sexually Transmitted Infections, 79*(5), 408–411.

Fortenberry, J. D., Tu, W., Harezlak, J., Katz, B. P., & Orr, D. P. (2002). Condom use as a function of time in new and established adolescent sexual relationships. *American Journal of Public Health, 92*(2), 211–213.

Hayden, J. (2009). Chapter 4: The health belief model (pp. 31–44). In J. Hayden. (Ed.) *Introduction to health behavior theory.* Sudbury, MA: Jones & Bartlett Learning.

Heiman, J. R., Long, J. S., Smith, S. N., Fisher, W. A., Sand, M. S., & Rosen, R. C. (2011). Sexual satisfaction and relationship happiness in midlife and older couples in five countries. *Archives of Sexual Behavior, 40*(4), 741–753.

Hochbaum, G. M. (1958). *Public participation in medical screening programs: A socio-psychological study.* U.S. Department of Health, Education, and Welfare: Washington, DC.

Janz, N. K., & Becker, M. H. (1984). The health belief model: A decade later. *Health Education Quarterly, 11*(1), 1–47.

Kazemi, A., Ehsanpour, S., & Nekoei-Zahraei, N. S. (2012). A randomized trial to promote health belief and to reduce environmental tobacco smoke exposure in pregnant women. *Health Education Research, 27*(1), 151–159.

Lewis, M. A., Kaysen, D. L., Rees, M., & Woods, B. A. (2010). The relationship between condom-related protective behavioral strategies and condom use among college students: Global- and event-level evaluations. *Journal of Sex Research, 47*(5), 471–478.

Lewis, J. E., Malow, R. M., & Ireland, S. J. (1997). HIV/AIDS risk in heterosexual college students: a review of a decade of literature. *Journal of American College Health, 45,* 147–158.

Masaro, C. L., Dahinten, V. S., Johnson, J., Ogilvie, G., & Patrick, D. M. (2008). Perceptions of sexual partner safety. *Sexually Transmitted Diseases, 35*(6), 566–571.

National Center for Education Statistics (2011). *Digest of education statistics: 2011.* Retrieved from http://nces.ed.gov/programs/digest/d11/tables/dt11_283.asp?referrer=report.

Noar, S., Carlyle, K., & Cole, C. (2006). Why communication is crucial: Meta-analysis of the relationship between safer sexual communication and condom use. *Journal of Health Communication, 11,* 365–390.

Oncale, R. M., & King, B. M. (2001). Comparison of men's and women's attempts to dissuade sexual partners from the couple using condoms. *Archives of Sexual Behavior, 30*(4), 379–391.

Quick, B. L., LaVoie, N. R., Scott, A. M., Bosch, D., & Morgan, S. E. (2012). Perceptions about organ donation among African American, Hispanic, and White high school students. *Qualitative Health Research, 22*(7), 921–933.

Rosenstock, I. M., Strecher, V. J., & Becker, M. H. (1988). Social learning theory and the health belief model. *Health Education Quarterly, 15*(2), 175–183.

Sheeran, P., Abraham, C., & Orbell, S. (1999). Psychosocial correlates of heterosexual condom use: a meta-analysis. *Psychological Bulletin, 125*(1), 90–132.

Silk, K. J., Bigbsy, E., Volkman, J., Kingsley, C., Atkin, C., Ferrara, M., & Goins, L. A. (2006). Formative research on adolescent and adult perceptions of risk factors for breast cancer. *Social Science & Medicine, 63*(12), 3124–3136.

Welch Cline, R. J., Freeman, K. E., & Johnson, S. J. (1990). Talk among sexual partners about AIDS: Factors differentiating those who talk from those who do not. *Communication Research, 17,* 792–808.

Welch Cline, R. J., Johnson, S. J., & Freeman, K. E. (1992). Talk among sexual partners about AIDS: Interpersonal communication for risk reduction or risk enhancement? *Health Communication, 4,* 39–56.

Widman, L., Welsh, D. P., McNulty, J. K., & Little, K. C. (2006). Sexual communication and contraceptive use in adolescent dating couples. *Journal of Adolescent Health, 39*(6), 893–899.

CHAPTER 26

College Students' Sexual Safety: The Verbal and Nonverbal Communication of Consent

Diana K. Ivy

KEY TERMS

Sexual safety	Consent	Verbal communication
Sexual assault	Bystander intervention	Nonverbal communication

ABSTRACT

Sexual safety is of extreme importance among the college student population in the United States and abroad. Although the rate of *reporting* sexual assaults among college students has increased, the rate of these campus crimes occurring has not decreased, despite widespread educational efforts. At the core of sexual safety between partners is the communication of consent. In this chapter, verbal and nonverbal mutual consent to sexual activity is discussed, including case studies that portray a sexual encounter gone terribly wrong. The chapter provides research on the challenge of expressing sexual boundaries and desires with a partner. Recommendations are offered in an effort to improve both the quantity and quality of messages college students receive about sexual safety.

She Said

What. Actually. Happened. I don't feel good; my head aches and I feel like I started a new exercise program and overdid it. Every part of my body hurts. I remember that girl from down the hall giving me a ride home after the party, but most of last night is fuzzy.

Must not drink. Must not drink. Okay, must not drink so much next time. I need to eat something but the thought of eating makes me nauseous all over again.

"Wow, what happened to you? You look like warmed over dog shit."

This is my roommate's favorite greeting to me after a hard night of partying. It's weird, too, because I'm not that much of a partier—which is probably why it hits me so hard when I do party. I mumble something to her, like "Don't talk so loud; I feel like crap but don't need you giving me hell right now."

"Oooooh, so sorry for offending your ears and pointing out the obvious. Seriously, you okay?"

My roommate's great, so now she's being my friend. I immediately regret barking at her. I start to tell her about the party, then I stop—fuzzy things are coming into focus and I get scared. I tell her about the kegger, about the shots I drank—more out of wanting to fit in and not be so nervous than wanting to get drunk. Then I tell her about the cute guy I met—the one who flirted with me and kept bringing me drinks. The one I went upstairs with to just "mess around." The one who likely raped me.

It's all coming back now. I start to cry. My roommate drags the story out of me, even though I'm crying and gulping and horrified with my own story. But I have to tell her—I have to tell someone what happened; and she's the one I trust the most. As I tell her, her face changes. She starts to cry too. Then she tells me that we have to call the police—or at least the campus cops. We have to report it or this guy will do this again to some other girl. Some other girl he feeds drinks to and then takes advantage of against her will when she's passed out dead drunk and can't even mumble a "yes" or a "no."

"Did you want to have sex with him? Did he force you? How much do you remember? What did you say to him, when you were alone, I mean? Like, did you actually say yes to him? Did you touch him or kiss him back? You need to be really clear about this, if only for your sake, much less reporting it to the cops."

She's hounding me with questions. I'm trying to answer, but it's painful to remember. It's painful to think that I'm now one of "those girls." Those stupid girls who don't watch their own drinks, who don't stay with their friends at parties. Who saw the pamphlets and heard the RA warn about date rape. I thought I was too educated to fall for that crap. That it couldn't possibly ever happen to me. Now I'm one of those stupid girls who was too drunk to say no or yes or stop or anything. I. Didn't. Say. Anything.

He left me there, half dressed in someone else's bed. To stumble downstairs and look for a ride home.

I liked him. I thought he liked me. So now it begins: the aftermath. The recovery.

Sexual exploration is confusing; it's not always pretty, in fact it's rarely pretty. It's certainly not how the media predominantly portray it—glossy and romantic with everyone looking attractive and things turning out wonderfully. The reality is that sexual exploration can be awkward, especially when it involves people in the earlier stages of their sexual lives—those stages where they're experimenting and learning new things, including what they like and do not like, what kind of sexual person they are and perhaps want to become. Each of us experiences a learning curve when it comes to expressing our sexuality. What we can all likely agree on is this: sexual exploration should not be devastating; it should not involve abuse. It should not signal the end of life or even the end of a *phase* of life. Sexual exploration should not damage our soul and our future relationships, and yet we know that sexual exploration that involves abuse can do these things. It has the power to change a person, usually not for the better.

Scholars, counselors, clergy, and educators tend to agree that the key issue related to sexual activity is consent (Beres, 2014; Hust et al., 2014; Jozkowski, Peterson, Sanders, Dennis, & Reece, 2014; Peterson & Muehlenhard, 2007). At the core of appropriate, enjoyable sexual functioning is mutual consent—both parties agreeing to sexual activity. The purpose of this chapter is to explore the communication of consent in sexual situations, with the goal of improving the messages college students receive about sexual exploration, sexual communication, sexual desires, and sexual boundaries—in short, each person's *sexual safety*.

He Said

I don't feel good. My head aches. Heck, everything aches. I want to throw up again, but there's nothing left in my stomach. Another night of hard partying. Story of my college career.

"Dude, you had quite the night last night."

My buddy is impressed with me—he's always impressed with me. He thinks I'm some kind of chick magnet or something. He doesn't know that my drinking turns me into someone else—someone way cooler and smoother with the ladies than I really am. If he knew how nervous I actually am around girls, he'd never let me hear the end of it.

"Saw you head upstairs with that hottie. You two have fun?"

He wants details.....again. My buddies always "debrief" the morning after a party: Who scored, who tried to score but didn't (and now has blue balls). Who was too dead drunk to remember anything, or who the teases were at the party. Who got into a fight in the back yard.

My dad taught me not to "kiss and tell," so I always hate these conversations, but I tell my friends about what I do with women so they'll keep thinking I'm cool—even if I have to make shit up.

"Yeah, she was hot. Never seen her before last night, but I knew I wanted her right when she walked in the door. She had that innocent thing, you know? And she wanted me too—she was way more in to me than I expected. Like, really playful and physical with me. It surprised me, but it was a good surprise. Know what

I mean?" I embellish the story to keep my buddy interested and to make myself look good.

The truth is that last night was damned confusing. This chick acted like she wanted me, like the night was going to turn out great. She drank every damned thing I brought her—like a pro, her drinking. Every touch, every kiss I gave her, she gave back. When I suggested we go somewhere private, she looked at me with those big eyes and followed me up the stairs. Clearly, she wanted to have sex. We were making out and it started getting crazy.

Then she started changing. Like, she was really getting drunk. I've seen that look before—the look they give before they start throwing up. I knew if we were going to do it, it had to happen fast or she'd be passed out or throwing up or something, and the sex would suck. When I was done, she laid there with her eyes closed—not moving at all. I knew I had to get out of there, so I went back downstairs and then left the party a few minutes later. I was wasted. Time for my own bed.

I really do hope she's okay. I'm not a monster or anything—I was scared. But I hope I don't ever run in to her again on campus.

Thank God I don't have any classes with her. That would be weird. Unless she can't remember anything about that night…

Note to self: Must not drink so much.

Campus Sexual Assault: A Good News/Bad News Situation

The heading for this section might seem strange—how can there be "good news" about campus sexual assault? The good news is, rates of reporting sexual assaults have risen in recent years, due in part to bystander intervention programs (Bennett, Banyard, & Garnhart, 2014; Hust et al., 2013, White & Malkowski, 2014) and enhanced efforts to combat what has been termed "rape culture" on college campuses (Anderson, 2014; Blaney, 2014).

One such bystander intervention and anti-sexual assault campaign, "It's On Us," was launched in 2014 by President Obama (Grasgreen, 2014). The primary goal of bystander education is to encourage intervention *before* a situation escalates into sexual violence, by teaching students to be aware of their surroundings, to recognize the potential for behavior to cross over into bad behavior or criminal activity, and to monitor the actions of their friends and others in social situations, even if it involves removing someone from a scene if the person becomes intoxicated or incapacitated (Nyhan, 2014; Winerip, 2014). A secondary goal is to encourage bystanders to report abuse to authorities or counselors, so that help can be offered to survivors of sexual assault should they request it.

The bad news is, reporting rates are on the increase, but the rate of these crimes being committed has not decreased (Anderson, 2014; Breiding et al., 2014; Krebs, Lindquist, Warner, Fisher, & Martin, 2009). Educational messages about "what date rape is" and "what not to do because it can ruin your life" seem to not be heard, are not taken seriously by many college students, or are viewed as being about something that could only happen to someone else (never oneself). An air of invincibility contributes to the problem; some students think it impossible or highly unlikely that they could be victimized.

Despite decades of concerted, innovative efforts to educate students about sexual safety and the need for clear expression of mutual consent and boundaries in sexual situations, sexual assault remains a serious problem on college campuses. In January of 2014, the White House Council on Women and Girls (*Rape and Sexual Assault*, 2014) report documented the following statistics/facts:

- 1 in 5 women experiences sexual assault while in college.

- These sexual assaults/rapes are perpetrated predominantly by someone known to the victim.

- Some dynamics of college life (e.g., drinking; drug use; being passed out or otherwise incapacitated, typically at parties) fuel the problem.

- "Serial" assailants predominate the rapist profile (63% of men who admit to committing or attempting rape commit an average of six rapes each).

One study found that two-thirds of college students surveyed reported knowing one or more women who were victims of sexual assault and over half knew one or more men who perpetrated sexual assault, leading the researchers to conclude that most college students arrive on campus with considerable knowledge of sexual assault (Sorenson, Joshi, & Sivitz, 2014). The role that alcohol and drug use plays in sexual assault has been documented widely (Lannutti & Monahan, 2004; Meyer, 2010; Palmer, McMahon, Rounsaville, & Ball, 2010; Testa, VanZile-Tamsen, Livingston, & Buddie, 2006). Many, if not most, campus sexual assaults involve the use of alcohol or drugs that compromise partners' ability to clearly communicate consent or non-consent (Krebs et al., 2009; Wente, 2014).

A Closer Examination of Communication and Consent: Is Instruction Effective?

Bystander intervention programs and sexual awareness training sessions are laudable methods to try to reduce campus sexual assaults. Some universities have women's centers and gender studies programs that offer more targeted sexual safety education. At universities across the country, no doubt some well-meaning professors talk to students about communication in sexual situations. Some communication scholars address it in their textbooks and other publications, hoping that students beyond those at their own universities will be exposed to information on communicating sexual desires and boundaries. Here's one such passage from a gender communication textbook, currently in fifth edition, aimed at potential perpetrators of sexual violence:

> If you read and retain nothing else in this entire chapter, please remember this: Consent is everything. Being too drunk or high to give consent isn't consent—it isn't a reason to assert your will and assault someone. Not hearing no doesn't mean yes. Hearing nothing at all doesn't mean a person has consented. People must voice their consent for you to have consent. If your sexual partner says no, you do not have consent. If the person doesn't say anything at all, you may or may not have consent—you need to ask for clarification to make sure the sexual activity is desired, lest you be in a position of taking advantage of someone and later accused of assault or rape (Ivy, 2012, pp. 284–285).

A passage from a nonverbal communication textbook (currently in second edition) is more explicit on the issue:

> When anyone says no to sex, that means no—no matter what the body is saying or if that person expresses it without conviction in his or her voice. When anyone says no at any point in sexual activity, activity *must stop*. Throughout this book, we've advised you, when the verbal and the nonverbal contradict, to believe the nonverbal because it usually carries the truer weight of the message; however, in this context, the verbal should override the nonverbal. Translation: If someone's words say no but her or his body says yes, the no should take precedence, sexual activity should stop, and partners should seek clarification before any further action is taken. Beware of sending mixed signals, because it's hard to stop sexual activity when one's partner seems as though he or she is still into it. But if one's partner verbally or nonverbally requests either a breather or for the activity to stop, that request simply *must* be heeded, no matter if any sort of physical affection continues (Ivy & Wahl, 2014, p. 494).

In a recent senior level gender communication course, a discussion ensued that was especially memorable, if not for the right reason. It surrounded conversation between potential sexual partners regarding sexual desires and boundaries. The instructor emphasized the need for clear verbal and nonverbal communication (functioning in tandem, not contradictory) as sexual activity begins (or preferably, *before* such activity begins), especially the clear communication of mutual consent to sexual acts. At that point, two male students vigorously balked at the notion that consent had to be verbally expressed or the resulting sexual activity could be considered rape. These students held the view that if one or both partners were "having a good time" and had "had a few drinks and were feeling good," *so* good that one or both people were unable to verbally express consent, going ahead sexually was fine—no harm, no foul. The attitude was, "how dare someone call that rape." Although some students expressed gall that their classmates seemed so uninformed, it's possible other students either agreed with the two men, but were muted by the discussion and afraid or unwilling to say that they agreed, or were reticent to reveal that they did not know exactly how consent worked. In an even more recent nonverbal communication class session in which verbal and nonverbal sexual consent was the topic of discussion, students again revealed misunderstanding about the need for mutual consent in sexual activity. Male and female students alike seemed surprised to learn that, without expressed consent, sexual activities could be considered assault. It appears that some students recognize the potential for confusion and negative outcomes to ensue when sexual partners rely solely on nonverbal cues or such nebulous indicators as "getting a vibe," but they also admit that nonverbal cues about sex are more comfortable to convey than verbal messages.

Why is this the case? Does talking openly about expectations for sexual activity brand one a "nerd," "inexperienced," "uncool," or too cerebral to enjoy a good time? Humphreys (2004) offers several explanations for this communication difficulty:

> Most of us do not verbally communicate our wants, needs, desires, or our consent to engage in sexual activity to our partners. Sexuality has overtones of shame and guilt attached to it. The sensationalistic nature of media images of sex tells us little about how to negotiate our daily sex lives with partners whose reactions actually matter to us. The perpetuation of a belief in the unequal sexual power of women and men hinders the ability of either to effectively communicate sexual intentions to a partner. We also tend to believe that sex is perfectly natural so we will automatically know what to do in a sexual encounter, that somehow we will magically know how to please our partner and ourselves when the time comes. This widely held attitude about sex leads to the assumption that the best sexual experiences require little communication (pp. 209-210).

Powell (2010) suggests that attempting to teach young women to be more assertive about expressing sexual boundaries and desires is well-intended but mostly futile, in that many young women do not want to risk being perceived as unfeminine by a male partner. Traditional heterosexual scripts of male-aggressor/female-submitter are alive and well, despite attempts to encourage women to be proactive in their sexual communication and men to be more accepting and less threatened by or judgmental of assertive communication from a female partner.

We Understand the Problem—
What Do We Do Better or Differently?

It's important to recognize the many educational efforts on multiple fronts that college and university personnel, including professors, provide to help students become more knowledgeable about the role of consent in their sexual safety. But it's simply not enough; sexual assault on U.S. campuses is not decreasing. Colleges and universities need coordinated, concerted, fearless efforts on these topics across many fronts—orientation sessions as students arrive to campus; ongoing workshops for students; coverage in classrooms (not only in communication courses); one-on-one mentoring from RAs, teachers, and counselors; and continual information disseminated through a variety of channels about where students can go for help or to report an assault (or their confusion about a sexual encounter), either as a survivor of an assault, a bystander, or an accused perpetrator.

Such information needs to include details about verbal and nonverbal mutual consent, with special emphasis placed on what it means to verbally consent versus the perils of trying to read a partner's nonverbal cues and ascertain whether consent is given or not. It needs to be spelled out to students that nonverbal consent—reading someone's actions as indications of consent—is *no consent at all*. Nonverbal consent does not hold up legally; nonverbal cues are particularly prone to being misread when a person is under the influence of his or her own sexual arousal. Students need all of these important details about consent spelled out in language that speaks to them, not technical jargon or language that tiptoes around the problem. (Here is where the fearlessness on the part of professors and other educators comes into play, because university personnel might not be comfortable nor trained in how to talk explicitly, but appropriately, to college students about sexual activity.)

In addition, students need clear instruction about exactly how consent functions legally and personally, possibly using such techniques as roleplays in which students—again, using the realistic language of their own voices—work on communication skills surrounding "sensitive" subjects. Appropriate humor (the kind that does not diminish the seriousness of the topic, nor make fun of students struggling with sensitive content) is advisable in such instruction, because humor enhances the impact and retention of a message.

Faculty and staff are part of the culture that is squeamish, reticent, or puritanical about talking to college students about sex, so ongoing training is necessary to keep university personnel current and help them understand their role in combating campus sexual assault. In many parts of the country, the only messages public school students receive about sexuality surround abstinence, unwanted pregnancy, and STIs. These educational messages are important, but they're not enough. It's safe to say that many students arrive at the college campus gates knowing more about the downside of sexuality—unwanted or unintended outcomes and health risks— than they do about their own functioning as sexual human beings.

Communication educators must lead the charge on this front, because *consent is a communication issue*. It's time (past time) for professors to embrace this problem and teach students, across disciplines and course offerings, to think about themselves as sexual beings, to consider who they are sexually and what they want to express to others, and to encourage them to practice sexual safety messages. This challenge must be taken up even if such discussions are uncomfortable, unexpected, or risky in educational environments where frank discussions of communication and sexuality are not the norm. Special attention needs to be paid in such educational efforts to persuade college women that communicating their sexual desires and boundaries does not make them unfeminine or "ball-busting" women whom men will not find attractive (heterosexually speaking). Special attention should be paid to educate college men that asking a partner what she wants and does not want sexually will not detract from their masculinity or make a guy a "wimp" in a female sexual partner's eyes.

Perhaps a book like the one you're reading will make an excellent text for a course on the subject of communication and sexuality, taught across disciplines and across the country at college and university campuses. Perhaps bringing these topics into a classroom where the subject is expected to be sensitive will bring about more helpful, realistic advice through open conversations about a difficult, perpetual problem.

DISCUSSION QUESTIONS

1. What do you recall being taught, either by a family member, friend, teacher, or counselor at school about the role of consent in sexual situations? Do you consider the education you received adequate? If not, what was left out and why? Was this an awkward conversation?

2. Students often express confusion about verbal and nonverbal mutual consent in sexual situations. Was anything presented in this chapter surprising or new to you? What do you think is behind college students' lack of understanding about consent and sexual assault?

3. Discuss the benefits of verbal consent versus nonverbal consent. Discuss the challenges inherent in both forms of communication. Do you agree with the list of roadblocks to clear, effective communication about sexual activity, as provided by Humphreys in this chapter?

4. Some experts suggest that alcohol and drug use among college students is the leading culprit when it comes to sexual assault. But is it realistic to suggest that students should not drink, simply because drinking increases the likelihood of sexual assault? Should students be encouraged to have a "designated driver" type of person along when they attend functions or gatherings where alcohol will be present, almost as a pre-determined "bystander"?

5. Imagine that you have been tasked with talking to a group of students (younger than yourself) about sexual safety and communication skills. What would you include in such a lesson? How would you communicate the importance of mutual consent to these students, in a language they would understand—in a way that would not be accusatory, embarrassing, or that would elicit nervous laughter? What would be your goal of such a session?

References

Anderson, N. (2014, July 1). Sex offense statistics show U.S. college reports are rising. *The Washington Post*. Available: www.washingtonpost.com.

Bennett, S., Banyard, V. L., & Garnhart, L. (2014). To act or not to act, that is the question? Barriers and facilitators of bystander intervention. *Journal of Interpersonal Violence, 29*, 476–496.

Beres, M. A. (2014). Rethinking the concept of consent for anti-sexual violence activism and education. *Feminism & Psychology, 24*, 373–389.

Blaney, B. (2014, October 2). Student group protests "rape culture" on campus. *Dallas Morning News*, p. 2A.

Breiding, M. J., Smith, S. G., Basile, K. C., Walters, M. L., Jieru, C., & Merrick, M. T. (2014). Prevalence and characteristics of sexual violence, stalking, and intimate partner violence victimization: National Intimate Partner and Sexual Violence Survey, United States, 2011. *MMWR Surveillance Summaries, 63*, 1–18.

Grasgreen, A. (2014, September 19). White House: "It's On Us" campaign targets culture of sexual assault on campus. Available: www.politico.com, retrieved September 22, 2014.

Humphreys, T. P. (2004). Understanding sexual consent: An empirical investigation of the normative script for young heterosexual adults. In M. Cowling & P. Reynolds (Eds.), *Making sense of sexual consent* (pp. 209–227). Surry, UK: Ashgate Publishing Ltd.

Hust, S. J. T., Lei, M., Ren, C., Chang, H., McNab, A. L., Marett, E. G., & Willoughby, J. F. (2013). The effects of sports media exposure on college students' rape myth beliefs and intentions to intervene in a sexual assault. *Mass Communication and Society, 16*, 762–786.

Hust, S. J. T., Marett, E. G., Ren, C., Adams, P. M., Willoughby, J. F., Lei, M., Ran, W., & Norman, C. (2014). Establishing and adhering to consent: The association between reading magazines and college students' sexual consent negotiation. *Journal of Sex Research, 51*, 280–290.

Ivy, D. K. (2012). *Genderspeak: Personal effectiveness in gender communication* (5th ed.). Boston: Pearson.

Ivy, D. K., & Wahl, S. T. (2014). *Nonverbal communication for a lifetime* (2nd ed.). Dubuque, IA: Kendall Hunt.

Jozkowski, K. N., Peterson, Z. D., Sanders, S. A., Dennis, B., & Reece, M. (2014). Gender differences in heterosexual college students' conceptualizations and indicators of sexual consent: Implications for contemporary sexual assault prevention education. *Journal of Sex Research, 51*, 904–916.

Krebs, C. P., Lindquist, C. H., Warner, T. D., Fisher, B. S., & Martin, S. L. (2009). College women's experiences with physically forced, alcohol- or other drug-enabled and drug-facilitated sexual assault before and since entering college. *Journal of American College Health, 57,* 639–649.

Lannutti, P. J., & Monahan, J. L. (2004). "Not now, maybe later": The influence of relationship type, request persistence, and alcohol consumption on women's refusal strategies. *Communication Studies, 55,* 362–378.

Meyer, A. (2010). "Too drunk to say no": Binge drinking, rape, and the *Daily Mail. Feminist Media Studies, 10,* 19–34.

Nyhan, B. (2014, December 2). Reporting sexual assault is difficult, but a new technology may help. *The New York Times.* Available: www. nytimes.com, retrieved April 26, 2015.

Palmer, R. S., McMahon, T. J., Rounsaville, B. J., & Ball, S. A. (2010). Coercive sexual experiences, protective behavioral strategies, alcohol expectations, and consumption among male and female college students. *Journal of Interpersonal Violence, 25,* 1563–1578.

Peterson, Z. D., & Muehlenhard, C. L. (2007). Conceptualizing the "wantedness" of women's consensual and nonconsensual sexual experiences: Implications for how women label their experiences with rape. *Journal of Sex Research, 44,* 72–88.

Powell, A. (2010). *Sex, power, and consent: Youth culture and the unwritten rules.* Cambridge, UK: Cambridge University Press.

Rape and sexual assault: A renewed call to action. (2014, January). Washington, DC: White House Council on Women and Girls.

Sorenson, S. B., Joshi, M., & Sivitz, E. (2014). Knowing a sexual assault victim or perpetrator: A stratified random sample of undergraduates at one university. *Journal of Interpersonal Violence, 29,* 394–416.

Testa, M., VanZile-Tamsen, C., Livingston, J. A., & Buddie, A. M. (2006). The role of women's alcohol consumption in managing sexual intimacy and sexual safety motives. *Journal of Studies in Alcohol, 67,* 665–674.

Wente, M. (2014, March 1). Can she consent to sex after drinking? Available: www.theglobeandmail.com, retrieved September 15, 2014.

White, C. H., & Malkowski, J. (2014). Communicative challenges of bystander intervention: Impact of goals and message design logic on strategies college students use to intervene in drinking situations. *Health Communication, 29,* 93–104.

Winerip, M. (2014, February 7). Stepping up to stop sexual assault. *The New York Times.* Available: www.nytimes.com, retrieved September 15, 2014.

SECTION 6

Sex, Media, and Popular Culture

CHAPTER 27

Sexuality in Popular Culture: Is it "All About that Bass..."?

Lara Stache

KEY TERMS

Sexuality	Feminism	Media
Empowerment	Celebrity	

ABSTRACT

In this chapter, I explore popular culture as both a creation and reflection of cultural discourse. I draw on scholarly conversations that position popular culture as a way to provide the public with a language to talk about sexuality, and analyze the various conversations that contemporary music, television, and film texts and social commentators have about sexuality and the society in which we live. I argue that popular culture serves a communicative function, because it opens a dialogue that continues beyond the boundaries of the screen and airwaves, into public discourse. I conclude with a discussion of the implications of popular culture's representations of sexuality, focusing on both the progressive potential and limitations.

People like to talk about sex, and nowhere is this topic more heavily discussed than around popular culture narratives, such as music, television, and film. Megan Trainor's (2015) song tells us it's "all about that bass," as Nicki Minaj bounces her "buns" in "Anaconda" (2014). Not only do popular characters open up dialogues about sex and sexuality, like the *Sex in the City* ensemble that made vibrators and sexual positions topics of conversation at Sunday brunch, but popular culture narratives also spark discussion among the general public. These debates go beyond determining whether *50 Shades of Grey* is a sexy story, and instead get people to talk about whether young women can be both sexual and empowered, whether a man's number of previous sexual partners should be higher than a woman's, or what it means to be gay.

In this chapter, I argue that popular culture serves a communicative function, because it opens a dialogue that continues beyond the boundaries of the screen and airwaves, into public discourse. This is why popular culture matters and why so many academics, scholars, bloggers, and consumers spend valuable time critiquing the messages within and around popular culture narratives. Specifically, I critique the conversations that are occurring around women and sexuality in contemporary popular culture, and ultimately, I suggest that the messages reveal that there are some important discussions happening that are at least a baby step forward to offer broader ideas about sexuality for women in particular.

Popular Culture: The Past and Present

If you have ever had to defend your love of popular culture, then you are keenly aware of the feeling that television, film, and music matter in different ways to different people. From a critical perspective, many contemporary scholars view media, and popular culture in particular, as a way of understanding the society in which we live. This perspective resides in the theory that popular culture texts provide "the stories through which we make sense of ourselves," both as individuals, and as a society (Sinfeld, 1989, p. 23). When in 2015, *The Bachelorette*'s Kaitlyn Bristowe "shockingly" had sex with one of her suitors, Nick Vaill, viewers were not simply assessing Kaitlyn's individual actions to have sex with one man—when she was dating so many others—but also what it meant to be a young single woman having sex outside of a monogamous relationship. The opinions varied; some viewers called her a slut and others supported her decision, arguing that it is important to find out if there is sexual chemistry with a suitor. As scholars and students of popular culture and sexuality, the backlash, the explanation, and the feedback about this one popular culture narrative, reflects the swath of opinions voiced when it comes to women and sex, and also illustrates how popular culture moments like these offer an interesting glimpse at the way our society makes sense of and moral judgments about acceptable (gendered) behavior.

The importance of popular culture as a scholarly text began to be studied in earnest in the 1980s, with seminal work by scholars like Janice Radway (1984) and John Fiske (1986). Previously "popular culture was viewed as a site of entertainment and pleasure, whereas high culture was intended to inspire discussion and evaluation, thus placing the former as inferior to the latter" (Stache, 2015, p. 72). Rosalind Gill (2007) argues that due to the "collapse in the notion of a straightforward, unproblematic distinction between high and popular culture that is associated with postmodernism and with the increasing institutional respectability of media and cultural studies," popular culture provides an invaluable tool for critical scholars (p. 13).

The conversations that occur around, in, and about popular culture texts are rarely black and white, which makes the grey area fascinating to study. Contemporary scholars embrace the "complicated and often illuminatory statements about social institutions and formations" that popular culture can provide (Banet-Weiser, 1999, p. 5). There are a variety of scholars that have suggested that the communicative potential of popular culture that focuses on sexuality, which includes texts like pornography (Concepcion, 1999; O'Brien, 2004), romance novels (Radway, 1986), and film narratives (Read, 2000), is important, because it gives viewers a language through which to discuss their own ideas about sex and sexuality. It is in this way that popular culture serves a communicative function, when it starts a dialogue that continues into public discourse.

Critical study of popular culture reveals "how texts generate everyday, common-sense meanings and popular understandings" of conversations happening in the broader cultural landscape (Read, 2000, p. 5). If this is true, then I now ask, what does contemporary popular culture and critical commentary about these narratives suggest about sexuality in our society?

Sexuality in Popular Culture: Reflection and Creation

Contemporary popular culture has featured a lot of strong women prominently over the last few years, with characters like *Scandal*'s Olivia Pope, the protagonist of the *Hunger Games* series of books and movies Katniss Everdeen, and the only female member of *The Avengers*, Black Widow, showing what it means to be a powerful and sexy woman. Additionally, celebrities like Amy Pohler, Beyoncé, and Lena Dunham, openly embrace feminism and attempt to address women's issues through their creative choices, with 2015 predicted to be "the year of funny women" (Buchanan, 2015). Concurrently, gender equality advocacy groups remind us "only 7% of directors, 13% of writers, and 20% of producers are female" (Research facts, 2012). Although the steps are baby-sized, the conversations about women, power, and sexuality are occurring, both on- and off-screen, which makes popular culture narratives ripe for analysis.

One of the most prevalent social debates about women in music, television, and film occurs at the intersection of positive body rhetoric and female empowerment. In 2014, Meghan Trainor released the hit single "All About That Bass," which has been called a "body-positive polemic dolled up in a poodle skirt" (Markovitz, 2014) and "an anthem for the pleasantly plump" (Riley, 2014), as the song celebrates a woman with curves. Originally intending to sell the song, Trainor laughs about the fact that other female singers in the industry were too "teeny" to sing about their "bass" (as quoted in Markovitz, 2014). However, not everyone views the lyrics as body-positive, with some critics arguing that the song sets up an "us versus them" narrative against thin women, as opposed to embracing all body shapes and sizes, and also promotes a level of sexuality for young girls that is not about being happy with their bodies, but finding a heterosexual partner that will appreciate their bodies (Riley, 2014). Similarly, Nicki Minaj has received criticism for her song, "Anaconda," which is an example of feminist scholar, bell hooks' argument that "feminist women might be sexually liberating themselves 'against their own interests'" (as quoted in Stoeffel, 2014). hooks specifically cites Minaj and Beyoncé as artists who further the idea that putting sexuality on display is empowering, and she finds this problematic. Some social critics agree that songs that embrace sexuality, and encourage girls to display that sexuality, send the wrong message about the goals of sexual empowerment, when lyrics proclaim: "I got that boom boom that all the boys chase. And all the right junk in all the right places" (Riley, 2014). In popular culture narratives, encouraging young women to embrace their sexuality is positioned next to the goals of being on display, and critics of these messages suggest that these two goals cannot be combined with the result of female empowerment.

Not all of the discourse focuses on the pros and cons of featuring too much sexuality. For some women, an additional rhetorical qualifier has been introduced that places attractiveness as a gauge of agency and authority over sexuality. For example, Lena Dunham has received critical acclaim for her HBO series, *Girls*, which has also generated both praise and criticism for frequently featuring Dunham's (2014) self-described, "gummy bear" looking nude body. Dunham has credited her parents with her body confidence stating, "they…always made me feel pretty and cool and smart, even in the moments when I have known—and still know—that my body wasn't fitting into a traditional Hollywood idea of the female body" (as quoted in Barton, 2013). But, not everybody appreciates Dunham's vision, with Howard Stern stating about the show, "It's a little fat girl who kinda looks like Jonah Hill and she keeps taking her clothes off and it kind of feels like rape" (Chen, 2013). Stern has since publically apologized for his comments, but his original statement underscores the criticism against Dunham: who is she to think it is okay to be sexy? The critiques against Dunham question her authority to be sexual, and sexy; and as writer, director, and producer of her show, for her to be in charge of her image of sexuality on the show based on her appearance. Ultimately, cultural conversations like these about sexuality, particularly when it comes to women, result in what Jennifer Dunn (2010) calls a "regulation of identities and desires," wherein sexuality of women is limited to strict binaries of good and bad (p. 108). In Dunham's case, her sexuality as good/bad, empowering/disempowering is not being questioned, but instead the authority for her to put her sexualized body on display is doubted. The discourse against the representation of Dunham's sexuality suggests that authority of sexuality is gauged solely on attractiveness, and men like Stern can dismiss a woman's right to present her sexuality to the public, thus publically regulating the agency of women over their own sexuality.

Amy Schumer utilized parody to bring these types of conversations directly to the small screen, in season three of her series, *Inside Amy Schumer*, on Comedy Central (Cantor, McFaul, & Schumer, 2015). Responding to

CHAPTER 27: Sexuality in Popular Culture: Is it "All About that Bass…"?

425

conversations happening in the broader social discourse about the value of women and sexuality, Schumer uses the plot from the cinematic classic, *12 Angry Men*, to emphasize the absurdity of gauging the right to be a sexualized woman based on a perceived level of attraction. Schumer's name has made it into the cultural conversation, questioning her level of attractiveness and sexuality, with one critic describing her as a "chubby-cheeked, whipsmart, not conventionally attractive" woman, whose "wide facial features" are reminiscent of "Jennifer Aniston's somewhat heavier, not-as-lucky sister who watches a lot of television" (Wells, 2015). In the episode, an all-male jury of 12 men determines whether Schumer is hot enough to be on television. Featuring a star-studded cast, including Jeff Goldblum, Paul Giamatti, and *Mad Men's* Vincent Kartheiser, the skit beautifully details the cultural discourse about women's value, perceptions of attractiveness in association to sexual interest, and gendered double standards. In the end of the skit, Schumer is admitted to television on the basis that she gives all the men on the jury, "reasonable chub." Through this skit, Schumer not only reveals the range of cultural conversation about women and sexuality in particular, but also highlights the absurdity of the conversations, by emphasizing how seriously the men are taking this evaluation.

No woman is free of criticism, regardless of her perceived level of attraction. Even when a woman is deemed "hot" enough to be the sexualized leading character or pop music star, cultural conversations about her sexuality shift to a rhetoric of slut-shamming, as happened most recently with the new *Avenger's* release and the character of Black Widow. Jeremy Renner, who plays the character of Hawkeye in the Marvel franchise, called the character of Black Widow a slut, because, in the comics, she is sexually active with many of her fellow Avengers. He then pulled a #SorryNotSorry, with his interview on Conan O'Brien's show arguing, "If you slept with four of the six Avengers, no matter how much fun you had, you'd be a slut. Just saying. I'd be a slut. Just saying" (Michaels, 2015). Critics of Renner have pointed out that nobody is calling Tony Stark a slut, and he has actually been depicted in the films as sleeping with a lot of women, whereas Black Widow has yet to "hook up" with anybody in the film series (Hathaway, 2015).

Unfortunately, this is not a new conversation, where conventionally attractive women over the decades are disciplined against showing too much sexuality. Mylie Cyrus' infamous foam finger at the 2013 MTV Awards, offered an interesting moment to understand cultural perception of sexuality and age. Prior to her MTV Awards performance, Cyrus played a character named Hannah Montana on the Disney channel for years, and had always projected a rather wholesome image. Upon turning 21, Cyrus embraced her sexuality, breaking the image of Disney's girl-next-door at the MTV Awards, to don a skimpy satin bra and panty set, and a foam finger, which she used provocatively as if pleasuring herself throughout the performance.

After the event, some social critics labeled Cyrus a "sex-crazed twerkster" (Raven, 2014), but Cyrus argues in an interview with *W Magazine*,

> I'm trying to tell girls, like, 'F–k that. You don't have to wear makeup. You don't have to have long blonde hair and big t–ties. That's not what it's about. It's, like, personal style.' I like that I'm associated with sexuality and the kind of punk-rock shit where we just don't care (as quoted in Harris, 2014).

"Be yourself" is not a bad message, especially from pop culture idols like Mylie Cyrus; however, her tactics are similar to some of the criticisms against Meghan Trainor's song. In owning her sexuality and "personal style," Cyrus discounts women whose personal style is make-up, long blonde hair, and large breasts. One recurring message is that cultural discourse surrounding female empowerment and sexuality tends to unwittingly establish further boundaries and barriers, as opposed to breaking them down.

However, some popular culture narratives are breaking through traditional boundaries of socially acceptable sexuality. The previously detailed criticisms indicate that popular culture functions to embrace, or glorify a woman's personal sexuality; but we are also seeing more depictions of same-sex orientations and queerness in terms of sexual identities, which is a positive step forward for a more diverse representation of sexuality in the media. From Macklemore's (2012) song, "Same Love," to popular characters on television and film, like *Grey's Anatomy's* Dr. Callie Torres, discussions about sexuality and sexual identity have become much more prominent within popular culture narratives. The hit show *Modern Family* has won multiple awards and critical acclaim by representing a variety of different definitions of "family" on prime time television. Although the characters of Mitch and Cameron, the gay couple on the show with adopted daughter Lily, have received their fair share of criticism for reinforcing stereotypes about flamboyantly gay men, overwhelmingly the characters have been cited as a positive representation of queerness in a popular culture text (Pierce, 2014).

Arguably an even more important representation comes in Netflix's hit show, *Orange is the New Black*, which explores a gamete of sexuality, including queerness and transgender issues. Piper Chapman, played by Taylor Schilling, is the main character in *Orange is the New Black*, and she is in prison because she helped her ex-girlfriend smuggle drugs during their relationship. Upon entering prison, Piper is engaged to Larry, played by Jason Biggs, and her sexuality and sexual preferences are explored throughout the series, as she grapples with her attraction to her former lover behind bars. The series details the struggle with attraction to people regardless of gender, gives a glimpse of sexual loneliness, and generally embraces a queer spectrum of sexuality and desire. Within much popular discourse, sexuality tends to fall within a binary of "hetero versus homo" desire, but queer theory suggests that sexuality occurs on a much more fluid spectrum. Many of the characters on *Orange is the New Black* offer examples of sexuality in flux, just as others embrace the binary of queer versus straight; but the variety of representations sparks conversation. Additionally, the show tackles issues of transgender rights, when Sophia, played by Laverne Cox, has her hormone replacement medication reduced due to budget issues. Popular culture "tell[s] many different stories," (Read, 2000, p. 5), but this series can be read as a progressive step forward in providing an opportunity to open the dialogue about traditional binaries of sexuality, gender, and desire.

Conclusion & Implications:
A Language of Popular Culture

The above analysis of representations of sexuality in popular culture, and the cultural conversations that occur around these narratives reveals both progressive steps forward and potential limitations. On one hand, we have women, and particularly a young generation of women, who are actively proclaiming ownership over their sexuality and choosing to display that agency to others. Although some critics, like bell hooks would argue this is simply missing the point (see Stoeffel, 2014), or that this is an example of "enlightened sexism" (Douglas, 2010), other scholars might suggest that these representations of sexuality open the doors to breaking down binaries that restrict sexuality as good/bad (Dunn, 2010). Contemporary popular culture reveals a discourse about sexuality that continues to rely on binaries, with sexual empowerment always in opposition to social discipline. At times, this occurs with slut-shamming, where a woman can be sexualized, but not sexual. Other times, this occurs when only certain women are deemed appropriate to be sexual, and most often this means they must fit conventional beauty norms. Additionally, we have seen a queering of the lines of sexual attraction and identity that is refreshing and important in a social landscape that obsessed when former Olympian, Bruce Jenner came out as Caitlyn Jenner, a transgender woman in 2015.

At the same time, "cultural texts tell many different stories and, in negotiating a route through the text, the critic can only pretend to tell one of those stories" (Read, 2000, p. 5). The critic must be aware of the complexity within a text, and recognize the limitations of a single analysis. A popular culture text provides a specific telling of a social narrative, which, in addition to reflecting society, also functions to create a version of society. Different critics may find different stories within their analyses. Viewed through this framework, popular culture is not inherently a problem, nor a solution, but rather, an artifact that can be read by critical scholars as a representation of our social conversations about a given topic. However, the critic's analysis tells only one side of the story. In this chapter, I have explored the discourse of the producers and the critics, but now we need to look at the audience for these popular culture narratives and analyze how they are talking about it. It is the people through their engagement, appropriation, and circulation who are making these narratives popular, so the audience discourse is an important piece to reveal the larger puzzle.

The fact that these conversations are happening in mainstream popular texts is certainly a solid step forward. Both Lena Dunham and Amy Schumer embrace the social dialogue about their own bodies and beauty, but broaden those discussions to address the larger social landscape of women. Ultimately, the conversations are important, both those happening outside of the narratives in the broader social discourse, and the themes that occur within the texts themselves. In 1985, Alison Bechdel introduced what has become a feminist meme of sorts, suggesting that for a film narrative to be "feminist," it must feature two women talking about something other than men at some point during the film. Astoundingly, most films fail this colloquial test. In this sense, Bechdel's test echoes the critiques of the "body-positive" songs that seem to continually place women, and more specifically, young girls, as the object of desire, rather than active agents capable of thinking about more than men.

It is important for individuals to analyze how popular culture's representations of sexuality illuminate social expectations, boundaries, and conversations about sexuality more broadly. It is even more imperative that these critiques happen in conversation with others, both inside and outside of the classroom, thus highlighting the communicative potential of mediated narratives. In closing, I ask you to think about your voice in these cultural conversations about sexuality, and how popular culture has challenged and reinforced your ideas. Additionally, I encourage you to question whether the representations of sexuality and women in particular are empowering, and how they could be even better.

DISCUSSION QUESTIONS

1. Think about the popular culture narratives that you find most interesting or entertaining. What do you learn from watching these films or televisions shows, or listening to this music? As was discussed in this chapter, has it given you a language to discuss the way you see the world?

2. Where did you learn about sex and sexuality? Was it within conversations with your family and/or friends? Did you learn from the media and Internet? How have these discussions shaped your views on sexuality today?

3. Cultural critics argue about whether representations of sexuality, particularly, female empowerment, same sex relationships, transgender individuals, and the like are progressive or not. Would you agree that popular cultural narratives about sexuality are progressive and empowering, or that they tend to further stereotypes about marginalized groups within society?

4. Think of popular culture narratives that you do not like to watch, read, or listen to. What is it about these texts that make you not like them?

5. Do you find yourself reading articles about your favorite popular culture narratives online or in print? Do you actively seek out information about popular culture or is it something that you come across with little effort? What does your access (or lack thereof) suggest about the society in which we live?

6. What do you think of the statement that media both reflects and generates views about society? Do you agree or disagree? What are some examples of how popular culture both reflects and generates views on society?

References

Barton, J. (2013, August 29). Lena Dunham opens up about her body confidence in exclusive interview. *Marie Claire Magazine.* Retrieved from http://www.marieclaire.co.uk/news/celebrity/544142/lena-dunham-opens-up-about-her-body-confidence-in-exclusive-interview.html#index=1

Buchanan, D. (2015, January 11). The Girls legacy is here. Meet the female-led comedies you can't afford to miss. *The Telegraph.* Retrieved from http://www.telegraph.co.uk/women/womens-life/11336874/Girls-The-female-comedies-inspired-by-Lena-Dunahms-series.html.

Cantor, H. (Writer), McFaul, R. (Director), & Schumer, A. (Director). (2015). 12 angry men inside Amy Schumer [Television series episode]. In A. Schumer (Producer), *Inside Amy Schumer.* New York, NY: Jax Media.

Chen, J. (2013, January 12). Howard Stern calls Lena Dunham 'little fat girl,' likens Girls sex scenes to 'rape.' Us Magazine. http://www.usmagazine.com/celebrity-news/news/howard-stern-calls-lena-dunham-little-fat-girl-likens-girls-sex-scenes-to-rape-2013121.

Douglas, S. J. (2010). *The rise of enlightened sexism: How pop culture took us from girl power to Girls Gone Wild.* New York, NY: St. Martin's Griffin.

Dunn, J. (2010). HBO's *Cathouse*: Problematising representations of sex workers and sexual women. *Feminist Media Studies, 10*(1), 105–109.

Fiske, J. (1986). Television: Polysemy and popularity. *Critical Studies in Media Communication, 3*(4), 391–408.

Harris, M. (2014, February 3). Miley Cyrus is 'laid bare' for W Magazine. *Vibe Magazine.* Retrieved from http://www.vibe.com/2014/02/miley-cyrus-is-laid-bare-for-w-magazine-photos.

Hathaway, J. (2015, May 5). After apologizing, Jeremy Renner reiterates that Black Widow is 'a slut.' *Gawker.com.* Retrieved from http://morningafter.gawker.com/after-apologizing-jeremy-renner-reiterates-that- black-1702251229.

CHAPTER 27: Sexuality in Popular Culture: Is it "All About that Bass…"?

431

Markovitz, A. (2014, October 10). Meghan Trainor talks 'All About That Bass' (and all about Beyoncé, Swift, and Beiber). *Entertainment Weekly*. Retrieved from http://www.ew.com/article/2014/10/10/meghan-trainor-all-about-that-bass-beyonce-swift-bieber.

Michaels, L. (Producer). (2015, May 4). *Late night with Conan O'Brien* [television broadcast]. New York, NY: NBC Studios.

O'Brien, W. (2004). Qu(e)erying pornography: Contesting identity politics in feminism. In S. Gillis, G. Howie, & R. Munford (Eds.), *Third Wave Feminism: A Critical Exploration* (pp. 122–134). New York, NY: Palgrave Macmillan.

Pierce, S. D. (2014, December 28). Modern Family gay criticism misses mark. *The Salt Lake City Tribune*. Retrieved from http://www.sltrib.com/entertainment/1984592-155/modern-family-gay-criticism-misses-mark.

Radway, J. (1984). *Reading the romance: Women, patriarchy, and popular literature*. Chapel Hill, NC: The University of North Carolina Press.

Raven, D. (2014, May 9). Has Miley Cyrus gone too far? *Mirror UK*. Retrieved from http://www.mirror.co.uk/3am/celebrity-news/miley-cyrus-uk-tour-ticket-3518175.

Read, J. (2000). *The new avengers: Feminism, femininity and the rape-revenge cycle*. Manchester, London: Manchester University Press.

Research facts (2012). *Geena Davis Institute on Gender in Media*. Retrieved from http://seejane.org/research-informs-empowers/.

Riley, N. S. (2014, October, 19). The faux empowerment of 'All About That Bass.' *New York Post*. Retrieved from http://nypost.com/2014/10/19/the-faux-empowerment-of-all-about-that-bass/.

Sinfeld, A. (1989). *Literature, politics and culture in postwar Britain*. Oxford, Basil Blackwell.

Stache, L. (2015). When a man writes a woman: Audience reception of the avenging-woman character in popular television and film. In A. Trier-Bieniek (Ed.), *Fan Girls and the Media: Creating Characters, Consuming Culture*. Lanham, MD: Rowman & Littlefield.

Stoeffel, K. (2014). bell hooks was bored by 'Anaconda.' *New York Magazine*. Retrieved from http://nymag.com/thecut/2014/10/bell-hooks-was-bored-by-anaconda.html.

Wells, J. (2015, February 11). Apatow's funny-chubby community has new member. *Hollywood Elsewhere*. Retrieved from http://www.hollywood-elsewhere.com/2015/02/adding-funny-chubby-community.

CHAPTER 28

Sex *is* the Weapon: Sexualization and Heterosexism in Video Game Culture

Jennifer Mayo & Robert Alan Brookey

KEY TERMS

Gamergate	Gender	Boy culture
Video games	Online harassment	

ABSTRACT

On August 16, 2014, Eron Gjoni created a blog post about his ex-girlfriend and indie game developer, Zoe Quinn. Online users took Gjoni's accusations and harassed Quinn, assuming that she had sex with men in order to advance her video game career. This incident snowballed into #GamerGate, an online movement that claimed to be about ethics in journalism, but also included a series of attacks against women who disagreed with GamerGate, thereby revealing the underlying misogyny within the video game community. Over the years, a "boy culture" has been constructed around video games and has subsequently led to the assumption that these games are meant for males. With almost half of gamers being female, the masculine culture of video games no longer reflects reality. This chapter will examine the sexist and misogynist elements of GamerGate as a discourse that attempts to protect the boy culture of video games from the participation of women, by advancing implicit and explicit sexual threats.

433

Introduction

On August 16, 2014, a Boston computer scientist, Eron Gjoni, created a blog to chronicle his breakup with his ex-girlfriend and indie game developer, Zoe Quinn. The blog was created five days after Quinn had released her new game *Depression Quest* on the online gaming service Steam. Gjoni accused Quinn of emotional abuse and claimed she cheated on him with other men, including a video game journalist (Gjoni, 2014). Gjoni's blog sparked a YouTube video by InternetAristocrat (2014) who claimed: "I don't care that Zoe Quinn fucked five guys . . . However, when the people she's having an affair with, the people she's cheating on her boyfriend with, happen to be able to help her career through their actions related to the industry she's in, then it becomes a piece of public discourse." Later, actor Adam Baldwin (2014) linked this video on his Twitter feed with the hashtag "GamerGate." A group of gamers banded together under this hashtag and began to claim that ethics in gaming journalism had to be addressed.

The hashtag GamerGate went viral, and soon came to signify a decidedly divisive conversation across the Internet. Although many claimed that GamerGate was solely about gaming journalism, the discourse surrounding the controversy was often highly sexualized and violently sexist. After all, it was precipitated by a supposedly cuckold boyfriend who accused his former girlfriend of trading on her sexuality in order to win professional favors; not far from a charge of prostitution. Indeed, additional Internet texts would appear to malign Quinn's abilities as a game designer, and call into question her sexual practices. Quinn was not alone; other women have been harassed and sexually threatened for merely disagreeing with GamerGate.

Our purpose in this chapter is not to settle the controversy surrounding the real intent of GamerGate, and we concede that many identified with GamerGate might be sincerely concerned with journalism ethics regarding the video game industry. Instead, we use GamerGate as a starting point to discuss the implications of video game culture as a masculine culture. The masculine gendering of video game culture is a construction with a history, and we begin this chapter showing how the industry purposefully constructed a market targeted toward young males. More recently, however, the video game industry has opened up its marketing practices to encourage women to play video games, but as more women enter into the video gaming culture, there is resistance from those who believe it should be maintained as a "boy culture" where women do not belong. Therefore, we will review the theory that explains how video game culture operates as a boy culture, and then we will apply that theory in a critical analysis of elements of the GamerGate discourse. We conclude that the sexist and misogynist elements of the GamerGate discourse function to protect the male exclusivity of video game culture, and to discourage women from further encroaching on video game culture by issuing threats of sexual shaming and sexual violence.

History of Video Games and Marketing

1972s *Pong*, the first commercial video game success, did not have a specific gender demographic. Nolan Bushnell and his company, Atari placed *Pong* in bars and pool halls, with no marketing aside from the cabinet decoration (Kent, 2001). This event ushered in an era of coin-operated machines made for any patron, male or female. When Bushnell turned his attention to the home video game market with Atari's aptly named *Home Pong*, he marketed the game to any family that owned a television, not a specific gender or age. As Atari and other companies got involved in the home console market, their focus remained on the family as video games were often regarded as a type of toy.

When video games experienced a sharp decline in the early 1980s, most companies retreated from the home video game market (Kent, 2001). When Nintendo began introducing its Nintendo Entertainment System (NES) into the United States, it had to find a way to resuscitate a dying American video game market and create a solid demographic. The solution came in the form of gendered marketing, and Nintendo focused on boys between ages 8 and 14. Although parents actually bought the games, Nintendo relied heavily on the "pester power" of young boys to get parents to buy its products (Kline, Dyer-Witheford, & de Peuter, 2003). Nintendo's success brought on competitors also seeking the new demographic of young boys. Its first major competitor came in the form of Sega and the Genesis console in 1989.

Aiming for older teenagers and young men, and incorporating more violence and bloody graphics into their games, Sega soon surpassed Nintendo and consequently took games out of the world of children and into the realm of young adults. Later, when Sony entered the market, it marketed the PlayStation to males age 12 to 24 (Kline, Dyer-Witheford, & de Peuter, 2003). This choice allowed Sony to sidestep the oversaturated younger market while taking advantage of the disposable income of adult males. When Microsoft created the Xbox, hoping to bring the expertise of personal computer (PC) gaming to the console world, it carved out its market share in college-aged and adult men, skewing the demographic even further (Kline, Dyer-Witheford, & de Peuter, 2003).

Facing competition from Sony and Microsoft, Nintendo adopted a "Blue Ocean Strategy" with the release of the Wii in 2006, creating a new market for its console by targeting it to women (Brookey, 2010). Nintendo sidestepped the competition by going after an untapped demographic, and it succeeded as the Wii console would become the fifth best-selling console in the history of the industry (VGChartz, 2014). Males are still regarded as the primary market demographic for video games, but the expansion of the causal and mobile gaming market has made more women consumers of video games. In fact, according to the Entertainment Software Association (2014), 48% of gamers are now female. Although the video game industry is actively opening up video gaming to women, this inclusivity threatens the exclusivity of a video game culture to which many men and boys are heavily invested and identified.

Theory

Henry Jenkins (1998) tied the masculine identity of video game culture to 19th century boy culture, arguing that the digital world replicates the characteristics of boys' outdoor games, with an emphasis on competition, aggression, and a rejection of the feminine (Jenkins, 1998). These characteristics are not only found in video game culture, but are also present in the GamerGate discourse. For example, competition yields hierarchy in gaming culture, through high scores, achievements, and demonstrated game knowledge (Jenkins, 1998). In GamerGate, hierarchy functions as a tool of exclusivity and credibility, and those that challenge GamerGate are often accused of not being a "real gamer" (Bristol, 2014). Another characteristic of boy culture is aggression, which manifests itself in the violent threats sent to those who criticize GamerGate. Finally, the rejection of femininity can be seen in the sexual threats directed at women who work in the video game industry, and those women who challenge GamerGate and the masculine culture of video games.

Understanding how boy culture works requires an understanding of what it means to belong to the identity of gamer. In the book *Understanding Video Games*, gaming communities are described as being exclusive and requiring players to prove their worth (Egenfeldt-Nielsen, Smith, & Tosca, 2008). The exclusivity of the video game community, and the proving of worth through competitive gameplay, is enforced and perpetuated through gamer identity, and GamerGate has certainly drawn on a sense that the true gamer identity is decidedly male. If traditional boy culture can be witnessed in a "boys only" tree fort, then GamerGate's home base lies on the Internet. Hierarchy, aggression, and rejection of femininity can be found in some of the GamerGate discourse through the practice of "gendertrolling," which Karla Mantilla (2013) describes as ensuring "that women and girls are either kept out of, or play subservient roles in, male-dominated arenas" (2013, p. 568). The threats against women found in the GamerGate discourse can be seen as a type of gendertrolling, intent on keeping women out of the video game culture and industry.

These elements of the GamerGate discourse function as what Michal Foucault would describe as "discursive formation," a series of statements that define and enforce power relations. In *The Archaeology of Knowledge*, Foucault (1972) argued that a discursive formation is a system of dispersion, and "not organized as a progressively deductive structure" (p. 37). A discursive formation can be found "whenever, between objects, types of statement, concepts, or thematic choices, one can define a regularity" (Foucault, 1972, p. 38). In the GamerGate discourse, one "regularity" that is defined is power that men have to exclude women, and to enforce that exclusion through sexual threats.

As GamerGate continuously emerges online, analyzing it as a diffuse text presents a challenge. Yet, as we mentioned earlier, our intent is not to determine the ultimate purpose of GamerGate. Rather we will look at specific examples in order to illustrate how elements of GamerGate discourse reflect how video game culture reflects boy culture. Places such as YouTube,

Twitter, and blogs allow for individuals in GamerGate to create their own content. However, there are other places, such as the Reddit forum KotakuInAction, that serve as hubs for GamerGaters to organize and disseminate information. Analyzing these texts not as separate entities, but as part of a discursive formation, will allow for a cohesive look at how GamerGate reflects boy culture.

Criticism

As stated earlier, Eron Gjoni created a blog on August 16, 2014, five days after the release of Quinn's *Depression Quest*. After meeting each other online and then in person in November 2013, Gjoni and Quinn began a romantic relationship until their breakup in July 2014. Gjoni's (2014) purpose in creating the blog about his relationship with Quinn is "to warn you that she is overwhelmingly likely to do all of those things she makes active efforts to convince you she would never be capable of doing" (para. 1). While the first post details the high points of their relationship, Gjoni also lays out Quinn's supposed values that he later claims she broke: "What happened to the paragon of virtue I fell in love and set out to help fix the world with?" (para. 23). At the end of the posts, Gjoni (2014) accuses Quinn of being able to "lie in literally the same breath she is expressing remorse about having lied" and her propensity to ostracize him because "making it up to me isn't worth the risk that I might go public with any additional admissions if we have to talk things out online" (para. 196).

Gjoni (2014) claims that he does not wish for Quinn to be harassed, but his posts were created to call her credibility into doubt. He writes at the beginning of the first post, "I do not stand by the current abuse and harassment of Zoe Quinn or friends. Stop doing that. It is not in anyone's best interest" (Gjoni, 2014, para. 4). However, he uses sexually charged references throughout the blog, such as the metaphorical "cum collage" (Gjoni, 2014, para. 36). Gjoni (2014) also makes a "Burger and Fries" joke comparing the restaurant Five Guys Burgers and Fries to the "five guys" Quinn supposedly slept with. When a commenter on the blog questioned his reasoning for creating *thezoepost*, Gjoni (2014) replied, "You may not agree with my approach, and that's fine, but I had no other way to warn the people who would unwittingly come to trust her, as I did. Because she isn't just a liar, she's the kind of liar who uses people, while claiming to be hyper ethical." Here Gjoni claims a right and duty to warn other people about Quinn because she is not as perfect as her public image. Gjoni wishes to protect others from her, but his blog became the precipitous discursive event that would chain out in a variety of sexual threats.

Even though Gjoni (2014) acknowledges that Quinn is "a solid narrative designer" (para. 93), his blog becomes problematic when Quinn's detractors find it and use to discredit Quinn in the video game community. For example, critics latched on to Gjoni's allegation that Quinn had sexual relations with Kotaku game journalist Nathan Grayson. Gjoni's blog perpetuated the idea that Quinn's sexual relationship with Grayson yielded a positive review of *Depression Quest*, in spite of the fact that Grayson never wrote any reviews for *Depression Quest*.

Gjoni's blog also inspired a multitude of YouTube videos and forum threads reacting to his allegations. InternetAristocrat's (2014) YouTube video claimed that it did not matter that Quinn was a cheater, but that she had used her sexuality to gain advantages in the video game community. It should be noted that although he said his problem with her is not her sex life but her professional ethics, the title of his video includes the "Five Guys Burgers and Fries" joke made by Gjoni to cast aspersions on Quinn's supposed affairs (InternetAristocrat, 2014). InternetAristocrat (2014) also said that Quinn censored her detractors by removing an earlier YouTube video that discussed Gjoni's claims. Prior to InternetAristocrat's video, a user named MundaneMatt posted a YouTube video discussing *thezoepost*. Based off the information in *thezoepost*, MundaneMatt (2014) asked in his video, "How much of Zoe's coverage for *Depression Quest* lately has been from actual merits—you know, she earned it—or people she was fucking to get it? And I know that's kind of a broad assumption." Although he recognized that the information might be false, that suspicion did not stop MundaneMatt from comparing Quinn's ethics with her supposed sexual promiscuity. MundaneMatt (2014) ironically asserts that there needs to be a discussion about video game journalism without dissenters being called sexist or misogynist. While InternetAristocrat and MundaneMatt are criticizing the incestuous nature of the indie video game community, they both offer as evidence Quinn's alleged infidelity.

Soon after posting his video, MundaneMatt received a Digital Millennium Copyright Act (DMCA) takedown notice from Quinn for showing footage from *Depression Quest*. InternetAristocrat (2014) used the incident as evidence that Quinn is obsessed with protecting her career. He further went on to say that he and other detractors were being censored for being critical of her (InternetAristocrat, 2014). In addition to MundaneMatt's video being taken down, numerous forum threads about *thezoepost* and the YouTube videos were deleted. For example, threads and comments on Reddit relating to *thezoepost* were systematically deleted (el_chupacupcake, 2014). A vocal minority began to see this deletion as proof of collusion between Quinn, journalists, and moderators on Reddit (el_chupacupcake, 2014). InternetAristocrat's videos and the alleged censorship issue caught the attention of actor Adam Baldwin. On August 27, he tweeted two links to InternetAristocrat's videos about Quinn and used the Twitter hashtag GamerGate (Baldwin, 2014).

Reddit moderator el_chupacupcake (2014) explained that the deletion was happening because Quinn had her personal information leaked ("doxxed") by Reddit users. The moderator wrote, "Show your anger at the state of the video game industry, the trappings of publicity, and the lax state of games in general. But please, show it without making someone else fear for their life" (el_chupacupcake, 2014). However, this plea did little to quell users upset with the widespread deletions. To some users, the takedown of MundaneMatt's video, the deletion of Reddit threads, and the lack of mainstream coverage of *thezoepost* seemed to be further proof of a breach in ethics (el_chupacupcake, 2014).

After her personal information had been leaked, and accusations spread across the Internet, Quinn created a Tumblr post on August 19 addressing the controversy. She wrote, "The idea that I am required to debunk a manifesto of my sexual past written by an openly malicious ex-boyfriend in order to continue participating in this industry is horrifying, and I won't do it" (Quinn, 2014, para. 3). She then listed the harassment she has endured which included "(t)he proliferation of nude pictures of me, death threats, vandalization . . . sending my home address around, rape threats, memes about me being a whore, pressures to kill myself, slurs of every variety, *fucking debates over what my genitals smell like*" [sic] (Quinn, 2014, para. 4). Her final argument about the controversy is that it has little to do with ethics in gaming journalism and all about her gender. Quinn (2014) writes, "(i)f you are a woman, you are expected to constantly 'prove' yourself" and "I see major support thrown the way of my male colleagues when they are accused of any sort of wrongdoing" (para. 8). She ends that thought by saying, "Neither of these attitudes is correct, and they are patently unfair and reductive. Nobody exists in a vacuum, and anyone can change and grow into a better person" (Quinn, 2014, para. 8). Regardless of her call for humane treatment of others, Quinn would continue to be harassed over the coming months.

Boy culture relates to GamerGate to the degree that some participants in the discourse were using Quinn's gender and sexuality as a means to discredit her work. The belief that Quinn slept with Grayson and others to get favorable coverage for *Depression Quest* also implies that the game on its own does not merit success. It should also be noted that though Quinn does not divulge information about her relationship with Gjoni, his version of events are often taken as true. That is not to say that Quinn should be automatically seen as more credulous than Gjoni, but attacks against Quinn are based off of a he said/she said situation where she is held up as the alleged liar. When analyzing the animosity toward Quinn, boy culture comes to the forefront once again. Her detractors enforce a strict hierarchy that places Quinn's credibility beneath her former boyfriend, and her presence and status in the gaming community is subsequently questioned because she has allegedly used her sexuality to get ahead. The aggression comes forth through the threats she receives, but also through the threats to her friends and family. Finally, the entire controversy revolves around rejecting the feminine. One Tumblr user wrote that Quinn was setting back other women due to her infidelity, and perpetuating the idea that women can only advance in the gaming industry by relying on their sexuality (kc-vidya-rants, 2014). Yet the fact that this charge is being leveled at all speaks more to the resistance to women in video game culture, than it does about Quinn's supposed sexual impropriety.

The attacks against women in the GamerGate discourse were not exclusive to Quinn. Brianna Wu, after re-tweeting fan-created memes based on her GamerGate jokes, found herself subjected to violent rape and death threats (Stuart, 2014). On October 10, 2014, Wu and her husband left their home after Wu's personal information was released online and she began to receive death threats (Stuart, 2014). One series of tweets from an anonymous account read: "Guess what bitch? I now know where you live.

You and Frank live at [redacted]. I've got a K-Bar and I'm coming to your house so I can shove it up your ugly feminist cunt. I'm going to rape your filthy ass until you bleed, then choke you to death with your husband's tiny Asian penis" (Wu, 2014a). The anonymous user did not make any mention of GamerGate, but Wu ascribed the threats to the hashtag. Many Gamer-Gaters dismissed the tweets as a lone person who did not represent the movement, or argued that Wu made up the threats for publicity. Some of the tweets responding to Wu included, "That's one person, not the entirety of #GamerGate" and "You realize I could fake that in a minute? Let alone the fact there is nothing pointing at #GamerGate, stop defamating us [sic]" (Wu, 2014a).

After this incident, however, Wu continued to be targeted by anonymous users, some of whom explicitly aligned themselves with GamerGate. For example, the Operation False Flag II campaign encouraged users to create fake accounts to criticize Wu's game, *Revolution 60* (Wu, 2014b). The purpose of the campaign was to use feminist arguments against Wu's game for its sexualized portrayals of women (Wu, 2014b). Operation False Flag II claimed that Wu was falsifying the attacks to gain publicity, so the best way to take her down was not to harass her, but rather spread false information about her game (Wu, 2014b). However, GamerGate related harassment did not end there, and one particular self-proclaimed GamerGater, Jace Connors, sent Wu a variety of harassing messages and videos. Connors posted a video on January 30, 2015, claiming that he had crashed his mother's car on his way to Wu's house to confront her for supposed corruption (Park-ourDude91, 2015). In a strange twist, Connors revealed himself in February 2015 to not be a GamerGater obsessed with Wu, but instead comedian Jan Rankowski, who intended to satirize the movement (Bernstein, 2015). Unfortunately, Rankowski's attempt at humor contributed to Wu's company pulling out of a major gaming convention for fear of being attacked (Merlan, 2015c). For Wu, the GamerGate discourse has had a material reality, and has negatively impacted her both personally and professionally.

In another instance, Leigh Alexander published an article on Gamasutra in which she described games culture as a "petri dish of people who know so little about how human social interaction and professional life works that they can concoct online 'wars' about social justice or 'game journalism ethics'" (Alexander, 2014, para. 3). Alexander called on the video game community to take responsibility for the recent harassment by not pandering exclusively to "young white dudes with disposable income who like to Get Stuff" (2014, para. 11). Alexander concluded that companies and the overall community do not, and should not, listen to a vocal minority of gamers who choose to harass women. In short order, Alexander was subjected to some of the same online harassment directed toward Quinn and Wu. A disgruntled user on Twitter wrote of Alexander, "I actually live within a mile of this bitch. So tempted to pay her a visit and jam a screwdriver in her eyesocket [sic]" (Cross, 2014). Other online users actually threatened Alexander with violence as revenge for her claims that gamers are violent. Alexander's article became evidence to GamerGaters that video game journalism was indeed corrupt, and that they needed to rise up to defend the integrity of the video game community. This call to action, however, was martialled against a woman.

Defending the Tree Fort

The precipitating events of GamerGate involved anonymous online users harassing women in the video game community for perceived slights. As these users attempted to defend video games as a naturally male-dominated space, they defaulted to characteristics of boy culture to attack their targets. In terms of hierarchy, Quinn supposedly used her sexuality to get ahead and thus undermined the video game community. The threats against Quinn are aggressive in their language, and the criticism uses obscene language and disparages her for the alleged infidelity. Finally, the rejection of femininity occurs when the users criticize Quinn for her sexuality, but also harass her for daring to speak out about misogyny in the video game industry.

GamerGate's reaction to Wu and Alexander also possesses those three traits of boy culture. Both received explicit death and rape threats, demonstrating a fierce defense of the male-dominated game space. Even when GamerGate condemns such violence, they only do so to defend their own movement. Simply speaking out against GamerGate, and in essence boy culture, resulted in Wu's harassment. In all three of these cases, these women are not accepted as a part of the gamer identity. But as Alexander's (2014) Gamasutra article points out, the masculine gamer identity no longer reflects reality—video games are now for everyone. Although GamerGate claims to challenge journalist practices, elements of the discourse reflect a hostile reaction to the changing gender dynamics of video game culture. Yet, just as the construction of boy culture was a product of the industry, so too is the expansion of the video game market to include women. Although GamerGate might bring about change in video game journalism, the efforts to expand the video game market are motivated by economic forces that have often proved to be more formidable.

DISCUSSION QUESTIONS

1. How is gender a factor in the way the video game culture is divided? Are some genres of games considered more feminine than others?

2. When the term "hardcore gamer" is used, what assumptions are made about this identity?

3. Is there a way women can enter video gaming culture that would not be perceived as a threat to that culture? What would be the conditions of that entry?

4. Does GamerGate have a point about corruption in video game journalism, and if so, why was Quinn chosen to signify this corruption?

5. Accepting that GamerGate might have a valid purpose in challenging the practices of video game journalists, how does the attack on the women mentioned in this chapter hinder their cause? How do these attacks affect the greater video game community?

References

Alexander, L. (2014, August 28). 'Gamers' don't have to be your audience. 'Gamers' are over. Gamasutra. Retrieved from http://www.gamasutra.com/view/news/224400/Gamers_dont_have_to_be_your_audience_Gamers_are_over.php.

Baldwin, A. (2014, August 27). #GamerGate [Tweet]. Retrieved from https://twitter.com/AdamBaldwin/status/504801169638567936.

Bristol, D. (2014). Remove Anita Sarkeesian from Mirror's Edge 2 game development. Retrieved from https://www.change.org/p/ea-games-remove-anita-sarkeesian-from-mirror-s-edge-2-game-development.

Brookey, R. A. (2010). *Hollywood gamers: Digital convergence in the film and video game industries.* Bloomington, IN: Indiana University Press.

Cross, K. (2014, October 6). We must dissent: Intel bows to GamerGate campaign to silence feminist video game critics. Feministing. Retrieved from http://feministing.com/2014/10/06/we-must-dissent-intel-bows-to-gamergate-campaign-to-silence-feminist-video-game-critics/.

Egenfeldt-Nielsen, S., Smith, J. H., & Tosca, S. P. (2008). *Understanding video games.* New York, NY: Routledge.

el_chupacupcake. (2014). On Zoe Quinn, censorship, doxxing, and general discourse. Reddit. Retrieved from: http://www.reddit.com/r/gaming/comments/2dzrlv/on_zoe_quinn_censorship_doxxing_and_general/.

Entertainment Software Association. (2014). Essential facts about the computer and video games industry. Retrieved from http://www.theesa.com/wpcontent/uploads/2014/10/ESA_EF_2014.pdf.

Foucault, M. (1972). *The Archaeology of Knowledge.* New York: Pantheon Books.

Gjoni, E. (2014, August 16). Thezoepost [Blog]. Retrieved from http://thezoepost.wordpress.com/.

InternetAristocrat. (2014, August 18). Quinnspiracy Theory: Five Guys Saga [Video file]. Retrieved from http://www.youtube.com/watch?v=C5-51PfwI3M.

Jenkins, H. (1998). "Complete freedom of movement": Video games as gendered play. In J. Cassell & H. Jenkins (Eds.), *From Barbie to Mortal Kombat: Gender and computer Games* (118–135). Cambridge, MA: The MIT Press.

kc-vidya-rants. (2014, August 19). Zoe Quinn's Kotaku staff cheating scandal (and how she sets back women in gaming). KC Vidya Rants. Retrieved from https://archive.today/g3dTS.

Kent, S. L. (2001). *The ultimate history of video games.* New York, NY: Three Rivers Press.

Kline, S., Dyer-Witheford, N., & de Peuter, G. (2003). *Digital play: The interaction of technology, culture, and marketing.* Quebec City, Canada: McGill-Queen's University Press.

Mantilla, K. (2013). Gendertrolling: Misogyny adapts to new media. *Feminist Studies, 39*(2). 563–570.

Merlan, A. (2015c, February 24). Man who terrorized Brianna Wu for months says he was just kiddin around. Jezebel. Retrieved from http://jezebel.com/man-who-terrorized-brianna-wu-for-months-says-he-was-ju-1687689719.

MundaneMatt. (2014, August 18). Hell hath no fury like a lover's scorn [Video file]. Retrieved from https://www.youtube.com/watch?v=Equc1QnQ9rw.

ParkourDude91. (2015, January 30). Brianna Wu tried to assassinate me via street racing [Video file]. Retrieved from https://www.youtube.com/watch?v=jYPC-YMdJFI.

Quinn, Z. (2014, August 19). Once again, I will not negotiate with terrorists. Dispatches from the Quinnspiracy. Retrieved from http://ohdeargodbees.tumblr.com/post/95188657119/once-again-i-will-not-negotiate-with-terrorists.

Stuart, K. (2014, October 17). Brianna Wu and the human cost of Gamergate: 'Every woman I know in the industry is scared'. *The Guardian.* Retrieved from http://www.theguardian.com/technology/2014/oct/17/brianna-wu-gamergate-human-cost.

VGChartz. (2014). Game platforms. Retrieved from http://www.vgchartz.com/platforms/.

Wu, B. (2014a, October 10). [Tweet]. Retrieved from https://twitter.com/spacekatgal/status/520739878993420290.

Wu, B. (2014b, October 17). [Tweet]. Retrieved from https://twitter.com/Spacekatgal/status/523113644205555712/photo/1.

CHAPTER 29

Ephemeral Sex and Money: The Political Economy of Sexting

Danielle Stern

KEY TERMS

Sexting   Political economy
Snapchat   Ephemerality

ABSTRACT

This chapter explores the political economy of sexting practices, drawing on online documents such as terms of service, privacy policies, and public debates about the mobile app Snapchat as a case study. Snapchat promises disappearance and erasure of snaps. However, ephemeral intimate communication exchanges co-exist on the app with branded content, which I argue contributes to an ephemeral flow economy where sexting practices operate within a larger corporate production of audiences, thereby normalizing sexting as an everyday activity.

I begin this chapter with a confession: I struggled to start writing it, as I do not actively use the mobile apps I have set out to critique. Ethics led me to not want to engage with the users of the apps. I would feel like a fraud, "creeping" on people simply so I can write a chapter. Past research I have conducted started from my own pleasures and frustrations with media representations as they related to gender, race, and class in reality television; female-centered dramatic and comedic television programming; and Twitter activism, among others. Those were spaces I did use—interacting with participants did not seem so shady. However, when I saw a call for a chapter on sex and communication in this edited volume, I knew I wanted to contribute something about sexting. I had previously published an academic fictional case study about young adult sexting (Stern, 2012) and felt the need to return to the literature. Not surprisingly, academic research on sexting has increased tremendously in the past five years, just as the practice itself has gained popularity.

A search for the subject term "sexting" in peer-reviewed publications in the academic database WorldCat generated 316 results that demonstrate the interdisciplinary importance of the subject. The majority of sexting scholarship can be found in clinical, educational, and legal disciplines. Issues of privacy and bullying were the most common topics. When the search was further limited to the subject terms of "sexting" and "communication,"[1] 82 results were returned. However, many of these articles turned up the same as the previous search. In fact, according to the WorldCat database, only 13 essays about or including a section on sexting exist in the communication, media, or cultural studies titles, highlighting the breadth of area still available for critique or empirical studies. The majority of the research examined the moral panic[2] issues related to gender in adolescent sexting practices (Albury & Crawford, 2012; Chalfen, 2010; Curnutt, 2012; Draper, 2011; Lippman & Campbell, 2014; Ringrose, Harvey, Gill, & Livingstone, 2013), while one (Juntunen & Valiverronen, 2010) investigated political journalism coverage of sexting scandals, and two others (Manning, 2013; Wysocki & Childers, 2011) examined adult sexting practices. Jarc's (2014) research took a media ecology approach regarding "mobiliteracy" (p. 25), but only briefly reviewed intimacy issues and social norms in sexting.

---

1. I limited the search to the communication discipline due to the focus of this volume.
2. Moral panic is a concern about disruptions to the social order elevated through media reporting (Cohen, 2002) and intense user engagement in online spaces (Flores-Yeffal, Vidales, & Plemons, 2015). Recent examples include the perceived threat of Mexican immigrants contributing to crime in the United States or stereotyping Muslims as violent terrorists.

Manning (2013) investigated how adults define and experience sexting. Through interview and survey research with adults aged 18 to 54 years, he stressed the willingness of participants in the interactive exchange of intimate texts. Manning's sample included mostly White adults, though they were representative of the national population regarding gender and sexuality (55% female, 45% male, 13% identifying as lesbian, gay, or bisexual). Wysocki & Childers (2011) focused on the intersection of sexting and infidelity in committed adult relationships, finding that women were more likely than men to send intimate sexts, but that men and women were equally likely to seek partners outside of marriage online. Half of their survey respondents reported actively working to eliminate their cyber trail of sexts and other online intimate practices of infidelity. Ringrose, Harvey, Gill, & Livingstone (2013) took a feminist approach of pleasure and power in sexuality when they interviewed teen girls in the UK about their exchange of images on Facebook and Blackberry devices. Their study revealed a contradiction in a media culture that sexualizes young women, but then condemns them and in some cases criminalizes them for engaging in consensual sexual texting practices.

Albury & Crawford (2012) interviewed young people in Australia about ethics and consent in sexting practices. Similarly, Hasinoff & Shepherd (2014) completed surveys and group interviews with 18- to 24-year-olds regarding privacy expectations when sexting, and Bond (2010) completed unstructured group interviews with 30 young people in the UK about their relationships with mobile phones and practices, of which sexting was a major topic of conversation. Although these interpretive studies provide valuable data and understandings of sexting practices, there exists a need to examine implications surrounding the political, social, and economic contexts in which sexting has emerged as a popular cultural practice.

In this chapter, then, I explore political economy. Mosco (1996) defines the political economy of communication as: "the study of the social relations, particularly the power relations, that mutually constitute the production, distribution, and consumption of resources" (p. 25). In other words, the economic, legal, and cultural norms and practices that produce sexting are important to examine to begin to understand the lived experience of sexting communication. Questions might include the following: what firms produce software and hardware used for sexting, and how do their corporate policies and relationships with other powerful institutions impact our understanding of intimate sexual communication? The studies mentioned earlier in this chapter highlight how people actually engage in sexting, but scholars also must examine the relationship between these user-friendly platforms that encourage flirtatious and intimate communication and their actual production. For example, financially powerful, well-connected venture capitalists bankroll the physical production and marketing of mobile applications. Griffin (2015) articulated that venture capitalists have overwhelmingly provided the funds for social media startups in the hopes of "monetarizing" (p. 48) the social media sites via advertising. For distribution, one must examine the revenue models for these free mobile apps reliant on inescapable ads. Additionally, the legal policies and practices that define the parameters of using the applications provide important context for analysis of sexting production and consumption. Finally, although it is not explored in this chapter, information on the lived experience of sexting is a primary component of understanding consumption.

For the other goals of this political economic approach, and as a case study of sorts for this chapter, I turn to online documents such as terms of service, privacy policies, and public debates about the mobile app Snapchat (Snapchat, Inc., 2015), the most successful of the ephemeral mobile apps (Alluri, 2015) that have been used for sexting practices. Ephemerality refers to the promise of disappearance and erasure, which, as is further discussed later in this chapter, is complicated in Snapchat. I argue that Snapchat contributes to an ephemeral flow economy where sexting practices operate within a larger corporate production of audiences, thereby normalizing sexting as a mundane activity. Simply put, sexting has become an everyday practice and must be examined within the context of other culturally accepted, mediated experiences impacted by economics, for example television, which I expand on later. This essay responds to Curnutt's (2012) call to "keep in mind how a seemingly aberrant activity like sexting works in harmony with the institutional norms and cultural desires that are shaping the evolving relationship between old and new media" (p. 366).

Sexting, Snapchat, and the Ephemeral Economy

According to Manning (2013), "Sexting is the willing interactive exchange of sexual-oriented messages using a digital mobile communications device"

(p. 2510). Admittedly, I've had fleeting moments of exchanging consensual intimate texts with my spouse and past partners. However, the smartphone applications that promise deletion of online notes passed with the subtext of anonymous abilities to text sexually explicit language, images, and video are not useful to me unless I were to engage in an affair outside my marriage. As a 30-something academic in a committed relationship with three dogs, student loans, and a 60-hour-work week, I am not the target demographic of apps such as Snapchat, YikYak, or Facebook's Poke. Nonetheless, I am interested in the political, economic, and cultural environments that produce and sustain the desire for ephemerality in the polymediated (Calka, 2015) age. Polymediation examines the convergence and fragmentation in modern media forms and practices. "Poly" signifies the many forms media take, as well as our various interactions with them (Tyma, Herrmann, & Herbig, 2015, p. xx). The form at hand is that of ephemerality to protect our intimate technologically mobile activity.

According to Lenhart and Duggan (2014), 9% of adult cell phone owners have sent sext messages of themselves to others, while 20% of cell owners reported having received a sext from someone else they knew. Only 3% of cell owners reported forwarding a sext to a third party. Finally, according to the self-report study, married and partnered adults are just as likely as those who are not in a relationship to have sent sexts, while single adults are more likely to report receiving and forwarding sexts (p. 4). With the exception of sext forwarding, which held steady, the reporting of sexting uses across all age groups increased from Lenhart's 2012 study. The figures on forwarding of intimate texts is important in a communication context since these surveys indicate practices and perceptions of privacy, which this chapter addresses more closely soon.

Since it launched in the iTunes App Store in September 2011, Snapchat has garnered nearly 200 million monthly active users (Thompson, 2015). The application allows users to share photos and videos with select followers that automatically delete after a user-selected timeline, with the maximum length of only 10 seconds. Snapchat was listed as the No. 7 top free application in the iTunes App Store as of May 14, 2015. According to a researcher for the Pew Internet Project (Duggan, 2013), 9% of cell phone owners, and 12% of smartphone specific owners, use Snapchat. The same study demonstrated that of mobile phone owners aged 18 to 29, 26% use the app. The ephemeral architecture of the disappearing snaps is certainly an appeal, but according to

Snapchat's terms of use, the app does not track demographics of snaps, not even gender or age (Thompson, 2015). This anonymity to advertisers might certainly appeal to users saturated by surveillance in other digital environments.

Snapchat's popularity has led to a number of other online applications with built-in ephemerality, such as Armor Text (market enterprise), CoverMe (encrypted adult communication), Pluto Mail (email), and Wickr (encrypted messaging), among many other self-destructing messaging platforms, including the walled garden of Facebook, which premiered Poke in late 2012 after purchasing WhatsApp for $19 billion—upon a failed $3 billion acquisition of Snapchat (Thompson, 2015). Other apps used for location-based hook-ups, such as Tinder, have modified their design to include ephemerality to capitalize on the success of the feature (Sawers, 2014).

The creators of Snapchat assure that the application is not designed for sexting. However, co-founder Evan Spiegel shared that the app was partially inspired by the Anthony Weiner scandal and a "desire to create an app with expiring data" (Gallagher, 2012, para. 8). Snapchat users typically send snaps during the day (Taylor, n.d.), especially during school hours, which some supporters say indicates its appeal to youth who want to share funny, sometimes tasteless—but harmless—messages away from the watchful eyes of parents (Taylor, n.d.). Although the actual practice of sexting on Snapchat may be small, it is still important to examine the subtext and design of an app whose possible unintended consequences of ephemeral sexual intimacy provided a foundation for other apps and discourse related to ephemeral sexting practices.

In October 2014, following the quick rise of third-party applications intended to allow Snapchat users access to save photos outside the native app, insecurities in one or more of these apps led to more than 200,000 photos being leaked (Lunden, 2014). The hack did not limit Snapchat's popularity (Perez, 2015). An earlier security breach impacted 4.6 million user accounts, whose usernames and telephone numbers were published online (Shu, 2013), an event that also left Snapchat as popular as ever. In fact, the notoriety appears to have actually helped the tech company inside elite financial circles. A writer for online technology publisher Quartz summarized how the 2014 Sony Pictures' email hack revealed that Michael Lynton, the CEO of Sony Entertainment and Sony Pictures, sits on the Snapchat board (Frommer, 2015).

The emails exchanged between Lynton and Dick Costello, the CEO of Twitter, reveal Lynton's encouragement of Twitter to purchase Snapchat even before the public suggestion that Facebook might buy the company. Lynton also emailed to secure financing deals and advising from power players within tech and venture capitalist circles. One email shared the following about the app and its co-founder Spiegel:

> I really think he is one of the best product thinkers out there right now. Thoughtful, he understands what the shifts in the landscape actually mean for people, clearheaded about what the implications are for product and design. Great. The theme of communicating through media instead of around media is crystal clear and articulated simply. Really impressive (Frommer, 2015, para. 7).

Spiegel's discussion of *communicating through media* reinforces a polymediated view of the ephemeral sexting economy. This revelation of the ties to the Hollywood and Silicon Valley elite came at a time when Snapchat's revenue model had become increasingly compared to older forms of broadcast television. Not only does Snapchat deal in ephemeral photos and short videos produced by users, but also native advertising that users cannot skip (Ingram, 2015). In a digital landscape that allows television viewers to bypass the suffocating model of commercial breaks with the click of a button, Snapchat offers the promise of a captive audience to the tune of 200 million, including the lucrative 18- to 34-year-old market (Thompson, 2015).

Moreover, media partners such as CNN, Comedy Central, Food Network, People, ESPN, and more produce content on their own branded channels, replete with their own ads. For example, when I click on Cosmopolitan's channel, I can share an image that will lead my friends to their content. Comedy Central and Food Network provided teasers to their cable channel content. Before viewing images of celebrities in the "Who Wore it Best?" item from *People*, I had to watch a sponsored ad for the feature film *Pitch Perfect 2*. ESPN provided highlights and scores from major league sports, SportsCenter's #SCNotTop10, featuring a MLB outfielder's poor fielding, as well as a flashback to Michael Jordan's May 1985 Rookie of the Year award. Warner Music shared music videos of its featured artists, as well as childhood clips from pop UK superstar Ed Sheeran. The featured content changes daily for many of these media partners, further contributing to the ephemeral design of the app.[3]

---

3. The ephemeral nature of the content has proved a challenge for academic citations. Additionally, Snapchat's Terms of Use prohibit me from capturing and sharing archival images for reference. All of the snaps described here were accessed on May 17, 2015.

So what does all of this have to do with sexting? Ephemeral branded content of major corporations streams on the same platform to which users share their personal images and video. Whether users are sharing funny content or sexual exchanges, this user-generated economy co-mingles with slickly produced branded video and advertising. Snapchat introduced ephemeral ads in users' Recent Updates feature in October 2014 (Advertising on Snapchat, 2014). These ads, like the user-generated text and image content, disappear after they are viewed, allowing the user to move on to the content. As such, we are witnessing a domestication of ephemeral sexting within a broader ecology of the ephemeral media economy. Just as mobile television technology promised "privatized mobility" (Spigel, 2004, p. 121) in the 1960s, ephemeral smartphone technology invites us to share our private textual and visual selves alongside corporate content —in both private and public spaces. At the same time that entertainment and news outlets vilify celebrities and politicians for the public outing of their private sexual communications (Juntunen & Valiverronen, 2010), the design and revenue models of ephemeral technologies specifically encourage the act of sharing private intimate exchanges on a platform that risks making those messages public, or at least shared with someone else beyond the intended receiver. Ephemeral sexting makes privacy risk sexy. Moreover, it *monetizes* this risk. In sum, Snapchat fuels a cultural desire of risk in our intimate communication and has found a way to profit from it.

These videos also operate within a newer mobile economic system, Snapcash, introduced in November 2014. According to Snapchat (Snapcash, n.d.), the feature was created in partnership with Square (the mobile payment application created by Jack Dorsey, founder of Twitter and Vine) for users to exchange money within chat. The support blog for Snapchat explains that Snapcash is intended to help friends easily split bills at restaurants or "paying someone back for concert tickets" (What can Snapcash be used for?, para. 1 n.d.). Snapchat's terms of use prohibit Snapcash compensation for the selling or buying of snaps, access to usernames or accounts, adding friends, and "drugs, guns, or other unlawful things" (What can Snapcash be used for?, para. 2). A friendly reminder encourages users that "Snapcash is solely a peer-to-peer payment system; it may not be used for any commercial purpose" (What can Snapcash be used for? para. 3) and threatens action for any abuse to its terms, which is likely a response to sex workers' use of Snapchat to share video of erotic dancing and other sexual exchanges to drive traffic to their individual websites or offline performance spaces (Dickson, 2014; Flox, 2015; Yaverbaum, 2015). The architecture of Snapchat, which introduced the Stories feature in late 2013 to "enable users to share compilations of media publicly" (Flox, 2015, para. 15), was certain to encourage unintended uses of the app, which at that point had yet to be corporatized. In addition, this design speaks to the fragmented, yet converged nature of ephemeral sexual practices within a polymediated (Calka, 2015) practice, whether intimate sexting among consensual Snapchatters, or sex work from one to many: fragmented in the sense of a detached, hopefully deleted, perhaps anonymous communication via the app, yet converged in the sense of sharing intimate moments on a platform that reaches millions of users. The ephemeral design encourages private or public sharing in a structured, mobile environment that promises anonymity, but with the hopes of offline exchanges.

Williams' (1975) arguments about television flow are helpful to revisit here. He argued that advertisements and programmatic content became simultaneously blurred and distinct in that ads and original programming weave seamlessly. Commercial breaks used to demarcate our time, providing an opportunity to stretch, grab a snack, or use the bathroom. This was the old broadcast television viewing model, before remote controls and time-shifting technologies such as TiVo and DVRs transformed our viewing experiences. However, television executives did not want viewers to miss the commercials, which helped lead to examples of advertising as compelling storytelling or innovative branding to encourage consumption and connection to the television characters and stories—a desire for a better lifestyle. Williams also used examples of network scheduling and audience reception to build his theory of television flow, wherein audience market research became primary to setting the network schedule. Given technology forecasters' arguments about the potential for Snapchat to capture television's waning audiences (Ingram, 2015; Thompson, 2015), the ephemeral flow economy deserves more scrutiny in communication scholarship. This process is important to consider historically. According to Spigel (2004), who argued that mobile communications are, like the earlier traditional television era, "still structured around…binaries of space and sexual difference," (p. 135) scholars should examine the "structured absences" (p. 139) of what is not publicly debated about new technologies. There certainly has been plenty of popular speculation about the possibilities of sexting and sex work (Dickson, 2014; Flox, 2015; Hamill, 2014; Yaverbaum, 2015) on Snapchat. What remains unexamined, however, are the macro structures that afford the possibility of an ephemeral sexting economy. The next section theorizes some of these intersections and provides questions for future research that are beyond the scope of this volume.

Power Relations of Sexting as Production and Consumption

Hasinoff's (2012) arguments about sexting as a form of media production are useful due to the connotations of ownership and authorship in mobile environments: "Viewing sexting as a form of media production helps make it possible to consider the creativity and ingenuity of teens who consensually produce their own sexual images. If researchers saw sexting in this way, they might investigate whether consensual sexting could facilitate personal exploration or critical reflection on gender and sexual representations in mass media" (p. 457). Her claims build from rhetorical analysis of public dialogue about teen sexting practices that often lead to moral panic about young women's sexuality. This practice has been widely scrutinized in the courts. Although it is beyond the goals of this chapter to address all of the legal concerns around sexting, Hasinoff (2012; 2015) extensively summarized and countered the legal debates about minors who shared sexy images of themselves. The acts have often resulted in prosecution of teens, requiring them to register as sex offenders (See Leary, 2007, and Smith, 2008 for more complex discussion of these debates). While Hasinoff's focus on teens is not unique, her theoretical contributions provide a new framework for viewing texting as a practice of media production as opposed to interpersonal consumption. When combined with my arguments in the previous section about ephemeral mobile applications, production becomes a commodified creative endeavor.

Snapchat, although it has a policy of prohibiting users below 13 years of age (Terms of Use, n.d.), cannot guarantee the truth claims of self-report. Snapchat also offers "Snapkidz" for the under 13 set that provides the "familiar interface for taking Snaps, captioning, drawing, and saving Snaps locally on the device, but does not support sending or receiving Snaps or adding friends and, since the experience is local to the user's device, no Snapchat account is created" (Terms of Use, para. 6). Both of these terms indicate a level of embedded institutional protection against child pornography or statutory sexual abuse claims. Upon closer scrutiny of the Terms of Use, which constitute 11 single-spaced pages of printed text, legal matters related to Snapchat's liability in any use of or content on the app that cannot be resolved "informally or in small claims court" (para. 29) are bound by an arbitration firm of Snapchat's choosing. In paragraph 33 of the Terms of Use, Snapchat includes the following, all capitalized statement: "YOU AND SNAPCHAT HEREBY WAIVE ANY CONSTITUTIONAL AND STATUTORY RIGHTS TO GO TO COURT AND HAVE A TRIAL IN FRONT OF A JUDGE OR A JURY." In the same paragraph, the agreement explains that in the event of state or federal court litigation, "YOU AND SNAPCHAT WAIVE ALL RIGHTS TO A JURY TRIAL, instead electing that the dispute be resolved by a judge." Given that these explicit litigation issues follow a long list of prohibited activities, copyright infringement issues, as well as mention of the absence of any liability by Snapchat, it is clear that Snapchat executives know the risks their members take and want to absolve themselves from any responsibility. However, Snapchat's terms of use policies are in line with other firms that seek to limit liability by placing this burden on users (Braman & Roberts, 2003).

As such, not only does the architecture commodify potential sexting practices as explained earlier in the chapter, it also positions them within a legal context. Ringrose, Harvey, Gill, and Livingstone (2013) argued that sexting practices must be examined in the contexts of discourses of gender and power that commodify girls' bodies and contribute to the widespread moral panic surrounding the protection of girls' vulnerabilities and purity "where it is possible for such images to be traded like currency" (p. 319). In public debate about Snapchat, this discourse has been mostly absent. On one hand, this could be considered a step forward in that Snapchat might appear to not be contributing to the moral panic argument; but on the other hand, this silence speaks volumes about the privileged, well-connected, mostly white, and male board of directors who act as the gatekeepers of the app (Company overview of Snapchat, Inc., 2015). I am not arguing that the executives of Snapchat are misogynists or unconcerned about protecting children. Instead, they are simply operating by the laws of corporate governance in a capitalist system, which according to Meehan (2002) has always intersected with patriarchy and gendered power imbalances.

Lippman and Campbell (2014) summarized a Pew Research Center report (Lenhart, 2009) on the mobile phone behavior of teens:

> Four findings are common among these national surveys. First, sexts are often redistributed without the permission or knowledge of the original sender. Second, sexts are commonly sent to desired or actual romantic and/or sexual partners. Third, sexting becomes more common as adolescents mature. Finally, despite the gendered media coverage, girls are actually no more or at best, only slightly more likely than boys to send these types of images of themselves (p. 372).

Although my research is not focused exclusively on teens, Lippman and Campbell's arguments about teen sexting point to the circulatory practices of sexting, specifically the lack of control of the sharing of sexts with unintended audiences, as well as misconceptions about gender. They also operate with other research on the design of sexting communication. For example, according to Jarc (2014), existing sexting research confirms that mobile communication practices can provide the perception of increased intimacy, but also collapse our inhibitions due to perceived anonymity (p. 24).

As Curnutt (2012) argued, sexting "transforms a once relatively private activity into one that is always potentially public because of the ease with which digital content can be reproduced and shared" (p. 360). Misunderstandings about anonymity and privacy in ephemeral applications such as Snapchat become even more complicated in the context of popular discourse about surveillance society. According to Draper (2012), U.S. news coverage reinforces the surveillance narrative to discourage teen sexting: "With few notable exceptions, the experts, guests and anchors tend to agree that the courts are not the place to deal with issues of adolescent sexting. Rather, they argue parents and educators are primarily responsible for deterring young people from the practice" (p. 228). In their study of college-aged sexters, Hasinoff & Shepherd (2014) confirmed that young people do indeed expect privacy when sharing intimate texts. The erosion of privacy as an expected right deserves further study in the context of the ephemeral economy.

The role of bodies in the ephemeral design of apps like Snapchat is also understudied. Ringrose et al. (2013) built upon previous research (Manago et al., 2008; Siibak, 2010; Dobson, 2011; Ringrose, 2011) to explain that "the very architecture of digital profiles enables visual, bodily 'objectification' and intensified forms of rating and comparison of both women's and men's bodies" (p. 309). As Thomas (2004) explained, the cyberbody can be monitored and regulated via law enforcement and the courts (pp. 220–221), but the ephemeral polymediated body is also surveilled by corporations. Moreover, because of the user-centered design of the app, we all have the potential to be hackers and re-share private intimate moments with the click of a camera app against the will of the content originator. Snapchat encourages and romanticizes interactivity and the temptation of archiving while simultaneously prohibiting such behavior.

Another important context of ephemeral sexting regards the user-generated nature of the free labor (Andrejevic, 2009; Cohen, 2008; Terranova, 2004) of texters who create and distribute sexual communication. Mansall and Javary (2004) explained that the new media technology economy sometimes works outside the constraints of capitalism because of the shared, communal nature of content creation and curation. For example, we produce our own content in the forms of images, tweets, photos, short videos and then share, like, retweet, or pin our favorite user-generated content. However, my preliminary research indicates that the polymediated nature of sexting practices that blur the boundaries of production and consumption, private and public, and interpersonal and corporate, actually has the potential to reinforce capitalistic constraints of older forms of mediated communication. Chayko (2008) argued that the social dynamics of portable technologies encourage more flexible sexual norms, such as the pursuit of multiple relationships at once and increased online sexual discussion. However, when these otherwise sexual communication norms operate within a capitalist exchange, the potential for disrupting norms is limited. Sexting, evidenced by Snapchat's architecture, corporate policies, and commercial content, operates as one more media content exchange. Moreover, this content has both the promise of disappearing and the potential risk for exposing our most intimate communication. In this chapter I have demonstrated the beginnings of an ephemeral flow as it relates to the interactive, corporate economy that reinscribes traditional forms of audience construction. The next step is to examine representation and lived practices of users in such an ephemeral economy.

DISCUSSION QUESTIONS

1. What does the author mean by *ephemerality*?

2. How might expectations of sexting via Snapchat differ from sexting using a different communication technology?

3. Why do you think the author chose a political economy lens to examine sexting?

4. Have you ever paid close attention to the Terms of Use or Service in the mobile applications you frequently use? If so, what did you notice or find significant?

5. How does this article frame your thinking about your communication, intimate or otherwise in mobile applications?

References

Advertising on Snapchat. (2014, Oct. 17). *Snapchat Blog*. Retrieved from http://blog.snapchat.com/post/100255857340/advertising-on-snapchat.

Albury, K., & Crawford, K., (2012). Sexting, consent and young people's ethics: Beyond *Megan's Story. Continuum: Journal of Media & Cultural Studies, 26*(3), 463–473. doi: 10.1080/10304312.2012.665840.

Alluri, B. (2015, Feb. 23). Snapchat's secret to success. *Marketplace*. Retrieved from http://www.marketplace.org/topics/tech/snapchats-secret-success.

Andrejevic, M. (2009). Exploiting YouTube: Contradictions of user-generated labor. In P. Snickars & P. Vonderau (Eds.), *The YouTube reader* (pp. 406–423).

Ang, S. (2014, Feb. 13). 11 things you didn't know about Snapchat's founders. *Mashable*. Retrieved from http://mashable.com/2014/02/13/snapchat-founder-facts/.

Bond, E. (2010). The mobile phone = bike shed? Children, sex and mobile phones. *New Media & Society, 13*(4), 587–604. doi:10.1177/1461444810377919.

Braman, S., & Roberts, S. (2003). Advantage ISP: Terms of service as media law. *New Media & Society, 5*(3), 422–448.

Chalfen, R. (2010). Sexting as adolescent social communication: A call for attention. *Journal of Children and Media, 4*(3), 350–354. doi: 10.1080/17482798.2010.486144.

Chayko, M. (2008). *Portable communities: The social dynamics of online and mobile connectedness.* Albany, NY: SUNY Press.

Curnett, H. (2012). Flashing your phone: Sexting and the remediation of teen sexuality. *Communication Quarterly, 60*(3), 353–369. doi: 10.1080/01463373.2012.688728.

Calka, M. (2015). Polymediation: The relationship between self and media. In A. Herbig, A. F. Herrmann, & A. W. Tyma (Eds.), *Beyond new media: Discourse and critique in a polymediated age* (pp. 15–30). Lanham, MD: Lexington.

Cohen, S. (2002). *Folk devils and moral panics.* London: Routledge.

Cohen, N. S. (2008). The valorization of surveillance: Towards a political economy of Facebook. *Democratic Communique, 22*(1), 5–22.

Company overview of Snapchat, Inc. (2015, May 17). *Bloomberg Business.* Retrieved from http://www.bloomberg.com/research/stocks/private/board.asp?privcapId=224055283.

Dickson, E. J. (2014, Nov. 21). Snapcash is the new currency for Snapchat porn. *Daily Dot.* Retrieved from http://www.dailydot.com/technology/snapcash-snapchat-porn/.

Dobson, A. S. (2011). Hetero-sexy representation by young women on MySpace: The politics of performing an "objectified" self. *Outskirts, 25.* Retrieved from http://www.outskirts.arts.uwa.edu.au/volumes/volume-25/amy-shields-dobson.

Draper, N. R. A. (2011). Is your teen at risk? Discourses of adolescent sexting in United States television news. *Journal of Children and Media, 6*(2), 221–236, doi: 10.1080/17482798.2011.587147.

Duggan, M. (2013). Photo and video sharing grow online. *Pew Research Center.* Retrieved from http://pewinternet.org/Reports/2013/Photos-and-videos.aspx.

Flores-Yeffal, N. Y., Vidales, G., & Plemons, A. (2015). The Latino-cyber moral panic process in the United States. In G. Dinez and J. M. Humez (Eds.), *Gender, race, and class in media: A reader* (pp. 657–667). Thousand Oaks, CA: Sage.

Flox, A. V. (2015, Feb. 5). How Snapcash killed Snapchat porn. *Mikandi Blog.* Retrieved from https://mikandi.com/blog/news/snapcash-killed-snapchat-porn/.

Frommer, D. (2015, April 17). The hacked Sony emails show how Silicon Valley dealmaking really works. *Quartz.* Retrieved from http://qz.com/385742/the-hacked-sony-emails-show-how-silicon-valley-dealmaking-really-works/.

Gallagher, B. (2012, May 12). No, Snapchat isn't about sexting, says co-founder Evan Spiegel. *TechCrunch.* Retrieved from http://techcrunch.com/2012/05/12/snapchat-not-sexting/.

Griffin, P. (2015). *Popular culture, political economy and the death of feminism.* London: Routledge.

Hamill, J. (2014, Nov. 24). New Spapchat Snapcash service inspires amateur porn stars. *The Register.* Retrieved from http://www.theregister.co.uk/2014/11/24/snapchat_snapcash_micropayment_service_inspires_sale_of_adult_pics/.

Hasinoff, A. A. (2012). Sexting as media production: Rethinking social media and sexuality. *New Media & Society, 15*(4), 449–465. doi: 10.1177/1461444812459171.

Hasinoff, A. A. (2015). *Sexting panic: Rethinking criminalization, privacy, and consent.* Urbana, IL: University of Illinois Press.

Hasinoff, A. A., & Shepherd, T. (2014). Sexting in context: privacy norms and expectations. *International Journal of Communication, 8,* 2932–2415.

Ingram, M. (2015, Feb. 24). The $19-billion question: Is Snapchat the new television? *Gigaom.* Retrieved from https://gigaom.com/2015/02/24/the-19-billion-question-is-snapchat-the-new-television/.

Jarc, J. (2014). Mobiliteracy: Applying Ong's psychodynamic characteristics to users of mobile communication technology. *Communication Research Trends, 33,* 21–26.

Juntunen, L. & Valiverronen, E. (2010). Politics of sexting: Re-negotiating the boundaries of private and public in political journalism. *Journalism Studies, 11*(6), 817–831. doi: 10.1080/14616701003643996.

Leary, M. G. (2007). Self-produced child pornography: The appropriate societal response to juvenile self-sexual exploitation. *Virginia Journal of Social Policy & Law, 15*(1), 1–50.

Lenhart, A. (2012). Teens, smartphones & texting. *Pew Research Center.* Retrieved from http://pewinternet.org/Reports/2012/Teens-and-smartphones.aspx.

Lenhart, A., & Duggan, M. (2014). Couples, the Internet, and social media: How American couples use digital technology to manage lies, logistics, and emotional intimacy within their relationships. *Pew Research Center.* Retrieved from http://pewinternet.org/Reports/2014/Couples-and-the-internet.aspx.

Lippman, J. R., & Campbell, S. W. (2014). Damned if you do, damned if you don't...if you're a girl: Relational and normative contexts of adolescent sexting in the United States. *Journal of Children and Media, 8*(4), 371–386, doi: 10.1080/17482798.2014.923009.

Lunden, I. (2014, Oct. 10). Snapchat: Our servers were not breached in the "Snappening," blame 3rd party apps. *TechCrunch.* Retrieved from http://techcrunch.com/2014/10/10/snapchat-our-servers-were-not-breached-in-the-snappening-blame-3rd-party-apps/.

Manago, A. M., Graham, M. B., Greenfield, P. M., & Salimkhan, G. (2008). Self-presentation and gender on MySpace. *Journal of Applied Developmental Psychology, 29,* 446–458. doi:10.1016/j.appdev.2008.07.001.

Manning, J. (2013). Interpretive theorizing in the seductive world of sexuality and interpersonal communication: Getting guerilla with studies of sexting and purity rings. *International Journal of Communication, 7,* 2507–2520.

Mansall, R., & Javary, M. (2004). New media and the forces of capitalism. In A. Calabrese & C. Sparks (Eds.), *Toward a political economy of culture: Capitalism and communication in the twenty-first century* (pp. 228–243). Lanham, MD: Rowman & Littlefield.

Meehan, E. R. (2002). Gendering the commodity audience: Critical media research, feminism, and political economy. In E. Meehan & E. Riordan (Eds.), *Sex & money: Feminism and political economy in the media* (pp. 209–222). Minneapolis, MN: University of Minnesota Press.

Mosco, V. (1996). *The political economy of communication.* London: Sage.

Perez, S. (2015, April 3). Why your favorite Snapchat apps no longer work. *TechCrunch.* Retrieved from http://techcrunch.com/2015/04/03/why-your-favorite-snapchat-apps-no-longer-work/#.a7qrzz:82jB.

Ringrose, J. (2011). Are you sexy, flirty, or a slut? Exploring "sexualization" and how teen girls perform/negotiate digital sexual identity on social networking sites. In R. Gill & C. Scharff (Eds), *New femininities: Postfeminism, neoliberalism and subjectivity.* (pp. 99–116). Basingstoke: Palgrave Macmillan.

Ringrose, J., Harvey, L. Gill, R., & Livingstone, S. (2013). Teen girls, sexual double standards and 'sexting': Gendered value in digital image exchange. *Feminist Theory, 14*(3), 305–323. doi: 10.1177/1464700113499853.

Sawers, P. (2014, June 5). Tinder gets ephemeral with Moments, swipeable snaps that disappear within 24 hours. *The Next Web.* Retrieved from http://thenextweb.com/apps/2014/06/05/tinder-gets-ephemeral-new-snapchat-style-photos/.

Shu, C. (2013, Dec. 31). Confirmed: Snapchat hack not a hoax, 4.6M usernames and numbers published. *TechCrunch.* Retrieved from http://techcrunch.com/2013/12/31/hackers-claim-to-publish-list-of-4-6m-snapchat-usernames-and-numbers/.

Siibak, A. (2010). Constructing masculinity on a social networking site: The case study of visual self-presentations of young men on the profile images of SNS Rate. *Young: Nordic Journal of Youth Research, 18*(4), 403–425.

Smith, S. F. (2008). Jail for juvenile child pornographers? A reply to professor Leary. *Virginia Journal of Social Policy & Law, 15*(3), 505–544.

Snapcash. (n.d.) *Snapchat.* Retrieved from https://support.snapchat.com/ca/snapcash.

Snapchat, Inc. (2015) *Snapchat* (version 9.7.0) [Mobile application software]. Retrieved from: https://www.snapchat.com.

Spigel, L. (2004). Portable TV: Studies in domestic space travels. In M. Sturken, D. Thomas, & S. J. Ball-Rokeach (Eds.), *Technological visions: The hopes and fears that shape new technologies* (pp. 110–144). Philadelphia: Temple University Press.

Taylor, E. (n.d.). Snapchat – How did Snapchat reach a multi-billion dollar valuation? *GrowthHackers.* Retrieved from https://growthhackers.com/companies/snapchat/.

Terms of Use. (n.d.) *Snapchat.* Retrieved from https://www.snapchat.com/terms.

Terranova, T. (2004). *Network culture: Politics for the information age.* London: Pluto.

Thomas, D. (2004). Rethinking the cyberbody: Hackers, viruses, and cultural anxiety. In M. Sturken, D. Thomas, & S. J. Ball-Rokeach (Eds.), *Technological visions: The hopes and fears that shape new technologies* (pp. 219–239). Philadelphia: Temple University Press.

Thompson, B. (2015, Feb. 24). Old-fashioned Snapchat. *Stratechery.* Retrieved from https://stratechery.com/2015/old-fashioned-snapchat/.

Tyma, A. W., Herrmann, A. F., & Herbig, A. (2015). Introduction. The beginnings: #WeNeedaWord. In A. Herbig, A. F. Herrmann, and A. W. Tyma (Eds.), *Beyond New Media: Discourse and Critique in a Polymediated Age*, (pp. ix–xxiv). Lanham, MD: Lexington.

What can Snapcash be used for? (n.d). *Snapchat.* Retrieved from https://support.snapchat.com/a/snapcash-guidelines.

Williams, R. (1975). *Television, technology, and cultural form.* New York: Schocken.

Wysocki, D. K., & Childers, C. D. (2011). "Let my fingers do the talking": Sexting and infidelity in cyberspace. *Sexuality & Culture, 15,* 217–239. doi:10.1007/s12119-011-9091-4.

Yaverbaum, E. (2015, March 9). Is Snapchat peddling porn? *Huffington Post.* Retrieved from http://www.huffingtonpost.com/eric-yaverbaum/is-snapchat-peddling-porn_b_6826444.html.

CHAPTER 30

"This is a real job, man": Defining "Sex Work" In-Resistance to Dominant Discourses of Prostitution

Jennifer C. Dunn

KEY TERMS

Sex work	Reality television	Intertextuality
Prostitution	Rhetoric	

ABSTRACT

For this chapter, I explored experiences of women working at a legal brothel and their televisual representation in the HBO reality series, *Cathouse*. Using findings from my narrative rhetorical analysis of the show and observations and interviews at the brothel, I discovered a web of intertextual discourses of prostitution. This chapter provides methodological insights about using rhetorical and fieldwork to discover relationships between a media production context and its televisual representation. Additionally, it demonstrates ways seemingly marginalized women rhetorically define themselves in resistance to dominant discourses of prostitution by drawing upon an alternative narrative of sex work.

In HBO's reality television series, *Cathouse*, Deanna explains her experience as a sex worker at a legal Nevada brothel, the Moonlite Bunny Ranch: "I never do anything I don't feel comfortable doin'. I don't personally do anal sex, um, some girls do. I like oral sex. Some girls won't. It's too much contact. We do use dental dam, or we choose not to, it depends on…if I feel comfortable with the party or the guy" (Kaplan, 2002). Deanna's perspective complicates dominant portrayals of prostitutes by putting herself into the role of decision-maker. My narrative rhetorical analysis of *Cathouse*[1] revealed that the series overall constructs a counter-narrative of prostitution as "sex work" and its narrative suggests the women represented are safe, empowered by choice and money, and provide a service to the community (Dunn, 2010; Dunn, 2012). Typically, when prostitutes are featured on television, they are characterized as either dangerous fallen women from whom the general public needs to be protected, or, alternatively, as victims in need of protection from evildoers (usually men) who seduce innocent girls into this life of deviance (Hallgrimsdottir, Phillips, & Benoit, 2006; McLaughlin, 1991). In contrast, *Cathouse* exposes viewers to positive potentials of sex work in a legal context; which begs the question: Does *Cathouse* accurately represent the experiences of the women who work at the Moonlite Bunny Ranch?

To explore answers to this question, I spent five weeks in the winter of 2007 doing interviews and observations at the Moonlite Bunny Ranch. During this time I conducted interviews with 9 of the 24 women working, who ranged in age from 19 to 47, and had worked at the Ranch from one day to 6 years. Interviews ranged in length from 40 minutes to an hour and a half. Ultimately, I visited the Ranch a total of 16 days and averaged 6 hours a visit, during which I took field notes. As I concluded that *Cathouse* framed prostitution as "sex work," my interview protocol focused on how each woman defined "work."

Comparing the results of my rhetorical analysis to my narrative analysis of my field notes and interview transcripts, I found that the construction of prostitution as "sex work" in the show was also reflected in my observa-

---

1. Initially, I conducted a narrative rhetorical analysis of the first one-hour *Cathouse* special, which aired in 2002. Subsequent to this episode, HBO aired a total of 4 specials and 15 half-hour episodes (over two seasons) between 2002 and 2008. I used these other episodes to confirm my results and found little difference between the initial special and subsequent episodes. Re-runs of these episodes still air today.

tions and interviews (Dunn, 2012). This finding contradicts much reality television research that assumes that what appears on screen is edited to construct narratives that do not accurately reflect the participants without examining the production context (e.g., Andrejevic, 2002; Gillespie, 2000; Mendible, 2004; Stern, 2005; Waggoner, 2004). Using rhetorical and fieldwork together allowed me to compare this representation of these women with their lived experiences. Having the findings of my interviews and observations confirm what I found in my rhetorical analysis offered a way to confirm (or potentially deny) the validity of my results.

After doing my rhetorical analysis of *Cathouse* and fieldwork at the Ranch, though, I began to question the supposed one-way, directional relationship from production context (i.e., the making of the show) to textual representation (i.e., the show itself) that my comparison assumed. Rather, a web of intertextual relationships among historical, cultural, community, and individual discourses of prostitution seemed to emerge in both the textual and production contexts, which the latter revealed in the former. Kristeva (1980) describes intertextuality as any text being "...constructed as a mosaic of quotations" and is therefore, "absorption and transformation of another" (p. 25). In other words, when these women told their stories about working at the Moonlite Bunny Ranch, they were engaged in the process of constructing their identity/ies and drew on others' stories, negative and positive, to make sense of their self/ves. The purpose of this chapter, then, is to better understand these women's lived experiences, and their relationship with their televisual representation, by focusing on the intertextuality of their discourses as revealed through my rhetorical and fieldwork research.

Although a great number of readers of this chapter might not identify as prostitutes or sex workers, the relevance of this chapter extends to most young women (and men) in American society today. Tanenbaum (2015) points out that we live in "a contradictory landscape in which females are applauded for sexual audacity when they're not being humiliated and disgraced" as young women try to figure out how to deal with the divide between good girls and "sluts" (p. 2). This is especially relevant with the overwhelming presence of sex and communication about sex in traditional and social media. Should young women aspire to be seemingly squeaky clean Emma Stone or Keke Palmer? Or are Miley Cyrus and Rhianna role models for young women? Why must we choose? Add the idea of commodifying that sexuality, whether that means being a singer who wears little to no clothing in her music videos or charging money for sex, and then how do we as a society judge these women? Are they whores? Nonetheless, tensions have been created between what it means to be a good girl or a sexual woman in American society today. But why?

One of the major contentions of this chapter is that the ways society *communicates* about sexual women and commodified sexuality, in person and in mediated forums, affects these individual women and how they define themselves. Although college student Natalie Dylan's attempt to auction off her virginity through the Moonlite Bunny Ranch might seem extreme, it proves my points: 1) the lines between being sexually active, commodifying sex, and college students is not as distant as many might think, and 2) public discussion of young women's choices when it comes to sex are contentious issues that influence both how one defines oneself and how others define you (Dunn & Vik, 2014). The discussion that follows, of how intertextual discourses of prostitution influence these sex workers, should be considered in any discussion of women and sex in American society.

Intertextual Discourses of Legal Sex Workers

The organizational narrative of the Moonlite Bunny Ranch has been promoted vociferously by its owner/proprietor, Dennis Hof, on television, radio, and in the popular press (Mead, 2001; Pike, 2004)[2] and is encapsulated by a segment in *Cathouse*: "I'm not a pimp. I'm a businessman. I'm friends with these ladies. We're business partners. We are the most legitimate business in America because we know we're gonna be scrutinized. So we do everything right" (Kaplan, 2002). Research shows this is not the case with most legal brothels in Nevada (Albert, 2001; Herbert, 2007). Yet, this idea of prostitution as a business where women have choice, are safe, and provide a service, is one that Hof promotes in the media. In my interviews with and observations of these sex workers, their stories drew on this organizational narrative to define themselves *in-relation* to the "prostitution as business" narrative in order to define their experiences *in-resistance* to

---

2. Hof and workers from the Moonlite Bunny Ranch have appeared multiple times on TV shows such as *The Tyra Banks Show* and radio on *The Howard Stern Show*.

dominant discourses of prostitution as a coerced, unsafe, deviant, illegal practice. Although not exhaustive of my findings, from their stories the primary rhetorical strategies they used to define their self/ves *in-relation* and *in-resistance* emerged: defining what they do as "a real job" (Clair, 1996, p. 253) that provides a service. According to their stories, what makes what they do a real job is that it involves effort, provides monetary support, and involves more than sex.

It's "a real job, man"...

Cathouse defines prostitution as work. Dennis Hof asserts, "I don't like *prostitute*. I don't know where that word came from. I don't like it. And... whore is totally unacceptable. And slut, you're liable...We're gonna call the police on ya. K? So, working girl. That's what I think the girls should be called. They're working girls" (Kaplan, 2002). The accompanying visual demonstrates his point by showing women negotiating deals and having sex with customers. They also collect money, interact with the cashier's office, attend company meetings (in the form of the Thursday tea parties), and fulfill their obligations to be medically tested, pick up supplies, and other daily routines that do not involve sex.

These sex workers draw on the business narrative of the Moonlite Bunny Ranch to contrast what they do with the characterization of prostitution as a deviant social practice. In our interview on December 17, 2007, Kandi explained, "I don't really consider myself any different than any human working because it's a job. Does anybody else put a roof over my head or food on my table? You know...to criticize what I do? No. I'm not out on the streets. I'm not a homewrecker." Despite seeing what she does as a real job, she still felt the need to distinguish herself from street workers and clarify that she was not a homewrecker. Kitten made it clear in our interview on December 7, 2007, that if anyone wanted to criticize her choice of profession, she "doesn't give a fuck." She explained that she did care whether or not her mother supported her choice (she does), but, "Anybody else? I don't care...(T)hey can go pay my bills. So, I don't care what they say." She did not say that anyone did criticize her, but because of her knowledge of the criticisms sex workers face, she still felt the need to respond to such assumptions. These women justify their work as a real job based on the fact that it is their primary form of support (Clair, 1996). As Vivian West put it in our conversation on December

1, 2007, "I'm a firm believer that this is a real job because there are certain people out there, like my ex…who doesn't think this is a real job and I was like, oh, that's great. So, for the last eight years then, since I started stripping I've been making monopoly money. That's amazing! . . . No, this is a real job, man." Within the organizational narrative of the Moonlite Bunny Ranch, being paid for the hard work they do allows these women to define their work as a real job. The fact that it is legal in this context further facilitates their ability to define it in contrast to the deviant social practice of prostitution.

To further their characterization of prostitution as a real job, the working girls at the Bunny Ranch explained that what they do involves more than sex. When asked what "work" meant to her in our interview on December 10, 2007, Bunny defended her job against the assumptions of outsiders:

> (M)ost people…when they hear that we work 12-hour days, they're like "Oh my god! How do you do that?" And they think we're like havin' sex all day, with 500 people, and it's really not like that…(M)y 12-hour day consists of waking up, getting ready, watching TV, doing line-ups, doing bills, answering emails, goin' on the message board, posting comments…givin' a live chat, and…pretty much just bein' here. And, people come in, even if they don't come in to party, they come in. They've seen me on radio shows. They've seen me on TV shows. They want me to sign somethin' or take a picture or show 'em around. So, I mean, it's kinda like tour guide, and, like bein' on-call pretty much, but, you get to lay in bed.

She uses her description of a typical day that involves much more than sex with customers to legitimate what she does as work.

Despite the mundane daily routines, their work is promoted as fun as well. Dennis Hof said on *Cathouse*, "I don't wanna say 'sex act' or 'fuck' or 'suck.' It's 'party.' That's what we do. …We're havin' a party" (Kaplan, 2002). The perspective Hof promotes is also noted by Kitten in her definition of work:

> To me, seriously, havin' a good time and making money having sex. Or, not even sex. Some people think it's all about sex. We get guys who just want a massage. You get guys that…just want to spend some time with you alone and talk. You get guys who just wanna get in the hot tub…And it's all work. So, I would

say sex with fun…Partyin', and not necessarily meanin' sex. Just partyin' is work for me.

Unlike dominant discourses which discuss the horrific working conditions that prostitutes are forced to endure, Kitten, in line with Hof's perspective, focused on the fun she has entertaining customers and making money doing it.

Porn star and former girlfriend of Dennis Hof, Sunset Thomas, said on *Cathouse*, "Still every time I drive up here I still get excited… I still love it." On the same episode, Felicia said, "I can't lie. I would do this until I was 60 if I could. I really would. It's just that fun" (Kaplan, 2002). Yet, when a job is enjoyable, it is devalued as work (Clair, 1996). So, describing not only the fun but also the elements of the job that do not involve sex and enjoyment is important for these women and for *Cathouse* to note in order to be able to show that this is a business. Even though *Cathouse* includes both, it tends to focus more on the excitement of the job, likely due to the visual bias of television (Douglas, 2006).

Despite general agreement that what they do is a real job, Kayla strategically distanced herself from the concept of work when I asked what it meant to her in our interview on December 19, 2007. Kayla said, "I don't consider this like work. I consider this more like a lifestyle and this is just, to me it's just like another vacation that I take and then I just go back home." Prior to starting at the Bunny Ranch, Kayla said that she had never really worked. Between her divorce and her first visit to the Ranch, she was dating a professional athlete long-distance. As a matter of fact, she met Dennis while with her "friend" at a strip club. When Dennis suggested she come out to work, this friend told her that going to the Ranch would be like dating him. "He gives me so much money when I go out to see him…just the fact that I do go to see him in (his home town), he gives me money. He says it'll be kinda like that," Kayla explained. For Kayla, then, being paid to have sex with men at the Bunny Ranch was not that different than dating this man long-distance as both involved being paid to spend time with men.

Dennis promoted "work" as a "paid vacation" to Kayla and she talks about it not as a job but as a lifestyle. The issue, then, involves what "prostitution" is. Or more specifically, the issue concerns how society and the women at the Moonlite Bunny Ranch perceive prostitution. Kayla explained that she was extremely hesitant to accept Hof's invitation at first because it was prostitution. But the way that Hof described it to her, it sounded like a paid vacation. He offered to fly her out to the Ranch for a visit, during which she could work or not, depending on how she felt. But, as she explains, "I didn't feel pressured into it and it wasn't like, everyone's perception of it. I never look at like, 'Ohhhh, prostitution,' and I think that if I ever saw it as that, that I wouldn't do it. 'Cause I think prostitution, like on the street corner, is something that's worse." So, she went into the initial trip with an open mind and figured that if she saw anything negative, she would not do it. But, she says that within two days of her visit she felt comfortable enough to work. Despite being paid for what she does at the Ranch, Kayla describes it not as work, but a lifestyle. Like Kandi, however, she also strategically distances her "lifestyle" working legally at the Ranch from street prostitution as she was able to choose this vocation.

Characterizing what they do as a real job involves couching it as activity that provides financial support. For most of the women I interviewed, this is their primary means of support. *Cathouse* further emphasized how much money the Ranch and the working girls earn.[3] However, other factors, such as the ease of their work, the temporary nature of it, the idea that it takes place outside of "real time," and the fact that they have fun doing it, work against others seeing it as a real job (Clair, 1996, p. 253). So, the working girls feel the need to further justify their work as not "just sex." Even so, they still use the legal status of their place of business to distance their work from illegal prostitution.

...That provides a service

Hof's business narrative takes another step to define sex work as "not prostitution" when highlighting the service these women provide. Many women were brought to Nevada in 1859 by mining companies to provide sexual service and entertainment to the prospectors who flooded the area to capitalize on the Comstock Lode.[4] In this tradition, *Cathouse* also emphasizes

---

3. In *Cathouse*, they celebrate their best April ever, when they had bookings of over one million dollars. In our interview, Kandi told me that in a bad year she brings in about $125,000 and a good year can earn her $250,000.
4. The Comstock Lode was the discovery of silver near what would become Virginia City, Nevada in 1859. Just as the Gold Rush brought prospectors to California, the discovery of this profitable mineral brought large groups of (mostly) men to the area seeking their fortune. Mining companies brought women to the area to provide entertainment for these men. According to the 1870 census, prostitution was the number one way women earned money in pre-statehood Nevada. Even though prostitution dropped to the fourth most common occupation for women on the Comstock by 1880 (James & Fleiss, 1998), its impact on the Nevada economy remains present through today.

the services these women provide to the community. Sunset Thomas and Felicia argued that learning from a professional was the best place for men to learn how to perform sexually. One of the virgin men serviced on the show said that after his party with porn star Sunset Thomas, he had "a lot more confidence because before I didn't really wanna talk to anybody… Afterwards, it was like I was alive" (Kaplan, 2002). After his experience he said he was a different person and even felt comfortable with women. After helping a virgin get over his sexual anxiety, Felicia said, "Look at me, I'm a sex therapist" (Kaplan, 2002). *Cathouse* also showed a widower visit so that he could be intimate with a woman for the first time since his wife died. He did not have sex with Deanna, but had her hold him. He said that this experience may help him to come to a place where he could be intimate with a woman again and gave him comfort at the same time.

In our interview, Bunny Love explained that some men came for help with sexual problems:

> There's some guys that come in for therapeutic reasons…because they really need help…(T)hey need emotional attention…I have a guy who…flies in from way…across country… because when it comes down to it…he can't perform, and that's a real problem for him, 'cause he can't carry on any relationship…(I)t's just something that he's been dealing with since he was young and, so, we get his dick hard on cue, and…he needs that. He pays good money for it. And, some guys…they're virgins. They wanna learn what to do. They wanna learn how to touch a girl. What to do. What not to do.

Bunny recognized that her job involved helping men with their sexual dysfunctions and teaching inexperienced men about how to be with women.

Even those who do not have sexual dysfunctions can still take advantage of the services provided by these sex workers as shown on *Cathouse* and reflected in the way these women talk about their jobs. *Cathouse* also showed the Bunny Ranch as a place where men come to have fantasies fulfilled. Basic services, such as oral sex, are something Airforce Amy says many men cannot ask their wives for: "She (the wife) does enough around the house, I'm not gonna ask…Really, guys tell me that" (Kaplan, 2002). Kandi told me that fulfilling men's fantasies is part of her job. She said that she works out, tans, and keeps her hair blonde because she found that a majority of men who come in are partial to blondes, which means she does better business when she gives them what they want. She contended:

> It's what they come here to get: what they can't get at home…
> (A) lot of good men that come in…they may want a blowjob.
> They might wanna have oral or give oral, but they might also
> feel like they cannot ask their wife that 'cause it's the mother of
> their children. You know? 'Cause what if the mother feels like,
> you know, his wife feels like that's just degrading…Personally,
> I like givin' better than receiving (laughs). That's my pleasure.

Kandi recognized that part of the service she can provide in her job is fulfilling fantasies that men do not feel they can have performed at home. Interestingly, this assumption, that wives do not give blowjobs and that prostitutes do, merely reifies the good girl/bad girl dichotomy promoted in societal narratives of sex. In contrast to dominant discourses of prostitution that characterize such acts as degrading and coercive (Albert, 2001; Herbert, 2007), Kandi and Airforce Amy own the sexual nature of their business while characterizing sex as a service. Kandi adds that she enjoys it too.

Porn actress, feature dancer, and working girl, Vivian West, directly addressed these assumptions in speaking with me: "It's very empowering for a woman…I do whatever I wanna do…I've had a lot of guys come in here and be like, 'Teach me stuff.'…We'll play teacher. Then I'll show 'em somethin' new…. They'll be like, 'You're a porn star, teach me stuff.'" Vivian voiced the idea that providing the service of teaching men was empowering for her. Kitten also recognized the sexual nature of her work:

> I don't want to tell you this in the wrong way…I wouldn't call
> myself a nympho, which is an addiction. Oh my god, this is gettin' real deep. But…I love attention…I love to feel like I can
> take something from a guy with my sex appeal. That's awesome
> to me…I mean, I'm not the prettiest thing in the world, but to
> some guys I am like a goddess or somethin', and that kinda floats
> my boat…So, I think the sex appeal about it is amazin'. And,
> bein' open with yourself and your sexuality is kinda like great…

Kitten both felt the need to justify her enjoyment of sex and the fact that she found pleasure in being able to negotiate a good deal from a customer for the services she provided. This characterization both feeds into cultural discourses of transgression while undercutting the assumption that no one would choose, let alone enjoy, having sex for money.

Rather than being judgmental about the sexual proclivities of the people who visited the Ranch, both on *Cathouse* and in my interactions with the women who work there, these sex workers attempted to illustrate how they provided a service to their customers. The way Airforce Amy put it on *Cathouse* was: "It's service after the sale, during the sale. It's a business. I'm a business woman" (Kaplan, 2002). The way Kandi saw it in our interview was similar to how she viewed her military service. She concluded, "I was servin' my country then. I'm servin' my country now."

Discussion and Implications

Using textual analysis in conjunction with field methods served two purposes for my project. First, doing my fieldwork after I completed my narrative rhetorical analysis allowed me to use what I found in the field as a validity check on my insights from my textual analysis. The second purpose was to more carefully interrogate what the relationship between the lived experiences of the women who work there are in relation to how they are represented in the series. The latter purpose allowed me to see some of the ways they invoked intertextual narratives of prostitution in their stories about their work self/ves, including dominant media discourses that tell them they are in need of reform or punishment as well as that of the Ranch itself.

Both fieldwork and rhetorical analyses are subject to criticism for their focus on language at the expense of everyday, lived conditions that shape (and are influenced by) communication. I am not sure if we, especially in the Western world, make sense of our experiences outside of language. For this reason, the issue is not whether we can capture the social nature of that which we observe, but how do we *best* represent social experiences. Using textual analysis in conjunction with interviews and observations offers one way to "check" the validity of my analysis of the TV show and interviews and observations.

Taken alone, the narrative analysis of *Cathouse* suggests legal prostitution is safe, profitable, and useful. Since this is easily derided by dominant media and societal discourses, the probable response to *Cathouse* is that it is edited, fake, and airs merely to promote HBO's and Dennis Hof's business. The interviews and observations I conducted in the production context counter dominant perspectives of reform and punishment and confirm that the sex workers at the Ranch communicate their lived experiences similarly to that which is represented in this show. Considering these stories in relation to one another allowed me to address their intertextual nature. Working as a psychoanalyst, Kristeva (2002) reframed the concept of "textual plurality" as "a mental activity" in which "(t)he polyphony of voices accounted for...a subject *in process/on trial*, that unstable articulation of identity and loss leading to a new and plural identity" (p. 475). In this way, Kristeva took the concept of intertextuality beyond written texts to a person's communication about their self/ves. These findings suggest not only that these women's experiences are being represented in *Cathouse* and in my rhetorical analysis, but are also implicated in one another in the ways these women tell their stories in both forums.

My analysis also provides insights about the material (or economic) conditions that shape these women's lives. My use of textual and fieldwork revealed the importance of this representation to the lived experiences of the sex workers at the brothel. On one level, Dennis Hof chose to construct the narrative (and practices) of this brothel as a legitimate business to promote legalizing prostitution (Mead, 2001; Pike, 2004). On another, this narrative is enacted through words and practices at the Ranch. Although these practices are not beyond reproach, Hof's narrative not only resists dominant constructions (and practices) of prostitution, but shapes these women's material existence and how they produce their work identity/ies. In other words, promoting prostitution as legitimate "sex work" allows these women to work in a safe environment and make much more money than if they were working illegally. Constructing and analyzing this intertextual "text" revealed how these women assert definitional agency by legitimating their work in the face of discourses that operate to define them as deviant.

While this view contradicts dominant media representations of the reform/punishment binary of prostitution (Hallgrimsdottir, Phillips, & Benoit, 2006; McLaughlin, 1991), recent analyses of media representations of sexual women contend that claims to agency are dubious. Amy-Chinn's (2006) analysis of the prostitute-character Inara in Joss Whedon's *Firefly* "draws on patriarchal and colonialist discourses to reinscribe the body of a woman of colour as a site of white (predominantly male) hegemonic privilege" and therefore "her agency is undermined by the extent to which is she is subjected to limitations placed on her through regulation, discursive violence and her construction as the racialised 'other'" (p. 175). Pitcher (2006) contends that women's agency in *Girls Gone Wild* is undermined by the financial compensation the producers earn (millions) in comparison to what the women who participate earn (a T-shirt). Both Pitcher and Riordan (2001), in her analysis of the Riot Grrrl movement, additionally claim that the commodification of women's bodies in these contexts cuts against any potential challenge their claim to sexual agency poses. Although there is room for future research on the representation of race in relation to life at the Moonlite Bunny Ranch, I believe the ways these women rhetorically define their self/ves challenges the assumption that commodification of one's body necessarily results in the lack of agency.

Sex positive feminists claim that women commodifying sex (or even expressing the desire to do so) and profiting from society's (lack of) sexual morals poses a direct challenge to traditional conceptions of women as regulators of society's morals, in their roles of wife and mother, and the institution of heterosexual marriage itself (Nagle, 1997). Pendleton (1997) notes: "...the act of making men pay is, in fact, quite subversive. It reverses the terms under which men feel entitled to unlimited access to women's bodies...Rather than face sexual harassment in the underpaid straight work place, sex workers give men limited permission to play out their sexual fantasies and desires" (p. 79). In their words and actions, the women of the Moonlite Bunny Ranch clearly challenge ideas that what they do is not work, that it only involves sex, and in demonstrating the service they provide.

Merely expressing the idea that sex for money is a job, according to these discourses, combats limited expectations of the roles women are to play in society. Further, the fact that the narrative represented on *Cathouse* has led more women to come to work at the Moonlite Bunny Ranch demonstrates its effectiveness. Campbell (2005) asserts, "Whatever else it may be, rhetorical agency refers to the capacity to act, that is, to have the competence to speak or write in a way that will be recognized or heeded by others in one's community" (p. 3). The appeal this narrative has to the women working at the Ranch (or who want to work there) emerged in the ways they constructed their intertextual discourses. Additionally, the divisions they created between acceptable and unacceptable, legal and illegal prostitution demonstrates their ability to speak to their community, while at the same time creates a hierarchy of acceptable/unacceptable sex work/prostitution.

On one hand, the business narrative of *Cathouse*/Moonlite Bunny Ranch has positive material implications for the women who work there and for legal prostitution in general. Enforcing laws protecting the independent contractor status of the workers through the business narrative and practices at this Ranch means they have the right to choose their customers, decide what they will and will not do, and set their own prices. Not all legal brothels in Nevada do follow these regulations (Albert, 2001). The stories these women share demonstrate the choice and empowerment they feel working in this context and promote it to others as a positive model of legally selling sexual services for money.

On the other hand, this is not a feminist business model and the narrative these women invoke to resist characterization as deviant reinforces their definition as commodities. Independent contractor status in Nevada also means that 50% of what these women gross goes to the brothel and that they have to pay for their licensing, medical testing, supplies, room and board, etc. So, Hof, as the brothel owner, earns more than the individual sex workers do. To be fair, he also has more expenses, from paying other employees (greeters, cashiers, his general manager, drivers, etc.) to building maintenance, and from brothel and liquor licenses to business promotion, and he offers financial incentives for those who earn minimum amounts (free room and board) and are the best workers (bonuses). So, their agency is necessarily limited by the capitalist system within which they work (as are all Americans) and the systemic regulations of their business.

For nearly 25 years, scholars have posed challenges to traditional rhetorical criticism for the dual purpose of "cataloging often marginalized rhetorical action and representing these practices" in ways that highlight their emancipatory potentialities (Middleton, Senda-Cook, & Endres, 2011). Even so, it was not until I began comparing my narrative analysis of *Cathouse* to the interview and observation "data" I collected that I realized I would need methods beyond traditional criticism, fieldwork, or even Middleton, Senda-Cook, and Endres' "rhetorical field methods." Drawing upon Kristeva allowed me to reveal the intertextual nature of these women's stories about themselves. The contribution of this work is not theoretical in nature, but methodological and substantive. As a result of using textual analysis and fieldwork methods together, I found one way to address criticisms of both.

Additionally, I was able to explore the impact these various discourses have on how these women make sense of their lived experiences and rhetorically assert their agency. Ultimately, my analysis suggests material potential of how these sex workers define their self/ves *in-resistance* to dominant reform/punishment narratives of prostitution and *in-relation* to the safe/empowered/useful narrative of *Cathouse*/Moonlite Bunny Ranch. I hope that my examination of these women's narratives of sex work can help young women (and men) make sense of how history, culture, community, and individual discourses about sex, sexual women, and agency always influences the ways we communicate about and define ourselves.

DISCUSSION QUESTIONS

1. Give examples of television shows that have used prostitution in their storylines or that have featured prostitutes. How do those portrayals compare to stories told in *Cathouse* and by the women who work at the Moonlight Bunny Ranch according to the chapter?

2. Why do you think that most television shows portray prostitutes as "dangerous fallen women from whom the general public needs to be protected or victims in need of protection from evildoers"?

3. Why might Dunn's findings in this chapter be controversial to readers? Were they controversial or even surprising to you?

4. Do you believe that if there were more stories that showed prostitution as legitimate work on TV that more women would want to do this work? What advantages and disadvantages would there be to more of these stories in media?

5. What is prostitution? What is not prostitution? How do we distinguish between what is and what is not prostitution? Why do we make such distinctions? How do these distinctions impact women in general?

References

Albert, A. (2001). *Brothel: Mustang Ranch and its women*. New York: Random House.

Amy-Chinn, D. (2006). 'Tis pity she's a whore: Postfeminist prostitution in Joss Whedon's *Firefly*. *Feminist Media Studies,6*(2): 175–189. doi: 10.1080/14680770600645143.

Andrejevic, M. (2002). The kinder, gentler gaze of *Big Brother*: Reality TV in the era of digital capitalism. *New Media & Society 4*(2): 251–270. doi: 1461-4448(200206).

Campbell, K. K. (2005). Agency: Promiscuous and protean. *Communication and Critical/Cultural Studies 2*(1): 1–19. doi: 10.1080/1479142042000332134.

Clair, R. P. (1996). The political nature of the colloquialism, "A Real Job": Implications for organizational socialization. *Communication Monographs, 63*(3): 249–267.

Douglas, S. J. (2006). The turn within: The irony of technology in a globalized world." *American Quarterly, 58*(3): 619–638. doi: 10.1353/aq.2006.0057.

Dunn, J. (2010). HBO's *Cathouse*: Problematizing representations of sex workers and sexual women. *Feminist Media Studies, 10*(1): 105–109. doi: 10.1080/14680770903457469.

Dunn, J. C. (2012). "It's not just sex, it's a profession": Reframing prostitution through text and context. *Communication Studies, 363*(3), 345–363. doi: 10.1080/10510974.2012.678924.

Dunn, J. C., & Vik, T. A. (2014). Virginity for sale: A Foucauldian moment in the history of sexuality. *Sexuality & Culture 18*(3): 487–504. doi: 10.1007/s12119-013-9207-0.

Gillespie, T. (2000). Narrative control and visual polysemy: Fox surveillance specials and the limits of legitimation. *The Velvet Light Trap, 45*: 36–49.

Hallgrimsdottir, H. K., Phillips, R., & Benoit, C. (2006). Fallen women and rescued girls: Social stigma and media narratives of the sex industry in Victoria, B.C., from 1980 to 2005. *Canadian Review of Sociology/Revue canadienne de sociologie, 43*(3): 265–280.

Herbert, B. (2007). Legal prostitution does not empower women. *Columbus Dispatch*, September 12. Retrieved November 17, 2007, from http://www.dispatch.com/content/stories/editorials/2007/09/12/herb12.ART_ART_09-12-07_A13_BV7SFR6.html.

James, R. M., & Fleiss, K. H. (1998). Women of the mining west: Virginia City revisited. In R.M. James & C. E. Raymond. *Comstock Women: The Making of a Mining Community* (17-39). Reno, NV: University of Nevada Press.

Kaplan, P. (2002). *Cathouse*. Directed by Patti Kaplan. DVD (2005). Los Angeles, CA: Home Box Office Inc.

Kristeva, J. (1980). *Desire in Language: A Semiotic Approach to Literature and Art*. Roudiez, L. S. (Trans.). Gora, T. (Ed.). NY: Columbia University Press.

Kristeva, J. (2002). "Nous deux" or a (hi)story of intertextuality. *The Romantic Review, 93* (2002): 474–477.

McLaughlin, L. (1991). Discourses of prostitution/discourses of sexuality. *Critical Studies in Mass Communication, 8*(3): 249–272.

Mead, R. (2001). American pimp: How to make an honest living from the oldest profession. *The New Yorker*, April 23. Retrieved April 26, 2007, from http://www.newyorker.com/archive/2001/04/23/010423fa_fact_mead.

Mendible, M. (2004). Humiliation, subjectivity, and reality TV. *Feminist Media Studies, 4*(3): 335–338. doi: 10.1080/1468077042000251256.

Middleton, M. K., Senda-Cook, S., & Endres, D. (2011). Articulating rhetorical field methods: Challenges and tensions. *Western Journal of Communication, 75*(4): 386–406. doi: 10.1080/10570314.2011.586969.

Nagle, J. (Ed.). (1997). *Whores and Other Feminists*. New York: Routledge.

Pendleton, E. (1997). Love for sale: Queering heterosexuality. In J. Nagle. (Ed.). *Whores and Other Feminists* (pp. 73–82). New York: Routledge.

Pike, D. (2004). King pimp: Dennis Hof says he wants to clean up legal prostitution's image. *Reno News & Review*, January 22. Retrieved April 17, 2007, from http://www.newsreview.com/reno/king-pimp/content?oid=21703.

Pitcher, K. C. (2006). The staging of agency in *Girls Gone Wild*. *Critical Studies in Media Communication, 23*(3): 200–218. doi: 10.1080/07393180600800759.

Riordan, E. (2001). Commodified agents and empowered girls: Consuming and producing feminism. *Journal of Communication Inquiry, 25*(3): 279–297. doi: 10.1177/0196859901025003006.

Stern, D. M. (2005). MTV, reality television and the commodification of female sexuality in The Real World. *Media Report to Women, Spring*: 13-21.

Tanenbaum, Leora. (2015). *I am not a slut: Slut-shaming in the age of the Internet.* New York: Harper Perennial.

Waggoner, C. E. (2004). Disciplining female sexuality. *Feminist Media Studies, 4*(2): 217–220. doi: 10.1080/1468077042000251256.

CHAPTER 31

Misogyny and Torture Porn in American Horror Story: Coven

Kelly Wilz

KEY TERMS

Torture porn
Slasher genre in television

Sexualized violence
Rape culture

ABSTRACT

When looking at the intersections of sexuality and communication, the slasher genre provides a unique and complex place for serious analysis regarding messages surrounding the concepts of consent, rape, sexualized violence, and the ways in which these are depicted in popular culture. The mainstreaming of torture porn and sexualized violence send dangerous messages regarding myths and misconceptions regarding consent, rape, and assault, and contribute to a culture that systemically devalues and dehumanizes women. This chapter will analyze select scenes from the third season of *American Horror Story* to examine the formal and narrative elements that copy the slasher subgenre of torture porn. *American Horror Story: Coven* serves as a case study of how a series like this normalizes and trivializes violence against women in the same way slasher films have for years. Specifically, this chapter examines how the series uses conventions of the slasher film while simultaneously mainstreaming sexualized violence against women within the context of the medium of television.

The slasher genre in film is nothing new. The emergence of this type of entertainment often reflects the collective nightmares "circulating among the public, and therefore, in times of great stress or upheaval—when our collective nightmares push their way into the forefront of our conscious minds—there is often a resurgence in films that contain particularly violent content" (Kattelman, 2010, p. 4). As Valerie Wee (2006) notes,

> During times of social crisis, several sorts of cultural representations tend to emerge. Some idealize solutions or alternatives to the distressing actuality, some project worst fears and anxieties induced by the critical situation into metaphors that allow those fears to be absolved or played out, and some evoke a nihilistic vision of a world without hope or remedy (Ryan & Kellner, as cited in Wee, 2006, p. 55).

Many have argued that slasher films articulate the fears and concern prevalent in their respective eras. At the height of America's involvement in the Vietnam War, for example, a slew of films notorious for their graphic violence and brutality were released onto American screens. It was as if Americans, who were horrified at the real images of war and suffering needed "an opportunity to see those images in a different context, one that would keep them contained and give them some semblance of meaning . . . they were looking for some kind of containment and closure (Kattelman, 2010). Slasher films of the 1980s (mainly the *Nightmare on Elm Street* series and the *Friday the 13th* series) were said to portray parents and family as ineffectual protection against evil, and larger social problems were indicted for creating the films' monsters. In addition, these films were seen as taking a critical stance against reactionary patriarchal values (Wee, 2006). Films of the 1990s were seen as a reaction to school shootings and high school violence.

So it should be no surprise that post 9/11, a new age of slasher films emerged. Kattelman (2010), notes "the heightened sense of personal danger in the post-9/11 culture and the ongoing discussions surrounding the use of torture have certainly contributed to the revitalization of the horror genre and to the direction that this revitalization has taken . . . While the

American public had long been able to shield itself from a day-to-day fear of terrorist threats, the attacks of September 11 brought that fear screaming into consciousness" (p. 12). This fear translated brutal images on movie screens across the country. But why, during times of cultural crises would audiences seek out entertainment that frightens and terrifies them? What are the fears and concerns respective of this era that warrant such graphic torture and violence, particularly against women? Moreover, how is it that torture on the big screen is now mainstream viewing for American television audiences? It is possible that there is no "real" crisis motivating these mediated responses? Perhaps we have become so affectively invested in the rituals of undoing and resuturing (and the trauma/therapy cycle that these rites reflect) as our primary means of enacting the national imaginary. In either case, the mainstreaming of torture porn and sexualized violence send dangerous messages regarding myths and misconceptions regarding consent, rape, and assault, and contribute to a culture that systemically devalues and dehumanizes women. This chapter will analyze select scenes from the third season of *American Horror Story* to examine the formal and narrative elements that copy the slasher sub-genre of torture porn. *American Horror Story: Coven* serves as a case study of how a series like this normalizes and trivializes violence against women in the same way slasher films have for years.

Return/Revenge of the Slasher Genre

Slasher remakes have made a huge comeback in recent years. Ryan Lizardi (2010) states "In spring 2009, both *Friday the 13th* and *Last House on the Left* were remade and in 2010, *A Nightmare on Elm Street*. Other examples include *The Texas Chainsaw Massacre* (2003), *The Amityville Horror* (2005), *The Hills Have Eyes* (2006), *Halloween, 2006n* (2007), *Prom Night* (2008), and *My Bloody Valentine* (2008). This is a significant trend for a film genre that has never been shy about making sequels to their franchises" (p. 113). The remakes of *I Spit on Your Grave* (2010) and its sequel *I Spit on Your Grave 2* (2013) also show a cultural pattern of slasher revival. Lizardi (2010) goes on to claim, "since 2003, the horror film genre has fully embraced the cinematic trend to remake or reimagine, it's past" (p. 114). But there is more going on here than simply repeating a successful formula in order to minimize risk and secure profits in the marketplace. Constantine Verevis (2005) argues that "horror films are also a safe economic decision to make because of their relative inexpensive production budgets and predictable box office draw" (p. 37). Though these economic elements should not be ignored, they do not supersede the cultural elements including the question of their widespread popularity.

However, during this time, along with remakes, a new type of film emerged—one that turned out to be wildly successful. If the slasher films of the 1970s were a response to a cultural crisis regarding our involvement in Vietnam, a second wave of even more horrific films landed in a post 9/11 landscape and on the Hollywood scene during a time where Americans were deeply divided regarding support for the War in Iraq. Kattelman (2010) argues that this recent spate of mainstream, graphically-violent horror films reflects societal stresses circulating in the United States as a result of the 11 September 2001 attacks on the World Trade Center, and argues that the popularity of these films has been fueled by the American public's increased awareness of the threat of terrorism and a fear of random violence. In 2006, David Edelstein coined these types of films "torture porn" to describe this extreme sub-genre of the postmodern slasher (Lockwood, 2009). These films have also been variously labeled 'carnography' or 'gorenography' due to their emphasis on extreme violence and the prurient element that may be involved in their viewing, thus aligning them with pornography.

This sub-genre follows many of the formal and narrative techniques of the slasher, but differs slightly in its graphic depiction of torture, the prevalence and gratuitous amounts of rape and sexual assault, and its overall attempts to push the boundaries of what is societally acceptable. In these films, the narrative revolves around the attempts of an abducted character or characters to survive an ordeal at the hands of their tormentor(s) with graphic portrayals of sexualized violence and vivid displays of the body in torment. Indeed—what was considered too graphic to receive an "R" rating a few decades ago is now considered tempered or mainstream. One must ask, however, about the impact of such graphic media on viewers' attitudes and behaviors and the result of this type of desensitization, and why these types of films remain so wildly popular.

A new crop of directors also found fame within this sub-genre. Directors like Rob Zombie and Darren Lynn Bousman, were deemed the "Splat Pack." Rebecca Winters Keegan (2006) defines this as those "who are given almost free rein and usually less than $10 million by studios or producers to make unapologetically disgusting, brutally violent movies" (p. 2). *Saw*, for example, was an extremely huge hit, proving that mainstream audiences clearly were willing to witness and enjoy brutal and graphic spectacles of torture. The basic plotline and narrative for these films is displayed as such: the main characters become trapped somewhere and have to endure horrible things or do horrible things to each other to escape. Eli Roth's film *Hostel* was inspired by a website that claimed to let you shoot someone for $10,000. Steering away from slasher conventions, torture porn also gives us no Final Girl (Carol Clover's observation of the trope of the female character left alive to confront the killer at the end of most slasher films) and in some cases no final character at all. Instead, at times, we get all male casts (*Hostel*), or weak females who fail to save anyone. Maisha Wester notes, however, in almost all cases, even with this new sub-genre, we see the "traditional horror film monster that hides behind misogynistic, violent, white male anger extending from 'reactions against the emerging independent female of a [. . .] women's liberation movement and the corresponding erosion of power and gender identity associated with traditional patriarchy'" (Magistrale, as cited in Wester, 2012, p. 92).

One of the primary goals of this essay is to explore the kind of world in which torture porn makes sense. The appeal of torture porn provides pleasure in several ways. Beyond the tension-release found in all horror/slasher films, these films "loosely reference the extreme violence that is present in today's society and offers a sense of control over it. Unlike rampant violence in the real world, these films present what closely resembles real violence in a contained space where it can be kept under surveillance" (Kattelman, 2010, p. 10). Lockwood (2009), drawing on Benjamin Noys and Giorgio Agamben considers

> that new regulations emerging in the wake of the 'War on Terror' involving the suspension of certain rights are an indication of the ways in which Western citizens have entered into a permanent state of emergency in which they are held or suspended in a kind of limbo. The individual is constantly exposed to death, stripped of a sense of agency, of master over causes and effects. His or her identity reduced to mere bodily life (p. 44).

David Edelstein (2006) points out that where the spectator's sympathies lie at violent movies has always been a complicated one. "Post-9/11, we've engaged in a national debate about the morality of torture, fueled by horrifying pictures of manifestly decent men and women (some of them, anyway) enacting brutal scenarios of domination at Abu Ghraib" (p. 1). Part of these images exists in shows like *24*, in which the protagonist often uses torture in the name of an imminent threat.

Aside from their participation in the national dialogue on torture, these new brand of films somehow tapped into an undercurrent of anxiety about the place of gendered bodies in relation to torture as well as the connection between gender equality, torture, global capitalist venture, and the passive American consumer (Wester, 2012). In addition, as post-War on Terror narratives, the Splat Packs' films blur the line between torturer, victim, villain, and hero. At a time when the subject of torture was centered in political debates, these directors and writers visualized the difficulty of reducing such acts to acceptable and/or unpardonable.

If the sub-genre of torture porn was fueled by the American public's increased awareness of the threat of terrorism and a fear of random violence, how do we explain the popularity of the sub-genre making its way to the small screen? What's going on in the world right now that makes shows like *American Horror Story*, *Criminal Minds*, *Hannibal*, *The Following* and others so incredibly popular? Where are we as a culture that rape, torture, and brutal assaults have become common fodder for basic cable television shows? Some could argue that at a basic level, there are so many shows available that producers are all fighting for an audience that hasn't grown at the same rate. Others could say that at some basic level, the CGI technology has made it so the torture and explicit gore seems unbelievably real. I believe that most of the attraction (of torture porn and of the slasher genre in general) gains popularity *because* it is so far removed from our everyday lives. Sadistically or not, we live vicariously through torturer and the tortured—the only difference now is the level of brutality that has seeped into cable television from the big box office films.

Case Study: *American Horror Story: Coven*

According to an article in *New York Magazine*, 5.5 million viewers viewed the premiere telecast of the third installment of FX's *American Horror Story (AHS): Coven* Wednesday, October 5th, 2013 easily making it the most-watched episode in the franchise's three-year history. According to Josef Adalian (2013), "*Coven* was up a stunning 44% from the then-record premiere last year of *AHS: Asylum* and a whopping 77% over the original *AHS* (which FX has now tagged *Murder House*.) As always, *Coven* did particularly well with viewers under 35, beating everything on network TV" (p. 1). Ryan Murphy and Brad Falchuk, producers of *American Horror Story*, gave viewers a menu of slasher conventions including: slavery torture porn, a vagina-dentata-type death, a gratuitous and needlessly graphic gang rape of one of the principle characters, and, not to disappoint, a revenge-type rape and death of a comatose rapist by another female lead character in the third season.

Even before the show begins, the viewer is informed that the show is rated MA LSV, that it contains nudity, strong language, violence, sexual situations, and that viewers should be advised. The first episode of season three is entitled, "Bitchcraft," which immediately insinuates how the writers and directors are going to portray these women. Instead of focusing on the entire episode, I will analyze specific scenes that problematize healthy models of consent or glorify rape culture and sexualized violence/torture porn.

The first time we meet Zoe, a primary character in *Coven*, we see her walk slowly into her bedroom where we find out she will have sex for the first time. He asks if she is sure she wants to do this, and she nods her head, "yes." With no music but the pulse of a beating drum, her boyfriend takes her clothes off and the camera displays a series of quick shots of her body. He kisses her and the music begins, as if he is plunging inside of her. Though it is her first time, her face portrays exquisite pleasure until his nose starts bleeding. Within seconds, he lies on his back, convulsing while she kneels over him. He screams. The scene ends with Zoe on a train where we find out she (and her vagina) are the cause of her lover's death, and that her parents have kept the fact she is a witch a secret from her for years. The answer? Send her to witch academy. A Hogwarts of sorts, but with sex, violence, torture, rape, and murder.

This scene is problematic because a young girl, a virgin, is clearly traumatized by her first experience, harkening to the stereotypes and societal implications that for all young women, their first experiences with sex will be painful and joyless. While the scene portrays consensual and willing participants, the underlying message of the scene evokes societal messages about the dangers of premarital sex. Obviously not the "killing your partner with your vagina," but the pain, the scariness, and general subconscious warning that your first time is not going to be pleasant.

It is at dinner at the academy where Zoe meets Madison and the dialogue between the girls at the table is vitriolic. As they share their stories, the viewer discovers that Madison, a child star, was admitted to the academy for killing the director of a movie. As Madison defends her innocence, the four end up fighting, showing off their powers and hurting each other. Madison, given no other options for friends, invites Zoe to a fraternity party. The next scene portrays a party bus full of young men. The president of the fraternity encourages his brothers to get as drunk as humanly possible while he sacrifices and remains sober to drive. Madison is filmed from below accentuating her strength as she enters the party while Zoe meanders through the party as if almost in a dream. Zoe and the fraternity president see each other through an ice sculpture and he introduces himself to her. Immediately she is entranced by his charms. The scene cuts to a downward shot of Madison walking from upstairs. Looking irritable, she seductively puts a cigarette in her mouth and blows a cloud of smoke into one of the fraternity brothers' faces.

> Madison: "Want to be my slave tonight?"
>
> Fraternity brother: "What's in it for me?"
>
> Madison: "Are you stupid? Slaves get nothing. Now why don't you get me another drink?"

Within seconds, the fraternity brother slips a pill into her drink, finds another one of his brothers, and simply says "it's on." From there the episode depicts a horrific and gratuitous rape scene. Madison, severely affected by the drugs, wanders aimlessly into a bedroom. She can barely stand up so one of the fraternity brothers carries her into a bedroom. The scene then flashes to Zoe and Kyle (the fraternity president) as if to say, "he is one of the good ones." Realizing Madison is gone, Zoe goes to look for her. The sound of heavy breathing accompanies a close-up shot through Madison's eyes as if the viewer is getting raped as well. The faces change—quickly—to tell the viewer she is being assaulted by possibly more than a dozen men. There is no sound save for the grunts from the men, quick shots of their faces and then of hers. She weakly cries for help but is completely debilitated by not only the drugs, and the men inside who won't let her go. As one of the men zips up, signaling to the viewer that finally, this brutal act is over, *another* man climbs on top of her—her eyes glazed over, her makeup smeared. The camera pans to a shot of only his eyes, and another grunt to signal that he has ejaculated in her. Zoe and Kyle continue to look for her. Back in the bedroom, the camera pans to one of the brothers videotaping *another* man raping Madison on his camera phone—possibly a nod to the Steubenville rape case.[1] Finally, Kyle walks in and stops the assault, screaming at his brothers and attempting to get the phone from the initiator. The boys fight and flee to the party bus, leaving Madison still drugged and lying on the bed. Zoe tries to get help. The initiator rapist knocks out Kyle and tells everyone to delete the videos on their phones. We see Zoe running after the bus, crying, Madison behind her. In seconds, we see Madison flip the entire bus over and watch it explode into flames, killing all the boys on it, including Kyle. So, Madison has the power to flip an entire bus over killing everyone in it, but doesn't have the power over date-rape drugs and rapists? This message is essentially saying that no matter how powerful you are as a woman, you can't avoid/prevent rape, even with supernatural powers.

The next day, in the mansion, the television is on and a news anchor describes the horrible bus explosion. Zoe warns Madison that they need to come clean, while Fiona (Jessica Lange's character and an older witch)

---

1. The Steubenville High School rape occurred in Steubenville, Ohio, on the night of August 11, 2012, when a high school girl, incapacitated by alcohol, was publicly and repeatedly sexually assaulted by her peers, several of whom documented the acts in social media. The victim was transported, undressed, photographed, and sexually assaulted. She was also penetrated vaginally by other students' fingers (digital penetration), an act defined as rape under Ohio law.

   The jocular attitude of the assailants was documented on Facebook, Twitter, text messages, and cell phone recordings of the acts. The crime and ensuing legal proceedings generated considerable controversy and galvanized a national conversation about rape and rape culture. Two students and high school football players, Ma'lik Richmond and Trent Mays, both 16 at the time of the crime, were convicted in juvenile court for the rape of a minor. Additionally, three other adults have been indicted for obstructing the investigation into the rape, while Steubenville's superintendent of schools has been charged with hindering the investigation into a rape that took place earlier in 2012.
   Oppel Junior, Richard A. (March 17, 2013). "Ohio Teenagers Guilty in Rape That Social Media Brought to Light". *New York Times*.

reprimands Madison for being "sloppy" regarding the bus incident and whips her into a wall. There is no mention of the rape. No mention of "why" Madison flipped the bus. Rather, the only focus is Fiona's anger toward Madison drawing negative attention to the coven. No one, even Zoe, seems to be urging Madison to get help regarding the traumatic experience she just went through. Both girls are focused on revenge. This is problematic in that many rape narratives in the media depict that the first thing on the victim's mind is to get back at his/her rapist. As survivors will tell you again and again, many don't come forward because they are afraid of not being believed, they self-shame or blame themselves for what happened echoing the very same victim blaming we as a society engage in, or the event is so traumatic, they just want it to go away.

To reinforce this notion of "getting revenge," in one of the final scenes, Zoe visits the hospital to see if Kyle is still alive. In his place, she finds Madison's rapist. "It should have been you, asshole," she says, and without a second thought, Zoe closes the hospital room door and climbs onto the rapist. Prior to this, we know Zoe has only had sex one other time, and she has to essentially rape the unconscious rapist to avenge Madison. This is incredibly problematic in that in order to "make things right" neither participant truly consents to the sex act being performed. Zoe rapes him to kill him and avenge Madison, but not for her own sexual pleasure. And the rapist is unconscious, so he cannot consent either. Clearly, the producers of the season want the viewers to get a sense of justice, but is this really the best way? Throughout the final scenes the viewer sees Madison lying in a fetal position in the bathtub, bruised and sobbing, but that is all we see. Clearly, she has been traumatized and is hurting, and killing the men on the bus didn't help her deal with what she experienced, but this one shot is all the audience sees. Madison, we assume, will go on living and get past this as if it never happened. The audience then sees Zoe's shadow behind the curtain in the room climbing on top of the rapist and killing him through intercourse. The camera zooms in on his eyes—now covered in blood, the life pouring out of him.

It is important to ask ourselves, why include the gang rape scene at all? The audience already knows Madison has killed before, so the writers didn't need to show that she's capable of murder. If the goal of the rape scene was to show Zoe's character progression by embracing her powers and using them, again, there could have been many ways to do this without the audience having to sit through a graphic gang rape. Clearly the writers included the brutal rape scene with the specific intent of satisfying their audience through brutal sexualized violence. *American Horror Story* is notorious (and continues to be with each season) for pushing boundaries in terms of torture and abuse, and this was no exception. And, mimicking the slasher genre, this episode could fall into any number of "revenge" films in which the victim goes through a horrifying rape or assault in order for her then to get revenge on those who hurt her. In the 1970s, many saw these types of rape-revenge films as empowering and feminist and audiences enjoyed seeing the victim get back at her attackers. However, as Andi Zeisler notes, "why did slasher films and the female victim avenger character become such a staple of 1970s cinema to begin with . . . if the genre's popularity in the '70s and '80s indicates anything, it's that men who made up a large share of its audience got plenty of pleasure seeing women terrorized, sexualized, and killed" (p. 73).

It would seem as though the writers included this scene for nothing other than ratings and to please those viewers who still get plenty of pleasure seeing women terrorized, sexualized, and killed. In addition, the fact there was no public outcry regarding Madison's rape indicates desensitization to this type of sexualized violence. The show continued while ratings increased, and another season was produced after season three. Season five will air October 7, 2015 and a new series, created by the same writers and producers, *Scream Queens* debuts September 22, 2015.

The Problem with Torture Porn: Repercussions of Depictions of Rape and Torture

In the words of Gary Hoppenstand referring to *American Horror Story* (2012), "this program has completely destroyed any remaining limitations that television censorship has placed on the horror genre" (p. 1). As with any pop culture phenomenon, *AHS* deserves special critique due not only to its wild success, but also its widespread critique including those who argue that the show aligns itself too closely with slasher conventions and torture porn. Gaayathri Nair (2014) points out that "Ryan Murphy and Brad Falchuk have claimed that *American Horror Story: Coven* is an explicitly feminist season of *American Horror Story*. Previous seasons of *American Horror Story* have attempted to address sexism and misogyny in the horror genre. However, both *American Horror Story: Murder House* and *American Horror Story: Asylum* relied heavily on both the objectification of and violence against women as a plot device" (p. 1).

Most critics argue that *AHS* walks a knife-edge between feminism and misogyny. As Anne Helen Petersen argues (2013),

> In tales of abjection, the abject feminine manifests as the sprawling abyss — the mother who threatens to consume, to castrate, to make others into the gaping hole that is their lack. I always think of the massive vagina-dentata of *Star Wars* . . . In *Coven*, that's Zoe, who may look meek and non-threatening on the surface but whose inner void (re: murderous vagina) threatens to consume not just your penis, but your entire life (p. 1).

Zeba Blay (2013) and other authors have noted that despite *AHS*'s ability in producing complex female characters, the series perpetuates harmful stereotypes and regularly punishes women (i.e., all three seasons have used rape as a plot point) (p. 1). On the other hand, Joanna C. Valente (2013) notes, "There are hardly any popular TV programs that focus on women building (or destroying) relationships *with* other women, that do not hinge on the attention of men—it actually passes the Bechdel test" (p. 1).

So, is *AHS* feminist or misogynistic? Or both? There are several ways in which a critic could read a complicated text such as *AHS* and could argue that *Coven*, rather than promote violence against women, actually supports an alternate feminist reading because the witches are powerful and exercise agency. However, these questions miss the larger critique of "why has the torturing of women on the big screen and small still count as entertainment, and what does it say about our culture, men, and women, that shows such as this are so wildly successful?" Critics have long deplored the graphic torture and the abundance of eroticized violence against women within this film genre (e.g., Clover 1992; Cowan and O'Brien 1990; Linz et al., 1984). Andrew Welsh (2010) argues, "given the adverse effects associated with negative media depictions of female victims, the impact of gender expectations and sexual activity, and the continued popularity of slasher films, there is pressing need to examine the nature of violent content in this subgenre" (p. 762). However, although film has received much attention and criticism for these dangerous and problematic depictions of women, less attention (if any) has focused on the area of mainstream television. Torturing women for entertainment purposes is not a revelatory idea; however, the fact that this type of graphic torture, including gang rape, is portrayed on basic cable should cause us to pause. Through pushing the envelope of what is deemed an "acceptable" level of violence against women, *AHS* serves as a case study of how a series like this normalizes and trivializes violence against women in the same way slasher films have for years. The difference is that this show is popular amongst men and women—even those who deem it misogynistic and pushes the boundaries far beyond the sub-genre of torture porn whilst mainstreaming this type of graphic depictions for the small screen.

Over the years, many critics have argued that there is a greater need to study the effects of media violence due to its impact on its audience members. Sexual violence is and continues to be a significant public health issue and it is vital to explore all causes of sexual violence and factors related to its prevention. Lisa Cuklanz (2007) argues that while prime-time crime dramas are "the most fertile prime-time sites for the depiction of rape" (p. 304), assaults against women in mainstream television have become almost commonplace, yet the few studies focusing on non-pornographic media have primarily focused on film. It is therefore important that we take the medium of television seriously as a site that is perpetuating the sexual objectification of women and rape myth acceptance. Tara Emmers-Sommer, Perry Pauley, Alesia Hanzal, and Laura Triplett (2006) argue that the danger of torture porn becoming so prevalent in our country and in our media is that "information about women and violence in the media aids in shaping public opinion and public policy as well as reinforcing stereotypes that can affect the judicial process" (p. 314). Many studies have shown that repeated exposure to sexually violent films and other forms of media desensitize both men and women and increase the likelihood that both sexes will believe the rape was precipitated by the victim's actions (Emmers-Sommer et al., 2006). Also, as Stephen Kershnar (2004) points out, sexually violent depictions against women have resulted in more aggressive sexual fantasies, increases in the acceptance of rape myths, a fostering of sexual discrimination against women, and real life aggression against women.

In order to change perceptions of rape and assault, critics and theorists need to address a culture in which women are routinely devalued. If the devaluation lies in mediated texts, critics need to start there—with analysis, media literacy education, and consciousness-raising involving the direct correlation between depictions of women and our attitudes toward them. The persistence of rape myths in society are facilitated by rape myths in the media—whether on prime time television, film, or local news. The power of TV and other media to influence values, perceptions, beliefs, and actions cannot be overestimated. *American Horror Story: Coven* is dangerous because it sensationalizes torture porn and sexualized violence, it turns violence against women into benign entertainment, and it reinforces dangerous stereotypes and misconceptions regarding sex, rape, consent, and assault.

DISCUSSION QUESTIONS

1. Does the way television depicts sex affect your views as to what is "normal?" If so, how?

2. Do you agree that seeing so much violence against women in the media desensitizes us to this kind of violence?

3. What could we as a culture do to re-sensitize ourselves to these types of mediated violent acts?

4. Do you think the exposure to sexualized violence against women leads to real life violence and/or rape?

5. What would you have done in Zoe's situation? Could there have been more she could have done in terms of bystander intervention?

6. Do you think that portrayals of rape in mainstream television trivialize the act and reinforce victim blaming?

References

Adalien, J. (2013). Fly, my Nielsen's: *American Horror Story: Coven* debuts with huge ratings. *Vulture*, 1.

Blay, Z. (2013). *American Horror Story: Coven*: Slavery as torture porn? *Indiewire 17*, 1.

Clover, C. (1987). Her body, himself: Gender in the slasher film. *Representations 20*, 187–228.

Cuklanz, L. (2000). *Rape on prime time: Television, masculinity, & sexual violence*. Philadelphia, PA: University of Pennsylvania Press.

Edelstein, D. (2006). Now playing at your local multiplex: Torture porn. *New York Magazine, 39* (4) 63.

Emmer-Sommers, T. Pauley, P. Hanzal, A., & Triplett, L. (2006). Love, suspense, sex, and violence: Men's and women's film predilections, exposure to sexually violent media, and their relationship to rape myth acceptance. *Sex Roles, 55(5)*, 311–320.

Hoppenstand, G. (2012). Editorial: the horror of it all. *Journal of Popular Culture, 45*(1), 1–2.

Kahlor, L., & Morrison, D. (2007). Television viewing and rape myth acceptance among college women. *Sex Roles, 56.11/12*, 729–739.

Kattelman, B. (2010). Carnographic culture: America and the rise of the torture porn film. *The domination of fear. (At the interface/probing the boundaries)*. New York, NY: Rodopi.

Keegan, R.W. (2006) The splat pack. *Time*, 66–70.

Kershnar, S. (2004). Is violation pornography bad for your soul? *Journal of Social Philosophy, 35*(3), 349–366.

Lizardi, R. (2010). Re-Imagining hegemony and misogyny in the contemporary slasher remake. *Journal of Popular Film & Television, 38*(3), 113–121.

Lockwood, D. (2009). All stripped down: The spectacle of 'torture porn.' *Popular Communication, 7*(1), 40–48.

Nair, G. (2014). Exploring bodily autonomy on 'American Horror Story: Coven.' *Bitch Flicks*, 2.

Pearson, A. (2000). Rape culture: Media and message. *Off Our Backs, 30*(8), 13.

Petersen, A. (2013). The exquisite repulsion of 'American Horror Story:' an essay on abjection. *Los Angeles Review of Books, 21*, 1.

Valente, J. (2013). *American Horror Story: A feminist TV show? LunaLuna*, 1.

Verevis, C. (2005). *Film remakes*. New York, NY: Palmgrave MacMillan.

Welsh A. (2010). On the perils of living dangerously in the slasher horror film: Gender differences in the association between sexual activity and survival. *Sex Roles 62*(11/12), 762.

Wester, M. (2012). Torture porn and uneasy feminisms: Re-Thinking (wo)men in Eli Roth's hostel films. *Quarterly Review of Film & Video 29*(5), 387–400.

Wee, V. (2006). Resurrecting and updating the teen slasher. *Journal of Popular Film & Television, 34*(2), 50–61.

Zeisler, A. (2008). *Feminism and Pop Culture: Seal Studies*. Berkeley, CA: Seal Press.

CHAPTER 32

Celebrity Role Models, Social Media, & LGBTQ Youth: Lady Gaga as Parasocial Mentor

Sean Robinson

KEY TERMS

Advocacy	LGBTQ youth	Role model
Celebrity	Parasocial interaction	

ABSTRACT

This chapter explores the role that celebrities play in the lives of LGBTQ youth, as both role models and para-mentors. Given the ubiquitous nature of social media in the lives of youth, many youth are now engaging in parasocial interactions with celebrities, and see them as part of their larger support network. Drawing on Lady Gaga as an extreme example, I showcase how social media sites such as Twitter and Facebook can create parasocial relationships that become almost a mentorship in the eyes of youth.

In recent decades, cultural critics have explored how LGBTQ (lesbian, gay, bisexual, trans [transgender], and queer) people are becoming more and more visible in the public sphere, including in the entertainment industry and in campaigns for equality. These critics have considered a wide array of topics, including how representation and public figures relate to discourses about community, homophobia, and equal rights, among others. One of the lesser explored topics within gay visibility research is the important role that celebrities and media figures are playing in the lives of youth[1] who identify as gay, lesbian, bisexual, transgender or queer. Increasingly, we are also starting to see a number of LGBTQ-identified celebrity role models who are providing advice and support to younger generations through various mass media outlets such as film, television, magazines, and music, so that they can understand what it means to be queer within the world, and how to act in accordance with that identity (Bond, 2014; Gomillion & Giuliano, 2011).

For instance, we see queer mentors advise performers in TV programs, such as RuPaul's Drag Race on Logo. Likewise, LGBTQ role models are encouraging LGBTQ youth through social media campaigns, such as the Trevor Project and the It Gets Better Project. Fictive LGBTQ role models also are found in novels, such as Mayra Santos Febre's book *Sirena Selena Dressed in Pain*. Although LGBTQ youths look up to non-queer celebrities such as Tyra Banks for advice and guidance, many times they are looking toward LGBTQ individuals such as Lady Gaga, RuPaul, or Ellen DeGeneres for support and encouragement—despite the fact that they probably have no direct, tangible relationship to these individuals. Nonetheless, youth are following, learning from, role modeling, and being challenged by such media personalities (Gomillion & Giuliano, 2011).

Furthermore, a number of U.S. based television shows in the past few years have introduced characters that some LGBTQ youth might also see as role models (e.g., *Glee*, *Modern Family*, *New Normal*, *The Fosters*, and *Partners*). More often, however, LGBTQ youth turn to the Internet and various social media outlets such as YouTube, Vine, Facebook, and Twitter, as sources of support, guidance, and empowerment (GLSEN, 2013). In this chapter, I offer an exploration of how such social media outlets (also called "new media" by Ito, Horst, & Bittani, 2010) offer opportunities for the types of relationships with celebrities and media figures that go beyond mere role modeling. Furthermore, using Lady Gaga as a case study, I highlight how fan-celebrity relationships move almost into the realm of mentoring for, and to, LGBTQ youth via a process known as parasocial interaction. Media in the 21st century has taken on new forms; a continued understanding of the positive, affirming impact of these social media-based forms for LGBTQ youth offers us new modes of engaging with our youth based on representation, identity, and affiliation. As Brown and Bobkowski (2011) contend, "newer media provide unprecedented opportunities for selection and interaction that may be driven by and support identity exploration" (p.96).

In this chapter, I discuss the role of media in the lives of youth, present a discussion of mediated and parasocial relationships, and conclude by highlighting the mediated interactions of celebrities with youth. Specifically, I use Lady Gaga as a notable case study of celebrity-audience interaction.

Media in the Lives of Youth

Survey-based research offers compelling evidence that new media occupy a pivotal role in the lives of youth. According to a 2015 report by the Pew Research Center (Lenhart, 2015) 92% of teens ages 13 to 17 report going online daily, and 24% of teens surveyed claim they go online "almost constantly" (p.2). Facebook remains the most used social media site among teens ages 13 to 17 with 71% of all teens using the site, half of teens use Instagram, 33% use Twitter, and 4 in 10 use Snapchat. Young people also embrace multitasking by consuming more media in their daily lives than they are spending in school or with their parents (Rideout, Foeher, & Roberts, 2010). This generation spends more time with media than with any other activity except sleeping, putting today's youth in the vanguard of both a technological and cultural revolution (Heim, Brandtzeg, Kaare, Endestad, & Torgersen, 2007). New media therefore becomes a potentially critical element in the construction of identity.

Although little research has actively explored how celebrities can impact LGBTQ identity development, conceptual works by Dyer (1986), Chum (2000), and Gross (2001) suggest that LGBTQ identity and its exclusion from socio-historical perspectives in mainstream society might give rise to affiliation with media stars and celebrities. This contention, coupled with the rising use of social media by youths, strongly suggests that LGBTQ youths are more likely to use new media to facilitate the process of identity development and integration; and, it would stand to reason, are more likely to use celebrities for whom they have an affinity to do so. The few recent empirical studies that exist shed light on how LGBTQ individuals use various media and with whom they identify. Kivel and Kleiber (2000) found that gay and lesbian youth used media to learn about what it means to "be" gay or lesbian (i.e., what does a gay identity look like?). Furthermore, the youth in their study also found role models that they could emulate, and from whom they could seek ways to be successful and to overcome adversity. In their study of 56 college students, Bond, Hefner and Drogos (2009) found that during their coming out process, most individuals reported using various forms of mass media, rather than face-to-face interpersonal relationships, to assist them. An overwhelming majority of these students (70%) used the Internet to help them, and almost one-half used the Internet as their sole source of information during the coming out process.

According to Bond et al., participants often cited Ellen DeGeneres as a pivotal role model in helping them come to terms with their own sexuality. Furthermore, the authors found that the propensity of television to showcase LGB individuals in stereotypical ways often drove them away from such media to the Internet in search of more positive role models and information that was helpful. Bond's (2014) later work corroborates the fact that heterosexuality is overrepresented and LGB sexualities are underrepresented in mass media. When depicted, talk that involved gay, lesbians, or bisexuals often included stereotypes or insults and jokes related to sexuality and messages were rarely heard or seen about relationships; talk about sex or actual sexual behaviors between LGB individuals were nearly nonexistent.

The Importance of Role Models

What is a role model? And why are role models important for LGBTQ youth? Robert Merton is credited with coining the term role model in his seminal book *Social Theory and Social Structure* (1957). He defines a role model as a person whose behavior, example, or success is or can be emulated by others. He explains how individuals compare themselves with what he termed "reference groups" of people who occupy the role to which the individual aspires (Merton, 1957, p. 285). Examples include the way fans (oftentimes youth) will idolize and imitate professional athletes or entertainment artists. What happens when there are few role models for youth, particularly those already on the margins, such as LGBTQ youth? According to several researchers (Heubner, Rebchook, & Kegeles, 2004; Safran & Heimburg, 1999) the absence of supportive relationships and role models for LGBTQ youth increases behavioral and health risks, such as depression, suicide, and anxiety, among other issues; likewise, scholars have also documented the power that supportive relationships can have for all youth, not only those who are LGBTQ (e.g., Noam & Fischer, 1996; Resnick et al., 1997; Rhodes, 2002; Rutter & Leech, 2006). Thus, it would seem that the accessibility to role models with whom there is an authentic and supportive connection would decrease the risks associated with stigma and marginalization that many LGBTQ youth feel.

Recent research by Bird, Kuhns, and Garofalo (2012) offers a glimpse of the realities of LGBTQ youth and role models. In their study, 496 ethnically diverse LGBTQ youth between the ages of 16–24 were asked who they most wanted to be like, and answers were coded for how accessible the role models were for the youth. Youth were also given a battery of questions to measure various behavioral and emotional risks (e.g., AIDS risk behavior, depression, etc.). It is not surprising that almost 60% of the youth reported that they had a role model. What is surprising is that 42% of those with a role model claimed that the person was either a singer/musician or an actor/entertainer. Among those identified were Oprah, Beyoncé, Ellen DeGeneres, Angelina Jolie, and Queen Latifah. Furthermore, in their study, Bird et al. found that of those with a role model, 60% reported a role model who was inaccessible. Youths between 16–19 years old had the highest percentage of inaccessible role models (46%), compared with those aged 20–24 (34%). This research corroborates my own experience in working with urban LGBQT youth who view these same celebrities—plus others such as Tyra Banks and Lady Gaga—not only as role models, but in some instances see these media personalities as mentors.

In other words, LGBTQ youths are forming what researchers often call *parasocial relationships*. Originally developed by Horton and Wohl (1956), a *parasocial interaction* is defined as an illusionary experience of the viewer, who believes he/she is interacting with a media performer, despite the non-reciprocal nature of the actual situation; according to Horton and Wohl, it is a "simulacrum of conversational give and take" (p. 215) that occurs between viewers and [television] personalities (p. 215). In a follow-up study, Horton and Strauss (1957) further described the experiential nature a of parasocial interaction, by arguing that a "parasocial interaction is experienced by the user as immediate, personal, and reciprocal, but these qualities are illusory and are presumably not shared by the speaker" (p. 580).

Mediated and Parasocial Relationships

Parasocial relationships begin through parasocial interaction. A parasocial interaction (PSI) occurs between a media figure and an audience member (aka, "a fan") and is characterized by a perceived feeling of closeness by the audience member toward the media personality. Horton and Wohl (1956) originally defined the essence of a parasocial interaction as "intimacy at a distance" suggesting a one-sided sense of intimacy between a media personality that primarily occurs within some mediated source. In their research, this relationship was with a fictional television character. In contemporary culture, however, that mediated source moves beyond television and film personalities to include people and characters from various social media outlets including Facebook, Twitter, YouTube, and others. According to Horton and Wohl, typical indicators of parasocial interaction include feeling like we know a celebrity well, enjoying listening or watching a media personality or character, believing we are with a friend when we watch or experience them, and missing them when they are gone. Repeated parasocial interactions over time make up a parasocial relationship, which extends beyond exposure to the media figure. Parasocial relationships often involve learning more about the individual or character. In a digitally-mediated era, that can include active communication with a media personality (Hartmann & Goldhoorn, 2011). For example, a fan might tweet at Ellen DeGeneres—and, in some cases, even receive a response.

Celebrities as Role Models

Why are media personalities and celebrities so powerful as role models and in some instances perceived as advisors or mentors? As previously mentioned, researchers (e.g., Bird, Kuhns, & Garofalo, 2011; Chia, & Poo, 2009) have demonstrated that many youth identify celebrities and popular media figures as role models. According to Ivaldi and O'Neill (2004), youths use celebrity role models in several ways. First, celebrities are used as a source of empowerment; that is, celebrities create a powerful image of a possible ideal self for the youth to emulate, harkening back to Merton's (1957) definition. Second, youth use celebrity role models as a way to understand and negotiate group identities. In this way, youth can position themselves and others as part of a group that is perceived to have more power, prestige, success, or that is less marginalized. When considered together, all of the aforementioned studies suggest that celebrities help to create identities by allowing youth to develop an ideal image of themselves that is situated in the norms, values, behaviors, attitudes, beliefs, and schemas that are mediated not only through the traditional forms of media, but through newer forms, including social media.

One of the reasons that fans appear to like their favorite celebrities is indeed because they are viewed as role models for positive social change (Stever, 2008). Corroborating this work, Yurdakul-Sahin and Atik (2013) found that for young adults between the ages of 19–25, five dimensions impacted how much influence celebrities had over them: physical attractiveness, personality, ideology, success, and values-lifestyle. These can all be attractive qualities, and it stands to reason that if a celebrity's ideology were LGBTQ-affirming, then that celebrity might especially be appealing to LGBTQ youths. For example, Lady Gaga, who is featured as the case study for this chapter, explicitly enacts activism and advocacy for and with LGBTQ people. Research by Kivel and Kleiber (2000) and Ivaldi and O'Neill (2004) that demonstrates how role models create a sense of empowerment and support; help to develop an image of an ideal self; offer youth someone to emulate; and enhance one's sense of identity. Given her focus on uniqueness and her considerable successes, it is no surprise that Lady Gaga is a celebrity role model for many and especially LGBTQ youths. She also has a strong new media presence. As Keller (2014) contends, "celebrity culture created around new media is significant, as both 'average' citizens hoping to become celebrities and celebrities themselves utilize online spaces to make visible, promote, control, and rebrand their public image" (p. 152). She is one of the most notable celebrity role models who are LGBTQ or identify as allies. As such, this chapter's case study focuses on her LGBTQ fans' parasocial relationship with her, one that I argue constitutes a mentoring relationship.

Case Study: Lady Gaga as Role Model, Advocate, and Activist

This case study serves to highlight how Lady Gaga uses her position as a celebrity and pop music icon to influence her followers and fans through her social media platforms. The fans of Stefani Germanotta, aka Lady Gaga, are affectionately called "Little Monsters" by "Mother Monster," an alias Lady Gaga often uses. Through LittleMonsters.com, Twitter, YouTube, Vine, Instagram, Tumblr, and GagaDaily, Lady Gaga embodies, and thus transmits to her followers and audience the values, norms, behaviors, and particular identities that are built around perceived notions of feminism, equality, political activism, and even sexual freedom. Lady Gaga has been recognized for her use of online and social media platforms to both publicize her work and to engage with her followers and Little Monsters. Her social media presence has allowed her to "forge a reciprocal relationship with her acolytes unlike that of any other pop-music icon" (Wolk, 2012, p.58). In her own brief biography on her invitation-only social networking site, LittleMonsters.com, she emphasizes her own eccentricities and marginal status to create a safe space and show support and encouragement to her fans. Many of these fans also identify as outsiders. Her 2011 single "Born This Way" serves as a rallying cry for many of her fans, and her moniker of "paws up" acts as a physical expression of solidarity among her community of Little Monsters. Lady Gaga's relationship with her fans is built around empowerment and self-acceptance as well as her intense and seemingly constant online presence.

The release of her second single "Poker Face" from her debut album *Fame* was the true beginning of her rise to fame and her multi-million dollar musical empire. While her debut single "Just Dance" was a sleeper in some markets, including the U.S., "Poker Face" attained worldwide success, topping the charts in 20 countries, and is among the best-selling singles of all time, having sold over 14 million copies worldwide. The song has been certified nine times platinum by the Recording Industry Association of America (RIAA), and had 7.21 million paid digital downloads in the United States as of April 2015, according to Nielsen SoundScan. In numerous interviews following that song's release, Lady Gaga intimated that her song was a declaration of her bisexuality, of her fantasizing about women while having sex with men. This announcement gave her access to, and perhaps identification with, the wider LGBQT community in a way that a heterosexual ally might not enjoy. Indeed, her bisexual identity lends credence to her values, beliefs, and political activism within LGBTQ circles.

Since the release of "Poker Face," Lady Gaga has been a stalwart of pop music, but has also shown herself to be a dedicated advocate and activist for a number of social and political causes, including LGBTQ rights, anti-bullying programs, immigration reform, and promoting self-acceptance and confidence for youth and young adults. For example in June 2015, Lady Gaga partnered with New York Governor Andrew Cuomo to push for a new campus sexual assault policy at all of the state's colleges and universities. In a joint statement the two called campus sexual assault an unacceptable epidemic, and urged lawmakers to pass the bill called "Enough is Enough" to help reduce assaults and ensure justice for victims. Highlighting the impact that work is making, in 2015 Lady Gaga's Born This Way Foundation was honored by the Anti-Defamation League for championing positive social change and efforts to combat bullying, bias, and bigotry, particularly with youth.

In perusing Lady Gaga's media spaces—particularly her social media sites LittleMonsters.com and GagaDaily—one can see the values, beliefs, norms, and behaviors that her followers are appropriating and internalizing as their own. Beyond social advocacy and activism, however, one prominent ideology revolves around Lady Gaga's brand of feminism and sexuality. Discussing her own view of Lady Gaga's feminism and sexuality, a 23-year-old fan posted onto LittleMonsters.com,

> Gaga embraces authentic sexual expression and uses fashion to simulate different womanly body shapes and embraces different forms of sexual expression. Personally, I believe the sexual expression/sexuality is on a continuum and Gaga embraces all of it.

Yet, Fogel and Quinlan (2011) question the degree to which Lady Gaga's portrayal and discussion of sexuality "can be perceived as a sign of increased liberation for women" (p. 185). Lady Gaga pushes the boundaries of feminism and sexuality, and although Fogel and Quinlan take issue with her manner and style of feminism, many find her brand of sexuality empowering. Nonetheless, Lady Gaga does see herself as a feminist. Her 2010 interview on SHOWstudio offers a compelling description of her own beliefs about beauty and her appearance, and thus her notion of feminism:

> Yes. Yes I am a feminist. I reject wholeheartedly the way we are taught to perceive women. The beauty of women, how a woman should act or behave. Women are strong and fragile. Women are beautiful and ugly. We are soft spoken and loud, all at once. There is something mind-controlling about the way we're taught to view women… It's exciting because all avant-garde clothing and music and lyrics that at one time were considered shocking or unacceptable are now trendy. Perhaps we can make women's rights trendy. Strength, feminism, security, the wisdom of the woman. Let's make that trendy. (para. 8)

Marshall (2010) contends that celebrities today are maintaining and advancing their relationships with fans by sharing personal information and communicating with them online. Lady Gaga has become the embodiment of this phenomenon. The primary means that Lady Gaga connects with her audience is through her GagaDaily newsfeed (@gagadaily), and her personal Twitter feed (@ladygaga). As of this writing, GagaDaily has over 476,000 followers; has posted 5,536 tweets since 2008; and follows 2,663 others. Lady Gaga herself has over 49.4M followers, 6,823 tweets, and follows over 132,000 others. To the casual observer flipping through her media blasts, it might appear that Lady Gaga is indeed all sex, glamour, and fashion—and even, to some degree, anti-feminist. In reading some of her recent posts, fans see her dolled up in various outfits and costumes, covered in makeup and wigs, and perhaps wearing her new Alexander McQueen Armadillo high heeled boots—sexy, showy, glamorous, risqué, titillating fashion show online. Moving past the never ending fashion blitz, fans can take in scenes from her concerts and performances. Fans can catch glimpses of her recent performances with U2, photos and videos of her *Cheek to Cheek* tour with Tony Bennett, and even her presence in the audience at the George Washington University where Tony Bennett was awarded GWU's President's Medal for Achievement.

But beyond what one would expect of such a celebrity promoting her sex appeal, performances and public appearances on her media sites, Lady

Gaga also creates a sense of intimacy and reciprocal relationships by literally letting her hair down, sharing personal information, using photographs and language to increase affiliation, and publicly acknowledging fans and their creative endeavors, whether new artwork or a new dance routine choreographed to one of her songs. In a glimpse into the more mundane side of her life, one 2015 photograph showed Lady Gaga without any makeup sitting back, pensive look on her face, in an ordinary grey T-shirt reading, with the caption to the picture, "Lady Gaga is reading 'An Unquiet Mind,' a book on bipolar disorder by Kay Redfield Jamison." Another picture posted that very same day showed Lady Gaga up dancing around with the caption "Hey little monster, hope your [sic] having a great day, I am!" These types of postings make Lady Gaga appear accessible, ordinary, and even "normal" despite the juxtaposed postings of her in makeup, wigs, and costumes and her flagrant display of her beauty, talents, and skills as seen in her public videos and performances.

Not all of her postings appear self-serving however, and numerous posts are directed towards her fans either individually or collectively. One such post shows her wearing a T-shirt with the *Sound of Music* logo on it and the caption, "Did you know that the Sound of Music t-shirt Gaga wore the other day was a gift from a fan?" In another post on both Twitter and YouTube, in true Lady Gaga fashion, she engages with one of the audience members in the front row at a recent concert: Lady Gaga had to briefly stop the show to calm down this enthusiastic fan, who had been waving at the singer and taking photos non-stop. She exclaimed to him, "I'm gonna let you take one selfie, and then you're going to listen to the music," and, after kneeling down to take that selfie, remarked to the entire theatre: "My whole generation is high on their cell phones!"

Although her music already addresses issues of feminism, sexuality, and identity, Lady Gaga's status as a pop music icon also gives her the freedom to also openly discuss political and social issues in media and social media forums. Lady Gaga uses not only her concerts and public performances to spur action and advocacy by her followers, but she regularly uses LittleMonsters.com, GagaDaily, and Twitter feeds to talk about her own activism and to coax her fans into actions of their own. Several examples show her direct support of LGBTQ individuals. During Istanbul's annual Gay Pride parade in June 2015, Turkish police used tear gas, pepper spray, and rubber bullets to disperse the crowds and shut down the Pride event. In

2014 Lady Gaga had performed in Istanbul and had spoken about the need for gay rights in Turkey. During that speech she said, "I travel the all over world and I know that in some places it is really hard to be gay…. I wish for all my Turkish gay fans to hold your heads high. Be proud of who you are, you don't have to hide, it's time to rise up!" So it was no surprise then that when the police took action this summer, Lady Gaga posted on Twitter, "Istanbul? Who are these 'leaders'? Stop attacking innocent happy people who are celebrating. This is madness! This is inhumane!" She continued with another message, directed at the Governor of Istanbul, Huseyin Avni Mutlu: "Governor, set an example for people to celebrate both Ramadan and Pride in peace, instead of dividing with violence!" Such action is clearly an invitation to others to stand up for what they believe, to do what is right, and to take care of one another. In another show of support for LGBTQ youth, during her performance with Tony Bennett in their *Cheek to Cheek* show in Connecticut in July 2015, Lady Gaga decided to dedicate the Billy Strayhorn classic "Lush Life" to LGBTQ youth:

> I would like to dedicate this song tonight to all the kids that couldn't go out because they were too young, Mother Monster said. You know, the kids that are like 15, 16 years old that are at home or maybe here, wondering if they are gay, or LGBT, bi-curious. And they want to celebrate Marriage Equality but they don't know how because they haven't told anybody yet. But they're excited because they feel valued. I want this song to be for them.

Although Lady Gaga received accolades and thunderous applause from most in the audience for this, a few expressed their displeasure by her obvious politics and act of advocacy by leaving the theatre.

In reading the messages, posts, and tweets of both Lady Gaga and her followers, it is clear that many fans have similar ideologies; many of these fans either attribute their values to Lady Gaga, or claim that she helped further their pre-existing beliefs. But there is more to her music, her ideology, her values, and by extension to her fans than just a sexy pop star with postmodern feminist ideals and beliefs. Her number one song "Born This Way," off her third album, explicitly states her main ideology: love and accept yourself without conforming to sociocultural norms, and in turn love and accept others. The culture created, maintained, and perpetuated by Lady Gaga and her fan base stems from many of the circumstances of contemporary youth and young adults, many of whom are engaged with their own identity struggles. The use of identity struggles as a foundation for her message opens the door for any number of her social and political responses and activist activities—including LGBQT youth advocacy, touting the power of feminism, or teaching self-acceptance or acceptance of others. On the 4-year anniversary of the release of "Born This Way" in May 2015, Lady Gaga posted the following via Twitter onto LittleMonsters.com:

> Thank you for making the 4 year anniversary of Born This Way so special for me. Your online listening party, the positive tweets about self-confidence and pride in one's identity, I felt the soul of our fan base strong. And it wasn't related to anything shallow, our bond is based on our values. We value love and compassion of all things. Which is what that album was about. After a long tiring day I'm falling asleep soundly with you all in my heart. XXOO. I am going to bed dreaming of the Supreme Court legalizing LGBT marriage in America, dozing in gratitude that today it was legalized in Ireland. We are changing, if slowly. And while actions are important, faith is too. Let's keep our faith that change is possible, and keep our courage. Keep our bravery.

Turino (2008) suggested that the self encompasses all of the habits and traits "specific to an individual that develop through the ongoing interchanges of the individual with her physical and social surroundings" (p. 95). Turino further asserts that identity is both publicly and privately created and represented through the deliberate selection from among these habits and behaviors. Many of Lady Gaga's followers demonstrate particular traits and habits that emulate hers. Thus, most followers appear to have an affinity not just for her music, but also for the ideas presented through her work. These shared norms, behaviors, and values are reinforced through Lady Gaga's ongoing pronouncements and posts through her social media platform such as the ones above, and include notions of individuality, nonconformity, compassion, and self-acceptance. These publicly presented values help her followers choose ones to personally express themselves in order to create and project their own chosen identities; in essence Lady Gaga creates the space and the place where each person can become the Little Monster she was born to be.

As mentioned earlier, Lady Gaga often acts as an activist and advocate for LGBTQ rights. This social and political activism is also enacted by her followers, often using Lady Gaga's own actions and statements as a model for their own beliefs. In the LittleMonsters.com platform, one fan discussed how Lady Gaga had positively influenced the way he views the gay community, and another, a 19-year-old, was open in that Lady Gaga's work had taught him that it was "ok to be gay" and that he was "born this way." This young man also divulged although he might not have been entirely accepting in the past, she opened his eyes, and he was now more compassionate toward those in oppressive situations. Once a bully, he now posts images advocating LGBTQ acceptance and equality.

Through engagement with the texts and posts in LittleMonsters.com and the forums in GagaDaily, and in viewing the pictures posted by Lady Gaga's followers, it is clear that many of them have feelings of being the other, the outsider who is marginalized in many spaces and communities. They connect with each other through the various platforms Lady Gaga has established as a way to find their own community, a safe haven where they belong and where they can be themselves. Lady Gaga posts regular missives and affirmations to her followers, such as "Sometimes in life you don't always feel like a winner, but that doesn't mean you're not a winner," and "Good morning! Don't forget to be yourself today, that's true beauty!" Lady Gaga recently started following a fan whose handle is LittleMonster4Ever, and who claims "Since I heard and saw Gaga for the first time, my life changed. I am proud of being a Little Monster and I dream with [of] the day where I'll meet my Mother..." One female fan described being a part of the community as a "truly unique experience," and offered that it is a "space where you will be accepted and loved unconditionally for exactly who you are." Another fan remarked that joining the community helped her recover from severe depression, self-esteem, and body issues. They stated that being part of the community made them feel like they were "normal for once." These sort of coming-to-terms statements are rampant on LittleMonsters.com and in posts by her Twitter followers, and clearly demonstrate the feeling of otherness shared by a large majority of Lady Gaga's larger social media community. They also demonstrate the larger impact that Lady Gaga has on her followers.

The shared values, norms, beliefs, and commitments among Lady Gaga's fans allow them to function as part of a larger community, one which is established and maintained via social media not only by Lady Gaga herself, but by the members as well. These shared perspectives and values include feelings of otherness, a sense of non-conformity, self-love, a belief in equality, and looking to Lady Gaga as a role model for all of these things. Lady Gaga's own presentations of her personality, values, ideas, and sense of right and wrong serve as a foundation upon which her followers use to conceptualize their own beliefs and develop their own identities. Lady Gaga is not only an entertainer and musical icon; Lady Gaga is a celebrity in her own right, who serves as a role model, advocate, and activist, and who inspires, supports, and empowers thousands of her fans to stand up, be heard, and be loved.

DISCUSSION QUESTIONS

1. Consider the role models in your own life. In what ways have they impacted your own identity and behavior?

2. In what ways have media figures specifically influenced your identity or behavior, either in positive or negative ways?

3. Why do you think it is important for minority groups to have role models who are similar to themselves, rather than role models who are from the majority culture?

4. In what specific ways do you think LGBTQ media figures, other than Lady Gaga, have impacted LGBTQ youth and young adults?

5. In what ways do you think that social media helps, or hiders, one's identity development?

References

Arnett, J. J. (2004). *Emerging adulthood: The winding road from the late teens through the twenties.* New York: Oxford University Press.

Bird, J. D., Kuhns, L., & Garofalo, R. (2012). The impact of role models on health outcomes for lesbian, gay, bisexual, and transgender youth. *Journal of Adolescent Health, 50,* 353–357.

Bond, B., Hefner, V., & Drogos, K. (2009). Information-Seeking Practices during the Sexual Development of Lesbian, Gay, and Bisexual Individuals: The Influence and Effects of Coming Out in a Mediated Environment. *Sexuality & Culture, 13*(1), 32–50.

Bond, B. J. (2014). Sex and sexuality in entertainment media popular with lesbian, gay, and bisexual adolescents. *Mass Communication and Society, 17*(1), 98–120.

Brown, J. D., & Bobkowski, P. S. (2011). Older and newer media: patterns of usage and effects on adolescents' health and well-being. *Journal of Research on Adolescence, 21*(1), 95–113.

Chia, S. C., & Poo, Y. L. (2009). Media, celebrities, and fans: An examination of adolescents' media usage and involvement with entertainment celebrities. *Journalism & Mass Communication Quarterly, 86*(1), 23–44.

Chum, J. M. (2000). *Still acting gay* (Rev. Ed.). New York, NY: St Martin's Griffin.

Dyer, R. (1986). *Heavenly bodies: Film stars and society.* London, UK: British Film Institute.

Fogel, C. A., & Quinlin. A. (2011). Lady Gaga and Feminism: A Critical Debate. *Cross-Cultural Communication, 7,* 184–188.

GLSEN, CiPHER, & CCRC. (2013). *Out Online: The Experiences of Lesbian, Gay, Bisexual, and Transgender Youth on the Internet.* New York: GLSEN. Retrieved from: http://www.glsen.org/sites/default/files/Out%20Online%20FINAL.pdf.

Gomillion, S. C., & Giuliano, T. A. (2011). The influence of media role models on gay, lesbian, and bisexual identity. *Journal of Homosexuality, 58*(3), 330–354.

Gross, L. (2001). *Up from visibility: Lesbians, gay men, and the media in America.* New York, NY: Columbia University Press.

Hartmann, T., & Goldhoorn, C. (2011). Horton and Wohl revisited: Exploring viewers' experience of parasocial interaction. *Journal of communication, 61*(6), 1104–1121.

Heim, J., Brandtzæg, P. B., Kaare, B. H., Endestad, T., & Torgersen, L. (2007). Children's usage of media technologies and psychosocial factors. *New Media & Society, 9*(3), 425–454.

Horton, D., & Strauss, A. (1957). Interaction in audience participation shows. *The American Journal of Sociology, 62,* 579–587.

Horton, D., & Wohl, R. (1956). Mass communication and para-social interaction: Observations on intimacy at a distance. *Psychiatry, 19*(3), 215–229.

"In Camera- Lady Gaga". (May, 2010). *SHOWstudio*. Retrieved from: http://showstudio.com/project/in_camera/session/lady_gaga.

Ito, M., Horst, H., & Bittani, M. (2010). Living and learning with new media: Summary of findings from the digital youth project. Chicago, IL: John D. and Catherine T. MacArthur Foundation Reports on Digital Media and Learning.

Ivaldi, A., & O'Neill, S. A. (2004). Why adolescents admire famous musical role models: Implications for aspirations, expectations and identity. Proceedings of the International Conference on Music Perception & Cognition, Evanston, IL.

Keller, J. M. (2014). Fiercely real? Tyra Banks and the making of new media celebrity. *Feminist Media Studies, 14*(1), 147–164.

Kivel, B. D., & Kleiber, D. A. (2000). Leisure in the identity formation of lesbian/gay youth: Personal, but not social. *Leisure Sciences, 22,* 215–232.

Lenhart, A. (2015). Teen, Social Media and Technology Overview 2015. Washington, DC: Pew Research Center. Retrieved from: http://www.pewinternet.org/files/2015/04/PI_TeensandTech_Update2015_0409151.pdf.

Marshall, P. D. (2010). The promotion and presentation of the self: celebrity as marker of presentational media. *Celebrity Studies, 1*(1), 35–48.

Merton, R. K. (1957). *Social theory and social structure.* New York: Free Press.

Noam, G. G., & Fischer, K. W. (1996). *Development and vulnerability in close relationships.* Mahwah, NJ: Lawrence Erlbaum.

Resnick, M. D., Bearman, P. S., Blum, R. W., Bauman K. E., Harris, K. M., Jones, J., et al. (1997). Protecting adolescents from harm: Findings from the national longitudinal study on adolescent health. *Journal of the American Medical Association (JAMA), 278*(10), 823–832.

Rhodes, J. E. (2002). *Stand by me: The risks and rewards of mentoring today's youth.* Cambridge, MA: Harvard University Press.

Rideout, V. J., Foehr, U. G., & Roberts, D. F. (2010). *Generation M²: Media in the lives of 8-18 year-olds.* Menlo park, CA: The Henry J. Kaiser Family Foundation.

Rutter, P. A., & Leech, N. L. (2006). Sexual minority youth perspectives on the school environment and suicide risk interventions: A qualitative study. *Journal of Gay and Lesbian Issues in Education, 4*(1), 77–91.

Safran, S. A., & Heimberg, R. G. (1999). Depression, hopelessness, suicidality, and related factors in sexual minority and heterosexual adolescents. *Journal of Consulting and Clinical Psychology, 67*, 859–866.

Stever, G. S. (2008). The celebrity appeal questionnaire: Sex, entertainment, or leadership? *Psychological Reports, 103*(1), 113–120.

Stever, G. S. (2009). Parasocial and social interaction with celebrities: Classification of media fans. *Journal of Media Psychology, 14*(3), 1–39.

Stever, G. S. (2011). Fan behavior and lifespan development theory: Explaining para-social and social attachment to celebrities. *Journal of Adult Development, 18*(1), 1–7.

Stever, G. S., & Lawson, K. (2013). Twitter as a way for celebrities to communicate with fans: Implications for the study of parasocial interaction. *North American Journal of Psychology, 15*(2), 339–354.

Turino, T. (2008). *Music as Social Life: The Politics of Participation.* Chicago: University of Chicago Press.

Wolk, D. (2012, May 23). Monsters Inc. *Time*, 58–60.

Yurdakul-Sahim, D., & Atik, D. (2013). Celebrity influences young consumers: Guiding the way to the ideal self. *Izmir review of social sciences, 1*(1), 65–82.

Endnotes

1. Throughout this chapter I use the term youth to refer not only traditional pre-adolescent or adolescent individuals, but also to refer to young adults; this recognizes the lengthening time that individuals spend in emerging adulthood from the late teens into their late 20s (Arnett, 2004).

BIOGRAPHIES

Jace Allen (BA, University of Montana) is a graduate student in Communication Studies at San Francisco State University. His research focuses on sexuality and communication, representations of non-normative sexual identities in video games and new media, and sexual identity in cross-cultural settings, especially in comparing gay male identities in Japan, Korea, and the United States, within and outside of various forms of media.

Sara Baker (PhD, Ohio University) is an Assistant Professor in the Department of Communication Studies at Eastern Illinois University. Her work has been published in *Quarterly Journal of Speech* and the forthcoming book *Cases in Organizational and Managerial Communication: Stretching Boundaries.*

Linda Baughman (PhD, University of Illinois) is an associate professor of Communication at Christopher Newport University in Virginia. Her research on the sexuality of women started with the study of the birth control movements of the 1930s in America. More recently she is interested in how women construct their sexual identity via the media and their interpersonal relationships. She is currently working on a co-authored book on bisexual and queer identity among women. She has published several book chapters, as well as journal articles in outlets like *The Popular Culture Studies Journal, Communication Studies,* and *The Communication Law Review.*

Larissa Brian (MA, University of South Carolina) is a PhD Candidate in Communication Studies at the University of Pittsburgh and is also pursuing a joint certificate in Gender, Sexuality, and Women's Studies. Her research focuses on the relationship between communication, sexuality, and law, with a particular emphasis on the ways in which new affirmative sexual consent laws rhetorically work against a sex-positive feminist goal of being able to radically speak about sex and desire. Her work touches on such topics as pornography, court cases involving the interplay between speech and sex, queer theory, and the complex relationships between sex and violence, and sex and pleasure. She has previously received a departmental grant to undertake research at the Center for Sex and Culture in San Francisco.

Robert Alan Brookey (PhD, University of Minnesota) is a Professor of Telecommunications at Ball State University where he also serves as the Director of the graduate program in Digital Storytelling. His books include *Reinventing the Male Homosexual: The Rhetoric and Power of the Gay Gene, Hollywood Gamers: Digital Convergence in the Film and Video Game Industries*, and *Playing to Win: Sports, Video Games and the Culture of Play*. His articles have appeared in *Critical Studies in Media Communication, Convergence, Games and Culture*, and *Text and Performance*.

Randal Brown (MA, University of Nevada, Reno) is a doctoral student in social psychology at the University of Nevada, Reno. His research focuses on sexual communication in romantic relationships, communication and social cognition, and sexual health promotion. He serves as the student-faculty liaison for his doctoral program and is the recipient of the Janice M. Epp Student Scholarship Award from the Society for the Scientific Study of Sexuality. He is also a member of the International Association for Relationship Research, the National Communication Association, and the Society for Personality and Social Psychology.

Zelaika S. Hepworth Clarke (PhD, Widener University) is a sexosopher, sexual epistemologist, cultural and clinical sexologist, sexecologist, African-centered social worker, and decolonizing autoethnographer. Zelaika received a bachelor's degree in Sexuality, Culture and Oppression at New York University. In 2012, Zelaika obtained a Master's in Social Work and Master's in Education of Human Sexuality from Widener University as well as a certificate from the National Academy for African-Centered Social Work. Zelaika has studied internationally in Ghana, Kenya, Uganda, Trinidad, Jamaica, Netherlands, and Cuba. Zelaika is committed to intersectional mindfulness, counter-oppressive discourses, the decolonization project, empowerment, and increasing sexual epistemic justice and diversity.

Tina Coffelt (PhD, University of Missouri) is an Assistant Professor in the Communication Studies program at Iowa State University. Her research interests include sexual communication, privacy management, multigenerational family communication, and interpersonal communication. Her work has appeared in *Communication Quarterly*, *Communication Yearbook*, and *Journal of Sex Research*, among others. She is also a recent winner of the Federation Prize for a project related to sexuality and communication.

Shannon Criniti (PhD, Widener University) is an educator, researcher, and advocate with 18 years of professional experience in the field of sexual and reproductive health. As Vice President of Strategic Initiatives at AccessMatters, a sexual and reproductive health-focused non-profit, Dr. Criniti oversees the organization's research, quality improvement, and training programs. She holds an adjunct appointment in Drexel University's College of Medicine and College of Nursing and Health Professions, and is the developer and instructor for a graduate course called Introduction to Patient Sexuality. Dr. Criniti holds a BA in journalism and women's studies from Syracuse University, a Master's degree in public health from the CUNY School of Public Health at Hunter College, and a PhD in human sexuality education from Widener University.

Amanda Denes (PhD, University of California, Santa Barbara) is an Assistant Professor in the Department of Communication at the University of Connecticut. She received her PhD in Communication from the University of California, Santa Barbara, with an emphasis in Feminist Studies. Her primary area of specialization is interpersonal communication, with emphases in disclosure, sexuality, and identity. Much of her work looks at the association between communication in interpersonal relationships and people's physiological, psychological, and relational health.

Jayson Dibble (PhD, Michigan State University) is an associate professor in the Department of Communication at Hope College. He regularly teaches courses on interpersonal communication, communication and conflict, persuasion, and research methods. His research specialties include interpersonal communication, personal relationships, non-traditional dating and sex relationships, breaking bad news, persuasion, and social scientific research methods. Dr. Dibble has authored or co-authored several journal articles and book chapters on these topics, and his work has been published in *Human Communication Research*, *Communication Research*, *Computers in Human Behavior*, and *Psychological Assessment*.

Jenny Dixon (PhD, University of Missouri) is an Assistant Professor of Communication and Media Arts at Marymount Manhattan College in New

York City. Her research focuses on constructions of sexual and gender identities in the workplace and work/family balance advocacy across an array of family structures (e.g., single, childfree, LGBT, family of choice, etc.). Jenny's work can be found in *Communication Quarterly*, *Journal of Applied Communication Research*, and *Electronic Journal of Communication*. In addition to contributing chapters to edited volumes, Jenny's first book, *Enacting Family: Communication, Advocacy, and Work/Family Balance*—part of Routledge's Communication Studies Research series—is currently under production.

Jennifer C. Dunn (PhD, Ohio University) is an Associate Professor of Rhetoric and Public Culture at Dominican University. Her research centers on rhetoric, gender, and popular culture. Dr. Dunn explores how evolving understandings of women's roles, in general, and women's sexuality, specifically, are represented in media and their relationship with our understandings of their lived experiences. Her work has been published in *Feminist Media Studies*, *Communication Studies*, and *Sexuality and Culture*, among other journals and collections. She also currently serves as the Reviews Editor for *The Popular Culture Studies Journal*.

Shinsuke Eguchi (PhD, Howard University) is an assistant professor of intercultural communication in the Department of Communication and Journalism at the University of New Mexico. Prior to joining UNM in Fall 2012, Dr. Eguchi was a post-doctoral fellow on transnationalism, diaspora, and migration in the communication studies department at University of Denver. His research interests focus on critical intercultural communication, queer (of color) performance studies, Asian/Pacific/American communication studies, and critical autoethnography. His work has appeared for publication in various outlets such as *Communication, Culture, & Critique*, *Text and Performance Quarterly*, *Journal of International and Intercultural Communication*, and *Cultural Studies↔Critical Methodologies*, among others.

Tiffany Emerson (MA, Northern Kentucky University) is a professional event planner who provides services for the Kentucky State Parks system.

Sandra L. Faulkner (PhD, The Pennsylvania State University) is an Associate Professor of Communication and Director of Women's, Gender and Sexuality Studies at Bowling Green State University. Her teaching and research interests include qualitative methodology, poetic inquiry, and the relationships between culture, identities, and sexuality in close relationships. She has published research in journals such as *Qualitative Health Re-*

search, *Qualitative Inquiry, Cultural Studies↔Critical Methodologies,* and *Journal of Social and Personal Relationships.* In addition to two books on poetry with Left Coast Press, Sense published her poetry memoir of family stories *Knit Four, Frog One* and will soon publish *Writing the Personal: Getting Your Story onto the Page.*

Amanda Davis Gatchet (PhD, University of Texas at Austin) is an Assistant Professor in Communications at Montgomery County Community College. Her work explores the rhetoric of authenticity, popular culture, and popular music as well as oral history and rhetorics of alterity and persecution. Her work has appeared in *Journal of Popular Culture* and *Journal of Communication Inquiry,* among other outlets.

Roger Davis Gatchet (PhD, University of Texas at Austin) is a faculty member in Communication Studies at West Chester University. Dr. Gatchet's research interests focus on the rhetoric of popular culture and music, public memory, and social movements. He also incorporates oral history methods in his work, and he has spent the past several years interviewing blues musicians in Austin, Texas. His current research investigates how authenticity has become a principle category around which people organize and make sense of their lives and identities. His research has appeared in edited collections as well as the journal *Oral History Review,* and he is also a contributing writer for the magazine *Living Blues.*

Eli R. Green (PhD, Widener University) is an interdisciplinary sexualities scholar, Assistant Professor of Public Health at William Paterson University, and Adjunct Assistant Professor in the Center for Human Sexuality Studies graduate program at Widener University. Dr. Green is a nationally recognized trainer who helps non-profits, direct service, medical providers, and educational professionals expand their LGBQ and transgender-related cultural competency. Dr. Green's co-authored book with Luca Maurer, *The Teaching Transgender Toolkit: A Facilitator's Guide to Increasing Knowledge, Reducing Prejudice & Building Skills* is the first of its kind. Dr. Green is a Certified Sexuality Educator (CSE) through the American Association of Sexuality Educators, Counselors & Therapists (AASECT).

Kayleigh Grubb (BA, Northern Illinois University) is a Master's student in the Communication program at Northern Illinois University. She is director of the documentary film *Cosplay with Kindness* and does research about bullying in cosplay communities.

Richelle Hair (BA, Texas Tech University) is a graduate student at Texas Tech University. Her interests include interpersonal communication and romantic relationships.

Rose Hartzell-Cushanick (PhD, Indiana University) is a Licensed Marriage and Family Therapist and AASECT Certified Sex Therapist & Educator at San Diego Sexual Medicine. Dr. Hartzell has written multiple publications and has given over 50 presentations at international and national meetings on sexuality matters. She has conducted sex research with San Diego Sexual Medicine, the Kinsey Institute for Research in Sex, Gender, and Reproduction, and the Rural Center for AIDS/STD Prevention (RCAP). In 2007, Dr. Hartzell was awarded the Emerging Professional Award from the Society for the Scientific Study of Sexuality. She currently teaches graduate level sexuality courses at San Diego State University and twice served as the scientific program co-chair for the Society for the Scientific Study of Sexuality.

Dayna Henry (PhD, University of Indiana) is an Assistant Professor in the Department of Kinesiology and Health Education at Southern Illinois University Edwardsville. She received her PhD in Health Behavior from Indiana University, with a minor in Human Sexuality from the Kinsey Institute for Research in Sex, Gender, and Reproduction. She previously completed a Master's degree in Couple and Family Therapy with a specialization in sex therapy at the University of Guelph in Ontario, Canada. Her primary area of specialization is the impact of sexuality education on college student personal and relationship health.

Kathryn Hobson (PhD, University of Denver) is an Assistant Professor in the School of Communication at James Madison University. Her research lies at the crux of critical intercultural communication, queer communication, performance ethnography, and popular culture analysis. She focuses on intersectionality and identity, particularly how race, class, gender, sexuality, and ability operate in queer women's lives and experiences. Her work has appeared in *Liminalities, Kaleidoscope,* and the anthology *Glee and New Directions for Social Change.* She has performed at the Performance West Fringe Festival in LA and at the Eastern Communication Association Convention. Her dissertation recently received the Top Dissertation award from the GLBTQ Division of NCA 2014.

Diana K. Ivy (PhD, University of Oklahoma), known on her home campus as "Ivy," is a Professor of Communication at Texas A&M University-Corpus Christi where she has taught for over 20 years. Ivy is author/co-author of three communication textbooks (*GenderSpeak* 6e; *Nonverbal Communication for a Lifetime* 2e; *Communication: Principles for a Lifetime* 6e) and an upcoming book chapter on student sexual safety, specifically the communication of consent. She has published articles in *Communication Education, Southern Communication Journal,* and *Women & Language* and has held multiple offices in the National Communication Association and Western States Communication Association. She also hosted a call-in radio show, "Call Me Ivy," and has begun post-doctoral coursework at Oxford University.

Kristen Jozkowski (PhD, Indiana University) is an Assistant Professor of Public Health, affiliate faculty in Gender Studies, and Director of the Sexual Health Research Lab at the University of Arkansas. She is also a Research Fellow with the Kinsey Institute for Research in Sex, Gender, and Reproduction at Indiana University. Dr. Jozkowski's research interests include sexual consent negotiation, sexual violence prevention, sexual enhancement, and sexual function. This research has been supported by several funding agencies including the National Institutes of Health and has accrued over 50 publications in outlets such as the *Journal of Sex Research, Archives of Sexual Behavior,* and *Violence Against Women*, among others. She is currently the Secretary for the Society for the Scientific Study of Sexuality and co-chair for the Sexuality Task Force for the American Public Health Association.

Jessica Kratzer (PhD, University of Missouri) is an assistant professor at Middle Tennessee State University where she teaches courses in sexual communication and gender communication. Her areas of research include hooking up among college students, senior citizens' sexual activity and intimacy, and narratives about childbirth.

Pamela J. Lannutti (PhD, University of Georgia) is Associate Professor and Graduate Director in the Department of Communication at La Salle University. Her research focuses on communication in personal relationships. Dr. Lannutti is the author of *Experiencing same-sex marriage: Individuals, couples, and social networks* (2014, Peter Lang Publishing). Her work has appeared in many journals, including *Human Communication*

Research and *Journal of Social and Personal Relationships*. Dr. Lannutti has been named an Eastern Communication Research Fellow and has received the Randy Majors Memorial Award for Distinguished GLBTQ Scholarship. Dr. Lannutti is currently the editor of *Communication Quarterly*.

Ryan Lescure (MA, San Francisco State University) is a Lecturer of Communication Studies at San Francisco State University and an Adjunct Instructor of Communication Studies at Skyline College in San Bruno, California. He teaches courses such as Gender and Communication, Communication and Culture, Communication and Masculinities, Argumentation and Debate, and Public Speaking. His courses are taught with a special emphasis on critical theory and social justice. His research primarily focuses on the intersections between communication, gender, sexuality, media, culture, and power.

Tim McKenna-Buchanan (PhD, Ohio University) is an Assistant Professor in the Department of Communication Studies at Manchester University. His research focuses on the intersection of difference (or diversity) and organizational life, with an emphasis on the ways narratives empower identity and the stories that create, maintain, and change individuals' lived experience. His work has been published in journals such as *Communication Education*, *Health Communication*, and *Communication Teacher*.

Jennifer Mayo (MA, Ball State University) is a technical writer in Golden, Colorado. She completed her BA in English at University of Colorado Denver, and completed her MA in Telecommunications at Ball State University. Her Master's thesis focused on GamerGate and misogyny toward women in the video game community. Jennifer's spare time is consumed by non-technical writing, weight-lifting, and video games.

Michaela D.E. Meyer (PhD, Ohio University) is an associate professor of communication at Christopher Newport University. She is a critical identity scholar who uses critical/cultural and rhetorical methods to interrogate the relationship between media and identity. She is the author of over 40 academic publications in outlets such as *Communication Quarterly*, *Communication Studies*, and *Feminist Media Studies*, among others. Her most recent work interrogates communication patterns utilized by emerging adults (aged 18–30) in relational and mediated contexts. Dr. Meyer recently received the Randy Majors Memorial Award from the National Communication Association. She has presented over 100 professional conference presentations in a variety of national and international outlets.

Anita Morris (BA, Texas Tech University) is a graduate student at Texas Tech University. Her interests include interpersonal and intercultural communication.

Katrina Pariera (PhD, University of Southern California) is an Assistant Professor of Communication, with an additional appointment in Sociology at The George Washington University in Washington, D.C. She received her PhD from the Annenberg School of Communication at the University of Southern California, where she studied health and interpersonal communication. Her research focuses on issues related to sexual communication and sexual health, including how parents and children talk about sex, the influence of sexual norms on sexual well-being, and depictions of sexual health on television.

Brittnie Peck (MA, Northern Illinois University) is a doctoral student in the Communication program at University of Wisconsin-Milwaukee. Current areas of research include parent-child sexual communication, the relationship between a single-parent and child, and destructive communication practices such as bullying.

Narissra Maria Punyanunt-Carter (PhD, Kent State University, 2002) is an associate professor in the department of communication studies at Texas Tech University. Narissra teaches interpersonal communication, gender, nonverbal, and romantic relationships. Dr. Punyanunt-Carter's research interests include romantic relationships, computer-mediated communication, father-daughter communication, and mass media portrayals of romance. She is the recipient of many teaching and research awards. She is a consultant for several book publishers, such as Bedford St. Martin's, Rowan & Littlefield, Oxford, McGraw-Hill, and Wadsworth. She has published many articles, which have been featured in *Southern Communication Journal, Communication Research Reports,* and *Communication Quarterly.* n.punyanunt@ttu.edu

Tobias Reynolds-Tylus (MA, University at Buffalo, The State University of New York, 2013), is a PhD student in the Department of Communication at the University of Illinois at Urbana-Champaign. His research looks at persuasion in health contexts, particularly in the areas of organ donation and sexual decision-making. His work has been presented at national and international conferences, and in refereed journals including *Journal of Health Communication* and *Progress in Transplantation.*

Lance S. Rintamaki (PhD, University of Illinois at Urbana-Champaign) is an Associate Professor in the Department of Communication and adjunct Associate Professor in the Department of Community Health and Health Behavior at the University at Buffalo (SUNY). Dr. Rintamaki's research focuses on sexual communication and provider-patient communication. He has published over 50 articles and book chapters regarding stigma in health care interactions; health behavior promotion; and health behavior theory. He is the author of the forthcoming book, *The Science of Sexual Communication* (Hayden-McNeil).

Sean Robinson (PhD, University of Wisconsin-Madison) is an Associate Professor of Education and an affiliate of the Women and Gender Studies program at Morgan State University. His teaching interests include social justice in education, educational administration, organizational development, leadership development, and qualitative research methodology. His primary research interest is related to identity development and sexual orientation/gender expression of youth and young adults. He has published over a dozen articles and book chapters and regularly presents at regional, national, and international conferences on issues related to gender and sexual diversity. His research around LGBTQ youth and mentoring lead to the co-development of a city-wide mentoring program for LGBTQ youth in 2014, the first of its kind in Washington, D.C.

Annika Speer (PhD, University of California, Santa Barbara) is a Lecturer in the Department of Theatre, Film, and Digital Production at the University of California, Riverside. She completed her PhD in Theater Studies with a doctoral emphasis in Feminist Studies at the University of California, Santa Barbara and a postdoctoral fellowship in the Department of Communication at the University of Connecticut. Her main research interest is the critical study of sexuality and gender in the contexts of performance and communication.

Lara C. Stache (PhD, University of Wisconsin-Milwaukee) is Assistant Professor of Communication at Governors State University. Her research emphasizes media, rhetoric, and representations of gender in popular discourse. Lara's research has appeared in journals, including *Feminist Media Studies* and *New Technology, Work, and Employment*, and a book chapter in *Fan Girls and the Media: Creating Characters, Consuming Culture*. Lara's popular press writing has appeared on *The Feminist Wire*.

Daniel S. Strasser (PhD, University of Denver) is an Assistant Professor of Gender and Family Communication in the Communication Studies Department at Rowan University. He teaches courses in gender, family, and interpersonal communication. Strasser's research examines identity and relationship construction and negotiation, and the intersections of gender, sexuality, and family using interpretive, qualitative, and critical methodologies. His work has appeared in *Journal of Family Communication*; Dunn, Manning, and Stern's (2015) *Lucky Strikes and a Three Martini Lunch: Thinking About Television's Mad Men*; and Floyd and Mormon's (2014) *Widening the Family Circle: New Research in Family Communication*. He currently serves as Chair for the Eastern Communication Association Voices of Diversity Interest Group.

Danielle M. Stern (PhD, University of Ohio) is an Associate Professor at Christopher Newport University. Her scholarship explores themes of feminism, popular culture, polymediation, and digital culture. She has been actively involved in the communication discipline and has received several awards for her work including the Ellis-Bochner Autoethnography and Personal Narrative Research Award.

Morgan Summers (MA, Ball State University) is a doctoral student in the Communication program at Michigan State University. She studies interpersonal/relational communication and health communication.

Sara L. Trask (PhD, University of Missouri) is an Assistant Professor at Randolph-Macon College. Her scholarship centers on interpersonal communication, emotions, and intimate relationships, particularly the role of affection and deceptive affection in close relationships including friends with benefits, cross-sex friendships, and romantic relationships.

Andrew Tri (MA, Northern Illinois University) resides in Minnesota.

Daniel Weigel (PhD, University of Nevada, Reno) is a faculty member in the Social Psychology, Human Development and Family Studies, and Cooperative Extension programs at the University of Nevada, Reno. He has been studying romantic and family relationships for several years with an interest in communication, relationship maintenance, commitment, and change. He also coordinates several community intervention programs for at-risk families, parents, and children. He is a member of the International Association for Relationship Research, the National Communication Association, and the National Council on Family Relations.

Kelly Wilz (PhD, Indiana University) is a cultural critic, writer at the American Association of University Professors' Academe Blog, and an Associate Professor of Communication/Theatre Arts at the University of Wisconsin-Marshfield/Wood County where she explores the intersections of education, media literacy, gender, politics, and pop culture. The focus of her research is on rhetorical constructions of gender, violence, and dissent within the context of U.S. war culture and how dehumanizing and demonizing rhetoric extend beyond war to issues of social violence based on discourses of race, gender, sexual orientation, ethnicity, and other identity markers.

Gust A. Yep (PhD, University of Southern California) is Professor of Communication Studies, Graduate Faculty of Sexuality Studies, and Faculty in the EdD Program in Educational Leadership at San Francisco State University. His research examines communication at the intersections of culture, race, class, gender, sexuality, and nation, with a focus on sexual, gender, and ethnic minority communities. In addition to three books and a monograph, he has authored more than 70 articles in (inter)disciplinary journals and anthologies. He is recipient of numerous academic and community awards including the 2011 San Francisco State University Distinguished Faculty Award for Professional Achievement (Researcher of the Year) and the 2015 Association for Education in Journalism and Mass Communication (AEJMC) Leroy F. Aarons Award for significant contributions to LGBT media education and research.

CPSIA information can be obtained
at www.ICGtesting.com
Printed in the USA
FFOW01n0650120917
39866FF